As the paratroops trotted forward, vaulting the fences or cutting their way through them, they shouted a battle cry...

A stranger from another world must have thought life cheap on earth had he been witness to that charge; for to stand up was to be hit - it was almost a certainty - and young Americans fixed their bayonets and moved crouching toward the enemy to kill... There are no American fanatics – none in this outfit, anyway – only men who have so much confidence in their own strength and in their buddies and such a contempt for the enemy that they forget sometimes how sweet it is to be alive.

Private First Class David H. Whittier

A FINE SENSE OF HONOR

AT WAR WITH THE MEN OF THE
504TH PARACHUTE INFANTRY
FROM SICILY TO THE FALL OF GERMANY

© Tyler S. Fox, 2019

First edition
ISBN: 9781072101789

Front cover photo: Thomas Lane in Africa, shortly before parachuting into Sicily. *US Signal Corps*
Rear cover photo: Lt. John E. Scheaffer, unkown and Captain Adam Komosa in Germany around VE-Day. *Author's collection*

TO EDDIE

Captain Herbert Kaufman and his family stand outside their home near Fort Bragg, NC shortly before the 504th Parachute Infantry Regiment departed for overseas service to fight in World War II. Captain Kaufman, serving as the Operations Officer for the 3rd Battalion, 504th PIR was probably the first paratrooper of the regiment to be killed by enemy fire in World War II. Well over 600 more of his comrades in the 504th, over the next two years, would share his tragic fate to help defeat NAZI Germany. (Roy Hanna)

1

DRAWING FIRST BLOOD

Second Lieutenant Roy Hanna and two of his fellow paratroopers hid in the bushes alongside a road as a horse came roaring by. Mounted atop it, an Italian officer. Although the officer was not in uniform, it was clear he was out inspecting positions for the coming Anglo-Americans. Little did the officer know, but they had already arrived, and the enemy was closer than the Italian thought: Lieutenant Hanna and the two men could have quickly dispatched the Italian at their leisure.

Roy Hanna was but one man, one man of thousands who called themselves part of America's elite parachute troops. For days now, all across the isle of Sicily, thousands of men like Roy Hanna had descended into the countryside on silk parachutes, each of which carried a highly-trained soldier. Over these days, these elite men were supposed to prove their quality to the Allied efforts in World War II. And it had been a debacle, in a certain measure. Men were blown and scattered as they dropped, like leaves in the wind. Isolated paratroopers, like Hanna, fought the Germans where they found them. Men by the twos and threes waged individual wars on German columns across a 60-mile front like guerrillas fighting a hit-and-run battle. When Roy Hanna stopped to ask a Sicilian where he was located on the maps he had in his case, they found they had been dropped so far away from their intended landing zone that they weren't even on the maps he had been issued.

Another member of Roy Hanna's company was Corporal Russel Looney. When he first made contact with the earth after parachuting from his plane, near the Comiso Airport miles from his assigned drop zone, it was with a cactus plant which temporarily knocked him out, until the bullets of an Italian soldier brought him back to. Looney hurled two hand grenades, killing the Italian. He walked alone all night before finding members of the 45th Infantry Division the following morning.[1]

The airborne component of the Sicily invasion – Operation HUSKY – was a precursor to an extensive operation involving airborne, ground, and naval components from both the American and British Armies. The first wave of parachutists dropped into the Sicilian countryside on July 9, followed by extensive beach landings by the Anglo-American armies on the 10th, with another parachute reinforcement on July 11 to bolster the foothold gained by the seaborne troops. All paratroopers in the American sector were furnished from the US 82nd Airborne Division. The division's mission would be to seize vital crossroads, and form strong roadblocks to prevent the Germans from counterattacking the venerable seaborne forces as they consolidated a shallow beachhead.

The first paratroopers to land in Sicily were those of the 3rd Battalion, 504th Parachute Infantry Regiment. Lieutenant Roy Hanna and Corporal Russel Looney were among them, parachuting in on July 9. The drop was badly scattered by intense anti-aircraft fire. On the flight over, Lieutenant Roy Hanna had fallen asleep. Having been up for nearly a day and a half studying detailed sand table models of the road they were to secure, Hanna was already tired, able to sleep despite the roaring Pratt & Whitney engines and sucking wind coming in through the open door. Suddenly Hanna felt the man next to him nudging him with his elbow. "Lieutenant, the red light is on," he said. Across from Hanna, next to the door, the red light brightly glowed in the dark. It was approximately 11:25. Hanna stood up. "STAND UP AND HOOK UP!" the twenty-six-year-old lieutenant yelled above the oppressive drove of the engines. "INSPECT YOUR EQUIPMENT!" The men checked their parachutes and harnesses one last time. Hanna stood in the door, assuming his jump position. He turned his head, "STAND IN THE DOOR!" he yelled. The men closed up and went back to belly, waiting for the green light, poised to jump into German territory. As Hanna had predicted in a letter home he had written two months' prior, his family would soon be reading about he and his men. "Average age 23 to 24," Hanna wrote in the letter, "all athletic and energetic (except for work); but they sure can handle our light machine guns and forty rifles. You'll read about them, keep watching."[2]

While still over the Mediterranean, Roy Hanna watched as the shores of Sicily came into view when suddenly, *WHACK*. The sky was suddenly set ablaze like wildfire. Streaks of what seemed like small, glowing fireballs were coming up at them.

Donald Zimmerman and Lawrence Neumeyer H/504

One of the leading planes in the formation was the C-47 nicknamed, "Naught One," piloted by Lieutenant Colonel Willis W. Mitchell. Near the tail of the plane, Lieutenant Richard Aldridge was standing at the door, waiting for Mitchell to give him the green light, signaling him to take the men out when they were over the drop zone. Standing up two men behind the lieutenant was nineteen-year-old Private H. Donald Zimmerman. Known as "Zimmy", he watched as planes banked to the east, and another plane, seemingly gliding atop the water, passed underneath. Mitchell took the plane straight into the anti-aircraft fire. From inside the fuselage, it sounded like someone was throwing dozens upon dozens of pebbles at the plane, as shrapnel tinged against the fuselage.

In the plane, Don Zimmerman was struggling with his equipment; he was trying to put his reserve 'chute back on, which he had taken off to breathe easier during the flight with the .30 Browning air-cooled light machine gun that he was carrying pressed against his body. The crew chief, Sergeant Minor F. White, came up to see what the matter was. He began to tug and pull in an attempt to help Zimmerman get his reserve 'chute buckled over the machine gun. He couldn't and returned to his position. Zimmerman threw his reserve in the aluminum seat in disgust and as he turned around, the green light flashed on.

Lieutenant Richard Aldridge immediately leapt down into the night, disappearing. Right behind Aldridge was his radio operator, and in an instant he had taken his jumping position. Zimmerman was excited. He was next. Suddenly the radio operator stopped and braced himself in the door; he was obviously having second thoughts about jumping into German territory. The men were eager. Each second that passed meant they would be further and further apart from each other once they hit the ground. Zimmerman, with the men behind him pushing, ran into the radio operator from the side. The operator was hit with so much force by Zimmerman that he flew back into the tail of the C-47, crashing through the door leading to the cargo hold.

Zimmerman jumped, with his close friend Private Lawrence W. Neumeyer following right behind.

Private H. Donald Zimmerman at Fort Bragg, NC (author's collection)

Upon landing, Zimmerman immediately found Bucky Neumeyer. He was ensnared in a grapevine and had a compound fracture on one of his legs. Nobody else was around. Lieutenant Aldridge, Zimmerman figured, was quite some ways away and he wasn't sure about the rest of the stick, probably a few hundred yards away, he presumed. They both had landed in a grape vineyard not too far from an asphalt road. There was a small bridge not too far away that spanned what appeared to be a seasonal creek. The four equipment bundles from their C-47 had landed near the bridge, on top of the asphalt road.

Zimmerman went back to Bucky to examine him closer. He was so tangled up, there was no way Zimmerman could extricate him. Zimmerman took Bucky's M-1 rifle, and then took Bucky's three-colored camouflage parachute and covered him up with it to give him some concealment in his venerable position. Zimmerman would stay and protect Bucky.

They had only been on the ground about a half an hour when Zimmerman heard a vehicle coming down the road. It was a jeep full of Italians. Zimmerman laid down on the ground and hid under his parachute. All the Italians hopped out of the jeep near the bridge and cautiously gave a quick look to the equipment bundles. They never touched them. "I was under my parachute," Zimmerman recollected, "and you could tell which one was in charge. I had them zeroed in and everything, but I didn't want to shoot them because I didn't feel I could get them all at one time." After a few minutes, the Italians hopped back in their jeep and drove off. They must have thought that the bundles were explosives meant to blow the bridge, Zimmerman presumed, and that's why they didn't want to touch them. "That was quite the experience," he later reflected.[3]

Roy Hanna LMG Platoon 3/504

Clutching his Thompson submachine gun, the glowing moon revealed the gently rolling Sicilian landscape as Second Lieutenant Roy Hanna peacefully swung back and forth under his open parachute canopy, rapidly approaching the earth just after jumping from the C-47. Suddenly he fell through the branches of an olive tree, his parachute wrapping itself around the branches. "This was an experience in itself," he wrote many years later. "Here I was all alone, in enemy territory, hanging in a tree, in the middle of the night." Hanna reached up to the collar of his jump jacket and pulled down on the small silver zipper to the secret compartment just below his neck, which held his knife. Grasping the small, bone handled switchblade, Hanna depressed the button and the blade shot out from the handle and clicked into place. He reached up and began cutting his suspension lines.

Hanna fell just a few short feet as he cut free of his parachute risers and unbuckled the hefty medal clip on his chest, dropping his parachute harness. Tommy gun in hand, he waited and listened. It was eerily silent, except for a dog barking off in the shallow rolling hills at a distance. He was a long way from his hometown back in Lock Haven, Pennsylvania, and far from doing what he enlisted as a private in the Pennsylvania National Guard for back in October of 1940.

The lieutenant made sure his Tommy gun was undamaged and loaded, and set off into the night.

"George!" came a faint whisper.

"Marshal," Hanna replied, giving his correct countersign.

Sitting there was a private trying to assemble his standard issue M-1 Garand. "He was just sitting there," Hanna recalled, "scared to death, trying to assemble his M-1 rifle. (When making a jump the M-1 was disassembled into three sections, placed in a flat canvas container, and strapped to the soldier's leg). I put his rifle together, loaded it, and sent him in the direction of where I thought my men would be and I went searching for our machine guns and machine gun ammunition... I hadn't searched more than five minutes when I heard a rifle shot – the only one I heard that night." Hanna had no luck finding his bundles, and went back to look for his men.

Joseph Gwiazdoski of Company A displays the equipment worn by a paratrooper while jumping into combat. (Roger Mokan)

As Hanna was walking through the area in which he had landed, he again heard the word of the night: "George." It was one of the men from his stick: his runner Norman Salter. The lieutenant inquired as to the shot he had heard. "He told me that someone had come through there and when he challenged him, the person fired a shot and took off." It was the man whose rifle he had assembled and sent to look for his men. "At least I had put his rifle together properly and it worked."

Shortly after that, Hanna had found seven men under his platoon sergeant, Staff Sergeant Elbert Claunts. Only five were from his Machine Gun Platoon. They traversed a hill as Hanna tried to spot their objective in the moonlit night across the Sicilian landscape of olive trees, grapes, streams, and rolling grasslands. They could see further and much clearer in the daylight. Hanna bedded his men down to wait for dawn.

The next morning, the sound of rifle fire awoke a sleeping Lieutenant Hanna as he gathered his seven men and headed towards the sound of battle. Suddenly Hanna stumbled across two young paratroopers (from another company) attempting to attack a small building filled with the enemy. Hanna decided to form a skirmish line and move through the concealment of a grove of small olive trees, all aligned in near perfect rows:

As we headed toward the building we were passing through a small olive tree orchard when we suddenly came face to face with two enemy soldiers manning a machine gun. As this machine gun started to strafe across where we were, I jumped behind a small olive tree. The only problem here was that I was the third man in line behind that little tree. The first man in line got shot through the side of the neck, the second man through the right thigh, and me they missed. Luck again! Before the machine gun fire started coming back I ran to the right, jumped through a hedge, ran up the far side of the hedgerow and tossed a hand grenade over the hedge in the direction of the machine gun. I will never know whether I was lucky, they unlucky, or they were just scared, [but] I do know the machine gun became silent. By this time many, many enemy soldiers started pouring from these buildings. I called my 'nine-man combat team' to my side of the hedge and we made a strategic withdraw – got the hell out of there. I later found out that these buildings were the barracks that housed the troops that manned the artillery that protected the coast in that area.

As we worked our way away from that area we ran across an Italian farmer. With his help and that of my platoon sergeant, who spoke Italian, I discovered that we were about 20 miles from where we were supposed to be – we weren't even on the maps that I was carrying.

From there we worked our way down into the valley and continued down a small stream with bushes growing along each bank. About midmorning I heard voices up ahead. I halted my team and went to investigate. As I approached I realized the voices were speaking English and stepped out of the stream and met up with about eight or ten troopers from the 505th that included a first lieutenant. [4]

The 505th lieutenant led the group across an open field down to a large stone house at the base of a large hill. Shortly, German fire poured into their skirmish line. Hanna, Sergeant Alvin Yocum and a bazooka man from the 505th fell into a ditch to their right, while the 505th officer took men and began to peel off to their left. Hanna and the two others crawled through the ditch towards the house. Behind him, Hanna laboriously drug the bazooka ammo through the dirt. Finally they approached the house, and the firing died down. The 505th officer was missing.

The three men got out of the ditch and Sergeant Yocum covered Lieutenant Hanna from the other side of the road as he went to inspect the house. Hanna went and pounded on the door. Inside, he found about ten Italian civilians all hurriedly talking to each other. Hanna couldn't understand what they were discussing, so he led the Yocum and the bazooka man up the hill as night fell. They stopped half way up to bed down for the night.

About an hour before midnight, the area around Gela lit up with bright light as yellow, white and blue streaks flung into the air like a polytechnic show. This gave Lieutenant Hanna a direction in which to travel. After daylight, he went to the top of the large hill and found a column of Germans going by on the road. He, Yocum and the bazooka man went back down the hill and crossed across the field and ran into an onion patch. As they had consumed all their rations, they rested in the onion patch and picked some juicy, fresh onions to eat before moving on. They passed onto the road into Gela, where Hanna saw Germans up close for the first time: dead, bloated bodies of the enemy. Shortly after, Hanna ran into Lieutenant Peter Eaton where the remnants of the battalion was reorganizing.

When Lieutenant Hanna saw the fire breaking into the sky the night before arriving in Gela, Hanna became a witness to the greatest tragedy in the history of the 504th Parachute Infantry Regiment. When the blistering sun began to set over the airfields in Africa that night, heavy-laden paratroopers who would make up the second wave began to laboriously clamber up small aluminum steps, through a small doorway, and into the fuselage of a C-47 aircraft. The intoxicating smell of gasoline greeted their noses as the men stepped down the narrow isle. The ribbed, barrel shaped fuselage of the airplane was lined by aluminum depressions on either side. Here they would sit for the two-hour flight.

Little did the men know, but they were about to fly headlong into some of the deadliest and most effective anti-aircraft fire of World War II. For Private First Class William H. Schrack, this was his 30th birthday. Schrack would die that night, not living to even grow a day over 30.

This second wave of paratroopers principally consisted of the 1st and 2nd Battalions, 504th Parachute Infantry Regiment, and the 376th Parachute Field Artillery Battalion.

After take-off, the serials of C-47s bearing these paratroopers turned over Malta, and headed for the Sicilian coast. As they began passing over the DZs, the American anti-aircraft artillery opened fire on the paratrooper's transports – friendly fire – downing 23 planes before mission's end. When Private First Class Donald Giguere jumped from his assigned C-47 transport, the left wing was shot away, and the motor set aflame by the fire of his fellow Americans. "But we're here," Giguere said, "so what the hell."[5]

Flight of the 1st Battalion

The first serial of C-47 transports on the night of July 11 bore the men of the 1st Battalion, 504th Parachute Infantry Regiment. At the head of the formation, Captain Willard Harrison witnessed the start of the 'friendly fire' disaster, when a .50 machine gun from the sand dunes opened up on the transports. With each passing second, the fire grew more intense as the skyline lit up as more guns from the beaches, the ground and the water began spurting up their fire, augmenting the already deadly deluge of bullets.[6]

From his C-47, Joe Gardner of C Company "could see the Sicily coast over the shoulder of the man ahead of me. It was 10:47 P.M. We saw the ships spread out for miles below us. Then we saw hundreds of red-flickering lights down there. Then it hit us… Planes caught fire and spun down too fast for the troopers to jump. Guys in some hit planes bailed out and went down like stones into the sea."[7] When Ross Pippen, another member of Gardner's company, made contact with the earth after his jump, he landed on a house and gave a poor Sicilian family the greatest scare of their life when they heard the tremendous noise of him hitting the house under his canopy. "I guess the people in the house thought they were being bombed," Pippin later wrote to his friends back in Panama, Florida.[8]

Jimmy Eldridge perhaps gives the most poignant account of the days and hours leading up to this tragic incident:

The day of the jump everyone was up real early in the morning and seemed to be in high spirits. Just after we had finished breakfast (that is, the formation following reveille, known to us as chow call. But any resemblance between it and breakfast that morning was purely coincidental), our company commander gave us a talk, then we checked and packed our gear and moved to the airport. We stayed there all day and we were supposed to jump that night but just as we were putting on our 'chutes we got word that a lot of enemy activity was taking place in the area where we were supposed to jump. Several of the fellows were pretty burned up about the matter but others said they were sure the Germans didn't expect us this early or they certainly could not have been so rude as to be maneuvering around in our landing sector just at the time when we needed it the most.

Anyway, the officers got together and decided that since the Germans were already there that rather than cause hard feelings we would stand by and take what was left. Well, we stood by on alert all through the night and next day. Then about 6 o'clock that night we got the word to get into our 'chutes, and got into the planes.

We circled around for about 40 minutes, getting flight formation and then all the planes turned noses out across the Mediterranean Sea. Everyone seemed to be feeling great and I might stress that 'seemed', because if they were like me, you could call it 'whistling in the graveyard.'

Not near as much was said about the jump we had ahead of us as you might think. The talk was about band leaders and it was pretty well agreed that Harry James was tops as far as we were concerned. And the talk finally drifted around to baseball and boxing, of course.

I let everybody know that Frank Melton, Buddy Lewis and Crash Davis were from Gastonia and that at the present time Lewis was flying a paratroop transport like the one we were in. As we neared Sicily everyone felt it more and more. About 15 minutes before we were supposed to jump we got the command to put on our helmets. As time grew shorter we got the commands "stand up" and "hook up."

Well, I would like to tell you that I walked up and down that plane floor with a big grin on my face, feeling like I was about to enter the Friendly Tavern. But the way it was, it was quite different. The jump master gave the command, "Stand in the door." I remember having a rather sickly feeling around my fifty-yard line as I stood there looking down. (By this time the anti-aircraft had opened up, and it looked like a Fourth of July celebration).

I must have stood in that doorway about eight minutes while the pilot was trying to locate our area. I kept trying to convince myself that my feeling came from something I had eaten, but I knew I was wrong. I was the number one man and was supposed to go when I was hit on the leg by the jump master. I remember him asking, "Is everybody ready?" Everyone says, "Yeah." Then he asked, "Is everybody happy?" Everyone says, "Yeah." Then he said, "Okay, let's give them hell!" Then the light turned green and he hit my leg.

I jumped – and the next few seconds seemed awfully long.[9]

Marvin Courtney B/504

Marvin R. Courtney looked out the window, and saw the fire coming up at them. Bullets began coming through the bottom of the plane. The pilot of his plane pushed the throttle to increase the speed and try and gain height. When the men of the stick began jumping, Courtney had no trouble getting out because of the increased airspeed. As he descended under his open canopy, he could feel though his hands, which were grasping the parachute risers, the jerking of bullets and shrapnel as they were ripping through the taunt silk of his parachute. He could also feel shards of metal coming back down, from already exploded anti-aircraft rounds. "Everybody that had a gun was shooting at us," Courtney felt, "probably a few spit balls to go along." Courtney landed in a grape arbor near Biscari. "The grapes were ripe," Courtney recalled, "but I wasn't interested in eating grapes."[10]

On the final jump before leaving the United States, Howard Gregory of Company B took this photograph of his dangling feet as he floated down to earth underneath his parachute after jumping from a C-47. (Authors collection)

Norm Maffei was a member of an artillery unit. After moving inland a few miles from Scoglitti Beach, where he had landed by boat, his battery set up near Comiso Airfield. He recalled the night the paratroopers jumped: "We were nervous, new in battle, and touchy… Men yelled and scrambled for arms and ammo, while machine gunners stood by their weapons. Our guntruck machine gunner jerked his gun into ready position, swinging it around toward the approaching airplane."[11]

Marvin Courtney's close friend Edwin Decker also parachuted into the same grape arbor near Biscari. "The night we landed, everything seemed pretty strange," he recalled. "There was a stone wall going through the orchard with a ditch with running water on top of it for irrigation I guess."[12]

Just after getting out of his parachute harness, and ensuring the 60mm mortar tube was safe, a scared paratrooper ran by Marvin Courtney. "Where's that fool going?" Courtney wondered. Less than a minute later the man sprinted back by, and Courtney put his arm out to stop him and calmed him down. Two or three more men soon joined, and another man ran up. He said, "The Germans have captured four or five of our men. They have them under a bridge down there. Let's go get them back out."

Courtney thought, "Well, this don't sound like war. This sounds like playing hide and go seek."

The small band of paratroopers ran the Germans off, and freed their men. When daylight broke, their group had swelled to about fifteen paratroopers, and they met up with a colonel from the US 45th Division who had orders to take Biscari Airfield. Courtney, looking for an excuse to leave, had lost his helmet on the jump.

"I don't have my helmet," Courtney told the colonel.

"Right over there," the colonel said, "my jeep driver's over there. He isn't going to need his helmet anymore. He's dead."

Courtney walked over to the dead soldier, who appeared to be an American-Indian, and took his helmet, with Pocahontas beautifully pained on the side.

They came to a hill, and the colonel left a radio jeep with the paratroopers, and told them to hold the T-intersection at the rear of his regiment as they went in for the assault. Several other miss-dropped paratroopers from B/504 were with the group. Private Goddard and Private Art Matthews manned a .30 caliber machine gun sighted down the road, and Courtney and his buddy George Meyer dug a foxhole together at the T-intersection.

Not long after, a small convoy of three German trucks came roaring down the road. Goddard opened up on them with his machine gun. The trucks stopped. One of the drivers was slaughtered by the paratroopers' fire as he tried to escape the cab, half his body still in the truck, the other half dangling out of the open door. Behind the trucks, German infantrymen were closing fast. Goddard was shot, and soon after a grenade exploded next to him, wounding him severely. The small band was being overrun.

George Meyer tapped Courtney on the shoulder and told him that the other paratroopers had run and left them. Courtney and Meyer got up and ran for all they were worth. So close the Germans had been, that when the two paratroopers looked to their left and right, they were running alongside the attacking German troops. Courtney and Meyer slowly started easing off to the left until the Germans "saw we weren't Germans. We got two or three hundred yards out running just all we could and they started shooting at us. Well, we hit the ground, and they were getting too close to us so we jumped up and run again. So we ran again, and we ran as far as we could run. We stopped and they cut a few limbs off the trees [with gunfire] above us. We just hit the ground there and stayed there. They left."[13]

Flight of the 2nd Battalion

After the 1st Battalion's plane serials passed over the Sicilian coast on the night of the jump, the rest of the airplane train came crossing parallel to the coast over Sicily, making their way to the drop zone. With each passing minute, the volume of fire seemed to increase, leaving the serials following the 1st Battalion especially hard-hit. Captain Robert Halloran was a member of the Medical Detachment, and served as the Regimental Dentist. "Tracer bullets riddled [the] plane," he said, "sky lit up and it seemed exactly the way Hollywood portrayed combat… and later discovered combat [is] not like that."[14]

Two planes of Headquarters and Headquarters Company were downed, one, which crashed into the Mediterranean just off Gela Pier with disastrous effect, killed the 19 parachutist which it was transporting, including Private William E. Chapman, or "Chappie", who had helped found the regimental newsletter *Prop Blast* and became its first editor in September 1942. But his contributions to recording the early history of his regiment didn't stop there. Chapman authored newspaper columns telling the public-at-large about what it was like to be a paratrooper and trying to dispel the myth that they were just a group of lost souls in a "suicide squad."[15]

The plane in which Colonel Reuben Tucker was riding flew along the coast of Sicily two times trying to find the drop zone, all through heavy flak. They flew first over Gela and then came in low over the 1st Division's beaches heading west. On those beaches was Lieutenant Jack Brooks, who remembered the low-flying aircraft going over their positions. "God," he recalled, "it seemed to me I could reach up there and touch them."[16] His men fired on the planes, thinking they were German bombers. Colonel Tucker's plane continued to fly until they reached Licata, where they then turned back towards Gela after getting their bearings. One officer, Colonel Tucker recalled, "was shot between the legs and remarked, 'I feel like I've wet my pants.' Actually the floor was damp but that was caused by the fact that the round had smashed an oil container that was in his musette bag."[17] They jumped near the drop zone into heavy fire, and after Tucker landed he stopped the crews of nearby tanks from firing their .50 caliber machine guns. When Tucker's plane returned to Africa, it was counted to have 2,000 holes from the flak.[18] Flying through the thick flak was one of Tucker's most memorable experiences of the war, and it was the beginning of a saga of many acts "of real heroism that will never appear in print."[19]

Private Howard Gregory landed so far away from the DZ that he ended up in the Canadian sector. After linking up with Canadian forces, he joined their unit and fought as a corporal in the Canadian Army, going so far as to disguard his American uniform and take on the uniform of a Canadian corporal. Here he is during the fighting in Sicily, pictured in his corporal uniform. (Author's collection)

Edward Soloman, an infantry officer with the 1st Division, was also on the beaches of Gela that night when the paratroopers jumped. "A paratrooper – one of the more fortunate ones – landed in our immediate area," Soloman recalled. "We reached him just as he was rolling up his 'chute. His chagrin at the latest turn of events was aptly expressed with liberal usage of expletives that have no place in this monograph. His opinion of his brothers-in-arms was not complimentary to say the least. His point was well taken."[20]

Lieutenant Chester A. Garrison had come to the parachute troops from Wall Street, New York. When Pearl Harbor happened, Garrison was listening to a symphony over the radio when it was interrupted by the news of the Japanese attack. "Disturbed acceptance," he later wrote of his reaction. "I knew I would be involved." After being drafted, he was sent to Fort Belvoir, Virginia to be an engineer. Because of his college education, he applied for Officer Candidate School and then volunteered to be a paratrooper after being commissioned as a second lieutenant because "the best was what I wanted."[21] As a student of English literature, Garrison had prepared himself for Army life and the war by reading books such as Leo Tolstoy's *War and Peace*. Another book which he had read in his younger years was Stephen Crane's *A Red Badge of Courage*. At the time he felt the book was overrated, but after what the coming months of combat would bring for him, his view would change; he would go on to say that Crane successfully captures the confusion of combat and its psychological effects.

On the fateful night of July 11, 1943, Lieutenant Garrison was standing in the open door of a C-47 with men of E Company lined up behind him, poised to jump on the Sicilian isle. Garrison stood watching out into the night, when he saw a plane fly in the opposite direction about 50 to 100 yards distant. The plane had a swastika on it. Then came the anti-aircraft fire from the US Navy and ground forces below them.

Standing in the door, Garrison waited for the green light. He felt a tap. Garrison jumped into the black hole. Just as he exited the door, he felt an explosion. His parachute opened up with such force that it snapped the hunting knife from his boot. Garrison watched as a C-47 glided down in flames, assuming it to be the plane he just left.

Garrison touched down on a hillside, which made his right leg take most of the impact from the fall, injuring his knee. The night was utterly quiet – no shooting nor animals or people. He began to stumble around in concentric circles, finding nothing. Finally, he yelled, "Hello?!" And out from the darkness came a silhouette. Garrison pointed his carbine at the silhouette, until he recognized the trooper to be from his company. "He kept shaking his head," Garrison would later write, "to clear his mind because he had banged his head from oscillating backwards." A short time later, Garrison found three others together in a group. They were heading to a collection point, which they reached. "The assemblage that we joined was neither large nor organized, and Col. Tucker had not been heard of. In daylight we moved to a more convenient location by way of a field full of bushes of juicy Roma tomatoes. I picked and ate as I walked – the best I have ever tasted, even without salt. The gathering gradually became a camp."

There, Lieutenant Colonel Yarborough – the 2nd Battalion's commander – was the ranking officer. Rumors were flying. Some said that Colonel Tucker's plane had crashed.

That afternoon, to our mutual astonishment, my plane-load of men wandered in. I had thought they were dead, and they knew I was. They reported that, even before I had left the plane, bullet holes appeared on the floor of the plane and that one of the plane's personnel was on the floor dead or wounded. From their vantage point in the dark of the plane, they said they saw tracer bullets entering the plane between my legs when I had jumped into their stream. As I left the plane, an anti-aircraft shell had exploded next to the fuselage and had knocked all of them to the floor. By the time they got to their feet again and jumped, the plane had traveled several miles farther along.

The last man in the plane was Sgt. Freddie James, the second in control. He had yelled for them to get out. But when one of the troopers reached the open door, on second consideration he decided to step aside. James and my squeaky-voiced Southerner grabbed him in the front and back, and all three tumbled out of the plane. On landing, the resister broke his ankle. They gave him a shot of morphine from a kit each of us had tied to a leg, and then they left him sitting and waiting for help. Actually the accident was fortunate in comparison to the treatment he otherwise would have been exposed to by his fellow paratroopers. In Africa he had been the loud-mouthed blade sharpener.[22]

James Sapp Parachute Maintenance

As a member of the 504th PIR's Parachute Maintenance Section, James Sapp was scheduled to jump with the 2nd Battalion's 81mm Mortar Platoon in the stick jump-mastered by Lieutenant Lauren W. Ramsey, of Council Grove, Kansas. The men from the Parachute Maintenance Section were to gather up all the parachutes they could find once on the ground, guard them, and then get them back to the base echelon in Africa for repacking and reuse. James Sapp tells his story of the friendly fire disaster:

We took off and the moon was shining bright – it was a full moon – and we were flying 1,200 feet and we all had our parachutes unfastened, we had the snap fasteners then, they were real uncomfortable, sitting there and one of the boys, I don't know if it was the one next to me, we could hear him. He said, "What is that?" Then the other boy, he said, "Oh, that's just sparks from the engine." About that time another one had heard it and said – and this is what he said – "Sparks, hell! They're shooting at us!" I mean, you seen a Fourth of July fireworks celebration, you measure that by thousands of times, and that's what was coming up at us.

Then the red light came on, and that was to get us ready and stand up, hook up and everything and we got up and we weren't even hooked up yet, and the green light came on. Lieutenant Ramsey told the crew chief, "We're still over water. We can't jump!" So we waited until we got over land and then we went out...

After we hit the ground, we didn't know where in the world we were at. They shot down 23 of our own troops, the Navy and stuff shot down 23 planes. We didn't know where in the world we were and I landed on the side of a tree and fell down and it knocked me out for just a while. But anyway [it was] long enough that the planeload had already assembled, and we didn't know who else was around.

When I got up and got out of my harness and everything I – everybody was gone. I couldn't hear nobody. It was kind of up on a little hill and it was a grape orchard, and I could hear vehicles down at the bottom and I went down there and laid down in the ditch and a couple came by and I said, the moon was still shining, I said, "I know those are American," what we call a six-by-six, our main trucks we had in World War II, and I said, "The next one that comes by I'm going to stop it." And before he got to me I saw a red cross flag on the front bumper waving and I stepped out the road hollering, "Halt!"

They stopped, and I told the two fellas in the cab I was an American paratrooper and I just jumped and I hurt my back. He said, "Okay, can you get up in the back of the truck?" I said, "I think so." They said, "Well, be careful. We got several injured German soldiers back there on stretchers." That was my first experience. They told me they were on the way to what we call a field evacuation hospital. I went there and when the doctors saw me they just taped my back up from my buttocks up and told me I could go back and join my outfit.

But anyway, right there at that hospital they had taken a bulldozer and pushed a long strip, it was about, I guess, twenty or thirty yards and probably three or four feet deep and down in there they had dug with a shovel a place just big enough to put a human being in to bury him. In there, those that they hadn't covered up yet, they were in mattress covers and what they did, they, on the dog tags, they buried with the body and also they [were] taking a fifty caliber shell casing and put the paper, the information and stuff on that and crimped the end of it and put that under the armpit and buried them. Then they, on the cross, they put one of the other dog tags and that was the way they buried our soldiers and that was the first I saw [of dead men].

And then the next morning my unit wasn't too far from there and a truck came in with wounded and I got on that and joined back up with headquarters and the Mortar Platoon. ... There was so much turmoil and everything, I just went right along with them. I asked Lieutenant Ramsey, I said, "Lieutenant Ramsey, you think there would be any possibility of me staying with the company." He said, "Let's go and talk to the colonel." We went over there and he knew that he had lost half the platoon and 23 of our planes were shot down between the two battalions. I told him what I wanted and he said, "I'll be happy to have you. I'll transfer you in on a field order and when we get back to North Africa we'll make it permanent."

That's how I joined the Mortar Platoon and Headquarters Company, Second Battalion.[23]

He Died of a Broken Heart: The Men of HQ/2 and the Crash of 32918

The left engine was flaming on the wing. The plane was losing altitude, but thankfully it was not rapidly going down. Earl Levitt heard someone say they had to jump. They were at only 450 feet altitude. One of the men was shot in the door as he tried to exit. Earl Levitt made it to the door and was swallowed whole into the blackness of the night. His parachute jolted open. The last man in their stick – Miles Houser – threw the wounded paratrooper out of the door so he would not be killed when the plane went down.

Levitt hit the ground with a thud. Frenchy Harview landed some 20 feet away. A German machine gunner, picking out the white-panels of Levitt's parachute gently reflecting the moonlight, fired his machine gun at Levitt's parachute. They landed only 100 yards from a German tank park. Harview and Levitt argued about who should take out the German machine gun. John Magee, who had landed a few feet from the two, ran over. "You know that was Bartow's plane, don't you?" he asked Levitt. "Yeah. I know, John," he replied.

Just before the men had taken off for Sicily, Technician 5th Grade Richard O. Bartow had come running up to Earl Levitt. Bartow took off his watch and gave it to Levitt. "Here," he said, "you need to wear this."[24]

In The Air

The planes of the 53rd Troop Carrier Squadron were able to keep in a good formation as they flew through the light haze over Sicily, after crossing the coast near Pozzallo. Lieutenant Gerald Parker, a co-pilot in the 53rd TCS, remembered that "we encountered a little firepower before we made landfall, and the search lights in our eyes made formation flying more difficult." Flying in the same V-of-V as Lieutenant Parker was Flight Officer John Ehnot, who was piloting C-47 #32918. Ehnot's plane was originally supposed to carry three officers and fifteen men from HQ/2. Two of the three officers who were to jump from the plane were First Lieutenants Hubert H. Washburn and William P. Jordan, the two parachuting physicians serving the men of the 2nd Battalion. Shortly before the paratroopers were going to embark on their crusade in Sicily, a man came up.

"Doctor Jordan," he asked.

"Yes," replied the physician.

The man told him that there were already two doctors jumping from the plane, and that he needed to find another aircraft. Doctor Washburn would remain with the plane.[25] Doctor Jordan's open slot on the jump manifest was filled by 1st Lieutenant Mack C. Shelly, the battalion's operations officer.

As the 53rd TCS formation approached the mountains at Medica, the white tops were reflecting the bright moonlight, and were clearly visible. Gerald Parker was watching Flight Officer Ehnot's plane, when he observed a bright flash from Ehnot's aircraft. The plane soared up through the air, gaining altitude. Parker watched, hoping Ehnot could roll out and head back the opposite way and land the plane. After flying a couple miles, Ehnot's plane rolled and dove back down, tumbling through the air, crashing. Parker later wrote:

I don't know if Ehnot was hit on the way in or not but from my position in the formation I think he hit one of the white mountain tops as we tried to clear them. The moonlight made the mountain tops quite visible. At any rate it was a horrendous crash. He seemed to bounce off of the mountain top and do a loop hitting the ground... After the first drop in Sicily we had donuts and coffee and everyone said it was a piece of cake. After the second mission we were very somber and they gave each pilot a bottle of whiskey. I was too young to drink so I put mine in my barracks bag. I don't know if the crew chief and radio operator received one too or not. Edgar Lanning stuttered a little and when he saw me he said, "How how did di did you get ba back so so soon?" He thought I had been the one that crashed.

Lieutenant Carl Patrick was riding in another C-47 of the three-plane formation. His thoughts immediately turned to his good friend Lieutenant Mack Shelley, who was the jumpmaster of the stick. "Poor old Shelley," Patrick thought as the plane went down. Patrick witnessed the plane explode when it hit the ground. "Imagine my surprise," Patrick later wrote, "when over a year later, Shelly came walking into my office at Parachute School."[26]

As the plane began to fall, Lieutenant Mack C. Shelley had the stick stood up and hooked up and ready to jump. He was standing at the tail end of the plane inside the open door when the nose of the plane hit. The next thing Shelley knew, he was in the branches of a tree with no idea how he got there. When the nose of the plane came down, the impact tossed him clear out of the door and into the tree. "I was carried away from the aircraft by Italian famers," Shelly later wrote, "who returned me to the aircraft the following morning; after finding no signs of life, I was taken by them to a hospital in Modica. The farmers told me I was the only one left alive."[27]

Twenty-one men perished in the crash. From the 504th PIR they were: Robert Barnes, Richard Bartow, Charles Clevenger, Newton Crane, Russell DeVore, John Durham, Adrian Fillion, John Guba, Alex Hardridge, Hugh Henderson, Henry Kobak, Joseph Kopstein, Delmar Morrow, Clarence Schwark, Wilbert Sheffield, Clinton Stevenson and Hubert Washburn. From the 53rd Troop Carrier Squadron, the killed were: Arnold Froom, John Ehnot, Albert Singleton, and Vernon Best.

John Guba of HQ/2 was killed in the plane crash. (John Guba)

Each one of those 21 men had a unique story. The pilot, John Ehnot, was from Pennsylvania coal country where he worked in the mines before the war like his father. "He was so happy to be in the Air Corps and not working in a coal mine," fellow pilot Gerald Parker remembered. Parker can remember his poor grammar and annunciation, probably tracing back to his time in the mines. "He didn't have the English teacher I had, let's put it that way... but a very nice person," Parker remembered. The co-pilot, Arnold Froom, was only with the squadron a short time before they left the States and had graduated in Flight School Class 43-B, from which the squadron had gotten almost all their co-pilots. He had recently been married to, as Parker remembered, "a beautiful wife... Quite a few of them were getting married at graduation. He was just a real nice person."[28]

Robert Barnes was a member of HQ/2 killed in the plane crash. (Steve Barnes)

    One of the most fascinating men who lost his life in the crash was Joe Kopstein. Born into a Jewish family in New York City, Kopstein grew up speaking German, Hebrew and English, which was a great asset when he arrived at the 504th Parachute Infantry Regiment after Jump School. But his journey into the Army was even more unique than most. Perhaps his feature in the *Prop-Blast* describes his background best, "He took a trip to Palestine, stayed and learned Arabic and Hebrew. As a result, he became liaison man between the Arabs and Jews and was a correspondent for Reuter's for a short period." Due to his unique background and language proficiency, he was immediately put into the Regimental Intelligence Section before being transferred to the 2nd Battalion's Headquarters Company. Later, he himself became first a reporter for, and then the editor for, the *Prop-Blast*. In his column for the February 1943 issue, he wrote:

In Europe, strongly entrenched behind deep fortifications, lies the bulk of the Nazi Whermacht. We'll have to go in and dig them out. The Japs with their string of Naval and air bases are strongly dug in in the south Pacific. We are going to have to go in and dig them out and only a small island in the Solomons took six months to conquer.

But we are still the guys who are going to have to do the fighting and do the dying. All of the newspaper victories won't do it for us. The man with the bayonet on the end of his gun will still have to do the job when the chips are down – forward a step – fire a shot – and forward again. Let's go!!!![29]

Little did he know, but five months later he would be the one to do the dying for the routing of the Nazi Whermacht.

Another of the killed, Staff Sergeant Clinton Stevenson, came from a family of Naval service. Before the regiment shipped to Africa, he was the last member of the family to be in the United States still. His father was in the Navy, his mom was a Navy nurse, and all of his sisters were Navy nurses. He had one younger brother, who wanted to be a Marine. Each of the 21 men had their own, unique life stories to be told.

Telegrams

Throughout World War II, families of slain paratroopers were notified in a way which was cold - telegrams. It was a simple few sentences, "The Secretary of War desires me to offer his deep regret…" It was a simple, short message sent over a wire which changed lives and families forever. There was no knock on the door, no chaplain present for comfort, many times just a small boy wearing a Western Union uniform delivering news which would tear the hearts of mothers, fathers, brothers, sisters and friends.

At the Pere Marquette Translation in Michigan, William H. O'Brien, Sr. was sitting at his old wooden desk in the train station, where he had worked for years, as the telegram machine clicked and clacked out messages coming across the wire. When one message was finished recording, he gave a long still pause. He went home to his wife with the telegram which read, "Mrs. Leta O'Brian the Secretary of War desires that I tender his deepest sympathy to you in the loss of your son, Pvt. William H. O'Brien, Jr. The report states he was killed in action on the 12th day of July in the North African area. Ulio, the Adjunct General." For Mr. O'Brian, unlike others, no delivery boy was needed to tell him that his son was killed in Sicily while serving as a paratrooper in the 504th.

In the small industrial town of Georgiana, Alabama, a young boy, with a telegram in hand, rapped on the door of the Joyner household. The news the young boy would deliver would change the lives forever of the people residing in the house. The telegram read, "The Secretary of War desires me to express his deep regret that your son, Private First Class Rufus A. Joyner was killed in action on nine July…"

When Private First Class Wilbert Sheffield was donning his parachute on July 11, and preparing to jump into Sicily, there was no way he knew that two days earlier his half-brother Rufus Joyner had been killed in the Pacific Theater. And there was no way he could have known that he too would only have hours left to live. As a member of the 2nd Battalion's Headquarters Company, Wilbert Sheffield was one of the fifteen enlisted men and three officers who perished in the crash of 32918. It was only two days after the news of Rufus Joyner's death came that notification of Wilbert Sheffield's death in Sicily while serving with the 504th came to the household. The young man who had delivered the first telegram was selected to carry the second one to the Joyner household, but he just couldn't do it and refused.

At 13-years-old when the two notifications came, James Joyner could remember happier times. While Wilbert and Rufus were half-brothers, they were very close and when Rufus was drafted, Wilbert voluntarily enlisted because he didn't want his older brother to go alone. Wilbert knew he wanted to be a paratrooper, and young James could remember his half-brother going out in shorts and bare feet to do calisthenics in the front of the house to get ready for Jump School. Their father lived a while longer before he passed away; the doctor told the family that he had "died of a broken heart."[30]

Telegrams to the families of the 21 men killed in the crash rocked families across the United States. One of the telegrams also rocked the Durham household. Private First Class John Chesley Durham, the only son in the family, was born in Lamont, Iowa on July 7, 1919. Killed four days after his 24th birthday, PFC Durham was one of the oldest men to perish in the crash. "When John died, his life was turned around," recalls Richard Mark, nephew of PFC Durham, about John's father. And on the night of July 11, 1943, he died on the inside with the passing of his son. In his later years, Durham's father went to live with young Richard Mark and his mother Dorthy, PFC Durham's sister. Even the slightest mention of World War II was "forbidden" in the household, and even the minor instances where the war, or PFC Durham, was mentioned "he cried. He could never get through it."[31]

Walter Hutkins of Company H fought alongside Lieutenants Ferrill and Watts and lost his eye while they were engaging a large column of the Hermann Goring Panzer Division, which would become the nemisis of the 504th PIR during World War II (Donald Zimmerman)

2

I'LL WALK ON BLOODY STUMPS FIRST

Timeline – The 504th PIR, 82nd Airborne Division on Sicily

July 9 – 3/504 parachutes into Sicily

July 11 – HQ-HQ/504, 1/504 & 2/504 parachutes into Sicily

July 17 – the 504th PIR moves to Agrigento

July 20 - Sergeant Moorehead helps capture Sciacca

July 20 - Baldino, Hirsch & Gaygan are wounded

July 21 – fighting at Tumminello

July 23 – Castellammare falls to 2/504

July 24 – the Italian 208th Costal Division surrenders to Colonel Tucker in Alcamo

July 29 – 504th PIR occupies the area round Castelventrano

August 19 – 504th PIR is flown back to Africa to refit and absorb replacements

---

Colonel Tucker began gathering his scattered regiment on the outskirts of Gela, and his half-organized unit moved to Agrigento on July 17. Many paratroopers were still fighting with other Allied units across the entire invasion front. Private Howard L. Gregory, for example, had ditched his jump suit and exchanged it for a Canadian corporal's uniform while he was fighting his own war with Canadian troops whom he had met after landing in the wrong area. When he returned to the regiment wearing the Canadian uniform, his superiors were less than impressed.

Those paratroopers who had made it to the collection points and made their way to Agrigento were being positioned to advance up the cost of Sicily. On July 18, they were moved to Realmonte, from which point the 504th would spearhead a drive up Highway 115. Starting out on the 19th, the regiment had its first contact with enemy troops when a small skirmish erupted in the vicinity of Ribera. That day alone, the regiment had advanced nearly 30 miles. During the five days between July 17 and July 22, the men of the 504th Parachute Infantry advanced some 150 miles, the overwhelming majority of it done on foot. With the summer Mediterranean sun beating down on the men, it was a challenging accomplishment showcasing the human endurance and physical capacity of the men. After their rigorous training at Fort Bragg, the men were stewing to get into the fight. They had trained long and hard in the States for just such a maneuver as the Sicilian costal drive. They would advance with full combat equipment through the pine forests of Fort Bragg at no less than a 15 minute per mile pace.[32] Sometimes they would march through the woods for upwards of 20 miles, with the nearly 32-year-old Colonel Tucker at the front setting the pace. On one march, the 3rd Battalion even incorporated crossing McKellar's Pond, some 100 yards wide, during the frigid North Carolina temperatures of November 1942. There was grumbling, but with the prodding of officers the men waded into the bone-chilling waters behind then-Major Leslie Freeman.[33]

Almost every day during training, they would run with full equipment for three to five miles. The men were proud of their physical prowess, which tended to be at a higher level compared to that of the normal infantryman of the era. The 504th's parachutists, as a unit, were clocked at a rate of 135 steps per minute, compared to a normal infantry unit of that era, which marched 120 steps a minute.[34] Their job, as light airborne infantry with no trucks or jeeps, demanded such abilities; and they were paying their dividends during the march up the coast of Sicily. "In our three-day non-stop push up the coast of Sicily," Edwin Decker wrote, "many were forced to fall out from fatigues and worn out feet. We all urged 'Red' Curtis to fall out as he was in terrible agony with his feet. He responded with, 'I'll walk on bloody stumps first.'"[35] For many a blistered foot inside stiff Corcoran jump boots, it was one bloody footstep after another under the beating of the Mediterranean sun. Captain Adam Komosa observed, "They prayed for the enemy tanks to make a stand so that they could stop and fight – and rest. For five days and nights this continued…"[36]

The five-day marathon of the 504th Parachute Infantry Regiment up the western coast of Sicily is filled with many small yet intriguing stories and anecdotes which are due mention.

Roy Hanna 3/504 LMG Platoon

As the paratroopers made their way up the coast they met very little resistance; most of the enemy soldiers they faced were Italians with some German advisors. Sometimes the Italians would fire a few shots, and then wave white flags in surrender. Many times the surrender would be en mass with Italian troops surrendering by the hundreds. Often times, the paratroopers didn't even take the time to disarm their new prisoners, nor guard them. Roy Hanna, because they were not even bothering to disarm the Italians, felt that such a gesture was "insulting" to the Italian army. They would just send them streaming back towards the rear as the paratroopers continued their lighting advance up the coast.

Occasionally, they would stop for short breaks. "We walked many miles in the hot sun around Sicily," said Hanna. "I remember sitting down alongside of Sgt. [William H.] White during a break. He had taken his boots off and changed socks because the ones he had been wearing were covered with blood from broken blisters. He was flat-footed (didn't know one could become a paratrooper if flat-footed) and, I assumed, that this is why all the blood."[37]

The Italian civilians they met along the way were jubilant at the arrival of the Americans. Sicily, a crossroads to Italy, had been the subject of military invasions almost since the beginning of mankind. To them, being conquered was almost a norm, and some of them felt that they would be annexed into the United States of America. They often had young children following their column as they advanced, and Hanna was able to get a shave and a haircut from them for the price of one penny because General Patton declared that the lire would be worth one penny in American money stating that any other money exchange would be too complicated for his soldiers.

At the time, the 504th Parachute Infantry Regiment, and the 82nd Airborne Division at large, was fighting under General George S. Patton's 7th Army. Roy Hanna had his first view of the famed General Patton as the regiment was moving across Gela to begin their marathon up the coast.

We were on both sides of the road when he come through, and these poor little Italians with one of their little mules and this poor rascal just tried to cross the road when Patton come through in his car standing up in the back all spit and polish. I had a lot of respect for Patton, but he was a show-off. He always dressed up, but had a crop in his hand, standing up in the back – no windows, it was open – and this poor Italian and his little mule and his big two wheeler crossed the road right in front of him. Of course his driver stopped. "Shoot that God-dammed mule and get him out of here!" Well, whoever the troops were along the side just sort of picked up the mule and the cart and pushed them off the road and off he went.[38]

Edmund Moorehead Captures Sciacca

Sergeant Edmund Moorehead was a sickly child who grew up in Michigan. Moorehead, who had a heart condition which prevented him from going to school as a young boy, would sit at the town square with "all the unemployed old men in the park and listened to their WWI stories and family problems, etc. Seems all agreed that medals were only worth less than a dollar at the hock shop. As a teen I saw these medals gathering dust in the hock shop windows." Despite these problems, he was a very smart young man. "He knew more than you'd think he would," Marvin Courtney, who was in Moorehead's squad, recalled. Courtney recalled that Moorehead was a skilled player at checkers and chess, and he taught Courtney how to play the games. "I haven't lost many games since then," Courtney said. Despite being extremely smart, Moorehead never had the lack of a strong work ethic.

Many of the men in their platoon had graduated Parachute School together in Class 22, which graduated on July 4, 1942. While in Parachute school, Moorehead was introduced to Edwin Decker during hand-to-hand combat training. "When I first met Ed," Moorehead later wrote, "he seemed quite old to me at 20 years of age to his 29 years. We were paired off of do some wrestling. My first words were, 'I'll take it easy on you old man.' Little did I realize then that he was the strongest man in the 504th, 82nd Airborne. I grabbed his arm but couldn't move it. Ed just stood with the same smile he had when I said the above words. I took the other arm but couldn't move either of Ed's arms. I grabbed his throat and he just pushed his belly and I fell flat on my back. I smiled at my stupidity at him with great respect and asked his name."[39]

This was only the beginning of a storied friendship that bonded them together like no two people could be. A short time later, their bond was welded even stronger by the inferno of World War II; it was a bond that was extended to their families even after the war.

By 0600 on the 20th of July, Decker and Moorehead, along with the rest of their 504th PIR, began marching along Highway 115 to the coastal town of Sciacca. The leading elements had reached the town by 0930, but were slowed by a demolished bridge and a minefield.

The town was heavily defended. Captain Adam Komosa stated that "there were many formidable pill boxes, some of which were three stories high with basements. There were one or two on every hill and in places where they could command the roads, all of them were expertly camouflaged and surrounded by double apron wire."[40] Despite these fortifications, the town was captured with hardly a shot fired.

Sergeant Edmund Moorehead explains how this was accomplished:

We were marching two days and two nights without sleep. I stopped the men and tanks, spotting a fresh mine, of which I ordered my point on leaving once more to warn of the field… I approached a small town that had only one narrow street into town; there was no way around this town. The sea on the left and a high ridge of mountain on my right. I saw only Italian soldiers [wearing] gray moving into the buildings. I stopped the men and tanks as I decided to become a 'token' for the Italians. I ordered my point not to follow me; as I entered the narrow street and with my Thompson Sub Machine Gun slung over my shoulder, I walked some 40 yards into the center of the circle town center.

It was a few minutes, when no shots were fired at me, did I use some 30 words in Italian that I learned just the three days before we were ordered into C-47s to fly and jump onto Sicily behind the lines, which of course was a military disaster for the 504 as our own Navy shot down some 24 of our C-47s... It was my first public speaking attempt where I told loudly the Italians that we Americans do not want to fight Italians – only Germans. I urged them to give up saying and pointing to my rear that we had many Italian-American paratroopers who will not fight Italian soldiers. This was repeated as more Italians came to all windows... After some 10 minutes I urged the Italians to come to me and celebrate the end of the war between Italy and the USA. It worked, Italian soldiers rushed to me dropping their arms, some 1,200 soldiers.[41]

Marvin Courtney, one of the men in Moorehead's squad, recalled all the Italian soldiers they captured. "We were marching them back four abreast," he said, "and you couldn't see the end of them."[42]

Company A Sustains First Casualties of the War

After moving through Sciacca in the afternoon, the 1st Battalion was on their way to Menfi. Having been the leading element to jump on the night of the friendly fire disaster, Company A was not badly dispersed, and they suffered no casualties thus far in the operations on Sicily, although several of their men were still listed as missing while fighting with other units.

On the ride to Menfi, Fred Baldino's platoon from A Company was being trucked. As they rode on the deuce-and-a-halves, a group of German ME-109s came screaming overhead, strafing the trucks. It was here that A Company suffered their first casualties when Fred Baldino was wounded in the right arm, and both Joe Hirsch and James Gaygan were wounded severely and evacuated to the States.[43]

James Sapp Parachute Maintenance

Although technically a member of the Parachute Maintenance Section, James Sapp was still traveling with the 2nd Battalion's 81mm Mortar Platoon. While they were racing up the coast, he also got a personal view of the famed General Patton around the 18th or 19th of July.

It was hot. It was July – it was like south Florida! We were walking, we didn't have any transpiration and like I say, we'd have a little battle and Italians would surrender and we'd go again.

We were all exhausted about lunch-time and we fell out on either side of the road and Colonel Yarborough was our battalion commander and we saw this Dodge command car coming and we saw the flag waving on the front. We knew it was a general, we didn't know how many stars. It got up closer, we saw two stars and it got a little closer and we saw General Patton was standing up. He had the windshield down on that Dodge command car and he was standing up and he had those riding britches and had those two .45's on and had a driver and he had a body guard in the back. Colonel Yarborough was right, he wasn't three, four or five steps from where I was at and he jumped up to attention – none of the rest of us got up at any time.

General Patton had a shill voice and the first thing he said, "Who's in command here?" Colonel Yarborough said, "I am, sir." And he said, "Don't you know military courtesy?" And he said, "Yes, sir." He said, "The next time you see me, if you don't call your men to attention and show me some military courtesy, I'll relieve you of your command." He said, "Yes, sir." And that was the end of that.

He wanted to know what was going on and the situation and then he told the driver, "Let's go." They turned around and went back down the road. Different things like that happened.[44]

The day of July 20 was an eventful one. Sergeant Moorehead captured Sciacca and Baldino, Hirsch, and Gaygan were wounded by the strafing ME-109s on the way to Menfi.

Once the main body of the regiment was able to negotiate Sciacca, the 2nd Battalion, meanwhile, turned north on the San Margherita Road at Sciacca while the 1st and 3rd Battalions of the 504th Parachute Infantry marched on Menfi. The 2nd Battalion's objective was to reach Tumminello, just south of San Margherita. They were delayed by minefields, and that night stopped some five miles short of Tumminello Pass. The advance of July 20th took the regiment a distance of 20 miles, an overwhelming majority done on foot, and they were credited with taking 1,000 prisoners at the cost of three casualties – Baldino, Hirsch, and Gaygan.

It was in the early morning on the 21st when a thick summer flog sat down on top of the grassy, low-rolling hills stretching on either side of the road as the 2nd Battalion continued north. The fog was so thick, the men could hardly see in front of them, nor those low-rolling farm fields on either side of them. To the left, the farmland continued to gently slope away from the road, but as they continued north, the earth to the right of the road gradually rose around them until they were approaching a small valley of low, rocky hills whose pockmarked white rock faces bore witness to the traffic which crisscrossed through the small pass. Two major highways – one running north-south and another running east-west – crossed each other in between the two small rock masses. The place was marked as "Tumminello" on the map.

Moving through the fog, Colonel Yarborough's men were marching in double file at close interval. As they approached the Tumminello Pass, the Italian outpost saw the paratroopers and fled the scene; while this was normal behavior for Italian troops, Yarborough was failing to recognize an aberration. There was a tank trap set up on the road. Captain Adam Komosa explains the way the Italians made their traps: "Tank traps approximately 15' x 8' x 10' with 12" spikes in the bottom were dug across the road. They were camouflaged with cross pieces placed over the tops of the pits, callahan matting or burlap placed on the crosspieces and strewn with dirt. The Italians apparently learned this trick from the natives in the Ethiopian campaign. No vehicles to my knowledge have been caught by these ingenious traps."[45]

During the trek through Sicily, the men of the 2nd Battalion 81mm Mortar Platoon captured these small Italian "Tankquettes" and rode them for a short time, until they broke down. (James Sapp)

As the battalion continued through the fog, F Company was ambushed and a sharp battle erupted. William Mullikin had a bullet pass through his helmet, but it miraculously did not kill him. The Germans had an artillery piece hidden inside a cave in the pass, and a piece of shrapnel wounded Mullikin in the shoulder. He recovered fully and returned to the company just three days later.[46] He was lucky – seven others were wounded and six paratroopers from F Company were killed. One of the killed was Private Edward Coen of Pittsburg, Pennsylvania. That fateful day of July 21 was his 25th birthday.

Colonel Yarborough ordered the men to fix bayonets, and they charged the Italian positions in the caves and rocks, built into the cliffs which stretched some 250 feet in the air. Most of the Italians surrendered, including an Italian colonel, a battery of 75mm guns and two 90mm guns.

James Sapp relates his view of events on July 21 at Tumminello Pass while with the 81mm Mortar Platoon:

Two roads met and went through a pass and the name of that pass was Tumminello Pass. So when we got there, we were close enough to that pass, the Mortar Platoon they [had] us right in the fork when we went through the pass, they had an artillery, anti-tank gun or something. We could see the blast. They called for mortar fire and we set up the mortars and we had that thing almost straight up.

They had caves on each side of that pass in the mountain and they fired. Anyway, they surrendered and then Colonel Yarborough, he didn't go through that pass. He stopped and set up a defense. Shortly after that, General Ridgeway came up. He wanted to know why in the world he stopped. He said, "You didn't know to go through the pass instead of stopping before you went through it?"[47]

They continued on, and that night the battalion stopped and occupied Sambuca.

That night, the rest of the 504th Parachute Infantry marched on St. Marguerita, completing their marathon. Their march had taken them some 150 miles. The men were exhausted and dirty. The soles of their jump boots were worn, weathered, and turned off-white with a dusting of the Sicilian soil married to the once brown, shiny leather.

Colonel Yarborough at Castellammare & Alcamo

Lieutenant Colonel William P. Yarborough was one of the founding fathers of the airborne forces of the United States. As a captain in the 501st Parachute Battalion – the Army's first parachute infantry battalion – he had designed the parachutist wings, which are still in use today, and the now famous Corcoran jump boots which the men were so proud of that if they caught someone wearing them who was not a paratrooper they would often beat the offender, or worse.

By the time he jumped into Sicily as the commander of the 2nd Battalion, 504th Parachute Infantry Regiment, he had already participated in America's first combat jump in North Africa while with the 509th Parachute Infantry Battalion.

John Thompson, a war correspondent for the *Chicago Tribune*, followed Colonel Yarborough throughout the Sicilian campaign and described Yarborough as "a strange mixture of military proficiency and battlefield toughness and political idealism. He conceives every American soldier as an ambassador from our country and a living example of what American democracy means."[48] Thompson first met Colonel

Yarborough the morning after his battalion had jumped into Sicily under friendly fire. Yarborough's plane had been hit, and Yarborough was visibly upset about what had happened to his battalion. Thompson later wrote of the encounter, "His eyes dark with fury, his voice almost uncontrollable, Yarborough said: 'They all jumped. Every man in my plane jumped although some could hardly stand up. I haven't found them all yet, but every man jumped.' That night we did not know the full extent of the tragedy."[49]

On July 23, Colonel Yarborough led an advance party into Castellammare de Gulfo and persuaded the Italian commander there to surrender his forces. Captain Adam Komosa described the situation, "The defenses were strong. The shore line was rocky and sharp; all beaches were mined. Costal guns were covered by small arms and automatic weapons; all approaches were covered, except those inland. The defenses were all pointing out to the sea. The approach to Castellammare was a winding road on the face of a steep bluff. An anti-fascist reported this road as being prepared for demolition. He disclosed the position of the charges before they could be blown… Had this road been demolished, Castellammare would not have been accessible by vehicle."[50]

Daun Rice, John Fowler, and Frank Cole of Company H eat and pose for a photograph in Sicily. Rice would be killed in action while fighting in Holland in September 1944. Fowler would be severly wounded a few days after Rice's death. (US Signal Corps)

The situation on Sicily was favorable. Palermo, some 25 miles to the east of Castellammare, had fallen. What little resistance the Italians could have put up was broken. On July 24, the commanding general of the Italian 208th Costal Division surrendered to Colonel Reuben Tucker in Alcamo, a short distance to the southeast of Castellammare.[51]

The occupation, rounding up of Italian prisoners and general policing of Castellammare and Alcamo became the responsibility of Lieutenant Colonel Yarborough until the arrival of the American Military Government; a military organization set up to govern areas recently liberated – and then passed by – by combat troops.

In Castellammare, Yarborough learned of a woman who had been imprisoned by the fascists for nearly 20 years without a trial. In another nearby village, there were 25 children, all under the age of 12, who had been in prison for five months for petty crimes, also with no trial. In one of the villages Yarborough was tasked to police, he found a local jail where the majority were political prisoners, who were jailed with no trial. "Through my interpreter," Yarborough described, "I stepped into the courtyard and addressed the prisoners, their faces pressed against the bars and their arms dangling through the bars. I told them American justice had come to Sicily, that each man's case would be examined by our officials, that those jailed for political offenses against fascism would be freed, and that violations of criminal law would be given a fair trial."[52]

The companies patrolled the villages and countryside, rounding up straggling Italians, and other general policing duties while the American Military Government was being established. James Sapp remembered one episode:

We were like police duty, you know. We went in pairs of twos and we were gone about four hours then off, and we had to be on at night and stuff too. There was this one Italian and he could speak English just as good as we could; didn't have an accent or anything, and we got to be friends with him and there was an orchard right at the edge of town. It had all kinds of fruit trees in it and that's where we were bivouacked. We were in pup tents, so this guy he, we befriended him, and he wanted us to come have breakfast with him one morning and we asked him, you know, where he learned such good English. He said, "I used to live in Chicago. I got deported." We found out later the Mafia came from Sicily...

I never have been a drinker of anything. They drink wine over there like it was, like we drink tea. So they poured like a tea glass of wine for each one of us for breakfast. I drank that glass of wine with my breakfast. I think we got off at seven o'clock or something like that. Well anyway, right after we got relived we went back to bivouac and the next thing that I remember it was about twelve or one o'clock. I woke up and in that orchard they had fig trees and everything in there, and I woke up and there was children and ladies and all that gathered there and stuff, and I only had on my shorts. Like I said, I never drank anything. Anybody that was used to drinking, that wine wouldn't affect them, but I passed out with that little glass of wine. I was really embarrassed.[53]

This type of duty was not exclusive to Colonel Yarborough's battalion. After a few days, around July 29, the regiment was moved south to Castelventrano for more policing duties, and then a rest period.

Jim Gaygen was the frist paratrooper from A Company to be wounded in combat during World War II, during the attack of the ME-109s on July 20. (Roger Mokan)

Marvin Courtney remembered they spent a couple days combing the countryside trying to see if they could find anyone "hid out." Everything was clear, and the men began settling into the area as July turned to August, and the dry heat persisted. Typically, the men bivouacked in pup tents, which were two shelter halves put together. Thus, with each man carrying one half of a tent, two men would put their olive drab canvas pieces together and bunk for the night. In their area, there were lots of discarded paracord, which had formed the suspension lines of their parachutes. The men got busy being creative, and constructing hammocks to hang from the small trees in the olive orchard they were bivouacked in. The men began hanging their hammocks up to bed in for the night. "Lay in that hammock," Courtney recalled of their idea, "everything going along good. It got really quiet about midnight and you hear one of them hammocks break. That hammock broke and this guy hit the ground on his back. Man he let out a big bunch of curse words. You'd think well that's the end of it. A few minutes more [another one fell]; it just kept getting worse."[54]

The 2nd Battalion eventually settled in the village of Partanna, where the battalion staff took over a huge castle atop of a hill. The Grifeo Partanna Castle was built in 1076. When the paratroopers moved into the castle to set up their command post, it was not the first time the castle had been host to soldiers. After Ruggero the Norman conquered Partanna and built the castle in 1076, he used the castle to help defeat Arab invaders. In the main doorway, there is a sculpture of Prince Grifeo, who once occupied the castle, which was made by the famous Italian sculptor Francesco Laurana in 1468. Inside, beautiful frescos adorned the walls.[55]

Due to his troublesome knee, injured during the jump, Lieutenant Chester Garrison was relieved of his rifle platoon and appointed as the adjunct for the battalion. As he was now on the staff, he moved into the castle with the rest of the headquarters. "I had my bedroll on a stone terrace that was wonderfully suited for the night-walking scene of Hamlet's father's ghost in Shakespeare's play. The low crenelated wall was high above the orchards beyond, and the stars shone in the smogless sky. In the overwhelming quiet, the structure was shadow gray. I searched for my paperback Shakespeare in my musette bag."[56]

The regiment's fight on Sicily gave the men experience. The men had performed as they said they would, no matter if they were with their own organizations or not; whether there were hundreds of paratroopers or two. And although outside of the fighting at Tumminello Pass, sustained combat with the enemy only came in isolated incidents, the experience they did glean was valuable. Major Don Dunham wrote to his younger brother, who was training to go overseas with the 10th Mountain Division, about some of the lessons he felt were critical to survival in the combat zone. "Take my advice. Learn to walk, to shoot and take cover. When a Tiger tank aims its 88 at you, get the hell out of the way. Shoot at enemy planes only when they shoot at you but not unless he does…. We did not lose a man out of our Intelligence and

Reconnaissance Platoon, however they had armored jeeps with .50 caliber machine guns. They were fired on more than any other outfit in the division. (Dale is in Int. & Recon)."[57]

The mission in Sicily, however, left some of the men bitter and angry. The men did not see it as an overwhelming success nor a dismal failure either. Roy Hanna said after the war that he felt the mission was "poorly planned." He was far from alone in this feeling. The letter he wrote to his parents from Africa after being relieved from the isle might bring insight into what some of the men felt at the time:

Another Sunday and another very hot day. Sometimes I wonder what the people would do over there if every time we felt impressed upon we would go on a strike for higher wages. By golly sometimes we sure deserve it. However, with the cooperation of some back there and all of us over here we'll get this thing stopped somehow. I wonder why "Uncle Sam" doesn't send all the trained divisions in the States over here to help get this thing over with before the comparatively few over here fighting get killed off. I always say large numbers is better than small.

Private Fred Baldino shortly after the invasion of Sicily. (Author's Collection)

3

MAJOR DON DUNHAM AND THE REGIMENT'S ROAD TO ITALY

In Lemon Cove, California, Deloris Dunham and her two children were awaiting the safe return of their husband and father, Major Don Dunham. Major Dunham and his bride were diligent in writing letters to one another nearly every single day. To make sure no military information that could be used by the enemy was disclosed, all outgoing mail was censored by an officer whose job it was to, where appropriate, cut out parts of letters which contained potentially sensitive information such as troop movements and locations, and casualties. Major Dunham, as an officer, censored his own mail and contrary to custom wrote home about his many experiences and observations in Africa and Sicily. Don Dunham's letters home tell his story as he landed into Sicily, regrouped, made the arduous campaign up the coast, and ultimately policed and occupied Sicily for a short time before moving back to Africa to regroup and prepare for the invasion of the Italian mainland.

Major Dunham Lands in Sicily

On July 11, 1943, Major Dunham's stick of HQ-HQ Company took off from Tunisia and headed for the drop zone in Sicily. In the midst of the friendly fire disaster, the aircraft in which Major Dunham and several other officers were to parachute from into Sicily crash-landed into the Mediterranean Sea some 300 yards from the beach. The airplane broke in half, and began filling rapidly with water. The aircraft was coming under a tremendous amount of machine gun fire. One of the other officers on board was Captain Harry Cummings. When he was about to exit into the water, he saw a fellow officer who was wounded and unable to cut loose from his parachute. Captain Cummings went back inside and cut the man free enabling him to escape. The action was at the cost of his own life, when Cummings was cut down by machine gun fire. For his action, he was awarded the Distinguished Service Cross posthumously.

North Africa – July 4

We had a prop-blast party last night. We had rum and wine mixed to drink. As Jack Dempsey would say, I really took drunk. There were a few British and American nurses there – about one for every ten officers. I danced twice.

Yesterday it was 130 degrees here. We drink several gallons of water and eat lots of salt tablets every day. In case this letter beats my last two, I received your first letter addressed to APO 469. I have also mailed you a package of jewelry.

We have had our ration of cigarettes and candy but I wish you would send me some every once in a while.

I am still fine and expect to stay that way. I am definitely going when we start our operation. I thought for a while I would have to stay at our rear base. You will be able to read all about it in the papers.

There isn't much news so I shall close for now. Tell everyone hello for me and you and the kids behave yourselves.

Sicily – August 1

I have written you 2 or 3 letters but his is the first V-mail I have been able to get. I have been on Sicily for 3 weeks. I like the country better than Africa. I am OK now. I was slightly wounded in the left thumb.

The regiment was on the move for the first two weeks, but now we have been here for 4 days. I am Regimental Supply Officer now. The one that jumped was evacuated back to Africa. I have lost everything I had including your picture. My watch is ruined. I broke the crystal and salt water got into it. Please get me another like it and send it to me. Soon we may get our baggage from Africa and we should get mail any day now. I have not heard from you since we took off from Africa.

I have been in all the cities from Tunis to Casablanca. I wish this was over so I could get home again. I miss you all very much. Keep writing.

Sicily – August 4

I received 3 letters from you today and one from dad. I cannot get paper so please send this to him. I hope you enjoy the nurses and business.

I am now Reg. S-3 or plans and training officer again. I am very glad to get out of supply. There is no chance of promotion over here. I am going to try and get back into a regular infantry outfit. It may mean even taking a reduction, but I am not satisfied here. Your letter written July 10 arrived Aug. 3. I am still in good health and am enjoying Sicily very much. You have probably read about the battle in the papers. I may not be able to write often but you keep on writing every day.

Sicily – August 7

I had my picture taken on our wedding anniversary and I will send one picture in each letter for a few days to be sure that you get them. We have set up our HQ in a hotel in town. I have a room once occupied by a German general. I can tell you now that my plane was shot down – we did not jump but landed in the Mediterranean about 300 yards from shore. Most planes were able to jump their men. I had to get my name printed on this paper in order to buy it from the printer – I received my bed roll from Africa yesterday with a change of uniform. I have one wool OD and one suntan now. I am doing fine and enjoying this present place very much. We have good food with plenty of fruit and even a sort of ice cream. This is whole lot better than Africa ever was. I received about 10 letters from you, 1 from dad. I will only write to you so keep them informed. Keep writing. Tell everyone hello and give my love to the kids.

Major Don Dunham photographed in Sicily on his wedding anniversary.

Sicily – August 7

I have mailed you a picture I had made on our wedding anniversary. More will follow in each regular letter.

I am S-3 now – was S-4 for first 3 weeks of invasion. We have sort of settled down now. It is getting dark and my Italian pen does not write good enough to send V-mail. I have mailed several regular letters and two telegrams or radiograms on Aug. 5

I am alright and will always be able to take care of myself. We had quite a battle, but most of us came back OK. Keep writing.

Sicily – August 9

I am writing a V-mail letter today too and sending some pictures with this letter. I hope you get all of them and send one on to dad.

I was able to get a haircut and a shave at the barber shop today. The barbers here are much better than the French in North Africa.

We are all going to hate to leave Sicily, particularly if we have to return to Africa – the people here are very friendly and most have relatives in the US or have been there themselves. I wish I could speak Italian, but there is no use trying to learn it because we will probably be in some other country before I could master the darn stuff.

I could use some good shoe polish – Kiwe or Nugget or something as good. We can't get it over here at all and I have lost mine.

Sicily – August 9

Only main highways paved and they are very crooked. Going through towns we have to disconnect our trailers making a turn from one street into another, as streets are so narrow, average 14 feet some as narrow as 5 feet. All towns are built on hills, orange trees are beautiful, and I like it a lot better than Africa. Do not know how much longer we will be here. Towns are very crowded and filthy. Everyone has a horse, mule, or donkey and no one cleans the streets. This is the dry season and we have city water only in the mornings. We have set up our headquarters in a hotel in this city. I have a room that was occupied by a German general. He left in a hurry and left behind a lot of imported brandy and Champaign.

Sicily – August 9

I wrote you a regular mail letter today with 3 pictures – one for dad. I need V-mail forms and some good shoe polish. The first is hard to get and the second impossible.

Most of the roads are bad except for a few main highways which are about like the road to Woodlake. Going through some towns we have to dismount the trailer in order to make a turn because the streets are so narrow. Some streets are only 4 or 5 feet wide and many streets are just steps because all towns are built on hills.

I do not know how much longer we will be here or where we go from here. Just keep writing and so will I. The mail always catches up.

There isn't much more to write now. I just got a shave and haircut. The barbers here are better than those in Africa. Water is scarce so I am going 5 miles out to a river which is dammed up by a blown up bridge and take a bath.

Sicily – August 10

I can tell you now that my plane was shot down, we did not jump with parachutes, but landed in the Mediterranean about 300 yards from shore. Most planes were able to jump their men. I was hit twice with machine gun [fire] the night we came in and have the Purple Heart. Wounds have healed or nearly so, and I am back on duty. I lost all my personal belongings and salt water got in my wrist watch through broken crystal.

Jake Cantelmo of Company B writing a letter home from Fort Bragg, NC in April 1943, just days before going overseas. (Cantelmo family)

Sicily – August 11

I have sent my watch to you for repairs. None of the jewelers here could open it up – the crystal was cracked and let salt water in. It ran for two weeks before the hands rusted up enough to stop it. I hope it can be repaired.

I am sipping some very fine Italian white vermouth, a light wine made from muscat grapes. It costs $1.00 a bottle here and would cost 3 or 4 at home. I have been receiving many letters from you, dad and Dale and Dorthy. It is sure nice to hear from you. I am beginning to understand some Italian – can't talk it though.

My thumb is completely healed now, but I think a nerve was cut because there isn't any feeling in part of it. Everything is going along OK, even the weather is wonderful.

I would be glad to stay here until they send us home. Maybe Europe will be a better place – who knows? Tell Donnie I have some more coins for him which I will send soon.

Sicily – August 11

Another day has passed. We are doing routine duty. I have made an inspection trip to half our area today. Tomorrow I will cover the other half. The Germans left behind a lot of brandy and champagne when they pulled out so our people have taken it over.

I am sending another picture with this letter. There is not anything to buy for you. All they have for sale is junk and I won't buy any. I received two more letters from you today. I would like to have clippings from the papers about the invasion or at least about our part in it. Every once in a while send me some V-mail and carton of Luckies. I am glad that the things I have sent have arrived – you will like the last bracelet and broach when it comes. This is all for now – I have no V-mail.

Sicily – August 12

My B-4 bag came in today so I have all my clothes now. Still in same place. There are movies here, but old American with Italian speech so don't go to any. Wish I could speak Italian as lots of the people have been in America or have relations that are in America, and they are very friendly. I went swimming in a river that is damned up where a bridge was blown up. Gee it was swell because the only bath we get are sponge bathes out of a wash basin. I have been complimented for the job I did of supply officer that I did during the invasion. I got a shave and hair cut in a barber shop today, they are much better than the French shops in Africa. I will hate to leave Sicily if we have to return to Africa. The people here are very friendly here in Sicily.

Sicily – August 14

I am sending a German coin for Donnie and a flag for Susan. I received a letter from you and one from Dale today. Yours was dated July 25. The V-mail comes through fine.

There is no news that I can tell you. I am still fine and doing OK in my job. I have been congratulated for the job of supply that I did during the invasion.

I am sending you two copies of the menu out of a 5 in 1 ration which is 3 meals for 5 men packed in one box. After the war, it would be swell stuff to take deer hunting or on picnics. All you need is a spoon and cup to eat it. Of course a plate and coffee pot help. We also have a "K" ration which is 3 meals for one man in 3 boxes and the "C" ration which is 3 meals in 6 cans. Keep writing and sending cigarettes.

North Africa – August 24

I am enclosing an article that will be published in some magazine at home. I think that it tells the story of the first few days in Sicily. It happened hundreds of times. We had men that joined other units and stayed in the front lines as long as the unit stayed and then joined the next unit that relieved them.

Some of our men never returned to us until after the fall of Messina. Several of our units saved other ground units from being wiped out by Germans.

We are having a review today to award the medals won over on the island. I have heard that I have been recommended for one in addition to the Purple Heart for being wounded. I do not know if I will get it or not.

I must close now for I have a lot of work to do. I shall write very chance that I get. Do not worry if you fail to hear for some time.

North Africa – August 24

I have just returned to my office from seeing Bob Hope and Frances Langford in a USO show of theirs that is touring this part of the world. It was really good, but it makes me pretty home sick to hear the songs and to see a white woman again. There are some nurses over here but I never see any.

I just came back to finish this letter; I started it several hours ago. I had to go out and watch a jump by a provisional battalion which we will break up tomorrow and take into the regiment now that it has completed its training. It was a good jump with only a few minor injuries out of five hundred men jumping.

This Italian typewriter is hard to get used to. A few of the keys are different than ours and I hit the wrong key sometimes. There is no news to tell. You do not know any of the people here so I cannot tell about them.

This place is beginning to get on my nerves again. It is hot as the valley is at home and the wind blows the dust into everything. It is also quite a chore to get a bath even though it is better than when we left it for Sicily. I will be glad when we leave again. Bob Hope said tonight that it was just like a lot of Texas except that you could get out of Texas. We all hope that this time we will not have to return to Africa again. I hope that the package that you have mailed gets here soon.

Tell everyone hello for me and pass this letter on to dad because I am really pretty busy and do not get much time to write. Be a good little gal and write often. It is sure nice to get letters over here.

North Africa – September 4

The British have already invaded the toe of Italy. You probably know more about it than I do because we do not get too much news.

It will soon be time for school to start again. I guess that Donny will be glad to get back. I am all set for the job that lies ahead of me. I won't write again until after the next job is over. I feel fine and should be able to come thru this time better than the last time.

Don't worry and keep on writing. The mail is rather irregular now and it has been several days since I received any. I guess that it will catch up again sometime.

Tell everyone hello for me.

4

STRIKE HOLD: OPERATION AVALANCHE

> Timeline – 504th PIR, 82nd Airborne Division in Italy
>
> September 9, 1943 – Operation AVALANCHE begins
>
> September 11, 1943 – The 36th Division reaches Altavilla
>
> September 14, 1943 – The 504th PIR parachutes onto the beachhead
>
> September 15, 1943 – Altavilla is evacuated by the 36th Division
>
> September 15, 1943 – 3/504th PIR lands by boat onto the beachhead
>
> September 16, 1943 – HQ-HQ, 1/504th & 2/504th begin attacking Altavilla via Albanella
>
> September 17, 1943 – Germans counterattack positions of the 504th PIR
>
> September 19, 1943 – The 504th PIR is relieved from the Altavilla sector

Private Francis Keefe was riding in a truck full of paratroopers down a dusty dirt road. The heat was oppressive. Francis Keefe was one of the men in the replacement battalion who was just joining the 504th Parachute Infantry Regiment upon their return from Sicily. "They were pretty outstanding," Keefe reflected of joining the unit. "The whole regiment."[58] As the replacements had not made a parachute jump since leaving the United States on the *George Washington*, the truck they were riding down that dirt road was airfield-bound.

Soon, a sedan came down the road from the other direction, heading straight for the convoy of paratroopers. It stopped. Then the trucks stopped. Out of the sedan came Frances Langford, Bob Hope's ravishingly beautiful co-star on the tour, clad in white. Langford asked the paratroopers where they were going. They responded they were off to jump. "So you're not going to see the show?" she inquired.

While Bob Hope and Frances Langford entertained other paratroopers, the replacements jumped. For the first time, Francis Keefe jumped with his M-1 rifle fully assembled. The standard practice was to jump with the rifle disassembled into pieces, placed in a padded bag, and strapped to the jumper behind the reserve 'chute or on the leg. However, they would be jumping the rifle by holding it in the left hand, keeping the right hand on the reserve parachute in the event the ripcord needed to be pulled in an emergency. Once the main parachute opened, the paratrooper would simply raise both hands above his head to grasp the parachute risers, and the rifle suspended by the sling would fall into a shouldered position. "Later on," Keefe recalled, "you could use the gun carrier, you can put it across your chest, or you could jump with it in your hands. It was up to you. Some outfits, I guess they have regulations – you got to do this, you got to do that – not in the 504. It was the most unregulated outfit in the whole United States Army."[59]

After joining the 3rd Battalion of the 504th Parachute Infantry Regiment, most of Keefe's time in Africa had been spent in training. The battalion was detached from the regiment and sent to the coastal town of Bizerte to practice amphibious landings. During this period, Francis Keefe and some of the men were trucked about five miles from their training area for some recreational swimming. They could see a ship full of new aircraft coming in, and up above they could see the small specks of German aerial photography planes observing. *It's going to be hot in town tonight*, Keefe thought. He was right. That night, after they were trucked back to their training area, a large German air raid occurred. The searing hot shrapnel from the exploded shells of Allied anti-aircraft guns rained down on the men; some, who had larger pieces fall on them from the sky, were wounded by them.

After several different scheduled combat parachute jumps into Italy were scrapped, the 504th PIR was flown back to Sicily to be stationed at airfields on the isle. Shortly after, Francis Keefe would see his first combat with the 3rd Battalion, 504th Parachute Infantry Regiment when they landed on the Salerno beachhead by boat.

On September 9, 1943, the Allied armies commenced Operation AVALANCHE. After landing on the beaches south of Salerno, the Allied forces intended to capture and hold the hills, then break out onto the plains and turn north to capture the deep-water port of Naples. Things did not go as planned. In the American sector, the hill mass above the village of Altavilla-Silentina became a critical focal point of the fighting, and a place of great worry for General Mark Clark, the 5th Army's commanding general.

The village of Altavilla, and especially the dominating hill mass on which it rested, overlooked much of the southern invasion sector. Additionally, the village was a hub of roads and trails by which troops could be quickly transited.

The village sat on the lower slopes of the hill mass, and specifically Hill 424, which made Hill 424 the lynchpin to the village. Without control of Hill 424 and the adjacent hills, Altavilla was an untenable position. "From various points on Hill 424," a post-war Army study observed, "it was later discovered that the Germans could observe east into the upper valley of the Calore, north into the corridor between the Sele and Calore rivers, west into the valley between Altavilla and La Cosa hills, and on over those hills to the sea. The enemy had superb observation of every part of the central sector of the Salerno plain..."

Around noontime on September 11, Americans from the 36th Infantry Division, known as the "Texans" for they were a division of the Texas National Guard activated into federal service, occupied Altavilla. The following morning, the Germans infiltrated around Altavilla, attacked, and pinned a company of Texans onto the forward slope of Hill 424. Other companies from their battalion attempted to counterattack, but in a series of failed communications, the Germans cut the entire battalion in half and enveloped them, forcing them to withdraw in confusion.

At 0700 the next morning, two companies of Texans overran and occupied the Unnumbered Hill, which sat adjacent to Hill 424, and was connected to Hill 424 by a draw. Another company went in to clean up Altavilla itself. Other units failed to come on line with them, leaving their flanks exposed and venerable. When the Germans attacked them from the direction of Hill 424 in the early evening, they found this weakness and continued to press hard against the Texans. Soon, they found themselves surrounded. "The Germans," one officer in the battalion observed, "upon locating the battalion flanks and finding them unsecured, continued his counterattacks along the entire battalion front thus keeping those forces occupied and prevented the battalion commander from shifting forces to either flank to prevent an envelopment. By now it was very apparent that the battalion could not prevent the enemy from enveloping its flanks, and it was necessary to reorganize into an all-around defense to prevent attacks upon the battalion rear."[60] The Texans were cut-off.

The situation at Altavilla was not the only place of worry for the 36th Division's sector. One flank of the division had a large gap in it where no American troops existed. The journal of the 142nd Infantry described the situation as "serious."[61]

At 5th Army headquarters, plans had been drafted for a possible evacuation of the beachhead.

A Renewed Stability

On September 12, while the Texans were being surrounded in Altavilla, Sergeant William G. Hauser was laying on the Sicilian dirt beside his pup-tent, under the shade of a fig tree. Hauser was writing to his parents about how he wished for a white Christmas, and of how strange of a sensation it was that he could just put his hand up and pull down a ripe fig from the tree he was finding refuge under. He reported in his telegram a few weeks ago that he was safe and happy. As Sergeant Hauser rested under that fig tree, it was the day before his 28th birthday, and the farthest thing from his mind was making his second combat jump.

The following day, September 13, Earl Levitt was attending an Al Jolson concert when a message came across the amplifier. "504 men, report to your companies immediately," the announcer stated.[62] James Gann was also at the show. "Just before the show got started," Gann recalled, "a sergeant got up and got on the microphone. He says, 'All 504s report back to camp immediately.' We didn't know what was going on. We got back and they said, 'Get your gear together. We're fixing to make a trip.' … We got everything together, formed out and they brought trucks in and picked us up and took us down to the airstrip."[63]

Around 1500 that day, Colonel Reuben Tucker received orders to prepare his regiment to help reinforce the Salerno beachhead by parachuting onto a secured drop zone. Shortly after 2100, the C-47 aircrafts carrying parachutists of the 1st and 2nd Battalions of the 504th Parachute Infantry Regiment, along with Headquarters and Headquarters Company, began rolling down the runway. They had little idea of what to expect. "Every man has different ideas of the fear in combat," Fred Baldino explains. "We all, of course, have fears. If we didn't we would not be in the paratroops but it is a volunteer role that we all have. Some have deep fears and some not so. I had fear but I just kept going along with all of our good buddies. One guy got on the plane with the rest of us on our way to jump in Salerno, but he feigned sickness and they took him out of the plane and put him packing parachutes. No more combat for him. He is lucky they didn't court-marshal him."[64]

At approximately 2300, the formation began passing over the ruins of Paestum in their C-47s, and the men began parachuting onto the beachhead. The paratroopers – alerted only eight hours previously – began peacefully floating down onto the beachhead while the Germans looked down on the Americans from Hill 424. The paratroopers' presence sent a message – not to the Germans, but to the Americans who were hanging on – that message was one of a renewed resolve, and of renewed stability. The paratroopers moved up to the front lines that night, and were placed to fill the gap in the 36th Division lines.

In Altavilla, the Texans of the 3rd Battalion, 143rd Infantry were having a rough time. They remained cut-off and hard pressed by German counter-attacks. The Texans held out in houses converted to strongpoints. When some of them ran out of ammunition, they threw rocks. Under darkness on the night of September 15, they were forced to evacuate in small groups. They had to leave their wounded and dying, and their brave battalion surgeon, Captain Krata, volunteered to stay with the wounded. They were captured by the Germans that night.

The Tide of Battle Turns

Down below, a cloud of fog drifted across the beach as men drudged up the sand. The 3rd Battalion of the 504th was landing by boat onto the Salerno beachhead. Also with these paratroopers was the famed war reporter Richard Tregaskis, who would remain with the 504th PIR for several days and experience first-hand one of the regiment's most significant contributions to the Second World War: the 504th PIR would assail the hills above Altavilla, and they would hold them. The actions which Tregaskis would bear witness to are an epic like which few other military organizations can boast. With a notice of only eight hours, Tucker's regiment was successful in equipping for, planning for, and executing a combat parachute assault and then following that up with decisive, offensive action just a few days later. It is an exemplary display of combat readiness.

On September 16, the 1st and 2nd Battalions of the 504th Parachute Infantry began the effort to take Hill 424. After making a long, arduous march to the village of Albanella, the battalions crossed the line of departure and headed down the backcountry trails towards Altavilla and Hill 424. With no ability for leaders' reconnaissance, and even a grossly insufficient number of maps, the paratroopers began the journey at dusk, down narrow trails which led through small valleys and gullies lined with grape arbors and other crops.

Accompanying the paratroopers were two war reporters looking for a story. They were Richard Tregaskis of the International News Service and Seymour Korman of the *Chicago Tribune*. They found Colonel Reuben Tucker and his advance CP group. Seymour Korman remembered Colonel Tucker explaining his general plan of attack:

The colonel explained and pointed to that fateful hill some five miles away in a straight line, but more than ten miles over the rock terrain. Low ground to the northeast gave it a saddle effect and it was by that saddle we had to mount in a flanking movement. "I've got two battalion units heading up there and this headquarters company has to meet them," he continued. "We've got to get there before daylight, or else the Jerry will pick us off like ducks on the low ground on this side. And there's no certainty he won't be picking us off the same way even if we're on the hill."

I told him I had seen a jeep crew laying wire for communications, but that it would probably be some time before they would catch up with us.

"Can't wait,' the commander said. "Our mission is to get there tonight."[65]

Darkness fell. Moving over hilly terrain on the trails, the two battalions were moving. The moonlight gently illuminated the surrounding countryside. Occasional artillery moaned overhead, bursting on surrounding hillsides near and far; most whistled towards the beaches. With few maps and no previous reconnaissance or study of the geography, their unfamiliarity with the area turned into what could have been disaster: the column broke into several sections, and officers without maps and without contact with superiors became lost behind the German lines.

Captain Stanley Dolezal, commander of Company D, leads his company through the village of Albanella to the line of departure for the attack on Unnumbered Hill. (US Signal Corps)

Here, Lieutenant John S. Lekson points out, so markedly displayed was the men's near-suicidal discipline. Even though they knew their leadership was utterly lost, and had nearly no knowledge of the situation, they continued without question, trusting their leaders' ability to cope with the situation, act in the best interest of the unit, ensure that the men were taken care of to the best of their ability, and most importantly that they would be there with them.

As the units of the 1st Battalion, traveling in a column formation down the trail, lost contact with one another, Lieutenant Lekson found himself on the trail with Captain Charles Duncan and his B Company, one platoon from C Company, and much of the Battalion Headquarters.

Lieutenant Lekson checked the forces, then resumed the march to the objective.

The march was resumed, and the point had gone several hundred yards, when machine pistol fire from the left of the trail stopped it. My orders to the point commander were to swing off to the right toward the high ground; bypass the Germans; and when the point got on the hill (Hill 392), halt, and the column would close in.

The point swung off to the right of the trail and to the east without returning the fire of the machine pistols. It dropped down into a steep gully and then climbed up the fairly steep slopes of the hill. When it reached the top, I ordered the point commander to guard the north side of the hill. As B Company came up, it was swung to the west and south of the hill. Headquarters Company was routed to the east and southeast. As Headquarters Company moved in, it was found that the 81mm Mortar Platoon was completely missing.

The moon had risen and was full. In its light I reconnoitered to the north, Captain Duncan to the west, and the battalion S-2 [Lieutenant William S. Jones] to the east. When we met to discuss the situation over the only map, Captain Duncan's, it was decided that Hill 424 was farther to the north. The march would be resumed again.

Further up the trail, Lieutenant Colonel Warren R. Williams, Jr., the 1st Battalion's Commander, was with Captain Willard E. Harrison and his A Company. They had continued on the trail, and near Hill 315 had breached the German's defensive line after a brief firefight.

Shortly after, they came to a hill. Captain Harrison and a small group went to reconnoiter the hill. When he came back, he summoned the platoon leaders and told them they had reached Hill 424. It was 0100, Friday, September 17.

Meanwhile, Lieutenant Lekson's column continued the march and led the column to another hill and went into a perimeter. Contact patrols were sent out. Lekson and Captain Duncan reconnoitered to the north and the west of their positions respectively, and when they returned Major Daniel Danielson, the commander of the 2nd Battalion, had come through his positions. Major Danielson said the hill they were on was Unnumbered Hill, his battalion's objective, and that his men would be arriving. That meant the next hill to the north should be Hill 424. The men under Lekson began to organize for a march yet again.

At 0200, Lieutenants Lekson and William S. Jones were reconnoitering ahead of the column along the trail when they ran into Lieutenant Colonel Williams. He said that A Company was with him, and they were getting set on the top of Hill 424. They held a short conference, and made a check of the forces.[66]

The German Counterattack

That night, Lieutenant Colonel Williams ordered the defense of the hill. Corporal Marvin R. Courtney had the 60mm mortar for the 3rd Platoon of B Company. He remembered a couple of men from headquarters came up to him and told him that he and his mortar were needed. They found Courtney a pit for the mortar and the rest of the men in the squad, under the charge of Sergeant Edmund Q. Moorehead, followed.

It was like a castle to a foxhole. You could sit down in there and your head would be below the ground, that's what we needed. So they put us in that hole and we got our mortar set up and Moorehead got us placed. So he got outside that hole and put a stake down. From where our mortar was to that stake was due north.

So we sat right there, and here they come again; they come with some ammunition. We got stacks of ammunition in the hole with us, and me and that guy got in the hole. Then they brought us a radio. I thought, well boy, I had nobody know me here, but I'm popular here! They know me.

So we get in that hole and they bring us the radio, a German radio, and Moorehead gets one, I get one, and they had one more down at the machine gun nest. And they said, "About daylight, all hell's going to break loose." And it wasn't long until daylight.

The moonlight was bright, and Lieutenant Colonel Williams and Lieutenant Lekson could see the men busy digging in and preparing the position. Lieutenant Reneau Breard took a four-man patrol into Altavilla, where they knocked on a door, talked to an Italian civilian, then after the Italian closed the door, heard Germans talking inside.[67]

Lieutenant William A. Meerman went with several other men to the front forward slope of the hill. From here, he was positioned below Sergeant Moorehead, on the crest of the hill, so he could yell targets and corrections up to Moorehead, who would then be able to relay them via radio back to Courtney and the mortar.

Lawrence Stimpson recalled that "the next day was real pleasant. The sun came out, and the clouds came out past the valley below us, and after the clouds came in, a German 88 start firing on us."[68] In his memoir, Ross Carter recalled the leader of the battalion's Communications Section happening by just before the barrage and saying, "Hell! A man just has to lie down under a tree when a shelling starts, and he's as safe as in them gopher holes."[69] This was Staff Sergeant Thomas Brown, who lost his right foot to the German mortar and artillery preparation.

Lekson and his wife on their wedding day in 1945. Thanks to Lekson's intiative, he gave his battalion commander a force with which to fight the Germans on the morning of September 17. (Lekson family)

Shortly after 0800, Colonel Williams and Lieutenant Lekson observed as two German elements moved out of the village of Altavilla in the valley below them. One headed almost directly for them in a frontal assault, while a smaller force swung to the south, moving around Hill 315.

Marvin Courtney has vivid memories of the ensuing action that Friday morning:

Man, when daylight come, it was bam, bam, bam, bam. Moorehead started giving me targets. Now I set that mortar, I knew right where to set it and everything. I'd fire one shot and [he] says [over the radio], "You not far off." Then he'd give me, "A little farther," or "A little to the left." I'd set my sight where it's supposed to be, and we'd put another shell in, fire it, and he said, "Fire at will." Then we'd fire about three shells, and it just went from that [to] just as fast as we could fire. As fast as we could get the mortars, we'd fire.

So the battle kind of eased down and here comes another big load of mortar shells. I never even seen that much ammunition the whole time I was in the Army until I was on that point there. We had another hole dug out there and put the ammunition in it, and we had it in that hole.

So he started giving orders and we fired all that morning. That mortar would get so hot we'd have to slow down. We'd fire about fifteen shots. Five, three at each [target] ya know. Moving from here to there. So we were getting closer in to where we were. There one time, we were firing that damned mortar near straight up. Those Germans were counterattacking, and they were pouring to that machine gun and that mortar.

So they withdrew and it wasn't over an hour, they counterattacked again. So we moved the mortar all that morning, and we fired I don't know how many mortar shells, 60 millimeter mortar shells. That mortar would get so hot we couldn't touch it. Then we'd just have to slow down and let it cool off a little bit. We fired that until that day, about the middle of the day, things quieted off. This guy in the hole with me [Demart Chamberlain] says, "They're overrunning us. I can tell they going to overrun us." He wanted to get out of the hole, and every time he wanted to get out of the hole, I put my arm on his shoulder and bring him back down. I already got out and run in Sicily. I wasn't about to get out and run now. I had my carbine loaded, I had that mortar, and I was going to stay there. Anything coming to that hole is going to be tough.

Courtney's heart was pounding. Adrenaline was racing through his blood veins. With no saliva left, his throat was bone dry and desperately itched, as all the moisture had zapped from his body in the heat of the battle as his body tried to cope with what he was experiencing. It was almost surreal. "You couldn't believe it," he described. "You just have to take it. It's like a dream. You just put everything else out of your mind."

Sergeant Moorehead began having difficulty attaining accurate locations for the German positions for him to relay back to Courtney. In an action which earned him the Silver Star, Moorehead took off his jump jacket and attempted to draw a large amount of fire onto himself as to see where the surviving Germans were located.

So then we changed directions, and Moorehead says, "I just got blown out of one hole myself, I don't know if I can make it to another place." But we changed directions and fired there. It was evening time then. We were firing away [and] Moorehead says, "We've called in fire from the Navy." So I thought, uh oh. The Navy's ten miles away. But anyhow, in a few minutes we heard this gun way off [in the distance] fire. That shell, you could see it coming in, it was about like a five-hundred-pound bomb. That thing come in, and it come right down the hill from us, and it was a phosphorus shell. Man, it went up in smoke and fire and everything.

Things finally got settled down and Moorehead called and says, "I'm going to fire on some tanks. I don't have a target, but they're moving some tanks in down there. I'm going to start firing on them." I thought, well, that's a stupid thing to do. We fired on the tanks and them darn tanks fired back. They couldn't get us, but they got all the dirt from all around our hole and everything.

After inflicting significant damage, including mortally wounding Emanuel J. Weinberger by blowing both his legs off and killing Henry P. Paquet outright, the German tanks eventually shot smoke shells to cover their withdraw, and things began to quiet down. Marvin Courtney remembered Lieutenant Colonel Williams coming by his foxhole with two men. "I just peeped up over my hole," he recalled, "and stuck my head up and saw the colonel, his eyes as big as saucers. These two guys, they were all worried. I thought, this guy's name was Chamberlain, who was in the hole with me, I said, 'They are fixin' to overrun us, cause the colonel's coming out.' I thought, *well, I'm not getting out, and I'm not going to let him get out*. So the colonel hollers out, says, 'Shut that damned mortar off!' So we sit there a little while longer. Come to find out, we'd taken the wrong mountain. After all that."[70]

When Colonel Williams and Captain Willard Harrison had first arrived at the large hill around 0100, they believed that it was their objective, Hill 424. However, they had mistaken the Unnumbered Hill for Hill 424. Lieutenant Lekson explains that Unnumbered Hill sits just to the south of Hill 424. While, he explained, Unnumbered Hill appears to have little merit, looks can be deceiving. "Closer inspection," he says, "would reveal that Unnumbered Hill, instead of being a satellite to Hill 424, completely dominates it…" When Colonel Williams and Captain Willard Harrison made their reconnaissance upon approaching the hill, they observed its dominating features, assumed it to be Hill 424, and A Company began to deploy on the hilltop, as did the men in the column under Lieutenant Lekson once they arrived.[71]

Edwin Decker and Henry Paquet evacuate a simulated casuality during training at Fort Bragg, NC. Paquet was a victim of the tank shellings after Ed Moorehead decided to fire on the tanks sitting on the edge of Altavilla on September 17. (Marcia Decker)

According to the plan, the 504th PIR's 2nd Battalion was responsible for seizing and holding the Unnumbered Hill, while the 1st Battalion seized and held the main objective of Hill 424. Where was the 2nd Battalion? When their commander, Major Daniel Danielson, arrived at Hill 344 – just south of Unnumbered Hill – overnight, met Lieutenant Lekson, and declared it to be his objective, he ordered his battalion to dig in. The night had been quiet for them, until 0830 when an American P-38 Lightning fighter-bomber pilot mistook troopers located on Hill 344 for German troops, unleashed two bombs from his racks killing five men. They were Private First Class John C. DiRinzo, Private James H. King, Jr., Private James E. Lechner,

Private First Class John C. Le Count, and Private John J. Monti. About an hour later, Sergeant George A. Ruff's squad captured a German water detail of seven men.[72]

Colonel Tucker Arrives

In the lull that followed on Unnumbered Hill after the German tanks retired, Colonel Tucker and a group of paratroopers entered through the perimeter. Colonel Tucker and a small force had been holding Hill 424 since the previous night and were awaiting Colonel Williams, and once daylight broke Tucker's group was driven off the hill and, with German gunfire chasing them, had made a break for the positions on Unnumbered Hill. "Where in the hell have you been?" Tucker demanded. A short conference followed.

Sgt. Ed Moorehead in 1942. For exposing himself to German fire while observing the fall of 60mm mortar shells on Unnumbered Hill, Moorehead would recieve the Silver Star Medal. (Kathy Dasani)

Tucker wanted forces to race to Hill 424 without further delay. Captain Willard Harrison's A Company would provide that force, with the rest of the battalion following shortly thereafter.

A message was sent to the 2nd Battalion, which was found to be on Hill 344, to come to Unnumbered Hill immediately. The message was signed at 0955, and when it finally arrived, it was met with great confusion and Lieutenant Chester Garrison wrote in the battalion journal that "we have not understood." It wasn't until early afternoon that the battalion began to move. They left 2nd Lieutenant William L. Wilson and his platoon to guard Hill 344. That afternoon on Hill 344, one of Wilson's sergeants, Dale Decker, was killed by an airburst from an artillery shell.[73]

Also during the short conference, a group of walking wounded was organized, which, under the direction of a wounded Lieutenant Colonel Leslie Freeman, would make their way back to the beachhead to a proper aid station. Also going back with the wounded were the two intrepid newspaper reporters, who had been with Colonel Tucker's beleaguered group on Hill 424 overnight. Colonel Tucker told one of the reporters, Cy Korman, to "go back with the wounded and write your story about us."[74]

This photo shows paratroopers of the 509th Parachute Infantry conducting a training jump onto the same DZ which the 504th parachuted onto on the night of September 13-14, 1943. (US Signal Corps)

5

THE COST OF WINNING

It was before 1100 when the paratroopers of A Company dashed down the slope of the hill, crossed the ridge and made their accent up the scarred, terraced face of Hill 424. The set of the battle was horrid; dead were scattered across the hill. In the September heat, the bodies were maggot-infested, blackened, and bloated to superhuman size. The stench was incredible. It was a ghastly sight. Broken rifles and equipment, and ammunition littered the ground told a silent tale of the bitter fighting that had taken place. In the 36th Division's hectic retreats from Hill 424, they had left everything. There were stacks of equipment, ammunition and mortar shells in stockpile awaiting use; men's packs and clothing were about; machine guns were in their original emplacements; foxholes and fighting positions were dug. It was like the soldiers which were supposed to occupy the battle space had been raptured, leaving everything behind and preserved just how they had left it.

The A Company paratroopers jumped into the holes and fighting positions. Louis Marino jumped in a foxhole already occupied by Ervin "Pop" Prechowski. At nearly 30-years-old, Pop was one of the oldest men in the company, where the average age was early 20s. Although older than virtually all of the men, his tall, lanky body had some of the fastest reflexes in the company, and Pop was among the most athletic. Pop hailed from Detroit, Michigan, and had played baseball in the minor leagues before the war. Marino remembered Pop doing different tricks with baseballs during downtime, which showcased his cat-like reflexes.

No sooner had Marino got in the foxhole with Pop, when the Germans began attacking. Pop froze.

Below them, the Germans were coming up the vegetation-covered, terraced hillside. It was these same terraces cut into the side of Hill 424 that the Germans had used to quietly infiltrate and overrun the positions of the 36th Division. From the top of the hill, the paratroopers could stand up and fire down onto the Germans as they attempted to ascend. Marino would fire eight rounds from his M-1 rifle down on the Germans, and duck back down into the hole. Pop was still frozen, and Marino tried go get Pop's gun into the fight, "but he didn't do anything." From observing his skills with a baseball, Marino knew Pop could throw a grenade a mile. "Get a grenade!" Marino yelled to Pop. Pop got out a grenade and threw it down the hill towards the attacking Germans.[75]

In the afternoon, the rest of the 1st Battalion arrived. With the waning of the final German attack that afternoon, the backbone of the German effort to retake the hill was broken.

Back at the VI Corps headquarters, little had been heard from Colonel Tucker's forces fighting above Altavilla. At 1105, a message from Colonel Tucker arrived stating that their losses were heavy, and the Germans were preparing for another counterattack. He requested further artillery bombardment on Altavilla, which was greatly effecting the German infantry. The message must have not sounded encouraging, and in the evening a message arrived from General Ernest Dawley which ordered Colonel Tucker to withdraw back to Albanella under the cover of darkness. The order was unnecessary, as they had secured the hills and had driven back the Germans. The order angered Tucker, and the staff in the CP was disgusted. Tucker said to Dawley, "Retreat? Hell! Send me my other battalion!" General Dawley agreed to let Tucker hold his positions.

The night of September 17-18 brought peace to the area, but the following day, September 18, was marked by German artillery shelling of the positions with a fierceness which could break even the strongest combat soldiers. "They averaged about 50 rounds an hour at us," Lawrence Stimpson recalled. "They would come in as a barrage, and then they'd quit. And you'd – after this barrage came in – you'd hear digging: 'Dig, dig, dig.' And pretty soon everything would get quiet – another barrage – then, 'Dig, dig, dig.' This went on for 24 hours at least… We were running out of food. There was a chicken running loose there one day and I laid down my rifle and tried to catch that chicken. I never did catch the chicken, and I never did find my rifle. There were rifles laying all over the place and there were dead bodies all over the place… And finally, one guy made a salad one day and brought it around. I don't know where he got the greens for us to eat, but we didn't have anything to eat."[76]

Water was at an even more critical low. There were many wells on Hill 424, but the Germans had thrown dead soldiers in the wells to soil its potablity. Louis Marino recalled one well being filled with dead goats. This, however, was not discovered until after many of the men had drank from the wells. Despite using purification tablets in their canteens, Marino felt he may have gotten sick from the water because when they got to Naples, he was urinating red.[77]

The Story Breaks at Home

Across the United States, newspapers published stories by Korman and Tregaskis which described for the American people the valor which they had seen in the small group of Americans who had clung onto the most vital objective on the Italian beachhead – Hill 424 – in the face of tremendous odds. They were published under titles such as, "How 60 Yanks Took All the NAZIs Could Throw: Heroic Little Band Holds Strategic Hill for 10 Hours."

The stories told of "a major from California" and described the heroics in his effort to secure help for the small group of beleaguered Americans. They described in detail the actions which cost the "major from California" his life.

In Lemon Grove, California, a telegram arrived from Oregon on September 26. It was from Ed Dunham – Major Don Dunham's father. He had read the newspaper article, and knew the slain major had to be his son.

In reply to the telegram, Major Dunham's brother-in-law pinned a letter describing what happened in the ensuing hours in Lemon Cove, California.

Lemon Cove

Sept. 27, 1943

Dear Mr. Dunham:

Words are so useless at a time like this to try to express one's feelings that a letter hardly seems worthwhile, but will try to give you a little of what happened here, in case Doris and others cannot bear to put it down in words.

After your telegram came last evening, I took Doris and Donny to Visalia and we spent several hours going thru all the editions of the Chronicle we could find even as far back as Wednesday, and every Sunday paper we could find, but could never find the story to which you referred and so hoped and prayed that you or your paper was wrong. Then this morning I was able to locate an edition in Exeter which was no doubt the same as the one you had seen, and after reading it and putting the two articles together, we all felt just as you did that that was it.

As I see it, there is only the faint hope that there could have been two majors in the group from Calif. and that will be our prayer until some word comes. Why this particular fight was allowed to be described in so much detail and the names of the men given, we will never know. How these two articles could have been taken the million to one chance and been brought to you, his father' attention, is one of those mysteries to which I think there is only one answer. We here certainly never would have been able to put the story together with our newspapers. I wonder, too, if the great liking these two writers had for Don and expressed themselves on may have caused them to write as they did with the idea of getting the story past the censors in the hope that it would reach some member of his family.

This present apparent condition of facts certainly puts an entirely different picture on things here so far as I am concerned. Since Don has been away, I have never counted on anything except that he would be home soon to go ahead taking charge of our Lemon Cove operations, and that in the meantime I would try to get along as best I could during these troublesome times. Now it looks like I have a real load to carry by myself, but I intend to do it and Doris and the children can count on me 100 percent for as long as they want and need any help that I can give them. One of the chief faults of the human race is that some of us at least are too dumb to realize how much others mean to us and how much we need them, until it is too late to be able to express our appreciation in words and deeds.

There isn't much else to say and nothing to do but wait and hope that by some miracle Don has come thru this better than we think. If he did not, Marion and I can only express to you our deepest sympathy in the loss of your son and our brother-in-law. He was just too damn brave and too good a soldier and had to always take the lead. I sincerely hope that the Allies do a real job this time, so that when we get thru with Germany this time that she will never again be able to start another war. I hope we bomb her country until it is completely destroyed and every German is destroyed along with it.

Sincerely yours,

Eldon Runeiman

J.E. Pogue, Major Dunham's father-in-law, also heard about the newspaper stories and in deep sadness and confusion, also wrote to Major Dunham's father in Oregon about what the future would bring.

Lemon Cove, California, Sept 29, 1943

Dear Mr. Dunham

It is with a broken heart I am going to try to write to you this morning. I never had anything to hurt me so bad in all my life. After reading all those paper clippings and then this piece was finally located in the Chronicle <page 2 Oct 3> miss print of date of paper of course, "How 60 Yanks Took All the Nazis Could Throw: Heroic Little Band Holds Strategic Hill for 10 Hours."

No Chronicle came to Lemon Cove on Sept 26. We telephoned [illegible] at Exeter; none, [illegible] called his son at Visalia, found the paper Sunday, Sept 26 but could find nothing, Eldon and Doris then got in the car and went up to Visalia thinking they just were overlooking the piece but no results.

Monday Eldon went to Exeter and found the paper in an extra edition, came in late, and dated October 2nd. Eldon immediately brought the paper out and that settled things. No doubt. I don't know what we will do, of course we will wait for official news which is only 1 chance in a thousand.

I have worked hard all my life for the future and have accumulated enough for my girl's future, and after they both got married to the best boys in the whole country I immediately started them out. I wanted to see them enjoying what I had for them while I lived. Then Eldon went in with his father in the cold storage business at Exeter. Eldon told me he could never have done that only from the profits of the orchards I have given them and the packing house profits I gave them. Eldon has done well in the cold storage business but it really needs all his time.

Therefore, I have been expecting Don to take full charge <after this cruel war> here and it was my hope that my grandsons would still carry on in Lemon Cove after Don and Eldon. Now everything seems dark. I can't see ahead; no man knows what we are coming to, it is an awful task to try to run a business now. And in the future it might be a great deal worse; I just shiver at the thought of what our grandchildren have before them.

My health is pretty good as long as I sit around and do nothing and that is awful hard to do for I have always done things. I went to a specialist at Sacramento last week and he told me the same as the doctors here only stressing it harder that it was up to me entirely that I had had enough warnings, even said I should not even drive my car. I told him that driving did not bother me a bit. I have drove since March 1908 and I don't intend to quit now. When Don left I told him that I just wish I was able to take his place as I had about lived my time and his future was all ahead of him.

Many times I have said that I never expected to see Don again but I really thought he would be back, but it would be myself that had passed on before his return. I think I have wrote enough, even too much but I just can't help getting things out of my system as I can't see the future.

Yours very truly,

J.E. Pogue

P.S. I expect you will have a pretty hard time to read this, but I usually write better but not this morning. I just feel like talking to you but my hand does not handle the pen as it should owing to the sad feeling I have.

Just nine short days before J.E. Pogue sat and wrote his letter in heart-wrenched confusion, Richard Tregaskis watched as Major Don Dunham drug his tommy gun and slowly bent his knees to-and-fro to propel himself up the bare crown of Hill 424 on September 17. "He kept low," Tregaskis observed, "for somewhere on the other side of the hill, very close, according to the sound, snipers were lurking. Don was looking for human game, and he moved like a practiced hunter."[78]

While Lieutenant Colonel Warren Williams and the 1st Battalion readied positions on the Unnumbered Hill, which at the time he incorrectly believed was Hill 424, in preparation for the German attack that would come on the morning of the 17th, Colonel Reuben Tucker had moved his advance command post towards Hill 424. At the time, he had no contact with his two assault battalions, but expected Colonel Williams to have Hill 424 by the time he arrived. Along the way, they found no units of the regiment until Tucker discovered only Captain Albert Milloy and two platoons of his company just across a draw from Hill 424. They had lost contact with the rest of the battalion while on the nighttime approach march behind the enemy lines. Rather than wait for contact to be re-established with his chain of command, Captain Milloy made the decision to continue to his objective on Hill 424. Colonel Tucker's group and Captain Milloy's men secured the hilltop. They were the first paratroopers to reach Hill 424.

Still with Colonel Tucker were Tregaskis and Korman, the two journalists. Seymour Korman remembered Colonel Tucker saying, "They'd better be here in a few hours. We'll try and hold it alone, but what chance have we got at daybreak?"[79]

And so, the small group would hold the most vital objective on the Salerno beachhead.

Among the group was Major Don B. Dunham. Some hours passed. The small group of paratroopers were surrounded on the hilltop. Some men, such as Lieutenant Forrest Richter, the Regimental Adjunct, and Lieutenant Colonel Leslie Freeman, the Regimental Executive Officer, had been wounded in skirmishes. Other paratroopers tried to go out to seek help, but were unsuccessful in breaking the German encirclement. The outlook was bleak for the beleaguered men.

"It was just 4 A.M.," recalled Seymour Korman, "when my major friend approached me with Sergeant Charles Furst. 'Say,' the major addressed me, 'we're going to try and break through the ring again and bring help. Otherwise you guys won't have a change at dawn. Take care of my map case and binoculars.'

"He handed them to me.

"'Okay, Don,' I said, 'I'll give them back to you in the morning.'

"'Maybe,' he said slowly."[80]

Richard Tregaskis watched as Major Dunham gave Korman his map case, drop his superfluous equipment, and pick up his tommy gun and two magazines of ammunition. "He shook hands with me and said simply, 'Goodbye,' as if he didn't expect to get back," Tregaskis later wrote.

"I'm going to try to get back," Dunham said as he left.

He and Sergeant Furst went into the vegetation and disappeared into the darkness.

Korman remembered what happened next:

It was five minutes later that I heard machine-pistol shots. Ten more minutes and Furst came sprinting back alone. "They got the major," he said. "They shot him in the chest, head and mouth. He's dead." I nodded helplessly, looked as the map case and binoculars and put them tenderly in my foxhole.

I crawled into my foxhole. Enemy bullets were singing overhead and shells were plopping every few minutes. The hours passed with no cessation of enemy missiles. Our other units were not arriving.[81]

Shortly after daybreak on the 17th, they made their way to the 1st Battalion's positions on the Unnumbered Hill after the German tanks had withdrawn. On the way, they passed the body of Major Don Dunham. "Somehow," Korman recalled, "in his last agony his right hand rested near his forehead. Thus he had met death – as one warrior saluting another."[82]

Victory

The days between September 13 and September 20 were days from which incredible pride were drawn for the 504th Parachute Infantry Regiment. In 1990, veteran Fred Baldino revisited Altavilla and Hill 424 and recalled being filled with "nothing but pride." Even when the regiment was in England in the summer of 1944 after their participation in the Italian campaign, they still drew pride from their victory at Altavilla when the "Strike-Hold" crest, owing to the battle, was drawn on the wall of the 1st Battalion mess hall by Staff Sergeant Sam D'Crenzo, a skilled sketch artist.[83]

The action highlights what well-disciplined and highly trained troops, coupled with apt leaders at the company-level, are capable of achieving even when they are put in a situation where they are allowed the minimum of preparation and resources with which to accomplish a magnanimous task. John Lekson wrote these words in a paper while a student at the Infantry School in 1948 when he was a major: "Much credit should go to the ordinary soldier. Though he knew that at times his commanders were lost and that he was within enemy lines he moved willingly and did not shirk his duties. Even when direct tank fire fell into the foxholes of B Company, he held his position, trusting in his commander's ability to cope with the situation. When his friend was wounded and, as on Hill 424, left without medical aid he did all he could to assist him. Orders that may have seemed suicidal to him were carried out promptly. Such was the case of the second scout in the 2nd Platoon of A Company [Ralph R. Young] and the volunteers on Hill 424 who attempted to get reinforcements."[84]

Sergeant Otto Huebner concurred, and felt that the outstanding leadership of their officers was a defining factor. "It was the soldier's skillful shooting, his maximum use of cover and concealment, his determination, will to fight, trust in leaders and his self-initiative that beat the enemy. Contributing to this, was the excellent leadership of the officers and non-commissioned officers, especially in making decisions."[85]

They both also pointed out the incredible initiative displayed in the paratroopers, which helped the mission to succeed. In that initiative was a display of the heart with which nearly every member of the organization cared about his duty, the pride in his unit, and the men within it. There is no better example than the action of Major Dunham who, despite the failure of other troopers to break the German's ring around the men on Hill 424, went willingly to a likely death to try and get help for his men. This kind of action and initiative was displayed from every rank in the regiment, from private to colonel. When Private Warren Zumwalt felt that a German machine gun team was too threatening to his squad-mates, Zumwalt took it upon himself to jump into the German's machine gun pit and eliminate the threat to his friends. He succeeded, at the cost of his own life.

As a good friend of Warren Zumwalt, Jimmy Eldridge retained vivid memories of the action which took his young friends life on September 17, 1943 above Altavilla. Back home in Gastonia, North Carolina, Eldridge was a well-known boxer, and throughout World War II his local paper *The Gastonia Daily Gazette* published several of the letters he wrote from the front to friends and family back home. One of them described the action in which Zumwalt was killed.

We have been informed that we could tell about things that happened in combat providing it doesn't give away any information of value. I hope what I am about to tell you will get by the censor and I only wish everyone knew this incident as the fellows in our outfit know it.

After the Sicilian campaign was over we flew back to Africa to prepare for the jump into Italy. We had to have replacements and one of them was a young, nice-looking fellow from a small town in the west. He had a funny sort of name, "Zoomwalt," so we naturally called him "Zoomie." Well, "Zoomie" had only been married about four months before he had to come overseas, but since he had been across he had become a proud father. He was a good all-around athlete and had a wonderful personality. He made a big hit in the company.

Well, when we jumped in Italy he was right with us. While we were in one of our hottest battles in Italy, a German machine gun kept giving us plenty of trouble and we had trouble locating it. A patrol of five men was picked out of our section and "Zoomie" was among the five.

The plan was to locate the machine gun nest, then split up and creep and crawl up at five different angles, and, when every man was close enough, toss a couple of hand grenades each, then charge in. Well, sir, everything went all right [sic] and every man was in position, but then the Germans turned loose another burst and "Zoomie" thought they had spotted some of the patrols, so instead of waiting on the grenades, he jumped into the machine gun nest alone, and tried to take it single-handed. But, another machine gun, located where it could cover this first one, opened up on him and nearly cut him in two. The machine gun was taken care of, but we lost 'Zoomie'. He was one of the swellest fellow I ever knew, and it will be a long time before we forget him.

Tell Mr. Bob Simpson, Gus, Jimmy the Greek and all the fellows hello for me and tell them that those dirty ——— have not stopped me yet, that I am only slowed up a little while, and from what the doctor says, it will not be long before I will be in the fight and it can't be too soon to suit me.[86]

More Heartbreak at Altavilla

When Private First Class Meyer Hesselburg was cut down by an artillery shell during the German barrage of Hill 424 on September 18, the loss hit Edwin Decker very hard. But it was no harder felt by anyone than his wife Ethel back home in the United States. After Edwin Decker was wounded in Italy in January 1944 and sent back to the United States to recover, he received a reply from Ethel Hesselburg to his sympathy letter. She received several letters from the men of Company B, which is a testament to the regard which they had for her late husband.

Monday, April 10, 1944

Dear Edwin,

It was most sweet of you to remember me and to send along your sympathy. At the risk of annoying you, I'm going to ask you to try and help me.

I have been heartsick and weary over the loss of my loved one. I have tried every avenue to gain some information regarding him. It is so very difficult to believe I will never see him again. He was everything to me. I have received so many conflicting stories I truly do not know what to think. Perhaps I should drop the whole thing, but loving him as I did I probably won't rest till I hear all I can from the boys of Co. B who contact me.

Lt. [Milton J.] Crochet advised my Mickey was wounded in combat and evacuated to a hospital. Bob Corvelli wrote me Mickey died in a hospital. Earl Goddard wrote he was wounded in combat – never got to Italy, and Bill Clay wrote me he had sent my letter on to Washington. No doubt you know all the boys I mentioned.

Weinberger's letter came to me marked, "deceased."

The War Dept. just advised me my beloved husband died instantly at Alta Villa, Italy from shrapnel from an enemy artillery barrage. They say my Mickey never was in a hospital. The War Dept. has mixed this case up so I don't know what to believe. First, in Oct., I received word Mickey was slightly wounded in the North African area, and in Nov a wire arrived saying the first one was sent in error – that on Sept 18 my husband was killed in action in the Med. Area. Of course, not receiving mail for almost 7 months I know it must be the truth now, but the news I get is so confusing.

Can you, Edwin, confirm any of the things I've written you? Did you see him fall? Did you know if he reached a hospital? I was always so sure nothing could or would happen to him. I am so heart-broken. He was such a gentle, wonderful person.

I know you are hospitalized, and I trust you will be up and about soon and can rejoin your loved ones.

If you find it too much of an effort to write or answer, perhaps you can get someone to write for you.

I will be so happy to hear further from you.

Again, thanks for your sympathy and I do hope you are in first class condition soon again.

Sincerely yours,

Ethel T. Hesselburg[87]

One of the men to whom Mrs. Hesselburg wrote a letter was Emanuel Joseph Weinberger, known as "EJ" to the men of Company B. EJ had worked harder to get into the war's action than almost anyone in the regiment. His love for his unit and brothers-in-arms was clearly seen by his family and through his early military career.

Born in 1917 as the middle child, Emanuel Weinberger was known as "Weinie" to his family. His brother Joe was one year older, and the two were very close, although they were almost opposites. "Joe was a scholar," Polly Brennan, sister to Joe and Weinie, recalled. "Weinie wasn't a scholar, but he was a heck of an athlete." Athletics was Weinie's love, and before the war he had worked in a famous sporting goods store in Detroit, where he would often come into contact with prominent sports players. When the famous

New York Yankee baseball player Lou Gehrig played his last major league game against the Detroit Tigers as a result of his disease, Weinie was the one who drove him to the train station.

In 1936, however, tragedy struck the Weinberger family when Joe was killed in an automobile accident. Because of how close the two brothers were, Weinie took the loss extremely hard. Two months later, unable to cope with the loss of their first son, Weinie's mother committed suicide.

Five years later, in 1941, Weinie enlisted in the Army and was sent to California as a coastal artillery soldier. There, they told him he would be stationed in California for the duration of the war. "When he heard that," Polly recalled, "he decided that wasn't for him." In California, Weinie began investigating the parachute troops, and he wrote a letter to his father back home in Michigan asking for his blessing to join the paratroops. Polly and her father sat down at the table. "Well, tell him no," 13-year-old Polly said. "No," her father said, "I can't do that." He then went on to explain that Weinie, in all likelihood, would volunteer anyway, and he did not want his son to feel that he was volunteering against his father's wishes.

At Fort Benning after parachute training, he was sent to Rigger's School, and he became very adept at folding parachutes and jumping. He was told that he was selected to stay in the States and teach at the Parachute School, but, as Polly said, "He wanted no part of that." On his last leave home, Polly and their father took him to the train station and said their goodbyes. "Oh my goodness, I was just beside myself. You have to understand, he was my hero," Polly said. Later, they found out that on the way back, he rerouted himself to Washington, D.C. and he went absent without leave. He did it, as they found out, because Weinie thought that if he went AWOL, they would punish him by sending him to a rifle company, and subsequently overseas. He was correct. When he turned himself in, he was sent to the stockade, and then back to Company B of the 504th Parachute Infantry Regiment. "He was so happy to be in that corps," Polly remembered. "It was like getting his brother back. He became part of a fraternity of men, and he was very happy."

EJ, as the men in the company knew him, had seen combat in Sicily before Operation AVALANCHE. On September 17 above Altavilla, he died of major wounds when he refused to let the doctor operate on him. Ed Moorehead visited the Weinberger's after he had recovered from his own wounds received in January 1944, and told EJ's father of the incident.

The end of the war in 1945 was a hard day for Polly, knowing that her brother was not able to celebrate. "The day the war was declared over in Europe, I will never forget… I came home from school and my father and I sat in the living room listening to the radio, hearing the celebration going on all over the world… It was the emptiest feeling in the world to know that he wasn't going to come home. Then all of a sudden the front door opened and friends and family came in, bringing food and drink, and threw a small party. They were telling us in a very positive way, that we weren't going to be alone."

Aftermath of the Battle of Altavilla

The stories of what had been witnessed by Richard Tregaskis and Seymour Korman on Hill 424 were widely published in September 1943, and again when Richard Tregaskis wrote his book *Invasion Diary* in 1944. However, due to wartime censorship, the unit which had been involved – the 504th Parachute Infantry – along with its size went undisclosed; the articles never mentioned the men were even paratroopers. What was not written in any newspapers, or written in any period books, was the other actions which occurred in the hills above Altavilla during those hours. Neither Tregaskis nor Korman witnessed any of the incredible actions which occurred during the German counterattack on Unnumbered Hill, or the repulsing of the further German counterattacks on Hill 424 during the afternoon.

Like Henry Paquet, EJ Weinberger, pictured above, was killed by the realitoy German tank fire on Unnumbered Hill on September 17 brought down by Ed Moorehead. After being wounded in the legs, and being told he would have to have both legs amputated, Weinberger refused to be operated on and succumbed to his wounds that day. (Polly Brennen)

Further, official Army historical documents published in 1944 appear to either underappreciate, misunderstand or, in the most malicious interpretation, disregard the significance of the action of the 504th

PIR. When then-Major Lekson wrote his monograph in 1948, he included a paragraph at the end in which he tried to jab at the commonly-sold idea "that the Germans only gave up Hill 424 when they were ready."[88] This was the narrative put out by the official Army historians during and immediately following the war. Specifically, Lekson took issue with what was implied in the publication *Salerno*, published by the War Department on August 26, 1944. In it, it is written that the paratroopers spent September 17 in "foxholes, with artillery shells exploding everywhere… Split into small groups, they had fought hard and had suffered heavy casualties, but had not recaptured Hills 424 and 315. The Germans were not ready to give them up. Finally, the enemy began to withdraw, and his artillery fire diminished."

While *Salerno* does say the 1st Battalion repulsed one "particularly heavy attack," the publication fails to mention the Germans committing tanks to fight the paratroopers, as well as multiple distinct and bitter German assaults against the positions of the 504th PIR with clear intent to regain the hills. The above-quoted statement found in *Salerno* may be true for how the regiment spent the day of September 18 (under heavy artillery fire), but it grossly mischaracterizes the situation on September 17.[89]

Historian Martin Blumenson admits in his work, *United States Army in World War II The Mediterranean Theater of Operations Salerno to Cassino*, that the action of the 504th PIR had brought "change at Altavilla," however he fails to highlight its importance, depict the bitterness of the action, or help to dispel the myth that the Germans only withdrew when they were ready by writing, "Since withdraw was now Vietinghoff's principle mission, he decided, despite Kesselring's request, to commit no additional troops at Altavilla," Blumenson writes. "Instead of attacking, the Germans began withdrawing."[90]

Some of the lines found in the 36th Division records seem to contradict this narrative. One entry for September 17 in the 142nd Infantry's journal records, "At 2330 the Division G-2 reported that an officer prisoner of war from the 29th Arty Regiment stated that their mission was to hold the hill around Altavilla at all costs, and 2 battalions of German infantry were dug in on the southeast slope of this hill supported by two batteries of artillery. G-2 requested that we notify the 504th AB battalion."[91] While Lekson unfortunately did not see these lines, it supports the argument he made in his monograph: "The losses the enemy took attacking the battalion would hardly justify a delaying action."[92]

Even within in the 82nd Airborne Division and the 504th PIR, the victory at Altavilla is rarely studied. It was a victory which cost the lives of nearly 25 men and approximately 127 wounded; but while the battle may have not been as costly as actions like the Waal River Crossing or the routing of Joachim Peiper's SS troopers at Cheneux, the Battle of Altavilla is rich in history and lush with lessons for the profession of arms which can continue to be employed into the present day. It showed that the ability and confidence of the junior leaders to take initiative, combined with the trust the troopers had in their leaders to make the best decision, paved the way for victory in a precarious situation.

Maiori

The beachfront of the Sorrento Peninsula was a beautiful place. With small resorts on the shorefront dug into the side of steep mountains, the Sorrento Peninsula separated the Gulf of Naples in the north from the Gulf of Salerno to the south. Up above the resorts were high mountain passes covered in lush green vegetation, roads cut into the earth, and awe-inspiring views of the rolling hills in the east. To the north was a view of the plains which led to Naples, containing the ancient ruins of Pompeii and, above it, the looming volcano Vesuvius which had destroyed the city in ancient times. On the verge of erupting in September 1943, smoke could be seen from points on the Sorrento Peninsula leaving the mouth of the volcano and wisping up into the Italian horizon.

The beach resort of Maiori, located on the south coast of the Sorrento Peninsula, was one of the first locations American troops set foot when the Italian mainland was invaded in early September. Maiori had a road which led north up the mountains and through Chiunzi Pass, a critical position some 3,000 feet above the sea. From Chiunzi Pass, the main coastal highway – Highway 18 – could be observed, and through Chiunzi Pass forces could be moved to mount a flanking attack on the Salerno beach. During the initial stages of the invasion, the task of securing this location fell to US Army Rangers. However, on September 23, 1943, the 3rd Battalion of the 504th Parachute Infantry was withdrawn from the Salerno beachhead and sent to Maiori to take up positions near Chiunzi Pass.

Second Lieutenant Roy Hanna remembered the movement and mission well:

A few days after fighting in the Salerno area the 3rd Battalion was withdrawn, loaded on LSTs (Landing Ship Tank) – not an LCI – and taken to Maiori. I can't believe the entire battalion was on one LST, so there could have been a couple ships. The LST is a pretty big craft and they fed us a hot meal as we sailed a bit north of Salerno. I know our unit was the lead unit – the first to leave the ship. It sailed right to the edge of the beach, lowered its front gate (the entire front end of the ship) and we stormed ashore, raced across this beautiful beach through this beautiful little resort town and into the hills full of grapevines east of the town. Not a shot was fired, no enemy soldiers had been there, and we were not replacing anyone – just flanking the area north of Salerno. The rest of the 3rd Battalion followed us.

After going through the hillside of grapevines, we followed the narrow road up the side of the mountain up to the top. This road led through Chiunzi Pass, down the mountain, and joined a large highway that led to Rome.

The entire 3rd Battalion spread out across the crest of this mountain where we overlooked the Salerno Valley that led from the city of Salerno to Rome. We were dug in from Chiunzi Pass on the north and thinly spread along the crest south. We had a panoramic view of the war as it progressed toward Rome, as our airplanes dropped bombs and our artillery pounded the area in front of the advancing infantry. The battalion headquarters established their command post along the road at the foot of this mountain. It was in this area that Major Beall got smothered in his foxhole – what a horrible way to die!

I and my platoon sergeant had our foxholes at the extreme end of this defensive line and kept the contact with the unit that occupied the mountain top on the south. Sergeant [Elbert] Claunts and I were playing cribbage in our foxhole when we received some mail from home. My letter from my wife Janice informed me that we now had our first child. Her name is Stephanie.[93]

Whenever Hanna got the letter informing him of the birth and naming of his first child, Hanna did not know how to properly pronounce his own daughters' name. Hanna looked at Sergeant Claunts and asked, "Who names a baby stef-fanny"? In fact, Hanna would not learn the proper pronunciation of his daughters' name until he returned home from the war.

"I don't know how many days we occupied this area," Hanna continued, "but the Germans kept harassing us with artillery the entire time. Most of the shells hit the front of the mountain or went over our heads and hit on the reverse side. At night a few Germans soldiers would climb the mountain to within a few hundred yards of our position and fire their machine pistols up in the air to harass us. If we thought they were getting too close we would lob a couple hand grenades in their direction and they would behave."[94]

In some positions near the road, the men dug artificial caves into the side of the mountain like gophers to protect themselves from the German artillery which, on the road, the force of Rangers were constantly drawing. "The Rangers had a half-track. They had it on the side of Chiunzi Pass, and every couple hours they would run the half-track out and they would shoot a couple shots out, just about two or three, and they would run back in again. Then the Germans would throw some shells at Chiunzi Pass to see if they could knock it out," remembered Francis Keefe. "There was something going on all day long."[95]

On the 25th of September, the rest of the 504th Parachute Infantry repeated the landing at Maiori and began moving to join the 3rd Battalion near Chiunzi Pass. It was in the late-afternoon when the men of B Company landed at Maiori. There were orange groves nearby, and a British soldier came up to some of the men and told them, "Whatever you do, don't pick an orange." Allegedly, a British soldier had gone to the grove to get an orange, when he picked a booby-trapped one which killed him. While awaiting orders, some of the troopers sat down and fraternized with the British over tea before moving up into the mountains.[96]

As the men of A Company were passing up the road that housed the 3rd Battalion's Command Post, they were told their former commander, Major William Beall, lost his life there when a German artillery shell buried him alive in his foxhole, smothering life from the 29-year-old Marylander. The high school educator and family man turned paratroop commander stood a head taller than many of his men, and in another life he had been a track star. His hard-lined facial features made him appear as though his face had been chiseled out of marble by a Greek artist depicting a handsome and masculine warrior. He was described by those who served under him in A Company as "a peach of a guy – [the] fellows all worship him."[97] For Private First Class Fred Baldino and the men around him, hearing that their beloved former commander's life was snuffed out was a hard pill to swallow. Everyone tried their best to keep their emotions inside during times of combat, but Baldino thinks he may have seen a couple fellow paratroopers shed tears at the news. "We loved that man," Baldino said.[98]

Naples is Liberated

It was nighttime when the regiment began descending down the northern slopes of the mountains which characterized the Sorrento Peninsula. Marvin Courtney remembered the pitch-black night where nothing was visible, and holding hands with each other as they went down the slope before his assistant gunner – Private Demart Chamberlain – came tumbling down on top of him. Earl Levitt remembered the descent was made in a terrible hail storm, with the hailstones the size of golf balls. "I think the only thing that made it bearable," he later said, "was the fact it was coming from our back, and of course we had our musette bags and steal helmets to protect the back of our neck and everything. But even so, we took a terrific beating."[99]

The boon of British artillery pieces – set up during the night – could already be heard violently hurling shells, whistling to their fiery destination, in the morning. And as day arose, so did the activity in the sky. B Company troopers watched as two American P-38 Lightning's came tearing through the sky chasing two German Messerschmitt's. One German plane was shot down immediately, while the other flew away with the two American pilots giving chase. When the troopers got onto the flatland which led past Pompeii and into the outskirts of Naples, they observed a human leg wrapped around an overhead power line, likely belonging to the other German pilot.

This flatland contained a number of small streams that ran off the mountain range whose dark gray faces loomed in the distance to the east. Not only was it beautiful country, but also it contained the ancient ruins of Pompeii, which Lieutenant Moffatt Burriss took the time to snap some photographs of as his company passed.

After marching eight miles through the great rain and hailstorm, the first but certainly not the last the paratroopers would see in Italy, the 2nd Battalion set up bivouac on the night of September 28 at the base of the mountains in a large orchard of citrus. "Rain was coming down and we dug our slit trenches, our foxholes, and we were in about three inches of water," Earl Levitt remembered.[100] The fruit trees which they had bivouacked amongst invigorated the taste buds of Major Melvin Blitch, a southerner from Columbus, Georgia, who was accustomed to the citrus fruits. They reminded him of the fruits which grew from the trees back home.

The following day the battalion moved again, this time they were just south of Vesuvius and only three miles from the Bay of Naples. Louis Bednar could remember looking out of his slit trench or foxhole at night while on the journey to Naples over these days and seeing something glowing red, high in the sky, contrasting the deep dark night. It was Vesuvius. On the verge of erupting yet again, wisps of smoke could be seen in the daytime billowing up from its fiery mouth. The battalion remained here for two days before moving into Naples. However, in the interim days before the move into the city, Lieutenant Chester Garrison and Captains Robert Halloran and Kenneth Sheek took an ambulance to visit the nearby ruins of Pompeii. The three men and the tour guides were the only people on the ancient streets. Lieutenant Roy Hanna recalled they were relieved and continued through Chiunzi Pass and after negotiating the mountain, "met a tank column, jumped on the tanks and rode into Naples. Citizens were lined along the roads and streets waving and cheering. We jumped off the tanks and were given hugs by the girls – my huggers seemed pretty old to me, probably 30 or more."[101]

It was October 1 when the men entered Naples, and citizens were lined along the street waving and cheering on their liberators.

Capodichino Airfield

Francis Keefe and Leo Muri were nearly opposites. Keefe was from the big city of New York, Muri from Altoona, a rural community in central Pennsylvania. After graduating from Altoona High School, Muri moved to the coast and went to work in a Navy Yard. Not only did they have totally different backgrounds, but they were nearly opposites in physical stature. Keefe, a tall, lanky paratrooper stood at six foot, three inches and tipped the scales at 135. Muri, on the other hand, while skinny, was short. However, the two paratroopers quickly became inseparable friends, and would almost never leave each other's side up until the moment Keefe was wounded and sent home in September 1944, and even then the wounded Keefe sat there "concerned about him" because he was not going to be able to help him anymore.

When the men of I Company – the company which Keefe and Muri were members of – entered Naples, they took "Via Roma" into the city until it split, then were billeted in houses. After entering Naples, the 504th Parachute Infantry was given occupation duty – conducting patrols, breaking up disputes and other associated policing duties. Keefe and Muri's unit conducted these policing duties for several days before moving to secure the Capodichino Airfield, located just outside of Naples. "Me and Muri went on different patrols down the streets [of Naples] day and night; every four hours we would go on a patrol. I think we were there for two days and then we moved up to the airport. It was coming down by buckets – pouring rain – it's coming down by buckets and we went into one of the hangers, otherwise we were going to sleep out in the rain. It was like finding heaven. We were taking our clothes off because it was so wet and whatnot because we marched up to the airport and hit the cemetery and on top of the hill is the airport to the left. Now I know it had to be Colonel [Emory S.] Adams, he came in and said, 'What are you doing in here?' Everybody looked at him, I Company was in there, and we looked at him like what are you crazy, it's raining out. So he says, 'Everybody out of the building.' We were wondering why and he said, 'The engineers have to check it out for explosives.' So we had to go out and sleep in the rain at the airport."[102]

On October 5, newspaper reporter Hale Boyle visited Capodichino Airfield and wrote a story about the weakening German Luftwaffe, and interviewed several officers from the 504th who were at the airfield, such as Adams and Lieutenant Moffatt Burriss. Lieutenant Frank Payne was quoted as saying, "They left behind three to five Messerschmitts, which some of our men said could be put into flying shape in a few hours. Much of the destruction here was caused by the Germans themselves. While they were setting off their demolitions in the city of Naples they blew up a barracks near here and dynamited the water and electrical installations in the whole area. They cut the wires and broke the pipes. They destroyed anything they thought might be of the slightest use to us.

"There's no doubt they did a hell of a lot of damage here, just as they did in Naples, but what good will all their fireworks do them in the end?"[103]

Resting in Naples

The regiment was given a period of rest in the city, for a duration of approximately two weeks. The men of the 2nd Battalion were quartered in the Dante Alighieri school building, located on Piazza Carlo III. Albano Tassinari remembered the school being bombed out, and at night could remember the Germans coming over for occasional bombing raids on the Naples Pier. "They would light up the sky with flares to try and bomb that pier," Tassinari recalled. "And they did a good job of it... Oh, they were bastards."[104]

Roy Hanna remembered that he and the 3rd Battalion officers were billeted together in apartment buildings. Hanna was roommates with his closest friend, 1st Lieutenant Peter J. Eaton. Eventually, the regiment's rear echelon caught up with them, bringing with it all their equipment which had been left behind in Africa. Roy Hanna had packed Hershey's bars, and was hoping he and Eaton could enjoy the American classic in Naples.

When we were preparing to go 'overseas' we were told that each of us had a wooden crate in which our individual parachutes were packed for shipment and there was a lot of space for some personal items – candy was suggested.

Why these 'personal parachute boxes' I'll never understand because we didn't have our personally packed parachutes [until] after the 'D' stage of Parachute Training.

To continue: I bought two or more boxes of Hershey bars and put them in a 'Roy Hanna's Parachute Box'. I never saw that box again until we were in a rest mode in Naples and housed in an apartment building with very sparse furnishings; straight chairs, table, gas burner, or whatever.

Somehow we got word that our parachute box was available and we could pick up our personal things. I don't remember where these boxes were or how we got the stuff.

Pete and I were roommates in this apartment building. After I got the Hershey bars, we each grabbed a bar and took a big bite and promptly spit it out – the only taste in our mouths was that resembling moth balls. I assume the parachutes were packed is some kind of bug control.

I got the dumb idea that maybe the moth ball flavor was volatile enough that we could boil the flavor out. And so, I got a pan and put several of the Hershey bars in it and brought them to a slow boil. Result: After the chocolate cooled down, the flavor was as pronounced as at the beginning.[105]

H. Donald Zimmerman described their stay in Naples as allowing them to feel "loose and fancy free."[106] While they did have policing duties in the city, it was also a period for them to have some rest and relaxation. Lieutenant Edward Kennedy sent home a photograph taken by a street photographer of he and his best friend 2nd Lieutenant John Magner, a fellow Irish-Catholic from Philadelphia, and wrote home that it was "right after this was taken we drank four quarts of champagne together. It was the first day off we had in a long while and we sure had a good time. The people over here are very friendly but stupid. No wonder their army was no darn good."

This photo of John Magner, the 3rd Battaion supply officer, and Ed Kennedy was taken by a street photographer in Naples. (Author's collection)

Mail correspondence from home for any paratrooper was always a huge lift to their morale in both combat and rest periods alike. Kennedy called getting mail from his family back in Holyoke, Massachusetts "certainty a precious thing over here… I am OK except for losing a little weight and feel pretty pooped out.

I wish I could write to you about some interesting things but we aren't allowed to," he had penned on August 31 while in Africa. "It's pretty hot right now Rose and I'm going to cut this short. By the time you receive this I imagine you'll have a lot to read about in the papers. Keep saying some prayers for me Rose – someone's prayers were certainly with me the other night. Regards to John and write soon."

From Naples on October 10 he wrote this letter home:

I received your letter of Sept. 13 about three days ago, which wasn't bad time at all. I am feeling good and think I am putting on a little weight. As days go by I see many more interesting things. Maybe later on I can write and tell you just where I was when I wrote this letter. I've seen some real beautiful things and some ghastly sights besides. Our censor regulations are as strict as ever. Only received five letters this week, which wasn't good. I'd appreciate it if you would send some more candy, so here it is in writing as you asked for it. We really don't need much over here. In fact, I haven't used half the equipment I originally came overseas with. I certainly would like to see Jimmy now; I guess he should be a lot of fun now. Well this is all for now. Love to all.[107]

Once Naples Harbor was cleared, war materials started flowing into the city in preparation for the advance to Rome. It became an area swarming with activity like that found in a beehive, with troops and equipment moving in every direction as ship after ship unloaded its cargo in an unending procession. Fred Baldino was once assigned to direct traffic in Naples. "They actually treated us as liberators," he remembered. "They cussed out Mussolini for getting them in the war, and no matter where you went in Sicily or southern Italy, it seemed everyone had a cousin living in Brooklyn. We were well received, but at the time there was hardly any food in Naples and the young Italians used to rob the American trucks whenever they got the chance. Hunger will do that to you."[108]

As Baldino stood in the main street directing traffic, the 12th Service Company of the US Army Air Forces came into the docks. When Baldino first enlisted in the Army, he was a clerk in the 12th Service Company at Tallahassee Airfield. It was here when, a few months after Pearl Harbor, Baldino and his friends gathered for drinks in the post exchange. "Hey," one of the men said, "we aren't going to get to kill any Germans in the ground crew of the Air Corps, so let's join the paratroops." Everyone agreed, but only three of the men passed the test to join the parachute troops.[109]

As his old company drove past him in trucks, Baldino directed them through and waived to all the men whom he knew from his service in Florida. "A couple days later," he recalled, "they were encamped near Naples and I went over to the outfit and got my friend John Pechanski and we did the town up celebrating."[110] Baldino and Pechanski had been friends well before their service in the Army, and had actually enlisted together in 1941 when they were working in the Pennsylvania coal mines. "War was on the horizon and they were drafting men who were 21-years-old or older, and I was 19 at the time, but my friend John Pechanski was 22. I told him he would be drafted anytime and I would be soon so I suggested he enlist. He surprised me and said okay. We went down to the county seat, Pottsville, PA, and enlisted. The sergeant there asked when we wanted to go and we said now. He then said, 'You guys didn't rob a bank did you?' and we of course said no. And so he signed us up. We went back to our hometown of Ashland, PA and our friends took us out on a drinking spree and we didn't get home until 2 AM the next morning. But we got up at 6 AM and went to Pottsville. From there they shipped us to Philadelphia, PA, where we were sworn in." They stayed with each other until Baldino volunteered for the parachute troops, and they had not seen each other since – until that day in Naples.[111]

Fred J. Baldino in Naples, Italy at age 22. (Fred Baldino)

Other paratroopers also did the town up celebrating when they were not on duty. Lieutenant John Lekson wrote, "The 1st Battalion laid claim to an Italian nightclub called 'The Garden of Oranges' – 'Degli Arancis'. Despite its prior claim, the battalion had to contest the Peninsular Base Section and the Allies for its right to use the establishment."[112] In another local, one company first sergeant from the 504th and several of his men found themselves in the stockade of a military police unit after some drunken escapades near the harbor. When Colonel Tucker came to pick his men up, the MP officer refused to release them. Colonel Tucker insisted that his men be released and if they were not, he would come back with his regiment and they would release their comrades themselves. When Colonel Tucker left, the MP officer phoned General Mark Clark and informed him of Tucker's demands. General Clark told the MP officer that he'd better release Tucker's troopers.

The war, meanwhile, carried north towards the Volturno River, which was crossed in mid-October. Ahead of the Allied armies were the vast mountain ranges stretching from Naples to Rome, crisscrossed by winding rivers and fertile valleys, and dotted with high mountain villages.

While the stay in Naples did have its ups, it also had its downs. In addition to occasional German air-raids on the harbor, the evidence of the war and the brutality of the Germans abounded. A German time bomb went off in one building, collapsing the entire structure and killing many. Even while the regiment was in garrison the war was never far. Leveled or bombed out buildings abundant on every street were visible signs but the invisible signs were the gnawing of starving Neapolitan stomachs for food which was nearly impossible to find, and the lacking fresh water works and gas and electrical utilities which were all destroyed by the Germans before leaving the city.

Officers started being whisked away to meetings at the end of October. "We almost cheered when we heard that we were scheduled to go back into combat," Lieutenant Roy Hanna said.

As the men prepared to move out, General Clark rode by in his Jeep and stopped to talk to Captain Arthur Ferguson of E Company. Clark remarked that their coming maneuver would be like an autumn hike, and that the men would enjoy the scenery.[113]

6

THE AUTUMNAL HIKE

Lieutenant Roy Hanna and his men were marching down the gravel road shortly before they were to reach the Volturno River when the screaming of shells overhead pierced through the air. They were coming close. Roy Hanna fell on his belly and buried his head into the gravel as the shells began to impact. It all happened so fast, he didn't even have time to get inside the drainage ditch on the side of the road, where he should have gone to provide protection from shrapnel. Suddenly his body was showered with dirt. A German shell landed in the ditch alongside him – right where he should have been.[114]

General Clark's autumnal hike would prove to be a long and difficult climb up the damp Apennine slopes north of Naples, although Clark was right about one thing – the scenery. "It's a nice looking country though," Sergeant David Rosenkrantz wrote home, "but looks don't count here."[115]

Some of the mountainsides which the men of the 504th Parachute Infantry Regiment would climb and traverse were deemed as nearly impassable. The lightly armed and physically conditioned paratroopers, however, were well-suited to the task. They would first enter the Matese range, providing a vital link of contact between their American 5th Army to their left, and the British 8th Army, on the other side of the mountains, to their right.

As much as the paratroopers fought the Germans, they fought the weather, or perhaps more so than the Germans. While the regiment was in the mountains throughout the month of November, it rained approximately 26 days out of 30, leading Francis Keefe to claim that his platoon being stuck out in the rain so much – even in Naples at Capodichino Airfield – was becoming a "conspiracy" against him. Keeping dry was nearly impossible. Each morning seemed to start with a rain shower, swelling the mountain streams and rivers they were to cross as they made their way through the mountains. The temperatures stayed around fifty degrees during the day, leaving a cool and damp atmosphere, and the men rarely saw their shadow; the sun came out only occasionally in small spurts.

The Germans were retreating, unlike the weather, and other than some delaying actions and patrol actions, heavy and direct contact with German forces was negligible. In fact, one lieutenant wrote that he didn't fire his Thompson the whole time they were on their autumnal hike. Generally, casualties were light for the paratroopers. One did have to remain extremely vigilant for booby traps and landmines, however, which were left behind by the retiring Germans.

The tragedy of the German occupation was also evident in the small mountain villages that the paratroopers passed through. It was often that scantily-clothed Italian children would follow the men to their bivouac areas and beg for food. And if they got little or nothing, they would patiently wait for the paratroopers to discard their scraps. One day some paratroopers under Lieutenant Donald Horton were advancing up a hill in the midst of a rainstorm under sporadic fire from the Germans. After summiting the mountain, Fred Baldino and another man, soaking wet, went up to an old Italian house while Lieutenant Horton was in his little pup tent in the rain. "The woman had us take our clothes off and she dried them for us and we gave her some food and some money," Baldino recalled. Food for the paratroopers – K-rations – were often a topic of grumbling and joking. On the side of a mountain trail, paratroopers made jokes of the food as they threw elements of their packaged meals behind and up over their heads in disgust. Some days they went without eating. Marvin Courtney remembered his more mountain-savvy assistant Demart Chamberlain looking down on the ground while moving rather than up the mountain like most of the others did as they went up a terraced hillside. Courtney watched as he would bend down and pull up vegetables from the ground. When they finally stopped for the night, Chamberlain took a tin can from a C-ration package and began cooking the vegetables over a small fire. Greasy canned hash was often consumed by the paratroopers, and Courtney once ate so much of it he ended up vomiting it all back up.

On the night of October 28-29, the 2nd Battalion led the regiment off on the great autumnal hike by passing through the positions of the 135th Infantry Regiment of the 34th Infantry Division and going down the road from Ailano to Valle. Meeting no resistance, the battalion seized Valle Agricola before the end of the 29th, and the parachute infantrymen took up positions on the surrounding hilltops.

Gallo Matese

It was just after sunrise on October 30, 1943 as the 504th Parachute Infantry Regiment's 2nd Battalion moved out of Valle Agricola. The day grew warm and the sky clear as Major Melvin S. Blitch, Jr. of Columbus, Georgia was led along by Italian boys along the rocky hill mass, with two companies of paratroopers following. They had come from a hill on the south side of Valle Agricola, down into the valley, and then laboriously climbed up the mountain before moving in the direction of Prata Sannita. Their objective was to get to the other side of the mountain towards Letino.

The battalion's commanding officer, Major Daniel W. Danielson of San Francisco, California, was accompanying the other half of his battalion as they too were led by civilians along the valley, taking a different route. Both forces reunited above the village of Prata at the entrance to the water main tunnel on the side of the mountain. Major Blitch and a few men went to investigate. He came up to the old gate guarding the entrance and pried it open. They passed word back for the rest of the battalion to follow, which they did in single-file. The tunnel was nearly a half-mile long, narrow, and pitch black. Since the battalion had been moving through the mountains in Italy the past couple of days, they had begun to take pack mules to help carry equipment, but they couldn't bring the mules through the tunnel.

As the battalion came out of the tunnel near the top of (what they referred to as) Mt. Capella, the mountains ceased and below them a basin-like valley of lush blue-green farmland appeared.[116] With the brilliant color of the lush, cultivated vegetation and the surrounding mountains, it was a beautiful sight made for a postcard. Below the paratroopers was the village of Letino, on the east side of the basin, and out in the distance the men could see Gallo on the far western side of the basin, back dropped by low rolling mountains. James T. Sapp remembered, "It was up in the mountains, but it was like a big basin. It was, the town of Gallo was down in it and it had farmland down around, but it was hill all around and there was just one road that went into Gallo."[117]

The troopers went down the mountain and captured the dam that created Lago di Letino. They stopped for lunch in this area and then, at 1400, moved into Letino, where they found the townspeople lined up in their best dress to welcome their liberators. As a sign of the appreciation and excitement, the townspeople threw banquets, and rang all the church bells (much to the officers' displeasure, as there were Germans on the other side of the valley in Gallo).

The battalion moved out again at about 1445. Destination: Gallo. The battalion Headquarters Company moved along the road on the south side of the valley, with D Company led by Captain Stanley Dolezal advancing through the brush above the road.

As Headquarters Company continued on the road, the Germans down in Gallo fired machine guns and 20mm guns on the paratroopers as they negotiated the hillside. The company went above the road and took cover in the brush, and the 81mm Mortar Platoon of Lieutenant Lauren Ramsey tried to fire on the Germans in town. The battalion journal recorded that "a German light tank was observed to enter the town from the other side and presently it poked its nose out of a lane facing the Bn and fired several shots; it repeated this four or five times."[118] Lieutenant Chester Garrison, the battalion's adjunct, was using Lauren Ramsey's field glasses and picking out German troops running about in the valley and relaying adjustments for the mortar fire. The little figures were at great distance, Garrison recalled, and the endeavor seemed "impersonal and game-like. We did not see the blood or hear the distress."[119]

As darkness fell, the battalion went back into Letino to spend the night. The night grew bad with a rain descending on the valley, which turned the temperature cool. Private Robert J. Finizio and four men took a patrol that night and snuck into Gallo and contacted a local priest, possibly Father Don Pasquala. The priest told Finizio that the Germans had pulled out just after dark, except for one squad armed with a machine gun. Finizio instructed him with great force not to ring the bells when they arrived (despite the fact it was going to be Sunday the following day). Sergeant John W. McGarrah also led a patrol to get the layout of the town.[120]

At 0500 on October 31, Lieutenant Virgil F. Carmichael led a small patrol into Gallo and contacted civilians. The battalion was a couple of hours behind him, with D Company advancing on the left of town and F Company maneuvering to the right of town. Once the first elements reached the far side of town, a small firefight broke out between the paratroopers and German soldiers.

The battalion journal best describes the situation:

One Polish refugee who had been on labor detail under the Germans and who had been hiding in the house of some prominent citizen, gave himself up to the patrol – he was immediately searched by Lt. Carmichael and sent under guard back to Lt. Gorham at Regimental Headquarters, now at Letino. Some natives from outlying farms made their way into the village with information concerning the approximate positions of German machine guns... Six enemy dead were reported and three wounded, and also one prisoner. Bn CP was set up in an old school house in town. The civilians have been most obliging and helpful. At night the enemy shelled the town at 1900 – hits to left rear and front of town, stopped firing after 3/4 of an hour.[121]

The paratroopers found the people of Gallo accommodating and welcoming. Like most Italians, they had suffered much from the Germans, especially in the last month with the Germans stealing foodstuffs and animals which left the people starved. Some took for the mountains until the arrival of the Americans. On October 29, while the paratroopers were still in Letino, the Germans summarily executed a 38-year-old artisan by a gunshot to the head for allegedly being an American spy.[122]

The people who settled Gallo, in the ancient volcano crater they now cultivated crops from, originated out of Bulgaria. Their secluded location meant that they retained much of their original culture;

their dress and their language, for instance. James Sapp remembered the people treating them wonderfully and found his experience in Gallo, and the war at large, extremely educational:

They treated us royal, but the people in Gallo, they were not Italians…. They had really colorful dress and they just dressed different from the Italians and Lieutenant Ramsey told us later that those people came over to Italy and settled there in Gallo… I was really blessed to go all those places that I would have never had [the] chance to go. I had to go at a terrible time – the war – but I went through those three countries in North Africa, and I went to those places in North Africa. People lived like they did back in Christ's time and we got to go those places over there and [see] how the Arabian people lived in the deserts and then we got to Kairouan – that's where we were stationed out [of] – Kairouan was the third most holy city in Islam and it was a walled city. It was off limits to Americans, but all the roads came just like spokes in a wheel come in there. It was at least a half a mile, might have been more than that, all the way around that town. It was mostly desert but just like little Roman hills and people had been buried there for ages. Almost every day you would see a camel caravan come in there and one of the camels would have a saddle with like a flat top and there would be a corpse on there and they would be wrapped like the wrapped Jesus when he was buried. All that was really educational to me.[123]

Macchia and Fornelli

On the morning of November 4, the 1st Platoon of I Company was ordered to the village of Macchia d'Isernia. The platoon dug in at the graveyard, which they felt was very "convenient," overlooking a valley.[124]

There were two men dug in with the platoon who were out of place. The soldiers wore standard field jackets and pants with no side pockets and pant legs which flowed down past the ankles, as opposed to the other men dug into the graveyard who wore baggy, tan trousers –with a big pocket on each leg – and bloused. The man's name was Charles O'Keefe, the brother of Francis Keefe.

Just before they started the autumnal hike, Charles and his childhood friend took leave from their unit in Naples, the 803rd MP Battalion, and came to where the 504th PIR was bivouacked to move up into the mountains the next day.

We were bivouacked at our jumping off point. We were behind, the 5th Army was up in front of us and the mountains where we were going were on the right facing north, as far as where the 5th Army went, and all of the sudden we heard this big, loud cheering and clapping way off in the 1st Battalion. The 1st Battalion was the first lead off, then the 2ⁿᵈ, then the 3ʳᵈ. We were all saying, "What in the world is going on over there." Then they come into the 2ⁿᵈ Battalion, then they head to the Headquarters, G [Company], H [Company], and then I [Company].

I looked out and there was my brother and his friend George Pagano. They had white helmet liners on and carrying two sub-machine guns and white leggings. They were all screaming, "The war is over!" They were making fun. So anyway, they come in and I said, "What in the world are you doing here?" They said, "We want to go see combat." I said, "What, are you crazy?" So he says, "No, we're going to see combat." I said, "Look, I got enough problems myself, but I don't even want you going off with us." Sergeant White was standing there listening to this. So he says, "If we won't go with you we're going to go with another outfit." So I am trying to talk them out of it. Well anyway, Sergeant White went over to [Captain] Warfield and he told Warfield Keefe's brother and his friend, they want to join the outfit and they want to go to combat. He said, "The more the merrier."[125]

At the time, Francis Keefe was not happy with his brother's decision to go to combat with the platoon, but Charles brought a camera with him and captured several photos of the men in action in the mountains. Many years now removed, Francis Keefe is happy his brother came – just for the fact that he took the photographs.

The 1st Platoon of Company I, under the leadership of 2nd Lt. Robert Blankenship moves towards the village of Macchia on November 2, 1943. (Francis Keefe)

While they were dug into the graveyard at Macchia, Charles O'Keefe sat down with one of the men in the squad, Private Forrest Pierce. Peirce, who was a large and strong man, yet gentle and quiet, pulled out a photo of his daughter and showed it to Charles O'Keefe. Pierce told O'Keefe he felt he was going to be killed soon.[126] Sadly, his premonition would come to pass about a week later.

The men spent some time with the children and Italian civilians in Macchia, and remained dug into the graveyard until they were ordered to the village of Fornelli on the 7th.

Surrounded by lush green rolling hills dotted with olive trees and grape vines, the Piazza was the heart of Fornelli. The stone and plaster walled buildings – topped by little clay tiled roofs – sat in a circular shape on the summit of a small green hilltop and stood overlooking the rolling landscape beneath it, boarded in by the rugged mountain terrain. The Piazza was the center of the community and provided vitality for the community of substance farmers who worked the vineyards and the fields in the surrounding low hills. The Piazza hosted the market within its streets, where the farmers traded their crops for other items they required. The church was where many of the children who were birthed into the local families were baptized.

Life was simple but hard, Tata Antonaccio, a local subsistence farmer, would explain. In October, the corn which was planted in May was harvested, along with grapes to make wine. In November, under normal conditions, the fields would be plowed and sowed with wheat, which would be reaped in the summer months. Potatoes were planted in February, which would be picked in June. In January, the pig is killed for meat which would cure until February and feed the family with sausage for much of the year.

War reached Fornelli with the arrival of Moroccan troops and their tanks; tanks which destroyed the farm fields which grew the crops the families used to feed themselves. These would be just the beginnings of even harder times.

The Germans followed the Moroccans, and with the arrival of the Germans came even greater hunger. The Germans stole the animals which the Italians relied on for meat and their tanks rolling through the fields destroyed the crops underneath the weight of their tracks and wheels. The Germans, however, didn't destroy the grapes on the Antonaccio farm. Wine was made, which was then traded at the Piazza for beans which were soaked in gasoline.

Later, it became safe only to travel at night, and soon the men fled the town and held out in the surrounding mountains. On October 4, the Germans rounded up six men, including Mayor Laurelli, and summarily executed them by hanging.[127]

Perhaps the first Americans to enter Fornelli was a patrol led by Lieutenant Floyd Fry on the evening of November 4. He estimated a German battalion was garrisoned in Fornelli, with more Germans in the surrounding mountains to the west. He observed a strong German patrol of 20-30 men moving along the road from Isernia to Fornelli and engaged them in a small firefight. The patrol made it back to report on the movement in the late morning of the 5th.

The night was damp and black when the men of the 3rd Battalion dropped down from Macchia. Men and mules heavy laden with the materials of war filed down onto the road to Fornelli as they moved through the valley of lush, green low rolling hills sliced up by groves and small fields of crops. Seen in the daytime, it was scenery as one would have envisioned on a postcard of rural Italy.

It began to rain, putting a bite in the cool mountain air.

Under the rainfall, the men of Company I, leading the way for the battalion, came to the La Vandra River. Under normal conditions, it was a small stream of pristine blue-green water but with all the winter's rainfall, it had become a rushing torrent of waist-deep water.

The I Company paratroopers plunged in. Beside where they were wading, the corpses of two Germans were sticking up. *I hope nobody drank this water*, Francis Keefe said to himself.

The men moved towards a hedge on the other side when suddenly a German artillery spotter unleashed an intense barrage. The mules went crazy, braying to the cacophony of explosions zeroing in on the hedge. The company took cover behind a small three-foot rise in the ground, their only protection from the shrapnel. There were several casualties. One trooper missing a portion of his arm came down. "Keefe, they took off my arm. I'll see ya. Take care," he said as he walked passed alongside the medic.

Keefe's brother decided he would go back to his military police duties Naples.

After making it through the barrage, Lieutenant Ferrill moved the men to the base of a ridge and ordered Keefe and a couple others to go and scout the ridge and make sure there were no Germans lying in wait on top. *If the Germans don't know we're here now, they're gonna know*, Keefe thought to himself.

The rest of the company strung out and waited.

Keefe and the others returned with a good report and informed Lieutenant Ferrill there were no Germans.

"Nobody?" he asked.

"Nobody."

"Okay, let's get ready to go," said the lieutenant.

Keefe turned to go talk to his best friend, Leo Muri, who was lying down and suffering from a bout with Malaria, like many others in the regiment.

"Keefe, that includes you. You can lead the way," the lieutenant said.

"Okay, lieutenant, just a minute. I want to talk to Muri."

"I'm telling you!"

Keefe went to go talk to Muri, but the company was shortly moving up the ridge and dug in with the Piazza to their backs.

Company I was lucky. "If it wasn't for that piece of ground coming up about three feet, we would have had a ton of casualties. I Company would have been cut in half," said Francis Keefe.[128]

Charles O'Keefe of the 803rd MP Battalion and his brother, Francis Keefe of Company I, 504th PIR, pose for a photograph with the villagers of Macchia. (Francis Keefe)

While Lieutenant Ferrill and his men were able to get across without becoming terribly disorganized, the rest of the battalion was not a fortunate, as the German artillery continued to bemoan their efforts at crossing the La Vandra. Earl Oldfather remembered that Company G reached the bridge crossing the river when the German shells began coming in so close that his ears rang and dirt was thrown at his helmet. One man, wounded, lay calling for his mother. At 2340, Lieutenant Edward Kennedy called from one of the 1st Battalion's outposts and reported that they were disorganized. Company G went across the river wading underneath the bridge, turning their feet into icicles, and waited for the rest of the battalion to get organized again. This would be accomplished by daylight, and the battalion was set in the defense. Later that morning, the regimental CP opened in Fornelli.[129] When the person who was responsible for calling in the German artillery was discovered, they were summarily executed.

Action on Hill 1017 Near Colli

It was a bright moonlit night as Lieutenant Payton Elliott led his platoon out of Colli. As they departed, the Germans began shelling the village. Elliott and his men dipped down into the waist-deep Volturno River and waded across. On the other side, Elliott formed his platoon for an attack. They were to slip up through a mined vineyard at the base of Mount 1017 and kick the Germans off in the night. Behind Elliott, the rest of the company was wading the cold waters of the Volturno.

Elliott moved to the front of his platoon to lead them. Sergeant Charles Hawkins, who had led a scouting party to the area during the daylight, was a few paces behind guiding the lieutenant on where to go. They reached the edge of the vineyard, guarded by a strand of wire. Elliott was passed the wire cutters and began to cut a gap, and Sergeant Hawkins held the freshly cut entanglement to keep it from making noise.

The platoon funneled through the gap and into the vineyard, resuming its attack formation on the other side of the gap that Elliott cut. The men moved through the vineyard until an S-mine – a nasty invention known to the men as the Bouncing Betty – was spotted.[130]

The German 'S' mine derives its name from its bouncing action: It was first triggered by an unfortunate soldier stepping on a short prong sticking out of the ground. A small charge at the bottom of the canister would detonate and propel the canister about two feet in the air, just at waist height. Inside the canister was another charge lined with ball-bearings. When it detonated, it sent the ball bearings in all directions. It was highly effective at killing and it was an agonizing way to die.

Captain Fred Thomas, the company commander came forward. They decided to veer off to the left. Just as soon as they got started, Sergeant Hawkins stepped on a mine, claiming his life. The men got down on their bellies and watched, waiting for the Germans to open fire or attack. Sergeant Heinz Graalfs gave account of the efforts: "We ran into a single strand of wire running along the foot of the hill, and behind that the Germans had laid booby traps and mines. We crawled along the ground on our bellies, feeling ahead of us for trap wires and mines, but there were too many of them for us to get through. Some boys never came back from the minefield – because they crawled onto mines or booby traps."[131]

Lieutenant Roy Hanna watched as Captain Fred Thomas tripped an S mine on the trail, and watched as it popped up from the ground and exploded, wounding Thomas.[132]

The company backed out of the mined vineyard.

The next day, the company moved back up with a team of engineers led by Lieutenant "Spike" Harris, who were to clear the mines. As they were working with their metal detectors, one of the engineers discovered two Germans asleep behind a boulder, who were promptly awoken and coarsely questioned about the locations of the mines. They informed that the northern slope was not as heavily mined, and the two Germans were impressed as guides.[133]

A firefight broke out as they doggedly made their way up the slope, which was covered in thick, heavy brush and vines limiting the ability for controlling the attack. Sergeant Leonard Harmon and his squad eliminated one machine gun nest. Heinz Graalfs recalled that Harmon "sent one rifleman around the right flank and another on the left flank. They opened fire on the Germans position and then Harmon led his men on a frontal assault that cleaned them out."[134]

A group of Company I also began a dogged fight up the mountain, skirmishing the Germans as they came. One of the first paratroopers to reach the top of the hill was Lieutenant Henry B. Keep. When the small group surged over the crest, they ran into a German bivouac and immediately attacked the resting Germans, surprising them, and quickly drove them off.

In the paratroops, the diverse nature of the men meant that millionaires and beggars alike served alongside one another. Lieutenant Henry Keep belonged to the former class, in the most literal sense. His father, Henry B. Keep, Sr., was a graduate of Yale, and joined the Army at the beginning of the US involvement in the First World War. He first saw action in July 1918, and in August was promoted to captain and given command of a company in the 10th Machine Gun Battalion. He was scheduled to be relieved for training, but insisted that he stay with his company to lead it in the coming offensive. On October 5, 1918 Keep and his company officers were sleeping in a shell hole when a German artillery shell landed in the hole, claiming the life of Captain Keep, Sr.[135]

Henry Keep, Jr. had been born on October 1, 1917, and his father was killed just a few days after his first birthday; they never met. Captain Keep's widow married Major Charles J. Biddle, of the influential Philadelphia Biddle family, in 1923. Charles Biddle had been a famous flying ace during the war, and he documented his experiences in the air war over France in a book entitled *The Way of the Eagle*, which was released in 1919. Biddle was a graduate of Princeton before going to Harvard Law School, and when the Great War broke out he was practicing law and terminated those efforts to join the Army. He returned to law after the war a hero fighter pilot and became an influential litigator.[136]

Lieutenant Henry Keep, Jr.'s family background made him the regiment's resident millionaire. It was rumored that he requested not to be paid for his services in the war and what was to be his salary used for the war effort, but law required he be paid some salary which became once cent.

Despite whether the rumor was true or not, Keep's generosity, even to the enlisted men under his charge, was fact. Always ensuring his men had some money when they went on leave, Keep would ask, "How much money you got?" as he nuzzled up to the man, "to go on furlough?" Sometimes no matter the reply, he'd say, "Here, take this."

While the men were training, Keep bought a 1942 Buick for his men because he did not like watching them have to wait for the bus into town. And when they left for Europe, he gave the Buick to the wife of Lieutenant Willis Ferrill and their two children. "He was always involved," Moffatt Burriss remembered, "he was our battalion S-3 and of course we had close contact with him virtually every day. He was very generous."

On the morning after taking Hill 1017, Keep was wounded when a burst from a German's Schmeisser machine pistol stitched him up the inside of the thigh with three bullet holes, almost in the crotch. Someone later told Roy Hanna that Keep observed men digging down at the forward slope of the hill below him, and he got above them to holler at them and tell them to come back up towards the top of the hill because they were too far down. They were Germans, not paratroopers as he thought, and his order was answered with gunfire.[137]

Keep wrote a letter from the hospital describing his participation in the fight on the hill and the wound which he received.

November 22, 1943

Dear Daddy,

If you can't read this letter I am not surprised since my index finger has a bullet hole in it and hence is incapacitated. I suppose you have by now heard from Captain Kitchin, our battalion medical officer. I asked him to write you and tell you the story. I was wounded for the second time on November 13th, somewhere in Italy by a German machine pistol. There is one bullet hole in my left foot, two in my left calf and one in the index finger of my right hand and a little shrapnel in my left cheek. Don't worry, they are not serious and the doctor says they are mending nicely. We had been fighting at the front for weeks (I can't say where or even describe the terrain). Someday I'll give you a vivid picture of it. On the 12th our battalion was given the mission of taking the corps objective, a hill. What was left of one company started up the hill but was stopped by mines on all the trails. Our company was sent for and when we arrived at the place where the other company had been stopped three enemy machine guns opened up on all of us. We dispersed and keeping off the mined trails and fields, set out under cover of the thick underbrush on the slope of the hill to get the machine guns. After a firefight of about three quarters of an hour the machine guns were stilled and two other officers and myself and three or four enlisted men found ourselves half way up the hill. We decided to continue to the top as it would be easier for our outfit to take the hill if there were already some of us on top.

The climbing was difficult, the undergrowth thick, and we didn't know what was on top. When finally we got there, we found ourselves in the middle of a German bivouac, occupied at the time. We had another firefight, killed three men, the Germans retreated down the ridge. There was about a squad of them. I decided it would be best for the six of us to get to the highest point on the ridge where we could make some kind of a defense and hold the hill. We made our way cautiously to the peak keeping an eye out for more Germans. We got there, strung ourselves out in a defensive line and I sent one man down the hill to tell the colonel what happened and to get reinforcements up immediately. About two or three hours later our company commander [Captain George Warfield] arrived with one platoon and that night we were able to set up a defensive position. That night all was quiet. Early the next morning under the cover of the heavy undergrowth and darkness a platoon of Germans got up the hill and opened fire on us. That was when I was hit. Another firefight of about an hour ensued and the Germans were driven off again. It was about 7:30 I was hit. About one o'clock more reinforcements arrived as well as stretchers for us wounded. A stretcher-bearing detail took me down the hill by the path now clear of mines to the aid station. We were shelled heavily on the way down. About 7 I got to the aid station. The next day I was evacuated until I finally arrived here. The six of us were the first people on the corps objective. It gave me quite a funny feeling. The men on the hill when we were up there did a superb job. My hand is giving out; so I'll have to close. Don't worry about me. I am all right. My thoughts are always of you and mother and the boys.

Continue to write me to the old address.

Love,

Henry[138]

For a great perspective on Lieutenant Keep's actions from others who were with him, and a great account of the fighting on Hill 1017 in general, Moffatt Burriss' memoir *Strike and Hold* is the best resource.

Tragedy on Hill 1017

By the morning of the November 15, the 3rd Battalion had been relieved, and the men of the 1st Battalion were firmly entrenched to protect Hill 1017. At around 1600 on the 18th, a call came into the Regimental Headquarters from Hill 1017. They reported that they were under fire, that there were causalities and they were requesting medical aid. An ambulance was dispatched to nearby Colli to collect the wounded.[139]

On the hill, Lieutenant Lyle Nightingale and 1st Sergeant Albert Henry lay dead, along with Sergeant William Jones of the 376th Parachute Field Artillery Battalion's liaison party. Several other were wounded; they were all victims of the German's artillery.

Ross Carter and Bill Murry were just coming back from taking their canteens and a large, five-gallon jug down the mountain to get water – which, along with rations, was in short supply at the forward position – for the men. While they were out, they watched as the Germans shelled Colli, and the hill which they had come from. When they returned from their water duty, they were told about Nightingale and 1st Sergeant Henry. Ross Carter recorded in his memoir the last trip of their beloved first sergeant: "Next afternoon donkeys were brought up on the mountain to carry off the dead men… First Sergeant Henry, the last to be carried down, was one of the best men who ever served his country. He was always fatherly and thoughtful of his squad's well-being. We stood looking at Henry, whose short, black curly-haired, blood-matted head hung on one side of the donkey and his shrapnel-mangled legs on the other. More than one man had tears in his eyes as Henry disappeared around the bend."[140]

Lieutenant Harold Gutterman and the Regimental Reconnaissance Platoon

Since the regiment's breakout from Salerno, 29-year-old 2nd Lieutenant Harold Gutterman and his paratroopers of the Regimental Reconnaissance Platoon had been on the cutting edge of the regiments advance though southern Italy. On the advance to Naples, Gutterman and some of his troopers had been the first Americans to reach the ancient ruins of Pompeii after they attached themselves to a British armored column.[141]

Gutterman, of Jewish decent like many others in the platoon, was born in 1914 in Devil's Lake, North Dakota to a father who had emigrated from the Crimea. The Gutterman's moved to a farm in Bristol, Indiana when Harold was a young boy, where he and his two brothers grew up. Harold graduated from Elkhart High School and went to Purdue University to study agriculture. After graduating, he enlisted in the Army on September 23, 1941 and was inducted at Ft. Benjamin Harrison, Indiana. After service in Hawaii, Texas and California, he graduated Officer Candidate School as an infantry officer and was commissioned on November 19, 1942. And after volunteering for, and completing, Parachute School at Fort Benning, he was assigned to the 504th Parachute Infantry Regiment.

Troopers of the 504th PIR negotiate the steep terrain in the mountains of central Italy. (US Signal Corps)

The men in Gutterman's platoon were specially trained for the job they were to carry out. James Gann was one of the men who served in the platoon. "Say we are going to take a village," Gann explains, "we would go in, maybe three of us, we'd go in and reconnoiter to find out the German movement in there. Then come back and report…then we'd go from there. We did a pretty good job of snooping, I'd call it. We were all checked out before we were in [the platoon]… They put us in a room one at a time and we'd look at everything in there, then go out. If they had moved something and added something, you had to know what had been added or what had been taken away. So, we had a pretty good memory as far as [that goes]." A lot of the men were of German decent, or could speak German.[142]

The Regimental S-3 Journal gives an idea of the actions of the platoon as it recorded their findings and the messages which Lieutenant Gutterman would send back. The Regimental Staff Journal also recorded some of Gutterman's messages from his advance patrols. As a testament to the quality of the work the Reconnaissance Platoon was conducting, Gutterman was even sending back the names of the German officers in the area. A sampling of his messages recorded in the Staff Journal follows:

November 6

Message to S-2, 504 - Germans left their headquarters in Cerro Berger. A nest of machine guns between Pizzone and Castel San Vincenzo. Two to seven days ago tanks and infantry passed through Scapoli towards Cassino - Lt. Gutterman

November 7

Message to S-2 from Lt. Gutterman: All bridges blown along highway thru Cerro and Pizzone. Two tunnels blown. German tanks, armored cars, trucks traveled road between Alfedena and Cerro several times. Two days ago passed through Cerro, Colli, Volturno to Cassino. They have boasted of defenses either just north or south of Rome

Message to S-2 from Lt. Gutterman: Alfedene, Casteldi Sangro civilians had to evacuate. The informer believes heavy guns in area. German officers mentioned Opi, Rocca, Rieti, Termi as their area.

The work behind the enemy lines could sometimes be dangerous. James Gann and a couple other troopers were discovered while reconnoitering one village, and then pursued by the Germans. They escaped only by hiding inside of a mausoleum inside a graveyard. "It started raining," Gann recalled, "and we could hear them all around us, and it started raining then they gave up I guess but we spent the night in there. The next morning, we started going out one at a time and made it back." Since the war, Gann has continually asked himself why the mausoleum was unlocked; he has come to the conclusion that it was nothing short of a miracle.[143]

On November 14, Gutterman and several of his men were making a reconnaissance of Rocchetta when a German heavy weapons platoon came into the village. Held up in a white, three-story stucco house, one of the men yelled, "Krauts!" Subsequently, a battle ensured. On the steps leading to the third story, Lieutenant Gutterman was firing on Germans who were in a blind spot beneath a window. "I'll take care of the devils," Gutterman said. He leaned out to throw a grenade. Before he could get himself back inside, a bullet tore through his head, killing him instantly. The platoon sergeant, Staff Sergeant Donald Greaber, took command.[144]

For three and a half hours the paratroopers held the Germans off, before Sergeant Theodore Bachenheimer, who had escaped from the house to get help shortly after the fight began, brought paratroopers of the 2nd Battalion, who were three miles away in Cerro, to provide relief for the beleaguered paratroopers. In addition to Gutterman's body, there were two Germans who had been killed inside. The 2nd Battalion troopers took Gutterman's body to their battalion aid station, before Lieutenant Joseph Forestal claimed Gutterman's remains to move them to regiment.[145] Today, 2nd Lieutenant Harold Gutterman lies in the Sicily–Rome American Cemetery and Memorial in Nettuno, Italy.

The Problem of Supply

The regiment pushed past Rochetta and continued the march north to Cerro. The skies continued to pour rain, making the rising Volturno River problematic not only for the advancement of the forward echelons, but also the rear echelons trying to keep pace. In the forward echelon, Lieutenant Herbert Norman lost most of his equipment when he tried to cross the Sorgente Capo Volturno (the spring out of which the Volturno River is born) to lead his company to seize Castel San Vincenzo. The men even tried to use felled trees to cross, but the current was too swift and strong for them to cross as planned.[146]

In the rear echelon, the going was just as difficult with the continually rising water as the Volturno flowed south meeting its tributaries, now rushing with rain runoff. The same day that Lieutenant Norman lost his equipment trying to cross, a meeting was held at regiment to discuss the supply problem. The regiment was handily the furthest forward element of the Allied armies. This distance, over such terrain and coupled with rising water levels from the rain, making the river – in normal conditions wadable – strong, swift and deep, threatened the supply lines much more than the Germans did. Even without the weather, the terrain alone was a force to be reckoned with for the regiment's logisticians.

Lieutenant John L. Watson had been a supply officer in the 504th since Sicily. Positions in the Army were not necessarily given because of a person's background, but usually because of a person's availability at the time. For example, Watson had been an excellent horseman and a stunt man for Paramount Studios.[147] But he adapted and became an integral part of the success of the mission of removing the enemy from the rough mountain areas of central Italy.

Troopers of the 504th PIR, using mules to carry their 81mm mortars, negotiate a mountainside. (US Signal Corps)

As the paratroops raced through the high mountain trails, removing the enemy from the small villages and encampments, they discovered that resupplying rations, ammunition, and other supplies became a major problem due to the arduous terrain. Everything needed to be carried, and much of it was heavy. For example, two cases of rations weighed 90 pounds, and the machine gun weighed 30 pounds without the tripod mounting. The Italians had small pack mules they used for moving crops, but in a very short time soldiers 'borrowed' them for their use. These mules could carry up to 180 pounds up the mountains, and so were a big load off the soldier's backs. That became even more important as time, weather, and decreased rations degraded their bodies.

In short time the complaints from the farmers caused our government to issue instruction that a farmer be given a written receipt indicating that the soldier took his mule. Lieutenant Roy Hanna remembered one instance: "While in these hills we took the small pack mules from the Italian farmers to carry our machine guns and ammo. We were cleared to do this, but were told to give the farmer a receipt. One farmer came to me questioning a slip he had. Sgt. [John D.] Antanori had given him a slip in which he had written: 'I owe you one mule.' and then had the farmer sign it. I shook my head yes – OK. I often wondered if he ever got paid for the mule."[148]

The supply of ammunition had priority followed by food. At times no food would arrive and the soldier had to revert to the emergency food that each soldier carried. This was a hard textured bar, called the 'D' Ration, of chocolate that had was so hard it had to be gnawed to consume. Cigarettes were delivered at a ratio of one pack per day person. This was an oversupply because a large percentage of the paratroopers were non-smokers. Some took up smoking because it tended to stave off hunger. However, despite this, Captain Robert Halloran remembered that mail was still "brought to front religiously, even by donkey in the mountains of Italy." That alone was a tremendous boost to morale.[149]

Paratroopers of the 2nd Battalion 81mm Mortar Platoon hand-carry the pieces and ammunition to the 81mm mortars. In the foregroud, carrying a tripod, is James Duckett. Following him, carrying a tube, is Robert McNally. (US Signal Corps)

James Gann and troopers from Regimental Reconnaissance were enlisted to help with the mule trains at times during the mountain campaign, when they weren't reconnoitering the high mountain villages ahead of the battalions. He recalled how frightened of the German artillery the mules would get: "They couldn't get containers of ammo up to the troops on the mountain, and we went up there with pack mules taking them up – taking food and ammo up to the troops – and that wasn't very much fun either. The secret to trying to calm one down was to sing to it in a low voice, or talk in a low voice and they'll calm down, but you don't want to start jerking them around trying to make them behave themselves. Of course I learned that from growing up on the farm." Gann remembered one of the men trying to yell at a mule in Italian, before saying that he didn't understand Italian. "You don't have to," Gann told the trooper. "She don't even understand it, but it's the tone that calms them down."[150]

Some men became endeared to the mules, and even began to give the mules their own dog tags. And the mule that was acquired by Lieutenant Robert Blankenship's men was promptly named, 'Eleanor', after First Lady Eleanor Roosevelt. At one point, Francis McClain told Eleanor that the First Lady was better looking than Eleanor the mule. Eleanor promptly bit McClain's hand.[151]

Members of the 1st Platoon of Company I pose for a photograph in the mountains of Italy with their mule, which they named Eleanor. Pictured from left to right are: Donald Emmett, Sam Cleckner, Francis Keefe, Francis McLane, Forrest Pierce (killed November 13, 1943), Vernon Evenson, unknown, Lt. Robert Blankenship (Francis Keefe)

After a short time of this type of uncertain delivery system, Lieutenant John Watson came up with a great innovation. He decided to pay the mule owner $3.00 per day to accompany his mule. Supervised by Lieutenant Watson, most of these farmers traveled six to eight miles up the Apennine slopes to reach the paratroopers' positions. But still some of the locations were even inaccessible by mules, and where the mules could not go, female porters were hired by Watson. Although he resisted the idea of hiring the females for the back-breaking work at first, they insisted and told him they were accustomed to such work for their own survival. Watson ended up paying each porter 100 lire per day (equivalent to $1.00). "They are hale and hearty, and can do more work than a man," Lieutenant Watson later observed.[152]

Rest in Ciorlano

November 23 brought relief in the high mountains for the men of the regiment's 3rd Battalion. They arrived in the village of Ciorlano, nestled in a damp, blue-green valley at the base of two towering mountains. The men from the battalion soon filled up the houses of the village. As the rest of the regiment continued to come over the successive days, the overflow was moved into barns, such as some B Company paratroopers who began finding refuge in one such structure. Both Jake Cantelmo and Marvin Courtney were "leery," as Courtney described, of the possibility of German booby-traps in such barns, and only went in after others had. However, it was not German booby-traps that soon found the paratroopers, but an infestation of lice from sheep, found after one of the men let out a loud cry of curse words and began snatching off his infested clothing.[153]

Other men, such as Donald Zimmerman, were relegated to their pup tents on the muddy ground. When Zimmerman found the hospital unit which his childhood friend was a member was nearby, he tried to get a clean place to sleep but was met with news that his friend and another soldier from the hospital were thinking of joining the paratroops. "I took them back to the unit," Zimmerman said. "They had to eat out of mess kits and stuff like that. It was muddy, and it was awful. I said, 'Are you guys ready to join up?' He said, 'We talked it over and we think we'd better stay with our outfit.'"[154]

Two days after the first elements of the regiment were relieved came Thanksgiving Day. Lieutenant Thomas Utterback had written his wife from Fornelli the week prior to arriving in Ciorlano that "I know, Honey, it has been a long time since you got a letter from me but am sure that you reading the circumstances, it has been some very hard work and frankly I'm surprised that the old man has held up as well as he has. Winter weather in Italy is no joke and I mean it."[155] On Thanksgiving in Ciorlano, he wrote a longer letter describing his holiday in Italy:

Today was Thanksgiving and I thought it impossible under the circumstances but we had turkey, cranberry sauce, mashed spuds and real butter and apple pie. We really and truly have lots to be thankful for. Sunny Italy is just about like sunny California. Ducked into a building the other night and ran into a unit from the home state. Talked to them on the phone and may go see them tomorrow...

A friend of mine brought up one of my xmas pkges and it was the box of candy. Honey, I can't tell you how much it meant. Didn't last long but uh-huh while it did. Of such is built up moral... Got your letter of Nov. 1st. Don't worry when you don't hear from me. Mail just isn't going out or in. Could do as several do – write once a day and sent all at once but you don't get news any sooner. I always write as soon as possible.

Saw [Lieutenant John] Pease today – looked OK and doing alright. [Lieutenant John] Randles is back with us after being sick, is doing fine. Haven't talked to him yet but he is close. By the time this letter reaches you the farming year must be about over. Kids shouldn't forget to write Santa Claus. Guess Old Nick will have a time getting around with much this year. You know reindeer may have been rationed. Well, this next one will be one to look back on and surely next year we can have a very merry one. Gonna miss it all this year but will be thinking of the ones to come. There will be lots of them, you know.

Well, Honey, news has done run out. Sherman was right tho, there are lots of soldiers going thru a lot worse than we have. Wish Adolph could see the light tho don't expect it.[156]

The men of the 2nd Battalion had less-pleasant an experience than did Lieutenant Utterback for Thanksgiving. Their relieving unit was late and the relief was not completed until the early morning hours of Thanksgiving, and when they arrived at Ciorlano, there was no room for the battalion. After much red-tape cutting at headquarters, they were finally allowed to move to Gallo long after nightfall. That night, the battalion lined up by flashlight as the cooks ladled their Thanksgiving meal of turkey and apple pie into upturned helmets, and the men were housed by the people they had first liberated a month earlier.[157]

During the stay, whether in Gallo or Ciorlano, showers were set up, and the men had the first opportunity to bath in nearly a month. New equipment and uniforms were issued, the doctors checked the men, and Christmas packages began to arrive as the regiment's weary bodies began to blossom back for the next mission.

7

THE REGIMENTAL MEDICS AND THE BATTLE OF MONTE CASSINO

> Timeline – 504th PIR, 82nd Airborne Division in the Battle of San Pietro
>
> Night, December 10-11 – G/504 & I/504 begins moving to Hill 950
>
> Evening, December 11-12 – the remainder of the regiment moves up the mountains
>
> December 12 – Captain Watts killed
>
> December 13 – Lieutenant Jordan wounded
>
> December 14 – Lieutenant Breathwit mortally wounded near Hill 950
>
> Evening, December 15 – 2nd Battalion attacks Hill 687
>
> Morning, December 16 – Captain Johnson killed
>
> Afternoon, December 16 – the truce
>
> December 17-18 – 1st Battalion relieves the 2nd Battalion on the crest of Monte Sammucro
>
> December 24-25 – 1st Battalion attacks Hill 687
>
> December 28 – the 504th PIR is relieved from Monte Sammucro

Taking care of the unit's sick and wounded was an arduous task in every environmental or battle condition the regiment found itself in. It was a difficult mission with which the Medical Detachment carried out with unparalleled dedication. Despite this, the Medical Detachment has received little recognition or study since the end of World War II.

The difficulty of the work is perhaps best highlighted in the regiment's fighting in Italy, especially in the mountains from October to December 1943. The steep, inhospitable terrain multiplied the difficulty with which they could provide adequate care to the wounded. This terrain also created large distance between a suitable place for an aid station and the front line parachute infantrymen. Evacuation times from the front to the nearest battalion aid station, and then an evacuation or field hospital, were sometimes extensive due to the distance, terrain, and weather. First Lieutenant William P. Jordan, one of the regiment's surgeons, remembered one instance where it took two men nearly 14 hours to reach an aid station, crawling on their knees over icy rocks with their wounded comrade.

Managing the regiment's medical needs for the duration of World War II was Major Ivan J. Roggen, the son of a minster from Maurice, Iowa. At full strength, Roggen's Medical Detachment was staffed with eight surgeons and one dentist, along with enlisted medics to go forward with the rifle companies, medical assistants for the doctors, and other support personnel. The detachment was staffed with approximately 115 enlisted men.

Captain Robert M. Halloran, the Regimental Dentist, was one of the few doctors along with Roggen who served in the 504th though all of its campaigns. Halloran felt that Roggen "was wise, fearless, and considerate."[158]

Halloran, an Irish Catholic from Connecticut, was attending dental school at Georgetown University in Washington, D.C. when the war broke out. Many of his classmates signed up for the Army while still in school, "hoping to contribute what we could to winning the war… I was gung-ho, but nervous because I knew so little about being an Army officer, and was so anxious to do everything well." Halloran said that on his first leave he was traveling in a lieutenant's uniform, but still "completely ignorant of how a lieutenant should act."[159]

While in the States, Halloran worked long hours providing for the needs of 2,000 men and ensuring that, dentally, they were ready to go overseas. And while in theatre overseas, the difficulty of his job was compounded by the lack of tools he found, but he put in hard, long hours to render dental care to the men while they were in reserve positions. Sometimes, he felt the care was inadequate, but he tried his best with what he had. "Dental field equipment [was] very obsolete and incomplete," he recalled. "I had dentists back home send me what I needed to perform just basic dentistry, and later improvised extensively." He found the same held true for the regiment's surgeons in the field, and while he felt the medical treatment they were giving was adequate, "supplies and equipment forced our M.D.s to render less care than they wanted to."[160]

Halloran described a 'typical' day of operations while the regiment was in combat, in addition to treating and evacuating the regiment's casualties, as being "briefed so we could support combat units, patrols, etc. We 'leapfrogged' our aid stations as the troops advanced so we were constantly on the move, searching for adequate buildings for aid stations, treating wounded and sick, and evacuating to field hospitals."[161]

In the mountains of southern Italy, Major Ivan Roggen was far away from the well-lit, sterile surgery rooms of Iowa Methodist Hospital in Des Moines. The fighting had been fraught with problems for the Medical Detachment, as evidenced by Lieutenant Jordan's story of two men crawling for 14 hours to reach an aid station.

Kitchen Surgery

On November 16, the regimental aid station was located in a small, cool and damp room in an old house. A fire was lit under the hearth to help take the dampness from the air. The kitchen was the dispensary and first aid room. Up the winding stone staircase, bedrooms were turned into wards, where a dozen wounded paratroopers were waiting to be taken to the evacuation hospital for further help.

The kitchen table was taken and set up in a makeshift operating room. Surgical miracles were performed on the rough wooden dinner table. "This is kitchen surgery in the rough," Major Roggen described. "We have to take whatever we can find and do a lot of improvising. I know it is difficult to believe, but we do major operations in places like this - operations such as chest wound closures and brain surgery."

No matter what they did, getting the paratroopers to the aid station was the most difficult maneuver. "We've tried everything, but about the only practical method of evacuation is to have eight men for each litter, and then they can alternate in carrying it. Sometimes it takes them from six to twenty-four hours to reach an aid station. Fortunately we have not lost a man because of slow travel from the front, but there have been complications which would not have developed had there been any way to get them to us faster. The litters are usually carried six or eight miles, but the trails are so narrow, steep and rough that the carriers have to crawl along. In the last fight we lost several of our men, and had to call troops out of the line to help with evacuation." For a short time, before having to start calling troopers out of the line to help evacuate wounded, Roggen enlisted the help of Italian civilians. "I remember the day," Roggen said, "there were two direct hits by enemy artillery near a path. The civilians ran away, and we pulled men from foxholes to carry comrades down the hill. Honestly, I believe the litter bearers have the worst time of all. They can't hurry, and must travel on difficult trails. Sometimes they crawl thru underbrush and often under terrific German shellfire."[162]

As vehicles, such as jeeps and ambulances, often couldn't travel the mountain roads, wounded were carried down by mule or by paratroopers, as Roggen described. Sergeants Eddie Miques and Brunche Curnick, and Corporal Richard Bertolette, some of Roggen's medics, used the pack mules to evacuate wounded. Private William Bruggeman, Roggen's jeep driver who was actually a member of another company, volunteered himself to help carry wounded up and down the mountains. When Bruggeman got 30 days leave to go back to the States in late 1944, Major Roggen sent him home with a letter for his parents which, in part, read, "Pvt. Bruggeman was the best man that I have ever had to drive for me. He has always proved to be dependable, reliable and efficient. He is a soldier of unfaltering courage and always places his buddies before himself."[163]

Regimental Protestant Chaplain (Capt) Delbert Kuehl and Regimental Surgeon (Maj) Ivan Roggen pictured in Germany near the end of World War II. (Moffatt Burriss)

December 1943 – Fighting Around San Pietro

Mid-December 1943 saw the regiment participating in the fighting around San Pietro, part of what would become known as the Battle of Monte Cassino. The difficulty and challenges faced by the Medical

Detachment in Italy were highlighted here, on high, barren slopes of numbered hills such as 710, 950, and 1205. It also highlighted the valor, determination, and persistence with which the medics and doctors carried out that difficult, yet vitally important job. "The medic's task, at best a difficult one," the regimental history recorded, "was increased ten-fold on the high, craggy, wind-swept, and shelter-less hilltops. Medical supplies were short when they were needed most, and there was no quick way of obtaining more."[164]

As the men of the 504th Parachute Infantry Regiment rested in reserve near Ciorlano, the Allied armies had their eye on the next major city north of Naples: Rome. The journey to the Italian capital had already been a costly path in terms of casualties, with no end in sight. The village of San Pietro would be the next mortal struggle in the bitter Italian campaign, and for many it would be their last.

The village of San Pietro Infine sat nestled at the mouth of a valley the Allied tanks intended to take to Cassino, the anchor of the German's Gustov Line. The strategic Highway 6, running at the base of Monte Sammucro through the village of San Pietro, necessitated its capture. Lieutenant General Mark W. Clark, who would command the attack through the San Pietro sector, wished to avoid a frontal assault on the village. The fore of the village, consisting of stout stone homes and walls, provided ample emplacements for guns which could prove to be a lucrative field of fire for a determined defender. The best route of approach, Clark concluded, would be a flanking attack on the dominating Sammucro hill mass, where two battalions would make the long climb up the mountain; one battalion would hold the hill while the other descended Sammucro behind San Pietro and attack from the rear. These two actions would, General Clark believed, make the German garrison in San Pietro untenable.

Under the cover of darkness on December 7-8, 1943, soldiers from the US 143rd Infantry Regiment began the climb up Monte Sammucro undetected. At daylight, the Americans surged over the crest and drove the Germans from their holes, seizing the heights before the Germans could tell what happened.

By December 10, the battalion which was holding Monte Sammucro reported being at a strength of 340 men – half its combat strength. Repeatedly the Germans were attempting to retake the hill in determined counterattacks. They were successful in routing a battalion of Rangers, holding the adjacent Hill 950, from their positions before it was recaptured on the 9th. And the exposure from the cold weather was also taking a toll. The units were hard-pressed. Once again, General Clark called on the men of the 504th Parachute Infantry Regiment to bolster his Army.

December 10 was a cool, overcast day which saw the paratroopers arriving near the village of Venafro. It seemed the earth was tucked in by a gray blanket as the boon of artillery echoed in the distance. Ahead of them loomed the towering Monte Sammucro. The mountain stood wide, the shadow of its rocky, jagged ridge line stretching across the horizon. The top of the mountain stood so high that there were days the summit was shrouded in a cloud. Here would be the sight of the regiment's next struggle.

Two companies of Lieutenant Colonel Freeman's 3rd Battalion were immediately dispatched the hill adjacent to Monte Sammucro, Hill 950, to relieve the Rangers who were under pressure. As they began the arduous climb up the mountains, the rest of the regiment closed into a bivouac area to spend the night. Over the coming 48 hours, elements of the regiment would gradually be sent up into the Sammucro hill mass to join the battle.

When the morning of the 11th dawned, the sky was gray and the air cool and damp. Marvin Courtney was walking along the road back to their staging area with a helmet full of gasoline for their small camp stoves which he had scrounged from a British artillery battery. Overhead, the artillery shells from the British battery he was coming from groaned, occasionally answered by a German shell.

Courtney was approaching a roadblock, formed by felled trees, when he heard the staccato anti-aircraft fire go into the air. Courtney looked up and saw a German plane releasing a bomb and watched as the bomb wobbled through the air. Courtney jumped into the ditch by the felled trees which provided protection. The bomb blast reverberated with an earthshaking force, showering him with dirt and rock. But he and his gasoline were safe.

When Courtney got up, he could see men running around their bivouac area. Courtney made his way back to the company. "Courtney!" one of the men said, "that bomb hit you on the head didn't it?"

"Yeah," he replied. "It just missed me."

Several men had been wounded in the air attack. One man was missing an arm. But with Courtney's gasoline, at least they would be able to have a hot cup of coffee.[165]

When the German fighter-bombers came over the regimental area, Donald Zimmerman was sitting on a tree stump reading a copy of *Stars and Stripes* he'd pulled from a pile of newspapers the men had collected. It was two weeks old. During combat in the mountains of Italy, newspapers had a low priority compared to ammunition, food, water, and medical supplies. By the time the men in the front lines received the paper, it was already old news.

About ten feet from where Zimmerman was sitting and reading, some troopers had built a fire to warm themselves. Suddenly the whine of an incoming airplane sounded overhead. It was one of the German Stuka dive-bombers. Zimmerman looked up in just enough time to see a bomb release from the rack and begin to wobble to the earth. Zimmerman rolled off of the stump onto the ground as the bomb exploded on the muddy road. Although the impact was about 25 yards away, Zimmerman was aching from the near hit. "The concussion was so bad," Zimmerman described, "that you kind of felt you were wounded."

Just a short time later, Private First Class Robert G. Anglemyer, a short, muscular Indiana farm boy came up to Zimmerman: "Hey, Zimmy, lookie here! I got two belly buttons!"

The cheerful twenty-one-year-old lifted his shirt, and just below his navel there was a hole the size of a dime made by a fragment from the Stuka's bomb. Zimmerman looked at the wound, which was not bleeding. The Hoosier did not realize how serious the wound was. The cheerful Anglemyer was helped into an ambulance and driven off. As the ambulance left a few of the men asked Zimmerman how he was. "I told the guys Anglemyer talked to me and he said he was in good shape."

Four days later the men learned that he had died from internal bleeding. The news shocked the paratroopers by the death of friend cut down during the prime of young life. Shortly after the war, Zimmerman heard that Anglemyer's family in Indiana was looking for someone who witnessed their son's death. Zimmerman talked to them on the phone. He did tell them all the details but he "didn't like to talk too much about it to them because I couldn't see them, I didn't know what kind of people they were. I know that he was a hell of a nice kid."[166]

While the planes were attacking the regiment's bivouac area on the morning of December 11, the two companies – G and I – of Lieutenant Colonel Freeman's 3rd Battalion were emerging out of a night of yeoman's work in dealing with the German infantry in the Sammucro hill mass, especially I Company who were continuing to check the German counterattacks into daytime on December 11. While the rest of the regiment spent the night in the bivouac area on the night of December 10-11, G and I Companies had made their way up Hill 950 to relieve the Rangers.

As I Company reached the hill in the dark, a large firefight ensued with German soldiers of the 71st *Panzergrenadier* Regiment, who were attacking up the hill just as the paratroopers were making their way on the trail. Paratroopers batted German grenades with their rifle-butts in the dark, and the battle continued well into the next day, December 11. Roy Hanna remembered one incident on Hill 950 which likely occurred around this time. "This [occurred during] one of the many attacks from the Germans to drive us off this hill. It was on the right flank and I was in the upper front slope of the hill firing at 'whoever might be in the way' when the man beside me suddenly stood up and started staggering around. I noticed a rather large blood spot in the center of his forehead. I grabbed him and pulled him back to the edge of a small cliff at the top of the hill and handed him down to the medics located there. After the skirmish was over I went to the area to check him out and found him standing there with a patch on his forehead. Apparently a rock or piece of shrapnel glanced off his forehead and stunned him."[167]

One 19-year-old German soldier, who was originally from Westphalia in northern Germany, was captured on December 11 by the I Company troopers. He was thoroughly embedded with "Nazi propaganda. Being young and in battle only three weeks, it was difficult for him to realize that everything he had been told for the past 10 years was not true. Despite the fact that his company was practically wiped out, he was still under the impression that they were winning. He was astounded at the number of vehicles which we had. He said that none of the Germans had any idea that we had brought so much equipment into Italy in such a short time. However, [he] says in a rather shrugging manner that food is good and so is morale. 'After all, you cannot beat an overwhelming power.'"[168]

Captain George Watts had led his Company G to an adjacent hilltop, and as I Company's firefight continued into the day of December 11, his men could hear the small arms fire popping off. Watts and his men remained here until after dark on December 12, when Captain Watts moved his men to relieve I Company, which had suffered many casualties over the past 48 hours, on the forward positions of Hill 950. When daylight broke the next morning, Earl Oldfather saw three dead bodies and part of a leg near the new position he had taken over – a silent witness to the fight which I Company engaged the Germans in during those first 48 hours on the mountain.

This shifting of forces was allowed because Company H had made the climb up to the hill, and were able to take over the positions Captain Watts's men had vacated when they moved to make the relief. Donald Zimmerman and his friend Peter Firing from New York got to the hill when it was dusk. "Pete and I found a hole in the top of the hill with stone built up around it... We [were] crawling in that hole and we felt that would keep us away from the shrapnel if any got hitting around that area. I was laying on something and I didn't know what it was. I said, 'Pete, did you take your boots off?' He said, 'No.' I said, 'Well, there's somebody else in this place!'" Zimmerman ordered Pete Firing to hold a bead on the foreign object with his M-1 rifle, while he promptly got out a raincoat and covered their rock palace, as to not attract artillery, before turning on a flashlight. What they saw was quite the scare to the duo: there was a German still sitting nearly upright with his back against the wall of the foxhole. Zimmerman had rested his head on his boots. The German was dead, thankfully, and stiffly frozen. It appeared that he had been wounded by shrapnel and subsequently sat there and bled out.

They had no choice but to sleep with the corpse in their foxhole: dragging the body out would silhouette them against the black night and attract German mortars or artillery. That night, Zimmerman slept with his head resting upon the German's boots, using it like a pillow. While even the thought of doing such a thing would be repugnant to most people, Zimmerman and Firing were unfazed. They got to a point where they just became emotionally disconnected with what was going on around them. They simply didn't care what happened to them one way or the other.

Peter Firing and his wife pictured shortly before the regiment shipped overseas. (Author's collection)

Right at dawn the following morning they nonchalantly drug out the German's lifeless carcass and put it on a pile with others whom had been met with similar fates. "They sent food up by mules," recalled Zimmerman, "and we would strap these dead guys on the back of a mule going back down."[169]

Had Zimmerman stopped to take in the breathtaking view, it would be one that would leave anyone touring Italy awestruck. With the hill mass dominated by the towering Monte Sammucro, located just across a large draw to the left, the paratroopers could see the Appian Mountains in all their glory - a vista of mountaintop after mountaintop as far as the eye could see. At the foot of the southern slope of Sammucro sat the village of San Pietro Infine. Imbedded in the deep valley, the small village, dominated by the Sammucro ridge line, would be the site of one of the bitterest battles in the Allied effort to break the German's Winter Line.

Both Mount Sammucro and Hill 950 were foreboding, gray and depressing places whose rocky slopes almost looked as if they were the home of death itself. The shale rock surface was covered only by a film of moss-like plant life; there was little in the way of vegetation, giving the wind a biting effect. The sun shone rarely, as it was always obscured by clouds which looked as if it wanted to add rain to the trooper's misery.

Living conditions on the front were often primal, scarcely better than the living conditions of Neanderthals. This was especially true of the windswept mountains in December. The sun went down at around 1700 and did not rise again until nearly 0900 the next morning, leaving the nights long, damp and frigid - and giving the wind an extra bite. Their thin cotton summer jump suits protected them none from the cold, providing no insulation or protection from the wind. Troopers would often develop coughs, severe colds, or illnesses such as jaundice or malaria; or develop problems resulting from exposure to the winter alpine environment, such as frostbite. When the men began being issued thicker tankers jackets and coveralls while they were on top of the mountain, they put them on to supplement their thin jump suits rather than exchanging them as was originally intended.

In the thin, chilled air on Hill 950, Lieutenant Roy Hanna had the same bed he had for the near-300 days of combat he was credited with – his one wool blanket would comfort him in winter and summer weather alike. "Our bed rolls," he remembers, "were one blanket that was rolled and tied with whatever and usually carried on our back just below our neck. Mine was an Italian military blanket that I took from an Italian soldier in Sicily because it was a bit larger and I believed was a bit warmer." Roy Hanna had been on Hill 950 since the beginning of the battle. Below the surface of moss-like vegetation laid the hard rock of the mountain, which made foxholes impossible. Most men tried to nestle themselves into the rocks for protection, or stack rocks in a way which they felt would protect them from shrapnel and rifle fire. "Rain off and on and cold nights stick in my memory," Hanna remembered. "This is where we had a large number of new replacements join us. One night I slept by a large rock and during the night it rained. The morning started with a bright sun. I stood up and was draping the blanket over the rock when an artillery round came in. I just leaned forward on the blanket and a piece of shrapnel took out a piece of the blanket right alongside of my head."

Especially during their first few days on the mountain, Germans tried repeatedly to retake the hill, scrambling up the hill out of the valley, frog-hopping from boulder to boulder and terrace to terrace. "I know I had a couple machine guns located on the right flank. My machine guns were scattered over that whole sector. They kept in touch with each other by tapping out signals with their guns – had great touch with the trigger. Example: One would fire a single and then two together, another would answer with two together and then a single, etc."[170]

Throughout the regiment's stay on the Sammucro hill mass, getting a supply of rations and water was a problem. Nearly every day, a trooper would have to collect the canteens of his platoon mates and go down off the mountain to fill them up at a well, and then make the arduous climb back up the mountain - a physically taxing duty for which straws were drawn, or another selection method decided upon. Cases of rations were even more difficult to bring up the mountain. Sometimes this was done with the mules, who, at the top, would offload their food and on load bodies, as Zimmerman described, for the return trip.

Captain Watts is Killed in Action

Lieutenant Edward Kennedy propped his boot up on a rock and watched as the mule stumbled down the rocky shale switchbacks of Hill 950. Lashed to the top of the mule was one of Kennedy's slain paratroopers who, with great labor, Kennedy and another man had wrapped in a wool blanket like mummy, took off the blood-soaked litter and lashed to the mule. The trooper had been killed three days earlier, on December 12, and in that time he had gone into such rigger that he was unable to drape fully over the mule's back. Kennedy watched as the other paratroopers and an Italian soldier prodded, guided, and pulled the uncooperative mule down the steep slope, taking their slain comrade with it. Perhaps it was sights such as these which caused Lieutenant Kennedy to write home often about how terrible and how unholy war is.

The paratrooper had been killed shortly after G Company had moved into the positions they took over from I Company. A shell – one of the most expensive shells the Germans shot during the war – had impacted G Company's command post. Most tragically, the shell killed several paratroopers, including Captain George J. Watts.

On the night of July 9, 1943, then-Lieutenant Watts and his men leapt from a C-47 and touched foot on Sicily inside a small valley. After gathering his supplies, Watts attempted to locate the road running from Priolo to Niscemi. Eventually, he joined forces with Lieutenant Willis J. Ferrill, and they established positions at Casa Nocera, a building up on a hill overlooking the SP31, which ran from Niscemi to the Gela Beachhead. The group was responsible for slaying over 75 German and Italian soldiers, an extraordinary feat for a small group of lightly armed paratroopers.

Many miles away, in the village of Vittoria, 1st Lieutenant Marshall C. McOmber, Watts' inseparable friend, was presented with more tragic circumstances, which resulted in his death. The loss of 'Mac' hit Watts especially hard and the loss was never far from his mind.

Watts was given his slain friends command, that of commanding Company G, and promoted to captain. While Watts was leading Mac's old company in Italy, McOmber's widow wrote to him for news of her husband, who had only been declared as missing in action. Captain Watts replied, and gave her the tragic news.

Italy Oct 10, 1943

Dear Francis,

I received your letter a few days ago but the Jerries were occupying all my spare time. For a month now I've attempted to write to you and give you some news. This will hurt, it is straight from the shoulder. Your husband and my best friend is dead. Please believe that I know how you feel. I always took pride in not being sentimental but I was wrong. I am just like anyone else and the shock of Mac's death was a terrible blow.

On July 9th we took off for Sicily. I was in "X" BN. with Mac but he was to take some hills and protect me while my men and I laid a minefield. Coming in over Sicily we ran into heavy anti-aircraft fire. The planes spread out in an effort to avoid the flak and some of the ships were lost. Mac was in one of these but he had come to fight so he jumped anyway. They landed at a place called Vittoria in the midst of the enemy. Entirely surrounded and hopelessly outnumbered. Mac and some of his men held back the Germans while a couple of men escaped and went for help. It didn't get there for two days, they couldn't hold out that long. In the meantime, I landed in the right place and gathered my supplies. We held out for five days and then were relieved. I had gone in with Malaria and due to the lack of food and poor water I was terribly ill when I was relieved. I was sent back to Africa to a hospital. It took me a month to get back up to Sicily and since I had been told Mac was missing in action, I went up to Vittoria. The Army cemetery had no record of him so I went to the civilian cemetery. It was then that I found his grave. I got the rest of the story from the medical card that had been on his body. It said wounded tenth of July and an Italian priest brought him to an aid station at Vittoria. He died on July the eleventh and was buried by an unknown parachute SGT. on July 12.

The civilian cemetery could not compare with the Army cemetery at Gela, Sicily so I left orders at Gela to have the body moved. It is much better that way, where Cal will be taken and if ever any remains are shipped home they know where he is.

You may not be notified for some time by the War Department. They check everything carefully and have to be absolutely sure. For that reason, please do not contact them or the Red Cross until you are notified. I would lose my official head if they knew I wrote you first. I don't care much though. It is the least I can do for you. Please write if there is anything more I can possibly do. Offer my deepest sympathy to Mr. and Mrs. McOmber. I know they thought I was wild, but I loved Mac.

Since the battle of Italy I have again landed in the hospital this time with malaria. While in the hospital the first time in Africa I was given my promotion. I asked for Mac's old company. I lead them here in Italy and believe me, Jerry is paying for killing Mac. He will continue to pay as long as I can get near him.

Once more let me tell you how sorry I am, and let me say Mac did die like and officer and a gentleman. It was in the service of his country and he was doing the job in the best way he could.

He and others like him made the Sicilian invasion possible. You feel justly proud to have been his wife. Be brave.

Yours,

George

P.S. I've read this and it seems pretty mixed up but I guess you get the gest of it.

Geo[171]

Lt. Marshall McOmber, the commander of G Company, who was killed in the Sicilian village of Vittoria shortly after landing on July 9, 1943. (McOmber family)

It was 33 days after Watts typed this letter to Francis McOmber that he too would die in the service of his country, when the artillery shell impacted his command post claiming his life and the lives of several others. One of the troopers killed with Captain Watts was Corporal Fred Clare Streeter, Jr. of Marshall,

Missouri. In 2003, Streeter's sister wrote a moving piece describing the day the family received the gut-wrenching telegram, informing them that Fred had lost his life on Hill 950.

Even today I occasionally daydream that this 82-year-old man will walk into my life saying, "Oh, Mindy, I've had amnesia, at last I am home with you."

Christmas, 1943, Mildred and I are aimlessly driving around the square seeing the bright lights and decoration, board in our thoughts. Playing on the radio of the 1937 Chevie is the song, "I'll be home for Christmas – if only in my dreams." Fred is overseas, a paratrooper in Italy, fighting the evil empire. We sent him the cigarette lighter he requested and numerous other meaningless things.

Christmas came and went. I had been working in Jefferson City at the state Constitutional Convention, a plum job but terribly lonely for me. It was time to catch the C & A train from Marshall to Jefferson City to return to work.

The doorbell rang. I answered it to see the Western Union boy in uniform with a pained look on his face. I drew back and screamed, "Mom, come to the door." With trembling hands, she signed for the telegram and we opened it together.

"We regret to inform you .... Killed in Venafro, Italy ... December 12..."

Mom clutched her chest and said quietly, "Call the doctor, call the doctor." I told her again and again he could not help her. She lay down on the floor weeping and I lay besides her cradling her in my arms.[172]

Fred Streeter, pictured in Sicily, was killed in the shelling of the G Company CP on Hill 950. (Katy Vargas)

Lieutenant Peter Eaton was with Captain Watts just an hour before the shell hit the CP, and Eaton was "all broken up about it." Eaton was very close friends with both Watts and McOmber. When Eaton got back to the States after being wounded himself, he visited with McOmber's widow Francis, and Eaton said he heard that "Mac dived over a wall after a German machine gun. He was so mad he was going to take the machine gun and the Germans with his bare fists."

On Hill 950, Lt. Edward Kennedy (far left) ties down the body of one of his slain comrades killed in the shelling of the G Company command post. Lt. Kennedy would be killed in action in Holland less than a year later. (US Signal Corps)

Flanking Hill 950 to the left was the large saucer-like saddle which, on the other side, abruptly rose to the summit of Sammucro. The summit of Sammucro was vacant from paratroopers, but the positions of the 2nd Battalion, 504th PIR were on the opposite side of the summit, on the western crest of the hill. On December 14, a German was sighted across the saddle on Monte Sammucro. The paratroopers poured fire at him. The German fell on his face, and Earl Oldfather looked through a set of field glasses at the fallen enemy soldier. Later, one of the company's outposts was pinned down by fire. Second Lieutenant James Gulley Breathwit, of Monroe, Louisiana, led a combat patrol out. During the patrol, Lieutenant Breathwit was shot in the face. Lieutenant Roy Hanna watched as a stumbling man was being held by his arms by two flanking men. He had bloodied bandages across his eyes. It was Breathwit. When Hanna asked the medics, they said he had been shot in the eyes. Although after all these years Hanna thought he had survived, Breathwit actually died shortly thereafter. Breathwit had been wed in Fort Benning, Georgia in February of that year. He was 23-years-old, and less than two months away from his first wedding anniversary.[173]

The following day, another patrol went up Sammucro. They found Germans in a dugout. The rumor was that the patrol killed six Germans, and that the Germans would watch the paratroopers by day and travel back to their own lines at night.

Germans were again spotted on Sammucro on the morning of December 16. Finally, that afternoon, another patrol of paratroopers pulled three live enemy soldiers out of some bunkers near the summit of Sammucro. John Zence was able to converse with them and found they were Polish conscripts.[174] Later, when they were formally interrogated, they said they were part of a group of 10 men sent to reoccupy those outpost positions on Sammucro. They were new replacements who had only entered combat three days previous to their capture.[175]

This photograph taken by Lt. Moffatt Burriss gives a good view of the Sammucro ridgeline and the valley. Note the rocky foreground, showing the difficult conditions in which the troopers lived. (Moffatt Burriss)

Donald Zimmerman remembered that later the Germans would fire artillery, normally 88mm or 105mm, down into the depression of the saucer-shaped saddle between Sammucro and Hill 950, and when they shot off the artillery, it was almost always at the same time of day. "This thing was like a big oval," he recalled. "We were kind of on the point of the oval – Pete [Firing] and I – and we could watch both directions. They would set off a volley at certain times, and it all go down in the big dip way, 100 yards away from us… Maybe they didn't know we weren't there. They sure were missing us."[176]

Hill 710

Corporal Marvin Courtney awoke from a slumber in his rock cubby on the summit of Hill 710. Occupied by Courtney and the men of B Company, Hill 710 was smaller, but no less steep and rugged as the other surrounding mountain peeks being occupied by the paratroopers. Corporal Courtney overlooked a deep valley from a perch so high that he said, "I can see every which way. If anybody's coming up that mountain, I can see them a day before he gets there because that side of the mountain was nearly about straight down."

That morning, Courtney observed everything to be quiet, until the fog clouds, which socked in the damp atmosphere, lifted. "Everything's quiet," he remembered. "Fog clouds lift, and I start seeing things. Below me, I can see tanks; I can see a war going on – I can see planes dogfighting below me! I wouldn't mind staying here the rest of the war, I feel safe here! Nothing's bothering me!"

The journey up to the top of the mountain the day before was long and arduous. Courtney vividly recalls the movement, which illustrates the difficulty of mountain warfare:

We go pretty smooth for half a mile or so, then it starts getting really steep. So where it starts getting steep, we set up a CP there and the doctor moves in and sets up [too]. We got mules and stuff that takes stuff up to where we're going, and it helped. Well, we get there and we have to have ropes. We take the ropes and part of the mountain we had to be pulled up, or pull ourselves up, with all of our equipment and everything else we've got. So we pull on up, we had been shelled off and on all through this, and we get near the top and some units go to the right, some to the left, and we go straight on up. We go straight on up all that night and we got up there the next day and we're still a long way from being to the top. We walked, going on up, shelled and shooting, and everything going on. We finally reached the top of the mountain.

We reached the top and we peep over and we see guys with guns pointed at us; oh, four or five hundred yards out in front of us. But we pull on up, no firing going on, everything's quiet, so we go on up and find out "Are they Germans?" These guys were dead Americans with their guns. They got stiff and they [the Germans] propped them up to where they look like they're a soldier in the kneeling position or the standing position pointing his gun at you. So there's three or four of those.

So we go on up a little farther and we see some dead Germans. We see six or eight dead Germans in kind of a piled group there, and on top of that group this one soldier that's not dead all the way, he's just blinking his eyes a little bit, and on his finger he's got a brand new gold band, and you could tell he's a young guy, not an old guy, and they pile their dead. So we go on past them and we get by and one guy tells me, "Courtney, you get that ring off that German's finger." I said, "That looks suspicious to me. I wouldn't touch that because he's probably booby-trapped."

So we go on and the unit gets there. Everybody kind of gets up on that level so they start placing guys out...They find me a spot really quick right there. So they set me up there and everybody else goes on in different directions and everything. So they come back and they said, "We are going to have to leave you here by yourself. We hate to, but we just don't have the men. We're short of men. But we're going to get somebody for you." Getting somebody's not no easy job, because it's not no easy job getting here!

So I set up; find me a nook in the mountains. I sit there and get the mortar set up and everything made comfortable. So the next guy ahead of me, he's half a mile away! But I pulled off of the main path that leads up there. I pulled off and found kind of a safe place to set up the mortar, a safe place to lay. So I sleep there that night.

Two days later, a fellow paratrooper came around to issue the daily water and food rations. With him was a replacement to stay with Courtney and assist him with the mortar. The following story gives an illustration of the difficulties it took to get wounded and injured paratroopers from the battlefield, to the aid stations, and finally to permanent care facilities.

The Journey of the Wounded

One night, Courtney heard an explosion very close, and felt rock shower around him; it aroused him from his sleep inside his nook but he didn't get up. The next morning Marvin Courtney awoke to find his foxhole buddy missing. *He must have got scared*, Courtney thought, *or maybe he went to visit somebody down the line*. In the morning, the mule train arrived and the supply man brought around the rations and water. "Where's the man that's supposed to be with you?" he inquired.

"I don't know," Courtney said. "He wasn't here this morning when I got up."

A short time later another couple of men came by. "We hear somebody hollering down there," they said. Courtney listened intently, and couldn't hear anybody, except what he thought were some sheep down in the valley. *Baaaa, Baaaa*, it sounded like. "I have seen sheep or goats or something way down the mountain. I had a pair of binoculars, I could draw them up pretty close. There couldn't be anybody down there."

The following day Lieutenant Colonel Warren R. Williams, Jr., the commander of the 1st Battalion, 504th PIR, came up to inspect the positions. "He had a carbine over his shoulder," recollected Courtney, "and he had about three German prisoners walking right close to him, and they saw me and they got a little closer. The colonel come by and he looked down that mountain, way down there, and he looked down there with binoculars and he said, 'I see a man way down yonder. Go down there and shoot him.' I wasn't about to leave. He had three prisoners there, and I had the mortar, and I wasn't about to leave and go shoot nobody. If he had given me a direct order, I'd [have] thought something about it, but I was under the impression that he wanted to let those prisoners know that he was in charge of everything up there."

Another night passed with Courtney's foxhole buddy still missing. Sometime during the day, three medics came by with a litter. "We're going down there to get him," one of the medics said. Courtney still had his doubts that a man was down the hill. *They must have seen him from somewhere else*, thought Courtney. With their olive drab green collapsible canvas litter, the three medics started down the nearly 80% grade, scurrying and zagging. Surprisingly, there was a paratrooper down there – Courtney's missing foxhole buddy. "I don't know how they got him up, but they got him up out [of] there, and said, 'You gotta go with us.' I said, 'I can't leave my mortar and stuff. This is my post; I'm supposed to stay here.' So they checked around and said, 'It's OK for you to go with us. We got to have you help us take him down.'"

The four of them carried the injured paratrooper, who had apparently fallen off the cliff, down the hill. This was not an isolated incident. The 2nd Battalion, for example, reported multiple men falling off small cliffs and severely injuring themselves.

When Courtney and the medics reached the aid station of the 1st Battalion's surgeon, Captain Charles Pack, halfway up the mountain, the four men were exhausted and took a break. Although they had reached the first line of treatment, the journey still continued for the wounded and litter bearers alike. The next step was to get them to the regimental aid station or a casualty collection point, where they could be taken to a field or evacuation hospital with more robust facilities. The four men, including Courtney, lifted the man on the litter again to finish the journey. "I'm going down with you boys," Captain Pack told them.

Down the barren cliff they went with the wounded man. It was ten o'clock at night when they reached the field hospital, set up right in front of an artillery outfit. There were large tents containing wards, and lit operating rooms for the multiple doctors who worked in the mobile hospital.

The five paratroopers were completely exhausted from their arduous journey. "You all might as well just lay down here," one of the hospital staff told them. Courtney and the men took their clothes off and drifted off to sleep on the canvas floor of the tent.

After a few hours – "way before daylight," Courtney is quick to note - the paratroopers were awoken. There was a bustle of activity as men were being moved in and out. Courtney went to where he'd left his clothes only to find them missing. Courtney complained to Captain Pack: "Well, I come here with no basic training, and here I am in the middle of this darn war, somebody's got my clothes, all I got is myself and my dog tags."

"Well, don't feel bad about that, son," Captain Pack said. "My first jump was in combat."

Come to find out, Captain Pack had been assigned to the parachute troops without attending Parachute School at Fort Benning, GA. After this journey, Captain Pack, who was from Milan, Tennessee, would never return to work at the 504th PIR.

The 2nd Battalion Joins Battle

It was evening time on December 11 when the 2nd Battalion of the 504th Parachute Infantry Regiment began a slow climb up a "long, muddy tortuous trail with all equipment back-carried. Destination – Hill 1205, Monte Sammucro." In some spots, the mud on the trail was six inches deep. Lieutenant Chester Garrison remembered, "The night was as black as could be with a mist setting in early and turning into rain… A place was reached where ascent was possible only by pulling oneself up by a long rope… Loose and rolling rock also hampered the climb."[177]

The trail took them along the razorback ridge on the southern part of Monte Sammucro. Below them, at the bottom of the cliff, lay the fortified village of San Pietro where the Germans were burrowed in like ticks. As the battalion slogged their way up the precipitous terrain, they captured seven Germans along the trail. They were from the 15th *Panzergrenadiers,* who were holding with tenacity the village of San Pietro down below against the Allied onslaughts. They had likely run astray during the fighting. The men were nervous wrecks owing to the American artillery, so much so that when one of the Germans was interrogated a few hours after falling into the hands of the paratroopers, he broke down and wept openly. One had fought with the unit when it was on the Russian front and had seen service at Stalingrad and said, "There was never anything like it at Stalingrad."[178]

The battalion finally nestled itself with the soldiers of the 143rd Infantry Regiment, occupying positions on the crest of Sammucro, and poised for a renewed attack.

Wounded Surgeons

Back home in the small North Carolina town of Windsor, Dr. William P. Jordan practiced small-town medicine in an office on Main Street in Windsor. Although most cases could be handled in the little office hospital, more serious cases encountered in the town of 2,000 required travel to larger cities, such as Greenville or Norfolk.

The war had taken him far away from his comfortable workspace in Windsor, which had to be exchanged for more austere conditions. The first casualties of his battalion began to trickle in on December 13 – the regiment's first full day occupying positions around Monte Sammucro. As artillery on the ridge line increased, so did the casualties. And when shrapnel didn't wound men, falling rock would; the German artillery dislodged boulders which then raced down the gray, steep, rocky slopes with enough force which would break bones. The battalion reported 13 casualties for the day. Lieutenant "Jocko" Thompson narrowly missed being the 14th when a stray bullet thudded his left chest, striking the bowl of his spoon which he carried in the upper left pocket of his jump suit likely saving his life; he would survive the war and have a career in baseball as a pitcher for the Philadelphia Phillies.[179]

When word was received at the aid station that there was a wounded paratrooper near the summit of Sammucro, and no litter-bearers were unengaged, Jordan unhesitantly went forward, alone, to render aid. As he was making his way, a piece of flying shrapnel from an 88mm shell tore through the doctor's left wrist. Over the scared, rugged terrain, the 3,000-foot descent back to his aid station, the doctor later said, took him 18 hours.

Due to his wound, Jordan was evacuated back to the United States. He was told that his hand would need to be amputated, but Jordan fought his fellow doctors. After being in a brace for quite some time, his hand reached full capacity after several years. After the war, Jordan returned to his small-town practice, and was the quintessential country doctor. Thankfully, the wound was in his non-dominate hand, and while you could tell the wrist was smaller than the other there was only a subtle deformity. In 1993, a large birthday party was held for him. Nearly the whole town of Windsor turned out, and Dr. William Jordan had delivered into the world nearly every single person in attendance.

Upon returning home in 1944, Jordan wrote that "there's something to remember about an experience like that, and I am glad to have had it. It makes you appreciate comforts when you have them. A cigar once a week, hot food if you ever get it, just a chance to sleep – you really know how to appreciate them when you get them at the battle-front, if you are lucky enough to get 'em. And I'm glad to be back here out of it, seeing friends and away from the hard work, enjoying the comforts of America. But, I don't know, somehow I think about the boys of my outfit."[180]

William Jordan, the surgeon for 2/504 who was wounded on December 14. (Carl Jordan)

As dawn broke on December 15, 1943 the 504th PIR's 2nd Battalion had already reported 75 wounded and 15 killed, but the path for a renewed assault seemed ripe. Throughout the day, coordinated attacks all along the front were to be launched in an attempt to bring the full weight of the Allied armies on the Germans occupying San Pietro and its surroundings.

The official history for the Fifth Army describes how the attack was to be made by the soldiers of the 143rd and the paratroopers of the 2nd Battalion, 504th PIR from the hills around Monte Sammucro on the evening December 15: "The 143rd's objective was Hill 730, from which fire could be directed on enemy movements along the road between San Pietro and San Vittore. To reach it, the assault troops had to cross a deep saddle with precipitous sides. A less difficult approach would have been from the north, but this route was blocked by the enemy on Hill 687, which the parachute troops had been ordered to capture."[181]

At the time news of the renewed attack came, Captain Francis G. Sheehan was working in the battalion aid station with the Assistant Regimental Surgeon, Captain Kenneth I. Sheek. The two seasoned surgeons, veterans of the Sicilian invasion, had known each other well before their time in the Army. Both native Hoosiers, Sheehan and Sheek were classmates at the University of Indiana Medical School. (Sheek graduated in 1937, and Sheehan in 1938).

Both doctors had already seen much combat togeather in the fight for Italy prior to the fighting around San Pietro. Captain Sheehan had set up medical clinics in Naples after its liberation, and had nothing but praise for the Neapolitan people: "They were particularly helpful in leading us to shelter where we could immediately establish aid stations. Very often the citizens would drop in to be treated for one thing or another, and leave excellent wine and fruits - and one time a patient left a gallon of honey, the first we'd seen since we left the States."[182]

As Lieutenant Walter Van Poyck led his Company E of the 504th PIR into the attack on the night of December 15, the rest of the battalion followed. Their objective: climb down the weathered and creviced northwest face of Monte Sammucro into the narrow valley, and climb Hill 687. The brave Captain Sheehan went with the advancing troops. The men were met with withering fire from the Germans. Tracers, deflecting off rocks, emitted beautiful red and silver streaks across the night. Sometimes there were so many tracers in the air it would have emitted enough light to read a book. As the men met the German fire, Captain Sheehan was wounded when a machine gun slug tore through his chest.

The men became disorganized in the night. One officer, who was hollering out for his men which had gone astray, kept being answered by a German, "Vot you vant, captain, vot you vant?" The parachute officer would yell back, "Shut up, you son of a bitch, we'll take care of you in a minute."[183]

The attack stalled.

The famed war correspondent Ernie Pyle – a favorite of the 504th PIR – was nearby, and met Captain Sheehan shortly after he was wounded in the attack: "There was an old stone building sitting on the bare mountainside at the top of the mule trail… It was used as a medical-aid station, but even so the Germans put a few score shells around it every day… One day, when I was at the top of the mule trail, a wounded paratrooper captain walked into the aid station in the old stone building. He was Captain Francis Sheehan, of 22 North Grey Street, Indianapolis, a man with a finely sensitive face, who almost seemed out of place in such a rugged outfit as the paratroopers. He stood out among the other wounded because he was cleanly shaven, and although his face was dirty it was recent dirt, not the basic grime that comes of going unwashed for weeks and weeks… He got a machine gun bullet in his right shoulder, but it apparently missed the bones. He walked on down the mountain without help, and said that the wound didn't actually hurt much."[184]

They Were Killing Our Men Coming and Going

Pink rays of light, streaming through the complex silhouette of the eastern mountaintops, began to illuminate the barren ridge line of Monte Sammucro as the dawn of Thursday, December 16 broke. Near the summit of Sammucro, James T. Sapp, from Rincon, Georgia, and his platoon was laboriously making their way to the other side of the mountain, where the parachute riflemen of their 2nd Battalion were still pinned by withering automatic weapons fire, and heavy artillery fire.

James Sapp and his platoon was one of the battalion's two heavy weapons platoons. With their platoon's eight large 81mm mortar tubes, they had the ability to quickly lay covering fire with the many different types of shells they stocked, such as high explosive or white phosphorus shells. These heavy mortars were extremely deadly - they could throw up a large shell at a high arch, making them capable of hitting an enemy in defilade, and drop them right into the pocket of the Germans.

The way over the crest, Sapp remembered, was arduous when carrying their 81mm mortars, which weighed in at 136 pounds each. They were moving up to give supporting fire to their heavily-engaged battalion on the other side of Monte Sammucro, still trying to break the bastion of Hill 687. "The engineers went up there and anchored big ropes. One morning we went over in the attack, over the top of that mountain, and the Germans could see us," Sapp remembered.

They descended to the slope and began to get orders for fire from the rifle companies. When they got the coordinates and began setting up the fire mission, the tubes were nearly straight up and down. The men dropped mortar shells into the 50-inch tube. *PUMFF! PUMFF!* sounded the mortars as the shells bucked up out of the tube with a dull anger, heading for the German positions.

Then came the German counter-battery.

Under one of the most blistering artillery barrages James Sapp had seen to date, shells were bursting all around him in a deadly cacophony. Shrapnel and fragmented shale wrenched from the barren, rocky ground, and flew in a thousand different directions. James Sapp and his foxhole buddy, James C. Duckett, just laid down next to each other, as everybody "just tried to get as close to the ground as possible, or by a rock." The artillery seemed to be coming in at "point blank" range, and the artillery was "killing our men going and coming."

To Duckett and Sapp's right, Privates Otho Liles and Raymond E. Hinshaw were attempting to dig through the rocky ground next to a small tree. An artillery shell bursted the tree into pieces, sending flying tree fragments across the space and passing through the bodies of Liles and Hinshaw. Sapp got right up and went over to them. The tree fragments, Sapp recalled, "went through them like a bullet." Both were dead.

Under the barrage, which lasted two hours, James Sapp also watched with horror as their company commander, Captain Robert N. Johnson, suffered a direct hit from an artillery shell. He was only six or eight feet away and Sapp watched as the shell just "disintegrated the lower part of his stomach." One of his last acts in life was acquiring water for his men, as he was killed shortly after delivering it. "He was one of the finest men I ever met," Sapp said.[185]

Sapp felt that Captain Johnson was killed instantly, but Lieutenant Chester Garrison heard that he lived a few moments after the shell rocked his foxhole. "Dying," Garrison heard, "he exerted strength enough to yell to nearby foxhole occupants, 'Write to my mother that I was a good soldier!' That he was. He also was a most likeable leader – tall, clean-cut, duty-minded – an American boy from Florida. I knew him only slightly. At Fort Bragg I had seen him with his neatly dressed, admiring parents and fiancée. Although I did not hear him shout, I was told about his last communication by a trooper in the next foxhole. I have wondered about his wish because I cannot imagine my making such a request, whether to my parents or anybody else. I do not know what I might have spilled out."[186]

About noontime, men began to fall back to the ridge. The attack had failed. One trooper came up to Captain Delbert Kuehl, the seemingly omniscient Protestant chaplain for the regiment. "We still have some wounded over on the German side," he said. They couldn't be left behind. Kuehl went and found Major Ivan J. Roggen, the regimental surgeon, and spoke with him about going over the ridge to evacuate their wounded. Major Roggen acquired an old four-by-six-foot white flag with the red medical cross on, and found a stick to post it from. Medics gathered to get ready to cross the ridge under the flag. "We all knew that if the German troops were from the fanatical SS," Kuehl explained, "or if they couldn't figure out our purpose, we wouldn't be coming back."[187]

Major Roggen and Chaplain Kuehl began walking over the crest of the ridge. Sergeant Irving S. Hollander, of Newark, New Jersey, was following close behind. Roggen was waving the flag as he went. A burst of gunfire crossed their path, impacting just at their feet.

Following close behind Roggen, Kuehl, and Hollander, Captain Kenneth Sheek, and the rest of the medics and litter-bearers came. There were nearly 21 men in all.

The other paratroopers were dismayed and amazed. Private George W. Beavers explains that "even our own men didn't recognize the flag at first. One soldier said, 'Are we surrendering' as I went past." And as Corporal Albert Creal made his way around a foxhole, he could hear a German holler, "So you are surrendering, yes?" Then Creal heard a paratrooper yell, "No, but if you want to surrender, come on out and we'll talk it over!"

"Nix!" replied the German.

"Don't shoot, they are medics!" a voice yelled.[188]

It was a terrible sight as the medics separated the dead from the wounded. Lieutenant Richard A. Harris of F Company was rolled onto a stretcher and carried back up the hill, along with 2nd Lieutenant Earl F. Morrison of D Company. Morrison would succumb to his wounds a few hours later. Richard Harris would recover from his wound, only to be killed in January 1945 during the Battle of the Bulge.

"The men themselves didn't know how many of them had been killed," Floyd Butler explained. "Guys who were wounded would say, 'I think my buddy over there got hurt too.' Then you'd walk over a couple yards and find his buddy was dead."[189]

Chaplain Kuehl would later say, "Many of the men who looked like they still were fighting were dead. Twice I started to offer cigarettes to men crouched in their foxholes, their rifles still out in front of them. They were dead."[190]

During the cease fire, James Sapp and the men were told to move positions: "There was a ridge that went down and we were on the right of that ridge [during the attack], and during the cease fire they told us to move off [to] the left of that ridge; there wasn't quite as much fire." When Sapp got to the other side, he saw a large rock that was shaped like a bench. Exhausted, he took his pistol belt off, and laid it a few feet in front of the rock, then set down his Thompson sub-machine gun on top of that. He then took a seat on the rock and laid his helmet down in front of him. Two other paratroopers soon joined him on the rock. Out of the view of Sapp, the red cross flag was removed. Suddenly, a mortar landed in front of Sapp, scoring a direct hit on his Thompson sub-machine gun and pistol belt. The equipment just seemed to disappear in a flash - "disintegrated," Sapp recalled. Shrapnel few into the trio of men sitting on the rock. The two troopers on either side of Sapp fell wounded. Sapp was unscathed. A short time later, Sapp pulled out the handkerchief he carried in his pocket with a piece of shrapnel inside it. There was a small cut which just drew a little bit of blood from his hip, but the handkerchief saved him from serious injury. "The Lord was watching over me," Sapp would later say.[191]

The war was now back in full swing.

Artillery continued to pepper the battalion off and on all day. Lieutenant Chester Garrison, a philosopher in his own right and student of literature, witnessed an act later that fateful day which later made him consider human nature. Years later, in 1996, he wrote about that day in his memoir, *An Ivy League Paratrooper*:

A notable incident occurred during a barrage on the ridge. A trooper on the forward side had been badly hurt. On hearing about this, a fellow trooper from the same platoon immediately and instinctively went over the ridge to help, in full observation of the Germans. He had made no second thoughts; a wounded friend was in need. He returned, panting from the weight on his back of the injured mate. His response had no regard for danger: this need required this action, which was awesome, heroic, and foolhardy.

Although I did not know the trooper, I knew who he was and had heard something of his background. In civilian life he had tracked bill collectors who went store to store for rent, loan payments, protection money, whatever. In late afternoon at some advantageous location, he would corner and rob the collector.

This ridge hero is a robber? He does "the right thing" in combat; he cheats in society? The good guy is the bad guy? What is the continuity or explanation?

The suddenness of emergency denies consideration whether at war, in a car accident, in a fire, in a hospital; the individual reacts by remote or instinct, both of which eliminate all pretentions and show the individual, for better or for worse, in the raw. Some take action, some cringe. Only afterwards, wonderment about the reaction – or lack of it – takes over.

The incident on the ridge might suggest that basic goodness exists in an individual. In the prolonged confusion of survival in society's business, politics, and human relations, this element may be obscured and held back. But in the stark setting of warfare, it tends to emerge more readily. This ridge tale, I suspect, has its equals wherever living is reduced to physical survival and is particularly on show in combat.[192]

Fighting of the 1st Battalion

Fred Baldino was one of four original paratroopers of the 1st Battalion, 504th PIR who originated out of the small coal towns around Columbia County, Pennsylvania. The other three were Leroy Doyle, John Piroc, and James Rupp.

Shortly after Baldino was assigned to the 504th, he got a leave to go home. While visiting, he attended a dance and saw another paratrooper with the vivid red and blue insignia of the 82nd Airborne Division, and introduced himself. It was none other than his childhood friend James Rupp! Rupp had just been assigned to B Company, and Baldino had been assigned to A Company, both within the same battalion. When they were kids, Rupp would accompany his father who would bring his foodstuffs to sell to Baldino's mother and others in their neighborhood in Ashland, and while Rupp's father would sell his goods, the young Baldino and Rupp would play together.

Visibly weary from the campaign on Sammucro, Al Clark and Fred Baldino rest on steps in the village of Venafro. (Fred Baldino)

Every chance they got overseas, Baldino, Doyle, Piroc, and Rupp would get together. However, on December 14, 1943, Rupp and Piroc were both killed. A mutual friend who had been with Rupp when he was killed said that he had been shot through the head by a sniper when Rupp looked over a stone fence they were taking cover behind. When Baldino got word that Jim Rupp was killed, it was the only time Fred

Baldino wept in World War II. "What a terrible blow it was to me." Doyle was killed at Anzio, making Baldino the only young man of their foursome to survive the Italian campaigns of the 504th Parachute Infantry.[193]

Under the cover of darkness on December 17, the paratroopers of Lieutenant Colonel Williams's 1st Battalion took over the forward positions along the ridge line of Monte Sammucro from the 2nd Battalion, whose men were suffering of frayed psyches, mental and physical exhaustion – and casualties. They moved back to front line reserve positions, where even there one could not feel an easing of the nerves nor escape death and maiming. As the battalion was settling into the reserve positions, two more men were seriously injured when the boulder by which they were sleeping was set cascading down the mountain.[194]

It was days of death and privation and nervous mental and physical tension just such as these which would take in smooth faced 19-year-olds and output them as square-chinned, haggard-looking men who appeared as if they aged years in days. As the torturous days on Sammacro's moist, wind-swept face drug on for the paratroopers of the 2nd Battalion, Lieutenant Chester Garrison would find himself nestled into his rocky foxhole reading Shakespeare's *Macbeth*, and memorizing Macbeth's soliloquy in Act 5, which reflected his thoughts and feelings in the trying conditions.

Tomorrow, and tomorrow, and tomorrow,
Creeps in this petty pace from day to day
To the last syllable of recorded time,
And all our yesterdays have lighted fools
The way to dusty death. Out, out, brief candle!
Life's but a walking shadow, a poor player
That struts and frets his hour upon the stage
And then is heard no more. It is a tale
Told by an idiot, full of sound and fury,
Signifying nothing.[195]

Between December 15 and 16, the attack cost Garrison's battalion 73 battle casualties and had fallen short of its objective of sacking Hill 687.[196] Their attack, however, had depleted severely the 71st *Panzergrenadiers*, reducing many of its companies to 20 men, making the unit a hull of its former self.

Feldwebel Kurt Kleinschmidt was one of those captured by Garrison's battalion during their attack. Feldwebel Kleinschmidt had seven years of service up to the time of his capture, and before the regiment's prisoner of war interrogator he was shivering cold and his belly had a want of food. Despite this, he continued to maintain that "the morale of the troops and of people at home is very good. Even more, he refused to think about losing the war."[197]

On nearly all fronts the German army was rearing from strategic defeat after strategic defeat, and the soldiers opposing the 504th were beginning to feel the strain. But, despite these things, many of the full-blooded Germans, like Feldwebel Kleinschmidt, were loyal to the cause - radicals, they would be called today - and determined to keep fighting, and, like Kleinschmidt, determined to keep their pride intact. This latter fact was something which the eingedeutscht fighters in the ranks of those units opposing the 504th bore witness to. A significant number of troops under arms in both the 71st *Panzergrenadiers* and the 132nd Infantry Regiment were from occupied countries and were recently *eingedeutscht* - Germanized - so they could fight in combat units. There were Poles, Slaves, and even some from occupied countries in Western Europe like Luxembourg. The full-blooded Germans, some of these eingedeutscht fighters observed, were beginning to show cracks in their morale. Food was coming to be less plentiful at the front, and they began to recognize that the future for Germany may be dark.

Their pride, however, was too strong to allow them to admit it, and many of the Germans were still fanatically devoted to the cause of Nazism and refused to think about losing the war. One of the more fanatical stated that the Italian front might prove to be drain on German manpower, but the thing which would ultimately lead to the ruin of Germany was that she was more and more obliged to call upon non-Germans, the eingedeutscht fighters, of occupied lands. These men, he felt, were a hindrance.[198] There was something to his point; some of them deserted at the first opportunity. Lieutenant Thomas Utterback, an officer in the 504th Parachute Infantry, remembered that "German patrols roamed through our lines. One night the switchboard operator, from his tent and in a hushed tone, told me that his tent was full of Germans. I thought he was crazy, so I told him to send them over to my tent. Soon the tent flaps parted, and about a dozen soldiers in German uniforms entered the tent. They were Polish conscripted fighters and were so happy to be 'captured.'"[199] Unfortunately, not enough of them gave themselves up so easily, at least in the opinion of the paratroopers of the 504th.

The same full-blooded German prisoner who talked of the inferiority of the eingedeutscht fighters was also questioned about his feelings on the inevitability of another front opening up in France. He was positive the Allies would fail because the French coast was so strongly defended. Here is a reflection of the fact that the German soldiery had not lost hope. Many were still thoroughly indoctrinated with propaganda of grand stands and battles to come which would turn the tide back in their favor. Another prisoner captured by the 504th "stated, with a knowing glint in his eye, said he heard that there were 3,000 paratroopers [less than 10 miles north] in the Cassino area all set to go in the line." This, obviously, was a propagandic fantasy fed to the German soldier by his leadership. The regiment's prisoner interrogator finally concluded, "It is possible that Hitler's fighting men receive morale and spiritual inspiration for continuing this war from the vigor and viciousness which characterizes the ever-continuing offensive of their body lice."[200]

Although the attack of the 2nd Battalion, 504th Parachute Infantry shot the companies of the German units opposing them to pieces, the paratroopers failed to achieve their objective of usurping Hill 687 from the Germans. Their attack had depleted severely the 71st *Panzergrenadiers*, reducing many of its companies to 20 men. The unit supporting the 71st was the 132nd Infantry Regiment, who had two companies manning the bulwarks of Hill 687. Before dawn on the 16th, one of the companies had been pulled out and forced to the slope of Sammucro to reinforce the hard-pressed 71st *Panzergrenadiers*, who were facing the brunt of the 2nd Battalion's attack.

The German's repulsion of the attack of the battalion can be analyzed in two different phases. Firstly, the night phase. When the battalion became disorganized on the slope by the German fire, the terrain and the loss of contact with each other in the night, the troopers lost their momentum and the weight of their attack. Now, with the paratroopers effectively halted on the northwest slope, pinned by fire and fraught with confusion, it left them sitting exposed to the German artillery on the morning of December 16, the second phase. The battalion, it would appear, was greatly disrupted by the German barrage in which Captain Johnson and Privates Otho Liles and Raymond Hinshaw were killed. This barrage seemed to effectively stymie the battalion for good.

While the 2nd Battalion's attack did not achieve its objective, it did alter the German lines drastically, including the German positions on Hill 687 which were being held by the 3rd Company of the 132nd German Infantry Regiment. Two prisoners from the 3rd Company later told how they could not understand the "American way of fighting." They described being plastered with artillery, which, by their description, beat them and left them frightfully clinging to the rocky bottom of their foxholes "fully demoralized" and waiting for the Americans to come – and nothing happened. By the end of December 16, the 3rd Company numbered 11 men. They had no ammunition left, and under the cover of darkness they abandoned Hill 687.

Gefreiter Joseph Rduch and Grenadier Joseph Sezesny were two stragglers. They woke up on the morning of the 17th all alone. That morning, they left the hill in search of water before returning again to their former positions on Hill 687, still virtually abandoned, on the morning of the 18th. They found it, much to their surprise, still unoccupied by the American paratroopers, something they could not understand.[201]

The intelligence officers of the 504th Parachute Infantry had gone to bed on December 18 with an un-confusing picture of the German situation. They knew who was opposing them, what they looked like, a general idea of their strength, and most importantly where they were. They had this knowledge until they woke up the next morning, and all patrols reported no contact with the Germans.

One of the men patrolling down at the base of Sammucro was Lieutenant Horace Carlock. Overnight, he had taken his platoon to Hill 687 with orders to occupy the hill. According to Ross Carter's *Those Devils in Baggy Pants*, they received fire from a German machine gun as they approached 687. Shortly afterwards, they were ambushed by another patrol - probably a patrol of engineers - in which Michael Ogonowski was killed.

The men came to small shepherd's huts at the base of 687 and began to search them. Carter and Sergeant Frank Dietrich detected the scent of freshly-burned wood and yelled out to the Germans they knew were inside. Two came out - most likely the two stragglers, Gefreiter Joseph Rduch and Grenadier Joseph Sezesny.[202]

The rest of the platoon got a toe-hold on Hill 687, but the Germans still held a spur, likely a position to protect the flank of the new defensive line which the Germans had been pushed to. Therefore, it was decided that before dawn on Christmas morning, the 1st Battalion would try their hand at attacking Hill 687.

This attack was repulsed by entrenched German positions – some dug into caves – on the terraced hill, and shortly after daylight the men began to fall back to their original positions. Lawrence Stimpson gives a vivid account of his experience on Christmas morning during the attack:

...There was absolutely no vegetation on it, except rocks about the size of your shoe, maybe. That happened to be Christmas Eve of 1943. We were taking this hill, but they had a machine gun set up there that was in the back of a pile of rocks that really gave them a lot of protection. Anyway, I know I was lying on my back that night watching the tracers go over my head and I could say, "What a heck of a way to spend Christmas morning."

Anyway, the sun started coming up – it started getting light – so we had to pull off that hill... [to] where we were protected. Later on, about 10:00 that morning, the battalion commander Colonel Williams came down and asked for sniper protection to go out with him on that hill. He said the Germans had pulled off from it, so I went out. I was about 30 or 40 yards ahead of him. I walked right past those pillboxes. Pretty soon, I heard shots, hollering back there and the Germans were still in the pillboxes. Why they didn't shoot me, I have no idea. Then he told me, he said, "Go check out that house." And that house was, oh, two or three hundred yards away, and I really didn't appreciate going to check out the house in enemy territory alone. On the way to that house, I heard somebody hollering at me. It was kind of a brick wall or a rock wall there. This German soldier was laying there by that wall and his buddy was hit and was dead with him. He kept pointing at his forehead and said "shoot." And I said, "C'mon." And he said, "Next boom?" And I said, "Next boom." And so I sent him back to the Colonel.

(...)

Well, in the meantime, I saw another German that was bringing supplies or something in the barrow. I started chasing him – I really didn't want to go to that house. While I was chasing him, I got away from the Colonel and whoever was with him – I don't know where they were – but the German finally started firing back at me with mortar fire. They will go and shoot at one spot to try and get your range. So I thought, "I better get out of here." I went over and up a draw there. Now I'm all alone – I have no idea where anybody else is at, any American soldier – and here I come up and there are three drunk Germans in a hole asleep. So I say, I wake 'em up, "C'mon kids, let's go." And I didn't know it at a time, but there were three more about 50 yards from them watching me. And so I got them and took them back too. And I was sitting that afternoon eating my K-rations, and I thought, "You know, this hasn't been too bad a Christmas after all."[203]

Christmas 1943

The war had taken a young, handsome lieutenant by the name of Edward Kennedy far from the snow-covered streets of his beloved New England hometown of Holyoke, Massachusetts. "Tonight is Christmas Eve," Kennedy wrote home, "and I am writing this on the floor of a shed covered with straw. This my second Christmas away from home, and I hope the last. I am sick and tired of this war, and all its miseries and killings. I am going to Mass in a Nun's Chapel tomorrow. Thank God I am able to go. It seems like a long while since the good old Christmas Eves at home. Do you remember that one in the Bronx when we were waiting for the bus at the Howard bus station? I would give a year's pay to be home. It is eight months now overseas, and it seems like a much longer time. Well, I'll remember you in my prayers tomorrow and I am convinced that God has placed special care over me as far as my personal safety is concerned. Love to all and the merriest of Xmases."[204] In a sad turn of events during the invasion of Holland when Kennedy would lose his life, this would be Kennedy's final Christmas.

On Hill 950, Christmas carols could be heard echoing out of the valley from Don Zimmerman's perch. He had lost track of time and date. "It was a distressing arrangement. It was fun to hear that, but I was all alone," said Don Zimmerman. "There were some foreign troops down there… They were playing them on the loud speaker and boy you could hear them raring through those hills. It was kind of a distressing thing because at least you weren't thinking about home [before and now] you were pitying yourself for being where you were."[205]

Just behind the front lines, a footpath cleared of mines, indicated by white engineers' tape lining either side like a runway, led up to a little Italian church, with its gray stone sides pockmarked by machine gun bullets. Inside, Chaplain Delbert Kuehl and Chaplain Edwin J. Kozak, the Regimental Catholic Chaplain, had been at work decorating the church, creating a small refuge from the disparaging situation. The weather was, for a change, clear and warm. It was December 25, 1943 – Christmas Day. For those able to get a quick respite from the war, Kuehl held Protestant services at 2:30 PM, and Kozak held his Catholic services at 3:00 PM.[206] Private William Brown wrote home, "There's no tree in the window, no wreath on the door - no last minute shopping, we don't have a store."[207] Brown would live through the next Christmas in the Belgian snow, before losing his life a few days later on New Year's Day, 1945.

Relief

Private Francis Keefe had been evacuated from Fornelli when he had to have an emergency appendectomy. He had only recently been released from the hospital in Naples and was able to rejoin his platoon while they were on Hill 950 at about the end of December. "The Germans would try and shell us and try and hit us," Keefe remembered, "and those shells would just come over – it's like a cliff – and they would hit down and they would roll, run right along the surface. All we had to do was stay down and they would land twenty-five yards over from where we were, more or less lying on the hard ground. Those shells would go spinning all over the place, and there was an awful lot of shells back there that didn't go off; I'm talking about thirty or forty shells so I don't know if the detonators were no good, or if they didn't hit that part when they hit. It was just unusual."

The First Special Service Force of Robert T. Frederick was set to relieve their positions on Hill 950. Francis Keefe remembers Frederick and a staff sergeant coming up to inspect the positions and terrain. "The staff sergeant," he recalled, "had a map case and he went out and stood wide in the open and they were looking at the map case and pointing to this. I said, 'We better get away from here because some German, if they can spot us, they're going to spot this guy and we're going to get an awful lot of artillery coming in.' And sure enough that's what happened. We were all smart enough to get away from Colonel Fredricks."[208]

The relief of the entire regiment was completed by December 28. They were weathered, worn, and drained; with short, scraggly beards and pitted faces, all had been unclean and unshaven. Portable showers were sent up. The mess crews prepared canned turkey for a belated Christmas dinner, and the men received their Christmas packages from home. "They were some of the finest people I ever met," James Sapp reflected. "Every one of them. I didn't have any problems. We were a close nit unit."[209]

The battles around Monte Summacro had a lasting effect on the paratroopers who fought there. Edwin Bayley was a later-war replacement to the 504th PIR who noted, "I remember the old guys talking about [Hill] 1205 right up to the time I left the division... The troopers from 1205 seemed to have an everlasting, special bonding with one another."[210]

For the 2nd Battalion, 504th Parachute Infantry Regiment, the fighting around Hill 1205 had been especially devastating. James Sapp, who did not miss one day of the front line time credited to the unit for the duration of World War II, remembered the fighting at Hill 1205 as the lowest point for him. And when Lieutenant Rexford Stribley tried to talk to Lieutenant Chester Garrison upon reaching the bivouac area after he was relieved on Christmas Eve, Garrison was unable to comprehend anything Stribley was saying; Garrison was dejected, empty, and exhausted, both physically and physiologically. Garrison had recorded in the battalion's journal as early as December 18, just after they had been relieved of their forward positions on the crest, that "the men who have come back from the forward slope are, for the most part, in an exhausted condition due to the severe mental and physical strain, the terrific barrages and the lack of rations, particularly water. The Bn personnel is drastically depleted."[211]

For his company – Headquarters Company – December 16 was one of the blackest days in all of the war with the loss of their commander, Captain Robert N. Johnson. James Sapp considered Johnson the finest individual he had ever met in his life. Sapp's close friend Earl Levitt, who "literally worshiped" his captain, also took the loss very hard. When the company got relieved in the middle of the night on Christmas Eve, Levitt became extremely distraught about the loss of the beloved commander – that night was the worst of his life. He remembered, "We each had one bale of hay to make our bed and I sat down on the bale of hay and I couldn't get my pistol belt off. I don't know why, but I struggled with it for about five minutes, and I just sat down on the bale of hay and I just stayed there for a couple hours. I finally got my pistol belt off and I lay down and I didn't sleep. Just about good daybreak I got out of the tent and I went out my tent and stood in the door and I looked up the street, and about six or eight tents away Major Blitch and Chaplain

Kozak [were] standing there in their tent and they saw me and beckoned to me and I went up there. They had gone into Naples and all they could find was gin, and it was probably at least a day old. They handed me the bottle and I took a big swig of it, and I am a man who hates gin, but it was the best drink I've ever had in my life."[212]

We Know What We Are Fighting For

Corporal William W. Bullock of Marion, North Carolina had been wounded for the second time since September and was on convalescence in a hospital. Bullock, trained in communication, was assigned to operate the switchboard while on light duty. While at the switchboard, he wrote to his parents about some of the activities in Italy while he was on light duty.

Dear Mom:

I'm at the switchboard again tonight, and that gives me a chance to write you. My buddy, Skip, and I have just had a good laugh out an experience we had on the front line recently.

We went to a little shack for some water, and it was snowing to beat the band. Pretty soon, here came two Jerries. Guess I best not say too much about it, but you see who is writing this letter, and Skip is right beside me writing to his mom too – that's two Jerries we won't have to bother with anymore.

Four of us went to church last Sunday. Couldn't tell much of what the preacher said, but we were welcome. Each of us gave $5 in the collection. The church is about the only building here that doesn't have a shell hole in it.

After church we visited an orphanage. The children were glad to have us. We bought $12 worth of fruit for them and gave them $40 in money – it was a happy bunch of kids.

Next day Skip and I took a little girl of five to a town about eight miles from here and dressed her up from head to foot. She was a cute biting thing when dressed up in her new outfit.

Her mother was so grateful to us that she cried for about 15 minutes. Then in appreciation, she washed out clothes for us. We who are over here and see what we are fighting for.

We have been invited to several of the better homes to eat. They gave us the best they had. I can talk to these people better now. We have a girl who is teaching us, and they like you better for trying to learn their language.

The people here still use horses and carts, and the sight of a car almost runs them nuts. There are thousands of things I'd love to tell, but guess it will have to wait for a while longer. Mom, please don't worry about me for everything will be O.K.
Believe me.
All my love to you. Your son,
Billie[213]

8

IT DIDN'T MATTER TO ME WHAT HAPPENED

To contain the weary bodies of the 2nd Battalion's paratroopers, sixty tents were erected, and straw was laid. Although late, the battalion's kitchen served a steak dinner. Their ranks mustered less than 350 men. The following day, Dr. Sheek examined half the battalion, and the other half the next day.[214]

On the cloudy day of December 30, Captain William Row of Marine City, Michigan, son of the town's doctor, took command of the 2nd Battalion's Dog Company, whose officers had been especially hit hard in the proceeding weeks. At the time of their relief from Summacro, the company consisted of only one officer, Lieutenant Wayne Hockett.[215] Captain Row wrote home to his parents about his men two weeks after taking command of the company.

You know, battle experience is a great thing. I wish there was a safe way in training to give men that something that only actual battle produces. In training, a soldier will moan loud and long if he has to train on Sunday, or if chow becomes a little monotonous, but the same fellow in combat will suffer in silence while going without food, or be exposed for days in the worst kind of weather. I must say it would enhance your national pride to see how really rugged and tough American soldiers are. News of what is happening in New Guinea reaches us quickly. The government not only informs the soldiers, but translates the news into German and sends it by plane or shoots it with heavy artillery across to the enemy. They know when they read it that we are telling them the truth.[216]

Over the coming months, their ruggedness and toughness would be tested to its extremes yet again.

Often times, when on the line, the men were not paid so when the unit was in the rest areas, all the back pay would be issued. There was little to do with the money but gamble. Blackjack and dice were most popular within the 504th. As the men were due back pay for the months of October, November and December, Lieutenant Colonel Freeman appointed Roy Hanna and Edward Kennedy to take a jeep back to Naples to get the men's money. They arrived in Naples, checked into their hotel, and went out to dinner together. Ed Kennedy, a dashingly handsome lieutenant from Holyoke, Massachusetts, talked about his

Catholic faith, and said how he was going to go to seminary when he got home from the war. After dinner they went back to their hotel and walked into the lobby to hear a male and female having an argument. It was none other than actor Humphrey Bogart, on tour with the USO. Bogart, as with many Americans, was a very popular actor with the paratroopers of the 504th, and they had his blockbuster *Casablanca* shown to them on many occasions. Roy Hanna remembered meeting the famous actor that night:

When we returned to the hotel that evening about eleven there was Humphrey and his wife on the other side of the lobby (not another person around) having a rather heated argument.

When he spotted us he hollered "Paratroopers" and rushed across the lobby, threw his arms around me and gave me a big sloppy kiss on the cheek and then repeated the same for Kennedy. He then took us across the lobby where his wife was sitting on a davenport and introduced us to her. I will add that they both had had a bit too much alcohol.[217]

Three days later, January 2, Bogart's USO show was attended by many of the men. Edward Kennedy wrote home on the 14th mentioning the experience. "We are resting after another spot of combat and really needed it. I had a drink the other evening with Mr. and Mrs. Humphrey Bogart, Lefty Gomex and Jack Sharkey. They don't want us to write about our combat experiences, however I'm proud to say I can remember way back one time when I was the most advanced soldier on our front lines in Italy. I have been recommended for the Silver Star Medal, but I won't tell Ma about [it] unless I actually get it as higher command has to approve yet."[218]

Rain and wind continued to be a problem in the rest area. On the morning of January 4, the regiment moved to another rest area in Mugnano, a suburb of Naples.

Men went into Naples for rest and relaxation, and found the city much different than when they had left it in October for the mountains. One evening, Lieutenants Chester Garrison, Edward Kline and Walter van Poyck went to the San Carlo Opera House, which was now reopen. "The theater was crowded; the orchestra and cast were energetic; the scenery had been resurrected," Garrison recalled. The "variations from routine inspired my psyche just as rest invigorated my body," Garrison described. "But the intermission from soldiering was not long. We dreaded an anticipated mission – any mission."[219]

This sentiment was not shared by Lieutenant Garrison alone. The grueling mountain campaigns since leaving Naples at the end of October had taken their toll on the youth and prowess of the regiment, and the effect was felt by all. The precipitous part of the campaign was felt in the Sammucro area, especially the last nineteen-day stretch before the relief, so that even the replacements who had joined in early December were war-weary veterans.

Shortly after their arrival in the Villarica-Mugnano area north of Naples, news of a new parachute mission called Operation SHINGLE fluttered through the formations.

Lieutenant Edson Mattice later wrote, "The badly depleted 504th Parachute Infantry Combat Team had been relieved from the heights of Mount Sammucro in the last days of December 1943. At the time of its relief, many companies were below 50% of effective fighting strength due to heavy casualties, the almost impassible terrain and the physical hardships endured by the difficulty of transporting supplies by pack animals over precipitous mountain trails under heavy enemy shell-fire. The combat efficiency and physical condition of the personnel available for duty upon relief was poor and impaired by mental and physical exhaustion and a deficiency of basic equipment and ordnance. During the short rest period, not all of the equipment shortages were replenished, neither was the Combat Team brought anywhere near basic [strength] in replacements and hospitalized men returning to duty. Were it not for the characteristic fighting spirit and mental aggressiveness typical of the 504th Parachute Infantry Combat Team the advisability of sending the Combat Team into another mission so closely following one of the type just finished might have been questionable."[220]

As the Operations Officer for the 2nd Battalion - one of the most hard-hit units in the Sammucro fight - Lieutenant William Sweet perhaps most poignantly described the situation facing their regiment as they were trying to get the men in better condition for the coming Operation SHINGLE.

In the last nineteen days of combat the regiment had lost 218 men through enemy action, and about half the outfit through sickness and fatigue, so that each battalion was composed of a very large percentage of replacements or men that had just been released from the hospital. In fact, the 2nd Battalion had been relieved from the line when it had only 120 men and twelve officers.

The period of 4 January to the 21st was spent in retraining and briefing the troops on the impending operation. Due to the lowered morale and physical condition this was extremely difficult. At the end of the training the men were only shadows of their former selves, and the only thing that carried them on was an intense loyalty to the unit. This loyalty was played upon by everyone in an attempt to make the men put forth the necessary energy to make the training and mission a success.[221]

Operation SHINGLE was the code-name for the surprise Anglo-American landings at the resort town of Anzio, birthplace of the Roman Emperor Nero. Bogged down at Monte Cassino, the Anglo-

Americans made the strategic decision to land forces amphibiously behind the German lines in hopes of pulling resources from the Cassino front, thus weakening it, to defend against the beachhead at Anzio. The forces on the Cassino front, now facing a weakened front, would break through to the beachhead, where both forces would then unite and drive to Rome, some 30 miles beyond Anzio.

The preparation for the impending operation was hurriedly executed, and the tone was one of rapid changes. Sand tables were constructed, showing scale models of terrain of the drop zone and objectives. Recognition crews to show regular infantry units the distinctive uniforms of the American paratroopers were sent avoid episodes of 'friendly fire', as had occurred in central Italy when trigger-happy GIs occasionally fired on the paratroopers due to not recognizing their uniforms.

A group of pathfinders were formed under the leadership of Lieutenant Colonel Emory Adams, Jr., the Regimental Operations Officer. The men picked for the mission were told to get on a truck with no knowledge of what they were volunteered to do. They were driven south of Naples past Vesuvius and over towards Foggia where the British airbases were located. Once they arrived, they were told they were going to be pathfinders, and were told where the mission was to be executed. The second day the detachment was there, British parachute officers came with radar sets – the "Rebecca's" and Eureka's" later made famous in the Normandy operation – and instructed the men how to use them. They also stressed that they wanted the sets back, but if they were to fall into German hands they were to be blown up. Each man was given lights which only weighed a couple of pounds, and they were instructed to make a cross on the drop zone to guide the pilots visually. The jump was scheduled for a clear night, and the lights were supposed to have been visible for 20 miles.

From the airbase, Lieutenant Colonel Emory Adams took a flight over the drop zone to survey the terrain from the air.[222]

Back in Villarica, preparations for the regiment continued when suddenly on the morning of January 20, a mere two days before liftoff, Colonel Tucker received word that the parachute mission was canceled in favor of an amphibious landing of the 504th. The regiment moved to the port of Pozzouli without delay, and the clear, sunny morning of January 21 brought a bustle in the Neapolitan docks as the men of the 504th Parachute Infantry Regiment prepared to embark upon landing crafts (LCIs). In the early afternoon, the men lined up by their boatloads and began boarding. Edson Mattice recorded that Colonel Tucker "was still without any well-defined mission other than that he was to land his Combat Team on Red Beach southeast of Nettuno, Italy as soon after daylight as possible."[223] Things had moved rapidly and hastily. The regiment was still well-understrength; Lieutenant Colonel Leslie G. Freeman's 3rd Battalion, for example, mustered approximately 536 men and officers.[224]

After some time, the regiment was aboard their respective landing crafts, and the 504th was out to sea by four o'clock in the afternoon. Waiting for them off the coast of Naples was a massive convoy of ships transporting the 5th Army, poised to strike at the beach resort of Anzio. Rather than parachuting, they would be sailing into battle. It had been just over 24 hours since notice of the amphibious landing was given to the regiment.

Embarking on his first combat mission was Lynd Neely of Daisetta, Texas, one of the new replacements. "Not the best time for a guy to join an outfit, as he found out later," Henry Hoffman wrote of the new paratrooper they would come know as 'Tex'. "As the LCI pulled out of the harbor and sailed for the beachhead, Tex was ready and anxious."[225]

LCIs loading troopers of the 504th PIR for the trip to Anzio. (US Signal Corps via Center for Military History)

The trip to Anzio was overnight. When they awoke the next morning, they had arrived off shore surrounded by ships. William Sweet remembered that "reports came through that five waves had landed, but from the ships no action could be observed on the beach. The enemy was very noticeable by his absence. All in all, it looked like a dry run for the 504th. Sprits began to rise, as it seemed that for once we would not be committed and that Fifth Army had told us the truth; surely the reserve wouldn't be needed in a quiet and peaceful situation."[226]

The men hung over the railing of the LCIs and got some sun, which they had seen little of over the previous months, and took in the Mediterranean air and the view of the Italian beach. But soon the men were ordered to prepare for landing, as the LCIs transporting the 504th Parachute Infantry Regiment lined up for a run at the beach. Al Tessinari remembered that several of the men were seasick. "Put your cigarettes in your helmet," he recalls someone saying. "We don't know how deep the waters going to be."[227] As the landing crafts in which they rode roared towards the beach and the morning sun hung overhead, the soldiers were still as formidable a fighting force as any.

As the landing crafts carrying the regiment raced into the shore, the medal ramps on either side of the deck dropped into the water at the fore of a gently sloping beach, patched with bushy grass and interspaced with wheat-like flora.

For most of the men, the ride into shore was a wet one. Lieutenant Reneau Breard remembered that his landing craft hit a shoal, which halted any further forward movement of the ship. "I mean it stopped," Lieutenant Breard recalled, "and we were kind of far out so they let those ramps down and we started wading in. We thought the water was going to be up to our waist. The water was over our heads… so consequently we waded in and you'd go so far then you'd jump up out of the water with everything you got on you and take a deep breath then go back down really fast."[228]

Captain John Lekson was disembarking the LCI just next to Breard's when he watched his radio operator, a jockey by profession, go off the ramp and disappear into the water. "Searching frantically under a floating helmet," Lekson described, "I found the radio and the operator – both still working."[229]

German Dive-Bombers

Under the sunny, clear blue morning, Private H. Donald Zimmerman and the men of H Company were packed onto the deck of the landing craft as it roared into the invasion beach in the long line of LCIs carrying the regiment. The sight was a strange backdrop to the once precious resort town. The screaming drone of two German Focke-Wulfe 190's was emanating from the air above. Then it happened. "It sucked the air out of you," recalled Zimmerman of the explosion. "You tried to breathe." A bomb had hit the craft next to theirs – LCI #20 – bearing Company G. Zimmerman got down on the deck and tried to "take some big breaths. It just sucked the air out of your lungs." There was no more time for lying down. They were back in combat.[230]

Henry Hoffman was on the inflicted LCI #20, and remembered the chaos. "The trip was rather nice and quiet considering everything," Hoffman wrote. "The trouble started just as the landing craft prepared to beach. About 100 yards off shore a couple of German planes came over and dropped a couple of eggs. One got a direct hit on the engine room and the boat caught fire and, since the back was cut off, it started to sink rapidly. Abandon ship was given and there was a mad scramble. Everyone went over the side and swam for shore."[231]

LCI #45 had grounded about fifty yards from shore, and took the engines under full power to get closer to the beach but had only gone another 10 yards along the bottom. As the troops left in three feet of water, the German Focke-Wulfe 190's came over and dropped a bomb on LCI #20, impacting on the after part of the deck house. The guns on LCI #45 began firing at the German planes, expending 149 rounds.[232]

Francis Keefe was also on a neighboring LCI and recalled how the beautiful morning soon turned to chaos.

We were floating out in the ocean, Mediterranean I should say, and all the sudden a bull horn comes up and I guess it was some kind of a signal to our boats, to the commanders of the boats, to say we're going to hit the beach. So they all lined up, got in a line and started into the beach together. I guess it must have been about eight o'clock in the morning, or just before eight and we hit the beach. The commander of the boat said, as far as our boat is concerned, they were all lined up by the ramps to go up, I was more or less in the back with Muri and Blankenship on the right hand side. He said, "We didn't get in there close enough. I'm going to back up and get you a good run up on the beach so you won't get your feet wet."

He just started to back up and all the sudden the planes came out of the sun. You looked up and you saw the planes coming, actually you could see where a couple of the bombs went. We hit the deck and of course one of the bombs hit near the side of the boat and went right into the sand because we were that close to the beach you know, and the boat actually rocked over. Like it turned over, that's how much the concussion was. Then it came back up again and he says, "Everybody off!"

Meanwhile, the other bomb hit G Company. Well, there was a couple guys floating in the water so I said, "Let me over there." ... I said to Blankenship, "Let me go over and give them a hand." I took off my equipment real fast and I dived in. I was swimming over to grab one of the individuals. All the sudden I see Muri next to me. He dived in. So I grabbed one guy, he went after another. There was kid, well he wasn't a kid. He had red hair, I remember him from North Africa and he looked out and all the sudden – plop – he jumped in the water and we grabbed ahold of one of the men, which I believe to this day was the medic, doctor. I forget his name now. We dragged him up on the shore and we left him there. Other people came running over so, you know, he was taken care off.

Then we went back into the water again and Muri was one of the other individuals. By that time, they got everybody out of the water and you know, during the excitement the water was a little chilly, again it was pretty cold, but you didn't feel it that much, know what I mean. The initial shock, that was it. We went up and sat on the beach to get our breath and some officer, I just don't recall who it was, but the LCI was dead in the water and nobody was on it. They said, "You guys are all wet," there was three of us there, "go up on the LCI and make sure there's nobody left on there." Meanwhile, it was on fire and the ammunition was popping off – they had cases of ammunition on there. So anyway, we went out and got ourselves wet again and went on the LCI, looked into the cabin. You couldn't see down into the holds and whatnot, you know, because there was flames and whatnot.

In the meanwhile, we come off the LCI and one of the longboats from the navy pulls into the side where they could look in and all the sudden we heard this screaming inside there. I guess the planes hit the person that was in there. One of the guys had a .45 and boom, boom, he shot into the LCI. A lot of people don't realize that he shot to kill him, otherwise I guess he was being burned to death.[233]

Troopers of Headquarters Company, 3rd Battalion emerge from the water on Anzio beach. In the right hand corner of the photograph, smoke billows up from LCI #20. (US Signal Corps)

Despite these early episodes of chaos, the men were still in fairly good spirits and things seemed to be going smoothly. The 481 men and officers of the 2nd Battalion, 504th Parachute Infantry under the command of Major Melvin Blitch landed without casualties and began drying out in a wooded area about a half mile inland to get organized, before marching two hours to their assembly area. The road was littered with discarded equipment from the units who had landed ahead of them. "The day was sunny and warm," Lieutenant Sweet wrote, "making it very hard to believe that a war was going on and that we were in the middle of it."[234] No German infantry was seen, but the German Luftwaffe continued to make an appearance in the skies above them. Major Blitch and Lieutenant Garrison were walking down a road to get their bearings when they heard the drove of a low-flying plane and ducked quickly.[235] Francis Keefe and his friend Bill McClain had also made it to the wooded area to dry out, where McClain had dug a nice large foxhole, when planes also buzzed their battalion. The short-statured McClain dove in his foxhole and Keefe, all six foot of him, came crashing down on top of McClain.[236]

The men of Company H plunge into the water as they disembark their LCI. (US Signal Corps via Center for Military History)

Colonel Tucker and Lieutenant Colonel Emory Adams reported in to higher headquarters, where they were ordered to prepare to assume positions on the right flank of the beachhead along the Mussolini Canal. The night of the 22nd and the morning of the 23rd was spent resting, with little activity, until Colonel Tucker summoned his battalion commanders and informed them that he had been ordered to move the regiment into positions the west bank of the Mussolini Canal.

There still had been only one vehicle assigned to the 2nd Battalion since landing – an ambulance. Captain Colville, Dr. Kenny Sheek and Lieutenant Chester Garrison piled in and went to conduct reconnaissance on the positions which the battalion was to assume.

That night, the entire regiment began moving out.

Colonel Tucker ordered the seizure of two bridges across the Mussolini Canal: Bridge #2 and Bridge #5, to be taken by the 3rd Battalion and 1st Battalion respectively.

Leading the race to Bridge #2 was Company I, spearheaded personally by the 30-year-old 1st Lieutenant Willis Jackson Ferrill. A family man who hailed from the rural Illinois town of Ullin, Ferrill was one of the oldest officers in the regiment, but one of the most respected. He had distinguished himself during the invasion of Sicily, where he and Captain George Watts fought an epic battle against a superior force of German *Fallschirmjägers*.

In his pre-teen years, his father had moved the family to Detroit for work. At the age of 12, Willis discovered he missed Illinois and took the family car (with his younger cousin in tow), and drove himself all the way back home because that's where he was the happiest. Willis's father decided if he wanted to be there so bad, he'd better let him stay. In the meantime, he had graduated from high school in Cobden, met his wife, and while she was pregnant with a second child, a daughter who would be named Jackie, he walked into their home and declared, "I am going to jump out of airplanes." He would later describe the act to his wife as the greatest thrill he ever had.[237]

As Company I proceeded down the SP42 in two columns, it was approaching midnight. Lieutenant Ferrill was at the head of his column. When they were about two hundred yards from the crossroads, where the SP42 intersected with the SP18, the I Company men challenged a platoon-sized force, which turned out to be a platoon of the US 3rd Reconnaissance Troop. Ferrill's orders were to replace that platoon at Bridge #2. "Where are you coming from?" Ferrill asked them. They told him, "Up by the crossroads we can hear Germans digging in all around up there." Ferrill seemed surprised to hear that. He called Sergeant William H. White to gather five or six men and go see what was going on. Ferrill was a very cautious officer and had a habit of sending scouting parties ahead to insure they were not walking into a trap.

Just a couple minutes later, Lieutenant Colonel Emory S. Adams, Jr. pulled around in his jeep. Colonel Adams asked Ferrill what the hold-up was. "Well," Ferrill told him, "a platoon of men came down and said the Germans were digging all around. I sent a patrol up to find out what was going on. I'm waiting for the patrol to report back."

Just at that time, some trucks came down the road. The men, who were strung out on both sides of the road, were highly disciplined and held their fire. They were challenged. The trucks were from a 4.2 chemical mortar outfit. Adams's jeep blocked the road, so Adams pulled his jeep out of the way and told Ferrill, "Look, the four trucks just came down. Nobody fired on them. Take your men up." Ferrill initially said he still wanted to wait for Sergeant White to get back, but Adams ordered Ferrill to get moving to the bridge. The four trucks, and Adams, drove off.

Ferrill turned around and said, "Okay, let's get the men together."

The 1st Platoon was in the lead, and Ferrill was walking at the front of it, leading the way to the bridge. They were about 40 yards from the crossroads and had just began to pass two houses – one on each side of the road – when a German machine gun opened up on the column. Private Francis Keefe could hear Ferrill yell, "GET OFF THE," and those were the dying words of Lieutenant Willis Ferrill.

Everyone was getting off the road already when Ferrill yelled, and were diving for the drainage ditches which were on either side of the road, or for the cover of the two houses.[238] Lieutenant Donald Holmes remembered, "We heard a challenge in German to hold for they would shoot – and they did. There was only one thing for us to do. We dove into the ditches on each side of the road."[239]

Corporal James Hopkins rolled into the ditch just as a bullet hit the ring on his finger, which was directly over his heart. The impact of the bullet melted the ring and smashed it into his finger, saving his life.

Lieutenant Holmes tried to get some of the men to circle around the houses to divert some of the machine gun fire, but it was to no avail. The company was pinned down.

Orders were received to pull back. Some of the troopers started drudging on their bellies through mud and culverts with deadly machine gun fire passing incessantly over their heads. A couple men started dragging the wounded Hopkins on a blanket, when they came to a culvert that was too narrow for him to pass through. "Leave me here," Hopkins said. "Go back and get the gang together, then come back for me. Otherwise, we're all finished." One of the men dressed Hopkins' bloodied hand and covered him with a blanket. "The Germans set up a machine gun position right over my head," Hopkins recalled. "Several times they kicked me and stepped on me, but I lay quiet and they thought I was dead. They fired over me all night." Hopkins didn't know the extent of his wounds. "I was really praying; man, I was praying." Thankfully he would later be evacuated to a field hospital, where his finger was forced to be amputated as a result of the German bullet. When he got home, he brought back the half-melted ring to the store which he had bought it and jokingly asked for a refund.[240]

I Company had pulled back about 100 yards to a gully that ran perpendicular to the road, and were to wait until dawn to resume the attack on the bridge. Francis Keefe remembered the night well:

We went into the drainage ditch, but it had started to pour rain. We were always getting stuck in that rain! That drainage ditch, later on in the night, it was up to our knees but anyway we were pretty orderly getting back and Lieutenant Blankenship said, "Anybody seen Lieutenant Ferrill?" Went from one platoon to the other, nobody saw Lieutenant Ferrill. So he said, "We got to get somebody up there to find out what happened and see if they can find Lieutenant Ferrill." I said, "I'll run up." So I went up the side of the road, the left hand side, and I started up the road. I got up to where the house was and I heard somebody on the other side of the road and I heard George Leoleis – The Greek again – and I yelled over, "Greek, did you see Lieutenant Ferrill?" He said, "No," and he says, "I'll follow the patrol that went up there." I said, "They're back at the drainage ditch." So anyway I said, "Wait a second, I'll come over." So I went across the road then the machine gun opened up again – that was on the other side. Blankenship must have had a heart attack. He figured maybe they caught me you know.

So anyway we worked ourselves back and I said to him, "Where I crossed the road," I says, "I didn't see Lieutenant Ferrill." So, the next morning of course we saw his body there dead.[241]

Lt. Robert Blankenship and Lt. Willis Ferrill shortly before leaving for Anzio. (Author's collection)

Shortly after midnight, a liaison officer from the US Navy reported into the 504th PIR. He was a forward observer, and had behind him the arsenal of the Navy's powerful deck guns. First Lieutenant Roy Hanna became his guide. Hanna and the naval artillery observer went into a house and set up a temporary artillery observation post. The house, which fronted the Mussolini Canal, was on the SP18 south of the crossroads. Out of a window, they could see through the dark down onto the farm fields whose crops were fed by the Mussolini Canal.

Behind them, on the SP18, a column of paratroopers from H Company came up the road. Hanna went to join the center of the column.[242]

H/504 Joins the Fray

After landing, H Company had taken a southern approach to the Mussolini Canal, taking the SP106b (which turns into the SP39 as it approaches the canal).

Just after Roy Hanna joined the column after it turned on the SP18, mortar shells fell around them. Hanna and a number of the men dove for the grassy ditch on the right side of the road and waited. It had just begun to rain as the men got out of the ditch and began forming up on the road again. Hanna got up and walked back to his temporary observation post in the house as they began to move. The rain poured into the gully which I Company was finding shelter in, and the water came almost up to their waist that night.

At 0300, H Company's 1st Platoon had been ordered to advance on the crossroads from the south, in order to bring the Germans under a crossfire. The naval deck guns had shelled the field to the southeast of the crossroads, which was the field in which the platoon was to dig in. "There was a lot of Germans lying about dying in the ditches and stuff because the Navy had worked that area over pretty heavy," remembered Donald Zimmerman. As he was wading through knee-high grass in the field, he came across a German soldier. He had his hands over his blood-drenched midriff. His blouse covered the bloody mess that was once his stomach. He was still alive. "He was asking for 'Vasa, vasa,' which is water. I tried to get somebody that had a canteen full. I didn't have one. I lost a lot of stuff trying to dig guys out of the water [during the landings]… I went back to him a couple of times and got him some water, but he died through the night. Graves registration came. We didn't sleep that night."

Zimmerman dug his foxhole closest to the SP18, which was elevated about three feet in relation to the fields on both sides, and approximately twenty-five yards back from a house.

Just at dawn, at 0640, the naval artillery observer was scheduled to start a concentration from the deck guns on the crossroads, in preparation for the 3rd Battalion's attack on Bridge 2. Just before the barrage was supposed to begin, Don Zimmerman was sitting in his foxhole when Leonard Harmon showed up.

Harmon was an original sergeant in H Company. He had been awarded a battlefield commission within the month, and rather than chevrons on his jump suit his helmet bore the bar of a second lieutenant.

The morning was beautiful and clear. The ground was still damp from the evening's previous rains. Zimmerman got out of his foxhole and Lieutenant Harmon and he were just making conversation when the whine of incoming artillery came in. They were big shells, zeroing in on the crossroads or the house that was in front of Zimmerman; he couldn't tell which. Harmon dove into Zimmerman's foxhole facedown. Zimmerman tried to do the same thing. He missed the foxhole and began rolling around like a worm trying to find it. He couldn't. The shells began to impact with ground-shaking explosions. They were German 88's. Zimmerman knew he was in trouble. Zimmerman laid flat on his belly and buried his face into the ground like a tick.

Flying shrapnel flew through the air, and Lieutenant Harmon had the cheeks of his butt severed off by flying shrapnel. Donald Zimmerman immediately discovered two holes in his leg, clogged by shrapnel. Harmon was in no condition to move, so Zimmerman went back to try and get help.

Zimmerman had just gotten up to the road when the whine of another volley of incoming 88-millimeter shells pierced his ears. He knew they were going to be close. He took cover by the ditch and buried his head and braced for the explosion. He knew if they hit the road, raised about three feet, he would be cut to pieces by the shrapnel. A second went by. No explosion. He raised his head in just enough time to watch two 88s as they skipped down the road "like bouncy balls." He took a second and thanked God his life was spared.

He got back up and continued to walk and finally found Lieutenant Richard G. LaRiviere, or more commonly known as "Rivers", taking cover behind a pile of building materials; they looked like scrap metal or something of the sort. He was with another man – a radioman, it appeared – whom Zimmerman had never seen before.

"What the hell is going on back here?" Zimmerman exclaimed. "Lieutenant Harmon got his ass blown of."

"WHAT?!" replied Rivers in his gravel-like voice. "Come on, go with me."

Zimmerman put his hand up as if to tell Rivers, get away from me. "I'll be Goddamned if I'm going with you," said Zimmerman, or something to that effect, as he rolled over to try and show Rivers his wounded leg and explain that he needed to get the bleeding stopped.

LaRiviere began to walk away and, raising his hand in disgust, it sounded like he mumbled, "I'm going up, the hell with you."

Zimmerman stayed put and a short time later a number of officers came around. Zimmerman went up to one. "What the hell should I do?" he asked.

"Go back and get patched up," the officer said. "Down this road there's an aid station set up." Zimmerman walked the quarter of a mile, where the aid station was, and got his leg patched up. He tried to go back to the company, but they wouldn't let him leave.[243]

The Battalion Seizes Bridge 2

Just after 0700, H and I Company began their attack. On the right side of the road, I Company's 1st Platoon was leading the way. As they began their attack, the naval gunfire was being walked down the road. To their right they, could see troopers from H Company coming up from the south.

A German machine gun concealed in some trees about 20 yards to the right of the crossroads was chattering away at the I Company paratroopers.

Earlier, a platoon of tanks had been attached to the company, and those tanks were preceding down the SP42, heading to Bridge 2. The tanks began firing into the houses. When interviewed, Francis Keefe says they were not receiving fire from the houses, and his group, about 40 yards from the road and tanks, which didn't leave the road due to the soft ground, couldn't tell what the tanks were firing at. However, Sergeant George S. Davis was pointing the houses out to the tank commander, who would then put one shell in the first floor and one in the second floor. Davis did specifically point out the two houses that Ferrill had just approached when he was cut down by German fire the night before, as he had felt they had been fired on from a second story window.[244]

Sergeant Raymond Gebo claims they only found three Germans inside the houses when they cleared them up. It was also rumored that an old, bedridden Italian woman was killed in one of the houses, by the tank's shell.[245]

The I Company men were in hot pursuit of the Germans. They waded the canal, and shot many Germans as they fled across the open fled on the other side. The naval artillery was still working down the road on the other side of Bridge 2. The tanks did not advance beyond the bridge.

Sergeant George Davis, an I Company communications sergeant, pointed out houses to the American tanks during the attack on Bridge #2. (Walter Hughes)

The men rounded up approximately 25 prisoners, wounded who had been left down in the canal by their fleeing comrades, and marched them out to the field, lined up in ranks. Almost all were wounded by small arms fire in the gunfight. Nearly everyone in the company was visibly agitated by the slaying of Lieutenant Ferrill (they had come upon his lifeless body lying on the road during their attack that morning). I Company men walked through the ranks of nervous prisoners, with a frightened look on their face. Many of them felt they would be shot. About this time, about six newspaper reporters came up, and the prisoners were shot with cameras and not bullets.[246]

Most of the prisoners were from the Panzer Division Hermann Göring – the same division which Lieutenant Ferrill had inflicted an untold number of casualties on in Sicily.

After the bridge was captured, the image of Bridge 2's cost was forever to be seared into the memory of Roy Hanna. "I do remember of standing at our side of Bridge #2 and meeting the GI truck coming back from the other side loaded with dead comrades, including Ferrill."[247]

Willis Ferrill left behind a wife and a son and daughter. A couple of the men went and visited Ferrill's widow after the war, and told her that they were so angry about her husband's death, that they wanted to kill anything in their path that next morning.

The Death of Sergeant Tokarczyk

Twenty-three-year-old Sergeant Stephen A. Tokarczyk, of Wabeno, Wisconsin, was killed during the attack on Bridge 2, while fighting with H Company. As he was approaching the Mussolini Canal, a shell from the naval deck guns fell short, killing him.[248] When the I Company troopers came upon his body, they could see bandages on the ground next to him, and white sulfa powder – used to prevent infection of open wounds – in Tokarczyk's grievous wound, which had ripped almost his entire side open. It was obvious a medic tried to save him, but the wound was too severe.

About an hour after Bridge 2 was taken, Sergeant Marvin C. Porter and a few other troopers collected Tokarczyk's body on a wheelbarrow and began wheeling him down the road, to a place where the remains could get proper attention. As they were wheeling him away, one of the troopers said, "Let's move his body. I'm getting blood on my pants." Sergeant Porter turned around and said, "Don't worry about it. It's good old American blood."[249]

Troopers of the 504th PIR are held up in a ditch while attacking the crossings of the Mussolini Canal. (US Signal Corps)

Throughout the previous night, the men of the 2nd Battalion had heard the fire and seen tracers streak across the sky, but their area was quiet. They had marched into a wooded area under the rain and set up local security. On the morning of the 24th, they moved into the positions on the west bank of the

Mussolini Canal. First Lieutenant Beverley Richardson's F Company was ordered to clear the crossroads at Borgo Santa Maria near Bridge #3. Here, the battalion lost its first men to enemy action on the Anzio beachhead, when snipers fired upon the men from the houses. The snipers were Italian sympathizers in German uniforms, or just Italians in civilian clothes. Jack Bishop was shot in the chest. Sergeant Alvin N. Corpe, whose section from the 81mm Mortar Platoon was attached, was shot in the knee by one of the snipers.[250] The most grievous casualty, however, was Private Harry Rabb of Kannapolis, North Carolina, who was killed. Rabb had been drafted in August 1942 before joining the parachute troops. From Fort Benning, Georgia, he wrote home to his parents about how good a job being a paratrooper was.

Today was my big day, mother. I made my first parachute jump. I passed the test, for I'm here to tell about it. I wasn't hurt at all. In fact, I had to make two jumps today. It was raining yesterday and we had to postpone the first leap. I must make two more before I get my wings.

I made a perfect landing in each of today's jumps. While sitting in the big transport plane I was OK. But about the time I was ordered to leave the plane I naturally became a little nervous.

We were riding along very smoothly, really enjoying the flight. Suddenly, the jumpmaster said, "Stand up and hook up." Then I started shaking. "Stand in the door," the boss said, and we moved a little closer to the opening in the side of the plane. I looked down. It gave me a strange feeling around the middle area. I knew then it wouldn't be much longer until I either passed or failed that vital test. "Go," the jumpmaster finally said. I thought my heart would stop. Then I stepped through the door. The next thing I knew I was in thin air and the ship was gone.

I followed instructions and the landing wasn't so rough after all. The second jump was nothing. Guess I was a veteran by that time... Suppose I had better close for this time. I have to go down to the hanger now and pack my chutes – two of them. That'll take me until 1 o'clock. Be good and don't worry about me. Parachuting is a pretty good job after all.[251]

Monday Night Patrols

After General Lucian Truscott visited the command post of the 504th on the night of January 24, Lieutenant Colonel Adams began drawing up plans for the regiment to launch an attack to expand the beachhead the following afternoon. The orders from General Truscott required all three battalions to participate in the attack.[252]

While Lieutenant Colonel Adams was busy preparing the regiment's scheme for the following day, the foot-slogging paratroopers were busy tramping around in the German lines across the entire regimental front. At Bridge #2, William H. White gathered the men for a patrol. They had been taking sporadic fire throughout the day from a German half-track. "You know," White told the men, "if we run into that halftrack that was shooting at us all day, we're bringing it back." Francis Keefe remembered that everybody "looked at each other [like] *here we go*." They passed the bridge and ran into an OP from another company and talked to the troopers and gathered any information they had about German activity, which they said was plentiful. "On the way back in," Francis Keefe remembered, "White said, 'Look, it's dark, we're going to come in there and somebody's going to be trigger-happy and wind up killing us and nobody is gonna know what happened to us.' So he says, 'What we'll do is wait here. We're not too far from the bridge' – I guess we must have been 200 yards away from the bridge – so he said, 'We'll wait 'till it gets light then we'll come in.' That's what happened. Somebody saw us coming in and they reported we were coming in. He was smart."[253]

Troopers of the 504th PIR inspect a recently captured German paratrooper from the HG Panzer Division in the opening days of combat operations on the Anzio Beachhead. (US Signal Corps)

While Sergeant White's patrol was traversing in the south, the northern sector of the regiment's line was a flurry of activity as the men tried to deny the German armor a crossing of the Mussolini Canal. The plan called for engineers protected by two platoons of paratroopers to demolish the bridges. Lieutenant Reneau Breard led his platoon through the night up the canal and located his assigned bridge. Behind them, a firefight erupted. "We waited all night for them to blow the damned highway bridge…The engineers got shot up behind us, so finally we had to send somebody back down the canal and find out what the hell was going on, and they had already moved back," Breard recalled.[254]

Accompanying the engineers was another group of paratroopers from Company B. While Breard was awaiting them, the Germans had driven them back. Around dawn the B Company paratroopers were approaching the friendly lines near the canal. They came under fire from German 20mm flak wagons and mortars. Marvin Courtney and four or five others broke out at a run for a house which he thought was the one they had left from. Just as Courtney got to the house, a volley of 20mm rounds came in and chased Courtney into the house. Courtney knew German mortars or artillery was soon to follow. He hurried into the attached barn to look for cover. "I figured I'd lay down by this cow, but I figured that cow roll over and kill me too!" Courtney exclaimed. Courtney saw a dead cow laying against the wall of the barn, and squeezed down between. It was the last thing he remembered. "I never knew what hit me," Courtney said. He remained unconscious until he woke up in a hospital in Naples and later learned that after a German mortar dropped on top of him, Private Samuel Tomilinson carried him back to get aid. The company suffered heavily on January 25, and the incident at dawn was only the beginning of a bloody day for them, and the regiment as a whole.[255]

The Push to Expand the Beachhead

All these things happened as Monday turned to Tuesday, the day of the attack to expand the beachhead. The major objective was the seizure of Borgo Piave by the troops of Major Blitch's 2nd Battalion. The other two battalions, supporting, would launch diversionary attacks.

Sergeant Moorehead had become hardened, like many of the other men, to his experiences. "War is aptly called hell," he would write, "and to degrees it was… Each day and night we lost men who were killed and wounded; some of the wounded lived, some died. We had near 70% replacements - so many times that I lost count… I never knew many of the men in my squad or platoon as few lasted long. The way you survive was by luck or God, and to stay focused one had to be hardened. It's called battle hardness where you realize that it's only a matter of time that you will be shot… It's hard for any never involved in war to believe that since time men have adjusted to wars."

The wounding of Marvin Courtney early in the morning had set in motion the breaking up of the gang of close friends who had all come from Parachute School together to help create the company at Fort Benning - Decker, Courtney, Moorehead and several others.

The men of Company B strung out in a file on the bank of the Mussolini Canal in one of the diversionary attacks that afternoon of 25 January, marching on the bridges crossing the canal near Sessano. Soon rifle fire began to break. "We didn't pay too much attention to it, but we knew they knew we were coming," Sergeant Lawrence Stimpson recalled. "I came to one spot and I could look out and thought, 'Man, I'm really wide open here.' I just stepped back and the lieutenant stepped in my place and he got it. That's the first person I actually watched get hit and die at the same time."[256]

Heavy fire from machine guns erupted. Edwin Decker was wounded in his right shoulder, destroying his nerve. Sergeant Moorehead was also wounded at the same time, when his upper body was machine-gunned. "My shoulder bones were split apart," Moorehead recollected. He fell into a three-foot feeder canal and played dead for several hours while the battle raged above him. "Actually I fell asleep well knowing we lost our asses, and a crawled on my back… until I was discovered by our own forces."

Meanwhile, Lawrence Stimpson pulled up on the bank of the canal and watched as the German machine gun fire cut the leaves off the trees. "I could watch the leaves fall off there, and they threw one of these what we called potato masher grenades at me," he recalled. "It was only about 10 feet away, but I don't know why it didn't hurt me. I don't know how long I was there, but the other lieutenant called me back and asked me if I could go get some artillery support from the battalion commander… So I started back, but I would run and hit the dirt, run and hit the dirt. That's where they [had the] machine gun, just every time I'd get running, it was firing. I don't know why it didn't hit me, and I swear it was coming down the bank, it seemed not much closer when I got to the end than it was when I started. I finally got to the battalion commander and explained where they're at and he said they were too close. He didn't think we could adjust the artillery because the troops were too close to it."[257]

Moving on the main objective, the village of Borgo Piave, the men of Captain William Row's Dog Company were moving at a dead run through the low-cut, open farm fields towards the village. After crossing the SR148 – the main road running from east to west into the town – Captain Row's men came under heavy fire from 20mm flak guns.

Lieutenant Louis Fern was moving down the road with a group of Captain Row's men when the fighting began to break out. Fern was talking to his friend Corporal Al Slaubaugh, who Fern had seen rise through the ranks in the parachute troops since the early days of the unit, when a German flak wagon began firing on their group. Fern turned to his left to say something to Slaubaugh when he saw a black spot in the center of his forehead. Slaubaugh was dead.[258]

Soon, more German flak guns materialized, much to the surprise of the paratroopers, and with fire coming from the north and from the town itself, the Germans caught Row's men in a crossfire. Company E, following Captain Row's men, immediately sprang into action and went around the right to flank the town. They were successful in getting into the town in just enough time to be caught in between German tanks, as they came roaring from the north and the east in a pincer movement, breathing fire. Captain Row's men were left cut-off, and E Company was now left isolated in the village and holding on by a thread.

Fox Company was in the canal as reserve. Major Blitch immediately ordered F Company to get anti-tank weapons and help D Company, exposed in the fields and facing German tanks with no way to fend them off. It was getting dark before F Company could do anything for Captain Row's men. All the regiment's anti-tank weapons were left in the supply area in the rear and had to be located first.

While the anti-tank weapons were being retrieved, Lieutenant Sweet was with E Company inside Borgo Piave. "E Company was having a bad time in town," Sweet recalled. "They had been hit hard twice by three medium tanks and two flak wagons plus about two companies of infantry. Lt. [Hanford] Files at last withdrew to the west side of town and set up a perimeter defense on the three roads leading towards the canal. The town was shelled by using the 526 radio to the CP, then relaying the directions through the normal channels. By these means the companies held out until 2020, when they were ordered to withdrawal to the canal."[259]

D Company was being overwhelmed by the tanks. Louis Bednar, an attachment from battalion headquarters, was there and spent the rest of the war as a guest of the German government after he, like many others, were captured.

They told us we would have our tanks supporting us. They never got across the canal. We got across the canal because we could wade across on these little concrete things, but the tanks couldn't get over there. So here we were left over there, rangers and paratroopers were left over there... That was kind of depressing, and I think that's why a lot of us wound up as prisoners there at Anzio because they, for some reason, they didn't get the Bailey bridge across to get the tanks over on the other side... The tanks were sitting over on the other side of the canal; but the German tanks just came and ran right over us. And it's kind of scary when the tank, you see it off about a hundred yards away and you see the gun pointing at you. They used to tell us in basic training that, well, [the Germans] don't ever fire a tank at one soldier because the tank shells cost too much money. I mean, that's a lot of hot air. If they saw one soldier, they figured there were other soldiers nearby, and they saw one head or one movement, they'd fire that tank shell. What's the difference? They weren't paying for it themselves. And the Germans had that 88 mounted on their Panzer tanks, and I remember seeing this one just before I was taken prisoner. I could see that it fired, but the shell got to me before I heard the sound from the gun. I could see a puff of dirt around the tank and I heard a boom right behind me where the building got hit, and then one of the fellows out from

D Company got hit in the neck and it just about tore his head off. And it was – wasn't anything I could do for him...

The shell got there before the sound. And that was kind of scary. And then when I looked at that fellow and he was looking at me and his blood – I could see there was nothing I could do because his head was just almost severed, and, I don't know, it took something out of me there. What could you do? We had nothing to fight a tank with. Our carbines were popguns to fight those. But, anyway, I've relived some of the deals. Well, then a few of us had to get down in the ditches there because the Germans would spray the machine guns, and we had nothing to fight them with in a tank.

If you're infantry, you have nothing to fight a tank with unless you have a bazooka. We didn't have a bazooka there. A machine gun or rifle isn't going to do you any good because that tank is buttoned up and they just mow you down. So they came rolling through the town there and there wasn't too much we could do except get down in the ditches, in the water, and kind of hope they wouldn't see us...

I mean, their infantry was a little cautious about sticking their heads up too. So it was just us against the tanks, and I tell you, it's kind of an uneven match anytime. Then, we lasted that night, that night we tried to get back. We got together with a few of the fellows in the ditch and we tried to get back and we got separated, and that's when I got caught trying to get over an embankment, and the German hollered at me, "Halta," and I couldn't see him, but I figured halta meant halt, so I stopped, and that was it...

I didn't give a damn really. I was so depleted, disgusted, it didn't matter to me what happened really.[260]

Only 28 men from D Company returned at first, but men infiltrated back through the German lines and dribbled in throughout the night. Captain Row himself came in the following morning shortly before 0900 with nine more men. This brought the company to a strength of 40 men and officers. Lieutenant Sweet recalled that Row said "he had gone all the way through Borgo Piave and had tried to hold the enemy from entering the town from Littoria and the northeast. He had no idea what had happened to his company when they had been hit, as he was with the point at the time. All he was concerned with was why no one had come to help him hold the enemy off."[261]

The battalion captured three Germans in the battle, all from the 7th Battery of the 2nd Hermann Goring Flak Regiment. One of the captured prisoners was their battery commander, Lieutenant Werner Jentzech. He told that they were rushed to the front after the landings and entirely "ignorant of the situation." Jentzech stated that his unit had not received replacements for two months and that he had been "told to go into position west of Borgo Piave and stay there… This gun crew was in position for 3 days. During this time, they had no communications with other units and PW had not eaten for 2 days." Jentzech said that when the American's pre-attack artillery barrage came down, most of his unit pulled out, including the flak wagons, but unable to move his gun position, Jentzech stayed behind. The flak wagons which pulled out later returned to counterattack the paratroopers.[262]

Aftermath & Hard Lessons

The town of Borgo Piave had been established in the early 1930s and was named after the Piave River in northern Italy. The river had become a piece of sacred ground to the Italians during the First World War, where the Italian armies routed the Austrians in an epic battle during the summer of 1918. The Piave was referred to as *Fiume Sacro alla Patria* – Sacred River of the Homeland – and after Mussolini was deposed and the Italians defected to the Allies, their national anthem became *La Leggenda del Piave*, written after the Austrian defeat at the hands of the Italians on the Piave, which became considered as the fatal blow to the German ally in the war. In a village that was named to pay homage to a defeat of a Central Power, it was almost ironic that it would be the scene of such a costly battle for the paratroopers of the 504th Parachute Infantry.[263]

The battle had been the first time the regiment had engaged a strong German force in open, maneuver combat. While the terrain in Sicily had largely been flat, the resistance was weak and undetermined. And while they had met resolute resistance from the Germans before, and the paratroopers were experienced, the fighting had been on rocky mountain slopes with highly defined fields of fire and places of limited maneuver for both German tanks and large infantry forces. Likewise, the men were inexperienced with the limitations in working the American tanks. The Battle of Borgo Piave provided the regiment some hard-learned lessons. "The tanks," Lieutenant Sweet later wrote, "might just as well have stayed in their assembly area as they could not shoot over the dyke and would not get on top of it, for fear of hi-velocity fire."[264]

Lieutenant Colonel Adams also observed the problem with understanding the capabilities of attached units for the planning process. The week following the battle, he wrote:

When new units are attached to major units every effort should be made to effect the attachment as early as possible so that the units which will actually fight together may work out their coordination, communication and detailed plan. An example of this is the attachment of armor to an infantry unit. Unit prior planning must include providing the method and material to exploit success. As an example, required bridging material to cross tank barriers should be held in readiness when armor is necessary to support infantry advance. A most effective joint employment of armor and infantry is to maneuver the infantry deep into the flank of the enemy, cover his flank and rear with machine gun fire, then push frontally with tanks supported by tank destroyer... When unsupported by armor or tank access, infantry cannot hold positions and will suffer heavy causalities if enemy armor has access to [the] sector.[265]

Lieutenant Sweet wrote on reflection after the war several problems which set his battalion up for failure, from the corps level on down to the decisions of the battalion commander and the battalion staff, of which he was a member.

The attack orders on Borgo Piave were confused. Corps wanted a diversionary attack made and the orders we received were to make an attack, seize and hold; be prepared to continue on order. This was due to verbal orders and the chance that is taken in their being misunderstood. Corps should have had someone on the spot to supervise the attack.

The battalion should not have been committed in a column of companies as it allowed the enemy to defeat us one company at a time. Also too much faith was placed in the G-2 report that no armor was in the area, some anti-tank weapons should have been carried. This was a very serious mistake on the part of all commanders and the staff... The battalion commander should not have gone with the lead company as he lost contact with the rest of his battalion and could not control their actions... Captain Row likewise got too far forward in his company and lost control of them, as well as not knowing what had happened to them. All communication was in a terrible state. It never did work properly and caused untold confusion.[266]

Poor intelligence assumptions were also made. In the Regimental S-2 report by Captain Gorham published at noon, just hours before attacking Borgo Piave, he wrote, "It is the opinion and belief of this S-2 that the German has no organized defenses between Canal Mussolini and Littoria," a town some two-and-a-half miles beyond Borgo Piave. The report makes note of a battalion of tanks in the area, however in the S-2 report it was noted, "They may be employed against this [Combat Team] by attacking west to Canal Mussolini in an effort to seizure a crossing. However, they may probably be used to prevent the cutting of Highway 7."[267]

It would appear that, as noted by Lieutenant Sweet, that too much confidence was placed in the reports of no armor in their immediate vicinity, but it was a lack of planning which resulted in the inability to have the men carry the right equipment with which to fight a possible counterstroke by the Germans. Had they seized Borgo Piave, a seizure which would have also threatened Highway 7, they would have been just as unprepared to defend it had the Germans committed the tanks to retake Borgo Piave to eliminate the threat to the highway.

A Renewed Attack

On January 29, Colonel Tucker was served orders to make an attack north along the Mussolini Canal. The new attack orders were to be executed that night under darkness. The attack was made to shift the sector north and seize other bridges across the Mussolini Canal. The 1st and 2nd Battalions formed into columns and at 2 AM the final elements were on the march north. The whole beachhead was eerily illuminated by the glow of a flaming ammunition ship out in the harbor, making the men bulge against the black night fantastically as they marched. Enemy flares intermittently shot up and glowed gentle soft white.

As soon as daylight came, each minute thereafter increased the German activity. Minute-by-minute, the entire area became further and further embroiled in ordinance being shot through the air from seemingly all directions. Germans which in the night hid in the many irrigation ditches lacerating the land, which were like capillaries moving water from the main canal to every corner of every farm field, began firing into the rear of the assaulting paratroopers. A dual 20mm flak gun crackled to life and began firing directly on the headquarters group of Lieutenant Colonel Williams, who promptly climbed aboard a buttoned-up tank, under a fusillade of exploding shrapnel from the German shells, and personally directed the tank's fire which silenced this dual gun. Lieutenant Colonel Williams continued to personally direct the tanks around the area, supporting his troops which were doing yeoman's work throughout the whole sector.[268]

Along the Sessano-Cisterna road, an intense firefight was happening as the paratroopers tried to wrestle control of a row of houses from the Germans. In that action, Fred Baldino's platoon captured about 20 prisoners when they surrounded them in an open area after jolting them from the houses. "They were smart enough to give up and surrender," Baldino said. Otherwise, they would have had no choice but to shoot them. "I was in about a group of 5 A Co. guys that took them back behind our lines," remembered Baldino. "Most of them were cooperative. They showed up pictures of their relatives, but we did take their watches off them. On average, they were like any bunch of guys; some decent and some very uncooperative where we had to push them along with the butts of our weapons." On the way back, they ran into Colonel Tucker – "a brave, wonderful commander," Baldino felt – who yelled at them for walking the Germans on top of the road in view of German artillery. "Get the hell off the road before you all get killed!" Tucker ordered.

Baldino got a lot of souvenirs from the group of Germans. Looting souvenirs from prisoners and the dead was common. One instance Baldino remembered was taking an American watch off a German who had looted the watch from a dead American. In 1990, Baldino got a job helping to take the US Census, and struck up a conversation with a former German soldier who had since immigrated to the United States. "When he was captured the American sergeant took his watch and he was amazed. He said here the Americans are all rich and this sergeant took his watch. Ha! If he only knew how many things we took off dead Germans. One time I had about 6 or 7 watches, German helmets [and] German money. We were just as bad we would take anything off the dead Germans; one time I was searching a dead German on Anzio and COL Williams came running down hollering, 'What did you get? What did you get'? I laugh about it now as he was an officer and he was just like us. Of course after the war I felt bad about it at times, but war is war and all is fair in war and peace."[269]

9

I SWEAR I'LL NEVER GET WOUNDED AGAIN

It was just after daylight on the 30th of January when the last elements of the 1st Battalion peeled off into the canal to seize the bridges. The 2nd Battalion now leapt through the 1st to continue the pressure on the Germans and seize as much area as possible.

The 2nd Battalion, which was to seize three bridges (7, 8 & 9) near the juncture of the Mussolini Canal and the Fso di Cisterna, formed up in two single-file columns (one on each side of the dirt road), and started marching down the via Toree Astura. They turned right (to the east) and went a short distance on the via Conca, before moving north by cutting across a farmer's field, and wading across the Mussolini Canal above Bridge 5. They then got on the via Macchia Pantano headed east, before they turned left (to the north) on the road via John Marshal. (For clearer understanding in the 21st century, I have used modern names for these roads).

Soon, E Company was committed to clear the banks of the Mussolini Canal of Germans, which had brought the battalion column under fire. F Company continued east past the intersection, before encountering a strong German force in a couple of houses near the fork in the road. (One direction, left, led to Bridge 8, and one, right, led to Bridge 7).

With E and F Companies committed, the battalion Headquarters Company was now in the lead. At the intersection of the via John Marshal and the Str. Acque Alte, the company turned left (north) on the Str. Acque Alte, and began rushing to the last bridge, Number 9. Leading out the column was 1st Sergeant Alvin Tway. As he approached the bridge, he was shot and killed by a German sniper. Hearing the commotion, Staff Sergeant Bennie M. Weeks ran to the front of the column, and was immediately made the acting first sergeant of the company. The 81mm Mortar Platoon deployed their heavy mortars in the Fso di Cisterna just below Bridge 9. To the men, the Fso di Cisterna became known simply as "The Ditch."[270]

The 504th Parachute Infantry was instructed to hold what it had taken. The next few days were quiet. From their positions in the Ditch, the 81mm mortars, observing traffic on Highway 7 at the base of the mountains, began shelling the German vehicles driving in the distance to pass the time. "They called them autobahns [that] ran along the foothills of the mountains," James Sapp explains, "and it was open country and we could see the Germans, the vehicles, trucks and stuff, traveling on that road and 3,290 yards was our maximum range, but we could put a, there's six charges, what we call increments. You could add the fins on the mortar shells and we could add two, which we weren't supposed to do but we did it, and hit that road and we just said there was nothing else to do and we'd have a man sitting on the mortar and the other one sitting there with his binoculars and we figured out where they had those light poles that were along the road, and we would figure out, they would run about the same speed all the time and when one would get to each numbered [pole] we'd tell the guy on the mortar to drop the round in and they would meet! I don't know if we ever knocked any out, but we were close enough that we let them know that we were there and we saw them."[271]

Troopers of the 2nd Battalion 81mm Mortar Platoon photographed in "The Ditch" shortly after deploying. The spot where 1st Sergeant Alvin Tway was killed is just out of frame. Bridge #9 is in the background. Little did the men know, but they would be stuck in the positions until their relief from the beachhead in March 1944. (US Signal Corps)

After several days, orders came for the men to prepare the Ditch for the deliberate defense. Because the battalions were so understrength, there was not enough personnel to effect a defense in depth where multiple lines and points of resistance were constructed, one of the biggest keys to slowing down assaulting forces. Thus, they made their positions in the Ditch as formidable as possible, and constructed small outposts on the opposite side, most often by sending a small contingent of paratroopers into a house to watch for the Germans.[272]

The German Reaction to the Allied Landings

Timely intelligence as to the enemy's location, strength and morale was as important to the 504th as it was in any combat organization. That is why all prisoners captured by the men of the 504th PIR were brought to Lieutenant Irvin Bushman. Lieutenant Bushman was a member of the Army's new Military Intelligence Service. Men like Irvin Bushman were charged with embedding themselves within combat units for the purposes of interrogating enemy prisoners of war, in hopes of gaining tactical knowledge of the enemy which would support the units to which they were attached. In November 1943, the first five interrogation prisoner of war (IPW) teams from the Military Intelligence Service were shipped to the Italian front to gain practical experience, as IPW teams had never before been used in combat. One of these interrogators was Irvin Bushman, and his attachment to the 504th was the beginning of a long combat career with the 82nd Airborne Division. Throughout the war the 504th's IPW team, which would grow and become even more well-established as the war progressed, would make valuable contributions to the regiment that have gone unrecognized.

Hailing from Cleveland, Ohio, Bushman was born a child to Jewish parents who had immigrated to the United States from eastern Poland, and he had dreams of being a journalist. He grew up speaking not only English in the home, but also Yiddish, a European language spoken by Jews which is similar to German. Although Bushman originally dreamed to be a journalist, he pursued the study of music after high school after discovering his naturally beautiful voice and attended Oberlin College where he learned all aspects of music. And because he wished to sing German Lieder, French Art Songs, and Italian operas, he studied the French, German, and Italian languages. When the war broke out, his adept writing ability coupled with his knowledge of European languages made him a unique asset. It was his knowledge of the German language which was put to use for the war effort when he became the 504th Parachute Infantry Regiment's Interrogation Prisoner of War Officer. His efforts were highly valuable to Colonel Reuben Tucker, the regimental commander, who wrote to Bushman, "It was through your tireless efforts, regardless of the time of day or night, that much valuable information was secured from captured enemy personnel. This information contributed in no small part to our success in the operation."[273]

The information Bushman was able to extract from the Germans captured by the regiment's paratroopers chronicle the German response to the Allied landings.

Some of the first Germans to be captured by the 504th Parachute Infantry Regiment on the Anzio Beachhead were those prisoners marched or carried back from the area around Bridge #2 on the morning of January 24. Shortly after their capture, they were brought to 1st Lieutenant Irvin Bushman. The Germans were from the elite Hermann Goring Division. From them, Bushman gleaned that "all prisoners of war seemed to agree that things were happening too fast for them to comprehend. They were bivouacked… when order came that an Allied landing had been made south of Rome and they were to proceed to the area and attack at once." It was clear to Bushman that their landing at Anzio was a complete surprise. From the best Bushman could determine from reading captured German papers and talking to the prisoners captured that day, it appeared that their company was the only company of their unit that had yet arrived, and that their commander, Hauptman Schultze, had been slain by the regiment. But, as Bushman warned, "It also seems probable that as soon as they can bring them up, more elements of the Hermann Goring Division will come into [the] area."[274] Bushman was correct.

As the paratroopers fought on the Anzio Beachhead and captured German prisoners, Lieutenant Bushman would interrogate each one of them; and using his writing abilities, he would draft reports containing the knowledge he was able to glean from the prisoners. His interrogation reports detailed life on the other side, down to what the German soldiers felt of their situation. One wounded prisoner was drug in on the 26th and told Bushman that they had come to the front "in a great rush and were not fully equipped. PW rather bitterly pointed to his severe wounds and stressed the fact that as a vehicle driver he was sent out on a foot patrol." Bushman's reports detailed everything from their feelings about their immediate commanders to general morale, what kinds of food they were eating, the history of their unit and the people in it, and perhaps most importantly their strength, organization, armament and locations.[275]

From them, Bushman learned that many of the men they were opposing had been scouted from labor centers in Germany and sent to the Hermann Goring training center because they "looked like good soldier material," and that, for many, opposing the 504th was their first combat duty.[276]

The situation developed rapidly for the Germans, as Bushman learned, as more units were rushed every hour with great haste to the front to oppose not only his 504th PIR, but also the Allies as a whole on the Anzio front. On January 30, German counterattacks began falling upon the entire regimental front. All were quickly broken up; one large attack came in the evening by a battalion of German Luftwaffe troops who had just been rushed to the front, arriving the afternoon before. Several members of the unit were captured and Bushman, through his interrogations, found their officers had been told "that the sector which they were taking over was so lightly manned by the Allies that 12 men… were able to defend a 1 ½ kilometer sector. They were further told that they would be fighting against British Negro troops who would surrender at the first round fired."[277]

Day-by-day the German forces increased, and the stress was mounting as the paratroopers of the 504th went into the deliberate defense and the time drug. It was a battle of nerves – of "wait and see" – of waiting for one side to make the next big move. Each action had a reaction and the Germans were very easily excited; a single man exiting his position in the daylight would bring massive artillery bombardment. The psychological strain manifested into edginess.

Attachments came to the 504th Parachute Infantry. One of the most used and most valued attachments came from the attachment of C Company, 84th Chemical Mortar Battalion. Their unit history describes the situation poignantly:

Small-arms fire across the roads and flat fields, although undirected in most instances, was nevertheless a constant source of danger – often hitting the houses and coming through the screen doors.

Unlike Salerno, the almost constant alerts at Anzio seemed always credible, indeed, too much so. Defensive measures were continually being taken within sight of the mortar positions: mine fields and barbed-wire entanglements planted in the adjacent fields by engineers; dynamite set under the road bridge 500 yards up the road, and a guard there 24 hours a day; a thin, strung-out secondary line of infantry in a ditch 200 yards in front of the mortar positions…

That particular psychological state of one-foot-on-the-beach-one-foot-in-the-water was intensified not a little by the tremendous concentration of defensive power that gradually accumulated in each of the houses.[278]

In the 2nd Battalion's area, the Str. Acque Alte ran parallel to the Ditch, which constituted their main line of resistance. The Str. Acque Alte, the men referred to as "Red Top Road." Red Top Road had several houses along which the companies and platoons set up their command posts inside. These houses soon became a dangerous place to be. On February 5, the house which was hosting men from the 81mm Mortar Platoon came under an artillery barrage. One shell came into the house, killing Walter M. Wallace. He was 21-years-old. Lieutenant Ramsey wrote his mother that he died on the way to the hospital and "didn't suffer too much pain."[279] On the 7th, the F Company CP – also in a house located on Red Top Road – was subjected to direct fire which killed Corporal William Jewel and Technician 5th Grade Jasper Byrd, and wounded nine others.[280] On the evening of February 12, the battalion staff was reading by candlelight around a marble-topped kitchen table inside of the house which they had set up their command post when a plane droned overhead and dropped a bomb just outside the house. Hearing it coming, the men slid underneath the table for protection, and a bone-shaking explosion occurred busting out windows and showering dust. The house was evacuated that night and the CP moved into another house further behind the lines.[281]

In the Ditch, the living conditions were primitive and uncomfortable. "Continued rains made the foxholes damp and in many cases untenable," William Sweet wrote. "Also the blown bridge at 7 formed a damn and threatened to flood the battalion out of the Ditch. New holes had to be dug on the side of the dyke above the water line. The Ditch floor turned into a sea of mud, and mud became each man's bosom companion whether [he] wanted it or not. Clothes were cleaned by trench knives and what were once shinny boots became blobs of mud… All the trees were cut down to prevent tree burst. Shade was unnecessary as the sun was a stranger that called only seldom anymore. The final touch had been added to make us all living pictures of what the First World War must have been like."[282]

If the strength of F Company's ranks were any indication, the units were like a revolving door as men went into the hospital and came out of the hospital. Between February 1 and February 16, F Company sent 20 men to the hospital, most for ailments or trench foot, due to the moist and muddy life they led in the water-logged ditches, rather than enemy bullets. The company received 28 men back from the hospital in the same period. Statistically, for the month of February as a whole, the company averaged 97 men present for duty of the 147 assigned, which left them operating at approximately 54% strength. Two days, the 6th and the 19th, the company was at its lowest numbers with only 90 men present. Other companies fared worse, others only marginally better.[283]

Counterpunch

Company D under the command of Captain Andrew W. Row had been hard-hit by the fighting in Borgo Piave, after which the company numbered some 50 men. On February 16, the men had been on the line for 25 days, and in that time the numbers in D Company had become fewer and fewer.

To help give fire support to Captain Row's men, Lieutenant Lauren Ramsey was ordered to move one of his 81mm mortars and a crew behind Row's company. The crew was provided by Paul Pannell and Marcus Young. Although they were only two men, as opposed to a full crew, Pannell was glad Marcus Young was with him. "If I ever go to war, I want Marcus Young to be on my side," Pannell said. "He was a tough one. He'd always do his share."[284]

Over the preceding week, small German probing attacks had been hitting the positions of the 2nd Battalion and the rest of the regiment. Mental and physical strain begin to take root in the men. "We were scared," Fred Baldino said. "I'm not going to tell you that we weren't ever scared. I think you would be lying to yourself if you didn't have fear in you. When the Germans attacked us at Anzio a lot of times I'd have to rout the guys out, 'Come on! Get up here and get on the firing line!' You have to keep after them, sometimes the guys would not pay attention and you have to get after them."[285]

Small, local attacks on the positions of the 2nd Battalion came on the 13th and 14th; on the latter date, the D Company troopers killed 18 Germans the attack. During the course of these small German attacks, the locations of the American's defensive positions had been revealed. In the farmland laced with known canals and ditches, there was nowhere for the battalion to change their positions. They knew it was only a matter of time before a large German assault came.[286]

As one of the few officers remaining in F Company, 1st Lieutenant James D. Simmons had been with the regiment only since December 1943, but already found himself to be a company commander, albeit temporary while Lieutenant Richardson was in the hospital. Simmons hailed from the small town of Seven Springs, North Carolina, not far from Fort Bragg, and had been educated at North Carolina State, where he had been in the university's first marching band. Immediately after college and his commissioning, Simmons volunteered for the parachute troops. As Simmons's mother drove her son to the train station as his final leave before going overseas came to an end, he asked her to stop for a beer. His mother never knew her son to drink, but she stopped and Simmons got one beer. While there, he said, "damn." Simmons's mother had never known her son to curse before. As the train pulled out of the station, she watched as her son ran to the back of the train as it began to pull away, with tears rolling down her sons face. Right then, she later told family members, she knew her son would never come home again. At Anzio on February 16, her motherly senses came to pass.

That morning, grazing German 20mm cannon fire flew over the farmland, and whizzed and snapped and cracked overhead. Mortar and artillery fire added to the cacophony of death and terror. Germans, in formation, started moving across the field opposite D Company, crashing into their fire. As the Germans attempted to overrun the D Company positions by crossing the field, their left flank was exposed to a dogleg in the 2nd Battalion lines. From the dogleg, Simmons's F Company fired heavy machine guns. They mowed the Germans down like a farmer cutting down wheat in his field for harvest.

The battle raged. Supporting fire from Paul Pannell and Marcus Young's 81mm mortar was being directed by their platoon sergeant, Staff Sergeant Laurel M. Parks; Peter to those who knew him. From his forward outpost on the other side of the Ditch, Parks would observe the fall of the 81mm mortar shells and relay adjustments to the gun crew to walk the rounds forward and backwards, or side to side for maximum effect on the Germans as they crossed the field.

Despite taking heavy casualties, the Germans continued to clash with the paratroopers. On the forward position, Sergeant Parks caught a burst from a Schmeisser sub-machine gun across the top of his head, taking the top of his skull off. The position became untenable, and the other men had no choice but to pull out, leaving Parks behind.[287]

Thankfully, Pannell and Young had targets preregistered and marked by stakes, so they could fire without a forward observer. "We could detect where it was coming from because there's a little depression, little ditch approaching our area – D Company – so we knew what target they were on. So we began to fire. We fired for about two or three hours constantly. *BOOM*! You'd wait a few seconds, drop another round, *BOOM*! Those machine gunners were shooting until their guns would get so hot it'd start slowing up."[288]

The fires from the attached 4.2 chemical mortar company helped tremendously, to help make machine gun and small arms fire as effective as possible. Sergeant Milton Orshefsky of the mortar company later wrote:

Everyone knew they were coming; the men had been cautioned for days to sleep with their shoes on. On the paratrooper sector the attack struck just before dawn - the favorite hour apparently for counter-attacks – on February 16. The enemy left no doubt as to his intentions. He started out with only a short preparatory barrage, but brought up several flak-wagons – half-tracks mounting batteries of 20mm guns – and began sweeping the fields, lofting tracers against the front-sides of every house in the sector that faced the canal. Then he began pouring troops towards the 504th's positions in the ditch running into the canal, with the main thrust coming down into the 2nd Platoon's mortars' zone of fire.

The first two gun crews of the platoon to go into action did so, because of the hail of 20mm, on their hands and knees. In the first half-hour, however, according to the paratroopers' commanding officer, they build up enough of a smoke-screen, punctuated with HE, to slow up the German attack to a point where our small-arms fire could be most devastating. The platoon was later given credit for getting off the first effective fire on the counter-attack and one enlisted man at the OP was later awarded the Silver Star for directing that fire, and also heavier artillery fire against the attack.

The fire was kept up intermittently all day long by both platoons, and when the enemy mounted another thrust from a different point in the sector, it too, was thrown back. By nightfall, the company had expended almost 650 rounds, next to the largest single day's fire it did on the beachhead.[289]

The Germans came across the field drove after drove, fully exposed, seemingly indifferent about casualties. Company D's paratroopers were pinned down in their holes by mortar and artillery fire landing on the reverse slope of the Ditch. This, combined apparently with shear weight of numbers, allowed a small number of Germans to break into the company's lines, where another miniature battle began to take place.

Meanwhile, the German reserves massed together and took into the ditches alongside the road. The artillery observer fired concentrations from the big guns by walking them up and down the road to prevent tanks from approaching, and his artillery found the Germans gathered in the ditch all bunched together, massacring them.[290]

The enemy who had broken into D Company's lines were repulsed. The Germans asked for a respite and a two-hour truce was put in place. German bodies were literally stacked up in front of the east bank of the Ditch. One man counted 36 German bodies, and at least the same number of wounded. But this infliction on the German superman was not without cost to the paratroopers. D Company suffered six dead and eight wounded, including their commander, Captain Row, who had been shot in the hand.[291] Row was eventually evacuated to a hospital in Africa. "I've been blitzed," wrote to his parents from the hospital. "Here I sit in my new address. Furthermore, when I look outside this fine hospital ward, I see those original sad sacks. (I'm back in Africa). I swear I'll never get wounded again. Those medics believe with physiotherapy I'll soon have complete use of my right hand. It's the silliest thing. I feel guilty staying here and I'm still plenty burned up about being evacuated to Africa. Except for the ruins one would not believe that less than a year ago, battles raged here. I am in a ward with some fine officers, most of them as restless as this captain. If I had lost a leg or an arm, I could understand and be quite contented here." In another letter from the hospital, he wrote, "I'm getting sick of this inactivity. Furthermore, when I was on the front, not changing clothes for a month, getting wet and keeping dirty, I never caught the cold I have now. Since I am mostly left-handed anyway, I know I can get along just as well. I do not want you to get the absolutely wrong notion that a German could put me out of this game for good. I do have to join my men."[292]

After the end of the truce, the spirit of the German attack was broken and they never returned to try and tip the scales back in their favor.

That evening Bennie Weeks heard about the fate of his friend Peter Parks. The men who had been on OP with Parks said that he was dead, and they were forced to leave his body. That night, Weeks snuck across the Ditch and found Parks. He was still alive. Weeks drug him back across the Ditch. Eventually, he was evacuated to the hospital, where he died of his wounds the next day.[293]

After nightfall, the men of the 2nd Battalion were replaced on the front line by US Army Rangers. The battalion's troops fell back to an area about 1,100 yards behind the canal near Bridge 6, where the men were crammed into a line of roofless houses. Although over 1,000 yards behind the forward positions, the dangers remained nearly unchanged. Bridge 6, near to which was the battalion command post, was shelled heavily by the Germans during the day, almost constantly, as it was one of the main supply routes. Some 100 rounds of German artillery fell in the area each day. Major Melvin Blitch, the battalion commander, and Lieutenant Chester Garrison found a loft in the CP which had sheets and a mattress. The two officers flopped down, but German artillery shells soon started to rain. "We held out for a while," Garrison recalled, "although our nerves and bladders were sufficiently jostled to urge us to pee out the second-story window. Back on the bed we listened to the barrage accelerate, when we realized that the Germans were zeroing in on the house and decided that the slate shingles of the roof were inadequate protection, we reluctantly abandoned our bed and descended as the stone building shivered and shook."[294]

Even in this supposed "rest area" the men could not rest. After being in the line, the men wanted to get up and stretch after being confined to trenches and holes like gophers. In the primal living conditions on the canal, the men were forced to live like rats underground, for getting out would mean they were in the open view of the Germans, and with that would come artillery or sniper fire. Being forced to reside in the earth would drive the men crazy. Boredom set in. A few men would try and entertain themselves by building small shelves into the sides of their trenches which would act like a roadway, and then using objects to represent toy cars. They had little to think about but pervasive death and misery, empty stomachs, the coming patrol through the minefields, and the consistent rain and mud. Along with the boredom came psychological exhaustion and edginess from always being concerned that a German artillery shell may finally find its mark. Enemy counterattacks were almost welcomed as an opportunity for the men on the line to "blow off steam" as contrasted to sitting under an artillery barrage with no means of self-defense.

In the rest area the men wanted to stretch but with the dangers unchanged, this would remain almost impossible: even in the rest area the Germans on the high ground remained able to lay in artillery to smite one jeep or a lone soldier with God-like will. One of the "rest areas" used by the regiment was later described by headquarters as turning into an impact area, as it was constantly subjected to the German artillery fire intended to silence the American artillery positions located just alongside.[295]

In addition to stretching, the men wanted to shower and change clothes while in the rest areas. On March 3, Lieutenant Garrison had the chance to take his clothes off and shower. It was only his fourth chance to bathe since invading Italy in September. But at a rate of seven men per company per day, the men allowed this luxury were few.[296]

Edward Mokan observed that hot food, showers, clean clothes and new socks were the biggest factors that helped morale when they returned to rest areas. Not only were the showers and new socks in short supply on the beachhead, but also the hot food.[297] For these months, the paratrooper's diet consisted of K-rations; which consisted of canned hash, beans, or stew, along with cigarettes, gum, coffee or lemonade powder mix, and other items all packed into a rectangular wax box which could fit into the pockets of their jump suits; or C-rations, which was also canned food such as tuna or meat. "With the canned stuff," Fred Baldino remembered, "we learned to put them in a fire if we were in a secluded area and the cans would give a pop. We then would pull them out of the fire and juggle them some and open the can to a hot meal."[298] William Sweet wrote that lack of hot food had perhaps the biggest negative effect on the men's morale. "No hot meals were served while we were in the line," he wrote, "as we had only one kitchen per battalion, and it could not get the food to the men while it was still hot. With rare exceptions the men cooked their own food for the entire period. This had a very bad effect on the morale of the men."[299] Fred Baldino remembered once incident with a slain cow that turned sour. "A cow was killed by a shell behind the lines and our cooks made up a bunch of hamburgers and sent them up to us and the C Company guy took them all for his company and I found out and I went over to him on the Mussolini Canal and we fought and fought but he was tougher than me and beat me, but I didn't care because at least I fought for my squad."[300]

On the forward positions dug into the canal, the wax cardboard which contained their meal also doubled as the men's toilet in many cases, as the sanitary conditions endured by the men on the Anzio beachhead were nothing less than abhorred. If a paratrooper had to urinate in during the day, it was often done by using a wax K-ration container, then throwing it out of the hole. The men couldn't even leave their holes to urinate, and neither could the Germans. One day, William J. Rothweiler observed a German on the other side of the Mussolini Canal get up during the daytime to urinate. After he got started, Rothweiler dialed in his sights and shot the German dead; and while shooting a urinating German may sound imprudent, the rational the men operated under was the more Germans they killed, the faster they could go home.[301]

Earl Morin wrote home about the unpleasantries of the Anzio beachhead. "Your little man thought his duck was indeed well done (cooked, I believe the expression is) on the beachhead at Anzio, where he spent some odd days of delightful hell, and I will not erase that word. I don't mind their bombing the ship from under us – it was due for the scrap heap – and the days and night of artillery and air bombardment, but the living conditions were simply abominable. Can't our Congressmen alleviate the lack of clean sheets in foxholes?"[302]

Robert Righthouse also wrote home about the conditions on the beachhead:

Maybe you would like to know some of the things we do over here besides shoot at Germans. Well, we sleep in a hole that we dig in the ground at night. We go for a week without washing, and our beards grow long and we get disgusted to think that people at home complain because they can't get all the steak they can eat. And to think there are so few fighting this war, an army of nine million and about 60,000 doing all the fighting while the rest make all the USO dances and pictured shows. How in the hell can you win a war like that? The papers may sound good, but we fight for weeks to gain a mile. We see our buddies get hit and can't help them. And we grow hard and cold and love no one only the soldier in the battle with us.

People at home complain because they can't get the kind of clothes they want and we wear the same ones for a week without being washed. So you know the reason I don't write home more often.[303]

The letter which Righthouse wrote home expresses the effect that continuous combat had on the men; not long after writing the letter he would be wounded on March 21, and later killed in action in January 1945. While morale was something that had been forgotten and ceased to exist in the trenches of Anzio, it was intense pride in the unit that kept them going in the face of adverse weather, sickness and a hardened enemy. Captain Robert Halloran, of the Regimental Medical Detachment, felt that the men "got tougher and more able to tolerate the conditions" as time drug on. Bad weather, rations and extended time on the front contributed to declining morale. Sometimes, it would be too much for men and they would suffer from 'shell-shock'. "We often saw it," Halloran wrote, "and sometimes treated it with sodium amytal, or got them some sleep." However, in totality, their combat performance, he felt, was unequaled. "Here, I know I am prejudiced. We were the best – never lost a fight or gave up a bit of ground. It was the direct result of 'esprit de corps' which was unbelievable."[304]

Lieutenant Chester Garrison provides a vignette of life on the Anzio beachhead as a battalion personnel officer:

Anzio Beachhead was the epitome of the watch-and-wait anxiety... being the essence of war – not the continuous carnage that movies feature. We were restricted to our safe places during the daylight day after day. Our having time on our hands – to use one cliché – and fear in our hearts – to use another – were unsettling. We became edgy. Some of the men along the damp canal began to crack up from *exhaustion-related illnesses... Paper work kept me busy, as the turnover and changing of personnel were constant. Returnees from the hospital in Naples rejoined their companies, and forty or more recruits periodically arrived. Eight new officers arrived on March 1, and our standing officers were moved from company to company as needed. Orders for promotion, both for officers and enlisted men, also came through. All of these matters had to be processed through my "desk", the Army-issued writing board. I even had to supervise the collection of money ($938.45) from men who wanted to pay for telegrams and flowers for Mother's Day in May, some of these senders would be dead by then.*[305]

This extended combat – the stress alluded to by Lieutenant Garrison – became wearisome, and that combat even extended to those in the "rest areas" 1,000 yards behind the canal. When Fred Baldino's platoon was sent back to stay in an abandon Italian house a few hundred yards behind the Mussolini Canal towards the end of February, Fred Baldino, Fay Steger, William Rothweiler, Albert Sebastian and a couple others decided to go scrounge for some food. They walked about two miles and found a large pig inside a stable. An Italian farmer came out of the cellar of his home, and Baldino, who could speak Italian, asked if the famer would sell the pig. The farmer told Baldino, "If I say no you will take him anyway, so I will sell him to you." The six troopers took up a collection and got $32.00 together and gave the man the money for the pig. The men put the pig on two poles and trekked back to the house they were staying at. Like emaciated men, they wanted to eat the meat right away as Fay Steger, a farmer from Iowa, began butchering the pig. He said the meat needed to be hung overnight, but the liver was okay to eat. It was gone in mere minutes. For the next two days, the 2nd Platoon ate better than anyone else on the Anzio beachhead.

Just because they were behind the lines a few hundred yards, did not by any stretch mean they were safe from danger. While they were staying in the house, a shell from the German's feared railroad gun dubbed "Anzio Annie" passed overhead, sounding like a freight train, and wiped off the face of the earth a house just across the street from the one they were sleeping in. "Blew the house to smithereens," Baldino recalled. "Boy, were we lucky it didn't hit our house. It would have wiped out the entire platoon."

February 1944 was not the only time the men indulged in this act. Many years after the war, some of the men were at a reunion in Philadelphia, Pennsylvania. Al Sebastian, who lived in Harrisburg, invited the men over to his house. About 12 of the old gang showed up. Sebastian went out and bought a pig and rented a split roster. "And after much drinking, laughing, and telling war stories we all dug into the pig and had a ball doing so," Baldino reflected.[306]

From these "rest areas" the platoon went on patrols and raiding parties into the German lines.

While at all times no less than two-thirds of the regiment was occupying the most forward positions on the line, one-third was in one of these supposed "rest areas" on alert and tasked with conducting patrols and raiding parties into the German lines. All these things made the "rest area" a busy place, and the unit in reserve was not spared and the men were kept anxious and frayed both by German artillery and by thinking about what the night's raid into the German lines would bring.[307]

Since the end of World War II, the 504th Parachute Infantry Regiment has hence been referred to as the "Devils in Baggy Pants." The sourcing of this moniker comes from its nighttime perils on the Anzio Beachhead, its forays into the German lines for which the regiment has become famous in post-war history books and contemporary Army lore.

By post-war observers, these nighttime raids have been portrayed as entirely successful raids of offensive military action during a period of static warfare, which inflicted casualties on the enemy. Although these were of a byproduct of the raiding parties, the true reality was that they were a masterful deception. While the patrols had 'objectives' these were secondary to their chief purpose: fool the Germans. In reality, the line the regiment was holding was only a thinly held hull with little to nothing behind it. The chief purpose of the patrols and raiding parties were to trick the Germans into thinking the line was stronger than it truly was, for if they knew the reality the results would have been catastrophic. And the regiment pulled off the deception with great skill through their fighting spirit and aggressiveness.[308]

To understand the need for the deception, one must look at the causalities sustained by the regiment, combined with the swath of land the regiment was responsible for defending. And while much has been mentioned in previous histories about the casualties, few have been able to ascertain or emphasize the seriousness of the personnel situation.

At the time the 2nd Battalion was relieved on February 16, for instance, the battalion had a strength of 228 men, a mere 47% of the men who had originally landed on Red Beach in January. The personnel situation reached near-desperation around this period. The 1st Battalion numbered only 214 men, and the 3rd Battalion was cut to a staggering 35% of strength. In essence, the 504th Parachute Infantry, a proud organization which once had nearly 2,000 paratroopers in its ranks, was with less 1,000 troopers.[309]

These 1,000 paratroopers were responsible for defending from German counterattack a distance equaling the length of 50 football fields. That meant the regiment had one paratrooper for every five yards of length for which it was responsible, and many of these men in less than stellar physical condition as many were suffering from the illnesses which ran rampant in the damp environment which served as a breeding ground for disease and infection.[310]

The amount of area combined with the casualties rendered the regiment unable neither defend in depth nor concentrate force, both fundamental military principles. There was considerable distance which existed between the companies on the line; this also applied to the problem of coordination between the units. While the regiment was at Anzio, it laid 865 miles of wire, which would stretch more than the distance from San Diego, California to Denver, Colorado.[311] Thus, it became necessary to trick the Germans into thinking the line was stronger than it actually was.

The solution was the patrols and raiding parties, which were sent out aggressively each night. "On the whole," the regiment's report of operations commented, "the results of these patrols were not altogether satisfactory except that they kept the enemy in a constant state of bewilderment, and their aggressive tactics served to hide the salient facts of the [unit's] extremely thin line and badly depleted strength."[312] Their pride in the unit - their fighting spirit - was played upon to produce the aggressiveness which made this concealment a success. In one of the most fundamental documents of western warfare, Carl von Clausewitz often wrote in *On War* about the moral powers and forces behind an army. If, he argues, there is an inferiority of numbers and force, there must be a supremacy in moral power to compensate.[313] In this, the regiment was extremely successful, and it was a success for which the unit became famous.

With the transit of patrols, the Mussolini Canal and the Fso di Cisterna became like covert interstates. Originally built to drain the Pontine Marshes, the Mussolini Canal, which formed the paratrooper's front lines, had built up berms on either side standing almost as tall as a man from the level ground, and sloping at an approximate 45-degree angle. The water, at its deepest point, came up to an average man's waist. It was these funnels of water which the men would have to cross to enter no-man's land and, beyond that, the German lines. The area smelled of death and destruction. One night Albert Clark and Fred Baldino were crossing the canal to go on a nighttime patrol when they nearly stepped on the body of an American artillery observer missing one leg. Baldino searched the body, and found a coveted all-steel compass, which was much more accurate and durable than their plastic compasses. Al Clark wanted the compass, so Baldino gave it to his buddy.[314]

The patrols varied in their size – they could be few men or a few dozen men. For example, a 16-man patrol which was led by Corporal Baldino was successful in killing one German soldier and capturing two others. Edward Hill was on a patrol comprised of eight paratroopers, and was wounded. "I have again stopped a Jerry bullet," Hill wrote to his mother from the hospital, "but it only grazed me through the arm... I got one Jerry this time and that's a total of six for me. I hope this war will be over soon – as everybody else does. You know this war is like a football game with the consequences greater."[315] Another patrol raided a house on the German side of the line, and, shooting a tommy gun through the ceiling of the first floor, wounded several Germans in the upstairs. It was out of actions just like this one on the Anzio beachhead during the months of February and March 1944 that prompted a German officer to pen in his diary, "American parachutists – devils in baggy pants – are less than 100 meters from my outpost line. I can't sleep at night; they pop up from nowhere and we never know when or how they will strike next. Seems like the black-hearted devils are everywhere." From this quote, the moniker of the 504th PIR was born.[316]

A Typical Foray into the German Lines

It was a moonless night when a handful of paratroopers blackened their faces with soot. Their mission was to investigate a house on the German side which fronted the Mussolini Canal, and try and capture a prisoner. In absolute silence, Sergeant Bernard E. Karnap led the men across the canal, and slipped under a barbed-wire strand fronting a German machine gun nest. The patrol crawled on their bellies nearly 200 yards, in pitch black night.

As they approached the building, they found a sandbagged machine gun emplacement concealed by a shelter half, which sat between the main house and a tiny outhouse. Sergeant Karnap left the patrol, and crawled to within 15 yards of the main house. He could hear the Germans talking and walking around, by the distinctive thud the German's hob-nailed boots made when crossing the floor. Karnap came back to his men and pointed a pacing German sentry out to Private First Class Robert R. Lanier, and told him to keep him covered with his M-1.

"Let me shoot him now," Lanier whispered.

"No, wait until I give the signal," Karnap whispered back.

Sergeant Karnap deployed the rest of the patrol in a skirmish line, then crawled silently to the German machine gun emplacement. He got to within arm's reach of the gun, so close he could tell it was a barrel of an MG-34, even in the moonless night. Two Germans talked silently in the pit, and he could hear a third snoring. Karnap grasped the shelter half roof, and was about to yank it off, when eight Germans came slowly walking around the corner of the house. The eight Germans approached the machine gun nest. Sensing something afoot, the man leading them stopped. The following Germans tripped over each other's heels as if in a cartoon.

Karnap depressed the trigger of his Thompson sub-machine gun, letting loose a fusillade of bullets at the leading German.

Karnap nearly cut him in half.

Swinging his fully-automatic Tommy Gun to and fro before the eight Germans, Karnap hosed the rest. One wounded German staggered a few yards, heading for the door of the outhouse, and fell dead on the dirt like a sad sack. Karnap, his magazine empty, ran for the outhouse. He jumped over the dead German and slipped and fell.

Responding to Karnap's rampage, five Germans came out of the main house. The other men of Karnap's patrol killed them. One paratrooper fired rifle grenades through the window of the house. Bone-chilling screams, echoing through the pitch black night, could be heard from the wounded Germans inside.

Karnap ran back to the men, who were already running across no man's land back to the canal. Whistles and yelling could be heard behind them, and suddenly every German machine gun in the area set ablaze with fire, kicking up dirt around the swiftly retreating patrol. They sprinted back to the canal and jumped in. They were home free.[317]

In addition to patrols, the regiment also maintained an extensive network of outposts set up in houses on the opposite side of the canal. The men would rotate in and out of these outposts to stand watch. Along with the troopers on the rotation schedule was a young Italian teen named Antonio Taurelli.

When the men of the 504th Parachute Infantry Regiment landed on January 22, young Taurelli had gone to the Martufi Dairy Farm with his cousin Rolando before dawn to get milk for his family – his mother, two sisters, and an aunt with five children – who were all living in a wooden hut on the family's vineyard at Seccia. There were already Americans there, heating up coffee, and Antonio was intrigued to hear them speaking Italian of the Abruzzo and Neapolitan dialects.

After landing on the beaches around 1000, the men of the 504th PIR had fanned through the area inland from the beach. F Company turned up the wide dirt Frati road that led through a field, and approached a junction with the Velletri Road. Leading the F Company column was Lieutenant Stanley R. Navas. Twenty-four-year-old Lieutenant Navas, originally from San Juan, Puerto Rico, had graduated from the Virginia Military Institute as the vice-president of his class with a degree in civil engineering in one hand, and a commission as an Infantry second lieutenant in the other hand. Navas was highly athletic, and played baseball, football, polo, and wrestled, all in his career as a cadet at VMI. All of these athletic events made him fit right in with the nimble, athletic parachute troops of the 504th PIR, who he joined in December 1943.

Along the Frati road, shortly before approaching the Velletri Road, young Antonio and his cousin Rolando spotted a column of men, wearing distinctive tan jump suits, coming up the wide dirt road. Lieutenant Navas spotted young Antonio and his cousin Rolando.

"Where are the Germans?" Navas hollered at the boys.

Antonio and Rolando approached the Hispanic-looking Navas.

"Down there, at Le Ferriere," Antonio told Navas. Navas pulled his map out, and Antonio saw a bridge along the Mussolini Canal marked, "Number 2."

"Take me with you," Antonio said to Navas.

Navas looked at Antonio from head to toe with studious eyes. "Okay," he said. But, Rolando was to go home. "He's too young," Navas remarked, shaking his head, "send him home."[318]

From then on, Antonio stayed with the men of the 2nd Battalion. Despite the mortal dangers, which he endured just like any paratrooper of the battalion, he stayed, even when he could've gone home. For the duration of the 504th PIR's stay on the beachhead, Antonio largely remained with Company F, but he also assisted the 81mm Mortar Platoon, and used his invaluable local knowledge to help them identify targets to shell. James Sapp remembered this of young Antonio: "We got him a uniform that fit him and everything, and when he was up there with us on the front, I was in the Mortar Platoon, and he would, it was flat country and he would go out and find out the houses the Germans were in and he would come back in and tell us, you know, point them out, and we would shell them with the mortar fire."[319]

The nighttime transit of patrols and raids from across the Mussolini Canal made the front as busy as a covert interstate. The paratroopers set up listening outposts in a virtual 'no man's land' on the other side of the Ditch and Canal. Young Antonio explains:

There were some frightful scenes in the dark, one ambush after another. They killed each other in silence, the paratroopers with their daggers in their mouths and their faces blackened. The paratroopers had to take it in turns to go to a farmhouse in no-man's land, stay there 24 hours, and signal by telephone the nighttime transit of the German patrols. This watch duty was indispensable if we didn't want to end up with our throats cut, and I did it three times.[320]

There was one man in particular who distinguished himself above all others in this period of patrolling action. Birthed to Jewish parents in Germany in 1923, Theodore Bachenheimer and his family fled the country when he was 11-years-old as Jewish persecution increased, and the Bachenheimer's eventually settled near Los Angeles, California. His mother became an actor, his father was a musician, and Bachenheimer himself had studied drama at Los Angeles City College before the war broke out. Having grown up in Germany, he spoke the German language at a native proficiency.[321]

Lt. Navas of Company F being decorated with the Silver Star Medal for his actions on a nighttime raid into the German lines on 27 February 1944. During this action, Navas was wounded by a grenade which severed his left arm. He would lose his left hand, which was replaced with a wooden hand which can be seen in the photograph. (VMI Archives)

After Ted Bachenheimer joined the 504th, he would use that knowledge of German first at Fort Bragg, where he taught an intelligence class. He would read out of German field manuals, and show all the training, tactics and signals the Germans used in their infantry.[322] But it was on patrols at Anzio where he found his niche, and his skill as an actor, orator and linguist all came together. At night, Bachenheimer would go out into the German lines alone and, because he lived in Germany for 11 years, could easily carry on conversations with unsuspecting German troops before trying to talk them into surrendering. By

February 17, he had talked eight Germans into surrendering, and killed three others who refused to give into his oratory. "You should give them a chance to be taken prisoner without resorting to rough stuff too soon," Bachenheimer once said. "Those three I killed just wouldn't go for my oratory. I wanted to take them prisoner but they wouldn't listen. We had to fight it out with bullets instead of words." When he could not convince Germans to surrender, he almost seemed to feel it was his fault. "Sometimes my German language persuasiveness doesn't go over and the argument breaks off in rifle fire. It was that way the other night. I told a fellow to stick his hands up, and he yelled back in the darkness, 'What for?' I gave him plenty of good reasons why but he wasn't convinced. He fired at me and missed. I got him. But that was a weakness in my oratory..."[323]

On one night, he and one other paratrooper attached themselves to the rear of a column of German wounded. To help conceal their infiltration into the German lines, Bachenheimer's comrade pretended to limp and Ted 'helped to steady him' before they hid behind some bushes inside the German lines and ambushed a column of Germans. "I called out to them to put their hands up or I'd mow them down," Bachenheimer told. "That meant my Daniel Webster act had worked."[324]

Fred Baldino remembered one patrol with Bachenheimer where Baldino witnessed him get inside a foxhole with two Germans, ask them for a light of his cigarette, and then explain to the Germans that they were now his prisoners. On the return trip, Baldino said, "Bachenheimer got ahead. He knew that territory better than we did, and he got ahead of us with the prisoners."

Fred Baldino got to know Bachenheimer a little bit at Anzio, and after they were relieved from the beachhead and sent to England, they were both hospitalized together for minor ailments and got to know each other even more. Baldino remembered how smart Bachenheimer was. Baldino asked him what he thought of the idea of a group of paratroopers jumping in to shoot Hitler, to which Bachenheimer simply replied, "Fred, that would only make him a martyr."[325]

James Gann served with Bachenheimer, and remembered him as a wonderful soldier, but a quiet man. Baldino recalled that Bachenheimer did not have any real close friends, and kept to himself most of the time. Some of the other troopers in the section, Gann recalled, used to make fun of him for his German heritage and accused him of offering sauerkraut and wiener schnitzel to convince the Germans to give up. "I don't know whether it really happened or not," Gann said, "but we accused him of it... I don't know, a lot of stuff that he did we didn't even know about... He was a good soldier. He was obedient – an officer or whoever would give him an order, it was carried out and he never griped and grumbled."[326]

Bachenheimer would carry out his Daniel Webster-like acts until October 1944, after the regiment jumped into Holland, where he went missing. During the Battle of the Bulge, Fred Baldino was in the hospital recovering from wounds received in Holland when the regiment's causalities from the Battle of the Bulge came flowing into England. These men told Baldino that Ted Bachenheimer had gone missing. Later, Baldino was evacuated back to the United States to recover from his wound, and arrived in New York on the *Queen Elizabeth*. As he was getting off the ship, a woman spotting his 82nd Airborne Division patch came running up to him. "When I got off the ship the *Queen Elizabeth,* when I came back to the States, a woman in a Red Cross uniform came up to me and asked me if I knew Ted Bachenheimer, and naturally I told I did and also told her about stories I knew about him. She in turn gave me the address of his mother who was living near Hollywood, Calif."

After getting a leave from the hospital, Baldino went to Elizabeth, New Jersey and called his sister. "I called my sister at my house in Pennsylvania. I knew although she lives a couple miles away, that every Sunday she would go down to visit my parents; and this sister – Helen was her name – was like a second mother to me. She was 19 years older than me and she took care of me as a baby, as my own mother was busy taking care of the cooking and washing, etc. running the house, and when Helen answered the phone she just broke down as I didn't tell anyone I was coming home. She to write her congressman to tell them I had served enough and to send me home. We loved each other so much as brother and sister could. I got home about 9 PM that night and we all stayed up for hours – my mother, father and Helen. We talked until after midnight and cried a lot."

Later, because of the nerve damage he suffered from his wound, he was moved to a special hospital in Louisville, Kentucky, and about a year after meeting Bachenheimer's aunt, he went to California and visited Bachenheimer's mother. "Well, when I got put in the nerve hospital in Louisville, they were pretty crowded and they gave me a 10-day leave of absence, so I visited my sister here in Burbank, Ca. and after I was here a couple days I called his mother on the phone and then went over to see her only about 10 miles away and we had a real long talk. Meanwhile, it was known that Ted was, at that time, missing in action. She was confident that he would get back to friendly lines because he knew Germany pretty well. She then drove me down to Los Angeles to view a lot of the town."[327]

Eventually, Baldino would settle in the Burbank area, near where Ted's parents lived, and remained in touch with them. Nothing was known of Ted Bachenheimer's whereabouts until 1946 when his body was discovered in a civilian cemetery in Harde, Holland with a gunshot wound to the back of the head and another to the back of the neck, as if he was executed.[328] Today, Theodore Bachenheimer rests in Hollywood Forever Cemetery alongside his mother and father in the heart of Hollywood, California. Dozens of famous actors and singers – all with large, decorative and colorful statues and headstones – surround them. In Bachenheimer's true modesty, his flat gray headstone simply reads, "Theodore H. Bachenheimer 1923-1944." Fred Baldino, like James Gann, felt that many of Theodore Bachenheimer's feats were never recorded, and nobody knew the extent of his actions beside Bachenheimer himself. "Bachenheimer never got the recognition that he deserved," Baldino wrote, "and I think that it was that he was of Jewish origin, and people are biased against Jews in many instances... One thing I will say is that the Dutch people admired Bachenheimer very much."[329] And so did Colonel Reuben Tucker, who would often tell his sons about how good and brave a soldier Theodore Bachenheimer was.

10

THEY HAD A LAUGH, BUT IT COST THEM THEIR LIVES

As the men of I Company marched to the front, artillery shells came in. Francis Keefe watched as one shell hit the ground right underneath the feet of one of the men. The trooper flew in the air and came tumbling back down like a ragdoll. Lieutenant Colonel Freeman was with the men and went up to the trooper. They were all expecting to find a dead man. Miraculously, he got back up. "You alright?" Colonel Freeman asked. He didn't even have a shrapnel wound; everyone was looking at him like a museum relic, in disbelief. Unfortunately, that kind of luck would not permeate the rest of the men over the coming, trying days.[330]

As they continued to move up, Francis Keefe watched as the battalion peeled off and began establishing their positions. He watched H Company go to the left, while his company went to dig in just in front of a group of buildings known to the Allied forces as "The Factory."

For the men under Lieutenant Colonel Freeman, their battalion's attachment to the British forces on the western sector of the Anzio Beachhead did not begin with such violence. After being detached from the rest of the 504th Parachute Infantry Regiment, the 3rd Battalion, under the command of Lieutenant Colonel Leslie G. Freeman, spent the first few days of the month of February in reserve in the Podiglione Woods while the British troops attacked past the Factory into the hamlet of Campoleone, which created a large salient in the German lines sticking out like a thumb.

Violence shook the positions as the Germans plastered Colonel Freeman's men with artillery shortly after midnight on February 4. Up in the Campoleone Salient, the Germans began a counterattack on the British to reduce the thumb into their lines, and the German artillery preparations were felt by Freeman's troopers. "Our Lt. Col. Leslie Freeman has just been inspecting all parts of our position," Lieutenant Edward Kennedy told a reporter that day, "and he said we haven't been budged one inch."[331] Kennedy also sat down to write a letter home on February 4 and said that it was "impossible to get our mail. I suppose you read about the new developments in Italy. Well, we are in on it and though it was tough at first things are going pretty good now. I hope the next time I write it will be from Rome."[332]

But little did Lieutenant Kennedy know that February 4 was only the beginning of what the Germans had in store. The successive days would bring hard, pitched battles, and some of the worst artillery barrages experienced by the 504th PIR during World War II as hundreds of German troops tried to overrun their positions. The German plan was to drive down the center of the salient while also sending pincer movements at the base to effectively cut-off, trap, and liquidate the British troops inside the salient. With the salient reduced, the Germans would then regroup around the Factory and mount an all-out counteroffensive, attempting to drive into Anzio down the Albano-Anzio road.

Lieutenant Roy Hanna remembered that at one point British soldiers moved through their positions with haste. "The Germans were right on their tail," Hanna remembered, "and I was running out of ammunition. I had the Tommy Gun [and] it didn't take long to run out of ammunition. They had .45 ammunition with them… They would not leave us one damned piece of ammunition. I stopped one of them. 'Let me have your forty-fives.' 'No, can't do that.' They weren't going to use it."

For most of the period between February 4 and February 8, when Hanna would become wounded while leading a bayonet charge as the hordes of Germans came, he was attached to G Company which was "dug in in a wide area of very nice farm land – reconstituted by draining swamp land."

About 200 yards behind them along the small highway was a single house which housed Lieutenant Colonel Freeman's headquarters. Hanna recalled that one day "there was a tank destroyer parked behind the building that was housing the 3rd Bn Hq. The tank man was out of the tank and we were just talking when he spotted a German tank along the horizon quite a distance away. He jumped in the destroyer, moved the tank forward and I, like a dummy, stood under the muzzle of the 105 (I believe) to watch him fire. He fired one round, enough to change the direction of the German tank, and then backed the destroyer around the building. He jumped out laughing as I'm holding my ears. I asked him how he could stand the noise inside the destroyer. He laughed and informed me that the noise is all on the outside." The incident left Hanna deaf for an hour or so.

"From that location I took a patrol of a hand full of men to contact the British. After walking quietly for what seemed like a mile or so I found the British. The British soldier on outpost duty took me to his 'Leader'. The 'Leader' was a Left Lieutenant and he was stretched out in a cattle trough filled with hay and reading by candle light. I got their general location and returned to Hq." On the 5th of February, Roy Hanna was sitting in his foxhole when he observed Private Earl Oldfather get out of his foxhole. He "dug a little trench," vividly recalled Hanna, "so he could go to the toilet and while he was squatted down a sniper took the end of his nose off. He came back and jumped in his foxhole before he was finished – holding his nose."[333]

Private Oldfather tells the story a bit differently:

At Anzio, the Germans had all high ground and seemed to fire on us at will. The weather was miserable, even hailed, and lots of rain. Being in a wet muddy foxhole sure was no fun... Later we had to move out toward the front where artillery was really coming in, German[s] did that. Near our position was a house and a well, where we got our water... On February 5, 1944, I left my foxhole to get water. There was a straw stack nearby, so I went over to it to have a bowl movement, I did not feel so conspicuous with the straw back between me and the Germans. The sun was out so after I had my B.M. I took my combat jacket off and laid it out to dry, cleaned the mud off my boots.

Started to write in my diary, shells began to land close by. I put my helmet on and flopped over on my stomach. I looked up too soon, something hit me in the nose and mouth, at the time I thought it was a large piece of dirt but found out later it was shrapnel. I ran for the house and was told there was a medic in the cave at the rear of the house. It was a very large cave and several civilians were in there. The medic was there and he bandaged me up and called for a jeep.[334]

During the days at Anzio, when not checking up on his machine gun crews, one could often find Lieutenant Hanna with his closest friend, Lieutenant Peter Eaton. Towering at over six-foot, Pete was a trim, imposing figure with a dark complexion. Despite his impressive outward appearance, there was no better man to be around during these stress-filled hours. No matter the situation, he was always able to get Hanna to crack a smile and lighten, to some degree, the mood for everyone around. "I spent a lot of time with him," said Hanna. "A good officer and a lot of fun – a great sense of humor that helped a lot in combat. I'm sorry I didn't track him down after the war." In front of them, where the British were, the battle raged.[335]

Francis Keefe I/504

Like all infantry rifle platoons, Lieutenant Robert Blankenship's platoon was composed of people of all types, as well as Catholics and Protestants. Private Francis Keefe and his inseparable friend Leo Muri were both Catholics, but several of their friends were Protestants. Within the platoon, it was a competition to see who was practicing Christianity in the correct way based on who was wounded.

Francis Keefe was one of the few men of Company I to survive the fighting at the Factory without ever having to go to the hospital, and his story gives one of the greatest insights into the gruesome battle endured by the 3rd Battalion during their attachment to the British.

When we first moved up, the first day we moved up, we moved in front of the Factory. That was I Company, and from there, there was a tank destroyer right next to a house dug in there. So we happened to see the tank destroyer there, [and] went over talking to the tank destroyer crews. They had a radio and what not. We listened to the radio – German propaganda – and we were pretty well relaxed. The Germans threw a couple shells at us but nothing really heavy. I remember in front of the Factory there was Hawkins mines – a British mine – they placed them on top of the ground… Oh, it was only a matter of, I guess thirty yards in front of it. It could have been a little bit more. I remember walking through the mines. There was a tower there. I wanted to see the tower, what was inside there, there was steps going up to the tower. I guess the Germans spotted me. They threw a couple shells at it and I got myself back out again. So it was, it was like a good cover where we were at so we were pretty well – we knew the German's weren't that close, I'll put it that way. So, we were pretty well relaxed. We hadn't dug any holes or anything. We did behind this mound. There was a road that was running outside, in front of the Factory.

It started to poor rain and all the sudden the tank destroyer got orders to pull back. I said, "Here we go." We had some great protection and all the sudden our protection started to leave us. We didn't feel good about that. Why they were pulling back we still didn't know. Then we got orders – Lieutenant Blankenship – got orders, we only had two officers left, he got orders to move up to this new position. It was pouring rain and we move up and meanwhile there was all kind of fire going with the British and the Germans – the Germans attacking the British. And we moved up a road, from the road we crossed the railroad tracks and we went into a position there in front of a house and on my left there was a burning tank – one of ours that was knocked out.

So anyway, Lieutenant Blankenship [and] Lieutenant Mandle, he was the other lieutenant that was still with I Company. So anyway, it started to pour rain, then it turned into ice rain and it got very cold. The foxholes started filling up with water. And even if you, it started to fill up, we were sitting on the edge of the foxhole because, you know, it was nice and dark so it started to turn into ice the water was so cold. We were pretty well beat because we hadn't slept since the night before, and you can imagine – with coldness – you can imagine how miserable we were and then we were lined up from the road and there was one – his name was [Loyd V.] Engebretson – he was closer to the tank and when you see the night's fire [but] you can't go near it, it drive you out of your mind a little bit. So then Lieutenant Mandle would come down the line and say, "Keep awake." I guess they were expecting an attack. Well, there were attacks going on the left of us and there were attacks going on the right of us.

This was the situation for most of the night. Flashes of light could be seen in the distance where fierce battles between the Germans and the British were occurring. Immediately at the break of day, the Germans pounded a fierce artillery barrage upon the paratroopers' positions. The earth was shaking around Keefe's foxhole. Occasionally he would poke his head up – but not too long – to keep in check the four-foot tall hedge, which was about thirty to forty feet in front of their positions, making sure Germans didn't come pouring over the top of it behind the barrage. Because of how Blankenship and Mandle had been acting, they knew there was an attack coming. *Why weren't we dug in behind that?* Keefe thought. He could see small clouds of smoke erupting as the artillery impacted the Italian dirt. He buried his head back into the ground. He checked the hedge in front of him again, watching as the Germans shelled it. Thankfully, they weren't behind it now. The Germans had thought the same thing Keefe had: *I bet they're behind that hedge.*

Francis Keefe in Naples, Italy (Francis Keefe)

Over near the road where Engebretson was dug in near the tank that had fantastically burned through the night, there was a lot of wounded from the barrage. Keefe thought some ambulances may have even come up, but he didn't dare put his head up out of his foxhole to see what was going on.

Suddenly the British guns opened up with a fantastic counter-battery in front of the hedge. The shells moaned low overhead, racing towards the Germans and going over the small mound.

I guess they broke up the attack because nobody got that close to us and that continued on most of the day with the artillery.

That night, as soon as it got dark, we got orders to pull back. We pulled back into the edge of the Factory. What a relief that was! Right in front, where our positions were before, so we bedded down pretty much for the night and me and Muri and Bill McLane, he was from California, Muri was from Pennsylvania. Everywhere it was dry. It was cold you know but at least we were dry. We had a halfway decent night of sleep. But as soon as day broke, I guess it must have been about a half hour after daybreak, Muri was making coffee and that artillery opened up on us and this Factory, the rooms we were in, they had big windows. I'm talking about six foot windows. Of course there was a chapel where we were – not a big chapel, it was a small alter in there, so we dived in the back of the alter and I mean that artillery, it made such a loud noise coming in. Of course the ceilings were high and the rooms were big and they opened up and it made such a noise. Your head started to rattle around after a while.

So we heard some yelling going on from another room on the right of it, so the three of us got out and ran over to see if anyone was wounded or anything. We went out to the next room and Sergeant [William] White was there. He was all white from plaster from the walls, and he was running around in circles. I guess one of the shells really go into the area where they were at and a fellow by the name of Tison, he was laid out on the floor. I went over to Tison. He didn't move. Anyway, Muri and Bill McLane calmed down Sergeant White. There was other people – medics that went to other positions – so I run back and I figured Lieutenant Blankenship most likely would be back where he made his CP. I run back there but he wasn't there. He most likely was up in front somewhere. Things like that happened, you didn't know where everybody is, you know?

So I asked, I can't remember his name, I said, "You got to get the communications. We got wounded here." So he said, "OK." I went back and I got, all the sudden the artillery started in again and my buddy Bill McLane he was laying down and Muri was leaning over him, seeing what he could do for him. But he was wounded and he was pale [from loss of blood]. I went back up to see if he could make communications with anybody back at battalion headquarters, the medics up there, and he said, "Oh, the line that they put in was broken." So it had to be cut somewhere, I guess from the artillery. Anyway, I decided to take off myself to get some help. So I had to go about one hundred yards when I was going that way, then the Germans spotted me, and they didn't waste ammunition. They were after me all the way. Some of them shells hit in front of me and when they made a big hole I jumped into that and then they most likely figured they got me and they'd stop firing. I'd get up and run again. I'd run maybe thirty yards, forty yards and they opened up again and the same thing. So they were pretty badly tuned with that artillery, trying to just kill me.

Anyway, I spotted the red cross outside the building. It was like a quantize hut and I popped in there and there were so many shells hitting outside the quantize hut so I saw Captain Kitchin [the battalion's surgeon] in there, and the medics, and I told him we have wounded up in front of the Factory and he said, "We were in the Factory! Overnight!" Then Lieutenant [Colonel] Freeman come in through another back door and he come in and he said, "What's going on up there?" And I told him we had a lot of wounded and as far as the artillery was concerned. I said, "Lieutenant Blankenship and Mandle, I didn't see any one of them." He said, "You get back up there again and you tell them to pull back in back of the Factory." So everybody that was alright. So the ambulance went, they even fired at the ambulance. They went back down and they had to go around the back to get back to the road to get to the front of the Factory. If they went up the other road, who knows? They might have really knocked them out. They threw some shells at them going the other way as a possibility, but they stopped after a while.

So I took the long way back. I didn't go the way I went going up there. I was too lucky getting there the way I came, so anyway I went back down towards the back of the Factory and to the sides of the road and I was getting the artillery shells thrown at me.

By the time I got there the ambulance had left and I ran into Lieutenant Blankenship and I told him what Colonel Freeman had told me; so anyway he put the men – but I didn't know Lieutenant Mandle had been seriously wounded so Blankenship was the only officer left – so they couldn't see where we were inside that Factory so we pulled back pretty orderly.

The British had dug some deep holes right next to the road, there's a road going east and west in the back of the Factory so we had some holes dug so we would use them if we had to but we didn't get nothing coming at us at that time – no artillery – but we were fortunate.[336]

H Company Committed to the Grenadiers

When I Company pulled out of the Factory on the evening of February 6, they had had a busy day with casualties inside the Factory during the German artillery barrages. H Company had no-less an action packed day. On February 6, H Company was attempting to crash through the Germans. After being repulsed by heavy German fire four times, Lieutenant Edward Kennedy watched as Lieutenant Richard LaRiviere, a fellow Massachusettsan, led his men to make a fifth attempt at cracking through the German line.

As Kennedy watched LaRiviere attempt to negotiate the German's nasty barbed wire entanglement, the seat of LaRiviere's jump suit got caught on a piece of barbed wire. Yelling to urge his men forward through the fire, and trying to disentangle his pants, Kennedy heard LaRiverie yell to his men, "I'm not stopping even if I have to leave these blankety blank pants behind!"

Lt. Richard LaRiverie of Company H pictured in New York City in January 1946 shortly after returning from Europe. (Richie Blankenship)

The men, watching their lieutenant's personal battle in the midst of the chaos of the firefight, broke into laughter. The men's change in attitude reinvigorated them as they continued to charge the German's positions.

Around that time, Lieutenant Kennedy watched as Private Grady Robbins manhandled his 31-pound Browning machine gun off the tripod – a system typically needed to be operated by two men – and in a feat of heroism and human strength, stood erect and began firing the belt-fed weapon from the hip as he walked forward through a gap in the German's barbed wire entanglements. Combined with the humor of LaRiviere's battle with the barbed wire, provided the men an edge. "The laugh came at the right psychological moment," Kennedy later said. "Maybe we never would have got through on the fifth charge if it hadn't been for the humor of it."[337]

On the evening of the 7th, the Germans reinvigorated their attack and the brunt began falling on the positions of the North Staffs when at 2200, the North Staffs announced over the radio that a German attack in strength was befalling their left flank. The call over the radio was heard by the 1 Irish Guards. Their War Diary recorded that "the situation in this sector, to the north and northwest of us, rapidly deteriorated and the enemy was reported to have overrun all but one of the North Staffs company positions. Their battalion HQ also reported themselves to be surrounded although still operating. The threat to our own forward and left hand positions thus became very real and a general stand-to was ordered. Every man capable of bearing arms and not urgently required as a runner or signaler was allotted a defensive position… Our right flank was being reinforced by the withdrawal to posts south of the bridge of the 504 U.S. Para Regiment. Contact between ourselves and the Americans was immediately established by means of line telephone."[338]

Tied into the left flank of Colonel Freeman's paratroopers was the 5 Grenadier Guards, holding the line along a raised railway bed. At 2130, the North Staffs reported to the Grenadiers that the Germans had broken through "on the road, past the sub-unit. The duty officer on the Bn set reader testily asked, 'What sub-unit and what road?'" The question was answered when a group of Germans were spotted in the left rear of the 5 Grenadier Guards's reserve company, 4 Coy. A few minutes later they were attacked. "This placed the Bn in an awkward position as 4 Coy were considered to be in reserve and it would obviously be wrong in any eventuality to switch 1, 2, or 3 Coy to its help, as they were in position guarding the railway bed." Between 2200 and 2300, the German attack had gained momentum across the entire front, including in the rear of the Grenadiers. "At 2304," the Grenadier's War Diary recorded, "the coy commander reported that the coy was being overrun and ten minutes later the N. Staffs came up again with the information that their 1 Coy (next to our 4 Coy) was overrun, their 2 Coy was surrounded (in a wadi half a mile to the north of the road) but that their 3 Coy was holding out."[339]

The War Diary of the Irish Guards wrote that "the Grenadiers on the line of the railway bed were being engaged from all angles with the enemy endeavoring to isolate their company positions and to break between them and us and to cut the main road."[340] And it was amongst this chaos that Lieutenant Colonel Freeman ordered Company H of the 504th PIR to move to the assistance of the Grenadiers. The Grenadiers sent their Intelligence Officer to meet Lieutenant LaRiviere – known as "Rivers" – and his 55-man company at a signal box and lead them down into the Grenadier's headquarters inside a large, question-mark shaped gully. The Grenadiers wrote that Rivers "expressed the greatest confidence in dealing with any number of Germans" with his 55 men.

While they were making their rendezvous with the Intelligence Officer, the situation continued to develop as the German hordes attacked the Grenadiers:

During the half hour before midnight the tempo increased even more. Enemy surrounded the Bn HQ of the N. Staffs with whom were two platoons of the reserve coy. The rest of the Bn had apparently gone. The N. Staffs commanding officer was heard to say calmly that "everything's alright, we'll just sit here till morning then sort things out." Our own 4 Coy, in view of this development, was ordered to fight its way back to Bn HQ, a distance of about 600 yards...

Hitherto nothing had been heard from the other coys but it came as no great supervise to learn from 3 Coy that one of their platoons had been overrun; on them was falling the brunt of the main attack... Ten minutes later, L/Cpl Emery, the signaler at Coy HQ, said that there were Germans all around him and that he thought the Coy as a whole was surrounded. After a five minutes running commentary he smashed his set to prevent it from falling into German hands...

As the American Coy [H Company, 504th PIR] arrived at Bn HQ in the gully the enemy laid a tremendous smoke screen from what appeared to be a very large bomb. This exploded scattering dozens of smoke canisters in a ring all around and thus making an area about 70 yards in diameter in a matter of seconds. Two of the American platoons were held close at hand, while a third was sent by the commanding officer to hold the hill at the back of Bn Hq. (That is, due south). It was decided at once in view of the direction of the German attacks, to put the whole H Coy on the ridge in front of Lieut E.D. Collie. This ridge stretched a good deal further to the N.W. than the comparatively small hillock held by Lieut A.J. Courage, and was covered with scrub which could conceal hundreds of men. It was at any rate beyond the capabilities of a single platoon. The commanding officer showed H Coy Comd this particular ridge and sent the Intelligence Officer off to each of 4 Coy's platoon commands to tell them what to expect. By the time this small group had returned to the gully and the whole of H Coy had been gathered, there was an astonishing amount of German small arms fire and Germans appeared in great numbers on the ridge just opposite to the gully. This ridge was a continuation of the hillock on which Lieut A.J. Courage's platoon had last been seen digging in, and there was no option but to consider that this platoon had been overrun. A moment later a solitary guardsman from No 4 Company said that he had just escaped, having seen Lieut E.D. Collie surrounded by a party of Germans whom he was bayonetting vigorously.

In the gully the sounds of battle grew more violent every moment. On the ridge in front several German machine guns appeared, all firing a good deal of tracer, some of it more accurately place than is usual in a German attack. The one platoon of H Coy which had been at the back of Bn HQ was caught on the forward slope and its best machine gunner, his No 2 and a rifleman were all killed. In fact, the Germans were searching all likely defense positions with great skill...

Throughout the night, pitched fighting occurred as the hordes of Germans tried to break through the positions. As the 8th dawned, Rivers and his men were "spread along the ditch by the side of the track leading into the gully from the North... The American parachutists, who had done yeoman work all night, continued to bang away at any enemy head which approached. It was now pretty clear that the N. Staffs had been liquidated although several had escaped through us."[341]

They had a Laugh, but it Cost them their Lives

After Francis Keefe passed along Colonel Freeman's order to Lieutenant Blankenship after the shelling of the Factory on February 6, I Company began to fall back to the railway embankment behind the Factory. In an orderly fashion, they proceeded to move towards the southwest behind the protection of an old single-track railway embankment, a distance of approximately one-quarter of a mile behind the Factory. Tied in on the left along the railway embankment were the positions of the Grenadiers.

Shortly after their arrival here, Muri – who carried the squad's small camp stove – tried to brew up some coffee, as "he was always doing," Keefe notes. No gas remained and water, supplemented by some cheese and crackers, was consumed in its place. "You just go through the same routine you know?"

The evening of February 6, Sergeant Samuel Cleckner's squad, which was on the far side of the Factory, was found to be missing. "I'll go see if I can find them," Keefe told Lieutenant Blankenship, who was the final remaining officer in the company.

"Come on Muri," Keefe told his friend, "let's go and get them." The distance to the Factory was not far, and Keefe found Sergeant Cleckner inside "all bedded down nice and comfortable" in the buildings. "Are you comfortable?" Keefe asked.

"Yeah," Cleckner said.

"You gotta pull out and get in the rain like we are," told Keefe.

Remains of The Factory looking out towards the German lines. (US Signal Corps)

For I Company, the dawn of February 7 came fairly peaceful. Francis Keefe describes the events that day and night:

The next morning where we were, the English – you know when they build a foxhole you can stand up in that foxhole – so we were in that foxhole there. It seemed very calm. A couple of British soldiers came up in one of their command cars and they stopped and talked to us, we spoke to them, and I remember I had a German small weapon and I pulled the trigger and everybody jumped because I shot in the air, so they had a laugh, but it cost them their lives because after they left there they were going down the road [and] a German shell hit them and killed them.

I don't know where G Company was, but I figured G Company [was] next to us. We didn't have too many men left so they must have been in-between, and then H Company was inside with the British – that was to the east. They went up to reinforce the British soldiers that were up there. You could hear the firing going on all over the place, and only I think two or three of them come back.

Anyways, we dug in not at the overpass, we were back a little bit from the overpass maybe 50 yards or a little bit more. Then the Germans infiltrated next to the overpass, and we were standing around more or less talking because we weren't getting hit with too much artillery and they start firing on the British, then we fired on them so the British sent up a couple of soldiers to reinforce that position, so the Germans infiltrated right down to the overpass. Now, H Company had pulled back along the lines where we were but the Germans had hit them pretty hard.

We must have been there about two days and they were throwing off a lot of artillery on us and first of all they started hitting G Company, which was up on the right of us. That's when we were down by the road underneath the culvert there. We had a couple guys got wounded inside the culvert. I was on that side so I walked to the other side [of the road]. Lieutenant [Payton] Elliott came down into the overpass, but the Germans spotted him and threw all kinds of artillery on him. I said, "Lieutenant we got wounded on the other end." So he says, "Well, I'll have to go back." I said, "No, they'll meet you here. I'll go back."

As I walked out of that hole – I want to tell you something – they hit us with EVERYTHING. They were trying to kill me for sure. I mean, they put a blast on me. I think Elliott thought I got killed. But I dove in a hole and we had so much rain and the water kept going inside my neck and down my pants and whatnot. As soon as it let up I took a b-line up to the house where I knew Blankenship was and there was Muri with him. So, they pulled me in. They had a heavy job because I had all the water in there, in my clothes; I was loaded up with water. So, I told them what Elliott told me and he told Muri, "Go back to the medics to get an ambulance up there." In the meanwhile, he says, Blankenship says, "Take off those clothes because you gotta dry off a little bit. You can't go running around like that." That's what I did.

The ambulance – we could look out the window – the ambulance come up where the culvert was and they were collecting some of the wounded but it was being blasted something fierce... Muri and a guy we call Pops, he was in the house too. So he told Muri and Pops, "You go out and get yourself a hole." It was facing more-or-less northeast and I said to Blankenship, "I'm going out." He said no, your clothes are all wet and whatnot. I said, "I'd feel better if I went out." He said, "That's up to you," and I went out and joined Muri so I didn't see Blankenship after that...

I gotta tell you, while we were in the house that night we had ponchos or whatever over the doorway and who come in but Lieutenant Colonel Freeman and we said, "You're letting the air in and the Germans will throw artillery at us." So he says, "They've been throwing artillery at you all day." So he said, "What's going on?" So I said, a couple of us all said it, that we can't heat nothing here and we'd like to have some hot coffee. So, while we were there he got the stove up there and some British soldiers come in and they were making their hot tea. I remember the tea that they were making. It had milk in the tea, I don't know *about the sugar though, but I liked it. Anyways, the gas ran out in no time so we were right back where we started from but Lieutenant Colonel Freeman had left.*

Lt. Payton Elliott in England after the battle of Anzio. Elliott was wounded shortly after Keefe left him at the culvert. He would recover from the wound and return to the regiment, only to be severely injured in a training jump in August 1944 which would end his Army career. (Dwight Elliott)

That was the night. Then the next morning, and then the next morning [of February 8] we went out, Muri and the other fellow and myself went out in a hole. So Pops left us. Somehow, he got a 30-day furlough because his mother was dying. We called him Pops because he looked like an old man. Little things like that are humorous, you know? ...

In fact, when Pops left, we moved over towards English foxholes that you could stand in, and one of the guys come over and wanted to talk to us and see whether we could get cigarettes and back and forth. On the way back, the Germans had spotted him. Now, he was only about, his foxhole was only about five feet away from mine and they laid in a barrage but he got hit somewhere and the guy that was in his foxhole *with him got out there even with the artillery. I went out and pulled him in and then me and Muri tried to relax them. I don't know what happened to him after that. I didn't see any ambulance come but maybe the medics got him out.*[342]

Roy Hanna Breaks the German Backbone

On February 8, H Company, after the night of repulsing the Germans with the Grenadiers, was still on the line along the railway embankment with the British troops. The rest of the 3rd Battalion had spent the day of February 8 attacking but were unable to get far due to the heavy German small arms fire. Lieutenant Roy Hanna was attached to Company G and remembered that evening that they were withdrawing to their original defensive positions as tracers flew over their heads. The battalion had established "a general line of skirmish," wrote Hanna, "running from west to east and facing north with 'I' [Company] on the east end near the Factory. Freeman and staff [were] near the west end of the line, but back maybe a hundred yards or so and I'm quite sure in a house." Eaton's 81mm mortar-men were scattered through the mixture firing over the men's heads from just behind the main line of resistance.[343]

Sometime in the evening, Private First Class Bonnie Roberts, a runner from Battalion Headquarters, found Lieutenant Hanna. Colonel Freeman was summoning him. It was a short walk, as Hanna was just to the front left of the headquarters. There, Colonel Freeman appraised Hanna of an extremely critical situation: the Germans had re-infiltrated to the west, leaving Lieutenant LaRiviere's men cut-off and virtually surrounded. Additionally, Lieutenant Blankenship had been wounded by artillery and I Company was being commanded by the first sergeant. Colonel Freeman directed Hanna to leave his Machine Gun Platoon and lead I Company in an attack to try and pull H Company back to the battalion.

Lieutenant Hanna proceeded to the house that contained the company CP and met with 1st Sergeant Odom. Hanna instructed Odom to collect some men from their foxholes and line them up along the back side of the railroad tracks.

Somebody came up to the foxhole Francis Keefe and Leo Muri were sharing. "Lieutenant Hanna," they said, "wants to see you right away down by the little gully from the road." *Who is Lieutenant Hanna?* Keefe thought. What Keefe and Muri didn't know, was that Lieutenant Blankenship had been wounded. Arriving at the gully was, as Keefe remembered it, about another fourteen men or so.[344]

Lt. Robert Blankenship was the last officer standing in Company I before Roy Hanna was sent by Lt. Col. Freeman. Blankenship would leave the hospital the next day and return to the company. Blankenship became one of the most respected officers in the 504th PIR. (Richie Blankenship)

The I Company command post was a two-story house that was sitting on the west side of the railroad tracks. And while the men were gathering in the small gully, Hanna began planning his attack:

I went to the second floor of the building that housed the command post. The enemy artillery had knocked a large hole out of the north side of the second floor. Looking through this space I used my field glasses to make my plans for our counter attack.

Let me try to give you a description of the terrain and my general plan of attack. Perpendicular to the railroad track, a dirt road ran directly into the wooded area where the Germans that had H Company pinned down were located. Approximately three hundred yards straight out the road from my position was a house where I had spotted German snipers. A large drainage ditch ran along the left side of the road for about 100 yards where there was a British armored tank that had been knocked out and vacated. This was going to be our first stopping place.

Hanna looked out across the space through the hole in the shelled out roof, observing the terrain and the low rolling hills on each side of the dirt road and the ditch. On the way to the tank, they would be completely exposed to the snipers inside of the house. He also realized that as they advanced along the railroad bed, his right flank would also be exposed. Lieutenant Hanna summoned Corporal Conover and his machine gun crew. He instructed Conover to position himself in a large shell hole that the enemy artillery had ripped into the ground to cover this venerability.[345]

Hanna joined the men that 1st Sergeant Odom had collected and instructed the men to fix their bayonets. "There was no formality," Francis Keefe remembered of Hanna's arrival, "how we were going to do it or anything else – he was going to lead and we were going to go and see what we could possibly do."[346]

Hanna led the men off.

They advanced across the field towards the burnt-out tank in open view of the German snipers in the house. Two grenades flew out of a German outpost, wounding John Gallagher and Marvin Porter. Roy Hanna remembered what happened next:

When we got to the disabled armored tank I sent two troopers up on a small knoll with instructions to fire as rapidly as possible into the house when they saw us in position to attack the house.

Just a bit beyond the armored tank the ditch ended and a concrete culvert ran under the road that was too small for us to crawl through. We crossed over the road and continued up the ditch opposite the house. We again crossed the road and attacked the house. The Germans inside must have been distracted because up to this point there was no evidence that they knew we were coming. After throwing a few hand grenades through the windows we removed that obstacle; two dead German soldiers and one wounded.

About this time, I saw the two men that I had placed on the knoll running toward the house with their rifles held in front of them. As I watched, the rifle suddenly flew out of the one man's hands, up over his head taking his helmet off. He never broke stride. When he arrived beside me he had no trigger finger. A sniper had shot at him and hit in the trigger housing of the rifle, knocking the rifle out of his hands and cutting off his finger. How about that for luck!

Our next objective was the wooded area back of the house. As I was running out a hedgerow a rabbit ran across in front of me making me pivot. As I pivoted a German rifleman shot me.

To give you a couple examples of how luck can play a big part in survival during war time;

1. When we went into combat we carried two hand grenades hooked on our harness, one on the right side of our chest, the other on the left. When we attacked the house I had used the one off my right chest.

2. I was shot through the upper part of my right chest with the bullet passing through my lung and exiting through the lower back. This happened when I ran along a small path that followed a hedge row. I hadn't run more than 25 yards from the house when a big rabbit ran across the path in front of me. I got shot just as my reflexes caused me to track the rabbit with my Tommy Gun. If the rabbit had not caused me to pivot?

3. The bullet entered my chest area and exited through my rib cage in my back. Fortunately, it was a steel jacketed bullet and didn't hit a bone. If the bullet had hit a bone?

After the bullet tore through his chest, Lieutenant Hanna didn't fall; he turned around and went back to where the rest of his men were to warn of the Germans behind the house. Hanna then collapsed and fell to the ground.[347]

Lt. Roy Hanna shortly after graduating Parachute School. (Roy Hanna)

Francis Keefe and Sergeant George Leolis – "The Greek" – were towards the tail-end of Hanna's men. As the men charged the houses, Keefe and Leolis took cover behind a large, five-foot-tall brick oven positioned just outside one of the homes as the rest of the men flowed to their left. Keefe, over six foot and skinny as a twig, had to crouch down a bit. Suddenly, from 50 yards up on the right side of the road, a German machine gun opened up. The gun was positioned up on a slight mound of dirt, and was likely the one that Hanna saw just when he was wounded. "I'm going up to throw a grenade at them," Keefe said to The Greek in his thick New York accent.

Crawling up about 20 yards, Keefe pulled the bolt of his M-1 rifle back and put in a blank cartridge in the chamber, then he put the oblong-shaped rifle grenade on the special adapter on the muzzle of his M-1 Garand. Firing the rifle grenade, it was a hit and the machine gun fell silent. Keefe headed back to the oven. "Greek," Keefe yelled, "I'm coming back in behind that oven!" The Greek was gone.

I just get behind there and the Greek wasn't there. He was with the rest of them attacking the other house they held the British officer in, and they made contact with H Company. Well, I don't know what was going on then and there. All I know is that machine gun opened up again. Either they thought I was that close to them or else I hit that gun and a replacement, somebody else took over. It was either one of the two. But the machine gun bullets, they knew, when I yelled, "Greek, I'm coming back," they knew the direction that I was in, or somebody was in, and they fired their gun and they hit the oven. Of course hitting the brick oven, the fire was all over – tracers all over the place! They must have figured, well, they're hitting something and there was no yelling from anybody getting hit, so they moved the gun to my left across in like the middle of the road – it would be to their right as far as their concerned – they were firing and them bullets were going no place. It wasn't going to harm anybody. I went up and joined the rest of them.[348]

Meanwhile, Hanna's right lung had collapsed from his bullet wound. Despite this, Hanna would continue to get back up and lead the men into the attack. "Every so often," Lieutenant Hanna stated, "I would wake up on the ground – passed out because of 'oxygen starvation' caused by the collapsed lung." Lieutenant Hanna would refuse medical treatment until his force broke through, breaking the siege on Company H and facilitating their withdraw.

"After the mission was completed and we were ordered to withdraw," Hanna wrote, "I again lost consciousness as we crawled across the dirt road under the overhead fire of a German machine gun." By now it was past dark and Hanna could see the gun's colorful stream of tracers streak across the road like bolts of lightning, passing just over his body. "A couple of the men drug me off the road and eventually got me back to that disabled armored tank.

"I was conscious as the men carefully placed me on a stretcher. As I laid there I could feel my back against the stretcher, but I could see my body floating up through the air. The higher I went the smaller I got. I remember thinking, *I must be dying and this isn't too bad.*"[349]

By the time Francis Keefe arrived, Hanna was already on a stretcher and they just began their withdrawal. "I don't know where the medic came from but they had a stretcher and they had him on a stretcher and I was pretty close too, when they were carrying him out, four men carried him out. Just as we started back again, one of our men stepped on a mine, he was killed... But anyway, he was killed and we were all out pretty orderly, moved back into our old positions. Of course Roy Hanna was taken to the farmhouse. From there he was taken out with the medics."[350]

As Hanna laid on the stretcher outside the shelled out I Company CP awaiting an ambulance and looking at the night's sky, he could feel the raindrops impact his face and cool him down.

Roland Gruber was a member of Lt. Hanna's Machine Gun Platoon, and was also wounded on Feb. 8. (Gruber Family)

They Finally Got Me

Thousands of miles away, all was calm in Altoona, Pennsylvania. At the local Western Union telegram office, the teletype could be heard clacking away at its normal pace. It was just business as usual when a telegram from the War Department in Washington, D.C. came through that read, "The Secretary of War desires me to express his deep regret that your husband, First Lieutenant Roy M. Hanna, has been missing in action..." It was intercepted by a friend of Mrs. Roy Hanna who worked at the Western Union station, and who decided that she would deliver the terrible news. She headed right over to Jan's parents' home at 419 25th Avenue, where Jan was living while Roy was away. With tears in her eyes she rapped on the door. When Jan asked what the matter was, she spit it out. Jan, however, knew it wasn't true: her husband had already sent a letter of his own.

While in the hospital, Lieutenant Hanna found life boring and with little to do. He had a little pain from his wound when the soldier occupying the bed next to him – a comedian – in the critical ward was not making him laugh, because when "I laughed it hurt like hell. Not really funny in my opinion at the time."[351] The downtime gave him a chance to catch up on correspondence. On February 17 he wrote his sister and her husband about his wound, letting them know he was in the hospital.

I received your 2 sheet V-mail yesterday – it sure was a nice long letter. That's exactly what I need now – lots of long letters, because I'm in the hospital and have plenty of time on my hands. Yes, they finally got me – but not seriously. I'll tell you exactly where but believe me it's not serious because I'm already walking around. A rifle shot entered on upper part of right chest and made its exit through the small of my back just to the right of my backbone. I know it sounds bad but it just made two little holes and didn't hit a bone. It did, however, penetrate my right lung causing it to collapse and making me a bit short winded for a while. But now I'm recovering rapidly and will be back to duty in a few weeks.[352]

With the end of February 8, the backbone of the German attack in the sector was broken, but it came at a terrible price. When the battalion landed on Anzio, it was 536 paratroopers strong. By February 10, there was around 213 still standing firm on the line. First Lieutenant Moffatt Burriss remembered that Headquarters Company was down to about 13 men at one point. In such a situation, the battalion was lucky to have Leslie Freeman. A black-haired, tall and lanky New Yorker, he remained determined and iron-bound, and he expected nothing less from his officers. When one officer cracked under the stress of these February days, he told the officer to leave allegedly saying, "Go find yourself another outfit." The officer, one eyewitness reported, was very shaken up over the whole situation and was acting like a "banshee." A rumor circulated that two officers were discovered hiding during an attack and Freeman had them escorted on a boat back to Naples with instructions to "find another home."

Freeman took everything that was going on "in his stride," observed Burriss, who was almost always within yelling distance from Freeman, "he really did. He was not the nervous type, and he was a good commander… Colonel Freeman was more calm and collective."[353] Roy Hanna was also happy to have him: "Freeman was liked," he said, "because he was an integral part of our combat team, always with us, always looking after us, and we could depend on anything he said."[354]

The battalion's resolute performance in the face of overwhelming casualties and uncertainty in the overall situation is an exploit that rivals Greek legends. There were many small, local epics of incredible feats of arms over the period the battalion was in action in the British sector which, due to the extraordinarily chaotic situation, went unseen and will likely never be told. Had the German attack succeeded, the beachhead may have utterly collapsed and the Anglo-Americans driven into the sea. For the period of February 8-12, the 3rd Battalion, 504th Parachute Infantry Regiment was awarded one of the very first Presidential Unit Citations awarded in the European Theater of Operations for their gallant stand in the face of fierce attack.

11

I DON'T THINK SUNNY ITALY AGREES WITH ME

Growing up on a farm in rural New Mexico, Thomas Utterback was not accustomed to being confined to a bed with time on his hands, but that is just what he had while his regiment was fighting on the Anzio Beachhead. On January 22, while the regiment was making the amphibious landing on Red Beach, Lieutenant Utterback was confined to a hospital bed in Naples. After his unit was relieved from the mountains above Venafro after Christmas in December 1943, Utterback reported to a hospital for illness. The scraggly, brutally cold, windswept peaks took their toll on the 30-year-old lieutenant. On January 5 he wrote his wife that it was "a hell of a way to start the New Year. Finally managed to get into a general hospital. Had a high fever for almost a week with chills, etc. Wanted nothing on my stomach but water. Am beginning to eat a little now and last night they brought the fever down to 101. Feel awfully weak and sore. The doctor asked me what was wrong with me. Personally I think it's the old story again only greater strain for longer lengths of time."

Utterback had been with the regiment since Sicily, and by the time the New Year dawned, he was still in the hospital. Utterback had been away from home so long that he wrote to his wife that he had now "forgotten how 'cokes' taste. The lushness of a strawberry sunday I can hardly bring to mind. But my mouth waters every time I think of a good cold glass of milk." At the outset of the war, Utterback, the holder of a reserve commission through the Reserve Officer Training Corps, was called up and sent to Fort Huachuca, Arizona to join the 93rd Division. In January 1943, Lieutenant Utterback and two of his friends, Lieutenants John Randles and John Pease, decided to volunteer for the parachute troops. On the 27th their orders were cut relieving them from the 93rd, and on February 24th they reported to Fort Benning for parachute training. All three were eventually assigned to the 504th.

Like most of the men, letters were his umbilical cord to his family back home. Utterback was probably one of the most faithful correspondents in the regiment, writing to his wife and two young children, Tommy and Jeanny, nearly every day. "You can't just imagine what letters mean to me over here," he wrote. "Your first ones contained these little things that don't mean much there but give me part of home over here. Just anything that happened that day makes interesting reading." Utterback would daydream about building a house for himself and his family on his New Mexican farm upon his return from the war. "Here it is almost '44 and as you know," Utterback wrote his wife at the end of December shortly before going to the hospital, "the war is going to end in that year. At least it gives a fellow something to look forward to… In my daydreaming I had 2 new houses down by the road. Cleared off the 'hilltop' and put in modern stuff. Cleaned out all the fences and installed electric ones. You know, made the place pretty…More than ever I'd like to be home and resume a normal life. Until then I'm with you all in my thoughts."

Lt. Thomas Utterback (Laurie Utterback)

On January 8, he was still waiting for the doctors to give him a definite diagnosis: "Well, the smoke has rather dried away and I'm almost clear-headed for a change. From Dec. 30-6Jan had a high fever, etc. Doc took x-rays and were ready to swear either the old fashioned flu or pneumonia. So now I lie around with tendency to fever and am taking gallons of sulpha drugs to clear up my chest. I am not leaving here until they feel clean. Really believe I have a weakness in the bellows someplace… Poor beginning - good ending. Am hanging on for that good ending. Have plenty of time here to dream and think of you. All seems to add up to the same thing - I love you."

As his time in the hospital continued to drag on, he became more and more homesick. He wrote several days later that he was "still an awful lonesome little boy… The doctor says that my chests appear to be dry but wants me to stay a few days longer and have another x-ray made just to be sure. But I've got to hear from you, Honey. And just to lay here and think of you naturally makes it worse… Yes, war news does sound good but Honey, the devils aren't licked yet by a long ways. Oh, but Lord please make it soon.

I want to see the sunshine start. Have I offered my happy birthday greetings? … Bet Tommy & Jeanny are lovable little tykes and I'm missing all that. Ah, to hell with the damn Jerries. This shouldn't happen to anyone. My humor will surely improve when I get back with the outfit."

Utterback continued to grow anxious to get back with his unit. But his physical condition was not improving rapidly. On January 14 he took a 1/2 mile walk and wrote that "it dinked me out. The doc says another week for me. What I wouldn't give to be able to have you folks drop in on me while resting here. It will be best to get back to the outfit. I do too much thinking laying around here."

The day after that, his x-rays showed his lungs were still half-filled with fluid and that the doctor said that he would not be released until they were clear, and he was still weak from the fever. On January 21, the day before the regiment was to land at Anzio, Utterback was confined to the hospital for two more weeks. "Don't think 'sunny' Italy agrees with me," he wrote his wife that day.

As January turned into February, he began to hear about his regiment's actions on Anzio. He continued to take walks every day and became ever anxious to get back into the fight. On February 14 and 15, he wrote two long letters which are good examples of life as a lieutenant in a parachute infantry regiment during World War II:

February 14

Honey, my mind is a complete void this morning. Am still in the institution of medical recovery or something. Will surely be out in a day or two. I don't know whether I'd know how to live out in the cold cruel world. And this morning it is really cold too. Ice laying around in spots and all of this in sunny Italy. Phhhhtttt.

Went to a show here last night and enjoyed it very much. It was "This is the Army." A very good show. See it if you have a chance.

As you may have guessed, the outfit is again in the line and holding a few tight spots. Randles and Pease are still OK, I just heard this morning. Makes me feel crummy to be laying around here while they are up there. Yet I'm not hypocrite enough to say that I wished I was there. I agree to your point, sweetheart, so don't worry.

So that's the news, Honey. Do I need to tell you that I'm still homesick? That I miss my family? … This outfit may go to the States - after they walk down the Wilhelm Strasse. I wouldn't mind marching in that parade. Or even Rome. Is Tommy going to have a garden this year? Let me know how it turns out. Hi Tommy.

February 15

Think I wrote a V-Mail last night with the same date. Dates mean nothing to me. The only one I have in mind is the end of World War II. To drive down a street with you, lights on, and the street all lit up. To go where you want to with no fear of getting into "enemy" territory. Have had that fear on a night or so. I have nothing to write about, Honey. [Ex]cept my love for you, so will shoot the breeze with some moments I won't forget:

One night the colonel phoned me up & said they need ammunition as they were expecting a dawn counterattack. Was night, black as a deuce of spades & raining as it only can here. So I collected a carrying party and headed up. Now, the only route I knew to that position led up thru a valley then up the mountain. German artillery had that valley zeroed in and kept pasting it with shells. In fact, it was on day and night and the valley (farmland) was almost one big shell hole. The men were loaded heavy and the trail was slick and unkind. It seemed we crawled up thru there. Believe it or not, just one shell came in. Hit the side of the mountain above us and bounced clear over our heads. Coming home in the early morning we all ran a footrace thru that place. - P.S. I won.

(2) Col. X gathered his company commanders and we started out over the valley - up the mountain that was to be our new position. We arrived there just at night. Going up the side of the mountain firing of all kinds broke out above us tho some of it was from American guns. Pretty soon an American lieutenant came from on top and yelled for someone to come up there.

My orderly & I went up. This lieutenant had 9 men and had just stood off a large party of Jerries. He wondered what to do. I reminded that his orders were to stay until our troops arrived. OK. The orderly and I went back down the mountain. It was now dark. Just as we got to the bottom we both saw something at the same time and hit the dirt. We each jammed a shell into our guns and 'over there' we could hear them doing the same. And there we stalemated for about 5 minutes. Finally, I asked someone to sound off over there. The col. answered, "Utterback, get over here and let's cut out this playing."

(3) In Sicily we necessarily had to spend several nights near a beach where lots of shipping was coming in. We all dug in… During the night Jerry dumped a flare exactly over our heads. Never saw so much light, then followed with his bombs.

As soon as that was over I hunted up my shovel and added 'several' feet to my foxhole. Felt ashamed until I stopped to rest and by the noise could tell that everyone was doing the same.

(4) Lt. Mc[Clain] had to answer the call of nature. When he got back, Jerry had dumped one in his hole. So Mc very promptly moved locations. Personally, I took on the theory that lightning seldom hits the same place twice.

(5) A scouting party went out into "no man's land" and when they came back to the CP the major wanted to know where they got the prisoners. Every man looked around to discover two Jerries who had decided to give up so just tagged up and followed in.

Lots of queer things happen that help to make this life endurable. And tho tinged with danger the men really get a laugh out of them. Questioning prisoners always proved to be illuminating.

Suppose farming is beginning to get into its stride. What is to be the set-up this year? I am getting out tomorrow to about a week's light duty which I am going to try to figure out as laying around taking life easy. Have the kids contracted spring fever yet? Regards to the clan. As ever, remember I love you.[355]

Utterback's situation was not particularly unusual. Throughout the Italian campaign sickness seemed to plague the regiment. Cases of jaundice were a dime a dozen, and malaria, while not as widespread, was commonplace. Many times these cases remained on the line, and the inflicted could sometimes be seen shaking in their foxholes from the symptoms. "Immunization was good against such things as typhus, tetanus, etc. but inadequate against malaria, hepatitis, venereal diseases and Vincent's [disease]," observed Robert Halloran.[356] In some cases, more men had to be pulled from the line from sickness than from enemy bullets.

Francis Keefe Returns to the Mussolini Canal

On February 18, the 3rd Battalion was reverted back to regimental control from the British, and they returned to the Mussolini Canal in a reserve area. "When this battalion returned to control of the Combat Team," Edson Mattice wrote, "it had been reduced to 35% of normal strength by casualties and sickness."[357] Because of I Company's personnel situation, by in large they were spared most of the patrolling actions the other companies in the regiment were subjected to. One night, the legendary Theodore Bachenheimer came through with two other men, and inquired about the layout of the land in front of them. They went out into the German lines, and never came back. No shooting was ever heard that night.

On another night, about ten men from G Company came through on their way out. Francis Keefe and Leo Muri moved down by a bridge which was the patrol's departure point. They gave them all the information they could of their observations, and the G Company men headed out. "After about fifteen minutes," Francis Keefe remembered, "we heard shooting and a scream, and we knew somebody got hit. We could tell there was a lot of confusion. We were told not to open up, but I said, 'The hell with that. They need help.' Muri was feeding me the belt of the machine gun and after about three minutes, which is a long time, a machine gun on the other side opened up on me. The bullet went right between me and Muri."

Francis Keefe was focusing his fire on the German machine gun which was firing at the patrol, even though the second German machine gun was firing on Keefe and Muri's machine gun. Finally, another American machine gun breathed fire at the gun that was shooting at Keefe and Muri. Now, there were four machine guns – two Germans and two Americans – dueling it out with each other while the patrol was trying to organize and withdrawal in the confusion. Thankfully, the fire from all the machine guns did give them the chance and cover they needed, and they came through with their wounded lieutenant on a stretcher.

Jack Lancaster of Company A stands before a .30 caliber machine gun. Lancaster was one of the largest men in the 504th and he was the regimental heavyweight boxing champion. (Roger Mokan)

About 100 yards to their right was a farmhouse where H Company had set up an outpost. Often times at night, they could hear a German machine gun firing in the vicinity of the farmhouse. "What the hell is going on," Keefe would say. Later, he found out that it was Lieutenant Richard LaRiviere. "He was trying to confuse the Germans, but he was confusing us more than the Germans!"

During the day, Keefe could see the Germans with their binoculars looking over from a farmhouse into their lines. Every day, Keefe would go to the same spot up on the berm on the canal and shoot tracers at them, to let the Germans know they knew they were there. "One day," Keefe recalled, "the Germans were waiting for me and I went up there to shoot and I hear, *PEW, PEW* going by my ear. I went down and said, 'I think we got some company coming over there.' One of the guys said, 'Let me go up and see.' I said don't go up there. He went up there and sure enough he came back. I said, 'I told you not to go up there.' He could have gotten himself killed. When you can hear the bullets going past you, you know they're close."[358]

It was on the Mussolini Canal that Lieutenant Utterback rejoined the 3rd Battalion. While he was recovering in the hospital, Captain William Kitchin, the battalion's doctor, went to Naples to "encourage anyone who was able" to return to Anzio to help. Lieutenant Utterback went. When he arrived, he reported in to Colonel Freeman and Freeman told him to go help their battalion supply sergeant, Staff Sergeant William Rankin. "Rankin was doing a good job," Utterback later wrote, "but needed some backing from someone who had more than stripes."[359]

"Plenty of valley up here," Utterback wrote in a letter home on March 2, shortly after assuming his new combat duty, "but not so very peaceful at the present time, thank you. Temporarily am working as supply officer and that means a lot of running around. Don't have a portable foxhole to send me do you? Plenty of fun, something to watch every minute… Mussolini built up quite a place here. Ground is a trifle damp. In fact, darn damp. And it will rain now and then. But in most ways everything is going OK. Got very sea sick coming up and am just getting back on my appetite. I Have $10 in a pool for the date of the big push. If I win will send you $300 – not bad but don't buy any fur coats yet."[360]

Running supplies for the entire regiment was Major William Addison, who ran his operations in the town of Nettuno near the port. Initially, Major Addison's office was in a building. Utterback later wrote, "I went down to check on something and found Major Addison in a wet dug-out behind the building. I asked him why he moved out of the nice building and into a wet hole. His reply was, 'Have you seen what that railroad gun did to the building across the road?' As I left the town, I looked and saw a hole in the building that you could drive a truck through."[361]

The 2nd Battalion Returns to the Ditch

When dawn broke on March 7, 1944, the men of the 2nd Battalion, 504th Parachute Infantry Regiment rediscovered themselves in the same positions inside the Ditch which they had captured on January 30, and had held until being relieved by the Rangers on the night of February 16, after the large German counterattack on their positions. Because of casualties, William Sweet had moved from the Battalion S-3 and taken over command of F Company. At the time, there were about sixty men and officers per company, as opposed to the 170 that were supposed to constitute a rifle company.

Physically, the area had changed little, but the Germans had moved closer to their positions. "When dawn came we found a much different situation than when we had left the Ditch. The Rangers were the remains of the Ranger Regiment that had been cut up at Cisterna and had lost their fighting spirit. So they had worked on the principle that if they didn't shoot at the Germans they in turn would not be shot at. This worked very well for the Germans, they had moved right on the position and set up machine guns less than two hundred yards from the Ditch and had fortified all the houses to the front. This caused a slight debate bright and early on the first day and resulted in our getting shelled all day long… In our minds, corrective measures had to be taken, and swiftly… The enemy had grown bold and careless in the area and in the first two days we were back on the line, he got a good idea that the situation had changed."[362]

12

DEVILS IN BAGGY PANTS ENDURE

The operations on Anzio had been costly for the 504th Parachute Infantry Regiment from the outset, and no element of the combat team had been unaffected by losing strength to battle, sickness, and weather. As the time in the trenches of Anzio drug on, the effect of the entire war and its killings and maimings began catching up to the regiment. Troopers who had trained with the regiment in the States, come over on the *George Washington*, and parachuted into Sicily slowly became the minority as they were killed and wounded, and new paratroopers took their places. "We lost a lot of men in southern Italy and a lot at Anzio," Fred Baldino, who had shipped over with the regiment on the *George Washington*, reflected, "but being realistic, I realized it was war and war kills people and we kill them, all so useless as after the war every country we fought became friends with us, or nearly all of them."[363]

Eventually, Lieutenant Chester Garrison became accustomed to replacements. "Gradual inclusion," he said of absorbing them into the ranks, "naturally old buddies preferred each other." Garrison observed they fitted in because "the situation demanded it."[364] Edward Mokan said the replacements were "very green, but were veterans in a week of combat if they lived."[365] And to Baldino, it seemed that replacements seemed to be lost quicker than the regulars, as, Baldino felt, "they are not aware enough of how dangerous it is in combat."[366]

William Sweet, who served as both a battalion operations officer and a company commander in the 504th on the Anzio beachhead, made some interesting observations when he stated that "esprit de corps can make up, in part, for a lack of conditioning and can assist new men in putting forth the necessary energy to become ready for combat… This esprit de corps should be given a full measure of the credit for the showing the unit made on the beachhead… Well trained and disciplined men can be depended upon in any situation for which they have been trained. A man's previous training will show up in battle, and if he is a well-trained soldier he will do the best he can under the conditions, be he enlisted man or officer."[367]

It was mid-1943 when a young Obie Wickersham had just joined the United States Army, and was in transit for training. Going through Union Station at Saint Louis, Missouri, young Wickersham saw a paratrooper. He was amazed at the uniform the soldier wore – a white parachute for a scarf and shiny, beautiful Corcoran jump boots. "Hey," Wickersham reflected, "if you joined the airborne, you were the best in the world." So, Wickersham volunteered to be a paratrooper. Earning the right to wear that uniform was not the easiest. Wickersham reported to to the oppressive heat that is seared into the memory of anyone who has gone through Fort Benning, Georgia for the rigorous Parachute School. The area lived up to the nickname many of the paratroopers gave it: the frying pan. "We had one canteen of water and I think we had one K ration. We had lemonade packets and I thought, 'I'm going to make lemonade.' It was so bitter I couldn't eat it and I had to go without water for the rest of the day."

After completing his five jumps and earning his parachute wings, Wickersham reported to Camp Mackall, North Carolina for further training as an airborne engineer. In January of 1944, a notice was put out for 25 volunteers to join the 82nd Airborne Division at Anzio. Wickersham volunteered, and soon he found himself traveling through North Africa with 24 other new paratroop engineers. From Africa they went to Naples, and on February 26, 1944 the volunteers landed on the Anzio beachhead and joined the engineer component of the 504th Parachute Combat Team: Company C, 307th Airborne Engineer Battalion.

There was no welcome party. Wickersham recalled, "My first night in combat they took the Second Squad out and each guy had a big box of TNT. I don't know, probably [weighed] about 50 pounds. It was raining, muddy, and we went through our lines and we'd slip and fall with that TNT – it's dangerous anyway! A few dirty words were going in and then we got there and the damned bridge had already been blown. I think the Germans. I think the Germans blew it…

"Going back – Herb Wendland, a good friend of mine – the Germans were firing twenty-millimeters. They're white and red, they're kind of pretty and they'll fire a shot with maybe eight or ten [rounds] at a time, just like they're floating in time. Herb was looking around this building, this damned barn, and one came real close. Some sergeant grabbed him and said, 'What are you trying to do? Get killed?' I was just a little old rookie."[368]

On both February 1 and March 1, infantry replacements came to the regiment. One of these was Hugh Wallis, from Louisiana, who came to the beachhead with the March replacement group. His welcome to combat was also a gruff experience.

It was crazy. When they're on the front line, I guess they assume you know everything. The jeep came and picked us up, we had to sit on the beach all day, on a hillside, because we couldn't move in the daytime, and right after dark a jeep picked us up, two or three of us. We rode for a while and came up to an old farmhouse and he said, "This is where you go, through that door there." We went through that door and someone said, "Welcome to the 3rd Platoon of H Company, 504th Parachute Infantry, 82nd Airborne." They gave us two bandoleers of ammunition, hand grenades and said, "Go with that guy there." So we slopped through the mud, and it was freezing on top but you break through it. We went over a big, high bank of dirt and walked a footbridge, which we didn't know but later I found out we walked across the Mussolini Canal.

We walked across then he stopped and talked to somebody in the bank of dirt and the guy said to us, "Stay right behind me on this path because there's mines on either side." We got out to the field, about 25 or 30 yards, and he stops and he says, "Hey guys, you better be a little bit quieter and stay right behind me. You're going to an outpost. That was our front lines we just passed back there." We didn't even have our guns loaded! We didn't even know we were at the front lines!

We went on out, and we were in an old farmhouse. I guess we were quite a ways in front of the front lines. The Germans didn't even know we were there, but we found out in the night along a creek bank they were on the other side in that direction. In the daytime we got in the house and got in the back room and there was a German that came in and walked in the front room, but he didn't open the door to where we were at. So, they didn't know we were there. ...

It was two stories [tall], and at one time or another it had been hit with an artillery shell and there was a hole in the roof, and that's where the artillery guys were spotting with the artillery; they could see through that hole in the roof... It was made out of stone, and the room we were in there was only one door, and that one door faced the German lines. So, we figured we had to get a way out of there, and it took us all day to cut a hole big enough for us to crawl through. Built on the back of it, what we had to go into, was where they kept their animals, but it took us all day with the little picks we had to cut a hole big enough. That was the first day we were in the house. It was about one or two o'clock in the morning when we, the replacements, got out there. All those farmhouses, their barns where they kept the animals were built on the house.

We were on the way back, we ran out of rations, and that night there was another squad that came out to relieve us, but they didn't get out early enough so it got light before we got back. We were going back to a barn where they had food so we could get something to eat, and after we crossed the Mussolini Canal going back, we were going to the barn and that's when the artillery shells came it. I really didn't know I was hit. I thought it was concussion, and when we got in the building the sergeant said, "Are you okay?" I said, "I think I am. I just feel numb, but I can't find any holes in my clothes." He said, "Sit down and we'll fix you something to eat." So I sat down and I felt the blood running down my leg. He said, "Well, I already called for the medics for the other guy. You just get in the jeep and go with him."[369]

Sometimes the replacements could be the brunt of some practical jokes for the older veterans. One lieutenant who joined the regiment in March would eat his five-in-one rations with two of the older veterans back behind their foxhole line a short distance. After they were finished eating, paper wrappers and cardboard was lying about on the ground. One of the veterans told the new lieutenant, "You can't leave them out there because a plane will spot them and they'll come over strafing, or else they'll throw artillery on you." The two veterans picked up their belongings and one of them said, "I'm getting out of here," leaving the lieutenant with all the trash, who promptly dug a hole and buried it while the two veterans returned to their foxholes laughing.

Private David Stanford also joined the regiment on Anzio in March, after a long wait in northern Africa. On March 19, he wrote home:

Dear Friends –

Thought had best drop a few lines to let you all know I am alright and thinking of you often. Have been assigned a unit and at present we are in the Anzio Beachhead, of which you have no doubt heard. Sunny Italy is not what it is cracked up to be, so far all I have seen is mud and rain, although the last two days have had sunshine and you may be sure it has been appreciated.

The country itself is very beautiful and picturesque. The farms here seem to use mainly man power, at least so far I have not seen even one tractor or machine implements. In the distance we can see snow-capped mountains, and on the other side of them is Rome, where we hope to be some day before too long.

There isn't much more I can say at present. Surely hope this letter finds you all in good health and spirits, with that thought in mind I will close.[370]

Relief

On March 23, the 504th Parachute Infantry Regiment began embarking ships to leave the Anzio beachhead and return to Naples. The operation had been especially wearisome and costly for the regiment. In the eight weeks the regiment was on the beachhead, 120 paratroopers had been killed, 410 wounded, and 60 missing. The 504th PIR's 2nd Battalion was relieved by a unit of the 34th Division. "The relieving battalion was amazed at the length of the front covered, and there were not nearly enough holes and positions to accommodate the battalion's personnel and weapons such was the difference in size between the two organizations," the 2nd Battalion's narrative recorded.[371]

"You don't know quite how close we came to losing that one," John Schwartz of the 3rd Battalion said. "It was a very close thing. Those Krauts used to drop pamphlets down on us, telling us we would all be pushed back into the sea, and drowned. Darned, if there weren't a lot of days when I believed them." Francis Keefe also remembered the propaganda pamphlets being dropped when they were near the Factory. "During the day they would shoot propaganda leaflets over and it was for the British, and what it said on the leaflets was, 'While you are over here fighting the Yanks are going out with your wives and girlfriends.'"

John Schwartz, who was from Rochester, New York, joined the parachute troops for the extra $50 per month, so he could get married. "We did get that double pay. But you know, come to think of it, we earned it. Being a small outfit, we couldn't be relieved like a regular infantry unit, and they'd keep us up there, earning our double pay, sometimes for as long as 60 days at a stretch. I think my wife prayed me out of the war in safety.

"And listen, mister, when they tell you about there being atheists in foxholes, charge it off to malarkey. I was in there a long, long time, and tough as they come, I never saw one of those birds in all my three years away. It was always, 'Please God get us out of here' whenever they were in a jam. It's alright for these guys back home to say that isn't true, but you couldn't find a thorough-going atheist on the lines with the help of the whole FBI."[372]

Father Edwin Kozak

For the duration of World War II, the 504th Parachute Infantry Regiment had two extremely dedicated chaplains, who are loved, respected and appreciated by every single member who served in the regiment throughout its combat time. The two chaplains seemed to always come out of the woodwork when they were needed most, at the right place and at the right time. It seemed for both men that danger never fazed them, and they would go anywhere the normal infantryman would in even the worst situations.

Father Edwin J. Kozak hailed from Baltimore, Maryland. Before joining the 504th, Kozak had been the first Catholic priest in US Army history to complete parachute training. "Up there you're close to heaven," Father Kozak told the *Stars and Stripes*. "It's a most unusual way of coming to church." The combat jump into Salerno was his 12th parachute jump.[373] Even in the worst conditions, Father Kozak made an effort to gather all the Catholics in an open field to conduct mass. Private First Class Leroy Doyle of C Company served as his alter boy until he died of wounds at Anzio on February 10.[374]

When Father Kozak wasn't conducting mass, he may have been found at the aid station giving last rights or comforting wounded paratroopers. As for both chaplains, the men and their families were always forefront in their minds. To help comfort the families of these paratroopers, a story was written by Don Whitehead and published in newspapers alongside the news of the airborne invasion of Sicily. "The parents of these boys have nothing to worry about," Father Kozak told Don Whitehead. "Their sons are well taken care of wherever they are, even if we have to fly to them and jump from a plane to reach them. If they can't come to us, we go to them."[375]

Father Kozak often encouraged the men to write home every chance they got. James Gann remembered the first time he met Father Kozak: "He came walking up, I don't know about 2 o'clock in the morning, and he came walking up. I knew who he was, but I never had any contact with him. He just stood there and would talk just about anything you wanted to talk about, and just about the first thing he'd ask you when you met him was, 'Did you write home today.' If you didn't, he'd want to know why." If Father Kozak wasn't satisfied with the answer, he would say, "Do you need a pen and paper? I got plenty of it."

Father Kozak was a gifted letter-writer in his own regard, and one of the efforts he made, along with the Regimental Protestant Chaplain Delbert Kuehl, was to write letters home to the families of paratroopers from the unit who were killed or missing. When James Gann was trapped behind the German lines while on patrol in Italy and listed as missing in action, Kozak was the first one to notify his father by letter. Kozak told Gann's father not to worry, and that his son would turn back up. "Sure enough I did," Gann says. But Gann's father found the writing from Kozak such a comfort, that he kept the letter in his wallet until Gann returned home after the war.

James Gann felt that Father Kozak was "one in a million," and Kozak was one of the biggest factors that brought Gann to Christianity.[376]

After the regiment arrived in Naples, the men arrived in Bagnoli and were housed in a large complex of huge dormitories on the hill overlooking the coastal town. In the square of the complex, an awards ceremony was held with General Mark Clark presenting the medals and ribbons. Both Chaplain Kozak and Chaplain Kuehl were decorated with the Bronze Star Medal. Kozak's citation was for holding masses at the front lines and assisting the medical personal in both treating and evacuating causalities at the risk of his own safety.[377] Also at the ceremony, General Clark personally decorated the 3rd Battalion's guideon with the Presidential Unit Citation – the highest award a unit can receive – for their legendary stand in the British sector in February.

Chaplain Edwin Kozak (US Army Fort Knox via Frank Leon)

At Anzio, the regiment had succeeded in a situation for which it was not trained, equipped, or suited. The very nature of parachute troops was a nature of aggressive action, and shock warfare. This was not what they found in the static trenches of Anzio, and thus they were not mentally prepared. When the men landed on January 22, they felt they would be in Rome within a few days. Once they reached the Mussolini Canal and both sides started fortifying their positions, it became a stalemate and that tolled heavily on the mental state of the men. However, the individual's tremendous espirt de corps, initiative and adaptably made up for the difference. "All of the credit for the success of this operation should go to the individual soldier," William Sweet wrote. "His adaptability, initiative and understanding of the situation, along with great fighting heart, made the mission a success, as great as it was. Here we have seen a special unit used in a roll that it was untrained for, unequipped for, not mentally prepared for and placed in situations it knew little or nothing about and yet, through stoutness of heart and initiative, has done a job to the very best of its ability."[378]

13

THE HEALTHIEST, SHARPEST-LOOKING BUNCH OF MEN I'VE EVER SEEN

The amphibious landings of the 5th Army in and around Anzio had been long in the making, and Operation SHINGLE was a personal brainchild of British Prime Minster Winston Churchill. What was also was a brainchild of the Prime Minster was the 504th Parachute Infantry Regiment's participation in the operation.

While the regiment was in the mountains of Italy in November 1943, higher headquarters was already busy planning for an amphibious landing south of Rome, and at that time the regiment had already been earmarked for the duty of conducting an airborne landing in support of the operation to prevent the Germans from reinforcing the beach defenses, which the 5th Army assumed to be strong.

With the rest of the 82nd Airborne Division already departed for England to begin preparing for the invasion at Normandy, the 504th Parachute Infantry Regiment was under orders to leave the Italian theater in early January so that it too could participate in the invasion of northern France. When the men were relieved from one of their hardest slogs of the war at the end of December 1943, the men thought they were going to leave Italy for England, but shortly after the turn of the new year it became apparent that a ship ride to England to rejoin their 82nd Airborne Division was not going to be the case.

As January dawned, Field Marshall Harold Alexander signaled Prime Minster Winston Churchill that the usual shortages of men were plaguing the SHINGLE operation. Specifically, and by name, Alexander singled out the fact that they would not have the 504th Parachute Infantry Regiment at their disposal for the operation, and that General Dwight Eisenhower was reluctant to press for their retention in Italy; he further stated that the use of a British parachute brigade was impossible as it was in action on the line and there were no forces with which to effect its relief and refitting in time for the operation due to their infantry shortage. There was also concern about the inexperience of this unit in that it had no operational experience in air-landings. With the commitments of the British parachute brigade firm, this left the 504th PIR as the only other parachute unit in the theater, and the emigration of the 504th from the Mediterranean Theater meant losing the ability of a parachute assault in support of the beach landing.[379]

This is when Prime Minster Winston Churchill personally intervened to keep the 504th in Italy for the purpose of parachuting into the SHINGLE operation. On January 3, 1944 Prime Minster Churchill signaled British Field Marshall John Dill, the Senior British Representative on the Combined Chiefs of Staff in Washington, D.C., to press for the retention of the 504th. "Eisenhower is now with [General George] Marshall," Churchill cabled. "Will you appeal to them and let this 504th American Brigade do this one fine and critical job before they come home for 'Overlord'? It is so rarely that opportunities for decisive air action by paratroops present themselves, and it seems improvident to take them from the decisive point just when they might render exemplary and outstanding service… Let me know what happens."[380] General George Marshall, Chief of Staff of the US Army, agreed and shortly thereafter orders came down direct from the Combined Chiefs of Staff keeping the 504th in Italy for the operations at Anzio. When this decision was made, it was under the assumption that the Anzio operation would swiftly seize its assault objectives, after which "the unit would be released and could arrive in the United Kingdom by the 16th March," according to the report submitted by British Field Marshall Henry Wilson, then Commander in Chief in the Mediterranean.[381] When that stated date came, the regiment was still fighting on the frontline at Anzio, and would remain on the front an additional week past that date.

On or about February 1, when the regiment, along with the rest of the beachhead, was ordered into the deliberate defense, a reconsideration of all plans and resources occurred. It was decided that the current situation made it impossible to withdraw the 504th from the beachhead. A further extension of the regiment's attachment to the 5th Army was granted likely around mid-February. Field Marshall Wilson wrote around this time, "Further retention of the 504th Parachute Regiment had been granted by the Combined Chiefs of Staff until the April convoy, but we still could not guarantee their release on this date, until the situation had been reviewed."[382]

The shortage of men to complete the Anzio operation was commonly touted by veterans of the 504th PIR after the war for the failure of Operation SHINGLE to achieve its objective of breaking through to Rome in a timely manner; however, very few of them knew even after the war that the shortages of paratroops was the decisive reason for their extended presence in Italy after December 1943, when the 2nd British Parachute Brigade could not be relieved, and that a general shortage of infantry kept them on the line until March.

When, on January 22, Operation SHINGLE first came to pass it was the beginning of a 62-day slog for the 504th. Prime Minster Churchill was immediately unhappy with the way the regiment was utilized writing in his 1951 memoir that "this sacrifice [of lobbying for their retention in Italy] was wasted."[383] On February 6, 1944, while the regiment was dodging artillery shells at the Factory and on the Mussolini Canal, Churchill cabled Field Marshall Henry Wilson and asked why the 504th was not employed "as proposed" in a parachute mission. Churchill then received word from Wilson "that the 504th Paratroop Regiment was seaborne and not airborne because of a last-minute decision by General Clark."[384]

The parachute drop of the 504th Parachute Infantry in support of SHINGLE was long-planned at the strategic level but down at the regiment's level all the preparations were relatively fast-paced and hasty, as the regiment was understrength both in men and ordnance, and the sudden cancelation of the parachute drop in favor for the amphibious landing threw the regiment into even further haste to account for the change in plans. Interestingly, General Mark Clark's 1950 memoir only contains one reference to the 504th's retention. That reference was in regards to the initial extension granted in November 1943 for the mountain campaign.[385] Clark fails to mention the fact the regiment's further extension in Italy was for the purpose of the parachute assault at Anzio; he also does not discuss his reasoning behind canceling the parachute mission.

In the summer of 1944, Field Marshall Wilson submitted a "Report by the Supreme Commander, Mediterranean to the Combined Chiefs of Staff on the Italian Campaign: 8 January 1944 to 10 May 1944." Here, Wilson omits the fact the decision to cancel the parachute mission of the 504th was last minute, and also does not mention who made that decision. He claimed, "This plan however was abandoned as likely to give early warning of our intentions to the enemy. Moreover, the place chosen for the drop was so close to the planned objectives of the 1st British Division, that the hazardous mission appeared to offer too few advantages to offset the risks, amongst which was that of danger from our own antiaircraft fire, should this drop and the main assault be launched together and be attacked by enemy aircraft."[386] A multi-volume Fifth Army history started in late 1944 states the exact same reasoning. This reasoning, however, is quite different than what the men of the regiment were told. The 1945 regimental history *Devils in Baggy Pants* records that the men were told of heavy German opposition on the drop zone, with bayonets pointed skyward, was the reason for the cancelation.[387]

Both the 504th and the 509th Parachute Battalion were committed as regular infantry on the Anzio beachhead, and with the continued engagement of the 2nd British Parachute Brigade in the mountains, this left no parachute units not engaged in combat duty in the entire Mediterranean Theater. This presented several problems on a strategic level. One being the fact that, with the combat commitment of all airborne units, there was no airmobile reserve in the theater if a crisis were to arise. However, the biggest problem of a strategic nature which was felt by the regiment directly was the acquisition of qualified replacements. The regiment was understrength by 122 enlisted men even before entering the Anzio beachhead, and the 62-day grind proved to cut the regiment down even further as the influx of qualified replacements could not keep up. According to statistics compiled by Captain Edson Mattice in 1945 from company morning reports, 153 paratroopers were killed or declared missing at Anzio and 359 were wounded - a total of 512 casualties. Mattice's statistics, however, did not count the casualties sustained by the 3rd Battalion from February 1 to the 16th during their attachment to British forces at the Factory. When factoring in these battle casualties, the total rises to 624 killed, missing, and wounded. This total is still not fully reflective either, as it accounts only for battle casualties and does not factor into account those removed from the line for sicknesses, which was likely as numerous as the men lost in battle casualties. The fighting at Anzio was the regiment's costliest campaign in terms of battle casualties, accounting for approximately 17% of the unit's total wartime combat casualties.[388]

Milton O'Quinn of Company G was killed during the 3rd Battalion's stand at The Factory on Feb. 10, 1944. (Ferne O'Quinn)

This type of extended employment left the unit in their costliest campaign with little ability to replace lost personnel. Some historians may argue that the unit was used to operating under such a handicap as that of the lack of qualified replacements. However, it should be remembered that after the costly Sicily mission, the unit's replacements were from the EGBs, which were already in theater, allowing for quick replacement of casualties. In later fights in 1944 on the continent, replacement pipelines were much faster and shorter in distance than at Anzio. Large replacement depots in the United Kingdom served as pools for volunteers for parachute duty, and the 82nd Airborne Division's own jump school in England provided a source for qualification. This shortened the supply line of personnel, and rather than awaiting qualified replacements to come from the States, as the regiment had to do at Anzio, they could recruit, train, qualify and transfer for duty replacements all within Europe.

Towards the end of what would be the 504th's time in Italy, Major General Ridgeway continued to appeal to General Clark for the return of the 504th to the division so it would be ready for the invasion at Normandy. Finally, Ridgeway turned to the same person Field Marshall John Dill lobbied on behalf of Churchill for the retention of the regiment in Italy: he appealed directly to General Marshall in Washington, D.C., and through his intervention secured the return of the regiment to 82nd Airborne Division control and a swift trip to England.[389] But it was too late: even with the two 'sizable' groups of replacements from the States who joined the regiment at Anzio, it was impossible for the unit to rest and be brought up to full fighting strength in time for the Normandy invasion.

As the men prepared for the impending move to England, they were free to go into Naples. David Stanford, a replacement which had been on Anzio for 25 days, wrote home just after they returned to Naples.

March 27, 1944

Dear friends –

As I sit here writing this letter can glance up and look out over the sea. Sun is shining and is an ideal spring day. Can see a couple islands far off on the horizon. Behind me is a city, built upon the green hills of Italy, under me is the marble floor of a one-time college. Yes, all is quiet and serene. Would not know there is a war being fought.

Have just returned from the Red Cross where I filled myself with ice cream and cookies. Would not have believed it had I not seen it with my own eyes.

Of all the things the fellows here are having a political argument. Some for Roosevelt and some against, but soon the conversation will swing to the favorite subject of girls who were left behind and of night spots, mostly famous ones that most of the fellow have visited at one time or another. Then soon will be on the topic of what is going on in the old home town at the present hour, either you're getting up or going to bed, and how nice it would be to sit at the table across from our loved ones. Yes, it goes on for hours like this.[390]

When David Stanford joined I Company, he joined a company which had been through the ringer at Anzio, and had suffered heavily. The men soon began organizing a company party, amidst their other trips to clubs and bars which entertained the thirsts of the American troops crowded in the city of Naples.

Members of the 3rd Battalion 81mm Mortar Platoon on the steps of their billets in Bagnolli, just outside Naples. Lt. Allen McClain sits at the front far left, and his platoon sergeant George Suggs at the front far right.[391] (Clark family)

A few short days before the company's party, Francis Keefe and Leo Muri, attached at the hip as always, went to the Five O'clock Club in Naples with 1st Sergeant Odom.

"I'm going," Keefe announced.

"Where are you going?" Odom asked.

"Going down to see my brother," Keefe said, thinking of finding his brother George and his Military Police unit.

"Get back early," Odom suggested.

Keefe stayed with his brother's Military Police unit for two and a half or three days while officially being a wanted man when his status was changed to absent without leave.

When Keefe returned the day before the company party, he was immediately to be made the charge of quarters, meaning that he would not be able to attend the party despite the fact that he was one of the few men from the company who had made it all the way through Anzio without a scratch. During the night, the men came in "half shot," Keefe recalled. "They had a nice time." The company was billeted in a building with large room, and the men were sleeping on the floor using their blankets to make themselves comfortable.

In addition to finding out he was going to be the charge of quarters when he returned, he also discovered that Captain Fred Thomas had transferred and taken command of the company in his absence. As Keefe was soon to find out, Captain Thomas did not take kindly to Keefe going absent without leave. "The next morning, I got off duty and all the sudden about two or three hours later they said, 'You're wanted up in the orderly room.' It was just another big room. When I am going up there I see this guy in uniform with a rifle. I said, *this don't look good*. I went in and they told me, 'Get your stuff together. You're going with the soldier there.' So that's what happened." Keefe was taken to an Italian prison which was being run by Lieutenant Donald Holmes, formally of I Company but had been wounded at Anzio and recently appointed as the regiment's Police and Prison Officer.

Francis Keefe was taken down to the row of cells that was below ground, and found George Silvasey, the regiment's prized boxer, and bunked in his cell. Someone took Keefe, but not Silvasey, out to where Lieutenant Holmes was to lead the prisoners in close order drill.

When Lieutenant Holmes turned around and saw Keefe, he came up to him.

"What company you with?" the lieutenant inquired.

"I Company," Keefe answered.

"What platoon," Holmes asked.

"Lieutenant Blankenship's platoon," said Keefe.

"Go inside and make yourself comfortable," Holmes ordered.[392]

Meanwhile, the rest of the regiment was preparing for the ship ride to England. Many of the men were still in the hospital, including Lieutenant Roy Hanna. After he was moved from the critical ward into the general population, he was put in a bed next to Lieutenant Holmes, who would soon leave for his duties in the prison. When Hanna found out about the impending move of the regiment to England, he phoned Lieutenant Colonel Freeman and "insisted I not be left behind. Someone came for me in a jeep and took me directly to the *Capetown Castle*. I was not assigned to anyone and so reported to no one on the ship and so just moved around visiting and exercising."[393]

Missing from the ship, however, when it pulled out of the docks of Naples on April 11 was Lieutenant Colonel Freeman. He, along with 104 others from the 504th PIR, were transferred Stateside to join the 515th Parachute Infantry Regiment. Freeman and several others, however, eventually ended up teaching at the Parachute School at Fort Benning. Freeman was promoted to colonel and eventually assumed command of a parachute training regiment.

Just three days before the regiment left Italy behind it and closed that chapter of their storied history, Freeman had come to Hanna in the hospital and delivered him a letter which Hanna was extremely proud to receive.

HEADQUARTERS THIRD BATTALION
504TH PARACHUTE INFNATRY
APO 469 U S ARMY

8 April 1944

To: 1ST Lt. Roy M Hanna

I wish to commend you for your outstanding work while under my command. The Machine Gun Platoon, which you trained and lead in combat contributed greatly to the success of the Battalion in each of our operations, especially at Campania, Italy and at the Anzio Beachhead, Italy.

Your action at Carraceto, Italy when you took over a disorganized Company and lead an attack against overwhelming enemy odds to the effect that your mission was accomplished although you were severely wounded was an inspiration to myself and every man in the Battalion.

I am proud to have had you under my command and regret that I cannot have you as a Company Commander in my next Command.

(Signed)
Leslie G. Freeman
Lt. Col. 504th Prcht Inf.
Commanding.[394]

Lieutenant Hanna was not the only one to join the regiment as they boarded the *Capetown Castle* and sailed out of the docks. Francis Keefe and the rest of the men in the Italian prison were also marched down to the *Capetown Castle* to stay with the regiment.

They must have thought I was a bad character. When we were leaving, they marched us down through Naples to the ship. As we were approaching the ship, all the sudden the guys told them they were getting some of our men back. They all cheered! I think [Captain Fred] Thomas went nuts because nobody else said anything. I got court-martialed the second day at sea and [Major Julian] Cook was there and Thomas whispered something in his ear so he turned around and said, "You got to be a good garrison soldier as well as a combat soldier." I don't know what Thomas whispered in his ear. So he said, "I sentence you to a $50 fine and a thirty-day restriction." You know, they could have done that way back before we left and I would have been restricted to the company instead of the prison.

I got orders from Thomas - they sent orders - "Captain Thomas wants you to clean the latrine every day." So, I went down to see what the latrine looked like – well, I knew what it looked like – and there was a British sailor. He was cleaning the latrine so I said to him, "Do you need a hand?" He said, "No, we take care of this, Yank." I said, "Oh, that's good." So I went outside where you could see the staircases coming down, where the officers would come down, I sat there and watched who would be coming down. It was about the last three days. The afternoon it was my time to be finished with that, they had a regimental inspection. Nothing out of the ordinary, all had to have our clothes, our combat suits ironed and whatnot. But I had big P's on mine. When you get into the prison they put P's on it so they know you're a prisoner. They gave me two pair of those. My barracks bag was taken and thrown in with all the rest of the barracks bags so that was the only uniform I had. We're all in formation around the ship, and as they came down we had one guy Sergeant Porter – you'd point your finger at him, he'd swing at you, he was goosey – so I was in the second row... and all the sudden a British soldier with one of our officers came past. One of our officers put his leg out and goosed Porter and Porter swung at the British officer. We never had another formation after that.

Captain Thomas called me up on deck. "You finished cleaning down there?" I said, "Yes, sir." He said, "Let's go down and see what kind of a job you did." We went down there, and that guy [British sailor] does a terrific job, and he said, "Okay, go up on deck now."

On April 22, ten days after they left Italy, the *Capetown Castle* pulled into the docks of Liverpool, England. Francis Keefe recalled:

When we pulled into Liverpool, all the guys ran over to the one side of the ship. They had to go, "Get back on the other side of the ship!" The ship looked like it was going to turn over. You know, you get a couple thousand guys it's pretty bad. That night we're coming off the ship and it was foggy and rainy and we got to the train station. We got onto the trains but somebody forgot to tell them that I had my P's on my coveralls. As we get off the train station, there's a formation. I think General Ridgeway was there, and all the high command. They all started to laugh. They sent word down, "What is the meaning of this you have a man in there with all P's on." Captain Thomas, he went into a fit. So he had to report back up the line to them and they were all laughing. He looked at me and said, "You cock knocker, you got me again." So then we marched into camp.[395]

The foggy and rainy weather which greeted the men of the 504th Parachute Infantry Regiment was indicative of the next several months. The train station the men arrived at was the train station at Leicester, a thriving metropolis approximately an hour's drive northwest of London in the heart of England. The regiment marched to the small suburb of Evington and found their new home in the English countryside of open, lush green fields with pruned grass, intermingled with small, dividing hedgerows along a road known as "Shady Lane." The tent city which the regiment would call home was erected on a golf course.

Lt. Ed Kennedy of Company G on the golf course that was the home of the 504th. Two tents can be seen in the background. (Author's collection)

Western civilization was not something the men had experienced in quite a long time, and they soon fell in love with the cleanliness and the hospitality of the people. Every week numerous passes were issued to the ranks to enjoy furloughs to London or elsewhere on the British isle. Roy Hanna and Captain

Henry Keep twice buddied up and took leave in London together. Captain Keep was a fellow Pennsylvanian who hailed from the prominent Philadelphia Biddle Family. "His aunt (I believe) headed up the Red Cross Center in London at the time. She got us two great tickets to *Arsenic and Old Lace* – quite a treat," Hanna noted.

Lt. Ed Kennedy on pass in London, visiting a historic icon. (Author's collection)

Lieutenant Hanna was still on light duty from his wound, and was still unassigned. A morning report showed him as being the executive officer of Headquarters Company, but he conducted no duties and really reported to nobody but himself. His favorite thing to do was to play Bridge with two of the doctors, Captains William Kitchin and Hyman Shapiro, and their communications officer, Lieutenant Charles Snyder. Typically, Hanna and Shapiro constituted one team, and Kitchin and Snyder constituted the other.

The four officers would sit around, talk, play Bridge and drink Hanna's concoction of vodka and grapefruit juice. "We got the grapefruit out of the kitchen in #10 cans (3 quarts) free," Hanna wrote, "and vodka was the cheapest thing available at that time." The game of Bridge was a friendly one and usually ended with Hanna and Shapiro winning a few Pounds here and there: "Played for a penny a point and made some money… We had two great Doctors in Kitchin and Shapiro and everyone thought they were great."[396]

The month of June 1944 was a big month for the Allies in the fight against Nazi Germany. On the Italian front, the 5th of June saw the fall of Rome to General Clark's 5th Army troops after they began the breakout from the Anzio Beachhead on May 23. In mid-April, shortly after the 504th PIR had left Italy, one of Lieutenant Payton Elliott's friends who was serving at Anzio with the 3rd Division wrote Elliott a letter which finally caught up to him in England. "Still here and expect to be here until we get to Rome," he wrote Lieutenant Elliott. "I guess you are having a good time wherever you are. Things are about the same. I don't think it [will] stay that way long. How was [sic] things the last time all was on the front lines? We are back up now. If you went to England, I guess you are getting ready for the big show which will come off soon… As you know there's not much to write from the battle front. About all there is to say in letters is about the war. I'll be glad when this is over and we don't even have to think about it."[397]

The day after Rome fell, the big show to which Elliott's friend referred came off in Normandy, France on June 6. After the Normandy Invasion, training for the 504th Parachute Infantry increased. On June 7, Lieutenant Roy Hanna was assigned as the executive officer of G Company. "We began training and jumping again," Hanna recalled. There had been several other personnel shifts. G Company was now commanded by Captain Fred E. Thomas. "I remember being attached to… Capt. Thomas on several occasions through Sicily and Italy and knew him to be a strong disciplinarian, good leader and respected as a company commander," Roy Hanna recalled of his new company commander. "I remember him welcoming me as his executive officer while we were in England."[398]

The men followed the progress of the war, but rather than from being there, it was from newspapers and radio broadcasts. There were several large maps through camp where the latest offensives and advances were pinned. One of these was inside the 2nd Battalion's command tent. Lieutenant Chester Garrison explains:

My battalion C.P. was a sidewall tent on ground that slanted upwards from the entrance to the rear, where I had a desk with a field phone. My sergeant, Russell Stevens, was similarly equipped. Between us hung a bulletin board for notices and a detailed map of Europe with red-headed pins indicating front lines. Stevens and I had bought a table radio for keeping up with news as well as popular music on the US Army station. Corporal Abraham Bloomfield, my mumbling typist from the Bronx, had a small table with the portable typewriter that he took into combat. I regret not having been able after the war to locate him in New York.

There was also a phone switchboard with an operator. The runners for the four companies and my New Mexico Indian jeep driver congregated near the entrance. I was regularly on the telephone with Louis Hauptfliesch, who had become regimental adjunct...

My parents could never comprehend the variety of an adjunct's duties. I explained that he was the go-between among the four companies, between the four staff members, between the battalion and the regiment. He was the spokesman for the battalion commander. He was the encyclopedia and general directory. He was responsible for the battalion in parades and for knowing what was happening in the aid station. He supervised the paperwork of the battalion, including promotions and awards. The most important statistic he had to submit was the morning report about the number and disposition of the personnel, some 500 bodies. Supplies depended on it. He was personnel officer.[399]

Garrison was initially very unhappy when he was made the battalion's adjunct in August 1943 on Sicily. It was an assignment which ripped him away from leading a rifle platoon in the thick of battle. However, he made the most of his new assignment, and it became his chief objective to build rapport with as many of the officers in the battalion as possible, to create an environment of shared understanding and cohesion between the staff and the company commanders and platoon leaders. This almost came crashing down when Edward Wellems became the battalion's commander in England. Wellems was not well-liked by the officers of the 2nd Battalion, and, as he told Garrison in later life, it was one of the darkest days of his life when Colonel Tucker informed him he was to take command of the 2nd Battalion as he knew many of the battalion's officers had feelings about him. The enlisted men were also not fond of him when he first took command, writing that he was a stickler for military discipline, courtesy and appearance, and not one to give compliments where they were not due. The regiment may have been known for its appearance and combat discipline, but it was not renowned for military courtesies.

One of the things Garrison tried his best to do was to build good rapport with the staff and the company commanders. Wellems, by his leadership style and personality, undermined those efforts. Wellems, who possessed a biting sarcasm, could often speak clippingly and dismissively; and as they soon found out could have an occasional flair for public shaming which soon greatly angered Captain Walter van Poyck when his company was publicly singled out for an indiscretion. Lieutenant Garrison remembers that the first time Wellems visited the S-1 Section after taking command he came into his CP tent and "he was cold, controlled, expressionless and factual. We had no personal exchange... When he left, I imagined that the tent, like the enlisted men, sagged. The first meeting between him and the officers of the battalion went no better."

Wellems proved to be a good combat leader, and the officers became able to work with him after a few months in England and Garrison's rapport-building was not terribly disrupted as time continued; despite this, however, there was still friction at times.[400] During the Battle of the Bulge, Captain Victor Campana, who at that time was the battalion's operations officer, complained of "the neglect of the battalion commander to continually acquaint members of his staff with the current situation… Had any accident befallen the battalion commander, the battalion as a whole could have suffered because the staff members were ignorant of the situation."[401]

Later in the war, Garrison got to know Wellems better as a person. Eventually, after getting to see sides of Wellems that most did not see, Garrison came to feel that his gruff exterior personality was "a cover-up for a sensitive and considerate personality… I do not know how far he could establish rapport with other people, but I was honored to have his friendship, and I gave him my full support."[402]

The 3rd Battalion was also going through a change of command with the departure of Lieutenant Colonel Leslie Freeman for the USA. Major Julian A. Cook was to take command of the battalion while they were in England. For Cook, this was to be his first combat command in the regiment, although he had been with the unit since it left the States. Freeman had left big shoes to fill. T. Moffatt Burriss was a company commander when Cook arrived to his new command. There were apprehensions about the new commander, Burriss remembered. "You had different opinions from the different commanders," he remembered. "Colonel Freeman was more calm and collective than Cook… There was apprehensions."[403]

The regiment occasionally paraded, and on one occasion Lieutenant Thomas Utterback was marching in his proper place behind their new commander, Major Julian Cook. "It was a morale builder, especially for the lonesome newly acquired recruits," Utterback wrote. "As S-4 (supply) staff, I was in my proper place behind Major Cook in parade position. Running across the parade ground came a captain of Colonel Tucker's regimental staff. He ran directly at me and ordered me to follow him. Away from the ceremony, he said that the 82nd needed our service weapons (machine guns and mortars) because so many had been lost when dropped into Normandy. I was to gather up all of the 504th's weapons, get them to the airport, and into a plane to be flown to southern England. As I delivered the load to an officer loading up a glider for delivery to Normandy, I was a very happy soldier. Maybe we were in reserve, but they couldn't plan on using us—not without weapons."[404] Utterback was correct, but that would only keep the 504th Parachute Infantry away from combat for so long.

The reaction to missing the Normandy Invasion was mixed within the regiment. "I am still in England," Lieutenant Edward Kennedy wrote home after news of the invasion broke, "so there is no need to worry about me for the present. A lot of us are sore 'cause we didn't get to go in but glad also. Our regimental commander tried hard but it was no dice. Our division, the 82nd, is really doing a grand job from all reports – even without us."[405]

The training continued to intensify with field problems and training jumps. The men knew they were going to be returning to combat eventually. One exercise was a nighttime parachute jump with a follow-on objective to attack an 'enemy' headquarters. Another problem saw the men on the moors upon which Sir Arthur Conan Doyle set his famous Sherlock Holmes novel *The Hounds of Baskerville*; and, true to inspiration, at night steam would seep out of the mossy ground so thick the men could not see each other, forcing them to have to hold each other's shoulders as they negotiated the problem. Additionally, two paratroopers from each company were sent to a British intelligence station in Nottinghamshire, located in an old royalty estate known as "Robin on the Pit Top," to attend an intelligence school. The students trained in patrolling techniques and other such trades in the adjacent woods.[406]

Lieutenant Thomas Utterback remembered one training jump the regiment conducted, this time at twilight.

The drop was with the last light at sunset. The troops, under full battle load, were to march several miles after the drop, and after a short rest to be on a battle line by daybreak. Each battalion was allowed a jeep and trailer for supply of basic ammunition. I was not to drop, but was to join the troops at the drop zone and march along with them. Well, things went as planned, but as I passed the Mortar Platoon the soldiers complained of the fast pace of the march while they carried heavy mortars, 60 to 75 pounds each for base plate or tube. I said, "Well, put them on top of the trailer." Thus loaded, I went on ahead to a spot where I could pull off the road until the troops caught up. When they did, out of the marching column came a tall, lanky officer with stars on his helmet: General Gavin.

"What the hell is going on here?" he inquired.

I said, "General, I'm not trying to fight the problem; this is what I'd do in actual combat."

"Well," he said, "just give those things back to the men and have them carry them!"

I answered, "General, I can't do that, those men are going to be pooped."

The general said, "Lieutenant, I am not asking you to do it...I'm TELLING you."

So....[407]

On one occasion, the regiment paraded with British paratroopers through the village of Oadby, nearby to their encampment, in a spectacle observed by the residents. Corporal James Gann was in a tower watching the parade with Colonel Reuben Tucker as his regiment marched past. "I was up in the tower guarding the flag, I'll put it that way. I don't know who this English guy was and Colonel Tucker was up there and the guy said – the 504 was going by – and he said, 'That is beautiful. Not a hair out of place.' The colonel said, 'They wouldn't dare.'"[408]

While the training increased after the invasion, the men continued to enjoy themselves that summer. Around town, there were numerous pubs to satisfy the men's drinking. Don Zimmerman remembered, "They opened up at noon and then they'd shut down at two or three o'clock, then they'd open up again in the evening for a few hours." This was a most popular destination for the troopers to fraternize with the civilian population – mostly the girls. Many nights the troopers would be invited into the homes of the parents of these young ladies for dinner. Don Zimmerman was invited into a number of houses and carried fond memories of the warmness of the English.

Overall, the unit was well-behaved. Sometimes there would be confrontations with the local Military Police, as most paratroopers made little note of the orders of non-paratroopers, be they officers or Military Policemen. So, to combat the problem they organized a program where a paratrooper would accompany an MP. "That way," Zimmerman said, "a drunken paratrooper will listen to his own before he'll listen to an MP. I can remember working it on the street many a night."[409] Although problems did occur, the unit had very few court-martials.

In July 1944, Lord Gillot, the mayor of Leicester, organized a party for the troops of the 504th at the de Montfort Hall. He invited 500 men of the regiment, and representatives from all the 504th's three battalions were present for the party and dancing. The local newspaper in Leicester, the *Leicester Mercury*, then sent the photograph and an article about the party to newspapers in all 50 States and explained how much they enjoyed the presence of the American paratroopers. The letter sent out by the Mercury's editor, H.W. Bourne, reads in part:

> *This party, given by the Lord Mayor of Leicester, is one of many happy occasions which afford citizens opportunity to share the good fellowship of our splendid guests from the United States and to repay in some measure the kindness the British people have received at your hands.*
>
> *We have the greatest admiration for the American boys.*[410]

James Gann was a quiet Texan who did not enjoy the large parties like many of his comrades, and frequented an out-of-the-way pub called The Moon where he, like many others in the regiment, would meet his eventual wife Florence Shenstone. "I didn't like going to crowded places, and I found a pub that was just a civilian pub and I started going in there and mingling with some people, you know, and these two girls came in one day and one was my wife-to-be and her friend. I never got to talk to her; she was in the British Land Army and she was only in on weekends. I finally got to talk to her and we ended up getting married. Best thing that ever happened to me."[411]

James Gann back in England in 1945. Gann would survive all the campaigns of the 504th in World War II. (James Gann)

Lieutenant Reneau Breard met Anne Goodman, and they would marry in 1945. The only downfall was she lived quite a long distance from camp, which meant that Breard "had a long and fast run back to the coffee shop near the railroad station to make the last 2-1/2-ton truck back to camp. Missed it several times." Another man in the company, Albert Clark, "had it easy," Breard wrote, because his wife-to-be lived so close to their encampment on Shady Lane.[412]

In late August, James Gann and Florence "Pat" Shenstone were still seeing each other. Gann would return to England and they would be wed on November 7, 1944.

England

August 23, 1944

Dear Aunt:

I thought as I have nothing else to do it would be a good time to write you a few lines. To see if I can get a letter from you. It has been a long time since I have got any mail from you. But I guess you have been too busy to write.

Well, it is wet here in the ETO tonight, and a bit cool. It has been raining for the past three or four days, but that isn't unusual for England. It has rained most of the time we have been here. Rain or no rain I like it here better than Italy or Africa.

I had a letter from dad yesterday, and he said everything was about normal there at home. He wrote like he was lonesome with the girls gone from home and Jr. working. Boy, I sure would like to see him. It has been two years since I last saw him. It doesn't seem like it has been that long, but when you get to thinking about it, it's a heck of a long time...

Pat and I are still getting along swell. I saw her last night and she was just as sweet as ever. I don't know what I will do when we move some place where I can't see her. I see her almost every day. It only takes me about ten minutes to ride from here down to her house on my bicycle. If we stay here much longer I will have to get me a new set of tires.

Well, I guess I better bring this to an ending and get some work done or it will be time to get the prisoners up and no work sheets made out. I know they will be awfully mad at me if I didn't have anything for them to do, the sergeant also.

Bye for now, and answer soon.

Lots of love,

Jim[413]

    That day of separation which Gann wrote about was not far off when he typed the letter to his aunt on August 23, which was a busy month for the regiment as they prepared to re-enter combat on the Continent. On August 24, the 504th executed a regimental field problem which included a parachute jump. First Lieutenant Payton Elliott, a quiet 23-year-old Alabaman and veteran of the regiment's Italian campaigns, was standing in the door of his C-47 poised to jump into the problem when he received the green jumping light too early. Lieutenant Elliott's parachute became entangled with those of the equipment bundles. Elliott was able to fight his way from underneath a bundle, but landed on his back making a "terrific 35-mile to 40-mile-per-hour lick at the ground," Elliott later described, receiving serious injuries. Both of his ankles were almost totally crushed and his "first lumbar was broken," he said, "and about six or eight other vertebrae were mashed in like an accordion." Elliott was immediately sent to the hospital where casts were applied to both legs, and nine days later a full body cast was applied. After evacuation to the States, Elliott's body cast was removed and he remained in a steel back brace for nearly four months. Subsequently, Elliott was in-and-out of hospitals for two years and ten months; he was required to undergo nine surgeries as a result of his injuries. His left ankle was fused, his entire right foot was fused back together, and one leg was permanently an inch shorter than the other as a result of the accident.[414]

After the war, Payton Elliott returned to Birmingham and began working for New England Mutual Life Insurance Company. Elliott had a love for football, which he played through high school and for a year in college, and while in his 30s he refereed high school football. Although he continued to have terrible back pain associated with his war injuries, he had a long and successful career with New England Mutual, where his record of sales for the year 1961 went unbeaten for many years. He retired in 1986 before passing away four years later at the age of 69.

Also in August 1944, the division paraded before a contingent of general officers, including the Supreme Allied Commander General Eisenhower. "Except for the 504," Chester Garrison wrote, "all the paraders had been in D-Day invasion; now we displayed our united might. We were proven candidates for involvement on the Continent. I had now been 2nd Battalion adjunct for four commanders in a year. I had overcome my initial resentment of my assignment and accepted my status. Learning the complications of the duty made the job easier and more productive. True, I was less exposed to front-line involvement, but certainly I was not out of danger. I was the sole survivor of the staff I had joined, and some positions had changed several times. I believe I had good rapport with many, if not most, of the battalion officers. I began to feel like an older uncle."[415]

Lieutenant Garrison would continue to feel that way as September came, and the regiment re-entered combat on the Continent, and the ranks of his 'old' friends continued to dwindle. Some of the old men continued to be replaced my new faces within the regiment, with a new batch of replacements coming in August shortly before the coming combat mission. One of them was 18-year-old Walter Hughes, who would join I Company as a wireman/SCR300 radio operator. Hughes had nothing but respect for the veterans who came from Italy, and when he asked about staying alive, Ed Hahn, one of the other wiremen, told him to stay by their new company commander Captain T. Moffatt Burriss because, Hahn said, "he's bullet-proof."[416]

Shortly after joining the company, he wrote home to his mother that "I am in a regular outfit at last and it is [the] best parachute outfit that was ever formed. It made history in the beginning of the war and is making it now. Well, how's everything there in God's country? I hope everybody is in the best of health and especially you… We had a train ride during the day here and the country reminds me of upstate N.Y. It is cold here and we're living in tents but I like it though."[417]

The first days of September, the regiment practiced loading and unloading equipment at the airfields, and on September 15 the men of the regiment found themselves enclosed in marshaling areas. Briefings began, and a new mission had been hatched and its name now etched into history: it was called Operation MARKET.

Several prominent officers of the 3rd Battalion just prior to a jump in England. They are: Lt. Robert Blankenship, Lt. Charles Snyder, unknown, Lt. Roy Hanna, Lt. Bernard Karnap, Lt. Moffatt Burriss, and Lt. Thomas Utterback. All would play vital roles in the coming Holland operation. Lt. Charles Snyder would be killed. (Moffatt Burriss)

14

JUMP DAY

September the 17th dawned in the marshaling areas. Part of the regiment was marshaled at Cottesmore Airfield, and others at Spanhoe Airfield. The day began as rainy and overcast, but soon the sun began to break through. The mission was on. The men drew parachutes and began to load themselves down with equipment. Morris Holmstock had joined the regiment at Anzio, and was preparing for his first combat jump. His platoon sergeant, William "Knobby" Walsh, a veteran of the jumps in Sicily and Salerno, advised Holmstock not to jump with his M-1 in his hands. "He said, 'Put that thing in a griswold [bag].' I said, 'Hell, no. I'm going to carry it in my hands so I have it when I land. He said, 'If you jump with that in your hand I'll make you a PFC.'"[418]

First Sergeant Kogut recalled, "We were seasoned in Africa and Italy and when we jumped into Holland, we carried only ammunition and weapons. The replacements asked us why we didn't carry the other stuff and we said, 'There'll be plenty on the ground.'" Kogut was referring to the equipment of casualties.[419]

Walter Hughes, also about to make his first combat jump, was loaded down with communication gear and food, recalling one of the veterans telling him to take as many rations as he could. When Hughes was sent to England, he was originally supposed to be assigned to a parachute field artillery unit, and subsequently had no weapon. He was told to go to supply and draw "any God-damned thing you can shoot. So, I remembered seeing the movies of James Cagney shooting the Tommy gun. I said if the Germans are gonna shoot at me, I want a gun that's gonna shoot a lot of bullets back."

For rations, Walter Hughes had packed extra K-rations under his reserve 'chute, and a can of orange juice in his jump jacket. In his pants pocket he had more K-rations and a brownie box camera, the latter something rarely carried by paratroops. For ammunition, he carried four magazines for his Thompson on his harness. He had a reel of communication wire clipped to his belt, as well as a bowie-style knife and a first aid kit. To top it off, he had a leg bag, which was a large duffle-bag strapped to the leg of the jumper containing large equipment. In his leg bag, Hughes had the SCR300 radio, extra batteries, a long antenna and a couple of sound-powered telephones.[420]

That afternoon, the men began climbing aboard the C-47s. At 11:04, the churchgoers that Sunday were just getting ready to end service when it was suddenly interrupted by the drone of hundreds upon hundreds of aircraft in the sky above them. For almost the past five months, England had been 'home away from home' to the men of the 504th Parachute Infantry Regiment, and many troopers had found their wives and as they crossed over one last time, some men wondered if they would ever see it again. Most of the replacements were eager to see action. The older veterans just knew they were going on another mission and were contemplating if they would beat that law of averages this time or not. Replacement or veteran, they all had a one-way ticket to Holland to participate in Operation MARKET GARDEN, a joint airborne-ground offensive.

Lieutenant Roy Hanna briefly describes the mission:

The main purpose was to establish a path across the Netherlands to allow the rapid advancement of troops. The 101st Airborne Division's mission was to secure all bridges and highways in the Eindhoven area. The 82nd Airborne Division's mission was to secure the bridges across the Maas River, clear the highway leading to Nijmegen, and secure the bridges across the Waal River (Upper Rhine), and the British and Polish paratroopers to secure the roads and rivers around Arnhem.

The mission involved the entire Allied Airborne Command. On September 17, 1944, 4,700 aircraft departed from 24 separate airfields in England and headed out over the English Channel.

The operation had begun in the predawn morning when 1,400 Allied bombers had taken off to pound German antiaircraft positions and German troop concentrations in the "Market Garden" area. The next group was the 18 planes carrying the pathfinders. Following this were paratroopers and glider men packed in 2,023 troop transport planes and 478 gliders. 800 fighter planes flew escort.

I would have loved to have been on the ground and seen this display of strength, but I was in one of those troop transports. It took us approximately 2 ½ hours to reach our drop zone.[421]

During the mission's briefing, Captain Carl Kappel had been chucking and viewed the briefing they had been given on the mission with much skepticism. And Colonel Tucker was also reading what he had been told to say with much skepticism as well. "We were given the overall plan," Kappel related, "and I vividly remember [Captain Henry] Keep and [Lieutenant Colonel Julian] Cook and I laughing out loud when the colonel said: 'I'm supposed to tell you - and I'll quote - "we will have the world's greatest concentration of armor with us on this operation." The old man said this was supposed to be the heaviest concentration of armor the Allies ever put together and he added something like, 'One Bren gun carrier might show up.' We had a good laugh." Although they were proven to be too skeptical of the claims when it came to the British armor concentration – as they would all be pleasantly surprised over the coming days at the amount that reached them – the cynicism of the intelligence report they had been given turned out to be more than justified. It was, as Kappel recalled, "the usual old-men-too-weak-to-pull-the-trigger and ulcer-battalion stories. I remember the colonel giving us the rundown on what we could expect, then looking up at us and saying, 'And don't you believe a word of it.' I think, though, we felt, all in all, fairly confident about the operation… We were kind of contemptuous of the Germans as fighters, I'm afraid, and a bit oversold on our own prowess."[422]

Outside, it was a clear, sunny day as the armada made its way to the drop zone in Holland. Lieutenant John Holabird was allowing his men to get up and look out the window at the scenery one at a time. When Holabird looked out the window, a burst from an anti-aircraft gun flew past him. He came back inside the door. "Man," he said as he turned around, "a guy could get killed here."[423]

In other planes, men slept, and those that had dozed off were awoken with a startle just as the armada was crossing the Atlantic Wall at 2,000 feet. *PING-PING-PING-PING*. A German anti-aircraft battery was firing at them. H. Donald Zimmerman watched as someone stood up and walked towards the cockpit. "Then [he] came back," Zimmerman recalled, "and when he come back his seat wasn't there. It ended up being hit."[424] The man Zimmerman saw was probably First Sergeant Mike Kogut: "I looked out and could see Dutch people waving orange flags. I sat down and a 20-millimeter shell hit the plane and got me in the back pack and knocked me across the aisle." When he finally jumped and his parachute canopy deployed, he could see holes in it from the German shell.[425]

William Hannigan was in the same plane as Zimmerman, looking out the window. He could see the plane beside them begin to catch fire, then two parachutes blossomed out the cargo door in the tail area. Hannigan looked down, watching as an American P-51 fighter plane dove in a furry towards the German guns. The pilot's machine guns were blazing as he swooped in low. "Took it right out," remembered Hannigan. "Beautiful."[426] The damage, however, was already done:

Hugh Wallis was the bazooka gunner for H Company's 3rd Platoon and remembers, "If I am not mistaken, the plane I was in had a number 33 on it. And there was a plane right to our left, we were flying in that little V formation, there was one in the middle and then there was one to the right of that and then the one to the left was shot down. We saw a flash and then a parachute opened and it was one of our guys that come out. I didn't count them, one of the guys did, all of our guys got out and the crew chief got out but the pilot and co-pilot went down with the plane… The whole front end of it was aflame."[427]

Donald Zimmerman, also peering out a window at the limping plane, watched as the trail of smoke became thicker. The plane began to fall out of formation, black smoke trailing. "It was a trail of smoke the whole way down," Zimmerman remembered.[428]

Touchdown on Dutch Soil

Private David Whittier was the 14th man in his stick of Regimental Headquarters Company. Looking out the window, he could see the rivers stretching and winding across the Dutch countryside like a snake. Whittier's thoughts turned to the rivers below, and the 'Mae West' life preserver he had underneath his bulging equipment. He thought about how he'd never be able to get to the cord to inflate it, and that with all the weight he was carrying, about how he would sink like a stone. He clutched his rifle even tighter. "Stand up and hook up," his jumpmaster yelled over the oppressive roar of the Pratt & Whitney engines. He grasped his static line and stood up, clicking it onto the steel anchor line running down the center of the plane.

Whittier and his stick was riding in a C-53 transport plane, virtually identical to a C-47 but the door was just smaller. Whittier, towering at six feet two inches, was wondering how he was going to get out the door loaded down with a pistol, rifle, bandoliers of ammunition, a pack, a bed roll, a dispatch case, gas mask, Mae West, two parachutes and sundry of other minor items.

"GO" the jumpmaster shouted. As the stick moved down the center aisle, Whittier could see the men as they turned and leapt thought a chink of daylight and disappear. The prop blast outside the fuselage was strong, and Whittier could hear at precise intervals the *PLOP* of the wind catching each parachute as it burst open.

Whittier made the turn and before he could think his face was covered in a tremendous rush of air before being violently jerked as his parachute opened and the prop blast caught the silk canopy and inflated it. "All in the world seemed suddenly quiet – as in a dream," Whittier said. "There was still a roar of engines but it sounded far away. I slung my rifle over my arm and reached up to grasp the risers in order to slip into a plowed field where I could see other paratroopers running around."

A gust of wind grabbed Whittier's 'chute, and he tried to pull down the risers to slip back into the field. The wind was too strong, and he was heading for a line of trees. He was coming down rapidly, and Whittier pulled his legs up into him and crossed his arms over his face and braced for impact.

When David Whittier crashed through the trees, a fellow paratrooper came up to help him out of his harness. "Where are we?" Whittier asked.

"In a turnip patch," the trooper said.

"I thought we were in Holland," a nervous Whittier strickenly replied.[429]

All across the drop zone, the men of the 504th Parachute Infantry Regiment were smacking into Dutch soil. Morris Holmstock "hit so damned hard I stayed there and rested and I finally got up."[430]

Jimmy Eldridge wrote home to a friend – "Fletch" – about his experience parachuting into Holland:

Sorry I have been so long in writing but it has been a little inconvenient lately, as you can probably guess. Everything is still all right with me but it's a long way from being swell, as it is customary to say.

The flight over here wasn't as bad as I figured it would be, although we hit quite a bit of flack and "ack-ack" and the Germans sent up quite a few fighter planes but we had a good fighter escort and, buddy, it was a real show. We 'hit the silk' at exactly 1:20, and before 6 o'clock we had taken our first objective.

I jumped with my Tommy gun in my right hand and more ammunition than I ever carried before and it was the smartest thing I ever did.

After we cleared the drop zone of them and started pushing them back a good looking sedan came zooming up the road with two German officers in it. I was lucky enough to see them before they saw me and in just a matter of a few seconds became sole owner of the best car I have ridden in, in the last twenty months, although I busted the windshield and the front seat was kind of messed up but I also got a nice watch and pistol out of the deal. Well, the sad part comes now, two officers of our staff took my car for official use, but if you want to take some target practice or want to know what it is just look me up. All in all, Fletch, it has been and still is rough, but we are a way ahead of them and I am pretty sure it won't take much longer.[431]

Roy Hanna G/504

Lieutenant Roy Hanna was standing in the door of the C-47, watching as they passed over lush green fields. His head was poked out the door, looking ahead alongside the belly of the green aluminum fuselage, the wind rushing across his cheeks. His men were standing close behind, ready to jump. Out of the corner of his eye, Hanna could see the red light glowing. Almost time now. As he watched, they passed over the 600-foot wide River Maas and into another lush green farm field. Hanna recognized the Maas – it was his checkpoint that he'd studied on the terrain model. Suddenly the green light flashed. Hanna leapt, his fourteen troopers close behind.

Hanna had the best landing of his jumping career when he touched ground on DZ "O." He gathered up the men around him, and rushed to the assembly area to report in. Along the way, Lynd "Tex" Neeley, of that company, was moving through a ditch when he came face-to-face with a German soldier, taking the first German prisoner on DZ "O."[432]

The 2nd Battalion was already moving on the Grave Bridge, and after a quick assembly, Hanna moved the men northwest across the field to set up a road block on the N324 (the highway coming from Nijmegen to cross the Grave Bridge). They cleared the houses in the village of Wijchen and dug foxholes. Not a short was fired. "It was a beautiful day," Hanna remembered.

Lloyd Watkins G/504

As Lloyd Watkins was descending, he could see two blonde females in their wooden shoes, about age 20 and wearing bright shawls and dresses, running onto the drop zone. Watkins hit the ground, and found himself tangled up in his suspension lines. The two girls ran towards him. Watkins pulled his pistol out and ordered them away. In his vulnerable position, he didn't want to take a chance. Watkins cut himself loose, and studied the two girls. They were wearing the orange armbands of the resistance. Watkins declared them as friendly, and the two girls gave him food, and even helped him dig his foxhole.[433]

Private Hugh Wallis was making his first combat jump on September 17, 1944. As a bazooka gunner, Wallis had more equipment than almost anyone. His 54-inch, 15-pound bazooka was strapped to his leg, protruding from a leg bag. When Wallis exited, he found himself coming down right on top of a fence. He started trying to oscillate himself to avoid hitting the fence. He succeeded in this, but when he made contact with the ground, he landed on his shoulder. Wallis got the bazooka ammunition out of the bundle and united with his assistant and one other paratrooper. They dug a foxhole at the end of an orchard along the N846 with orders "to blast anything off that came down that highway."[434]

Donald Zimmerman H/504

As Zimmerman struggled out of his harness, he heard woman hollering from the line of houses he had jumped alongside. Zimmerman went over to the houses, and tried to converse with them in German, but ended up using more sign language than anything else. He gathered that the women wanted the silk from their parachutes to make clothing, and Zimmerman, and the rest of the men that had come over to the home with him, consented to their being taken, knowing they would just be left behind. Zimmerman watched as they ran out and collected parachutes, including the colored parachutes from their para-packs, which identified what the bundle was carrying. The women were so happy, not only about their new clothing material which had been rationed during the occupation, but also their liberation that they told Zimmerman and his gang to come back later that day.

Charles Bady?, Edward Mokan and Albert Sebastian, all of Company A, shortly after landing in Holland. (Roger Mokan)

Around dinner time Zimmerman, Lawrence Dunlop and about three others went back to the Dutch home. "There was a whole row of little cottages along the field we jumped in… There was a dining room, a living room and there was a kitchen. Just like those little homes they have built around the country. The ladies in the neighborhood… were all gathered together to do that dinner." The liberators, warmly received, all sat down at a large table with their grateful hosts. "They each gave us a big part of a chicken," he recalls. "That was quite different than K-Ration!"[435]

The Taking of the Grave Bridge

Any book on Operation MARKET GARDEN typically abounds with information and stories from the now-legendary John "Jocko" Thompson and the role he and his small group of paratroopers played in the capture of the Maas River Bridge at Grave, a bridge still standing which is now most fittingly named in his honor. Because of the abundance of information covering Thompson's part in capturing the bridge, it will only be briefly summarized in a few short words: when Lieutenant Thompson, the jump master of his stick, got the green light later than the rest of his company and observed he would not land with the rest of his companions, he kept the stick inside until they passed the hamlet of Velp, and then led them out the door. Upon landing, he found that he was much closer to the bridge than anyone else, and took the initiative to start towards the bridge, capturing it with his small force.

While the rest of Thompson's company landed on the west side of the River Maas on a special drop zone, the rest of the battalion landed on the east side of the river in the lush green farm fields near Overasselt. If the drop was bad, battalion commander Wellems had ordered, the men would proceed to the bridge on their own accord. The drop, however, was good. "It was a very loosely knit organization," Wellems recalled, "but fell in tactically like the Pied Piper. The men were well trained and fell in in twos and threes. Soon you have a column."[436]

Groups of paratroopers from Fox Company under the command of Captain Beverley T. Richardson were among the first men to reach the approaches to the bridge from the east side of the Maas. After landing, Captain Richardson made his way to the H. Antonius Church, set in a small group of houses on the northern approach to the bridge known as the village of Nederasselt. Here, his company began to assemble into groups and the men began their assault on the bridge. Lieutenant Harris and some 17 men arrived at the church shortly after Lieutenant Middleton's group, which had already left for the bridge.

Captain Richardson ordered the 60mm mortar squad with Harris to set up in the churchyard. Lieutenant Harris with eleven paratroopers continued south to clear the open floodplain. After receiving scattered small arms fire, they moved through the lush green pasture to head for a house along the bank of the river. Caught in the open, machine guns and a 20mm flak gun open fire on Harris and his men from the other bank the Maas River. The men laid on their bellies and began to crawl. Had it not been for the horse and two cows following Lieutenant Harris with great curiosity, the German fire would have been undirected. One German slug grazed Harris's chin, but did not do more than draw a small amount of blood.[437]

Willard Tess F/504

With his tall stature, Captain Fordyce Gorham was one of the most physically imposing men in the entire regiment. As the regimental intelligence officer, it was his job to deal with enemy prisoners, make the nightly patrolling schedule for the battalions, as well as send out some special patrols to identify German units or gun positions which the regiment might find especially troublesome. "Maj. Wellems and Maj. Gorham had me as [a] sniper working patrols most of the war," Edward Mokan wrote. "Gorham scared the hell out of me on patrols. His big size 14 boots made more noise on patrol. He never wore a helmet. He was like a bull. But the greatest guy ever."[438]

As Captain Gorham with two men moved towards the bridge, they bumped into two Germans; one jumped on a bike and the other made for a run. Gorham laid down and killed the German on the bike. As they continued to the bridge, Gorham met Lieutenant William Watson and the 10 men with him. They were under heavy fire from a 20mm flak gun on the Maasdijk just off the bridge. Sergeant Edmond Bilby set up his squad's 60mm mortar and began firing on a house along the Maasdijk, from which house they thought the 20mm fire was coming from, while the rest of the platoon continued to try and move east to flank the gun. Bilby's squad demolished the house with their 60mm mortar shells. Sergeant Douglas Shuit, Willard Tess and William Sandoval moved along the river. For 150 yards, the three paratroopers were exposed to German fire from the 20mm gun.[439] Willard Tess earned the Silver Star for his actions while trying to eliminate the 20mm gun. "While engaged in this hazardous maneuver," Tess' citation states, "and being subjected to the full concentration of the enemy fire, Private First Class Tess was hit in no less than 32 different places by the flying shrapnel of the 20-mm. gun. Refusing medical aid, Private First Class Tess despite his numerous painful wounds doggedly and coolly pressed home the attack until he was able to bring his Tommy Gun to bear on the enemy. But skillful use of his gun and by throwing hand grenades, he personally killed or wounded the entire eight-man gun crew and completely reduced the position."[440]

In addition to the Germans in the 20mm position, there were some 10-15 Germans entrenched in dugouts. The three men, with Tess still refusing aid, continued in a grenade battle with the Germans. Lieutenant Heneisen and Corporal Tagus came with a bazooka and five more men. No prisoners were taken.[441]

Willard Tess, still refusing medical aid, continued to doggedly fight. His citation continued, "When the patrol was unable to reach one 20-mm. gun, Private First Class Tess retraced the exposed terrain to the remainder of his platoon and pin-pointed its location so that effective mortar fire could be brought to bear on it. Only after having delivered this information to his superiors did Private First Class Tess consent to be treated for his wounds and evacuated from the scene of the action."[442]

To the south, it took Lieutenant Harris's men - followed by the horse and cows for at least part of the way - two hours to cross the small field to the house on the floodplain. The work of Joseph Koss was praised by Lieutenant Harris, and he attributed their success to his commitment and scouting. Only 11 days later, Koss would commit a heroic action for which he would earn the nation's second highest award for valor, the Distinguished Service Cross; he would not live long enough to wear it.

After moving closer to the bridge, they met Lieutenant Middleton and crossed the bridge. That night around 2100, Lieutenant Heneisen and Sergeant Shuit also crossed the bridge and dug in outside of Grave, waiting for dawn to move into the city.[443]

Company I's Cows

Walter Hughes had a successful landing with all his communication equipment in the leg bag, and began running with the bag in his hands to where his company was gathering. "I was so scared I was just concerned [with] making sure someone was near me in case I needed help. It was my first combat. I remember running with Francis Keefe and running towards someone and they said, 'Drop that bag! Drop that Bag!' I dropped that and left it on the jump field. I was scared shitless and all I cared about was my gun and ammunition."[444]

Francis Keefe's inseparable friend Leo Muri turned 26-years-old the day he parachuted onto Dutch soil. After he and his squad landed, they began moving down the N846 near the church to locate a so-called 'baby factory', where German woman were impregnated to birth new Germans. Francis Keefe remembered:

We started down the road, all of the sudden we got word by radio, "Let's go back," and we started attacking the bridge. Then after the bridge was taken, they split [the company] up – one squad went one place, another squad went another place – so we were all over the place.

We went off the bridge all the way up there and had a roadblock there so me and Muri saw this cow out there and said to ourselves, maybe we can get milk from this cow. So Muri took off his helmet – I lost my helmet, that's another story – I always lose my helmet – Muri come from Pennsylvania so he knew how to milk a cow. So, he started up on the cow.

All the sudden – BANG. The dirt was flying all around us. Some farmer didn't like us fooling around with this cow. So we went back, there was a little farmhouse not far, maybe 30 yards in there, so we were drinking milk and the other guy says, "Where did you get the milk?" – "From the cow. Where else would we get the milk?" – "We'll go out there." – "There's somebody out there pot-shooting. They're not shooting the cow, but they're sure going to try and hit you." They wouldn't take our word for it. They went outside, started milking and all the sudden they come running back in.[445]

The night passed quietly along the entire regimental front. Patrols to the countryside were sent out, especially in Major Wellems's battalion, where his paratroopers were sending probing patrols to Grave.

City of Seven Sieges

The American parachute landings of September 1944 was not the first time the walled city of Grave had been the sight of battle. It was the sight of conquest from its beginnings, being on the banks of the Maas River, one of the most vial trade and transportation routes in the Netherlands. The city was born out of the 12th century, when the Lords of Cuijk built a castle on the land. Since that time, Grave had endured some seven sieges. The Romans and the Spanish Prince of Parma in 1586 are just two examples of the bountiful history which Grave was a witness.

During Napoleon's invasion of the Netherlands, French forces were unable to break the fortress of Grave at first, and bypassed it before it finally capitulated after holding out for ten weeks, and was well inside the French lines. Simon Schama in his work, *Patriots and Liberators: Revolution in the Netherlands 1780-1813*, states that many of Grave's houses were destroyed and took some 3,000 cannon shells.[446]

The German occupation of the city was slightly more agreeable to the structures, as few were destroyed in the Second World War. Louis Ficq, the mayor of Grave for some 25 years, was arrested in February 1944 for not collaborating with the Germans. He was sent to the Dachau Concentration Camp, where he died.

When Major Edward Wellems and his paratroopers entered the city on September 18, he set up his command post in the city hall in the center of town. The two-story town hall was of traditional brick masonry construction and classic Dutch architecture with a high-pitched roof was built in 1798. In the old days, the court used to be held in the second story. When trial would occur, the spectators would fill the front to discover the guilt or innocence of the accused. The town hall had stairs out of the second story going down to the street in either direction. If the accused was innocent, he would go down the left. If he was guilty, he would go down the right, where his punishment would be carried out immediately on the sidewalk. For thieves, it might be a hand cut off, or for a murderer, execution on the spot. During the

German occupation, the court had been moved into a small white building just across the street at the intersection of the Hoofschestraat and Hoofdwagt.

On September 18, Major Wellems stood in the large doorway on the sidewalk, underneath the apex of the two steps which at one time had declared guilt or innocence, and watched as the Dutch danced and sang in the streets, backdropped by the large Saint Elisabeth's Church - constructed in 1250 - which was across the street. The residents posed for photographs with their liberators throughout the city. After the war in December 1945, a resident of Grave wrote a letter to one of their liberators: "Many thanks for what you did," the Dutchman wrote. "Do you remember my little boy Cas who was standing the whole day in your foxhole? He is very well. The photographs are very bad but they are still souvenirs on the brave American troops who liberated us from a brutal enemy. God bless you."[447]

15

IT FELT LIKE A SUICIDE MISSION

When the British trucks carrying the boats arrived, Captain Burriss was about the first to run to them and pull a boat off.[448] He carried his down near the river's edge as the rest of the two companies and the parachute engineers began pulling boats off the trucks. They were canvas. They were collapsible. They were highly sinkable. Stacked like a deck of cards the boats' olive drab-colored canvas hulls were folded flat. The ribs were constructed of wood and, to hold the sides up, more wooden sticks were propped up into place widthwise and slid into the upper wooden rim where the canvas was sewed in. Put together, they stood at approximately four feet. They were light, puncturable, and they were flimsy and nothing short of pathetic. Fifteen men, with their weapons and all, were supposed to be able to fit into the boats. Obie Wickersham looked down at the flimsy crafts in disbelief. "I couldn't believe it," he said. "They folded flat, they had a plywood bottom [and] you'd put some kinds of sticks to hold it up. You were excited. At the time you didn't think too much about it."[449]

To add to the sheer madness of crossing the river, they would execute the operation in the middle of the afternoon in view of God and everybody - including the German's gun bores. Once the water's edge is reached on the north side, a wide sandy beach led up to a lush and green grassy plain flat as a tabletop used to graze cattle. Four hundred yards beyond laid the raised dike road. German positions were all across the raised dike road, which afforded them more than ample protection. It was almost a defenders dream. There were riflemen, machine gun crews, mortars and quad-mounted 20-millimeter flak cannons. The task of crossing in the first wave – consisting of 26 canvas 'boats' – fell to the 260-odd men of Companies H and I. Thankfully, most of the men hadn't seen the mighty Waal yet, but Captain Moffatt Burriss, who would be leading his Company I in the first wave, had. "It felt like a suicide mission," he thought as he peered at the vast river from the top of the factory, "and we would be lucky if any would get across."[450]

Such a daring and dangerous mission was required to keep the Market Garden timetable on schedule. The Allied armor advance to Arnhem, where the British paratroopers were being constantly attacked by German tank forces, was stymied by the failure of other regiments to capture the large highway bridge over the Waal River.

September 20 was a beautiful afternoon. The air was fresh and the sky was a crisp blue, with white, wispy clouds floating through the space above. The smell of the river was in the air. Absorbing 60% of the Rhine River as it flows towards the North Sea, the mighty Waal was an intimidating obstacle for any military movement, which made the seizure of its two crossing bridges – one railroad and one highway – absolutely necessary. They were still in German hands and couldn't be pried, so division decided the best way to attack the problem was by attacking the bridges from both sides.

As three P.M. neared, the men began preparing to cross. In addition to the riflemen, each boat was to have three engineers, whose role would be to row the boats. One of these engineers was Obie Wickersham, who remembered that his whole company was lined up in alphabetical order. The officers went down the line and divided them up in groups of threes and assigned boats. Wickersham, being near the end, was standing next to Private Herbert Wendland. There weren't enough engineers, and they would each be the only engineer in their respective boats, so Wickersham and Wendland could pick boats. Wickersham picked one, and Wendland the other. Wendland would die in the crossing. "I picked the right one," Wickersham said.[451]

When the crossing began, the men of H Company, on the right, were faced with a large embankment they were required to carry their boats over. Private Hugh Wallis had been told to expect a 100 round artillery barrage from tanks, and low-level strafing attacks from Allied fighters on the German positions north of the Waal River. Wallis never heard the tanks fire, and neither saw nor heard any planes.[452]

The current was moving swiftly and with nearly five foot swells, they could already tell it would be unforgiving to their plight.

Don Zimmerman of H Company climbed in the front right-hand corner of his boat and a number of men got in behind him. They were a mix of 1st Platoon and 3rd Platoon men. Many who got in the boat from the 1st Platoon were of the platoon's mortar squad. They were: Wilford Dixon, John Schultz, and Clem Haas. However, Bill Hannigan also climbed in, along with Zimmerman. Also in the boat was the platoon leader of the 3rd Platoon, 1st Lieutenant James "Maggie" Megellas and at least two of his sergeants: John Toman and Marvin Hirsch.[453]

There were hardly any paddles. Zimmerman started rowing, using his trusty M-1 Garand as an ore, as did most everyone. So far, hardly a shot had been fired. Then the water began seething – boiling like –

as if some mysterious evil force were about to come from the depths. Machine gun fire began to rip open the canvas hulls of the craft, complemented by geysers exploding up from the water, caused by impacting artillery rounds. Boats began to be thrown into violent spins. In Ralph Tison's boat, it was apparent to him that he was the only one who had ever rowed a boat before, the engineer included. The unorganized lunging of paddles began throwing them in circles. He went to the stern and chased the engineer off, and began yelling at the top of his lungs a rowing cadence.[454]

Yelling and screaming could be heard echoing from the flotilla, competing with the oppressive cracking and whizzing and whining of German might. First Lieutenant Roy Hanna watched from the southern bank in utter, jaw-dropping disbelief as they struggled through the hailstorm of German ordinance. To him, it looked like a "rain of bouncing bullets." He was scheduled to go over in the second wave, if any boats would still be serviceable enough to pick them up, provided anyone survived to even row them back.[455]

Rowing cross-current was hard, but the omnipresent cannon and machine gun fire from the Germans gave them an incentive – fear and a hormone and adrenaline cocktail drove their bodies to keep going. There was nothing between the Germans and the paratroopers but the crisp blue sky. The noise was overwhelming.

Bill Hannigan was struggling in the same boat a Zimmerman, driven by nothing but the hormone of fear. He felt utterly helpless. "Hell," he thought, "I got nowhere to hide!" Hannigan was getting down as deep in the boat as he could, rowing with his Browning Automatic Rifle. "I was seeing people get hit," he described, "falling out of the boat and machine gun fire ripping into the sides of canvas boats. It scared the hell out of me because I couldn't swim with all this equipment. I didn't want to drown, and I didn't want to get hit. It was a case of just doing the best you can."[456]

If there was ever an example of human desperation, this was it; men put in their mortal place, pathetically trying to cling to life by rowing to the other bank. "I can remember Maggie being on his hands and knees going across," Zimmerman recollected, "I can remember guys got killed, oh God!... We lost three. I could turn around to my left and see things happening. A lot of guys were laying down flat on their belly and a lot of them were along the boards using everything [to row]. They only gave us two paddles."[457]

The German's twenty-millimeter cannons were doing tremendous damage to the fragile flotilla. Quad-mounted two guns atop two guns, the point-detonating shells were bursting into hundreds of small, damaging shards meant to rip through muscle. The canvas gunwales didn't stand a chance against them. Bullets and shrapnel was flying through the air in every direction. Nobody was safe. William Hannigan just wanted to "Get out of the damned boat and get on land and take your chances." Some men, from all the bullets and shrapnel flying past, could literally feel the air heat up around them.[458]

As Zimmerman looked ahead of him, it was still a long way to go under the high sun. There were two others in the very front with him, all rowing. The closest boat was only about five to seven feet away. Inside of it was another fifteen desperate paratroopers jolting and splashing around with their guns. The fire was coming in sheets so thick it looked like you could walk on top of it. Zimmerman looked behind him, over his left shoulder toward Hannigan. He witnessed men sprawling themselves down to the hull on hands and knees, desperately trying to lower their profile; others rowing like jackrabbits. "Maggie was back about two or three rows and," remembered Zimmerman, this time, "he was rowing to beat hell to get across there."

Donald Zimmerman at Fort Bragg. (Author's collection)

The most haunting sight was the carnage, flesh violently ripped open or pierced, blood. "When somebody got shot, you just pushed them over; not out of bounds but on the [plywood] floor and hope the first aid man could help." Tech 5 Wilford Dixon from Saint Louis, Missouri was one of the killed in Zimmerman's boat. When Zimmerman looked over his shoulder, he could see Dixon's legs and stomach (his head was obscured by other men). His body was still sitting somewhat upright, his buttocks sitting on one of the cross members of the boat. "I was on the extreme front on the right, and he was back about three or four rows on the left. We had a hell of a time keeping that boat straight because it wanted to take off downstream."[459]

Very close – no more than two or three boats distant – to the boat Zimmerman, Hannigan and Lt. Megellas were in, was the boat carrying most of Megellas's platoon. Working a paddle (one of three in their entire boat) in the very back right corner of that particular pathetic canvas craft, Private Hugh Wallis was kneeling down, his upper body leaning over the gunwale. Stretched out for six feet in front of him, Wallis watched as his boat, overflowing with desperate troopers, struggled through the fire. A few men ahead of Wallis and to his left, could be seen one of his best friends – Pvt. Cletus Shelton; tall, full-profiled – ferociously trying to row over the powerful three-foot swells of water like everyone else.

Their boat, as Wallis recollected, was about the furthest boat on the eastern outcroppings of the flotilla. He could see the bridges in the distance. Suddenly, he heard word being yelled back that "THEY GOT THE MEDIC!" It was Private Robert Koelle, who was sitting at the bow.

Robert Koelle was the medic killed in the boat of Hugh Wallis. (Peggy Shelly)

Just then, a large caliber round – Wallis couldn't figure out what – flew straight between his legs, blowing a gaping hole through the plywood hull. Water started filling the back of the boat. Men in the front were floundering in shallow water, building up atop the plywood bow. There was another hole in the front. The entire boat was sinking right out from under them. "Gee," Wallis said to himself, a native Louisianan who just became a paratrooper to leave the swamp, "I got to stop that water from coming in." Wallis jammed his kneecap into the hole – the water was still rushing in. Raising just slightly up to move his other leg to plug the hole, Wallis suddenly found himself completely submerged in bloody water. "I don't know how I got in the water – if I was stupid enough to jump in or somebody knocked me in or what." He was sinking quickly – the two bandoleers of M-1 ammo and the two cumbersome bazooka rounds strapped to his leg (weighing 3.5 lbs. each) were taking him straight to the bottom of the Waal and to certain drowning. He got up for a quick breath twice while in the water trying to wrestle with straps and frantically peel equipment off. His right arm was limp – he had been hit by shards of a 20mm anti-aircraft shell at some point.

Finally, he came up for the third time, knowing that he wasn't going to have the power to come up again for oxygen. "That was it," reflected Wallis. Then he started sinking for the last time when suddenly he spotted his saving grace. Someone outstretched a boat paddle to him. Wallis reached out and grabbed a hold and tumbled into the boat, being helped by the unknown trooper. "I started back down," said Wallis, "when I saw a boat paddle and somebody pulled me in. I knew I wasn't ever going to get back up." He was worried he might be bleeding out as they continued through the hailstorm of plunging German ordinance and shrapnel.[460]

Bill Hannigan witnessed a number of men struggling in the water as bullets boiled it around the helpless paratroopers. No doubt some of these men were from Wallis's boat. "[We] couldn't do anything for them," he said. "They just floated down."[461]

Donald Zimmerman tried his best to keep his eyes forward, peering across the vast Waal towards the shore. Zimmerman just kept frantically rowing with his rifle as fast as his long, skinny arms would humanly allow. It was a slaughter. Many of the men lost all hope of walking away from this crossing unscathed and were just awaiting the warm, searing sting of a bullet ripping through their flesh. The shrieks from stricken men were spine-chilling. Zimmerman "just kind of felt this is the end."[462]

The 20-milimeter guns posted on the railway bridge were doing tremendous damage to the I Company crafts. Francis Keefe was in the front of his boat watching the fantastic spectical in front of him. The lightening-looking streaks of fire moving across the horizon reminded him of Italy. "One of the other boats in front of us got hit and went into a spin," he recalled. "It was like a race; we rowed hard trying to catch up with the other boats and get across as soon as possible. I never looked back at any time to see what was happening but, despite all the noise, I could still hear the chants of the troopers in the back boats on the right hand side of us saying, 'Heave. Ho.'"[463]

Keefe watched as the boat in which Captain Moffatt Burriss was riding in – just to his left front – slowed down and ran right into a streak of lightening-looking fire. Inside that boat along with Captain Burriss was Private Willard Jenkins, one of the engineers, who was working the rutter at the stern of the boat. Captain Burriss saw Jenkins's hand turn red from blood. "Captain, take the rudder, I've been hit," Jenkins said. Just then, a 20mm round made contact with Jenkins's head, nearly decapitating him. Half of Jenkins's body fell overboard, caught the water, and began acting as a second rudder. Burriss was forced to throw Jenkins into the water.[464]

Francis Keefe's boat slipped right under the fire of one of the 20mm guns. He remembered, "We rode right underneath the lightning which I figured I could have touched with my hand if I stood up. That's how continuous it was. If the elevation of the gun had been any lower, it would have cut us right in half."[465]

Moffatt Burriss, who led Company I during the Waal River Crossing and through the end of the war, photographed shortly before his promotion in England. (Moffatt Burriss)

Also in the boat with Francis Keefe was 18-year-old Private Walter Hughes, who was experiencing his first combat action. Hughes, a communications man, had his large SCR-300 backpack radio sitting in front of him in the boat. Suddenley, a 20mm shell tore clean through the man sitting in front of him and into Hughes's radio. The radio slammed into Hughes's chest and the trooper in front of him jolted up and nearly came down on top of Hughes. He was clearly dead, and his arm dangled down into the water. Hughes heared someone yell, "Pull him in! Pull him in!" Hughes was terrified. "I pulled him in," he later said, "and then I saw the whole front of his chest was gone. Scary. I felt very bad when I saw one of our guys die. What can I do for them? Nothing."[466]

16

WE JUST KEPT MOWING DOWN GERMANS

As Francis Keefe's boat slid closer to shore, he could see a steady stream of machine gun bullets popping in the water. He stopped rowing; there was nowhere to go. Then the firing machine gun suddenly stopped. They poured out of the boat. "The other troopers around me looked completely exhausted and fatigued with strange expressions on their faces," Keefe recalled. "Perhaps I looked the same way. We had approximately three feet of cover where we landed. I immediately climbed up to observe what was in front of us. All I could see was the dike road a distance in front of us and a wooded area to the left of the dike road. The road seemed to curve down toward the bridge. The ground between the river and the dike road was on a slope."[467]

Strung out for hundreds of yards along the northern bank of the Waal, boats were sliding into the muddy, sandy bank and men were lying and flopping around behind the protection of the small bank. Machine gun fire was ripping by. William Hannigan could hear men yelling, "Get down! Get down!" Others, Hannigan remembered, spoke words of encouragement. Someone behind Hannigan – a man whom had crossed in their boat – noticed a spot of water on the backside of his tan trousers. "You peed your pants!" he said to Hannigan. "No, I didn't!" Hannigan, gravely offended, said to the man whilst reaching to his right side, unsnapping the canteen cover. "I did not pee my pants!" Hannigan said, holding up his silver medal canteen. There were two large-sized holes through it, one on each side, the result of a machine gun bullet. The exit hole was characterized by folded metal.[468]

Francis Keefe knew that if they did not move soon, they would not stand a chance. "If we stay here, we'll all die. Let's move out!" Keefe yelled. He and Walter Hughes stood up. "There was a hesitation behind me," Keefe recalled, "so I turned around and yelled, 'Move out or you'll die!' I took off and everyone, including myself, let out this unmerciful cry. I know my personality had changed. God help anyone in front of us; they would pay."[469]

The men, moving across the grazing area between the bank and the dike, charged the Germans in an astounding display. The men, spread out over hundreds of yards, were totally disorganized and any level of unit cohesion was gone. Initiative took over, as men in small groups broke out at a dead run for the dike. Donald Zimmerman reached the dike road and peered over it into a vineyard. He thought that a lot of the Germans fire was coming from inside it. Finally, Zimmerman began to see the Germans move around in between the rows of vegetation. One turned to run away. "I shot him up through the ass hole, or back, and he didn't move anymore." Zimmerman began to fire and watched as Germans ran from one row to the next.[470]

Meanwhile, Walter Hughes and Francis Keefe, along with their platoon leader Lieutenant Robert Blankenship, reached the dike road. Sergeant Marvin Porter had already reached the dike.

When I got there, I figured the best thing to do was to go over to the other side, make a flanking attack towards the bridge and clean out anything on that side of the dike. I had seen this done successfully at Mussolini's canal at Anzio. I took a gammon grenade, which is an anti-tank grenade. It's made of a putty substance which I believe is composition "C." (The night before we left England, I put some British slugs in the putty to make it an anti-personnel grenade). I threw one of these on the other side of the road. It sounded like a bomb going off! Two of the other troopers did the same thing. Immediately we went over the other side of the road.

There was a house about fifty yards from the dike road and to the right front of us. I hadn't seen it because of the embankment on the other side. A machine gun fired out of the upper window of the house as our troopers came up from the river. I saw six Germans come along a hedge and run inside the back door. Sgt. Porter then let out a yell; he got shot in the leg. A couple seconds later, the man next to Porter was also hit in the leg. Both were only four feet away from me. Lt. Blankenship, Muri, [Walter Hughes] and someone else was to the right front of them. I was about a few feet in front of Porter when a German seemed to rise right out of the ground about seven feet in front of me. I was stunned that he was so close. Porter must have seen him because he killed him with a burst from his Thompson sub. It was then that I put a rifle grenade in front of my rifle and put in the blank cartridge. Blankenship moved closer to Porter and the other trooper to see if he could assist them. This put him pretty close to me on the right hand side. I got hit in the left wrist just as I had my rifle in position to fire at the window. My rifle dropped right down next to Blankenship; he was lucky that the grenade didn't go off. I said to him, "Lt., they shot off my hand." A bullet hit the bracelet I was wearing and did a lot of damage. It was one of the few that Emmett had made when we were at the airport in Naples. Some of us wore them; they were of a light substance.

[Walter Hughes] came over to help me. I told him that there was a first-aid kit in my back pocket. He went into the wrong pocket and pulled out my wallet. "What will I do with this?" he said. I told him to throw the wallet away and get the first-aid packet. He did. I held my hand and arm across my stomach as my hand hung off if I moved my left arm. Just then I got hit in the upper right arm. Then something hit me in the mouth and broke off my front tooth. Muri came over and helped the kid bandage my hand and arm. As Muri gave me a shot of morphine, somebody asked, "What do we do now?"

"Keep firing at the building," I said.

Blankenship, who knew we were in a bad position, went over to the other side of the road. Meanwhile, [Walter Hughes], who never seemed bothered by anything, asked me for my .45 and I told him to take it. I couldn't have cared less. I remember that Red Allen grabbed me around the waist and practically carried me over. When I looked down the road, it appeared that [they] were firing at the building a lot. My flanking attack didn't go too well.

Capt. Burriss, Sgt. Odom and about 12 troopers from I Company were there. Odom took out his canteen and gave me a drink of water. It was as if the war had stopped. Everyone was staring at me as I sat there. Someone said, "Give him a shot of morphine."

Muri said, "I gave him one on the other side."

"Give him another, it won't hurt him."

Someone wanted to look at my wound but I wouldn't let him. Capt. Burriss then told Sgt. [Alexander] Barker to take two men, go down, cross the river and bring back more ammunition.

He detailed two other men to help Porter and the other troopers down to the river. I sat there staring at the other troopers, especially Muri. I was concerned about him as we were together two months in Anzio. Neither one of us got a scratch physically. They used to say he was too small and I was too skinny. I guess tears came to my eyes when I realized that I couldn't be of any more help and would never be back. It was then that Capt. Burriss said, "I'll give you somebody to help you get back."

I said, "No, you need everyone you have here. I'll get back by myself."

Then he said, "Get yourself taken care of and we'll see you when you get back."

I said, "You won't see me again."

He replied, "Well, I will never forget you."

That was nice of him to say. To the rest of the troopers he said, "Let's go!" and they took off along the side of the dike road toward the bridge. I watched them go and then started down towards the river.

I could see in the distance on the right by the water's edge, a congregation of men coming up from the river. Six bodies were strung out about half of the way there. As I got closer, I could see [Robert] Dority, the medic, attending to one of the men who was lying there. The dirt was popping up; someone was taking pot shots all around him. As I got closer, they started popping around me. I believe the shots were coming from the wooded area on the other side of the dike road. Dority yelled to me to get down and then ran over to me. He said, "You better stay down or you'll get killed." I asked him about the condition of the troopers lying there. "Not good," he said. He asked if there was anything he could do for me. "No," I said. He told me that he had to get back to the other wounded and to "stay low."

As I got closer to the group, I saw some German prisoners, the Protestant chaplain (Delbert Kuehl) with some wounded and Sgt. Barker just getting into a boat to start back across the river with some of the wounded. It made me feel good that the German prisoners didn't get priority. I asked the chaplain why the wounded men lying up above couldn't get some help and he told me they would be all right. He was concerned about the German prisoners. I had to get away from there. I walked back to where we had landed and looked up. There were no dead or wounded lying where we had attacked. We were lucky. Someone with a head wound was coming toward me. I recognized him as Blacky. I don't know if he was from H or G Company. We went over to where the chaplain and prisoners were and Blacky got into a discussion with the chaplain about the prisoners. He came back to me and wanted to know if I had a gun. He said, "Let's see if we can find one."

I walked about forty yards along the shore towards the bridge that ran into a little inlet which was twenty feet in from the water, fifteen feet wide and about four or five feet deep. There I saw Lt. [Harry] Busby's body. His legs were still lying in the water. I thought about the argument we had earlier and felt bad. I wished I could have pulled him out of the water but it was impossible with my wounds. I called Blacky over but he couldn't get down there by himself. I decided to go back and ask the chaplain for some help. The chaplain told me not to worry about it; Busby would be all right. He spoke to me in a nice way. I must say he was very courageous for making the crossing under such conditions when I knew he didn't have to. I looked at the prisoners once again and I knew I had to get away from them.[471]

Francis Keefe's 1911 Saves Walter Hughes

After Walter Hughes bandaged the gnarled hand of Francis Keefe and claimed his .45 pistol, Hughes stuffed the handgun in his belt and ran after Lieutenant Blankenship and Captain Burriss. As Hughes was running, two Germans came around a corner near the bridge and fired their bolt-action rifles at Hughes. One round hit his harness and knocked him back, but was stopped by the spare magazines for his Tommy gun. The second round hit the wood stock of his gun, throwing it from his hands. Hughes was without a gun, and had two young Germans in front of him, working their bolts to finish the paratrooper off.

Then Hughes remembered the pistol he'd just acquired from Francis Keefe.

"It only had seven rounds in it, but I pulled it out and pulled that trigger fifty times," Hughes remembered. He collapsed on the bodies of the Germans he had just slain.[472]

Walter Hughes photographed in France shortly after combat operations in Holland. (Walter Hughes)

Meanwhile, small groups of paratroopers were swarming all over the north side of the Waal, moving to the bridge. Ralph Tison passed Doctor Kitchin treating wounded. "At the time [Darrell] Edgar had his pants down to his ankles. I said, 'Where did they get you this time?' He pointed below. I told him he might as well commit suicide, he wasn't going to be worth a damn anyhow… Who could want a better friend?" Tison ran to the Railway Bridge and met Lieutenant Richard LaRiviere, who began engaging the Germans on the railway embankment.[473]

The Second Wave Fights at the Railway Embankment

On the southern bank of the River Waal, Lieutenant Thomas Utterback, the supply officer, had watched as the first wave of paratroopers stormed up the cow pasture and headed for the dike at a dead run. To Utterback, it seemed like a movie. While not fighting with those troopers, he was their lifeline, busily lugging ammunition down to the river in preparation to get it across with the second wave.[474]

To get that ammunition over, however, boats had to be brought back. There, the intrepid engineers who survived the first wave began to turn around and row back to the southern bank to take another load of men and munitions across. One of those engineers was Obie Wickersham, who found his boat in such disrepair that he ran along the bank looking for a boat in better condition. When he finally located one, a wounded paratrooper was sprawled out on the wooden deck. The trooper had a tourniquet applied and he thought they had forgotten him and was left to die. Wickersham got in the boat and rowed him back across the river. When they reached the friendly shore, the wounded man was so thankful he pulled out his M-1918 trench knife, handing it to Wickersham as a token of his appreciation.[475] With all the excitement, and so much adrenaline coursing through Wickersham's blood stream, he did not even realize that his hand had been shattered by a German 20mm shell.

As other engineers began to return boats to the southern bank, Lieutenant Utterback realized that the engineers were drifting downstream away from the original point of departure, where they had been cacheing the ammunition. Utterback wrote, "We had been lugging ammo down to the river, but soon realized that boats weren't coming back to that spot, but further downstream. Sgt. [Clem W.B.] Calhoun and I ran around the factory where there was a little side bay, and found a boat with a wounded engineer in it. We pulled him up on the bank and paddled like mad back up to our cache. Here again, if we put in enough ammo to be worth the trip then we needed too many men to paddle. Finally Calhoun and I (with a supply corporal from H Company) started across. We were fired on from behind. Germans were in the upper floors of the power plant. I don't know how they missed. (On the return, I ran into the factory to tell the Dutch guards about the Krauts. They refused to believe; though the next morning they got 20 or 30 German Marines up there)."[476]

Most of the second wave contained men from Company G, including Lieutenant Roy Hanna. When Hanna first learned of the crossing, he could not believe they would actually be asked to do it, at least not in the daylight. When he first heard the plans, he said it "didn't scare me a bit because I knew damn well we'd never do it in the daylight. I still didn't believe it until I got in the boat!"

The German fire was still strong as the second wave made their way across. "All I remember," Hanna wrote, "is when I finally got a boat to cross I jumped in along with others and rowed very hard to get to the other side. I'm not sure if my rowing very hard was because the bullets were still bouncing off the water or I was just remembering watching 'H' and 'I' row through the rain of bouncing bullets. I do know that when I did disembark I was completely out of breath and dropped down on one knee for a minute or two. Other boats or boat beat me across and so I jumped up with the men from my boat."[477]

Lieutenant Utterback continued to stay at the crossing site, trying to sustain the fight on the northern bank. "In the middle of the crossing, I ran down to the river to get a boat to ferry ammo across and was fired on by a German machine gun from a nest right opposite the factory. The tracers from the gun just seemed to hose the river. Here the Germans made several mistakes: they had fired on a single soldier, they had missed, and they were using tracers. Because the power plant was coal-fired steam, there was a pile of cinders, and I dove behind it. From this vantage point I could see that the tracers were coming from a bunch of willow trees on the opposite bank. I ran to the nearest tank, banged the helmet of a British soldier sticking his head out of the driver's port, and pointed out the machine gun nest. As they swung their turret around, they kept their machine gun chattering until the bullets hit the trees. Thus lined up, they let loose with the 25-pounder. When the shell hit, two German gunners were blown up in the air. That was the end of that nest. I am sure that those Germans were the ones who caused most of the casualties in the river crossing. We lost one-third of the battalion in less than one half hour."[478]

Meanwhile, after landing, Lieutenant Roy Hanna and the men of Company G ran beyond the dike and kept to the east of the ancient Fort Hof van Holland. It was an ancient fortress surrounded by a drawbridged moat that protected the city of Nijmegen from armada invasions in ancient times. In 1944, the Germans were using its protection to bring to bear their large artillery guns upon the paratroopers. Just to the right of Hof van Holland was another grassy, open field bounded in the west by the fort and in the east by a hedgerow that lined the railway which led north toward Arnhem. As the men moved along the field they gathered near the railroad embankment, raised about 10 feet above the field. As they continued north, the men took cover and moved in a ditch at the base of the railway embankment, and as they continued north to an underpass, where a road went underneath the railway and continued north parallel to the tracks, they came into contact with Germans. The Germans were on the opposite side of the railway and were successful in pinning the paratroopers down into the ditch.

A hand grenade battle commenced, with the Germans throwing their distinctive 'stick' grenades, which the Americans dubbed 'potato mashers' for their uncanny resemblance to the cooking instrument, over the embankment at the paratroopers; paratroopers would return them and throw their own hand grenades at the Germans.[479]

Sergeant Henry Hoffman watched as Lynd Neely "stood up and waited until they threw another grenade; then he saw where they came from. He got his prized grenade known as the gammon grenade, which contains three pounds of TNT, pulled the pin and heaved, got a good hit and out flew Jerries and weapons. After examination he found them very dead, a P38 pistol was his prize."[480]

As the battle continued, the paratroopers were still pinned in the ditch. Lieutenants Roy Hanna and James Pursell were next to each other near the underpass where the road went underneath the railway and went north when they heard the clank of tank treads and running machine guns. Hanna got out his gammon grenade. The gammon grenade was a weapon of British invention. The main body of the grenade was a small green sack with a black screw-top detonator. The sack could be filled with plastic explosive or TNT to the specification of the user. The grenade was perfectly safe without the detonator, and Hanna had remembered the men playing catch with the grenades in the marshaling area in England.

The tanks came closer, their machine guns roaring. "I thought we were goners," Hanna remembered. "I should have known better, because the railroad track is a story higher than the road, and they had us pinned down in the ditch – we just couldn't move – and the only person I can remember with me at the time was Purcell, he was right alongside of me. We were pinned down by these guys and all the sudden we hear these tanks coming. I think they're German tanks and their guns are going, their machine guns are running, and they're running right into us… and there was no sense in shooting a BB gun at them. That damn gammon grenade didn't go very far. I guess I threw it and got down on my belly, but it knocked a couple links off and stopped them. Now we're firing at the tanks. The guy stuck his head out and yelled, 'Hey, Yank, we're British!' It's a wonder he didn't get shot."[481]

Massacre on the Railway Bridge

After moving away from the dike road, Donald Zimmerman ran into a group of H Company men up on the railway trellis that led onto the actual bridge, near where Ralph Tison had found Lieutenant LaRiviere fighting the Germans. Among them was Corporal John "Jack" Fowler of the 3rd Platoon; a fellow original which, by this point, was an endangered species.

Together they went out to the first bridge support and sat down, Fowler leaned his back against the first bridge girder, while Zimmerman sat with no back support. Below them, the river's powerful waves could also be seen gracefully flowing in whitecaps as if it were just another day in nature. Fowler pulled out a K-Ration from his pocket and offered to share it with Zimmerman. Zimmerman had only one box left, so he kindly accepted Fowler's offer. Over the cold ration they made small talk, discussing each other's trip across the river.

"My God," exclaimed Zimmerman, "we heard this loud stomping noise and there must have been 150 or 175 Germans coming across that bridge." Looking back, there were only about nine paratroopers. Zimmerman, turning to Fowler – thankful that he himself wasn't a sergeant – said, "What the hell you going to do?" Fowler seemed surprised at the sudden materialization of the Germans, and they knew what they had to do. Together they rose to their feet and began to fire their rifles. Fowler and Zimmerman were on the left side of the bridge near the superstructure. They were standing only two feet apart. Zimmerman – almost standing on the track – could see three other men out of the corner of his eye follow their example. They were standing on the right side of the tracks, firing incessantly at the Germans.

The Germans were in a less-than advantageous position. Bounded by the girders, there was nowhere to deploy their troops and skirmish without practically shooting one another in the back. For Zimmerman, Fowler and the rest of the men, it was like shooting fish in a barrel. "We mowed 'em down until they piled up on the bridge," remembered Zimmerman. "It was really unbelievable." This was the action for which he joined the Army. "We nailed them to the wall… We just kept mowing down Germans; that's what we were there for." He, Fowler, and the rest of the men emptied their rifles into the mass of humanity. Zimmerman only stopped to reload, out of the two cloth bandoleers he had crisscrossing on his chest. But here, on this bridge, Zimmerman wanted nothing short of annihilating the Germans. "I was happy it was happening," Zimmerman said.

Some Germans, seeing no other chance, resorted to committing suicide. Zimmerman watched one man, rather large, jump off the side of the bridge. His hands were up in the air above his head. Zimmerman tracked him with his sights, firing as the German fell. Zimmerman thinks he hit him once or twice, but couldn't be sure.

After shooting four or five clips worth of ammunition through his M-1 rifle, Zimmerman heard someone yell, "CEASE FIRE! CEASE FIRE!" Zimmerman turned around and, twenty-five yards to the rear, was Major Julian Cook standing erect atop the railroad tracks. "I thought we were here to kill Germans," he said to Fowler.

"I don't know what's wrong with him," Fowler said.[482]

I Learned a Lot of New Words

The aid station on the opposite side of the river was flurry of activity as the wounded began to work their way back across the river for treatment. After Hugh Wallis was wounded during the crossing, he and others hid behind a pile of rock for protection on the river's edge until they could be taken back across the river. After getting to more friendly shores, they were taken to a building and then to a tent. Still damp from the river, a Dutchman gave his clothes to Wallis and he dropped his jump suit and changed into civilian clothing. Having forgotten to take out his billfold from his jump suit, it was later found and turned into his platoon leader Lieutenant James Megellas. "The billfold got turned in to him, then later I got out of the hospital in England and he came back to England to pick up a bunch of recruits, replacements, to take back over [to Europe]. When he saw me, if he had had false teeth they would have fallen out because he said, 'Where in the hell did you come from?' I said, 'I was in the hospital.' He said, 'I thought you were dead. I got your billfold returned back to me. I know you aren't married so I took all the pictures out of it and cut it up except one I knew was your sister because her address was on the back and I mailed the billfold to your sister.' When I got home she had it."[483]

As the casualties were being processed, combat continued to rage north of the river as the last of the surviving German troops were cleared out. The British tanks continued to cross after the first ones arrived to meet Captain Burriss at the end of the highway bridge, and a few more pushed up the road towards where Lieutenant Roy Hanna disabled one near the railroad underpass. "I was convinced the war was over," Captain Carl W. Kappel later stated. "I was absolutely sure we had won it by that crossing. My unit had taken a beating and was all torn up, but we were across and we held both bridges. There was armor all around us and I could not visualize that armor not going through. It seemed to me it was merely a matter of rolling, but they never rolled."[484]

The furthest the British armor got up the road was around the area where Roy Hanna disabled the tank, mistaking it for a German tank. Captain T. Moffatt Burriss, who had lost over half his company, was boiling over with white anger; so much so that he attempted to kill the commander of one of the tanks in his sector, Captain Carrington. "I am not a profane man," Burriss later said, "but I learned a lot of new words to use on him: coward, SOB and other words like that. I got on the tank, put the tommy gun to his head and said, 'Get this blankity blank tank moving, or I'll blow your damn head off.' With that he ducks down in the tank, closed the hatch. Now I can't get to him! He stayed there all night."[485]

To Captain Kappel, the British excuses for not moving were invalid. "The enemy was behind them, sure, but to us it made no difference. If the enemy was in your rear, that was his tough luck because we were in his too. Keep, Cook and I were together that night and we discussed it. We felt our job was done and I'm afraid we were a bit careless about setting up protection around the British; but we expected them to move out, not stay there... I couldn't believe they were coming. I couldn't understand what they were waiting for."[486]

The men began to deploy around the bridge to hold their hard-fought gains, paid with copious amounts of blood. Ralph Tison found a dugout just next to the bridge to put his .30 machine gun in. "Nijmegen, the town on the other side of the canal, was on fire. During the night, I spotted German patrols. As I was adjusting the machine gun, Lieutenant Blankenship said he wanted to look at the weapon. He then began to fire the thing. There were several men [that] ran up to us with the white flag to surrender. The rest lay where they fell."[487]

September 21 Dawns

Outside the factory on the south side of the river, Irwin Soper helped load the body of his best friend Lou Gentile into the back of a truck, but not before taking his effects to mail back to his family in Springfield, Massachusetts. There were dozens of bodies lying out which needed to be loaded, Soper remembered. Obie Wickersham saw the scene shortly after he awoke the morning of September 21. Exhausted from fighting both the Germans and the water all the previous day, Wickersham had gone into the factory, crawled down on a piece of carpet and fell asleep. As he walked out the next morning, Soper and the others were loading the victims of the epic crossing into the truck. "It really got to me," Wickersham remembered. Later, the surviving engineers were all lined up by the power plant and the medics inspected each of them for wounds which still may have gone unaddressed.[488]

The previous night, Lieutenant Thomas Utterback decided to wait until full darkness to have his supply jeep ferried across the Waal by a British tug.

On the other side, rather than drive it into an unknown situation, Sgt. Calhoun... and I left the Jeep (and the rest of our men) at the river bank and made it on foot as far as the end of the highway bridge. When we got to the bridge we discovered that Smokey Lott, Regimental Munitions Warrant Officer, had delivered a truckload of ammo beside the knocked-out 88 gun. This took care of our resupply problem, and the pressure was off us to deliver. Calhoun went back to get the jeep, but reported that all he found were jeep tracks leading toward the enemy line. Apparently, the jeep, along with all of my supply sergeants, had been captured.

At daylight [on September 21], I went back to the crossing area and found our jeep and sergeants. When he had searched for them, Calhoun just hadn't searched far enough—they were still huddled below the river bank while the Germans controlled the flats above with 88 fire. The tracks Calhoun had seen were those of an antitank gun that had been ferried across before us. We had to make quite a run for it to get the jeep out; 88s were still firing, though for some reason they were pecking away at the top of the smoke stack across the river at the power plant.

After getting our jeep, men, and ammo up to the bridge, I started near the end of the bridge to look for the battalion command post. The little town opposite the city of Nijmegen was deathly quiet and no one in sight. I finally saw a GI coming out of a house, but he didn't know where the command post was, either.

I went on up the street and saw a German soldier (different helmet) duck back into the school house. It was too late to retreat. As I stood there, a German officer came out and signaled to me. I went up to the building to find a German doctor with medical orderlies trying to take care of about 50 wounded German soldiers. He spoke English, and told me he needed help. He was out of medicine, morphine mostly. He asked what he could do. I told him to stack all rifles and pistols outside, and disarm the medical orderlies. (The German army armed their medics; we did not). This was done, and I promised to pass the word. I contacted our battalion surgeon Captain Kitchin about it later. All day our jeeps went by with wounded Germans on the stretchers, and later that day I saw the last of the wounded Germans, with the German doctor riding up front, going across the bridge to the evacuation hospital. Mission accomplished.[489]

On the morning of September 21, one would have found Donald Zimmerman rummaging through the homes along the Oosterhoutsedijk. The Oosterhoutsedijk, the road running between the Highway and Railway Bridges, was characterized by a number of small one-story, single family homes. (These were some of the homes cleared by Hanna's company the previous day). Mostly they were of red brick construction and had black-shingled roofs and shutters decorating the perimeter of the windows. The road was a small asphalt road, barely wide enough to accommodate two-lane traffic. There was some room in-between the houses and small to medium sized trees brightened up the small riverside neighborhood. The houses practically came right up to the shoulder of the road, but some had a three feet wide gravel bed separating their home from the road. It was a small and cozy picturesque European neighborhood.

It was along this road that Zimmerman wondered into the company command post, set up in one of the small houses, to try and find some food. He hadn't eaten since just after crossing the river, with Cpl. Fowler on the Rail Bridge. Zimmerman entered the main room and found a number of familiar faces. Sergeant Albert Tarbell – a short, muscular Mohawk Indian – walked in and went over to the window, where Private Harold K. Shelden was sitting at a table writing on paper, the daily report, Zimmerman presumed, about ten feet away.

Lt. Thomas Utterback, pictured in England, worked very hard to ensure the paratroopers fighting on the north bank were supplied with ammunition, which was critically low on the north side of the Waal. In the days following the crossing, there was an instance where Utterback drove a jeep loaded with ammunition through heavy German fire to deliver the ammo to Captain Burriss and his men while they were engaged in a heavy fight. (Laurie Utterback)

Zimmerman wondered over to where Tarbell and Shelden were. Zimmerman and Tarbell shared a few words, and Zimmerman asked Shelden if there was any food around. He said there weren't any K-Rations, but he said there might be something on a shelf. "Look up behind me there," Shelden said, "and see what's in those cans." Zimmerman already knew what was in the cans: old, black German bread that had been left behind.

He was just reaching up to the shelf when suddenly they all heard the swish of a mortar falling out of the sky. Zimmerman saw Tarbell – between he and Shelden – lean down and turn; Zimmerman turned to follow Tarbell to the floor just as the mortar detonated outside the window. A shower of shrapnel flew through the window. The entire front of Pvt. Harold Shelden's body was suffused with shrapnel, instantly claiming his life. He saved the life of Donald Zimmerman, standing right behind Shelden, whose body absorbed most of the concussion and shrapnel. But Zimmerman wasn't unscathed. He caught a small piece of medal in his hip, making a good sized gash, just as he was turning.

"Where the hell is the dispensary?" asked Zimmerman.

"Just up the street," Tarbell said.

Zimmerman walked out of the CP, where he met 1st Sergeant Curtis Odom of Company I. Odom had been wounded by a mortar fragment in the leg or foot. "What are you going to do?" Zimmerman asked. "I ain't going back to damned I Company right now," Odom replied. "I'm going to look around for a while."

"Okay," Zimmerman replied. "I'll go with you."[490]

With battalions of the 504th Parachute Infantry now firmly in place and holding the gains, the bridgehead had expanded since the men of the first wave came across; and now that the critical Waal River bridges in the hands of the Anglo-Americans, the Germans needed a victory. At dawn on September 21, they tried to gain that victory by scraping together everything they had left for an all-out assault on the bridgehead that the 504th PIR had established. Shortly after daylight, the men of Company C began to see Germans weaving in and out of orchards and approaching their positions. The sharpshooters of the company lined up their sights and got to work doing what they did best: picking off Germans and mounting their casualties. Their success, however, had unwittingly earned the reply of German heavy artillery.

As the artillery began to pound down in earth-shattering expositions, the men burrowed into their holes. Behind the barrage, several German tanks loomed, bearing down on their positions. If the men could not hold, they would be slaughtered on the flat ground backed up to the river. With the danger imminent, John Towle, a 19-year-old private, slid down and collected his bazooka and ammunition bag and ran on the exposed dike road towards the outposts.

Towle had joined the unit at Anzio, and Dan Serilla remembered Towle as a "tall, blond, rugged lad that looked like a running back from the Army Football Team, whose home was located in either in or near Cleveland, Ohio. ... He was sort of a quiet, self-possessed trooper who quickly became our only bazooka man that had the skill and training of handling this type of firepower, and all during our training in England the bazooka was made for Trooper Towle."

As the tanks began their attack, Towle squatted exposed on the fire-swept road and fired at two of the tanks with his bazooka. Dan Serilla remembered the action: "Quickly [he] reloaded his bazooka and with his GI skill, disabled the second, and again with the speed and skill of operating his stove pipe (as the bazooka was often called) stopped the third tank dead in its tracks, whereby forcing the remaining tanks to withdrawal with the German infantry which we'd began chewing up with small arms fire. As we began to feel victorious a German mortar shell dropped on Trooper Towle, killing him instantly. Trooper Towle's bravery saved the left flank of the 504 PIR and prevented the Germans from a badly needed victory."[491]

Even with the bridgehead now successfully defended from the German's counterattack on September 21, the British tanks were still parked in the same place as the night before. And when the men of the 504th Parachute Infantry were relieved from the sector north of the Waal on September 22 and moved into division reserve to lick their wounds, the British tanks were still idle.

Photographed in Holland before the Waal River Crossing, Lt. Harry Busby, Capt. Moffatt Burriss and 1st Sgt. Curtis Odom pose outside a Dutch home. Lt. Busby got in an argument with Francis Keefe regarding his boat assignment for the Waal Crossing. Busby would be killed shortly after landing on the north bank. When Keefe discovered Busbys's body, he felt bad about their arugment. (Moffatt Burriss)

17

DEATHS AT DEN HEUVEL

Only two days after the 504th Parachute Infantry Regiment was relieved from action north of the Waal River, the unit was back in contact with the Germans, assuming defensive positions stretching a distance of over four miles in length. Almost immediately, hot spots for German activity were realized. One of these areas was the Den Heuvel Woods. From the outset of their arrival, the area was the scene of deadly skirmishes and patrol actions, and during the day on September 26 a piecemeal force of Major Julian Cook's 3rd Battalion occupied the woods and suffered several casualties. That evening, Captain T. Moffatt Burriss led his entire company into the woods. Captain Burriss had positioned himself about 100 yards east of the estate's farmhouse and dug a crescent-shaped trench at the base of a tree large enough to fit he and four men inside, and a radio.

At dawn on September 28, the Germans surprised the I Company men with a fierce shelling. Many of the men were still asleep, some even sleeping outside of their foxholes, when the barrage began. As the Germans, supported by tanks, began their attack behind the barrage, a large shell hit the tree at the top of Burriss' trench. Tree fragments showered down on Burriss, Lieutenant Robert C. Blankenship, Private Leo P. Muri, Sergeant Robert G. Dew and a medic that was with them. A piece of the tree impacted Sergeant Dew in the chest, putting a hole near his heart so big "you could put your fist in it," Captain Burriss remembered.[492] Lieutenant Blankenship was knocked senseless by the explosion.

With tanks crashing through the outposts and into the woods, two litter-bearers came to remove Dew to an aid station. They rolled the sergeant onto a stretcher, and didn't get three feet when they were hit by a shell. As the tanks drew in closer, Leo Blanchette, closely covered by Ernest Emmons, ran into a ditch and fired his bazooka at a fast-approaching German tank. He missed the first shot, and as the tank nearly ran him over, he fired again, knocking one of the tracks off.[493] Another trooper kept manning a machine gun until a German tank drove up on him. He rolled out of the way in just enough time to escape, as the tank crushed the machine gun with its track.[494]

Burriss's company was being completely overwhelmed, outflanked, and overrun. They were forced to make an unorganized mad dash for the Wylerbaan. Corporal Edwin Westcott walked backwards, firing an air-cooled .30 machine gun from the hip as he fell back, helping to keep the Germans at bay.[495]

Leo Blanchette shoots his bazooka at this German tank in Holland. Behind him, Ernest Emmons covers. (US Signal Corps)

One of the last to attempt to evacuate the Den Heuvel Woods was Staff Sergeant Leon E. Baldwin. When Baldwin saw a German kill one of his machine gunners and attempt to turn the gun on the paratroopers, Baldwin rushed the German, bayonetted him, and then turned the machine gun back on the Germans. As his position became untenable, he began to fall back behind the rest of the company. Baldwin then took charge of a group of prisoners to try and evacuate them.[496] When Ralph Tison, who had been temporarily knocked unconscious by a tree burst in the action, came to, he was surrounded by German soldiers and forced to surrender; but he witnessed Baldwin firing through a clip of his M-1 rifle from behind a tree. Baldwin ran to the cover of another tree, reloaded his rifle, and fired another clip on advancing Germans. He repeated this several times. Tison then watched as one of the German tanks let loose a fusillade of machine gun bullets at Baldwin, apparently wounding him. Sergeant Baldwin ran into some underbrush, and was never seen again.[497] Lieutenant Bernard Karnap thought that Baldwin may have been captured. A little over a week later, Karnap wrote that the last time he saw Baldwin he was "marching a group of enemy prisoners through the woods to the rear, but an enemy tank cut in between he and I and the prisoners scattered and I believe S/SGT Baldwin to have been captured for at this time we had been completely surrounded." Others believed him to be dead. In a 1945 report, Ed Hahn and Lewis Spalding said that Baldwin was dead when they last saw him, and Lieutenant Vincent Ralph stated, "Because he hated Krauts so much, was so seriously wounded, and dropped his rifle and head, reasonable to assume him dead." To this day, whereabouts of Leon Baldwin, or his remains, have never been traced definitively.[498]

Ralph Tison couldn't tell how many Germans Baldwin had killed in the acts he had witnessed, but the number was significant. Tison recalled a conversation with Baldwin just a few days prior, shortly after Baldwin was told his brother had been killed in action in another battle. Tison felt that Sergeant Baldwin should have been nominated for the Congressional Medal of Honor for his actions at the Den Heuvel Woods.[499]

David Stanford also went missing in the Den Heuvel Woods. Stanford was last seen by James Wallace as he was withdrawing. Wallace stated that Stanford was "slumped forward in his foxhole, and I could not tell if he was wounded, dead or alive."[500] David Stanford's last time home was Christmas of 1943, shortly after he had graduated jump school, where he had met William Benavitz. As Benavitz had no family, Stanford brought his friend back home to Ohio with him. Stanford's young nephew Bud Kaczor remembered the two paratroopers in the house, and he got on a chair and jumped off it, pretending to be a paratrooper for them. He also remembered several years later, the next time a paratrooper was at the house: when one came to visit Stanford's mother to tell her what had occurred in the woods on September 28 – "crying," Kaczor recalled, "while he was relating the story to my grandmother." The last thing his grandmother said before she died was, "What ever happened to my son?"[501]

Earl Oldfather of G/504 was positioned at the Wylerbaan Highway, and could see the action of I Company in Den Heuvel a half-mile forward of their positions:

About 5.30 or 6.00 this morning [Pfc. Edward J.] Owsianik came down and said the Jerries were breaking through Co. I's lines. It was not long until the battle began. Troopers started running back towards our lines – the Jerry artillery plus machine gun pistols let go. I saw one shell land right in a group of our fellows – most of them kept running. From this distance we could not make out our troops from Jerries – almost certain we let some Jerries get by.[502]

As Captain Burriss was making his dash to the Wylerbaan, he came across this scene, best put in his own words as he wrote them in his memoir, *Strike And Hold* (Brassey, 2001):

As we approached the aid station, a mortar shell went through the roof and exploded. I rushed inside and found Lt. Charles ("Charlie") Snyder... lying unconscious on the floor. I knelt down, lifted his head into my lap, and said, "You're going to be OK, Charlie."

He let out a groan and that was his last breath. He was killed not by shrapnel, but by the concussion. That was a hard one more me to take. Charlie was one of my best friends.[503]

Letter from Glenn Dew

Second Lieutenant Charles J. Snyder – the battalion's communications officer – and Sergeant Robert G. Dew were just two paratroopers of dozens who lost their lives in the Den Heuvel Woods. Reproduced here are two lengthy wartime letters. The first was written by Glenn Dew, the father of Sergeant Robert Dew, to Lieutenant Robert C. Blankenship. The second was written by Private Herbert H. Carney, Sr. to the family of Lieutenant Charles Snyder. These two letters give a unique and intimate perspective into the thought, feelings, and mentality of paratroopers while they were still at war, and the questions the families of the killed were left to ponder about what occurred to their loved ones, after receiving little information from the government.

Dike, Iowa

July 29th, 1945

1st Lieut. Robert C. Blankenship

504th Prcht. Inf. U.S. Army

Dear Robert:

Received your most welcome letter the other day, and as it was the first word we had received in reference to Robert's missing in action report. After reading your kind letter I feel as if we had almost known you personally, as you had censored several of Robert's letters from over there.

I was in World War I for sixteen months, so I have some idea of the goings on that you have to contend with.

I think I shall write to the adjunct general and give him the information regarding Robert's status as you stated in your letter, as he asked to be informed of anything that we might receive in any way.

All we ever heard was the telegram from the War Dept. was that he was missing in action, not a thing about him being wounded so you can see we were rather surprised when we read your letter.

I had intended to have the American Legion look into the matter if I hadn't received your letter about the time I did, so I am thanking you for being so prompt in answering as I figured that it should take at least a month from the time I wrote until I got an answer back.

We sure shall be glad to talk to Sgt. Dooley, as Robert had mentioned him several times in his letters.

We sure felt down in the mouth when the letters and packages started coming back as it didn't seem right some way, but it is rather hard to explain just what our emotions were in a letter and he had always seemed to be rather lucky up until that time, so it almost seemed as tho that telegram must have been a mistake but, as time goes on a person doesn't hardly know just what to think about the matter.

It seems as tho there must be someone somewhere that knows something about those five men, unless a shell dropped in their midst and wiped out the whole bunch at one crack.

Robert's brother, Kenneth, who is a Marine, has gone to the Southwest Pacific for the second time, which doesn't hardly seem fair when there are some who haven't hardly had a taste of the war as yet.

Thanking you again for your information and any other which you may send us in future. I remain

Sincerely yours,

Glenn R. Dew[504]

Letter to Snyder's Family

Herbert Carney had joined the parachute troops for the extra jump pay so he could support his wife and young son. He would later say, "My first jump? Hell, I was too scared and I don't remember anything about it. I just saw the door come up and took off. Next thing I knew I was floating to the ground as comfortably as if I were in a swing. That canopy above me sure looked good."[505] He broke his leg on a jump in training, and during one of the jumps at Fort Bragg he had landed on his face. He told people that being in the parachute troops was like being in show business. "You've never seen spirit until you've seen our outfit," Carney said. And he should know – at 14 he began a career as a traveling as a musician. He played multiple instruments, but was highly skilled on the drums.[506]

Herbert Carney had been with the unit since Fort Benning, and had joined them when he was 24-years-old which made him an old man compared to the others. When he caught up with the unit again in France after leaving the hospital, he was put off by all the new faces who had joined their ranks, replacing the men who had fought with him through Sicily and Italy. He also received news which surprised him: Lieutenant Charlie Snyder had been killed in his absence.

Somewhere in France

March 23, 1945

Mrs. Snyder,

You know I don't know exactly how to say what I'm going to try to put in this letter but bear in mind I've never written to anyone before under the circumstances, and then being strangers makes it twice as hard, but we all feel we sort of know you and can imagine what you are like because the relationship of our section and your husband was one of the most unusually close military setups that we have ever been fortunate enough and able to participate in.

The guys in the section seem to think I'm the one for this job, so here goes.

When Lt. Snyder joined us, we were on the Anzio Beachhead and at the time we hadn't had an officer for quite some time. Well, we had things pretty much our way and naturally when we got a new officer we all were skeptical, and some even a little resentful, and that is one purpose of this letter, to show how much we thought of him. You know as well as I that when a new man steps in a battle-wise crowd he is under a handicap. The masterful way the Lt. handled the situation is a legend with the boys now.

As you probably know now, everyone in the army has a nick name or title. Well, we called Lt. Snyder "The Man." We couldn't get a better name for him, for that's exactly what he was - a man, a man among men, a soldier and a soldier's soldier.

In the army, officers come and go, and in tough combat units the good ones are never forgotten even though sometimes they go. He will never be forgotten, not only did his section like him, the whole company did. He had an intelligence that was appreciated by all and equal to the best, and he used it to benefit the soldiers. Little tricks of the business we're into, if he didn't know than he caught on quick and then improved them.

A funny thing is no old soldier likes formations, especially combat men, but if you just dropped the word around that Charlie, or The Man, (that's what we called him when he wasn't around, it was always Lt. Snyder when he was around, and we didn't mind it a bit), well the company would fall out in force for his orientations or lectures.

What we enjoyed most was his news analysis, and sometimes he would get off the beaten path and say the Russians will probably do this or if it was me, I'd do this, and so help me, in a week or so those tactics and moves would develop. He had a brain that just wouldn't quit.

He wasn't just another officer to us. He was officer, mother, father, brother, Chaplain and everything else. If you had a pass and you were broke, he'd always help you out.

He was the most conscientious man I ever saw. Just before the Holland jump, we were all nervous naturally, but he tried so hard to be sure and positive that all his men were taken care of to the best of his ability that he almost cried and said, "Carney (that's me), they just don't realize the seriousness of the thing." What I'm driving at is he always fought for and took care of his men; he would never let anyone run over his men, and if you had soldiered in the unit as long as we have you could readily understand our deep appreciation for this.

I'm trying to make you understand how much we thought of him – I hope I don't bore you.

Lt. Snyder's communications section in Bagnolli, after being relieved from Anzio. Most of the troopers mentioned in the letter, as well as most of the signers of the letter, are photographed here. Carney, the author, is photographed in the front row, third from left. Lt. Snyder is at the far top right of the photo, along with Dr. William Kitchin, the battalion surgeon and Snyder's bridge partner in England.[507] (Patti Stevenson)

We have a fellow in the section named Ramsey. Well, every officer has a pet peeve, and every section has one or two characters or individualists – Ramsey and I were the latter. In spite of the many times he would bawl Ramsey out it didn't diminish his feeling for the "man." For my part, I consider myself a soldier, and not a bad one, and when the man jumped me it made me mad not at him but at myself for his having to. We all tried hard in our own funny ways to please him.

He wasn't only admired and respected in our own company and section, but he definitely made a lasting impression on the English people who met him.

He may have mentioned one of his men getting married in England. Lefty Lefaro got married, he's one of my best buddies, I was his best man. We invited the Lt. and he entered just at the right time, perfect conduction of all matters on his part, and he just left those English people with their mouths open. They said you would never see anything like that in the English Army. Imagine the toast we asked him to give. He wished Lefty well in a very impressive talk. And he wasn't one to dish out unnecessary compliments, and when he told Lefty how nice his wife was, and how sure he was that he would make her a good husband, well Lefty's buttons almost burst from his vest. He was just as proud and happy as anyone could be. I was too although I don't know why I was.

I could reminisce for hours and reams of paper about all the little things-

For instance, when we were marshalled to go to Holland, it was sudden, and we had spent a lot of money in arrangements for a section party, and when they told us it was off, naturally we were disappointed, but the "man" didn't let it go at that, he went through channels right to the top and he wound up with permission for us to have our party. What a party, but that's another story.

Then came the jump in Holland and the Man was just as efficient in the field as he was in garrison, and just as good. No kidding, we got a big kick out of soldiering for him. That man was cooperation personified. We got our first objective. Everything was fine. Then came the Nijmegen, Waal River Crossing. The Man – Fox, Kilcullen, Demetras, Delong, Rus and 2 engineers we were all in the little assault boat together – machine guns, rifle fire, mortars, tanks, burp guns, 20 millimeters, everything that the Hiene had he threw at us, including grenades and knives. Amidst all that, The Man started singing the Volga Boatman – he was a man – a man after my own heart, but he wasn't such a hot singer. When we hit the beach, he wasn't the kind that said, "Go get them men," and stayed behind. He said "Let's go" – and go we did. We hit the dyke and over the dyke past the burning flak tower into a ravine and followed the Col., so to set up communications for the C.P. On the way we passed a cow that was hit by shrapnel and its intestines were dropping out; busy as we were the Man stopped and put the animal out of its misery. He was hard but he was fair, just and kind.

I was just listening to Smitty talking, and he just said he was the only person that ever lived up to what the Army told EMs that officers would and should be. It didn't take an act of Congress to make him a gentleman.

Back to the crossing, and we continued on our way. The man first- I was covering him. He made a dash for the house we thought was the C.P. He made it O.K, I didn't, I got hit. Finally, we got to the house. The Man looked like it hurt him worse than me. He said to me, I'll never forget it. You see I'm a musician, and I was hit in the hand. "Carney, it had to be you, how bad is your hand?" You see, he was never too occupied, but what he couldn't consider his men as personalities and not numbers.

I would have liked to go on, and I was going to try, but I didn't honestly think I could because I was hit in the leg too, and The Man ordered me to be evacuated. Well, I was in the hospital three months, and when I came back about three weeks ago the news I got jarred me clean to my heels. The section hasn't been the same since, and I don't know the details of the accident, but honest we couldn't have helped it.

There's lots of new faces- I walked in the other day and I had to stop and look around to see if I was in the right room, and that's bad, as I'm one of the oldest men in the company.

There'll be a lot more next time. We know it, but can't help it because when you're in the Best Div. and the Best Regt. and The Best Battalion of that Regt. with a great section and leader, you're used a lot. You never know. Sometimes we wonder if it's fair, but being the best men in the Army over here we get lots of tough jobs and he was unlucky.

The French have a saying for it. "C'est la vie," meaning "It is the War." Now we are leaderless, and we miss him too.

You were a lucky woman, and in closing I wish you the best of everything along with regrets. If you think this effort is worthy of an answer we would surely, deeply appreciate it.

Sincerely,
Herbert H. Carney Sr. 35272787
Hq. Co. 3rd Battalion 504 Parachute Inf.

The following are or were members of his command:
Sgt. O. L. Davis
Herbert C. Lucas
William C. Levan
Martin J. Lefaro
Gabriel M. McNeel, S/Sgt.
Frederick M. Smits, Cpl.
Andrew Demetras
William L. Ford, Sgt.
James Kilcullen
James Normile
Millard E. Lindsey, Pfc.
Elmer A. Young
Stan Carpenter, Pfc.
Robert L. Moore, S/Sgt.
Paul E. Mentzer

(These signatures were by proxy)
Donald H. Fox - in hospital at present
Robert Ramsey

Robert Rees
Fred DeLong
Joseph S. Bell – evacuated to the U.S.
Jose A. Sandoval
John W. Creamer
Harrison L. Towne[508]

Herbert Carney, the author of the letter to Lt. Snyder's family. (Herbert Carney)

Further Fighting Around Den Heuvel

Ever since the evening of September 26th, the remnants H/504's 1st Platoon, under the leadership of Lieutenant Joseph Forestal, had been out-posted at the Heuvelhof Estate. Positioned just a few hundred yards due south of Den Heuvel Woods, the Heuvelhof was much smaller than Den Heuvel, and only consisted of one, one-story home and a barn alongside it, and a large outdoor hayloft in the back of the house. There was a small lane leading up to the house, lined by a row of tall, narrow evergreen trees and a barbed-wire fence which lined the entire estate. In peacetime, the likes of the estate would have been pictured on a postcard showcasing the modest farm life of the Dutch people. But on September 28, 1944, things were much different.

As Burriss and his men were being driven out of the Den Heuvel Woods, Lieutenant Joseph Forestal was becoming increasingly nervous. Being well forward of the main line of resistance, he knew that they were in trouble. As the German infantry infiltrated all around their under-strength platoon, continuing to press their attack on the 3rd Battalion towards the Wylerbaan itself, the platoon was effectively cut-off.

William Hannigan had joined the platoon on the Anzio Beachhead in March of 1944. Hannigan was on what he remembered as a patrol sent out from the Heuvelhof Estate with a number of other paratroopers, including the platoon sergeant, David "Rosie" Rosenkrantz. As the patrol continued down the dirt lane heading south, Germans were contacted. The patrol was caught in the open, lying in the grass around the small trees that lined the dirt lane. Staff Sergeant Rosenkrantz had already been killed (Hannigan didn't see it happen) when the order was given for the patrol to make its way back to the farmhouses. As they pulled back, Hannigan could see Rosie's body on the ground.

Suddenly, just as they were effecting their withdrawal, Hannigan watched as a bullet tore into the midriff of Private First Class John Baldassar. Baldassar immediately grabbed his stomach, appearing to attempt and stymie the blood. It was a fatal wound. A couple of men ran over to Baldassar and carried him into the farmhouse and laid him down. "If we had known better," Hannigan said, "we'd put moisture or something over it, but we didn't know any better and he just up and died." Hannigan and John Baldassar had both volunteered for the Normandy invasion, and served on the security team for the 508th PIR pathfinders.

PFC John Baldassar (Debra Talarico)

The Germans, flowing past them by the dozens towards the Wylerbaan, were threatening to overrun the petite 1st Platoon trapped in Heuvelhof estate. They were in dire straits. Lieutenant Forestal, as Hannigan remembered, was completely breaking down. He had no idea what to do and couldn't make any decisions. "This lieutenant just froze up and refused to lead."

It would take almost another day before the remains of the platoon made their way back to friendly lines.[509]

Lorry McCullough G/504

Twenty-four-year-old First Lieutenant Lory L. McCullough was a strikingly handsome, curly-haired G Company platoon leader, with a wife and young daughter, Patricia, in New Cumberland, Pennsylvania, waiting for his return. A native of Clarksburg, West Virginia, McCullough had been an infantryman since he was 18-years-old, before volunteering for the parachute troops in the summer of 1943 at age 23.[510] On September 28, 1944, during the German's attack on G Company at the Wylerbaan, 1st Lt. McCullough and much of his platoon was cut-off and captured. Melville Farrington was one of McCullough's men, and gives account of the critical position they found themselves in:

My platoon was cut-off by two Jerry companies for 72 hours. When they had us bottled up, they sliced through us with tanks. It was about 5 A.M., and my platoon of about 30 men was holding off the surrounding 300 Germans with our M-1 rifles and Tommy guns. Then the Jerries sent their tanks in against us, and we knew the game was up.

When the tanks started to run through us, it was every man for himself. I was lucky. We weren't too worried about the tanks because it is the foot troops behind the tanks who do the real damage.

Still, I shouldn't say I wasn't afraid of tanks; I was scared to death of them. Maybe that helped me get out. When they broke us up, I just ran as fast as I could for 200 yards or so through the ring where the enemy riflemen had us covered by fire. Very few of us got out of the trap. Most of the platoon were captured or killed.[511]

By the time Melville Farrington had regained friendly lines, he had already been wounded twice – the first time when a grenade went off near him at San Pietro, and the second time when a German ran a bayonet through his arm at Anzio. Staff Sergeant Melville Farrington would continue through the rest of the Holland campaign with G/504, before being wounded yet again in the Battle of the Bulge, the result of which got him evacuated back to the United States. Back home in New Jersey, Farrington had been a prominent golfer. Shortly after his discharge, Farrington won a golf tournament, coming back from behind by shooting five birdies in nine holes.[512]

The following day, just after noon, the regimental S-3 journal recorded, "Three-man patrol from Co G to contact platoon that was cut off returned one hour again. During night ten men drifted in. One officer and 10 men missing."[513]

Back at home, telegrams were being delivered to the families of the troopers from McCullough's platoon who were captured in the action. Although many of those men were captured by the Germans, the telegrams from the War Department stated that they were missing in action leaving families to wonder about the fate of their sons, brothers, and husbands. The ever present chaplains tried to be as diligent and as comforting to the families trying to seek answers and about the fate of their loved ones, but with so many parishioners it was a daunting task. And sometimes combat conditions would limit what they were able to do. Chaplain Kuehl explains, "If I knew, whatever I could, I would share with them, and sometimes I'd go to their platoon leader or their sergeant and get further information and share that. I think that was a real help and comfort to these people. But they, too, realized that in combat situations there's no way we could do all we wanted to do."[514]

One family that Chaplain Kuehl did get the chance to write was the parents of Private Junior Posey, one of McCullough's men who would later turn up as a prisoner.

Dear Mr. Posey,

We have hoped that word might have reached you by now from the International Red Cross in regard to Junior. As yet on our files he is carried as missing in action since September 28, 1944. The only word of encouragement I can give you is that some of our boys who were in the same action have been reported as prisoners. These fellows were in Junior's company. We are still hoping that further reports might have some word about your son. Junior is a very fine soldier and always carried on the tasks before him efficiently and showed the finest courage in all the hard and dangerous jobs. He helped to make the fine record the company and battalion have made and in which they are pretty proud.[515]

James Normile - far left - and Andrew Demetras - center - were two troopers of Lt. Snyder's Commo Section who signed their name on the letter to Snyder's family authored by Herb Carney. This photo was likely taken in Holland. (Normile family)

18

FIGHTING NEAR ERLECOM AND PATROLING ACTIONS IN GERMANY

The German effort of reducing the paratroopers at the Den Heuvel Woods and further attacking the positions along the Wylerbaan were part of a larger, coordinated German attack which was felt along the entire regimental front. On the night before the German attack, Major Willard Harrison called regiment and said that Captain Charles Duncan was "very uneasy," as was recorded in the journal, because the civilians were evacuating Wyler and claiming there was going to be a German attack. The civilians were correct, and Duncan's uneasiness was proved to be well-founded the following morning.[516]

When the 28th dawned, Cook's 3rd Battalion was not the only unit to feel the weight of the Germans. The northern sector of the line, Erlecom and Wercheren, were hit equally as hard. There, Lieutenant Colonel Edward Wellems and his men held firm. Light was beginning to break over the horizon when Raymond Fary was preparing to take over guard duty from Harold Richgels. On that fateful morning, their platoon, with their large 57mm anti-tank guns, was attached to Colonel Wellems's battalion to help the lightly armed paratroopers destroy any German tanks which might attack their positions.

Suddenly, thunderous artillery and mortar fire came bursting on the positions. Then, Fary remembered, the sound of squeaking medal wheels and the clank of tank tracks could be heard from their positions at Kerkdijk #50.

A paratrooper ran back yelling, "Anti-tank! Anti-tank!"

"It's one of ours," Fary said.

"No," replied the paratrooper, "this one's moving!"

Fary ran back to the foxholes of Robert Atkinson and Roland Boteler and awoke them.

The three men ran to their gun.

As the German tanks and infantry poured out of the wood line and across the lush green field, the glidermen's gun was pointed down the east side of the road. However, the gun crew on the west side - where the tank was - did not get out of their foxholes. "We had to remove the sandbags off the tires, camouflage tree branches off the gun, then we had to lift the trails off the ground and turn it 45 degrees," Fary remembered. Manhandling the gun was no easy task. The 57mm anti-tank gun weighed some 2,700 pounds.

The men fired at a German Mark VI tank, which stopped about 60 yards from the home owned by the Stappershoef family. With no tank support, the German infantry withdrew. Some of the glidermen formed in a skirmish line to help the paratroopers, but the German infantry never returned with the loss of their tanks.[517]

Awards and Citations in the 504th PIR

Several awards for valorous conduct were awarded to troops of Wellems's battalion in repelling the enemy and his tanks. Two soldiers were awarded Distinguished Service Crosses - one posthumously - for their actions, and German tanks are mentioned in both of the citations. As the adjunct for the battalion, Lieutenant Chester Garrison was responsible for writing the citations. Many times, he did this by conferring with soldiers and officers who had witnessed the actions in question. The citations would then be sent to regimental headquarters for rejection or approval. However, awards were not always well received by Colonel Tucker, who felt the men were just doing their jobs. Garrison noted that Tucker would often say, "They are all heroes!" when the subject of awards came up. "The 504 Parachute Inf. did not give many awards," Garrison wrote, "because the commander did not support them. I think award distribution can get out of control."[518]

Edward Mokan, who served with the regiment from 1942-1945, felt passionately that the number of medal citations awarded to 504th paratroopers was inadequate, and many acts of valor went either unrecognized, or under-recognized.

The awards given to airborne troopers were very poor to my estimation. Four Medals of Honor awarded to 504 Regiment was a disgrace. I myself with another trooper from A Co. 504, while attacking a road block, Trooper Jones was hit by 24 bullets across the chest and he still kept firing and tried to move forward. He received a Purple Heart. Of course most of the daring deeds that happened only a few were present and if an officer did not happen to be at a brave encounter, it was not mentioned or given credit. The airborne trooper was regarded as a one-man army and it was thought that bravery was a standard thing. At Anzio, A Company was on the line 67 days straight and down to 22 men in [the] company and still held off counterattacks day and night. There was so many brave acts, and all that any one received was a Purple Heart. We received numerous paper citations of which we threw away. The regt. lost over 680 KIA and only four Medals of Honor and 28 Distinguished Service Crosses was a poor estimation of awards given to men who were thought of as supermen.[519]

In his writing, sent to the US Army's Center for Military History, Mokan over-reported the number of Medals of Honors and Distinguished Service Crosses. In the 504th PIR, there was one Congressional Medal of Honor bestowed. It was awarded to John R. Towle. According to records dated through October 1945, there were 23 Distinguished Service Crosses and some 200 Silver Star Medals awarded to members of the 504th Parachute Infantry Regiment for combat actions in World War II. One of the Distinguished Service Crosses went to Joseph J. Jusek.

Before the war, Jusek was working in the iron industry in Ohio as a crane operator when he ran into legal troubles which gave him two options: jail or service to his country. Jusek said he would take the latter option, but only if he could join the paratroopers. Since that time, Jusek and his best friend Al Tassinari had been with the 504th Parachute Infantry ever since the unit shipped over from the United States on the USS *George Washington* in early 1943. Both Joe and his best friend Al Tassinari had been together since Jump School, and when they graduated from Class #13 and were assigned to the 504th PIR, they were both detailed to the same gun crew.

Tassinari's journey to the paratroopers was also by forced choice, although not in the same context as Jusuk's. When Tassinari was 10, his father died and he was soon forced to quit school to work and help support the family. He worked odd jobs, such as delivering Western Union telegrams and working at a factory that made pulleys. Tassinari enlisted for one year, and then tried to get out of the Army. "I said, "Well, look, I did my one year. I want to get out and join something else." So, I put in for aerial gunner on the B-17s. So they didn't accept me. I didn't have a high school education. I said, "What the hell does that have to do with anything." I said, "I want out. I don't want to stay with this division." I was getting jerked around because I wanted out. They said nobody's getting out because it's wartime. So I said, "What do you got that I could get?" We were getting $26 a month – A MONTH. I was broke! I went in broke and I got out broke! Then I joined the paratroopers and that was fifty bucks more a month, and I sent that to my mother. They wouldn't let me go to tail gunner [school] so I said, "What do you got that I could join. I want out." He said, "There's a brand-new outfit opening up." So I joined the parachute outfit and they rushed me right down to Fort Benning. I was in the 13th class."[520]

Class #13 would produce many paratroopers who would join the 504th, including pre-war friends Alvin Tway (killed at Anzio) and Emanuel Weinberger (killed at Salerno). It was also where Jusek and Tassinari began their journey in the American parachute troops.

At 30-years-old and standing at 5' 11" and 185 pounds, Jusek was among the oldest men in the regiment. Tassinari felt Jusek "was the luckiest guy in the world! Four Purple Hearts. We'd just go up one day, he'd get wounded, and off the line." On September 28, Corporal Jusek and his machine gun crew were attached to E Company near Erlecom when the German attack came.[521]

Joe Jusek after returning home. (Jusek family)

Staff Sergeant John Branca watched as the E Company positions began to be overrun by the German panzers and infantry. He sunk back into his foxhole, praying for God to let him live. At that moment, God spoke to him. "Have no fear for I am with you," He said. Peace fell over Branca. Later, when the danger had passed, Branca reached up and pulled out a six-inch piece of jagged shrapnel – likely from a German tank shell – which had lodged itself in the ground just above his head.

It was later reported that some 200-300 Germans, supported by the tanks, attacked the company's positions. German tanks attacked E Company's positions on two points. The first route was along the Erlekomsche Dam, which was a raised road on top of the dike lining the Waal River. After the Germans forced through E Company's roadblock, Roy Tidd earned the Silver Star Medal for running 250 yards through intense German fire to lead a British tank forward, and help direct its fire resulting in knocking out two German tanks.[522]

The second route taken by the German tanks was along the Erlekomscheweg. Here, Al Tassinari and Joseph Jusek were dug in. Tassinari was next to his friend Jusek, who was on the Browning .30 machine gun, when the tanks began to bear down on their positions. "Don't shoot them," Tassinari told his friend. "We can't hurt them. We don't have the equipment." However, Tassinari remembered that "Joe got really aggravated. Joe Jusek shot at them, he shot back, and Joe Jusek lost an eye there."[523] For his actions that day, Jusek was awarded the Distinguished Service Cross. The citation, in part, reads, "Despite heavy artillery and mortar fire falling near his position, Corporal Jusek, disregarding his own safety, continued to expose himself so as to direct effective fire on the oncoming infantry. Presently, tanks appeared on the scene to support the forward movement of the enemy foot troops, and one enemy tank moved within 200 yards of Corporal Jusek's position. The first volley of fire from the tank scored a near hit on his position, disabling the other three members of his gun crew and causing Corporal Jusek to suffer painful lacerations about the face and shoulder. Despite the acute pain of his wounds, Corporal Jusek refused to evacuate his position and continued to deliver effective fire on the enemy. He remained in position for approximately two hours, during which time he continually laid down fire against the foe."[524]

Born in Poland, Joe Jusek had come to the United States in 1920 as a 7-year-old boy, and at the time of these heroics was not yet an American citizen. On June 30, 1950, American citizenship was conferred. After the war, and despite losing his left eye in Holland, he went back to the iron works as a large crane operator and built bridges, and even had SCUBA dived while doing iron work on the bridges. Other than a false left eye, Jusek bore other physical wounds of his wartime service: a foot-long scar across his abdomen marked the spot where shrapnel had hit him, and his shoulder bore scars. Jusek had a love for golf and bowling, and his shoulder was prone to pop out of place; he would turn around wincing, go into a corner, and force it back in-place and continue to play. Joseph Jusek, the only man in the 2nd Battalion to live to wear his Distinguished Service Cross, passed away on August 31, 1971. He was 60-years-old.

Action of Koss and Maier

Activity for Captain Beverley Richardson's F Company in Wercheren had begun to increase the afternoon before the attack when their positions were shelled by the Germans. During the night they reported Germans moving into the woods along the German boarder only 150 yards east of where the Kerkdijk met the

Thornsestraat. In the morning, Richardson's men were faced with some 100 German infantrymen equipped with flamethrowers and supported by tanks.

Like Jusek, twenty-three-year-old Private First Class Joseph Michael Koss, of McKeesport, Pennsylvania, had been with the unit since it shipped over to Africa. At the opening of the melee on September 28, the thrice wounded veteran Koss directed Private First Class Robert Maier from their protected positions to an exposed position which allowed them to bring to bear more effective fire at the onrushing German troops. Maier fired the machine gun, whose fire helped to pin the Germans down to the ground. He had fired a belt and a half of ammunition through the machine gun as a German tank closed to within 100 yards of Maier and Koss. The tank fired nearly point-blank at their positions. The third shell temporary damaged the machine gun, putting it out of action, and wounded both Robert Maier and Joseph Koss.

The German tank continued to bear down on the two paratroopers while Maier field-stripped the Browning machine gun to restore it to action, and Joseph Koss continued to fire on the enemy with this Thompson. "Although painfully wounded," his Distinguished Service Cross citation reads, "Private First Class Koss fired upon the enemy with his Thompson submachine gun with telling effects while his gunner corrected the stoppage. Despite the continued point blank fire from the tank Private First Class Koss continued to fire for at least 15 minutes after being wounded until he fell mortally wounded from one of the tank shells."

Finally, Maier restored the machine gun to working order. "Ignoring the pain of his shoulder and leg wounds and refusing medical aid," Maier's Silver Star citation reads, "he maintained his effective fire on the attacking Germans. Another shell burst killed his companion, but Private First Class Maier stood his ground and fired his machine gun until anti-tank fire knocked out the enemy tank."[525]

With this grim determination and grit, the battalion was successful in foiling the Germans in the Erlecom-Wercheren sector. Eight tanks and one armored car had been knocked out, and approximately 200 German soldiers were killed or wounded, along with another 23 who were taken prisoner by the paratroopers.

Although well-supported by tanks and flamethrower-wielding pioneer troops, the German attack against Lieutenant Colonel Wellems's positions was put together with haste. Opposite the positions of Wellems's battalion on the night of 27-28 September was *Kampfgruppe* Levin, based in Leuth. According to a document captured by one of the paratroopers, *Kampfgruppe* Levin was ordered to be relieved on

September 28, but at last minute they were told to make the attack against Wellems's paratroopers on the 28th "to restore their former front line."

Outside the village of Grave, Holland, civilians share some moments with Joe Koss. (Graafs Kazemattenmuseum)

Kampfgruppe Levin was reinforced with a platoon of old, untrained men from 93rd Flak Regiment. The night before the attack, a flame thrower group of 16 men and a lieutenant from a pioneer unit based just east of Cleve – some 10 miles distant – was summoned to be attached to *Kampfgruppe* Levin for the attack. The 16 men were broken into four groups of four men. Two men to act as protection, one to carry spare parts for the flamethrower, while the fourth manned the flamethrower. Two of these flamethrowers were recovered by F Company paratroopers during the night, and brought back to headquarters.[526]

Evolution of Battle

As the days the men spent in the defensive phase of the Holland operations drug, the areas of activity would change. When on September 29 the men of the 3rd Battalion were trucked north from Den Heuvel to positions east and north of Berg en Dal overlooking the Wylerbergmeer, patrolling actions around the footbridge, crossing a small stream which fed into the north shore of the lake, were intense. As time pressed on, the patrols would migrate further south of that vicinity towards the village of Wyler, Germany.

But before the Germans reinforced the bridge so that it was denied to the Americans, that small area around the Wylerbergmeer was the scene of several casualties for the troopers of the 3rd Battalion. The Germans realized the importance of the bridge to their positions after Lieutenant James Megellas and his platoon was able to cross and "Surprise the Germans," which was the story Roy Hanna heard, and snag a number of prisoners on the second night the battalion was in the area, on September 30.[527]

The following night – October 1 – Lieutenant Charles A. "Hoss" Drew and his G/504 platoon was scheduled to furnish the night's patrol. Hoss would follow approximately the same route as Megellas. Corporal Earl Oldfather penned a lengthy diary entry describing the circumstances:

This afternoon the squad leaders and Sgt. Honey went with Lt. Drew in a jeep to Co. 'A's positions to look at a German town we are supposed to go tonight and try and get prisoners. The 3rd Platoon is supposed to do that little job. We got back just in time for dinner. We moved out about 7.00 PM for Bn. C.P. According to the major and the captain the patrol should be easy – no activity reported where we are going. We waited for a truck which took us to Co. I's C.P. from there we started for the bridge across the canal which we were to cross – proceed to the dike and then onto the little town.

My squad was to stay at the dike. The moon was bright – no good for patrols. We just got to the bridge and the Jerries opened fire. The 2nd Squad had to go to the left which meant going through the swamp – I have seen it done in the movies, but never thought I had been doing the same. We had to crawl on hands and knees – I got my rifle all wet but it fired ok.

We put up a little fight but had to withdraw. Lt. Drew was hit pretty bad. Hatcher – Walters and McLane were also hit. We came back to Co. I's C.P. Honey called Capt. Ferguson at Bn. – he said we would have to go out again. Most of the weapons were out of order – we went in a house I Co. had – cleaned our weapons and got more ammo. We moved out at 11.45 PM to try again.[528]

Lieutenant "Hoss" Drew was eventually carried back to the G Company position on a stretcher – his wound was grave. Hanna walked over to Hoss, who was lying on a stretcher outside a building. A bullet had entered into his skull; a wide strip along the side of his head was blown asunder, exposing an inkling of pinkish flesh. It was his exposed brain. Somehow he was alive, and thankfully unconscious.[529]

October 2 Retaliation

Sergeant Lloyd Watkins, known as 'Rev' to the men in his company, was the son of a minster from New Castle, Pennsylvania. Watkins had a love for boxing, which immediately made him a candidate for Colonel Tucker's regimental boxing team. In Oudja, Africa, Bob Hope, the famous, was observing a boxing match between Watkins and another man, when Watkins vomited upon Hope from his corner in the ring. Watkins would say that he "ate too much watermelon" prior to the match.

As an original member of G Company, Watkins was an experienced veteran of the Italian campaign by the time Operation MARKET GARDEN commenced. Lloyd Watkins celebrated his 22nd birthday on September 18, the day after jumping into Holland.

I remember sitting out in the field in my foxhole, listening to the German shells, just like the year before in Italy, I was sitting in a foxhole all day long, listening to the German shells. But Holland seemed to be even a gloomier place than Italy. I don't know why. It's flat county and people are happy and cheerful, they never expected us to jump and they were tickled to see us. But the wide flat fields are so empty and vast, it leaves you with a funny kind of loneliness.

Anyway, I was sitting in my foxhole when the two girls returned with my birthday present – two fried eggs on toast... Boy, that was something. You don't know what eggs taste like when you haven't eaten them for months. They were better than any birthday cake I ever tasted.[530]

Just before dawn on October 2, the Germans retaliated against the patrols by dropping a heavy mortar and artillery concentration on the G Company positions. Earl Oldfather was just returning to the company from a patrol when the first shell landed. "We just got back when a shell landed right among the pup tents," he wrote. "I did not hear it come, but saw it land. I do not know how many got hurt – several were calling for a medic. I started to dig my foxhole deeper. They continued to throw them in on us and I continued to dig."[531]

Lieutenant Roy Hanna remembered the shells exploding in the air, inside the canopies of the trees, and spraying molten shrapnel and splintered tree stumps down onto them from above; tree bursts, the troopers called them. "I thought we were in a rather secure area," Roy Hanna wrote of the shelling. "One platoon was hit quite badly. We had dug in, but had not built limb covers over the foxholes." Due to the fact they had not done so, these 'tree bursts' were devastating as the shells fell like rain, bringing death and maiming. He continued, "We received a lot of enemy artillery... Some of my platoon got seriously wounded and, I believe, a couple KIA. 'My buddy', Col. Cook, called me into the Bn HQ and chewed me out for not having the men dug in with 'covered foxholes'. This, because I was apparently in charge – again where was [Captain] Thomas."532

Earl Oldfather remembered Captain Thomas giving a talk about the incident later in the morning. "About 6.30 this morning we went back to the old area – the captain talked to us – said 17 were injured – some lost legs – others may die. Said we were moving a little ways and each man will dig a slit trench – lay limbs or something over the top and cover some with dirt. I dug a swell hole."533

One of the men wounded in the barrage was Sergeant Lloyd Watkins, who lost his right leg. That did not stop him from becoming successful in civilian life. After marrying a Civil Air Patrol pilot, he became the proud father of seven children and operated his own oil heating business, and then became a foreman for the GM plant in Lockport, NY. His love was tournament golfing, and he competed well into his 60s, and became a founding member of the Amputee Golf Association. "I didn't know him as a soldier," son Jeff wrote, "but I saw him live out a soldier's life by accepting the life God gave him with integrity."

Lloyd Watkins of Company G, who lost his right leg in the October 2 shelling of the company, after Lt. "Hoss" Drew's patrol returned. (Jeff Watkins)

After the thwarted German attacks on Erlecom, Den Heuvel and Wercheren, the paratroopers were on the defensive, but the shelling of G Company marked another shift in the campaign. The regiment began digging in for the long haul, and went into a deliberate, static defense. Hay or straw was absconded to cover the bottom of foxholes for added comfort. House or barn doors were put over slit trenches, and then dirt on top to protect from artillery and shrapnel raining down. Captains found small houses for their command posts, and for their squads to rotate in and out for sleeping when they would be relieved from the outpost line.

Some of the houses were more ornate than others, and some even had luxuries the men had become unaccustomed to while in combat. Lieutenant Colonel Wellems set up his battalion CP in a home set on an apple orchard which had electricity, beds and private rooms for the senior officers. There was even a Ping-Pong table. But despite these luxuries, these houses they slept in were not home.[534] Lieutenant Thomas Utterback wrote to his wife on the night of October 10, "Getting along OK, Honey, not happy but doing alright. Can't say how it's going or when it will end but not too soon. I too am about at the end of my rope on being lonesome. Uncle has just got to get us back together again. And soon. Remember I miss you folks plenty. Now have me two little Dutch boys who call themselves my boys. Jan is the baby age '3' and he has automatically become 'Jankee.' Nice boy but not like ours."[535]

In the Wylermeer sector, James Buskirk of the 3rd Battalion 81mm Mortar Platoon shows how the average paratrooper slept in Holland. Behind him, is visible is his log- and dirt-covered slit trench. (Mandel family)

Many small tragedies occurred in these houses, and the areas just outside them. It was outside a house that Lieutenant Hoss Drew was laid out on a stretcher. And it was inside the house that Captain

Walter Van Poyck was using as his CP that tragedy struck on October 3 when two German artillery shells came through the roof and exploded on a table which many were gathered around. Sergeant Walter C. Kitchen had just walked out of the room when the shell hit. Lieutenant Chester Garrison heard about the tragedy and immediately went to the aid station where the casualties were being treated.

Upon hearing about the shelling, I rushed to the aid station to check on the personnel damage – who and how many were hit and who had to be replaced. The jeeps, first with wounded and then with dead, began to arrive and unload. I discovered my two close friends on stretchers on the ground. Ed Kline was in shock from a severe leg injury; he was hospitalized for a year and had to walk even afterwards with a cane. Alongside him was Van Poyck. By the configuration of the blanket covering him, I could see that he was missing a leg. Even with additional injuries, he was not in shock, which would have killed him. He recognized me and gave me his wristwatch to care for; I later gave it back to him in the hospital. He was weak but conversant – too bullheaded a Dutch descendant to give in.

Sergeant Kitchen told me later that after the explosion Van had pulled himself into an upright sitting position against the wall. Seeing his loss of blood, he pulled off his belt and used it as a tourniquet. When Kitchen offered help, Van refused any and directed Kitchen to assist others in the room. When Kitchen got back to Van, he directed Kitchen to use scissors to cut through the thin stretch of skin that kept his leg attached to his thigh. Kitchen refused, and Van gave him a direct order, which meant court martial if not obeyed...

The aid station became so frantic from the number of incoming casualties that I was handed a bottle of blood plasma to hold over an unconscious trooper on a stretcher for intravenous feeding. I continued to attempt to estimate the personnel damage by questioning the coherent wounded. Five had been killed and six had been severely wounded. The administration of the company had been wiped out, and each of the three platoons had lost one of its two officers. I was standing in the midst of stricken friends.

I had to report the situation to Wellems and to arrange for replacements immediately. Wellems appointed Herb Norman as company commander, and I sent my typist Abe Bloomfield to do the paperwork. The company was being pulled together again, and the German artillery increased.[536]

The four men who were killed by the shelling were Sergeant Amos Overholt (succumbed on 8 October), Technician 5th Grade Romeo Hamel, Corporal John Morris, and Private First Class Kenneth Thomson. In addition to Captain Van Poyck and Lieutenant Kline, six others were wounded. They were

Lieutenants Carl Mauro and James Nelson, 1st Sergeant Edgar Dumas, Technician 5th Grade Floyd Johnson, and Privates William Gotts and Harold Roman.

Into the second week of October 1944, men were still fighting the Germans around the Wylerbergmeer and the footbridge near which Lieutenant Drew had been wounded, and they were still traversing the same paths. "Dumb plan," Hanna notes.[537]

As the regiment was now on the defensive, the men would rotate the duties along the outpost line regularly. G Company had since been relieved by I Company along the line. Earl Oldfather and several G Company men were guarding British artillery in Beek, near where Lieutenant Ed Kennedy's platoon was dug in. For chow – served daily at 9:30 AM and 5 PM – they would eat at a restaurant located just across the German boarder where the cooks were located. On October 4, the cooks had overslept and Oldfather and some of the others were outside eating a can of beans when Lieutenant Kennedy came to tell them the set-up and chow times. For the evening meal the following day, Lieutenant Kennedy told Oldfather that G Company was going to relieve them the next day. That night, October 5, Lieutenant Donald Holmes of I Company took a small patrol to the area around the footbridge.

On the following afternoon, October 6, Colonel Tucker visited the area and ordered that a platoon from G Company outpost the eastern side of the Wylerbergmeer as soon as they took the positions over.

At 3 PM on the 7th, Lieutenants Kennedy and "Booby-Trap" Blankenship came to Oldfather's positions and ordered him to move all their things to the I Company CP to begin the relief. Oldfather ate at Kennedy's platoon command post - steak, as one of the men killed a cow - before moving up.[538]

Executing Colonel Tucker's orders to outpost the eastern side of the Wylerbergmeer was Lieutenant Roy Hanna and the 3rd Platoon of G Company. That night, they were thrown back by the Germans who were lying in wait for the lieutenant as he was leading the men across the stream. "I do remember Cook sending me on a patrol with a few men to the area where he had sent Maggie and Drew," Hanna recalled of October 6. "That night I tried to cross the Wyler Canal short of the bridge. The water was up to my waist and I turned around and back tracked. About the time I got to the bank, German machine guns started strafing our area. All of us remained on our stomachs and I tried to radio Bn. Hq. All I got was Germans talking to each other – must have been on their frequency. When the strafing stopped I withdrew the men to our original jumping off place. No one wounded."[539]

Meanwhile, the I Company men were rotated back a short distance. On October 10, Lieutenant William Mandle wrote that "Bob Blankenship, Ed Kennedy, Don Holmes and I (the old gang) found a

Dutchman who could play and piano - and a piano for him to play; so we spent the evening listening to the Dutch version of American swing! He finally wound up the evening with some Italian songs, which was quite appropriate 'cause a year ago we were enjoying the sights of Naples."[540] The men had come a long way since Naples. On October 17, Francis Kennedy, a pilot in the Marine Corps, wrote to his brother Ed Kennedy to see how he was doing. "You sure are getting your belly full of this war," he wrote. "Don't get too confident of yourself because you were lucky to get through the African and Italian campaign without too much damage. You know it just takes one lucky shot by one German jerk to finish the job. Take it easy and use your training and experience to the best advantage."[541] Ed Kennedy would not live long enough to read the letter.

Fighting at Thornsche Molen

The Mosterd Dijkje separated the 504th Parachute Infantry's 3rd Battalion from its 2nd Battalion, which was north of the dike. Colonel Tucker's plan of out-posting the eastern side of the Wylerbergmeer was part of a larger strategy which was to be carried out on the 6th of October to help straighten out the northern sector of the regiment's defensive positions. While the fighting at the Wylerbergmeer was going on, Captain Richardson's F Company was ordered to clear the Germans out of a patch of woods to their front and connect with Lieutenant Hanna's G Company men. On the map, the woods Richardson's men were to clear were marked, "Thornsche Molen."

Richardson's F Company was still occupying the positions in Wercheren where they had successfully fended off the Germans on the 28th of September. The ground had been soaked with their blood, and they continued to receive heavy casualties in the first week of October. On the 4th, the German guns in Leuth and Zyfflich breathed fire, and what was estimated to be a 155mm artillery shell scored a hit on the command post of the 3rd Platoon led by Lieutenant William Watson.[542]

From F Company's foxhole line along the Werchensestraat, they could look behind them to the west and see during the day the skyline of Nijmegen on the bluff overlooking the Waal, and, looming in the distance, the two bridges over the Waal for which so much blood had been shed. In front of them to the east, they could see the woods at Thornsche Molen – occupied by the Germans – in the distance, across the long farm field. It was this same patch of woods which German activity had been heard the night before the attack on 28 September. Since that day the woods continued to be a hotbed of German activity, with several patrols from the company passing through to skirmish with Germans dug in there.

The task of clearing the woods at Thornsche Molen fell to the 3rd Platoon of Lieutenant Watson, which included Private Richard Gentzel, with the unit since they left the States. Gentzel sat down and wrote to his mother on the afternoon of October 6, just hours before he and his platoon went to clean Germans out of Thornsche Molen. "I am O.K.," Gentzel wrote. "Hope everything at home is the same. Can't tell you what I'd like to as time is limited. I wish I could come home." It would be the last letter she received from her son.[543]

Shortly before 2100, Watson's platoon began their attack. Heavy German machine gun fire caught them in a crossfire. Private Arthur C. Williamson was with the leading squad, along with Private William Sandoval. "As we went over a fence into the woods, Sandoval got hit," Williamson recalled. "The squad leader looked at him and said he was dead. I did not examine him."[544] Once their squad entered the woods, they soared over the dike road and a fierce, close-range battle ensued as the paratroopers became surround by what was estimated to be a German force the size of a company. The crossfire was deadly, and there was heavy machine gun fire. Williamson watched as Lieutenant Robert Heneisen "ran towards a German machine gun. [The] German shot him quite a few times thru the stomach and chest. Died a few minutes later."[545]

Behind them, the rest of the platoon was pinned down, leaving the squad exposed and unable to communicate with the rest of the unit. Williamson's squad leader sent a runner to reestablish contact with the rest of the platoon, but he was killed. Another runner attempted but was wounded, after which Williamson volunteered to carry the message. As he made it to the fence, a burst from a German machine gun walked across his lower body, striking his legs and his rifle, ripping off a finger. Williamson fell not three yards from where Sandoval's body was laying. "He was still there," Williamson recalled.[546] One of the first things Williamson did after being shot and falling, he would later say, was to feel and make sure his genitals were still in-tact.

For his subsequent actions that night after being wounded, Williamson was awarded the Silver Star. His citation reads:

During his platoon's assault on an enemy wooded strongpoint supported by a camouflaged pillbox and numerous machine guns, the leading squad in which Private Williamson was rifle grenadier managed to pierce the enemy positions and reached a dyke roadbed behind the wooded area. At this point all contact with the remainder of the platoon was lost and the squad, being completely cut off, faced certain capture or eventual annihilation. Recognizing the necessity for immediately regaining contact, the squad leader dispatched a runner to the rear. This runner was killed almost immediately, and a second runner was seriously wounded. At this point Private Williamson volunteered to carry a message through the enemy positions to his platoon leader. While en route he suffered two painful wounds in his leg from enemy small arms fire. Despite the acute pain which made it impossible for him to walk, Private Williamson, ever mindful of the necessity for delivering the message so as to save the lives of his comrades, crept and crawled approximately 100 yards through continued small arms fire until he reestablished contact with the remainder of the platoon. Upon receipt of the message, the platoon leader ordered the lead squad's withdrawal, and another volunteer runner delivered the order for withdrawal to the squad leader. By his heroic tenacity and unselfish conduct, Private Williamson rendered a service that enabled his squad to withdraw from an untenable position with a minimum of casualties.[547]

The volunteer runner taking the message into the hellfire of German arms was the square-jawed West Virginian Andrew "Dutch" Poling. Poling ran through the sheets of German machine gun fire. At one point, a machine gun bullet grazed his skull and caused him to temporarily lose consciousness. But he got back up until he reached the beleaguered men and led them back to the rest of the platoon. For his conduct, Poling was also awarded the Silver Star Medal.[548]

Paratroopers of F Company, 504th PIR in Holland. Standing at the far left is 1st Sgt. Jack Bishop. Kneeling left to right is James Churchill and W. George Benivitz. (Benivitz Family)

Due to the heavy machine gun fire, the entire platoon was forced back. When they returned to their positions, five men were missing: 2nd Lieutenant Robert V. Henieson, Privates Richard Gentzel, William

Sandoval and Ray D. Wilbanks, and Private First Class William K. Peirce. The bodies of Peirce and Henieson were put into a shallow field grave near where they were killed by the Germans. Their remains were found by two farmers in 1947 and interred alongside each other in the American Cemetery at Neuville, Belgium, where both troopers still rest. The body of Private Wilbanks was found in 1945 in an isolated field grave at a separate location. At the time of this writing, remains of Gentzel and Sandoval have yet to be recovered. They are both still officially missing in action.

The casualties in the 3rd Platoon were especially worrisome after the smoke settled. Shortly after midnight, the regiment's journal recorded that the other casualties were being removed.[549] In addition to the five missing paratroopers, six men were wounded, further cutting down an already depleted company. With the platoon sergeant being killed when the CP was shelled on October 4th and both of the platoon's lieutenants becoming casualties in the fighting at Thornsche Molen – Lieutenant Watson being wounded and his assistant Lieutenant Henieson declared missing – the entire platoon's leadership had been wiped out within three days.

Lieutenant William Watson had suffered a shattered femur when an artillery fragment tore through his right thigh, resulting in his spending a year in a body cast.[550] The other wounded men were Corporal Johnny L. Snow, and Privates Joseph J. Billott, John A. Patton, Herbert C. Rosser and Arthur C. Williamson. Andrew Poling never reported his wounds and remained on the line.

On the 12th of October, the regimental lines were shortened due to excessive casualties across the unit, and F Company left their positions to move further south. Despite these losses, and those suffered on September 28, Fox Company's lethality was not diminished. The company was home to some of the fiercest and most effective fighting soldiers in the regiment, and many of their heroics have received less recognition than others. Their first sergeant, Jack Bishop, was a stern disciplinarian. While he was a platoon sergeant, his favorite form of punishment was to instruct a trooper to carry his rifle over his head while running in circles around the barracks.[551]

Willard Tess was another of the company's many fierce fighting soldiers. After being wounded in 32 places by shrapnel during his heroics shortly after parachuting into Holland, he returned to the company only seven days later, and on October 25, 1944 Tess was wounded again in Holland during a company-sized raid on the German lines, during which the men of F Company were responsible for killing some 18 Germans in a single ditch as they attempted to flee. That raid cost the Germans heavily, and a divisional G-2 report stated, "The enemy suffered a severe blow from the raid made night 25-26 Oct. by 'F' Co, 504th Prcht. Inf. on Vossendaal Woods. It is estimated that 40-50 enemy were killed in their holes or attempting to retreat during the assault by our troops."[552] The raid was heavily coordinated with fire support from the battalion's 81mm Mortar Platoon. James Sapp recalled that they had been given a large amount of mortar shells from a German ammunition dump that was captured around Nijmegen. Supporting F Company's raid on the German lines with their own ammunition turned against them was the platoon's single-greatest volume fire mission of the war. "They were trying to capture a German prisoner to get information, and we had all four mortars firing... We zeroed in each mortar at certain place in the town and we'd fire twenty rounds at each location and creep forward... The mortar tubes had gotten so hot the olive drab painting on the tube turned brown." The mortars did tremendous damage, as the paratroopers found the German foxholes without log covers when they cleared the area.[553]

Patrols

There were many small, localized events that happened during the patrolling phase of the Holland campaign, which characterized October and November 1944. Sergeant Paul A. Mullan of G/504 explains just a couple of examples of what it was like:

[Germans] even bumped into us one dark night while we were on patrol, thinking we were their replacements. Fortunately for us, they spoke first, which also was their last. One of our fellows was in a foxhole when a man he presumed to be a German officer, spoke to him from behind. The paratrooper, with his rifle crossed in front of him, was unable to turn around and shoot, so he just replied, "Ja," which apparently was the right answer, for the Nazi turned and walked into the darkness.[554]

The actions at the Wylerbergmeer and in the woods around Thornsche Molen were on the northern sector of the regimental defensive line. As October drug and the calendar turned to November, many of the intense and pitched patrolling actions migrated south towards the village of Wyler, Germany, sitting buttressed up along the Dutch-German border. The regiment's patrols towards the German lines in and about Wyler traversed two main areas and paths. The first major path was along the Oude Kleefsebaan, a road which ran along the border and the southern part of Wyler. The patrols would commonly continue south along the road, and fracas with the Germans who were dug into the fields along the road to the south of Wyler, or, further along the road, with the Germans hold-up in houses in the small hamlets of Lagewald or Vossendal.

The second major path was along the Nijmegen-Cleve Road, now called the N325, which ran along the southern bank of the Wylermeer before passing by the village for which the Meer is named. The Wylermeer, separated by the Wylerbergmeer by a dam, was an oblong moat approximately one-mile-long.

Private First Class David Whittier provided acute knowledge of the terrain: "The Nijmegen-Cleve Road runs along the friendly bank of the Wyler Meer," Whittier wrote, "and as it approaches the southern end of the lake it passes into the German line where it is shrouded in a heavy copse of trees and tangle underbrush." Here, the Germans kept reinforcing their line making it grow stronger as time drug on. By October 23, the German positions along the Nijmegen-Cleve Road were formidable. The Germans laid concertina wire laced with grenades attached to trip-wires through the dense woods, ran the wire across the road and joined it to the bank of the Wylermeer. An outpost with an MG-42 machine gun covered a section of the concertina wire. About 100 yards beyond that was a heavily fortified roadblock on the road, just before the road forked into a spur that led into the village of Wyler. The roadblock was a wrecked vehicle, surrounded with teller mines and dozens of felled trees. A German platoon, equipped with at least three machine guns, was posted at the roadblock. These obstacles, and ones like them, were to be faced by the paratroopers on each night's patrol. "Our only avenue of entry into the German line lay along that one-fifth of our sector that was not fronted by water," explained Whittier. "Every patrol that left our lines, of necessity, had to pass through this area. With five or six patrols moving out each night, this particular sector of the front became about as busy as Macy's basement in the days before Christmas. Each successive patrol ran into heavier oppositions from the enemy."

Paratroopers of Company B's 1st Platoon in Holland. They are: Jenchowski, Ian McGee, Graham, Lee Cox and Amedo Castagno. (T. Castagno)

Lieutenant Reneau Breard and Staff Sergeant Otto W. Huebner led their platoon of 31 paratroopers into the teeth of the German roadblock on the Nijmegen-Cleve Road on October 23. With the coordination of 81mm mortar fire and artillery, as well as dogged tactics by rushing the Germans from tree-to-tree – and covering each other – and under the rolling barrage of mortar and artillery, they were successful in mauling the platoon of Germans at the roadblock, killing eleven and capturing two, as well as capturing two German MG-42 machine guns.[555]

The Perfect Officer

Back in the United States, telegrams continued to be delivered to the families of the 504th Parachute Infantry Regiment's many casualties. In Holyoke, Massachusetts, Patricia Kennedy was walking home with the family dog from a trip to the store she was making for her mother. Her elder brother, Eddie, was serving in Holland as a platoon leader with Company I. The neighborhood she walked was a well-established, New England, working class neighborhood with small two-story homes. Just a stone-throws away to the east was the river, where as a boy Eddie had jumped off rocks and swam in the river.

As the young Patricia got closer to home, she saw the Western Union boy ride past on his bicycle and turn down her street, Pearl Street. Many of the young men on Pearl were in the service, so she wouldn't connect it to her family until she came up on the Kennedy house as the Western Union boy rode out of their driveway. Patricia remembered, "I went in the house and there was my father, he had been shaving and he still had lather on his face. He was holding the telegram. He couldn't open it. He handed it to my mother who opened it, and the sadness began. We had learned Edward had died of wounds suffered in Germany. It was a terribly sad day."[556]

On the night of October 30, I Company's Walter Hughes, who had celebrated his 19th birthday the previous day, reported to where 1st Lieutenant Edward W. Kennedy's 3rd Platoon was dug in along the outpost line. Hughes had joined I Company's Headquarters Section in August of 1944 while in England as a wireman/SCR300 radio operator. He was already on his second radio for the Holland operations, the first destroyed saving his life during the death-defying Waal River Crossing in September. Kennedy would be leading a patrol towards the German lines, with Hughes and his SCR300 accompanying.

Staff Sergeant William H. White, a revered and experienced platoon sergeant in I/504, was joining Kennedy's 3rd Platoon men. He was a short man of 25 who had his upbringing in rural Arkansas. He had a round face and a skinny frame. What White lacked in size, he made up for in aggressiveness and determination. Although Walter Hughes didn't know Sergeant White on a personal level, he had recognized the toughness of this man from Arkansas from the first time they met in England. *If he can't get through this war*, Hughes told himself, *nobody can.*

But disaster would soon strike as the patrol continued in the pitch black night. Sergeant White stepped on a mine, setting it off in an explosion. Sergeant White's blood sprayed across the front of Hughes's jump suit. The explosion seemed to be "right in front of me," Hughes vividly remembers as if it were yesterday, "and then as soon as the mine went off, shit hit the fan. They had everything all covered and bullets [were] flying all over the place. I'll never forget the sound of a German bullet going past your head." As machine gun fire raked the area, there was little hope for organization in the dark. "People took off by themselves, more or less," Hughes continued.[557]

Amidst the chaos, Lieutenant Kennedy, in an incredible act of valor, rushed forward to Sergeant White to render aid. Kennedy was "carrying him to safety when he stepped on a mine which blew off his left leg. First Lieutenant Kennedy crawled out of the mined area and collapsed."[558] White was still alive. It was decided by White, Russell McDermott, who was lightly wounded, and another man to drag Lieutenant Kennedy back first, and then they would come back for White.

Meanwhile, Hughes made his way to the company CP as fast as he could. "I come [sic] strolling into company headquarters," Hughes explained. He was a nervous wreck. Inside the house Burriss was using as a CP was Hughes's close friend Paul Gurley, one of the company clerks. Sergeant White's dark red blood was all over the front of Hughes's cotton khaki jump suit. Paul grabbed a hold of Walter as he was walking towards his bunk. "Sit down," Paul said, "you got shot."

"No," Walter replied, "I didn't."

"I just started for my bunk and laid down," Hughes remembered, "I was shaking like a leaf."[559]

Outside the CP was Captain Burriss. "Three [men] came back bringing the lieutenant," remembered Burriss. "He said, 'Moffatt, my foot feels funny. It's kind of numb.' I said, 'Let me look at it.'" Burriss and Kennedy had a short conversation.[560]

Just a moment later, Lieutenant Roy Hanna was coming up with a squad of G Company in tow. They would be replacing Kennedy's depleted platoon along the battalion's outpost line. Just outside of the house, Hanna saw Kennedy still lying on the stretcher. "I reported into a building," Hanna remembered, "where Lt. Col. Cook, Col. Tucker and others where just sort of milling around. Kennedy was lying on a stretcher with Capt. Kitchin standing by Kennedy's head. I stood at the foot of the stretcher and had a few words with Kennedy."

Kennedy's left foot and leg to just above his ankle was completely blown asunder.

"He looked at me and asked, 'How bad is it?' I looked at Kitchin and he shook his head and so I said something like, 'Not too bad, bruised a bit, you'll be O.K.'" Soon an ambulance was off to the field hospital with Lieutenant Kennedy.[561]

Lt. Ed Kennedy (Author's collection)

Just a short time later, Walter Hughes overheard someone come into the I Company CP and tell Burriss that Sergeant White was still in the minefield. When they went back to find White, he was missing. White's remains would not be recovered from the field of battle until 1946. His death left a great void in not only Company I, but the entire battalion. Men would follow him to the very gates of hell in the thick of mortal combat. "Sgt. White," wrote Roy Hanna, "was one of the great leaders."[562] White was selected to receive a battlefield commission to second lieutenant, and it was an accomplishment that he was extremely proud of. In one of his last letters to his mother, he wrote how proud he was of being selected to become a commissioned officer. Sadly, White did not live long enough to receive it. He also did not live long enough to wear the Silver Star Medal, awarded to him for actions on September 17. His memory and hardness in combat, however, never faded from those who knew him.

Sergeant White hailed from Hamburg, a town of 2,000 in rural southeastern Arkansas. One day during training at Fort Bragg he sat down alongside Edward P. Haider – who served in the 1st Platoon with White – and a circle of other paratroopers, and confided to them about his youth:

"I was in Arkansas," White said. "We didn't have shoes until we got in the service. We were poor as church mice. We finally got in the service and we got uniforms, shoes, and nice slacks and raincoats.

Oh, God, we got everything! We had pretty good service." When questioned what kind of service he was in White replied, "Oh, we were rum-runners." It would seem that his artillery unit was running booze on the side. "Anything went well with him," Haider recalled. "The guys would pull pranks you know, and he thought it was fine. As long as they got away with it, and nobody caught them. He says, 'We did that in the artillery.'"[563]

Seemingly anesthetized to pain and pity, White would come to be respected as one of the most relentless, dedicated, and wisest fighters in the 504th. He had brains seemingly made for war. In fact, William White's cousin Nellie can still remember the outgoing young man they knew only as 'Willy' dressed in a uniform and wearing "black and shiny and creaky" jump boots, showing the family how to dig a foxhole. Men would follow him anywhere in the confusion of mortal combat. When he said something, men responded. "He wasn't scared of anything," Private Francis Keefe remembered.[564]

After the conversation with Lieutenant Kennedy, when he was on the stretcher awaiting to be evacuated, Lieutenant Hanna received his mission and continued towards the outpost line with a guide from I Company. "From here I and my squad were led through a minefield to the outpost where we stayed until relieved; believe two nights and a day. When I got back I was surprised and saddened to hear that Kennedy had died on the way to the hospital."[565]

The death of both of these men, greatly respected both as men and combat soldiers, weighed heavily on the men of I Company, and the 3rd Battalion at large. "We lost Sergeant White," Captain Burriss reflected, "who was one of the best sergeants, and a good platoon leader in Lieutenant Kennedy. Unfortunately, we suffered accidents like that time and time again."[566]

Kennedy, son of Irish immigrants, was described as "the perfect officer." In England, just days before the regiment jumped into Holland, Kennedy was presented with his Silver Star Medal, for actions in Italy on November 9, 1943. The occasion was written home by a Red Cross worker: "We saw the general present the Silver Star to one of our friends for gallantry in action in Italy. It was a wonderful experience to be standing by a hedge beside an English lane, and see stretched out before us, our favorite regiment, complete with regimental band, and then to see Ken march forward across the meadow to receive his citation… His men adore him."[567]

Edward Kennedy was a born gentleman. Even in his days as a young man in the Civilian Conservation Corps, in the late 1930s, he exuded a gentlemen-like countenance, which was a common theme in his many letters of recommendation from CCC commanders. He displayed this in the 504th as well. Roy Hanna said that Kennedy "was one of the real young gentleman in the 504, and a great loss to society."[568]

Kennedy, ever a devout Catholic, had been yanked from seminary when the war broke out and was planning on returning to seminary upon his homecoming to become a Catholic priest. One of his younger brothers would go to seminary to finish what Edward started, as a way of honoring his memory.

Like all soldiers, Kennedy's thoughts often turned to his home in Holyoke, Mass. on 39 Pearl Street. In a letter written in Holland to his father, just nine days before his death, Eddie wrote that he "was dreaming of home in my hole the other night, trying to keep warm in a puddle of water. Our boys are doing a grand job, and you just can't beat our parachute outfit. There isn't much to say except I miss home more than ever, and long to be there with you all. God sparing me – we'll all get back to Ireland. Love, Eddie."[569]

Lieutenant Kennedy hated war, but he fought with all his might because he believed in the Allied cause and felt distasteful of the Germans, saying they needed cleaning up. He wrote how he missed playing baseball, and lunchtime games at his former employer White & Wyckoff, his old Holyoke friends, and the privilege of gathering for mass without fear of being shelled. He often wrote home about how sick he was of war's miseries and killings. From Anzio, he had written about how, despite the killings and mortal combat, the farm life lived as they always had as though nothing was happening around them. The sheep and cattle grazed amidst the land mines, back dropped by barbed wire which would occasionally entangle the chickens. The birds sang in the sky. These little things reminded Kennedy of how unholy modern war is, and how desperately they must fight to bring it to an end. "There have been many a times when I didn't know what writing paper looked like," Kennedy wrote in one letter, "and wished it were a cigarette I had in my pocket instead of a pen... There have been lots of times I cried over the loss of a friend – have seen mutilated bodies – stiff and bloated – have gone for hours without sleep, slept in a pig pen to keep dry, and have marched till I couldn't lift my feet another step, they were so bloody and blistered. I was shell-shocked for one period. I can recall coming down from a mountain with my platoon of dirty, exhausted men, and how scared we were when we reached the bottom. A jeep pulled out in front of us – the first we had heard for a while. We all hit the mud together. We were so nervous we were ready to shoot till we realized it was American. They can say back in the States, there are so many Americans or divisions of American soldiers that are overseas in danger – well, it doesn't mean a damn cause there are only a few fighting and the rest sit on their ass in comfort. Excuse this letter but I just had it."[570]

Indestructible

Like all families in the same situation, the Kennedy household was rocked by the loss. Eddie's parents got to writing, searching for answers regarding the circumstances surrounding their son's death; on December 13 his mother wrote Major General Gavin.

Lt. Ed Kennedy shortly after graduating from Parachute School in 1942. (Kennedy family)

Meanwhile, Eddie's best friend 2nd Lieutenant John "Jack" Magner was working in the Internal Security Branch of the Army Service Forces Depot in Columbus, Ohio when news of Eddie's death hit. Magner had previously served in the regiment in Italy, until he was wounded on the day they made the amphibious landing at Anzio. He arrived back in the States in April 1944, and when he heard the news about Eddie, he immediately wrote a letter to Mrs. Kennedy. But finding that he had lost the home address, he sent his letter to the local newspaper, the *Holyoke Transcript-Telegram* (which Eddie had sent to him in Italy to keep up on news), and asked if they would be "kind enough to check your files and make certain that Mrs. Kennedy has been officially notified of her son's death, and if she has received the notification, please forward the enclosed letter to her."[571]

The letter, which was forwarded, read:

15 December 1944

My Dear Mrs. Kennedy:

One time in Italy when Eddie was missing for a few days I knew it would be up to me to write and try to explain the situation to you. I started several times but to no avail. Fortunately, Ken turned up safe and sound.

Now it has really happened, I can hardly believe it. There was something about your boy that seemed indestructible. In some sense of the word he was indestructible; I know I'll never forget him and there are many more in the Regiment that won't either.

He was a great soldier and an even greater son and I can only say that he was my best friend, and a good Irishman.

Enclosed is a Mass Card and I'll always remember him in my prayers.

Jack[572]

That was the beginning of an exchange between the Kennedy's and Magner and his wife. As Magner had hurt his hand making it hard to write, his wife Eleanor wrote the letters. She said that her husband "has talked about Eddie so much since I have known him that I feel as though I know him myself." Lieutenant Magner had written someone in the regiment and asked for the circumstances of Eddie's death, but as of January 3 had yet to receive a reply. He suggested to the Kennedy's that they write the regiment's Catholic priest Father Kozak as he "was a good friend of Eddie and if you wrote to him he might be able to give you the details." This, the Kennedy's had already done.

Eleanor Magner also wrote that "Jack is no longer hospitalized but has returned to duty. Due to the fact that he is not very strong he was transferred to the Quartermaster Corps. At present, he is trying to get back in the paratroops but since he heard about Eddie I believe he is changing his plans… In closing we assure you that Eddie will never be forgotten in our prayers. May God bless you all."[573]

Eventually, Father Kozak wrote the Kennedy's a reply, giving them account of Eddie's last moments on earth:

Belgium

Dec. 30, 1944

Dear Mrs. Kennedy,

Received your letter of inquiry concerning your late son, Edward. Really intended to write you sooner but recent developments forced us back into combat.

I have known Edward even before he joined the outfit. It was in Africa, one Sunday morning, I asked for a Mass server. A young and handsome lieutenant stepped forward. Hearing his Latin and the manner in which he served aroused my curiosity. After Mass, Edward told me his history. Shortly afterwards, Ed reported to the outfit and we have been close friends.

His religious fervor soon attracted attention both of officers and enlisted men. His example aided me greatly in my work. During combat at times, Edward was ordered to take a patrol out away from the regiment. Miles away, he would locate a church and take his men to Mass.

I'll always remember the day that Ed died. While on patrol he stepped on a mine receiving his fatal wounds. He tried to carry out his wounded sergeant at the time. He received prompt first-aid, and given priority, and sent immediately to the hospital. On the way, he asked for me. All this happened about ten at night.

About eleven thirty, as I was preparing for bed, a jeep driver came in and told me what had occurred, and that Edward wished to see me. Immediately I called the medical company who said that he was transferred to a larger hospital, and that his condition did not appear too serious. I decided to wait until the next day to make the long trip; besides, it was black night and blackout had to be observed.

I then spoke with the doctors who administered first-aid. They too, were surprised at Edward's condition. He joked and seemed as if he didn't feel his wounds. But, I couldn't rest, so summoned my driver, and we raced to the hospital.

I found him on the x-ray table. He greeted me with his usual smile. To me, he didn't appear to be in a too serious condition. I heard his confession, gave him Holy Communion, and, being in doubt, administered Holy Oils.

We chatted for a while, while the operating table was being prepared. Here I noticed a change coming over him. And he was rushed on the table. Shock set in, and, despite 1,500 CCs of blood plasma, he failed to rally.

His death was a shock to everyone. No one realized his popularity until after his death. The colonels called, officers asked, and enlisted men, outside of his company, asked about him, and mourned our loss, because he was loved by all and was missed by them.

He was buried with full military honors in an American cemetery in Holland, a Catholic priest of the division performing the service.

Our loss is heaven's gain, and Edward gave his life to obtain eternal life for which he was so well prepared.

Yours in Christ,
Fr. Edwin J. Kozak, OMC
Formerly of Granby, Mass.[574]

As for Lieutenant Jack Magner, he made a career out of the Army, which he had been in since his enlistment in 1940. In addition to his service in the 504th PIR during the war, he had also been present for the first shots fired on Americans during the war when he was in Hawaii during the Japanese attack on Pearl Harbor. In 1959, Major Magner was serving in Japan when he passed away at the age of 40. He is buried in Arlington National Cemetery.

By the end of the war, all four Kennedy brothers served in the armed forces. After Eddie's death, the youngest brother John forged their parent's signature and served in the Marine Corps. As Eddie had been in seminary before the war, John went into the seminary after he returned home to finish what his brother had started; he dropped out shortly before his final vows and wed. The Kennedy's became prominent in Holyoke, and John served on the Board of Alderman's. In 2001, Kennedy Park, located on the grounds of the grammar school Eddie attended, and only a few blocks away from the house on Pearl, was dedicated in his honor, and it is now a place where children play on the playground or on the baseball diamond; fitting, as Eddie was a star catcher.

In accordance with his wishes, First Lieutenant Edward W. Kennedy was returned to the United States and he is buried with his family in Holyoke, Massachusetts.

The Grind Effects Both Sides

Although it had been badly shaken-up, the roadblock on the Nijmegen-Cleve Road which Lieutenant Reneau Breard's men had assaulted on October 23 remained intact and a troubled spot for the regiment. On November 1, two officers and 25 men of H Company went to outpost the high ground on the ridge above the German roadblock, only some 100 meters away from where Lieutenant Kennedy was mortally wounded in the minefield two nights before. Telephone wire was laid and trenches dug along the ridge line. At 2100, 14 paratroopers moved out to contact the Germans and try and take a prisoner. They ran into the concertina wire and tried to flank it, when a German threw a grenade at the patrol. Bursts from close-range machine guns opened up, and mortar shells began to fall. The patrol, carrying captured German panzerfausts, fired them, and the Germans fired panzerfausts back. The paratroopers began to move back under mortar fire, which killed Private John Beyer as they were withdrawing. Captain Gorham wrote in the regiment's nightly patrolling report, "Enemy strongpoint is well developed and organized with [a] crossfire of machine guns. 50mm mortar began to fall in two minutes of first contact. Fire fight developed and enemy was pressed hard. Red flare went up, aimed towards Wyler, and prepared concentration of 81mm mortar [fire which] fell across [the] road to rear of patrol."[575] The following night, 2nd Lieutenant Robert S. Wright led two men to reconnoiter the roadblock. While they were observing the roadblock, they heard mortars fire and sought cover. Lieutenant Wright stepped on a mine on the southern fringe of the woods while looking for cover, and both of his legs were cleanly blown off on the upper thigh, not even leaving shrapnel. He was 30-years-old.[576]

Sus Gonzales was the Operations Sergeant of Company H in Holland. On September 20, during the Waal River Crossing, Gonzales was fighting with members of his company towards the bridge when they were pinned down by a German patrol not far from the railway embankment, near where G Company was later pinned down. Gonzales dashed through heavy German fire across 15 yards of open ground, climbed the railway embankment and ran through three magazines from his Thompson, killing 18 Germans and wounding several others. Gonzales was later killed in the Battle of the Bulge. (Gonzales family)

Between Anzio and Holland, the regiment became masters of patrolling; in Holland there were typically at least five or six patrols sent out each night, and many times more than that, and a majority were led by an officer. Although they did a lot of it, the enlisted men hated it due to the strain on nerves produced by walking through enemy territory in the middle of the night. The regiment conducted three types of patrols: combat, contact, and reconnaissance. Combat patrols were to eject the enemy from a certain position, perhaps a house or a small patch of woods, but most commonly to capture an enemy prisoner; contact patrols were sent to maintain a connection with adjacent companies. Sometimes, due to casualties or terrain, there would be gaps in the line where there was little or no physical presence. These gaps were covered by fire or patrols, usually at every odd hour. Reconnaissance patrols were to investigate enemy positions and see how the enemy might be shifting his forces or if certain German outposts or foxholes were occupied. Some small listening posts in the German lines also monitored vehicle traffic. Some of these patrols were ordered by division, especially when a certain area in question needed to be reconnoitered for their planning: road conditions for tanks, German troop concentrations, or other such matters of importance to the overall picture.

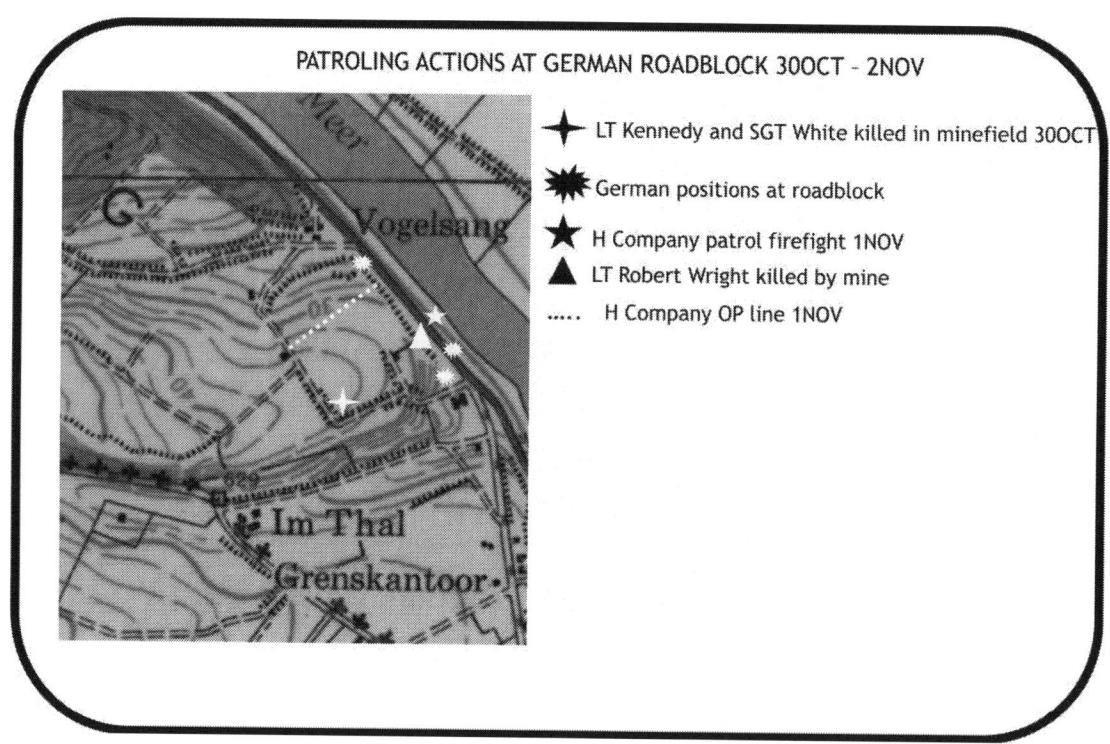

Typically, the regiment exceeded in the number of patrols required, which begs the question of why such actions were conducted in such volumes. Lieutenant Virgil Carmichael provides the answer:

Higher commands are always seeking intelligence of the enemy and regimental headquarters was pressing us for information from the enemy. We were patrolling constantly in an effort to capture prisoners because they were our best source of information concerning the activities of the enemy. In operating as a battalion, which is a rather small, compact unit (our airborne companies were rather small), there was a close comradeship between all the officers in the battalion, and usually a patrol was under the command of a commissioned officer. So that, the officers were very concerned about the taking of prisoners, since if we could take prisoners regularly, it would mean that we would have to patrol less often and the exposure of the men would be less. So that, we were very much concerned with the taking and keeping of any prisoners because it meant that our patrolling would not have to be as vigorous and dangerous.[577]

Collecting the patrol reports was Captain Fordyce Gorham, the regimental intelligence officer. Patrol leaders would go to headquarters and report what they had saw and done, or often times Gorham would go to where one of the patrols was operating and await their return. Gorham was one of the tallest men in the regiment, and a physically imposing figure due to his height and athletic physique. "Gorham scared the hell out of me on patrols," Edward Mokan wrote. "His big size 14 boots made more noise on patrol. He never wore a helmet. He was like bull, but the greatest guy ever."[578] With the collection of patrol reports coming in from the men each night, they would all be typed up in a nightly patrolling report and sent to higher headquarters. Often, Gorham could be seen by the men parading around freshly-captured German soldiers on their way to the regiment's PW cage.

At the PW cage, the mission of extracting the knowledge the German prisoners possessed fell to the professionals of Interrogation Prisoner of War Team #45: 2nd Lieutenant Alfred Landgraff, Master Sergeant Kenneth A. Nickels and Staff Sergeant Mercel Bollag. Virtually all of the troopers who served on IPW teams were first-generation immigrants, or had immigrated themselves, and many were Jewish. Staff Sergeant Bollag, for instance, had been born in Zurich, Switzerland and had immigrated to the US when he was 19, and enlisted about two years later. By virtue of the job, all spoke German, and many of them spoke more than one language. Lieutenant Alfred Landgraff was born to German parents who had immigrated to the USA from Russia. He hailed from Milwaukee, Wisconsin, and could fluently read, write, and speak German, as well as speak a little Russian; and Lieutenant Landgraff had an illustrious career before joining the 504th's team. He was one of the now famous "Ritchie Boys" – a veteran of the Army's Military Intelligence Training Center situated on the secret Camp Ritchie in rural Maryland. After Landgraff arrived in England, he volunteered for the 82nd Airborne Division and received his wings on March 30, 1944. On D-Day, Landgraff parachuted into Normandy where he was involved in astounding heroics on D-Day afternoon during the fighting at the Merderet River Bridge at LaFiere. He was awarded the Silver Star for standing fast under withering German fire while guarding an anti-tank gun as men ran for more ammunition to defeat the German tanks trying to overrun the causeway.

IPW Team #45 was a unique asset which many regiments did not receive. Between D-Day and August 1945, only approximately 72 such IPW teams saw service in the entire European Theater of

Operations. Although under the operational control of the 504th, the team and its personnel belonged to the Military Intelligence Service, and it was considered an "Intelligence Specialist Team." Being as it was assumed that freshly captured Germans would have the latest and most valuable information, some of the teams were attached to combat units on the front where they could interrogate prisoners and provide timely, detailed intelligence to combat commanders. This was the role IPW Team #45 played.

As at Anzio, the prisoners captured by the men of the 504th Parachute Infantry Regiment fell into the hands of the IPW team whose job it was to know the enemy; it was not uncommon for the team to know the names of the lieutenants and captains commanding the platoons and companies opposing the 504th. IPW Team #45 provided the regiment with German-speakers trained in interrogation, and the product they produced with that skill were views into the lives the Germans lead on the other side of the lines. And as at Anzio, the small group comprising the team interviewed every German who found his way into the hands of the regiment's paratroopers, and not only did they interrogate live prisoners, but also told the tales of dead ones when they translated documents recovered from the bodies of deceased enemy troops. Things such as letters, written orders, or pay books (a *soldbuch*) could help not only identify who was opposing the regiment, but also their unit composition, how long the average soldier they were fighting had been in the army, and what types of training they had.

Part of IPW Team #45 photographed in Holland. They are Lt. Alfred Landgraff (OIC), Sergeant Bollag, and Lt. Walter Spitzer. (Guy Condra)

The job for IPW Team #45 began immediately after they landed in Holland. By the end of the first day of Operation MARKET GARDEN, Landgraff and his men had already interviewed 20 Germans, from a mixture of units, which had been captured by the 504th Parachute Infantry. The Germans came from units as varied as soldiers from anti-aircraft companies, a German from an NCO school, and a few members of the regiment's old nemesis from Italy, the Hermann Göring Division. "At Grave," Landgraff wrote of the knowledge he gained the day of the jump, "expected enemy strength is about 100 men. Germans in this part of Holland came from all kinds of replacement and training units. Most of the men are very young, 17-18 years old, and inexperienced in combat. Some of the Germans coming in late in the afternoon were extremely old from 50 to 60 years, just drafted about 6 weeks ago. Many Germans had left their unit in Belgium and were on their own, badly equipped. Nijmegen is occupied by about 200-300 Germans. Some are replacements."[579]

Landgraff's reports were sent to division where they were met by Captain Irvin Bushman, the divisional IPW officer, where all of the information from the prisoners would be analyzed. Bushman, who Landgraff had replaced as the 504th's interrogation officer when he was promoted, would publish a periodic interrogation report to accompany the divisional intelligence report. At the beginning of Operation MARKET GARDEN, what Lieutenant Landgraff was seeing in the 20 prisoners taken by the 504th on September 17 – where no more than two men seemed to be from the same unit – must have been reflective of the prisoners captured by the rest of the division. In the first four days of Market Garden the division as a whole captured 2,000 German soldiers. "It is hardly an exaggeration," wrote Captain Bushman, "to say that for every four PW processed a new unit identification was made." From the Germans, Bushman and the IPW officers of the division were able to deduce the German's strategy and situation, and a three-page summation of the enemy's situation was written by Bushman on September 22. It, in part, reads:

The threat to the German border from our east flank was real, but not as important as the bridges which we had captured initially, and others taken later, which have enabled us to bring armor through with lightning speed. Therefore, he proceeded to fill up the gap on our east flank with motley groups of landesschützen. In these groups we find the dregs of Europe's manpower. We find men from 45-65 years of age, men who would under normal circumstances be retiring from active life to make room for their sons and grandsons. These men are carrying guns against the invading enemy. But Hitler knows his men. He knows that he cannot expect any great demonstrations of patriotism or combat efficiency from these people. He has put them in to fill a hole. Then he proceeded to round up all of the spare parts which he had lying around in his SS and parachute training centers, in replacement depots, in hospitals and convalescent homes, in straggler and collecting points... The one outstanding factor with this latter group is that their fanatical devotion to Adolf Hitler is just as rampant as it ever was. And their fighting is ample evidence of that. These people were chosen to turn the tide against us.[580]

As Operation MARKET GARDEN progressed, more in-tact German parachute units came to oppose the division. Although many of them were severely understrength, it brought lethal combat power to bear against the US paratroopers, including those of the 504th PIR. These were the men the regiment was facing in battles like those at Thornsche Molen on October 6, and on the nighttime patrols and skirmishes with the Germans. Although they were steadfast in holding ground, their aggressiveness was markedly lacking as October and November drug. Captain Fordyce Gorham, the 504th's intelligence officer, wrote in mid-October that the enemy capabilities would allow them to launch "limited objective attacks," but that was not a favored action. They did have favorable defensive positions, and were apt to hold it and "organize the low ground in the front against any possible break-though we might attempt to launch. This capability is favored in that the enemy shows no marked aggressiveness, lack of active patrolling (both combat and reconnaissance) and no apparent large scaled build-up of company, battalion or regimental size in front of this organization."

Captain Irvin Bushman, the divisional IPW officer, interviewing captured Germans on September 17, 1944 shortly after landing in Holland. (Robin Bushman)

By November 10, Landgraff's team had processed 919 German soldiers through the 504th PIR's prisoner of war cage since they landed in Holland. By that time, the Germans were tired and had no relief in sight. One prisoner captured by the 504th on October 26 stated that his unit – the 5th Parachute Regiment

– had been on the line continuously since the American parachute landings, and it consisted of only two platoons of paratroopers and one platoon of a parachute flak regiment, mustering up only some 100 men.

On the 10th of November, Landgraff's team interrogated prisoner #920. The German soldier had only been in Holland for five days, but had fought and been wounded in Normandy near Saint Lo, and had personally planned desertion for some time before he, as Landgraff wrote in his interrogation report, "wrote a note, a message, advising his comrades to do the same thing, place this in his helmet, took off his boots and sneaked out on hands and knees."

Capt. Irvin Bushman on a destoryed German tank in Holland. (Robin Bushman)

The German stated that there was only 61 men left in his company, and he heard they had been on the line five weeks. The prisoner reinforced what Gorham had written the month before. As Landgraff wrote, "PW claims morale of his unit to be extremely low. As an example he cited an instance occurring on the night of November 8th. On this night volunteers were sought for night reconnaissance patrol into our lines. No volunteers were forthcoming. The morale of the men was so low that the entire patrol was called off." Despite this, the German's resiliency to continue to effectively fight the paratroopers was impressive; this particular prisoner's decision to desert is not reflective of the rest of the Germans in his unit. Even after the regiment was relived, there would be no breakthrough in the sector until February 1945.[581]

The interrogation reports generated by the IPW team, such as the one chronicling PW #920, were sent to the regimental intelligence officer Captain Gorham and attached to the regiment's periodic intelligence report. They would ideally be read by the commanders so they could use the information gained from the Germans, information about their morale, armament and locations, in planning anything from patrols to attacks.

Members of the Dutch Underground and two paratroopers. Second from left is the legendary Theodore Bachenheimer of the 504th PIR, and third from right is another paratroopers, likely Lt. Walter Spitzer of IPW Team #45. After this photograph, Bachenheimer would go behind the German lines, be captured before subsequently being summarily executed by the Germans. (Guy Condra)

Lieutenant Landgraff's team was perhaps unique in that it did more than interrogate prisoners while they were in Holland: Landgraff and his men had become established with the Dutch underground movement. They also worked with Theodore Bachenheimer, who by September 21 had firmly embedded himself with the Free Netherlands Army and began to help run operations of the underground. By the end of October, Landgraff had his own network of some eight Dutch civilians, between the ages of 20 and 38, working for him. Landgraff was receiving intelligence reports of German activity from places as far away as Hertogenbusch, some 25 miles distant; he was told that Dutch and German SS were digging in. There, Landgraff also heard that all the farmers in the village of Roshalen, just to the east of Hertogenbusch, were forced to give the Germans their horses. While the prisoner interrogations were of great help and importance to the regiment in determining the enemy's motives, disposition and capabilities, much of the work with the underground was done in the shadows, and the totality of its contribution to the liberation of Holland will likely never be fully known.[582]

IPW Team #45 remained with the 504th PIR after Holland, and continued to provide the regiment with critical intelligence on the German units opposing the regiment until the end of the war.

Return to Sender

On November 9, Walter Hughes penned a letter to his childhood friend from Brooklyn Herb Brown, who was serving as a tanker with the 4th Armored Division in France. Little did Walter know, but Walt would again hold the letter soon after he dropped it in the mail, when it was returned with a stamp on it marked, "RETURN TO SENDER" and a note scribbled across the front of the enveloped reading "DECEASED." It was then he found out that his childhood friend had been killed in France in September. To Walter, the news was a shocking blow which upset him greatly.

November 9, 1944

Somewhere in Germany

Dear Herb,

How's everything going down your way pal, you still ducking 88s and burp guns? We are. Boy, I never thought I could get so close to the ground in all my life. Boy this combat stuff sure isn't cracked up like the movies make it is it pal? Have you heard from Joe lately? When I wrote him last he was at Camp Hood, Texas. I have not received any answer to my letters. I guess he was too busy with the women down in the Lone Star State. Boy, I sure would like to be strolling around the neighborhood with the old gang now. Well, I guess we'll all get together again as soon as this stuff is all finished with. Well, I have to hang now, Herb. Don't forget to drop me a line and let me know how things are.

Walt[583]

Relief

Ever since the men parachuted into Holland on September 17, the troopers of the 504th Parachute Infantry Regiment had been in continuous contact with German troops. While in the forests and farm fields stretching the Dutch-German border from Erlecom, Holland to Wyler, Germany, the men had seen fall descend on the countryside. The average temperature in September when they arrived in the country had been around 68 degrees, and as November set in the average temperature dropped to around 45 degrees. On November 10, word was received that the regiment would be relieved by the 8th Canadian Brigade within the next few nights, with the relief completed by the 13th. But before leaving Holland, Lieutenant Reneau Breard would see snow – a stark contrast from the beautiful weather he had experienced when he parachuted into the Dutch countryside nearly two months prior. "I had to wait and wait and wait because the unit that relieved us, I thought they never would get there, and I got orders just to pull out, and then stay and put the Canadian company in position whenever they got there. They got there at daylight, and going in they made too damn much noise and got shelled and everything. I got them all fixed up and I pulled out real fast and it started snowing."[584]

In the 57 days the regiment was in Holland, they had experienced the full breadth of weather, and the full breadth of the German war machine, which, as they experienced, was still alive and well. The German still had fight in him, and for much of the defensive phase of the Holland operation, stretching from September 23-November 13, the men were on edge expecting a large German counterattack, but it never came. What they had been expecting in Holland, they would experience in the Belgian Bulge a month later. But first they were given a chance to rest in the French military barracks of Sissonne, France and recuperate from the losses they experienced in Holland. Over the course of 57 hard days and nights, the regiment suffered 98 killed, 88 missing, and 443 wounded. However, the damage that they were credited with inflicting upon the Germans was nearly two-fold: they were credited with 920 prisoners and killed an estimated 1,110 enemy soldiers.[585]

This historical photo of Kenneth Nicoll and Hartwell Stoneham, of the 2nd Battalion's 81mm Mortar Platoon, showcases a well-established mortar pit during the defensive phase of combat operations in Holland, and the results of German counter-battery. Ken Nicoll himself describes the context of the photo:

"Sgt. Nicoll and Stoneham in Berg en Dal, Holland. Screaming meanie shell set fire to this position. Taken just after we put out fire and were getting ready to fire again. Note burned ammo. All burning equip. has been dragged aside. (Oct 44)."

(Thomas Nicoll)

19

I HAVE NOTHING BUT RESPECT AND ADMIRATION FOR THESE MEN

Disembarking the truck at the French military barracks at Camp Sissone, France was 22-year-old Morris Holmstock, who was happy to be alive and out of Holland. Standing in a crowd, Holmstock heard Colonel Tucker address a group of troopers. "Men," said the colonel, "no more combat. We're going to rest for two months!" The news was welcome as they were all understrength and in need of replacements to bring their ranks back up to combat strength, and the veterans, like Holmstock, had wearied bodies which needed to be rested after a hard-fought campaign.

Holmstock had a long journey to finally seeing combat with a parachute outfit, having volunteered for the parachute troops twice. Holmstock grew up on the north side of Philadelphia and voluntarily joined the Army on September 1, 1942. The recruiter asked him what he wanted sign up for as a military occupational specially: "I looked up at the posters on the wall and one was a paratrooper. I said, 'Either a bombardier or a paratrooper.'" He got more than he bargained for, as he was sent to the "Currahee's" of the 506th Parachute Infantry. After completing basic training with the regiment at Camp Taccoa, they began marching to Atlanta, destined for Parachute School at Fort Benning. "We got up at 8 o'clock in the morning and stopped at 7." They marched hundreds of miles in the hot sun of Georgia, and finally reached Benning where he graduated Parachute School with the 506th. "After I got my wings, there was [sic] a lot of gremlins in the outfit, and Colonel Sink was the commanding officer of the 506th and he had us fall out and he said, 'Anyone who doesn't like it here take a step forward and we will transfer you immediately.'" Holmstock stepped forward and was transferred to the 300th Infantry's Cannon Company. After a short while he missed the fast-paced paratroops and re-volunteered. As he had already gotten his wings, he was put directly in a paratrooper replacement depot and sent to the Airborne Training Center in North Africa before joining the 504th PIR at Anzio.[586]

Willard Tess Willard Tess of F Company was one of the hardest paratroopers in the 504th. During the assult on the Grave Bridge shortly after landing in Holland, Tess was wounded in 32 places by shrapnel, but continued to dash through heavy German fire and was responsible for killing several Germans. He returned to the company shortly after recovering from the wounds, and was wounded for a second time in Holland during the 25OCT company-sized raid. (Mike Tess)

As replacements were needed after Holland, newer paratroopers were sent to Sissone ahead of the regiment's arrival. One of these men was 23-year-old Edwin R. Bayley of Maine. He had training in the States with the 87th Infantry Division, and was sent to England with that division. After D-Day, he was transferred into a replacement depot near Liverpool, where he volunteered to become a paratrooper.

I joined the 82nd at their jump school at Ashwell near Leicester, England near the end of September 1944. Following two weeks of strenuous physical exercise, ground level training in parachute handling, mock door exercise, and qualifying plane jumps... our group received jump boots, shoulder and hat patches and wings and were trucked to the 504 camp at Evington, next to Leicester.

We were not yet assigned to company's as the regiment was in Holland. After a couple of weeks, we flew to France and helped set up the new 504 camp at Sissone.

Ed Bayley helped put up the large, canvas bivouac tents that enlisted men had become accustomed to during their short periods of rest in Italy and their extended stay in England. When the 504th arrived, Ed

Bayley found a home with the 1st Squad of Company A's 1st Platoon: "Chow time passed O.K.," he recalled, "and then it was doughnut line time. The first trooper noticing the newly arrived me was Harry Freeman who made me welcome and introduced me to the others. From then on, I was just another one of the troopers."[587]

The officers were billeted in old French military barracks. Roy Hanna remembered that his 3rd Battalion, which he had been a member of since it was activated, always had a great compliment of officers who almost always got along and associated with one another in the rest areas, and often held parties.

Lieutenant Thomas Utterback had been sent a toy jeep, and he wrote that he was having fun putting together and that "all of these geezers have fun helping too." Utterback wrote his wife about one of the parties they had on November 27, resulting in Lieutenant Robert "Bobby-trap" Blankenship deciding to marry Eulalie Sutherland, who he had met in Alexandrea, Louisiana before the war. To him, she was Lalee. "The boys are having a great time tonight," Utterback wrote. "A kangaroo court on whether to get married or not. The single boys, one at a time, bring up their problems (backed by other single bucks) and we just naturally settle all of his problems. It's all helped along by various bottles of cognac of course. Booby-Trap had just up and decided by golly that he's gonna marry that girl. Hasn't written much lately but he's going to write tonight. He has several fellows who want to add a line to help the matter along."[588]

Roy Hanna remembered another party some of the battalion's officers had in the barracks:

While we were in Holland the Army started issuing a bottle of booze each month (I believe) to each officer. We never received any while in Holland, but when we got back to the French Barracks the back log was issued to us - a bunch of all kinds of stuff. This led to a drinking party. We were billeted in a French barracks with concrete floors and three beds per room; two beds high and one single.

When we arrived there Murph [Lieutenant Ernest P. Murphy], Mac [Lieutenant Allen F. McClain] and I were assigned to live together. We tossed for bunks, Mac got the upper, Murph the lower, and I got the single.

Our party was in a very large unfurnished room at the end of the barracks. Don't remember much about this except a lot of drinking, talking and singing. Mac passed out and so Murph and I more or less dragged him to our room and decided to put him in his upper bunk (no reason we didn't just put him in the single - not doing much thinking at that time). Anyway, I had Mac's head/shoulder area and Murph his legs. We got him about half way up and started to laugh and I dropped Mac, but Murph still held his feet about shoulder high. Mac's head hit the floor with a bang. This sobered us up a bit and we managed to put him in the upper bunk. The next morning when I got awake the first thing I thought of [was] did we kill Mac? I jumped out of bed and shook him awake. He had a slight headache, but didn't even have a bump on his head.[589]

Shortly after, Roy Hanna was called into Colonel Tucker's office. Hanna was informed that he was selected to receive a 30-day furlough back to the USA. It was well deserved, and Hanna had much to go home for – he had a newborn daughter that he had not yet seen or held, although he kept a photo of his daughter in the clear custom handgrips of his .45 pistol.

Hanna was not the only person selected; there were several others including Sergeant Lawrence Stimpson, also an old veteran who had been with the regiment from the beginning. Sergeant Stimpson was sent home with a letter from Colonel Tucker:

Sgt. Lawrence W. Stimpson:

You have been selected to represent your company in the United States. It is a reward which you justly deserve, and I both congratulate you and thank you.

It has been your devotion to duty, your ability, and your cheerfulness in the face of hardship that have contributed so much to the success of this regiment in its more than 200 days of actual combat. You have molded this regiment into what it is today - outstanding in the allied army.

Thank you, good luck and happy landings.

— R.H. Tucker
Colonel, 504th Prcht. Inf.
Commanding.[590]

Others who were not quite as lucky to go back to the USA were handed out passes to go to nearby Rheims or Paris on leave. The time in Sissone was also a time to catch up on correspondence.

Next-of-Kin Letters

Many letters went out to the families of friends, comrades, and respected leaders which had been lost in Holland. Although some have been quoted in previous chapters, personal letters to the next-of-kin of deceased paratroopers were not relatively common, contrary to popular belief. When such letters were written, they were often responses to inquiries made by the family, where they would write one of the company's officers or a friend of their deceased son or brother. One such letter was written by Captain George Warfield in response to an inquiry from Lieutenant Clayton Johnston, whose 18-year-old brother Warren Johnston had been killed in the Waal River Crossing on September 20, 1944. Clayton had last seen his brother when Warren was in the hospital in England recovering from wounds he had received while the regiment was at Anzio.

France

30 Nov. 1944

Dear Lt. Johnston:

Am in receipt of your letter dated Nov. 9th, inquiring about your brother, who was recently killed in action.

Pvt. Warren Johnston was killed during an attack after crossing the Waal River, near Nijmegen, Holland. You probably read in the paper or heard over the radio about the crossing of the Waal on Sept. 20, which will go down in military history for the bravery and initiative on the part of every man with which the mission was carried out.

Pvt. Warren Johnston was buried in the American grave yard several miles south of Nijmegen, Holland. His personal effects have been forwarded through military channels for disposition.

If I can be of any further assistance to you drop me a line.

Sincerely yours,
G.W. Warfield
Capt., 504th Para. Regt.
Comdg. Hq. 3rd Bn.[591]

The cemetery which Captain Warfield referred to in his letter was the Temporary American Cemetery about five miles south of Nijmegen. The cemetery was located on the grounds of a brewery in the village of Molenhoek. Here, all the soldiers of the 82nd Airborne Division who lost their lives in Holland were temporarily put to rest. After the war, families would have the decision to either have their loved ones moved to permanent American cemeteries overseas, or to have their loved ones repatriated to a domestic cemetery of their choosing.

One of the paratroopers resting in Molenhoek was the close friend of Seymour Flox, Private Robert T. Koelle who was also killed in the Waal River Crossing on September 20. Flox had instructed his mother to call Koelle's parents, and when Flox wrote a long letter home describing his experiences in Holland during Operation MARKET GARDEN, Flox's mother transcribed the letter and forwarded it to Koelle's parents. Flox also visited Koelle's grave at Molenhoek and took photographs of the cemetery, which were also eventually forwarded to the Koelle family.

Hi Shorty:

Here's your wondering son again. I just had breakfast and now I'm sitting down and writing a few lines. We had a nice breakfast of grapefruit juice, hot cakes, sausage, and coffee. When I got back to my room I washed and made my bed and swept the floor.

There was a notice on the bulletin board that we can tell where we are and also say something about our experiences. Well, we jumped into Holland about one thirty on September the seventeenth. We had a pretty smooth ride over and encountered some flak over the flood area in Holland. We were lucky and only had one plane shot down on the trip over, but one of my good friends was hurt pretty bad on that plane. We were pretty well loaded down with equipment so I made a pretty hard landing. I just skimmed over a house and landed just beside a haystack, there were three Dutchmen sitting there watching the big show and when they saw I was coming down near them, they ran like the devil himself was after them. You have to give the Air Corps a lot of credit on this mission because they did a marvelous job. They dropped us right on our drop zone and in no time we were assembled and ready.

The first two days we met little opposition, in fact we mostly drank milk and stole eggs out of chicken houses. However, on the third day came the worst fight I ever hope to be in. We made the river crossing at Nijmegen and took the bridge. We made a forced march of about six miles up the river bank and there we assembled by boat loads of about fourteen men to a small canvas assault boat. We started out with twenty-six boats and ended up with six. The boats were about the size of a good size row boat and when you put that number of men in a boat with all their weapons and equipment you have quite a load. We had to paddle the boat ourselves and it seemed as we were going around in circles. The Waal River is only about two hundred yards wide, but it seemed we would never get to the other side. When we got down the bank we started to catch hell. We were the first wave, and rifles, machine guns, and mortars opened up on us as soon as we stuck our heads up. But we couldn't go back, so we just started moving and I do mean fast.

Shorty, making that crossing was the worst hell I've ever been through. There have been a few tough spots where I thought I'd met my maker, but then I could almost see him reaching out for me; but I guess our prayers were heard and that's why I'm able to write about it now.

When we started across the bullets were coming so close that if they wouldn't hit you they splash water in your face. We were all paddling like mad, but you just couldn't paddle in time with each other and that doubled the job. When we finally did get across we were all tired out, but there was no resting then, we started up the river bank. We fought our way to the railroad bridge about four hundred yards away making several dashes across open fields under machine gun fire.

When we got the bridge someone said Jerry's were coming across it, so the captain took three men and myself to the top. I stuck my head over the top and saw two Germans coming, and the captain told me to hold my fire because he wanted them prisoners. I stuck my head up again and saw two columns, one on each side to the track, and then the fun started. They refused to surrender so we opened up on them. They got about seven feet away and we started throwing grenades at them and only got one in return. But it was only a concussion grenade and did no harm except knock us off our feet.

Well, we captured one of them, and a fellow who could speak German told him to go back and tell them to surrender or else. Well they refused to give up and we really lowered the boom and poured the lead into them. You have to give those monkeys credit, they fought to the last man. When the fight was over they counted over two hundred and seventy dead. We also captured three anti-tank guns which enabled the tanks to cross the main bridge. When we got them for support, the rest was mop up. So, you can tell Bud I did what he asked me to and got a couple for him.

We then marched down to the main bridge which crosses the river to meet the rest of our buddies who had taken the bridge, and the Limey tanks which had crossed the bridge. The main purpose of taking the bridge was to clear the road and let the Limey tanks push through to Arnhem to relieve the British paratroopers, but you know the English, they just weren't ready, and you read what happened to the English boys up there. All the loses were unnecessary, because if the tanks had gone up there like they were supposed to, those boys could have been saved and the war might have been shortened.

Our work was finished for a while so we set up a C.P. in an old brewery and reorganized. While the rest of the company came in, in one's and two's, we drank beer and ate. We found some preserves and made a meal out of them, we even found some German cigars which most of us smoked, but give me a good old American rope anytime.

We were lucky. Our casualties were light this time; they were only about fifty percent.

That's where the Koelle boy I wrote you about got hit, on the river crossing. (Thanks for calling Koelle's parents up for me). I gave an officer friend of mine the roll of film I took out at the division cemetery and he is going to get them developed for me. As soon as I get them I will send Mr. and Mrs. Koelle a set. Thanks again.

From then on most of our work was limited to patrols and holding the ground we had taken, and yours truly had one other narrow escape. One night during a shelling I was completely covered by flying glass and timber when we got two direct hits on our C.P.

All in all, it was an experience I wouldn't trade for the world, but no matter what anyone tried to offer me would I do it again. I never was with a better or fighting bunch of fellows, they really were swell.

At the airport after we were briefed, and we knew definitely it would be Holland, you would expect everyone to be on edge and sweating it out. But not this bunch of men, we were playing football and shooting crap for the invasion money we were given, and some of the fellows, after studying their maps, just went to sleep.

We really got a number one breakfast at the airport. It was pancakes, chicken, corn, potatoes, bread, cake and coffee.

The photograph taken by Flox of the grave of Robert Koelle in the temporary cemetery in Holland. (Peggy Shelly)

Then we got our chutes and got in the plane for a last minute pep talk.

On the way over we read magazines we had in our pockets and smoked and joked with each other. But it only took about nine seconds for all of us to get out, once we got the go signal. None of the men got excited when the flak started, or vomited up the breakfast.

Yes, Shorty, I have nothing but respect and admiration for these men. We were on the front fifty-seven days and that's a long time to have the same socks on your feet. I said I joined this outfit to see action and I'm getting my fill. This makes about two hundred and fifty days on the front, so I have no kick coming, although now I would like to go home. And let's both thank the Lord for listening to our prayers, and we said plenty for letting me get through it all okay. I guess I'll close

With love to all

Forever yours

Seymour

P.S. Keep the fires burning.[592]

The men continued rotations to places like Paris or Reims for some rest and relaxation. Some of the men who went to Paris were able to see champion boxer Jack Dempsey on tour. Bars were often subject to the troopers' visits, and copious amounts of vodka was often consumed. James Sapp, now a twenty-three-year-old veteran of three combat jumps, did not drink and was one of the best-behaved soldiers in the unit. When the regiment formed their own military police-like organization to take care of intoxicated paratroopers on passes in town, Sapp accordingly became one of the patrolmen in Reims. This was done, as Sapp recounts, so the regiment would not have to go through all of the Army's "red tape" to spring their men.[593]

Clarence Williams of Company A was killed by a German machine gun on October 2 in Holland while fighting over a house near the German roadblock that was subsequently assualted by Lt. Breard in late October. (Ray Watts)

In-between the passes, field training continued. Some of the companies trained at night, in platoon and squad field problems practicing patrolling and other such tactics. There were a few training jumps, where the men would land behind the tents which housed the enlisted men.

Things changed on December 17, and the following several hours were a whirlwind of rapidly developing events. W. George Benavitz and several other F Company men had been on pass in Laon that day, and they had returned to their barracks late in the evening. "I had nearly climbed into my bunk when we were awakened to the notice that we were moving out," Benavitz later wrote.[594] For the F Company men who were not on pass, they had trained that day at the rifle range with their small arms and machine guns. Speer and his squad was woken up at about 11 o'clock that evening. "We had to turn everything in at the supply sergeant's place. [We got] our barracks bag and weapons and clothes and what not and issued some ammunition for the machine gun and the rifle. We got on trucks and we rode on trucks the rest of the night."[595]

This photo of SSGT Williams's grave at the temporary cemetery in Holland was sent to his sister by a Dutch family which adopted and cared for his grave at the division cemetery. (Ray Watts)

At about 11:30 that evening, Colonel Reuben Tucker had been summoned to division headquarters, where he was instructed to prepare his regiment for immediate departure to Belgium, where the Germans had launched an offensive and cracked through the American lines and advanced some 50 miles.

Captain T. Moffatt Burriss began preparing his company by calling the platoon leaders together after being informed to the situation. Many of the men were still on passes to various cities in France. "We had a lot of them that were in Paris on leave so they were immediately recalled," Captain Burriss stated. "The MPs were noticed to pick up any soldiers that were there that belonged to our unit and get them back to us… Immediately when they got back they were issued ammunition and told to be ready to leave at six o'clock in the morning."[596]

Men who were in the regimental stockade for minor offensives were immediately released to go back to their companies as they began to try and organize for a quick departure back into combat.

Also arriving that evening from the port in LeHarve, France was a large group of new replacements who had just come from depots in England, along with some of the old veterans who had recently been released from the hospital in England. Many of these paratroopers thought they were arriving at a quiet and resting outfit and could hardly believe they were going into combat in a few hours. One of the new arrivals was Robert DeVinney of Lansing, Michigan. DeVinney and his friend Robert DeDoncker, who had recently found out his wife had given birth, had both recently graduated together from the 82nd Airborne Division's jump school in England. The NCO in charge of their replacement pool was 1st Sergeant Wayne Long, who had recently been released from the hospital. A tall - nearly six foot, five inches - and well-built man, Long would lie dead four days later. Some of the replacements who joined the unit that night would be killed within 96 hours; DeDoncker, the new father, among them.

For the new replacements, DeVinney remembered that everything was already packed for them, and all that was needed was for them to climb aboard the big cattle trucks which were to transport the regiment to the front.[597] The men had rapidly drawn their weapons out of the armories where they were being serviced and ammunition and rations; for the lightly-equipped but highly mobile paratroops, there was room for little else. "…We lived out of our pant and jacket pockets," 2nd Lieutenant Robert Bramson recalls, "and no one in the paratroops had space for anything but basic needs... I can't recall ever carrying a bag – those large pockets in the jump suit pants and jacket were what I think I used." Soon, the men were ready to move back to the front once again.[598]

The trucks the men would ride for the approximately 150-mile journey were mostly semi-trucks for transporting aircraft. Troopers packed on them like sardines in a can. Moffatt Burriss said, "They were loaded in what we call horse trucks. Big, long trucks and we were all loaded into those and headed for the front line and we met the Krauts."[599] Although they were really for airplanes, most men described them just a Burriss did – cattle trucks. Leading the regiment in convoy to the front would be the 1st Battalion under the veteran Lt. Col. Harrison, followed by the 2nd under Lt. Col. Wellems, and then finally the 3rd Battalion under Lt. Col. Cook. From the time the last truck of the 1st Battalion crossed the initiating point, the 2nd Battalion would wait five minutes before it pressed on, and the 3rd Battalion would follow suit so that between each battalion was a five-minute interval.

The men were headed to the crossroads town of Bastogne. Morris Holmstock de-trucked there. "We were there about an hour," recalled Holmstock. "They said, 'Okay, you guys, get back on the truck; we're going to the north end.'"[600] Although they didn't know it at the time, they were needed immediately in Werbomont to defend the road junction, as the 1st SS Panzer Division was rapidly advancing on the town on the northern shoulder of the German breakthrough.

20

WE KICKED THE BALLS OUT OF THEM

On the edge of the village of Rahier sat the machine gun position of F Company troopers James Churchill and Werner Speer. As Speer describes, shortly after noon SS troopers of *Kampfgruppe* Peiper came into view on the road from Cheneux. "We were just at the edge of a village next to a road that went up into the woods, and there was, guessing again, from our positions up to the woods probably maybe not quite a full mile, three-quarters of a mile, and the road went up there. It was a paved road, just two lanes about. We had our machine gun set up maybe 25 yards from the road, and we were at the last house in the village on that road. Churchill and I looked, and this was somewhere around noontime, and we saw these two lines of German troops coming down that road. We quickly passed the information along to our platoon sergeant, and it went on the line, and they immediately got some mortars in place, and fired some mortars at them and they pulled off the road."[601]

Not long after, the column of the 1st Battalion, 504th Parachute Infantry, bound to seize the bridge over the Amblève River at Cheneux, marched passed Churchill and Speer's positions in the direction of the Germans. As the battalion marched through the wooded road to Cheneux, intermittent artillery fire began befalling their formations as they progressed. In the B Company column, some of the artillery shells began exploding in the trees, creating a deadly shower of shrapnelled tree-splinters, which are devastating if one has no overhead protection. One of the new replacement officers, Morris Holmstock remembered, "ran around and said, 'Get a handkerchief over your nose and climb a tree.' We all looked at him and said, 'What? Are you crazy?'" This type of "chickenshit," as the men called it – or cowardice – was not tolerated in the slightest within the regiment, especially not from officers, yet somehow this particular officer was able to remain with the company, and his behavior continued. When the regiment was engaged along the Rhine River during the fighting in the Ruhr Pocket in 1945, this lieutenant was tasked with taking a patrol across the river. The lieutenant marched the men up and down the bank of the river for quite a while before Staff Sergeant William "Knobby" Walsh finally told the lieutenant that he would take the men across.[602]

The scenes on December 20, 1944 on the road to Cheneux described by Werner Speer and Morris Holmstock were the opening scenes to one of the regiment's most epically fought battles, which resulted in the destruction of the vaunted 1st SS Panzer Regiment of Joachim Peiper. The SS troopers were good, well-trained fighters who put up tenacious resistance as the as the 1st Battalion tried to affect their destruction. "Our boys," Lieutenant Colonel Williams stated, "practically beat them back with their bare knuckles."[603]

The short-statured Lieutenant Colonel Willard Harrison, the commander of the 1st Battalion at Cheneux, had commanded combat formations in the 504th PIR since parachuting into Sicily as a captain. Since promoted several times, he had become one of the most decorated officers in the regiment; what he lacked in physical size he made up for in courage. After the Battle of Cheneux was over, Sergeant Michael Jalowey said, "We had a hell of a fight, but our colonel stayed right up there with us. He's combat happy, but he's the greatest guy in the world."[604]

A few great accounts containing the bloody, dramatic details of this battle do better justice in both detail and breadth than what specific circumstances will be covered in the following paragraphs, which will be focused on a few supporting elements such as the aid station, the role the engineers played, and the rebuilding of the destroyed B Company. For a personal, dramatic account of this battle, Ross Carter's famous memoir *Those Devils in Baggy Pants* is as good as it gets. Robert Kinney's detailed account of the fighting can be read in Patrick O'Donnell's book *Beyond Valor*, and the 504th history written by Phil Nordyke has a great chapter on the fighting at Cheneux.

Overview

On the afternoon of the 20th, shortly after the battalion passed Werner Speer's positions, Company B came into contact with the head of Joachim Peiper's SS troopers at the fore of the village of Cheneux. After a sharp firefight, Captain Thomas Helgeson withdrew the company into the woods on the edge of a long field opposite the village. A meeting was called with the company commanders and Lieutenant Colonel Harrison, where a plan was devised to attack the village with two companies after dark. Down the field, bisected by a road, the companies moved with C Company on the left side of the road and B Company on the right. The night was foggy, the air damp and cool as the men, bulging fantastically in the dark, emerged from the woods and onto the field to make their nighttime attack. In an instant, a mass of fire erupted and light and pressure pulsed through the air. "The Jerries mowed us down with flak guns as we moved in but we kept going, hitting them with everything we had," Sergeant Samuel D'Crenzo explained. "They had heavy stuff against us - including three flak wagons, a half track, a reconnaissance vehicle with a mortar, an artillery piece and a couple of other guns. The Germans set up guns in the middle of the street and kept pinning us down with ack-ack."[605]

The men were stymied.

Knobby Walsh

Like their commander Willard Harrison, Staff Sergeant William "Knobby" Walsh, nicknamed after the character found in Joe Palooka, had not only been with the regiment from the beginning but likewise made up for his lack of physical size with an invisible trait: bravery. When the withering fire from the Germans began, the men got to the ground tight as ticks. The advance paused. The veteran Walsh, realizing that the casualties would multiply the longer they remained in the open, immediately arose into the stream of tracers as if he were bulletproof. Morris Holmstock was nearby and heard Walsh yelling for a grenade and heard him yell, "'Let's get these sons-of-bitches! They're going to kill us!' When I heard him yell that, I was in the middle of the field and I yelled, 'Where do you want it [the grenade], Knobby?!' He never answered and I just threw it down on the road."[606]

The Distinguished Service Cross citation for Walsh's actions that day read more like a work of fiction than an official Army document:

> *When his platoon was pinned to the ground by heavy grazing fire, Staff Sergeant Walsh, though seriously wounded, rose to his feet and voluntarily led a charge upon an enemy held village. Advancing three hundred yards, he encountered devastating flanking fire from a 20-mm. flak wagon. Unable to pull the pin from a hand grenade because of a severe hand wound, he moved quickly to a comrade who armed the grenade. Returning to within ten feet of the weapon, he tossed the grenade into the vehicle, destroying the gun and annihilating the crew. Staff Sergeant Walsh's intrepid actions, personal bravery and zealous devotion to duty exemplify the highest traditions of the military forces of the United States and reflect great credit upon himself, the 82d Airborne Division, and the United States Army.*[607]

Walsh's action began to jumpstart the men as they engaged the Germans in hand-to-hand fighting.

Establishment of the Battalion Aid Station

Morris Holmstock was in the first assault wave of Company B that departed the woods and entered the open field. When the blistering fire began, Holmstock was with his two best friends Edwin Clements and

Nelson Hudson. After Walsh's incredible act, there began a mad rush for town, where house-to-house fighting began on the edge of town as a toe-hold was gained. Clements, Hudson, and Holmstock got to what Holmstock believes was the first house on the right side of the road. Clements and Hudson opened the cellar door and heard a noise. "Komm raus! Hände hoch!" they yelled. With no response, they threw a grenade. Upon inspection, they had slain about four or five sheep that were cowering in the cellar. This cellar became the battalion's aid station, where medics began to gather and treat the wounded.

After killing the sheep, Holmstock became separated with Clements and Hudson, who were both later wounded in the battle. Holmstock swung around to the right and found a ditch along the tree line in back of a house which afforded him a clear line of fire at a German flak wagon which was sitting on the road in front of the house. "I got down at the back of the house and the ground was like steep decline in the backyard and I was on my belly and I was firing my gun at the flak wagon, where I thought the flak wagon was, and he whipped his gun around and I ducked down." The flak wagon began firing into the tree line above him, blowing tree limbs asunder and raining shrapnel. Finally, he was maimed him in the face. "After a couple seconds I just tasted blood and I said, 'Oh shit, I'm hit.' I wasn't hit that bad, but it hit me in the eyebrow. I said, 'Oh, fuck this war! I am going to quit.' I made it back to the house and the medics made the little room where the sheep were into a medical station." Holmstock got a patch put over his eyebrow where the shrapnel had hit him, and went back into the fight.[608]

The paratroopers of Company C, 307th Airborne Engineer Battalion, like always, were in the thick of the fighting with the parachute infantrymen of the 504th. Corporal Obie Wickersham and his squad fell in line along the road into Cheneux, which bisected the two fields where the infantrymen were pinned down in, behind a tank destroyer which was supposed to move forward along the road and support the attack. "All hell was breaking loose," Wickersham remembered. At arm's length away was his friend Al Niemeth, who he had been with since jump school. The tank destroyer began moving down the road towards the German vehicles, with the engineers following behind. "Everything was firing," recollects Wickersham, "talk about combat!"

By the end of the night, the battalion had only gained a toe-hold upon the village of Cheneux, and the men began to dig in for what was to be a long night. The battalion was well disorganized and had suffered severe attrition of personnel.

Eventually Obie Wickersham got the squad of engineers organized on a knoll and told everyone to dig in behind a fence with wood uprights. As they were digging in, the Germans began shooting the fence with 20mm shells, making the wooden uprights into tree bursts. Private Leo Cardin, a new replacement, was extremely disturbed by the shrapnel from the German 20mm guns. "Just dig your slit trench and don't get up," the veteran Wickersham told him. This firing on their positions continued through the night.

On the morning of December 21, Wickersham was running around and inspecting the squad's positions. "Somebody said, 'Look at your raincoat.' Some of that shrapnel was coming down [and had] put holes in my raincoat." As he kept the coat tucked in-between his pistol belt and back, it likely saved him from being wounded by absorbing some of the shrapnel. That same morning, Wickersham came upon the body of Private Cardin. By the hole sadly adorning the back of his head, it was evident that the young man had raised his head up and was killed instantly. Wickersham was saddened by the unfortunate event. The young private was so new Wickersham never even knew his name, a part of the incident which bothered him.[609]

Third Battalion Action at Cheneux

On the morning of December 21, the 3rd Battalion of the 504th PIR began to spring into action in support of the assault on Cheneux. They followed the forest trail until it adjoined the road entering Monceau from the south. Across sloping country to the north was the village of Cheneux. From Monceau, the battalion would help to try and encircle the SS troopers, blocking off any escape route to the south. That afternoon, the battalion began their assault on the village of Cheneux from the south. The men broke into a run as 20mm fire began to bounce around them. Sergeant Bill Hannigan took his squad up on a small hill and began to return the German's fire. He watched as one man was hit in the shin with a 20mm shell, ripping his lower leg into shreds. "We thought, 'Well, the leg will come off.' Doc said, 'No! They'll fix it.' So we put him on a raincoat and pulled him back in. He went to England. The next thing we heard, he was going up the steps drunk and he fell backwards and they had to redo the whole leg."[610]

Sergeant Ray Walker took his squad into the cover of a Mayberry hedge a few hundred yards short of Cheneux. Robert DeVinney set up his Browning Automatic Rifle next to the machine gunner. The German gunner, seeing the muzzle blast of the machine gun and BAR, whipped his cannon in DeVinney's direction. DeVinney dropped down and rolled over behind the protection of the hedgerow as raking 20mm fire flew overhead. Behind the Mayberry hedge, the German 20mm tracer shells were burning into the stone.

One of the buildings behind them was a house with a small barn attached to it, where the medics had chased the horses out and begun to use it as an aid station. Joseph Barnard, the veteran paratrooper which was helping to 'break in' the young DeVinney, was wounded in the head by the German 20mm gun.

"He came in and the blood was running," DeVinney recalled. "He had his hand over his forehead and the blood was running down his sleeve. He went into the building right there… and he had this band-aid across his forehead and he was white as a ghost when he went in there. He came back out, right into the fighting."[611]

One of the 20mm guns in Cheneux, photographed by Lt. Robert Blankenship of Company I. (Richie Blankenship)

Company I under the command of Captain T. Moffatt Burriss had moved right onto the edge of Cheneux under the 20mm fire. The Germans continued to fire their flak guns at Burriss' men, who were "out in the open practically all of the time," before they began to withdrawal after two or three hours. "That," Burriss explains, "would usually indicate that the troopers that were firing on us were getting pressured to move out… That they were losing ground when they were not firing."[612] That pressure was coming from the renewed attack of the remnants of the 1st Battalion, which were now attempting to drive into the remainder of the village of Cheneux from the west, destroy the remnants of the SS men, and finally secure the bridge over the Ambleve River.

It Wasn't a Pretty Battlefield

After the battle had been won that afternoon, the paratroopers of the 2nd Battalion began to provide relief for Willard Harrison's nearly-destroyed unit. As they passed on the road into town, they witnessed the aftermath of the bloody, bitter fight that Harrison's men had engaged the German SS troopers in. For Lieutenant Robert Bramson, the scene was a memorable one:

I recall the damage he mentions and also all the dead Germans - as I recall I was impressed with their physical size and quality of the men and their equipment - it wasn't a pretty battlefield.

I was called into company or Bn. Hq. in town just after they had a visit from English speaking Germans in a jeep - apparently one of the groups acting like Americans and trying to create as much confusion as possible. If you will recall, we were all instructed when these infiltrators made contact to ask rather silly questions like the names of famous football or baseball figures - information these men might not know. Anyway, I think these particular ones were taken into custody.

Getting back to why I was called up - it was to take a patrol into the adjacent area to look for further German activity - we found none.[613]

"That night," remembered Werner Speer, "there was nothing more going on. Pieper – I don't know where they went – but they didn't try to pull forward on us anymore that night."[614]

Reconstituting A Destroyed Company

When the 1st Battalion assaulted the village of Cheneux on December 20, Company A had already departed for the nearby village of Brume, where they were to occupy it, send patrols out, and set up roadblocks in the nearby countryside. After arriving in the town, Lieutenant Reneau Breard set out on a patrol in the late afternoon to the north towards La Gleize. "We located the rail bridge and a low water bridge over the

Ambleve River," remembered Breard. "We could hear the trouble at Cheneux. We returned to Brume about 2 AM on 21 Dec."[615]

That trouble that Breard heard while on patrol was the destruction of the rest of his battalion. "There was about 120 of us, and we kicked the balls out of them," Morris Holmstock said of their victory at Cheneux.[616] However, "was" turned out to be a very accurate term. Holmstock's Company B had only some 18 men standing when they were relieved. For the entire 1st Battalion, the casualties were near-devastating. In two days – December 20 and 21 – the 504th Parachute Infantry Regiment sustained 206 wounded through enemy action at Cheneux, with the overwhelming majority of those casualties being suffered by the 1st Battalion. "The boys - rather young men averaging 22-years-old - of the 504th used to tell about the luck of the First Battalion," wrote David Whittier. "Through the jumps in Sicily, Italy, and Holland; through the battles of Salerno, on the approaches to Cassino, during the long bloody months on the Anzio Beachhead, at Nijmegen Bridge in Holland where two-thirds of the Third Battalion fell; through all of this and more, the First Battalion had always managed to come out least hurt. But tonight was the payoff - almost the finish for the First Battalion."[617]

Shortly before they were relieved at Cheneux, Holmstock and several others were sitting down on the road into the village "counting our blessings that we were still alive" when some troopers came and began stacking bodies up in a pile like firewood. "Wow," he said, "that's the end of that."[618]

While all the companies in the battalion had suffered heavily, B Company was the hardest hit in the officers' corps with none of the company's officers fit for duty. Captain John M. Randles and Lieutenants Reneau Breard and Leo Van de Voert were set to Company B to begin to rebuild the company.

Morris Holmstock remembered that they "were blessed with" about 20 new replacements, in addition Breard, Randles and Van de Voert. In the company headquarters, Captain Randles took over as the commander and Amedeo Castagno was promoted to the first sergeant. The company was restructured into two rifle platoons, the 1st under Lieutenant Breard and the 2nd under Lieutenant Van de Voert.

Lieutenant Breard remembered the rebuilding of the company that night, and their first movements post-Cheneux:

The company consisted of about 70 men and 3 officers - after replacements. I remember my platoon sergeant was from the 509 PIR...

We reorganized with what we had and late in the evening, the BN moved to Trois Pont and went into positions in the town and along the Salm River. B Company was on the right in the bend of the river up steam near the RR bridge. BN Hqds. was set up just behind downtown Trois Pont.

If I remember correctly, most of the new men were from the 509 BN and 504 Service Company. Most of the NCOs from B Company who had not been wounded were still on the job. Actually, we did a lot in a very few hours. Morale was good; and we had very little bitching.

I will say that B Co. was reformed very quickly and was ready to move out that night of the 22nd. That night, we had a small skirmish with the enemy patrols trying to cross the Salm. Even some mixing it up with our three 60mm mortars in battery behind the Co. CP.

On the night of 23 Dec., we had a hard freeze and about 10 or 11 PM., we moved out back through Trois Pont, Basse Bodeau, and marched half way to Bra, but still got in the fracas, where the 1st BN went into reserve.[619]

Replacements continued to flow into the company throughout the Battle of the Bulge, but attrition to weather and enemy action also did not stop. "If they lived, they lived; if they died, they died," was the attitude Morris Holmstock exercised.[620]

Amedo Castagno became the 1st Sgt of Company B following the battle at Cheneux. (T. Castagno)

21

COMPENSATION FOR MISERABLE DAYS SPENT

Since Sicily, 2nd Lieutenant John Branca had been on the cutting edge of actions to wage war against what Winston Churchill so poignantly described in one of his most influential speeches, as "a monstrous tyranny never surpassed in the dark and lamentable catalog of human crime."[621] Lieutenant Branca saved a document distributed to the regiment, here reproduced in full, which documented a small piece of the monstrous evil perpetrated by the SS soldiers of *Kampfgruppe* Peiper before Branca's men could deliver some small semblance of justice upon them at Cheneux, where Branca himself was wounded.

The diary appears to have been written by a member of a flak unit attached to the SS men which formed the corps of *Kampfgruppe Peiper*. This translated diary provides a unique window into the German view of what occurred when the Peiper's men met their demise.

HEADQUARTERS 504TH PARACHUTE INFANTRY
APO 469 US ARMY

07 April 45

"TO WHOM IT MAY CONCERN"

The following accounts are reproduced for those of you who may have spent those trying days in the vicinity of CHENEUX, TROIS-PONTS, or RAHIER. If, during those days you had felt dismayed, then I'm sure these excerpts from a captured German staff sergeant's diary will compensate for those same miserable days spent.

****

19 December - We continue driving for a little while, till at dawn we come to a halt. Nobody knows why we stop, furthermore nobody gives a damn; for our bellies are empty and won't get filled by contemplations over offensive strategy. At daylight, there are a few nice bursts and then our how[itzer]s open fire on a couple of Shermans which dodge into the forest. Mortar fire proves to us that we constitute the forward lines. Later on, 200 Americans come out of town (STAUMONT). They gave up. But still I don't think we'll gain our objectives; the tanks are down to their last few gallons of gas.

At last we find some grub. They are "US field rations." Like animals we wolve down these delicacies (sic). Unfortunately, arty fire curtails our mealtime, and we have to dig in - only to change positions as usual when we have finished our entrenchments. This time we take new positions in LA GLEIZE. Behind a school building, in the worst possible bivouac area in the neighborhood, we dig in. We are supposed to surround the area with guards; the order came from the SS - the all-knowing SS who certainly knows better how to run a flak outfit than we do ourselves. Another night follows, a night such as I have never experienced before. I dive under our prime mover, but not even the devil could endure this, and I run in long spurts for the cover of the school walls. Apparently, this arty is shooting at us from three different directions. Without closing an eye, I live through this night. During the entire 24-hour period, no supply vehicle reached us. And I would not mind if they would provide some hot chow for a change. Latrine rumors from SS latrines have it that we are encircled.

20 December - With dawn I return to our positions. I can't believe it, but miraculously only one prime mover became scrap medal. Our bivouac area is punctured by arty craters.

Without warning, a monstrous, abhorrent picture presents itself to me. Its horror slaps me in the face. Corpses of murdered soldiers, soldiers, who after an honest fight, had surrendered to our paratroopers. They were then turned over to the SS who organized them into small groups of 6-8 men each for the purpose of the slaughter. Who of these SS bastards has even the slightest inkling of international law, or for that matter, of humanity? Nothing, absolutely nothing, is sacred to them. There they lie, those 7 or 8 US soldiers without weapons or helmets, about three paces apart; evidently shot from behind, mute witnesses against a system of murder. They are the witnesses, but where is the prosecutor, and where is the judge? I know, up above there is a higher tribunal, and I'm certain if we down here don't punish them, that a just Lord will do it unfailingly. In the afternoon we advanced in forced march tempo to a bridge in the direction of CHENEUX. In the beginning, our mission was defined as "bridge protection." But hardly have we reached our destination, when PEIPER requisitions one of our platoons for infantry commitment. To an ever-increasing degree of does the SS rely on the prowess of flak units, probably to refill their badly decimated ranks.

The din in the village (CHENEUX) is maddening, a fact to which I personally can testify as I am staying at the bridge. In vain do I try and point out to Herr SACKEN that an employment of our pieces near the bridge is plain and simple suicide. For an incessant arty and mortar fire seems to be zeroed in on this point. I inspect the first piece and already find one man of the crew wounded. He is evacuated. I return and hear that another man has disappeared without leaving a trace; probably was expedited into the murky river by a hit. And then I find Lt. POREP severely wounded. When I place the unfortunate guy at the major's feet, SACKEN become concerned over his own safety. In the meantime, I have already taken it upon myself to order the survivors of my platoon to retreat.

In the meantime, the SS was cajoled into new positions behind CHENEUX by threats, kicks, and curses of their officers. At night, American infantry [504th PIR] counterattacked twice. We suffer heavy casualties, while the *Herrenmenschen* sit in bunkers and basements. Prior to taking over, they displayed their courage by ordering the herding-together of all civilians in STAUMONT. Somewhere in the night we hear the anguished scream of woman.

John Branca, who saved this document, photographed shortly after receiving his battlefield commision to second lieutenant. He was posted to Company C and was wounded at Cheneux. (Deloris Branca)

21 December - A German counterattack at dawn is stifled by enemy fire. Nobody shows any inclination to fight - not even the SS. As a matter of fact, they are the first ones to withdrawal. Suddenly one of our tanks makes an appearance near the bridge. Again a frantic solicitation for gasoline. Draining all vehicles, including the Volkswagen, and the wrecked prime movers, we scrape 30 gallons together. The Tiger continues towards CHENEUX.

I am darned glad that I don't have to be in the inferno prevailing in that village. Down here the enemy arty bursts have somewhat subsided. In the morning hours two of my best comrades and I are elected to form a *Panzervernichtungstrupp* (AT [anti-tank] squad). 6 Pz Fauste, one machine pistol - and now we constitute a formidable force which will be able to stop all enemy tanks. Our battle plans [illegible] around the selection of the most favorable route of withdrawal.

Everything at our old AA position is quiet now. The piece lies by the roadside neatly segmented. I am just about to inspect one of my platoon's quadruple guns, when all of the sudden 12 Americans, southing continuously, their rifles and MP's raised above their heads, break out of the thicket. They shout, "Nicht schiessen" (don't shoot). At first I think this is a rouse and tell my men to go into firing positions, but then I recollect the GREIF boys. Yes, indeed, it's these lads who have returned, accompanied by some sizzling hot farewell messages from the Americans. They posed as the 88th Hq. Co., but the Yankees refused to swallow it. The "gangs" as they call themselves, at once change uniforms and the gagsters continue fighting as harmless anti-aircraft boys.

I don't know how it came about, certainly nobody gave orders to this effect, but suddenly everything on the CHENEUX highway is making a dash for our bridge. There is no more stopping; the situation has become hopeless. I swing aboard the first vehicle that comes along and we make a mad dash for LA GLEIZE. In front of a bridge, the S/P gun, overloaded with its human cargo, starts sliding and I pick myself out of a ditch. In the meantime, the Americans have been able to occupy the heights to the right (E) of the road and their guns pay careful attention to all vehicular movement. I barely succeed clamping myself onto a massing truck to escape towards LA GLEIZE.

The town has changed since we passed through here on our way to the grand attack. The old burg is aflame on all corners. I run into old acquaintances. Even the action GRIEF, those scalped Indians, whom I already saw at LOSHEIM, make another appearance here. Nobody even thinks of placing a gun into position although this constitutes a direct violation of the orders of Herr Major SACKEN. Fortunately for us, the American arty seems to be taking a break too. There is a cold drizzle and if somebody would have tapped me on the shoulder and said, "Hands up, come along" I think there would not have been a happier person in the world.

22 December - This morning we get some new orders; to throw a perimeter defense around LA GLEIZE. With this order the *Landsers* begin to realize that we are cut off and encircled. I had a premonition of this. Like a flash, I realized the deadly seriousness of the situation. Should the Yanks catch us here together with the SS - caught together, hung together, and those SS madmen may want to fight to the last man, including us…

The boys of my platoon have become taciturn; passively they have accepted their fate. Like robots they go through the motions of carrying out the orders which I pass down from the btry CO. I know darn well that only the utmost alertness and interest could see the men through in this critical moment, but these qualities are lacking as much as the motor fuel in the gas tanks.

We occupy the SE side of LA GLEIZE, facing the RR bridge. Everybody digs and claws to gain the slight cover mother earth can afford. With a wood saw we fell a few tress and roll them over our foxholes as protection against shrapnel. We add a few shovelfuls of dirt and place a prime mover right over a 4 man slit trench. This improvised bunker serves only as inadequate shelter against those Yank mortars…

On the other side of the river we spot American infantry. Our propaganda machine at once starts to work; "You see, boys, the Americans are retreating." In the evening the American arty cuts loose. We crawl into our trenches like moles. Hunger overpowers me, but in spite of this I don't dare go get one of my booty US rations only about 30 yards away. The arty shells fall as thick as hail into our positions.

During the night a plump JU 52 hums above us and throws down barrels with gasoline. Many of them land on the American side - where there is an overabundance of this juice without our involuntary contribution.

In the distance, behind our lines, we hear the grumbling of werfers; again a gala occasion for the *Herrenmenschen* to feed us a good line. "Hooray, they are coming." But nothing comes. Another morale booster is not long in coming. The SS Divs *Hitlerjugend* and *Hohenstaufen* will "box" their way through to us. But nothing came. Only the monotonous whine of the enemy arty assumes an even more intense tone.

In the small hours of the morning I find my blanket which I had stuffed into the foxhole. It is frozen board stiff. But our American comrades sympathize with us and obligingly send over a few phosphorous grenades to make it sufficiently hot for us.

23 December - For my breakfast we get a double helping of arty and mortar fire. We helplessly stand by as an AT gun is jockeyed into position. Just a few moments later it broadcasts its overtures for our benefit. And already the fourth round dissects one of our cannons. Then we became cognizant of the fact that only two of our tanks are still maneuverable, while just about 18 Sherman's race around firing relentlessly once from one, then from another direction. I straighten out my accounts with the forces above, for I have given up all hope to escape this hell alive. Herr Major SACKEN makes an appearance among us in the afternoon. The boys wink at each other knowingly; the good major is really scared stiff. Verbose through he likes to be, he now keeps his trap shut and silently cowers in his hole. Nobody in his vicinity may utter a loud word - "the enemy is listening."

Out of the 2,000 men which so proudly advanced through LA GLEIZE on the 19 Dec, approximately 700 dejected souls remained. Under these conditions and the face of the pleasant prospect of impending bomber attack, about which we learn through interrogation of a captured US major, Peiper decides to beat a retreat (*absatzmanoever*). But perhaps his prime consideration is that his valuable person has to be saved for his admiring Nazi contemporaries. If he could leave this town by himself, I don't doubt for a minute that he would gladly leave us in the lurch.

My comrade MEISSNER is assigned the mission of destroying all secret orders and after carrying out these instructions, to rejoin our ranks. Only too late did we learn that the charge had an instantaneous fuse. If the poor guy had carried out the order, and I don't think he is the type that would, he has become a victim of the SS murderers…

"On the command 'X-mas present' we will fight our way back to the MLR." Those are the instructions I get from the Old Man at 2200 hrs. It is possible that we will escape this inferno? Tense minutes crawl by. They add up to hours. Shortly before midnight, I awake from my semi-slumber. It has quieted down somewhat. I try to get to the SP to get my field pack which I have stowed behind the steel plating; but all I can find are the ragged remnants. It looks as if mice have gnawed on it. So I charge my underwear, toilet articles, etc to the account of the Yank arty boys. At the same moment the din of a dozen death spitting mortars breaks loose. I make a dive for my foxhole.[622]

22

ONE OF THE WORST THINGS A MAN CAN EXPERIENCE

In the previous chapter we have seen a narrative of the Battle of the Bulge from the point of view of one single German soldier who was opposing the 504th Parachute Infantry for a window of that time. In contrast, it may be beneficial to provide a similar narrative from the point of view of one paratrooper from the 504th Parachute Infantry. Between the years of 2013 and 2015, veteran Edwin R. Bayley, who joined Company A after their return from the campaign in Holland, wrote much about his wartime memories. Through Bayley's impeccable memory and attention for detail of daily events, Bayley's narrative provides a great account of one paratroopers experience as the Battle of the Bulge unfolded for his company.

Not only does he cover battle with the enemy, but also the daily life of a soldier: how they fought the cold to sleep, how they learned to dress; he also wrote one of the most horrifying and vivid accounts of what it was like to be subjected to enemy artillery.

As World War II enters history from memory, these incredibly detailed messages covering virtually every day of his time in combat during one of the most infamous battles in history become historic. As such, these writings have been complied and placed in chronological order by what they cover. Careful consideration has been exercised to ensure that, while rearranging them in order, nothing was taken out of context or otherwise misconstrued from the way in which Bayley originally wrote these memories.

December 19-20

A Company spent nearly the entire second day camped out at or near Werbomont. There was no movement from the previous arrival night. Sometime after darkness set in we were gathered together and told to move out. First we walked across brush land, cutting farmers' fences as we moved through. Then we came to a paved road. We turned off this road to the Rahier Road. We had gone some distance along this road when we heard machine gun fire close ahead. I was up front with the officers at that time. One said, "We're stymied." They then pulled us off the road and into some small hills and told to dig in. The ground was rocky and almost impossible to handle with our small entrenching tools. Most of us spent the night lying on the ground and trying to get some sleep as we didn't know what was coming in the morning. Soon after the break of day all hell broke loose in the valley below. Through the foggy atmosphere the noise of gun fire (rifles, tanks and artillery) was deafening. Not having any idea of who was winning, brought worries as what do we do if the Germans suddenly break through on us. This went on all day. At 2 PM First Battalion was ordered to come off the hill and hit the road. B and C Companies were told to turn to the left and proceed down the road to Cheneux. A Company mounted trucks and drove away from the battle sounds. We went on foot after coming to the main road and were on our way to take Brume, near Cheneux. We found Brume deserted and free of Germans.

We slept in houses and hay lofts and began our assignment in the morning soon after dawn. Our platoon set up a road block on the road toward LaGleize and stayed until after dark. There were two instances of flak wagon fire directed at us.

Afternoon, December 20 – Patrol from Brume to the Bridge at Trois Ponts

We saw the lone tank with the crew outside eating and telling us that there may have been German tanks inside the tunnel on the opposite side of the river. There were no other soldiers or persons in the area. [I've] often wondered if they were USA or Germans with a captured tank as they seemed so unconcerned about German tanks in local presence.

This bridge area is also interesting as told in my writings. Directly under this bridge across the road was a US Army truck loaded with wooden boxes of 155 ammunition. The front was up against a tree at the far side of the bridge and the load directly under the bridge. There were no soldiers or other persons at this point other than the patrol and the lone tank beyond. We steered well clear of the truck in the event it was booby trapped. At this time some houses along the river bank continued to be occupied by civilians. We stopped and went into one where I conversed in high school French and had a glass of water. They didn't seem to be concerned at all with what was happening in the countryside around them. At this point all was quiet and one would never have known a war was in progress. There was some rumbling and flashing of artillery in the mountains to the east.

December 21-25

At Christmas Eve the First Squad of the First Platoon, A Company was staying on the north side of Trois Ponts in the cellar of a two story house on the bank of the Salm River, a stream about 30 ft. wide. Germans

were on the other bank. We had been in the house for three days. In our area there had been no action and no enemy contact following an artillery attack in the early morning. We had a foxhole at the rear of the house. One of us would be in that foxhole during dark time on observation. We had our rifle and gammon grenades for armament. Starting about midevening of Christmas Eve, continuous artillery fire was passing overhead to the area uphill behind our house. At that time, I was in my two-hour assignment in the foxhole. One of the troopers came and informed me that we were withdrawing to an outdoor area [and said to] take all the blankets from the house as it was going to be cold. About half an hour later, A Company personnel assembled in the street in front of our house to set out on the route march. Some British soldiers were going in and out of the houses. They were easy to see by their different dress and hob nail boots scratching the pavement. At that time, we were under command of British General Montgomery.

There was a skim of snow and ice on the ground and roads. We made the climb of the steep winding hill road leading out of Trois Ponts. There was no enemy action against us – no artillery or rifle fire. At times we heard tanks in the distance without knowing whose they were. There were also pencils of light from searchlights in the distance. We passed through Basse-Bodeux and to the road toward Bras. On this road a convoy of apparent retreating soldiers passed through our area for some minutes. May have been the 28th Division but not sure. As dawn broke we came into a dead-end road at a small village with several houses and a church. As the residents became aware of our moving into the area they began evacuating. They had no automobiles. There may have been some horses. Many went walking down the road to some place of refuge. In some minutes the town showed no civilians. Our group passed to a sloping clear ground field to the south of the village and were told to dig in. At that time, I saw a civilian walking through the field toward the German area. I told an officer and he said he was OK and to let him go. This was a cold, clear cloudless morning. There were several dog fights in the air and it seemed so sad to see the planes shot down on Christmas morning. Off in the distance dive-bombers were dropping bombs on targets. After an hour or so we withdrew into the neighboring woods and were targets of incoming artillery. Apparently no trooper was injured. We were withdrawn deeper into the woods. At that time, a several hour firefight was heard several hundred feet distant. Outgoing artillery was passing overhead. After an hour or so we made another route march to another area in the woods. At this time, I noticed the medic carrying our Christmas turkey over his shoulder. Other troopers would spell him off as the turkey was real heavy. We finally settled into a new area with log-roofed foxholes having been made by previous occupants. This was where I joined with Harry Freeman as foxhole buddy. As of this time we knew almost nothing about the battle at Cheneux. We stayed at this place until New Year's Eve. There were some night time patrols. Most of the time we sat around a fire reading the Stars and Stripes, *and chatting... This pretty well describes the*

Christmas Eve march of Company A. It was a continuous march. We did not stop for an overnight rest. The march itself encountered no enemy activity or threat.

December 27

It was about two days after Christmas that some of our squad went down into the small village, lit a stove, and cooked the turkey. It was divided into a bunch of little pieces; a bit greasy, but it did taste good. No potatoes, stuffing etc., Just only turkey bits... When talking at night before going to sleep Harry [J. Freeman] and I agreed that if we both got home we would have a steak dinner together. Harry returned to the States long before I did and we lost contact.

Several years later, about 1949 or so, as a traveling fire insurance inspector, I was eating breakfast in a diner in Harry's home area. Looked to my left and there sat Harry. It was great meeting him. Due to time and travel it was not possible to meet the steak dinner promise. We got separated again as we were so busy talking we forgot to exchange phone numbers and addresses.

January 1

It appears that the Cheneux decimation of B and C Companies was a savior for A Company. As I previously noted, our First Platoon occupied a house in northwest Trois Ponts on the Salm River the night after the second day of Cheneux until late Christmas Eve. Except for three artillery shells early the first morning and sustained artillery from about mid Christmas Eve, there was no action with the enemy. In the Bras area we were encamped in the woods from Christmas day to New Year's Day. Then 3 days on the front after relieving the 325th.

Night, January 1

I was fortunate in being issued winter underwear and a sweater made by a ladies group in Pennsylvania. Also having been an avid all-weather hunter in Massachusetts and Maine from 12-years-old, where we usually had 20 degrees below zero days several times each winter, I knew how to take care of myself in the cold. Under the jump suit I wore my long underwear, the woolen OD pants and shirt and my knit wool sweater. I had learned as a boy to wear layers of lesser-weight clothing rather than heavy coats, etc., to keep warm. Only twice did I feel some cold. One was New Year's night in no man's land as a remote, beyond the line, night observer [outpost]. Then it was so cold our squad leader said to stand up in the sleeping bag with the rifle inside. I was out there beyond the mine field for two long hours.... Most every night in the field I got into the foxhole with my partner, got into the sleeping bag fully dressed, shoes and all, lit a cigarette and pulled the bag closed over my head. When the smoking made me sleepy I put the cigarette in the dirt and got some of the best sleep of my life even with the banging of outgoing artillery within hearing distance. If we were on the move with no chance of a foxhole the two of us would lay down fir or pine branches, then one shelter half, then the sleeping bags, and cover the bags with more tree bows. We always slept well and warm with this arrangement. In all the time in Europe I never dug any foxholes to stay in as always someone else had been there before us and left nice log-covered foxholes.

January 2

Harry and I had a narrow escape a day or so after New Year's at the front line position we had taken over from the 325th. At the time fortunately we were inside our log-covered foxhole. A five barreled mortar (nebel werfer) was firing into our area. A shell landed on the lip of our foxhole. The shock threw us into a corner of the foxhole with our arms and legs entangled. Took a moment to get separated.

January 4

A Company was on the front line near the crossroads at Bras going into enemy territory. We were waked up by a couple of big bangs as land mines in one of the roads tripped. We looked to our right and the road was jammed nose to tail with very slow moving invasion vehicles as far as one could see. There were some weapons firing in the distance - nothing local. Heavy snow on ground and sort of misty weather. About 4 or so the morning of the 4th we were relieved by an infantry division and we began a slow cross-country relocation march through the snow. Food was in short supply. We melted snow for drinking and coffee water. This went on all day with some short time stops for rest. We finally hit the road south of Trois Ponts along the river bank and went several miles along it. Saw some trees with explosive bundles wrapped around to drop them for road block if needed.

As dark came on we stopped and went into the woods to lay down our sleeping bags. We found ourselves amid the bodies of many dead troopers frozen as they fell in the snow from previous fighting in the area. Graves registration had not yet been by to pick up the bodies.

January 5-6

We set out through the woods. One non-com we met told us that German prisoners had said we were to be relieved at 3AM on a named date several days following. This relief occurred exactly as stated. Our relieving force was attacked I believe after taking position. At end of the morning move we stopped and some of us set up our shelter halves as tents. We stayed all that day and the following night.

January 7-11

We set out again with scouts at sides in the woods, moving through deep snow. Then [a] message came through that a German force was just ahead of us and we were ordered to fix bayonets for close encounter. They were gone when we arrived at the reported position. We advanced down a well plowed road to a sharp hilly area just short of the river. We went into the woods here where there were well made foxholes from previous occupants. There was heavy fighting with the 82nd vs Germans several hundred feet away on the river bank area. Very noisy with machine guns from both sides. We settled in with no threats facing us. The next day I believe there was more activity on the front in which we were not involved. That evening volunteers were sought to carry in ammunition to the front line guys and help bring out the wounded. I went with this group. The wounded had already been taken out. We were needed to replace them in the line. We hadn't expected this. I was placed in a position about 50 ft. from others with no foxhole and on snow covered icy ground where digging in was impossible with an entrenching tool.

It was a very cold night lying on top of the snow on watch. In the morning the A Company guys were sort of unhappy and cold. They did the unthinkable. They lit a big fire just behind the lines so we could thaw out. We had no water. Finally, an A Company trooper took some of our canteens and went down to the river and filled them. Often there were dead soldiers lying in the brooks and rivers. We relied upon our water treatment pills to keep us safe. About midafternoon we returned to the A Company area. About 3 AM the next morning our relief came and we drove to Remouchamps to stay with civilians in their houses. On arriving in Remouchamps we were awarded our Combat Infantry Badges and then went to our assigned houses where we stayed for about two weeks. The room I went to had no furniture or bed but sleeping on the hard wood floor was still a luxury.

January 12-January 24

The stay in Remouchamps was very nice. We stayed with a couple and child, the couple maybe in their thirties. We lived in the house as if it were ours, comfortable and warm. The civilians associated just like family. We shared our rations with the family, kept normal day and sleep hours. The local stores were all open for business. There were caves in the hills that had electric lights and we went through those with a local guide. The town's people were carrying on somewhat normal lives with assurance that the fighting was away in the distance. Buzz bombs came over and exploded in the general area but not in the town. One morning we were taken to an outdoor shower area, washed down and given clean used clothing to replace our real dirty clothes. A Stuart Cadillac engine light tank was brought to us, for everyone who wanted to do so, [to] learn to drive in case we managed to get one during combat. They were very light and certainly no match for a German tank of any size. One afternoon a couple of us were walking when a couple of girls invited us into their trailer parked beside the road. Just a social visit with no sex. There were other family in the trailer. Later we realized they were gypsies just being nice to us.

January 25

We were suddenly notified to pick up our stuff and get on trucks just before dark. Soon we found ourselves passing through Trois Ponts and up the winding hill road and on to just north of St. Vith. Arriving during the night we put our sleeping bags down on the snow. In the morning we had mail call and I got a letter from my brother B-24 navigator in the South Pacific. Religious services for those wanting to participate were held in the afternoon of a cold and bright clear day. Early the next morning we set out from Wallerode just north of St Vith for the approach to the Siegfried Line. It was heavy snow throughout the day. We received intermittent artillery fire, losing at least two men.

Troopers of the 504th move through deep snow in January 1945. (US Signal Corps)

Night, January 29-morning, January 30

A lot happened at Holzheim... The event started in the evening when we gathered with our squad leader and were told we were going out to capture a bridge. He said if we got the bridge we were to destroy it. I questioned this as I assumed if we captured a bridge we would want to keep it. We started on a moonlit route march with Sgt. [Frank L.] Heidebrink out front. There were no officers in the lead. This was a single file march. I was number four in the line. As we came to a turn in the road, shots rang out and the first three troopers dropped dead. I managed to roll into the ditch as tracer bullets passed just inches above my body. Two of Heidebrink's close friends rushed forward to help him if they could. I yelled at them to get down and stop or they would be killed. They kept on and both were shot and killed. After the two Germans were talked out [of] their ambush position, we continued to Holzheim where there were several black-uniformed Germans lying dead in the snow. We stayed for an hour so in Holzheim and then started for our objective three or four miles distant. What started as a rifle fight with Third Platoon leading in on attack soon became a slaughter as artillery fire scored direct hits on individual troopers. Then flak wagon fire took effect. The First Platoon was ordered in to assist. Finally, we were withdrawn. The medics went in to collect the wounded. Germans fired on the medics even though they were carrying a large red crossed flag. During the morning attack we were supposed to have artillery and tank support which never showed.

Afternoon, January 30

In the afternoon we started the attack again with support of several minutes of artillery fire and three tanks. We took the bridge which was little more than a paved crossing of a say 30 ft. wide river. One of the tanks tried to drive through the water and cross the river and got stuck. We captured about 200 prisoners. The attack stopped at a large farm complex on the top of a hill about two miles short of Manderfeld, the town that carries the name of the attack. Manderfeld was taken later by the 347 Rgt. of the 87th Division, the outfit I trained with in the USA before being detached and shipped to England as a replacement to the 82nd Div. and jump training.

(...)

In the afternoon attack from Holzheim there was no immediate artillery fire from the Germans. I led the afternoon attack down the road. A few minutes after the start, as I came down the curved hill to an area identified on commercial maps as a mill (a large house was here also), I looked far ahead up the hill in front of us and saw three Germans running to the artillery piece which up to that time had not been manned. I yelled up the hill behind me and quickly tank fire took the enemy gun and crew out. This gun must have been the one that killed and wounded so many of Company A in the morning. It was sighted right down the road. I am also surprised why in the afternoon it was not manned and also how long it took them to try manning it in the afternoon attack. (It could have been because of the heavy barrage from US artillery immediately preceding our afternoon attack). At that time the tanks less the one stuck in the river made a fast run up the hill and to the big farm buildings, and that was the end of the Manderfeld action. Shortly, *the prisoners came marching down toward us. I assumed the two Germans dragging the third in the road were bringing him in for medical aid. Our guys did not take a chance this was a ruse to move us off guard so they could shoot us. The dragged German was left lying in the road as the other two fled from the gunfire.*

The Germans must have thought our withdrawal in the morning attack must have finished us off for the day. I say this for two reasons. As I led the First Platoon in on the afternoon attack (I was first guy in), I saw a German truck parked at [the] roadside. Four Germans were slowly, calmly walking up the hill by the truck. They got into the truck which I promptly shot up. As I came down the small hill and leftish curve in the road, I saw the large house and mill arrangement. I fired many shots into the house. Civilian men, women and children came running out and stood facing me. There were two or three German soldiers standing with them. I don't remember seeing any weapons with these soldiers. Sure find it odd after the morning attack that these German soldiers would be calmly hanging out as I saw them.

Evening, January 30

The mill was on the bank of the small river. It was at the farm, about a half mile further on where the dragging [of the wounded German] was seen. I was there for about 30 minutes. Our platoon withdrew to the hill about a quarter mile before the farm between the farm and the mill. There we found some great quality foxholes left by someone else. Most of the dead troopers including the officers lay on the ground and at the side of Igelmondermuhle Road overnight, picked up after midmorning or so. Just beyond the mill the road to Manderfeld was named Igelmonderhof Road.

Reflections on January 30

The receiving end of an artillery barrage is one of the worst things a man can experience in life. If in a wooded area there are tree bursts that send shrapnel in all directions meaning many wounds or narrow escapes. If in the open some shells detonate when they hit a person. This tears the body into pieces with the upper and lower bodies torn apart and separated on the ground. Other events are gaping wounds and broken bones. In the Manderfeld operation, A Company was caught completely exposed while in a roadway with high snow plow banks at sides and in open fields as lines of skirmishers. Shells were seen landing on a firm snow surface and skipping along like stones skipping on water until they hit something and detonated. There is nothing one can do to stop the barrage until the enemy decides to stop or successful counter-battery fire can occur. The screams from stricken men are almost indescribable. They can be very loud and terrible to hear. In the afternoon attack in the Manderfeld operation, in which I was the lead soldier, there was no immediate artillery barrage on us. After taking the large farmhouse-mill I looked up at the hill ahead about 1,000 ft. distant and saw an artillery crew heading for the 105mm gun that had caused so much havoc and death in the morning. There was a US tank on the embankment behind me. I yelled up to as I remember Harry Freeman and others warning about the Germans. One shot from the tank stopped the Germans use of the artillery piece.

When men were badly wounded by shrapnel, aid men were not always nearby. Those of us with him would dust the wound with anti-biotic or disinfectant, put a gauze pad on it and leave him by the road or in the snow with his bayonet and rifle sticking up from the ground so following medics and others could find him for further treatment or evacuation. Sometimes they made it. Sometimes they didn't. One of the worst nights A Company experienced was Jan. 4, 45 during a route march to a new area when we put into a nearby wooded area for the night. The ground was covered with the numerous frozen corpses of fellow troopers who had been shot down en-masse. We slept with these surrounding our area.[623]

Henry O. Griffin, standing in the center of this trio, was the original first sergeant of E Company. His taciturn, steely sternness had control of the men, eliminating need for yelling and swearing. On the jump into Salerno, he and Lt. Hauptfleisch landed on a rock pile together. Griffin broke his leg, but Hauptfleisch was saved from injury by landing on his rifle stock, which shattered. After healing from the broken leg, Griffin became the Regimental Headquarters Company first sergeant during the Holland and Belgium operations, before becoming the regimental sergeant major. Standing to Griffin's right is the legendary "Knobby" Walsh, the original C Company first sergeant. He was the culprit of heroic conduct throughout the war and received the DSC for charging the Germans at Cheneux. (Maureen Wolf)

23

AN ANTHOLOGY OF PARATROOPERS IN THE BELGIAN BULGE

While Edwin Bayley's writings give a wonderful, detailed account of what life was like for one paratrooper of the 504th Parachute Infantry during the Battle of the Bulge, it admittedly gives a very narrow account of the experiences other paratroopers had during the period. Thus, it would be beneficial to cover in detail a few other, specific experiences different troopers had at the Belgian front throughout the post-Cheneux period.

With the conclusion of the 504th's violent fight at Cheneux to contain *Kampfgruppe Peiper* on the 21st of December, the northern sector quieted down as the crucible of battle shifted some 11 miles to the south. At Bastogne, the "Screaming Eagles" of the 101st Airborne Division had become encircled, and the 82nd Airborne Division was close to having the same fate befall it as the Germans, bound for Liege, began to press into the division's lines south of Lierneux. There, Colonel Charles Billingslea, who had served with the 504th in Italy, was masterfully manning an overstretched defensive line with his 325th Glider Infantry Regiment. Central to the fate of the 82nd Airborne was the village of Fraiture and the crossroads which sat a little over half a mile to its southwest. Running in between the forested hills, the road was critical, and while the rugged, abrupt hills provided advantageous positions for the defender, it was a double-edged sword: it required heavy troop density too because it also provided good cover for the attacker. With all the division's reserves committed, troop density was one thing the entire division was lacking, and the situation was foreboding.

The task of holding the village of Fraiture fell to Billingslea's 2nd Battalion. Shortly before nightfall on the 21st of December, as the din of battle broke in Cheneux for the 504th, Billingslea's men started for Fraiture. Trudging through the mud of a trail which was little more than the bank of a swollen stream, the men walked. Soon the gray, dismal skies began dropping a mixture of rain and snow and an all-consuming darkness fell over the glider men as night came on. At daylight, the men shivered a few hundred yards short of Fraiture.[624]

The task of securing the crossroads fell to a company of glider men under the command of Captain Junior Woodruff. Woodruff was a veteran who had been with the division's 325th Glider Infantry since it had left the States in 1943, and since the division's time in Africa had borne the brunt of jokes from his fellow officers stemming from his severe bout with dysentery in the desert; he became known to his fellow officers as "Woody of the Wadi" and was told that a book about their experiences would be written after the war under that title.[625]

If the Germans could break through the crossroads at Fraiture, which Woodruff's men were to hold, the Germans could run their tanks to Manhay, then to Werbomont and then to Liege - all while presenting a serious possibility of encircling the 82nd Airborne Division. Recognizing this, General James Gavin ordered the crossroads held at all costs.

The snow began to fall and dust the countryside.

Max Bach, scouting for the battalion's headquarters group, cautiously entered Fraiture. There, he found a jeep full of artillerymen. He entered one of the houses and was warmly received by the residents who took his clothes, wet from the rain and snow, and dried them near the fire and warmed his insides with coffee. He was told by a farmer that the Germans were on the heights overlooking the town. Bach immediately relayed the information as soon as the command post pulled into the village. Soon, Fraiture was under mortar fire from the Germans as activity just outside town heightened.[626]

Further up the road in Manhay that afternoon, a platoon of tank destroyers from the 643rd Tank Destroyer Battalion, under the leadership of Lieutenant John Orlando, was dispatched to Captain Woodruff to aid in his stand at the crossroads just southwest of town. As Orlando's tank destroyers approached the crossroads, they were forced to pull off into the berm of the road to make way for retreating columns of the 3rd Armored Division. After reading the crossroads, Lieutenant Orlando went to confer with Captain Woodruff while the tankers sat around in their halftracks. Three men from the 3rd Armored Division straggled by. One of them was a neighbor to one of the tankers; he said there was nothing around that was not occupied by Germans and said, "We may even be surrounded by Germans now."[627]

At dawn on the 23rd, elements of SS Panzer Division *Das Reich* began to probe Captain Woodruff's positions around the crossroads and artillery and/or mortars fell. Lieutenant John Orlando's tank destroyer men had dug into positions south of the crossroads. The gun position farthest south was that of Sergeants

Joseph Giordano and Frank Martilelli. When they dug in on the 22nd, they could hear Germans digging in within hearing distance; if either of them spoke German they could have known what they were talking about.[628]

Other chess pieces continued to move based on the fighting along Billingslea's 325th lines. Lieutenant Colonel Wellems's 2nd Battalion, 504th Parachute Infantry was ordered withdrawn from Cheneux on the morning of the 23rd. Having exhausted all reserves, General Gavin ordered Lieutenant Colonel Wellems to move across the entire division area, some 10 miles, to the wooded high ground south of Lierneux to bolster any critical spot on the 325th's front which may be overrun. Moving Wellems may have provided an opportunity for the remnants of *Kampfgruppe Peiper* to escape, but in the south, at the vital road nets of which the Fraiture crossroads was a part, the integrity of the entire division was at stake, and that took a greater priority for General Gavin. While Wellems and his men were being trucked to their new positions, General Gavin called 504th headquarters and instructed them to "keep well abreast of the situation" on the 325th front, and ensure there is a liaison officer between the two units. By the afternoon, the 504th PIR's 2nd Battalion was in position.[629]

Through the day probing attacks on Captain Woodruff's positions and artillery and mortars continued to fall around the crossroads. That afternoon the German SS troops came swarming, and with them at least four Tiger tanks breathing fire. Sergeant Joseph Giordano and T/5 Anthony DeFoster were killed from the attached tank destroyer unit, and the guns and halftracks of Giordano's squad destroyed, along with the gun and halftrack of Sergeant Frank Martilelli. The Germans swarmed their positions, taking 14 prisoners.[630]

The glider infantrymen of the 325th fought back with great tenacity as the weight of the Germans crashed down upon them. Their company was being attacked by a force three times their size. Captain Woodruff sent his runner, Private First Class Jim Bryant, back in a jeep to go northward and get more ammunition. The Germans had infiltrated around to the rear and the driver of the jeep was killed, along with the passenger sitting in the back seat by the radio. Bryant rolled out of the passenger side and onto the ground and ran for the woods and hid under snow and sticks, narrowly escaping with his life.[631]

Based on the weight of force falling upon Captain Woodruff's reinforced company, it was impossible to do more than delay the Germans, but this they did. Finally, Woodruff got permission to withdraw the remnants of his company by radio, and they came out fighting.

Up in the village of Fraiture itself, Company E of the 325th Glider Infantry had been staying in houses with fires to keep them warm, but things began to change when the crossroads fell as they found themselves now on the forward line. Throughout the next day, the E Company men had to be cognizant of where they were shooting as Woodruff's men straggled back to their own lines.[632]

From their positions up the road to the north, the men of Colonel Wellems's 2nd Battalion, 504th Parachute Infantry had no idea what was occurring. Suddenly, Werner Speer and the rest of the paratroopers under Wellems's command were called out of their foxholes and onto the now snow-covered road. A low, dismal fog began to form, and the paratroopers told to get ready to march. They were told they were going to take a crossroads; the men did not know it, but the crossroads they were to take was the ill-fated crossroads at Fraiture.[633]

The outlook for the attack at battalion headquarters was bleak. The only reconnaissance which could be done of the rugged terrain was by the map, and the attached artillery observer could promise no support from the gun batteries, which were busily firing all along the division's defensive front. At the meeting of the battalion staff before moving out, 1st Lieutenant Chester Garrison asked Colonel Wellems what the order of succession would be for command if he, the commander, were to fall.

The battalion, with the succession of command now stated at Garrison's request, began moving towards Fraiture in the dark of the night. Suddenly, the column was stopped. The men were instructed to return to their positions. The attack was called off - they had been saved from the brink. When Lieutenant Chester Garrison and Colonel Ed Wellems met for the first time after World War II, the meeting prior to that called-off attack was among the first things that crossed the mind of Garrison's then former commander.

In July of 1947, the 82nd had in New York its first reunion. At the hotel where we gathered, Wellems spotted me as I joined the gathering of 504 officers and he called out to me. On second thought, he pointed at me and fiercely announced, "Do you know what that Chester did to me in Belgium? As I was about to face certain death in leading the battalion down a hillside [to Fraiture], that son-of-a-bitch had the nerve to ask me about the chain of command!" Insult, but delivered with the slight edge that close male friends banter with. The seeming insult translates into an avowal of camaraderie. We hugged. When I visited him several weeks later, we went fishing early one morning at a secluded lake. I rowed and he cast – far in geography, time, and mood from the sound of battle that we had known together.[634]

In the meantime, the 3rd Battalion, 504th Parachute Infantry was joining Colonel Wellems and his men on the Lierneux Ridge. As H. Donald Zimmerman marched south of the town, a large contingent of retreating troops from the 28th Division began marching past them in the other direction. A lot of them,

Zimmerman thought, looked familiar until he spotted a kid he went to high school with back home in Scottdale, Pennsylvania. It was the National Guard unit from their area, Service Company of the 110th Infantry. "What are you doing?" Zimmerman finally asked. "The bulge is this way!"[635]

With two of the regiment's battalions now in place, it appeared that the 504th might be preparing for a major confrontation. "The situation is so fluid that orders are dependent on future activities," the 504th Regimental S-3 journal recorded.[636]

These facts - of the threat to the division, the shifting of forces and the reasoning behind them - were mostly known but only to the most senior officers. The privates and junior officers had only a rudimentary idea of where they were going, and no idea why. "As a lowly 2nd Lt.," Bramson wrote, "I didn't have any maps – to be blunt I was just told where to go. I know that doesn't sound very romantic."[637] Werner Speer likened their role as to that of a firemen moving from one area to another from day-to-day to put out fires here and fires there. There was one move, however, that the men well-understood: the order of retreat from the area, given by Field Marshall Bernard Montgomery on Christmas Eve. Werner Speer remembered that they had not been in their positions for too long after returning from the canceled attack when the new order came.[638] The men of the 3rd Battalion had only been in position for less than a day, and for that battalion Hugh Wallis was one of a handful of men ordered to remain behind to act as a covering force while the rest of the unit marched north towards the Belgian village of Bra to set up their new defensive line.

We pushed ahead, we was first on defense, and then we was pushing them back and we pushed ahead of the division that was to our left and we had to pull back to straighten the line. They left me and two other guys as rear guards. The one guy had a radio and they said, "We'll radio you guys when we get in position for you to pull back. Don't get in a fight you don't have to." It seemed like forever that we was there and finally there was a road down to our left where the German tank up there, we could hear them, and there was a farm field but there was a big bank and there was a road that came around that farm field and I was right on top of that bank in some bushes.

I heard something and I looked up and here come what I call a flak wagon right around that farm road. I could have stood on them. They didn't know I was up on top of them, but they told us don't do anything. It was tempting to drop a hand grenade but I didn't.

After that went on, the radio guy crawled up to me and he said, "My radio's been dead and I didn't know it. Do you think we should stay any longer or pull out?" I said, "I think we'd better go." Because it was probably after midnight. They had told us to go to a house on a little crossroad village. There wasn't many there. It was a big white house on a corner. When we got [there] there was guys from another company that was there and they said, "Where in the world have you guys been? We've been waiting hours for you. There's a jeep on the way after us. If you wasn't here we was going to leave you." Well that jeep pulled up just about the time we got there. I think that was on Christmas Eve. We got back to our company Christmas morning. That was a pretty good Christmas present![639]

Silent Night

Out on the new frontline, just outside of Bra, James Churchill and Werner Speer were sitting in their machine gun pit when Christmas morning dawned. Wearing from the past two days in which they had marched much and slept little, they were taking turns napping with their machine gun in their new position.

That morning, it was Christmas Day, I don't know how long or what time it was, but we got to where we were going, dug our positions and we were taking turns – Churchill would take a nap and I wasn't so happy that he was taking a nap and I was on guard with the machine gun. It started to get light. Very, very indistinct and there were trees and I guess it was about 75 yards to our front and there were small trees. It could cloud a division but I could see movement and I thought, Oh, here we go. *There were, it looked like large enemy group coming through those woods and I woke Churchill up and he cocked the machine gun and wanted to fire. I mentioned, "Hold on. Hold on. Please don't fire. Let them get closer." They were crossing in front of us, not towards us and they came out on the trees and brush and they weren't Germans, they weren't military at all. They were Belgian civilians and they were carrying bags of stuff, I guess whatever they could carry to get away from the enemy, the Germans, and I'll never forget it: Churchill and I looked at one another and thought,* boy, oh boy, I'm glad we didn't fire on them.[640]

Just a short distance away, James Sapp awoke to find the sun was finally breaking through the gray, dismal fog which had depressingly tucked in the Belgian countryside. The sun had been a fugitive from the men's lives since they left France, and it was a welcome change from the deep frost which had set in the night before. As the blue skies opened up, they revealed another battlefield high above them. Sapp looked up and could see so many bombers flying towards Germany that their vapor contrails almost occluded the sun; they laced through the blue sky like white ribbons.[641]

Rations for the day was a special treat for front-line combat troops: turkey. The rear echelon issued one turkey for each squad in the regiment. In preparing the Christmas turkey for his platoon, Lieutenant

Robert Bramson was far away from the halls of law school which he had known at the University of Nebraska. The turkey he received for his men was of such low quality, he was not exactly sure what kind of meat it was. "I do remember the rear area sending up food containers I think for the holiday – the meat, whatever it was, was too cold to eat," recalled Bramson. "We didn't have any stoves and the food was brought up in I think marmite barrels or containers and we had to use some kind of explosive material we had to make a fire and heat up a mess kit cup of snow to warm up the meat. It was probably too dangerous where we were for the mess crews to do more."[642]

A short distance down the line, an Army photographer by the name of Emil Edgren was walking around the regiment's front line. He had been sent from Paris to link up with the division and take photographs of infantrymen fighting on the front line. Edgren walked his way up near a road to the forward positions to take photographs. He had walked up past one of the machine gun pits when suddenly someone yelled at him, "Krauts! Get down! Get down!"

Edgren jumped in a ditch.

A hail of machine gun bullets slipped above him towards the German patrol.

A German machine gun replied.[643]

The men in the American machine gun pit belonged to Lieutenant Robert Blankenship. Relatively unaware of the skirmish that was taking place with the German patrol, Lieutenant Blankenship had not been able to contact that position all night through the sound-powered telephone, and so Blankenship decided he would crawl out to the forward position with Private First Class Walter Hughes to try and repair the telephone line if it was broken, and ensure the men in the position were still alive. It was the setting to what would become a widely-published photograph of a lone paratrooper flanking a German machine gun crew. Hughes remembered the vividly:

I was one of the two wiremen in the company. Cpl. Ed Hahn from Lexington, Ky was the other wireman. He had been up most of the night repairing sound power lines to several of the other forward positions. There was some small arms activity over toward several of the other holes but only an occasional burst of gunfire as we crept up toward the machine gun hole. I was following the wire with one hand and just as Lieutenant Blankenship got to the hole one of the men in the hole raised his head and yelled, "Jesus, you guys almost got shot." I had found where the wire was broken just before the hole and looked for the other end to splice them together when the Germans opened up on us with a heavy machine gun. Lieutenant Blankenship fell into the hole with me on top of him. After a few minutes the firing stopped and we discovered two of the men in the hole were wounded and the other [Leroy Simmons of Iowa] was dead. Lieutenant Blankenship took over the machine gun and sent a burst out toward the Germans. Then it got quiet. He called back on the phone that I had connected and said he would hold the position until the men could be evacuated and replacements sent out. Noting that my job with the wire was finished, he noted I had my Thompson. He said, "Hughes, do you think if I keep those Krauts busy you can crawl out and get behind them and shut them up." I smiled at him and said, "Hey, lieutenant, ain't that a job for a sergeant?" He laughed and said, "You're right Sergeant Hughes. Now go put them out of business." I was scared but hell if I'm gonna die at least I'll die a sergeant.

Ed Hahn shortly before the Battle of the Bulge started. He was the second wireman in Company I and had spent most of the night of Christmas Eve repairing phone lines. (Walter Hughes)

I crawled out of the hole and back toward the ditch along the road. I had one clip in the Thompson and two clips in my left hand. If need be I could hit the ejection with my right hand and shove another clip right in with my left hand.

Rolling under the barbed wire at the fence, I got the fright of my life. There was someone laying in the ditch! It was a Stars & Stripes *guy scared to death. He had heard the shooting and crawled up to take pictures but didn't realize he was almost shot - not by the Germans, but by me. I waited a few minutes 'till he crawled back along the ditch, then started easing my way toward the German gun. They had resumed shooting at the lieutenant and with the noise of their gun and Lieutenant Blankenship they never even heard me. There were four Germans in the hole and no other German soldiers near them to protect them. To make sure they were taken care of, I used two clips on them then headed back toward Lieutenant Blankenship. He was a good officer, and I kept the sergeant stripes until after the war ended and we were sent to Berlin, where I got in a hassle in the Club Famina and went back to a private.*[644]

The photograph of Walter Hughes moving to attack the German machine gun, taken by Emil Edgren. (US Signal Corps)

As Christmas night approached, there had remained only light activity across the front on that hallowed day. W. George Benivitz was providing over watch over the front line, armed with a telephone which led back to the F Company 60mm mortars.

One parachute infantry company consisted of about 100 men, no mess or kitchen, one jeep, and one two-and-one-half-ton supply truck. At this time, I was the forward observer for our 60mm mortar section, which consisted of three tubes located on the reverse slope of a hill overlooking a valley and the enemy on the opposite hill. My position was on the forward slope where I had an excellent view; however, the position was exposed and I dared not leave my foxhole during the daylight as it would be hazardous to my health. I had a small radio and a sound-powered telephone. Any movement and we would drop a few shells on them which was devastating because of the tree burst.

I had lost track of time and date. During the night I received a call that I would have a visitor. The only way he could find my position was to follow the telephone line by grasping it. The country-side was covered with ice and snow. I felt tugs on the line and got prepared to meet friend or foe. It was our supply sergeant. He said, "Merry Christmas" and handed me a canteen. It was filled with cognac. I took two swallows and my body temperature elevated many degrees. He also handed me a semi-frozen fist-sized piece of turkey and departed. I gnawed on that turkey for some time.[645]

W. George Benivitz, Werner Speer and James Chruchill in June 1945. (Werner Speer)

Mortar Duels Around en Florêt

In the woods looking out towards the village of Floret, Kenneth Nicoll was up before dawn trying to draw a bead on the German's artillery observation post using the 81mm mortars. "Sure have been raising hell all night," Nicoll confided to his religiously kept diary.[646]

Nicoll and his entire platoon of 81mm mortars were keeping close watch over the village of Floret, a small farming hamlet situated on the gentle slope of a hill, one in a series of low rolling hills characteristic of Belgium's Ardennes region. Floret had been occupied by the Germans for three days, and their bid on the town was won when they drove out a platoon of paratroopers under the charge of Lieutenant Harry Rollins. His men were overrun and scattered and when the Germans swarmed, Rollins used his pistol and fired an entire seven-round magazine at 12 Germans and tried to run for it while reloading. An explosion knocked him down and before he could recover, he found himself surrounded by a party of Germans and became their prisoner.[647]

Nicoll spent the day of December 29 using the 81mm mortars to hit a house just before dinner, and then rake the treeline, where the German's main line was. "Enemy seems to have shot its load," he wrote in his diary that day. "I don't think their offensive will go any farther. Now we will have to push them back again. What a hell of a war. No future."[648]

All night the artillery went back and forth. "This is getting to be an artillery duel. Can't move without drawing those screaming memies," Nicoll wrote in his diary in the morning. At noontime, Kenneth Nicoll and the rest of the men in the Mortar Platoon turned their attention to Floret itself. Nicoll saw three Germans run into a house, and the men decided they would burn the house down around them.[649]

James Sapp had a field telephone on which he would relay the fire missions and corrections directly to 1st Lieutenant Lauren Ramsey, their platoon leader, who would in turn relay them to the gunners on the mortars. Sapp began to shell the houses with a delayed action fuse, where rather than detonating on impact the shell would fall through the roof and donate on the bottom floor of a house. Sapp watched as the doors blew off and the windows blew out. On the livestock buildings, where there was a hayloft, he called for phosphorous shells which would catch the hay on fire.[650]

When the Germans would run to a different house, they would use the white phosphorus shells and burn that one down too. "Jerries running everywhere. We are having a field day with our mortars. The machine guns drive them into ravines and we finish them off. Dead Krauts everywhere," Nicoll wrote in his diary around 1400.

Sapp continued to call corrections back to Lieutenant Ramsey over the field telephone, which he was talking into with his left hand. Suddenly, the Germans fired a counter-battery on Sapp's observation post. A shell landed in the foxhole Sapp was in, throwing him on his back and covering him with dirt and snow. "When I got up," Sapp said, "the receiving end of my phone was gone." Due to the explosion, communication was abruptly cut-off with Lieutenant Ramsey. "He was on the phone on the other end and he could hear the explosion on the other end, and the phone went dead," Sapp recalled. "I got a radio and he asked what happened and I told him." Sapp was miraculously uninjured in what would have typically been a fatal explosion. Staff Sergeant William Kirkland and Private First Class Robert McNally were wounded. Sapp's close friend Casmir Klamut was wounded severely, and he would die of his wound on January 8, 1945.[651]

A member of the platoon holds a sound-powered telephone during the Battle of the Bulge. (James Sapp)

Kenneth Nicoll wrote in his diary that night, "The skies light up with all the town burning. One Jerry waved his handkerchief trying to surrender but of course I couldn't take him prisoner. His own men would've shot him."

The following morning - New Year's Eve - at daylight, Ken Nicoll wrote that he thought the town looked deserted. They watched closely as a three-man patrol went in to investigate unmolested. Around 1100, a platoon of Company E under Lieutenant Patrick C. Collins went to try and occupy Floret. They were ambushed, and Collins was killed and two others wounded. That evening, the 1st Battalion went in and raided the town, with Ken Nicoll and the Mortar Platoon firing in support.[652]

Two hours later, after dark, the Germans unleashed a hellacious barrage of 155mm shells on Nicoll's observation post and the 2nd Battalion's command post. At the command post, Lieutenant Chester Garrison was walking to confer with Colonel Wellems, the battalion commander, about taking an emergency patrol out when a shell landed near Garrison. The explosion threw the lieutenant into a flip like a toy, sending him violently crashing through the tarp covering the double foxhole being occupied by Wellems and his executive officer. Garrison, landing atop his two superiors, was bleeding from the mouth and after being given a morphine syrette was evacuated.[653]

James Sapp just before jumping into Holland for Operation Market Garden. (James Sapp)

"Boy we caught hell for two hrs," Nicoll wrote in his diary. "I laid under a barrage. One hit over my hole, two hit beside (155mm). This place looks like it had been through a meat grinder. How I ever lived through it I don't know. Buzz bomb dropped close by. Happy New Year."

The village of Floret would not be recaptured from the Germans until January 3, when it was attacked by elements of the 3rd Armored Division.

Attacking the Crossings of the Salm River

The men began moving out of their defensive positions around Bra on January 3, and began marching east through the Belgian snow to reclaim the German gains. The 2nd Battalion of Lieutenant Colonel Edward Wellems moved out the morning of January 4 and set out marching on hilly, ice-coated roads through the forest in deep snow. The march pace was slow, owing to the up-and-down terrain and knee-deep snow and ice. Soon the men left the roads and began traversing down the large, snow-filled firebreaks in the evergreen forest. The pine branches, like the men, sagged under the weight of the white snow which adorned the green nettles of the branches as they marched in the firebreaks between an infinite wall of snow-dusted green trees.[654] Second Lieutenant Robert Bramson of Company F remembered the conditions of the relocation marches: "As I remember it was pretty miserable – the main problem was frozen feet ('trench foot'). Being young then it really didn't bother [me] too much – but today at my age it would be near terminal."[655] The weather was so cold that the wet web gear worn by the paratroopers froze onto the clothing of the troopers. The moisture in the wool of damp overcoats would freeze, making the coat stiff as cardboard.

This photograph, also taken by Emil Edgren around Christmas Day, shows a trooper from Company H in a prepared fighting position looking out towards no-man's land. The German lines are in the opposite woods. (US Signal Corps)

When the men departed for the march on January 3, they had dropped their bedrolls with the battalion supply section, who would then truck them to their destination. The battalion arrived in the village of Foose in the late afternoon, where they were ordered to advance another four miles through what Captain Victor Campana described as "dense woods, void of any good roads except a few trails and fire-breaks covered by waist high snow." After getting to their objective with much confusion on the forest trails, the battalion arrived at their objective after 0100. "It was a black, dreary, wooded area void of everything but snow and one or two firebreaks," Campana described.[656]

Robert McNally was a member of the 2nd Battalion 81mm Mortar Platoon and was wounded by German mortar retaliation during the duels near en Floret, Belgium. (McNally family)

During the night, D Company was subject to six mortar rounds falling into Captain Adam Komosa's CP group. Komosa immediately called for litters and medics to treat his several wounded paratroopers, but no litters were on hand and the battalion's aid station was forced to the village of Foose, a distance of over four miles. Half an hour later, the wounded came through the battalion CP on their way back to Foose. Private Paul Nageley, Komosa's runner, was severely wounded in the head and was being hand-carried on a makeshift litter formed by tree limbs and overcoats. He would later die of his wounds.[657]

After marching sixteen hours that day through the snow, the men were unable to get hardly any sleep, and the men nearly froze to death as the battalion supply was not able to get through with the bedrolls. "We didn't have any blankets," James Sapp remembered, "so we nearly froze to death. We shoveled the snow down to the ground and we'd get four or five of us and huddle all together; then we'd have to get up and double time in place." In the morning, the men in Sapp's platoon were so cold they did the almost unthinkable in combat: they lit a fire, which in normal circumstances would end in a German artillery barrage. "In the morning," Sapp said, "we'd get big fires and the Germans started coming up and surrendering when they saw all the smoke and stuff, they were freezing also."[658]

Officers of Company I consult a map in one of the many firebreaks during a march in January 1945. (Richie Blankenship)

The marches conducted in the first days of January put the 504th Parachute Infantry Regiment in position for the attack on the villages overlooking the Salm River. On January 7, 1945 the regiment attacked the villages of Grand Halleux, Mont, Petit-Halleux and into the woods north of the village of Rencheux. The 2nd and 3rd Battalions met stiff resistance. Lieutenant George Amos' feet were wounded when a mine went off while he was leading I Company into Petit-Halleux. Captain Burriss and his two additional platoons were waiting the in the woods to mop up the Germans that Amos had bypassed. When Burriss got into the village, he went to see Amos. "He did have some foot damage but he kept on going," recalled Burriss. "It kind of messed up his feet for several days."[659]

Fighting in the Woods North of Rencheux

As the regiment began their attack on the crossings of the Salm, the 1st Battalion met little resistance as the unit moved out in the attack through deep snow. They encountered no Germans as they went down a well-plowed road to a sharp hill just short of the river. They occupied previously prepared positions, probably made by Germans. The A Company positions were just on the northern outskirts of Vielsalm, where elements of the 505th PIR were located. As they were getting settled, heavy fighting was occurring not far to the south – only about 200 yards – in the 505 sector. The fighting was extremely noisy, as the sounds of heavy machine gun fire could be heard bouncing off the hills.

Company B dug in on a steep hill overlooking the Salm River, just north of Renchueux, with the 2nd, 1st, and 3rd Platoons abreast from north to south. Lieutenant Reneau Breard's 1st Platoon was down to about 16 men, and they dug in where the river bent, meaning that part of the platoon was facing south in the hills inside the arm of the bend.

In the mid-morning, Lieutenant Leo Van DeVoert's outpost overlooking the railway bed was attacked by a German patrol. Breard remembered that shortly after Van DeVoert's outpost had been hit, his outpost was also probed.

It was still morning and my outpost was attacked while overlooking the railroad bed. The bed of the RR had been cut thru there along the high ground to the west of the railroad. The cut was about 15 feet high. On the west side there was no motorway on either side of the river, only the railroad on the west side. There was a foot path uphill but you still couldn't see the RR because of the forest (thick).[660]

Lieutenant Breard was up the footpath near his platoon CP when the Germans attacked the B/504 positions in force at about 1720. Germans started pouring out of the railway cut and climbing over the embankment. A contact patrol from A Company led by Sergeant Ignatius W. Wengress had come up to Breard's positions shortly before the Germans had begun their attack.

We had a fire up the hill about 50 to 75 yards as the men could come up to get warm. So I gave them coffee and a little bull when all hell broke loose down [the] hill from the path. They, the patrol from A Co., helped with a base of fire while my small platoon attacked down the hill yelling off like crazy. No need to say – I thanked the A Co. (4 men) and their base of fire.[661]

The immediate area to the south opened up into a large clearing in the woods which gently sloped down the river and towards a building the Germans had occupied. Further south of the clearing was the 3rd Platoon, and to cover this clearing was an automatic rifleman. William Bonning and Paul Graham had been in the platoon's outpost a short distance away when the German's attacked. Bonning, hearing the fracas, ran through the snow towards the clearing; approaching it a German machine gun opened up from behind the embankment and up in the woods. Looking fast, he saw a Browning Automatic Rifle leaning up against a tree. With machine gun bullets singing past him, Bonning dove for the hole next to the rifle and landed on another paratrooper. The trooper was pinned down in his hole and unable to reach his weapon.

Suddenly, Second Lieutenant James G. Douglass and his runner came running out of the tree line.[662] The machine gun turned on Douglass and zipped across his hands and arms. The gun fell from the lieutenant's hands; he and his runner turned back into the tree line. Then Fred Faidley emerged from where Douglass had disappeared, charging out towards Bonning as the German gun stitched him across the legs. Faidley fell into the snow like a sack of bricks. Bonning pulled him into the foxhole. Bonning turned his Browning Automatic Rifle towards the Germans, its barrel smoking with fervor as he fired back, killing three as they advanced.[663]

At the top of the hill in the clearing sat Morris Holmstock. From his foxhole, he could hear men yelling. "Come down this way, the Germans are down here!" Holmstock felt he could not leave his position, as he was on the uppermost point on the extreme left flank of the platoon. If he left, Holmstock felt, there would be nothing to protect their rear. Holmstock sat with his M-1 across his lap in a cold and miserable state, and listened to the battle below as Hilton Holland, Thomas Holliday and 'Turk' ran down the hill and counterattacked the Germans.

Not but a few minutes later, Holmstock observed two German grenadiers emerge from the tree line about ten or fifteen yards to his front, presumably attempting to flank their positions. Holmstock rose the wooden stock of his M-1 up to his cheekbone and dialed in with the sights. Holmstock pulled the trigger. One of the Germans collapsed and fell into the snow. Holmstock rounded the other one up, taking him prisoner. Sergeant Paul V. Mann came up. Holmstock inspected the German which he had wounded and he coveted the great big fur coat that he was wearing. Holmstock and Mann tried to talk to the Germans. They took the coat off. Holmstock's bullet had passed through his ribs, but it didn't look like it would be a fatal wound. "Take these two prisoners to the rear," Sergeant Mann said. As they were taking them back, Mann said, "Come on, let's knock them off and we won't have to take them back." Holmstock argued against Mann. They took the wounded man to the aid station, and Holmstock never did take the fur coat.[664]

Meanwhile, Hilton Holland, Thomas Holliday, Turk and others were still down at the bottom of the hill trying to chase the Germans back across the Salm River. Lieutenant Breard couldn't tell what was going on.

I then went alone downhill to see what was going on and foolishly crawled up to look south down the railway. I crawled up to the embankment when an enemy soldier raised up and shoots at me point blank with a rifle. Fortunately, the snow was waist deep and I started to back track. The soldier was a bad shot. He missed me and I lost my two grenades carried in my harness (like Ridgeway). I went back to the left crawling and made him give up. There was still shooting and darned if one of my men shot my prisoner in the shoulder so I had to give him first aid and sent him under guard to the company C.P. We did get some prisoners that day, but not many.[665]

Lt. Reneau Breard on his wedding day. (Reneau Breard)

As darkness began to fall, Corporal Hilton M. Holland was missing. It was getting late, and the men were forced to abandon their search until the morning. When they resumed their search for Hilton Holland in the daylight, they found him lying down next to the railway tracks, holding his intestines inside his body. He was still alive, but had suffered a grave wound during the gunfight the previous evening. A burst of the German machine gun had cut across his midriff, virtually ripping his stomach out. The men got him back, and were awaiting an ambulance. "We were standing around kidding him. That was the last time I saw him," Holmstock remembered. Hilton M. Holland would later die of the wound.

Later that day, Holmstock observed one of their medics wearing the fur coat from the German he had shot during the firefight previous day. "What did you do, kill him?" Holmstock asked.

"No, you shot him in the chest and he died," he replied.

It was a little bit of a shock to Holmstock, as he didn't think the wound looked that serious. However, he was thoroughly angered that the medic bequeathed the German's large, warm fur coat. What Holmstock told the medic, he could not repeat.[666]

For the actions of Reneau Breard and Hilton Holland actions on January 7, they were both awarded the Silver Star Medal.

A Wet and Miserable Night

On January 7, Robert DeVinney and another paratrooper were trudging through deep snow along the edge of the tree line on top of the ridge looking for a spot to dig in when a German artillery spotter witnessed them. The spotter called a German 88mm shell down onto them. The shell impacted the snow next to the two paratroopers as they were walking – a typically lethal occurrence. However, the shell went into the snow and slid underneath the snow surface and skated back into the woods where it detonated. "That," DeVinney stated, "made us pretty jumpy." Down below, they could see the Germans evacuating a village, probably Grand Halleux.[667]

Robert DeVinney of Company H, who joined the unit in France on the eve of the Battle of the Bulge. (Robert DeVinney)

The following night, Earl Oldfather was charged with leading a patrol to the village of Grand Halleux to see if there were any Germans still occupying it, now that the regiment held the other side of the river and could look down upon the village. Oldfather provides an account of their experiences between January 5 and January 8 as they attacked towards the Salm River.

January 5th [we] spotted Germans in front of us and captured some [in] back of us. Guess we were surrounded. From our position we had a view of Petit Halleux. On January 7th at 5:00 AM, the 2nd Platoon attacked the town. A staff sergeant [John D. Hamilton] and medic [Woodrow Yarborough] were killed. The lieutenant in charge and several others were wounded. Our lieutenant from the 3rd Platoon took over the attack. He returned later okay, but no details.

January 8th I was picked to take three men with me on a patrol that evening to see if the Germans occupied Grand Halleux. This is what I wrote in my diary:

Stopped at Co. H CP, the CO gave me what information he had. A guide took us through Petit Halleux to the river that divides the two towns. We crossed the River Salm over a blown out log bridge to Grand Halleux. It was snowing and the wind blowing, heard all kinds of noises - shutters and doors banging. The snow being on the ground made it light as day. I walked, the fellow following along a green fence to the main drag. Passed a large church onto the road junction, turned around and came back. Not a sign of a German for which I was very thankful. Came back across the bridge and reported to Co H and had a cup of coffee. Sure was a long grind back to our Co CP. Then I was told to report to BN. Took one of the fellows with me and back in the snow we went. Reported to a lt. col. and a capt. Was given two cups of coffee and piece of jelly. Back into the snow topped off with a dark, dark woods. We had quite a time finding our positions. Finally got in a foxhole by the end of a wet and miserable night.[668]

2nd Battalion Casualties

In the 2nd Battalion, casualties were disproportionately heavy in D and F Companies during the attack on January 7. The battalion was to make a secondary attack on the village of Mont with two platoons. Lieutenant Richard A. Harris' 1st Platoon of F Company was moving through the small hamlet of Farnières, sitting on hilly terrain and surrounded by forest-lined sloping fields. They killed three Germans, and as they began moving out from the hamlet to the northeast, the platoon was brought under heavy machine gun and rifle fire from the forest-line along the road leading into Mont. Firing as he advanced, Lieutenant Harris charged the German positions and was wounded severely by German fire. He continued to drive forward to get within grenade-throwing distance when he was shot to death. A few troopers went out to the exposed terrain to recover Harris' body, but they too were killed.[669]

Observing the difficulty of Harris' men, Lieutenant Martin Middleton immediately, on his own initiative, organized a patrol to locate the hidden enemy machine gun. They too were brought under fire, and Middleton went back to get smoke shells to blind the enemy. Upon his return, he fired several rifle grenades into the area, putting the German machine gun out of action. Under fire, he moved to help evacuate the wounded and carried one seriously wounded man back himself, and killed two Germans attempting to loot dead paratroopers.[670]

Lawrence Allen of Company I shaves during the Battle of the Bulge. (Moffatt Burriss)

The following day, Lieutenant Robert Bramson heard of Harris' fate. "I joined the regiment in Holland after being transferred from the 508 – being a new replacement officer you can understand that close relationships don't occur quickly which is perfectly normal. I can't recall how I [first] came into contact with him but he apparently was a friendly sort, a nice person – although I don't think we ever worked closely in any [combat] situations. At the time when I heard of his death I just wanted to see him and pay my respects as he had been one of the few officers I had gotten to know." Bramson said he went to a nearby collection area. "There, the bodies of those killed recently were laid out in the snow and I saw him – I wanted to pay my respect to him."[671]

On January 9, tragedy struck the battalion yet again. The engineers had inserted anti-tank mines into burlap sandbags and placed them on the road. When an officer came and told some of the men to remove the mines, the men picked them up with their hands and tossed them to the side of the road. The mines detonated, killing four.[672]

Rest in Remouchamps

Just a few short days after those tragic events, the entire 82nd Airborne Division was relieved for a much needed rest. Nestled between two rolling hills, the riverside town of Sougne-Remouchamps was to be the home of the 504th for the next several days. Surrounded by the two forested hills, the old Belgian town was a picturesque scene, and the snow made the village look like a beautiful diorama. The streets gently sloped down to the River Ambleve, where it formed the town's southern border.

Remouchamps had been largely unaffected by the war in terms of property destruction; the shops were open for business and the citizens went along as best they could ignoring the war.

The trucks offloaded the dirty, combat grizzled paratroops, and began moving into the town's homes, hosted by the families.

The townspeople, before long, became endeared to their paratroopers and forged strong, friendly relationships with the men of the unit. Robert DeVinney and members of his platoon were billeted with a mother and daughter, who slept downstairs while the men sacked out upstairs on the floor. The following day there was a formation, after which DeVinney went to the aid station to have his frozen feet looked at; he was later evacuated due to his condition.[673]

For 2nd Lieutenant Robert Bramson, the stay in Remouchamps was a fond memory of the war. The mentioning of Remouchamps "stirs memories," he wrote.

I remember those few days fairly clearly. Why – because it represented civilization, warmth and comfort for a few days after hardly ever getting into a house or barn and mostly sleeping freezing cold in the snow or in a dugout or whatever we could scrounge.

I don't remember numbers of men [in each home], but I was billeted with a couple of officers in a house on or near the center square of the town – just across the street from the Mayor's house. I seem to recall that the company's officers may have eaten meals at the Mayor's house, but I'm a little hazy on that point. We did use it for meetings and briefings – and more important we had a nightly poker game in his parlor. That I definitely remember.

The house we were billeted in was wonderfully warm with bedrooms and with indoor plumbing, etc. Of course [it was] nothing like we were used to at home. The occupants were pleasant and did all they could to make us welcome.

For the troops the Army set up a large portable trailer in the town square with showers, but it was so godforsaken cold outside that I never tried it.

Two or three officers and I took a jeep instead to Liège, shared a bed in some kind of hotel, with the missiles or bombs serenading us, and we all visited the public bath house where we were able to bathe and use the steam room – unbelievable luxury. We even had steaks in a cafe that night (we soon learned it was horse meat), but it was delicious to us that evening.[674]

Company B was still being reconstructed after its losses at Cheneux, and while they were in Remouchamps a new group of replacements joined the company. Morris Holmstock was summoned to the company CP, where he found 1st Sergeant Amedeo Castagno waiting. "He was tough," Holmstock recalled. "He didn't stand for any bullshit. He used to say, 'Let's go out behind the mess hall and I'll give you some boxing lessons.' Castagno called me up to the CP and says, 'You're going to be corporal.' I said, 'I don't want to be a corporal.' He said, 'Well, if you don't want it I'm going to give it to one of these new guys and they can tell you what to do.'" Holmstock didn't like the sound of that, and he reluctantly walked back to his platoon a corporal.[675]

This family hosted members of the 2nd Battalion's 81mm Mortar Platoon. (James Sapp)

For approximately two weeks the men of the 504th Parachute Infantry Regiment had dwelled among the citizens of Remouchamps. When the regiment began to pack their belongings and head to the front, it was a tearful occasion. For James Sapp, who had been with the regiment since it left the States in early 1943, it was one of the fondest memories of his military service. "That was wonderful people," Sapp recalled. His section stayed with a man and his wife, and the men would go out and scrounge flour and the wife would cook for them. "They didn't have much, but they took us in." For them, the goodbye was especially tearful. "We started to leave to go up on the front again… and she didn't have a lot to put in them but she made each of us a little bag and put waffles in it. She shed tears like it was her relative going back on the front."[676]

Battle of Herresbach

As the afternoon of January 28 came on, the weary column of the 504th Parachute Infantry Regiment was halted in the deep snow about a mile outside the village of Herresbach. For hours the men had been laboriously marching through the deep snow with one single-file column on each side of the road. At the front of the regiment, Sergeant Albert Tarbell, a radio operator in Company H, was halted by Colonel Reuben Tucker so Tucker could contact another battalion using his SCR300 backpack radio.[677]

A short time later, Private Harold Sullivan saw the 3rd Battalion commander, Lieutenant Colonel Cook, standing in the middle of the road talking to a group of officers. Shortly thereafter, Sullivan's platoon leader Lieutenant Richard LaRiviere came and gathered the men and told them "that if we took the town up ahead, we could sleep inside and that sounded good."[678] Across the entire regiment, attack orders on Herresbach were being issued to the men with the same incentive. James Sapp, with the 2nd Battalion column, heard an officer ask, "Do you all want to stay here, or go in town?"[679]

The men resumed their march along the road in double fire, bound for Herresbach. Leading the way for the regiment was the platoon of Lieutenant James Megellas. Unaware of each other's presence, Lieutenant Megellas and his platoon walked head on into a large column of several hundred Germans coming up the same road. In a matter of seconds after the discovery of the Germans, the calm march erupted into a violent firefight. Neither force had a chance to deploy. The men fired from the hip into the mass of Germans.

Lieutenant Richard LaRiviere's platoon moved up behind in support, joining the fray. "Everyone was doing a lot of firing in all directions - to the front, to the woods off to the left," Harold Sullivan recalled.[680] Suddenly, a German Mark V tank took the paratroopers under fire. Many in Lieutenant LaRiviere's platoon took cover, as the tank's machine gun roared to life. "I saw," Staff Sergeant Charles Crowder recounted, "a tank firing its machine guns, and saw Lt. Megellas running toward the tank, shooting from the hip then stopping to throw a gammon grenade… The grenade hit the tank and knocked it out. The tank stopped and Lt. Megellas jumped onto the tank throwing a hand grenade down the open turret, killing the entire crew."

By Staff Sergeant Crowder's estimation, from the start of the engagement to the end was approximately 20 minutes. A mad dash started for town, and the men went house-to-house clearing the Germans out.[681]

James Sapp remembered there was a German artillery unit in the town when they arrived. "Everything happened so fast evidently they didn't realize we were there… They stared running out of those buildings and the riflemen and machine guns piled them outside those buildings." The regiment slaughtered some 100 Germans that day, and captured 182. That night, James Sapp slept in a church in the village.⁶⁸²

It seems that during the Battle of the Bulge more than any other time in the war, the men discovered the type of treatment German prisoners sent to the USA were receiving. To the men, the treatment was luxurious. They could date American woman, something the men could only daydream about, and were afforded good, hot food and other amenities.

Several of the troopers were so disgusted at the revelation that they took to the pen to publicly announce their dissatisfaction with the plush treatment the German prisoners were receiving in the US. Peter Zucco wrote for his squad of G Company, and wrote a letter to the editor of *The Eagle* newspaper in Pittfield, Massachusetts about a German marrying an American girl while he was in captivity.

To the Editor of The Eagle:

The Stars and Stripes, the US Army newspaper, arrived at our foxhole today and we read about an American girl becoming engaged to a prisoner of war.

That stops us cold. We have been giving and still will give our best efforts to win the war. Our buddies who have died and others who were disabled never fought to capture our foes and send them back to the United States to marry American girls. We captured them to bring the war closer to the end. What a blow this girl has given to our morale.

For our part, we hope she sails back to Italy and sees the thousands of American graves which these very same PWs pulled triggers to make. We are wondering whether or not she plans to have Jerries at her wedding as ushers and Goebbels as best man?

We paratroopers wish your paper to publish this denouncement in full.

SGT Peter Zucco

*Somewhere in Belgium.*⁶⁸³

Morris Langhoff, who had been with the regiment since it left the States in 1943, read about how well the German prisoners in his hometown of Tampa were eating.

I have just read the Jan. 13th issue of The Tribune. I am a native of Tampa and expect to come back some day and continue living there. That's what I and 15 other Tampans are fighting for. I am speaking for them all in this letter: they have all read it. Most of us have four or five years of service in the Army and 23 months overseas. Twelve of us came out of the

116th Field Artillery of Tampa. We have fought the Germans in Sicily, Italy, Holland, France, on German soil itself. I have seen some Tampans fall on the battlefront.

On the front page of the Jan. 13 Tribune is a story, "German Prisoners Eating Better Than American Civilians." We read the prison camp menu for Jan. 7-13. We are all burned up about it. We just wish that the officer in charge could take a trip over here and see what our prisoners of war are eating. He said it was the Geneva Convention. That gave us a good laugh. Do the Jerries know that there is a convention? The bayoneting of our boys hung on trees in Sicily and rolling of our boys up in their parachutes and putting on gasoline and setting them afire - is that in the Geneva Convention? The Germans have broken every rule in the book.

Do you know what the boys are eating who have been captured by the Germans over here? The stuff they get you wouldn't feed to a dog. Censorship prevents us saying what the Germans are doing right now.

How about putting a piece in your paper just what the boys from Tampa are burned up about? The 16 of us want some action from this letter. If we don't get it we'll write the highest authorities. The other 15 fellows are not putting their names to this letter, but in the second letter, they will, with their street addresses.

Last Christmas we had "C" Rations and "K" for Christmas dinner.[684]

Trenchfoot

The wet snow combined with the bitter cold was a trying and painful combination for the men. The relocation marches in early January took their toll. One morning Robert DeVinney reported to the aid station for his feet because he was unable to put his boots on due to their frozen state. The aid station sent him back to the line. A day or two after they arrived in Remouchamps, he went back to the aid station where he was finally evacuated to a hospital.

In previous battles, Colonel Tucker wrote that trench foot was "successfully controlled in this unit by carrying a change of dry socks for each man and after a daily change, having one man carry the wet ones to a house in the rear to be dried."[685] This method was less successful in the Belgian Bulge. From the 2nd Battalion alone, 65 men had to be sent back to the rear due to the condition on January 5.[686]

Later, as the men began to assault the vaunted Siegfried Line in February, trench foot still effected the men. That's when James Gann became inflicted with the condition. He may have lost his feet, if it were not for the work of the regimental surgeon, Major Ivan Roggen.

The medic said, "Oh, you need to go to the hospital." I said, "I don't want to go to the hospital, they'll cut my damn feet off." About that time Major Roggen came in. He was the doctor. He looked at them and he said, "I'll tell you what. Put his socks back on" - he turned to me - "and go out there and walk up and down that path in that snow until you can feel them, and come back in." So I did. I couldn't feel them and I come back in and he says, "Can you feel them?" I said, "Yeah, I wish you won't cut them off." Man, that was terrible. He got me some dry socks and said, "You come back in the morning and I'll take another look at them." I said, "Okay." The next morning, I was on outpost and my relief came out and I went back down there. He said, "How's your feet?" I said, "I guess they're alright. I'm still walking on them." He looked at them and man, my feet were black up to my ankles. He said, "You got lucky." I thought okay. That's as far as it went. He said, "You go back to the hospital, you've got a Purple Heart." I said, "Who wants a Purple Heart?" Not for something like that. Of course, some got one for cut fingers.[687]

While in the Battle of the Bulge, the regiment nearly lost as many men through conditions such as trench foot as it did through enemy action.

PW interrogators of the 82nd Airborne Division confer in the village of Stavalot in January. They are: Lt. Walter Spitzer (504), Lt. Hans Losher (325), Unknown, Capt. Irvin Bushman (DIV IPW Officer) (Robin Bushman)

24

LAY THE LEATHER TO THAT COLUMN OF KRAUTS

When the men were awoken on February 2, empty trucks were idling nearby, eagerly waiting to take on their cargo. The paratroopers of the 504th Parachute Infantry, loaded down with ammunition, began to board the trucks to destination unknown. A small group of men were called aside and informed that they had won a furlough trip to the United States; they were literally being saved from the possibility of being chewed up by the dragon's teeth of the Siegfried Line.

After a short ride north, the men began to disembark at a traffic circle in front of a strongly constructed concrete house. In front of the house, General Gavin was standing with the trusty M-1 Garand rifle in hand as he watched the 504th paratroopers disembark one truckload at a time. To the left, a snowy, open field poured out filled with the concrete dragon's teeth, an icon associated with photographs of the Siegfried Line.

The troopers were in the town of Losheimergraben, Belgium, straddling the vaunted Siegfried Line which they were now to assault. Behind the town lay a maze of sharp and steep hills shrouded in thick forest crisscrossed by small brooks and steams which, in better circumstances, would likely have proved to be a serine environment for a day of fly fishing in seclusion. However, the sharp hills and forests had been turned into a labyrinth of interconnected concrete bunkers, pillboxes and prepared fighting positions.

The regiment continued to disembark the trucks and the paratroopers began to congregate and talk as they awaited orders. One of the African-American truck drivers spoke loudly in his southern phonics, "Them there boys are gonna crack that Scrachfried Line wiiiiiddde open!"[688]

Captain Herbert Norman and Private First Class Eugene Strutzenberg slipped into the woods to scout their area. "After about 30 minutes we spotted pill-boxes through the trees. Our captain thus informed us that this was our objective: the Siegfried Line. As we sat there watching, three scouts came back from that area. They were from an engineering battalion. I questioned them as to what they found. They said they found no one in the pillboxes. I asked them if they had left someone out there. They informed me that they did not. I told my company commander I was very suspicious and believed that we were being led into a trap. My company commander informed me then that we would have to cross the minefields to get to the pillboxes. We returned to our area and informed our men what was ahead of us."[689]

Through the deep snow and the raw, chilling air the men left Losheimergraben and "the regiment pushed slowly east through the somber, forbidding shadows of Forest Gerolstein," described David Whittier.[690]

At 0625, the first troops started through the forest up the snow and ice covered trails, wading through the white as they went. The snow was so deep, it funneled the battalion into a single column. Their mission was to attack through the forest and enter the Siegfried Line, then attack up the ridge leading to the Jagerhauschen Farm, where they would set up defense of the ground overlooking the Neuhof Road.[691]

Accompanying the leading battalion was Colonel Reuben Tucker and his Operations Officer, Captain Mack Shelley. Tucker was in constant radio contact with Captain Gorham back at the command post and sending updates on the progress of the forward elements. Gorham, in turn, kept Tucker apprised of what was happening in the assembly areas, where Lieutenant Colonel Berry's battalion was assembling, along with the 3rd Battalion of Lieutenant Colonel Julian Cook, whose battalion was to making a flanking maneuver far to the north and come onto the heights from the south. "Julian wants to know if he is to follow Berry or wait," Gorham came over the radio. "Wait till I say," Tucker replied.

Shortly before 0900, Colonel Tucker heard the crack of battle erupt ahead with the lead elements, as cacophony of machine guns, machine pistols and rifle fire pierced the crisp, chilled air. Colonel Tucker began to move towards the sound of battle. The point of the battalion was engaging German pillboxes guarding a large draw with a creek running through it. The German fire intensified and Captain Norman sent a runner back to say the point was held up. Colonel Tucker and Lieutenant Colonel Wellems reached the scene of the skirmish. As the battle developed, Tucker came over the radio fifteen minutes later and ordered that Berry's 1st Battalion needed to stop "where they are."[692]

Wellems called forward Lieutenant William Sweet, and Sweet was ordered to immediately take the pillboxes under a frontal assault. Sweet called for Lieutenant Stuart McCash, and instructed his platoon to make the assault. As the officers conferenced and McCash waded through the snow to get his men, the German fire intensified. Wellems later said it was the most effective concentration of small arms fire he had seen since Italy.[693]

Major Henry Frank, Captain William Sweet (Commander of F Company) and Captain Victor Campana (2nd Battalion S-3) enjoy drinks in Berlin at the end of the war. (ASOM Archives)

McCash's platoon had been depleted severely through the Bulge, but surviving through all of it was his assistant platoon leader, Lieutenant Robert Bramson, who remembered the frontal assault on the concrete pillboxes.

My platoon was down to about 10 or 13 men by this time - we were climbing up a narrow, heavily wooded trail in the snow on what I now know was the Mertesrott Heights. The trail was well mined and the trip-wires were not well concealed but potentially lethal. As we later emerged into an open area, with no trees or cover, we were facing a pillbox some 35 or 45 yards directly in front.

We were alone and there were no other troops nearby that I knew of – I sent half of what I had to flank and take the pillbox while myself and the rest of the men did what we could to keep the pillbox's attention from the flanking men.

I was wounded – first a bullet thru my abdomen and exiting out my back. While on my back on the ground they kept firing at me and finally hit me in the right groin after several misses. When the pillbox was taken, because the area was impassable to vehicles, they used the captured prisoners to carry me out of there under guard until they could reach some transportation.[694]

The assault was textbook. The bazookas were used to close up the apertures of the two pillboxes and the men charged the instillations and overwhelmed the defenders.

The Siegfried Line was now breached.

The 1st Battalion Moves into the Draw

As one of the scouts who had been sent out in the morning, Sydney Redburn waded through the snow towards the German positions. Redburn had been no stranger to the 504th when he joined Company B as one of the men who had been broken up out of Service Company; but in that capacity his experience to combat was limited. As he scouted, Redburn spotted a German machine gun. Bill Bonning watched as Redburn dropped into the snow and rolled over on his back to hold his rifle in the air with both hands, signaling the men of the danger. Suddenly, Redburn erupted into a shrill scream as the Germans opened fire on him, and a bullet tore through his shoulder and down through the rest of his body. "One of the guys, my wife and I went to Sydney Redburn's mother in Kentucky and told her what happened and she said, 'Oh, yeah, somebody was already here.' We didn't tell her what happened; we told her he got killed at the Siegfried Line and like that. She said somebody was already there. He told Sydney's mother that he died of shock from hitting his shoulder. Well, he didn't die of shock. He screamed his head off for about thirty seconds because the machine gun [bullet] came in his shoulder and went out his side - went right through his body - and he lived for about thirty seconds and he screamed his head off."[695]

Behind the trail which was blazed by Edward Wellems' battalion, was the men of Lieutenant Colonel John Berry's 1st Battalion. Ahead of their battalion, a trooper with a mine detector was followed by a bulldozer trying to clear some of the snow. German prisoners began to walk past them in the woods, walking the other direction, apparent victims of a fight occurring ahead.

The battalion's column came into a clearing down in the large draw, which the Wilsam Brook flowed through. Guarding the draw were a couple large concrete bunkers, one of them two-stories high. "In this area," Lieutenant Edward Shaifer recalled, "signs of a recent violent firefight remained. Dead Germans were spread everywhere, and interspersed among the enemy dead were a few American bodies. Sporadic mortar and artillery fire was interdicting the area."[696] These were the same pillboxes where Lieutenant Robert Bramson of F Company was wounded.

Around eleven that morning, the rest of the 1st Battalion began their attack on the German fortifications. The battalion was to tie in with Edward Wellems' men on the right, who had moved on and assaulted the high ground. That afternoon, as the 1st Battalion began to assault, German counterattacks coming up the Neuhof Road began to befall Wellems. For the 504th PIR, the cutting of the Neuhof Road to the Germans was of the most critical importance. From this road, the Germans could continue to foster resistance to the north, where the 325th Glider Infantry Regiment was making advances on the village of Neuhof itself.[697]

Soon, B Company became entangled with the enemy.

Bill Bonning and his ammunition carrier David Amendola were moving through the fog behind John McLaughlin, who was banging away at the Germans with his Browning Automatic Rifle up ahead.

I said, "Man, this guy's really good." He'd fire a blast and then he'd fire another blast. He was only about thirty, forty feet ahead of me, and I would see a magazine on top of the snow, and I kept getting closer and closer and all the sudden I saw a hump - I don't know how to describe it - it was a body, you know, but he wasn't laying on the ground. It was all kind of hunched up and I thought he was still alive. I went up and he was dead, but his BAR was stuck in the snow and he was hunched up and he was shot right smack in the forehead, right from a sniper - it had to be a sniper because it was one shot and there was no ammo carrier there unless he didn't have one.[698]

As Company B peeled off into the woods to engage the Germans, Company A was following up. They reached the brook and the bunkers, where paratroopers from B Company were congregating around the two-story bunker on the opposite side of the brook. "There were open top zig-zag trenches to the right hand side of the bunker as we faced it," Edwin Bayley of A Company remembered. "They were empty."[699]

When A Company finally reached the draw, Captain John Pease noted that, from across the other side of the draw, Germans were firing on the 2nd Battalion positions to their left. Pease, seeing speed as paramount, committed the 1st Platoon to attack up the draw. One of those men was Edwin Bayley, whose squad followed the same path as John McLaughlin.[700]

There was a brush-covered sharp hill behind the bunker. A Company was told to climb the hill and advance against the enemy. My area was hard climbing because of snow and ice cover and some climbing was by grabbing bushes. As I reached the top, I found several log-covered foxholes with carefully prepared firing slots. Thank goodness they were empty. A bit more into the woods and we were face-to-face close to Germans. My BAR was a brand new issued and had never been test fired by myself. It wouldn't work. Here I was without a gun in the midst of a firefight. I looked around and found an old BAR leaning against a tree. It worked and I was in business... I could see smoke trailing from bullets fired at me. Finally, I was hit in the left shoulder rendering the arm almost useless. Immediately after I was hit other troopers shot and killed the German hat shot me. He was crying for his mother as he died.[701]

The time was just after noon.

After being wounded in the firefight, Edwin Bayley got up and began an about-face back to the line of departure and began to go back down through the deep snow and slippery ice, in search of the aid station. On his way back, he met another trooper who had been shot through the throat, also calmly trying to find aid. The two, helping each other with their respective wounds, found the trail that led to the bunker and the Wilsam Brook, and continued down the slope. They got a view of the bank of the small Wilsam Brook near the knocked out bunkers where Bayley saw a number of men congregating. "In my view," recounted Bayley, "was a battalion surgeon with a table who was assisting some troopers. About 25 ft. to the right of the surgeon and about 25 ft. closer to me was a circle of several troopers sitting on the ground. Next to the troopers was a standing group of POWs. Suddenly there was an explosion in the center of the trooper circle. Some were badly wounded. The surgeon was hit by flying debris and with a bleeding face continued at his table. A POW medic immediately began to help with the wounded. At this point I got on a jeep and was taken to an emergency center (evac hospital)." It is not known precisely what caused the explosion Bayley witnessed. There are, however, two possibilities: A German POW threw a hidden grenade in the center of the trooper circle, or one of the troopers hit an unexploded land mine. This is the most likely cause. "The explosion, according to what I believe I saw," recounted Bayley, "occurred when a trooper jumped over others and into the middle of the circle as if he landed on a land mine."

Eventually, Bayley was put on a crowded ambulance. "There were men from the 325th Glider [Infantry] and Germans from Neuhof action," he remembered. "The Germans spoke English. The Americans and the Germans were comparing their personnel losses in a friendly conversation. Both said their losses were sort of catastrophic. It was interesting that those who had been in mortal combat could sit together and have a friendly conversation about the fighting."[702]

Meanwhile, back at the draw, Lieutenant Richard Hallock had watched as Ed Bayley and his platoon disappeared into the trees and dipped down at the foot of the far slope as they began advancing against the Germans. Hollock began to think that if the enemy began shelling he and his platoon at their present location, that it would be disastrous.

Lieutenant Hallock listened as a light firefight began to develop where the 1st Platoon was advancing up the steep terrain. He began to think that once the Germans committed themselves to fighting the 1st Platoon, another assault, if done with speed, would surprise the Germans. Hallock immediately began formulating plans for an assault with his platoon. He formed the platoon with two scouts, followed by a first skirmish line. Behind that, he placed his two-man machine gun team, and about forty yards behind would follow a second skirmish line.

Up ahead, the firefight was raging as the pinging and zinging of battle echoed through the chilled, overcast air. The sounds of battle seemed to be emanating from the same place. Thus, the 1st Platoon, Hallock assumed, was stymied.

Captain Pease ordered Hallock and his platoon to take the enemy under assault. The men racked their bolts to make sure the chilled air had not frozen them, and they started out though the 14-inch deep snow.

The two scouts made their way into the sparsely-wooded slope of the draw when Hallock began to move out with the first skirmish line. The men steadily fired as they heaved their bodies through the deep snow. Up ahead, Hallock could see the scouts came out on the open bottom of the draw and start up the steep slope. The Germans began to fire at the two scouts, who returned the fire at near point-blank range. Hallock could already tell they had achieved surprise.

The Germans shifted their fire on Hallock and the skirmish line, but Hallock could not even hear the German fire over the oppressive noise of his men's automatic weapons fire. The skirmish line went into the scattered trees and a real firefight began to develop. Bark flew off the trees. Slowly, the German fire increased in its noise and the flanks of Hallock's skirmish line began to bend. The aggressive firing of the BAR gunners brought them back on line again. At this time, Richard Hallock remembered, "As I moved abreast the lead scout, who was crouching by a tree, the scout shouted that his rifle would not fire. I told him to wait and get another from a casualty. Suddenly the scout's helmet flew off and he slapped his head as though he had been stung. A stream of blood an inch in diameter arched out from his temple and continued to run like an open spigot, melting a hole in the snow. The scout gradually relaxed and died in his crouching position."

The first skirmish line reached the level ground above the draw. Forty Germans in the prone position were seen. The first skirmish line, nearly on top of the Germans, fired point-blank at the ground into German flesh. The skirmish line nearly stopped, each man firing down into bodies. As the men slowly worked their way forward, firing, Hallock worked his way slowly across in front of the skirmish line and to the right. He called the light machine gun team to the left and told them to flank the Germans. The gunner expertly kneeled in the snow fired into the German's backs. Tracers, even visible in the overcast daytime, from the machine gun tore into flesh like lightning strikes.

It was a slaughter. Occasionally the men would slack off their fire and yell, "Komrade! Komrade!" to try and get the Germans to surrender. There were none offering up their weapons, so the men continued on with their rampage.

Two Germans broke and ran. A rifle grenadier, running and cursing as he came forward, fired a rifle grenade at one of the fleeing Germans and hit him square in the back with it. The other escaped as a trail of bullets from a Thompson Sub-Machine Gun chased him into the trees. "In the center of the enemy group," Hallock recalled, "a German lieutenant got to his knees, looked about at his dead comrades, and quit hesitantly as though reluctant to live. He lurched by, dazed, with bullet holes showing through the nape of his helmet and laced through the back of his overcoat. Suddenly all firing ceased and the woods were still."

As the fight ended, the men congregated amongst each other and began talking excitably about the action. Surrounding them were over 35 Germans, many with holes in their heads, lying about in the red, blood-splattered snow. An officer who had been in the regiment since Sicily later said he had never seen so many victims of head wounds. Lieutenant Hallock saw Harold Freeman, who was missing his helmet and had a deep bullet crease on his head, still clutching his BAR as he was being "restrained from running into the woods to take on the whole German army alone."[703]

Moving Down the Neuhof Road on February 3

Overall, the regiment's situation was less than ideal when the dawn of February 3 arrived. Lieutenant Colonel Berry's 1st Battalion was still short of their objective on the Neuhof Road, and the Germans counterattacked in force the regiment's penetration of the Siegfried Line. "The failure of the battalion to secure its objective the day before was a sin of the worst sort," recounted Lieutenant Edward Shaifer, "and much commotion [at Regimental Headquarters] was caused thereby… Throughout its colorful history, the 504 had excused many understandable shortcomings in its subordinate units, but failure to deliver the results called for on the field of battle had not been one of them. In one way or another the unit had always accomplished its mission, and from a morale standpoint it was also going to accomplish this one. A wide gap existed between First and Second Battalions and because of the unremitting German counterattacks, it was essential that the First Battalion's position be improved."[704]

That morning, Captain Randles' Company B was given marching orders to pull back and swing through the 2nd Battalion's area. After reaching the Neuhof Road they would attempt a flanking maneuver and head south, where the rest of their battalion was heavily embroiled in repelling determined German counterattacks, making it all the more important that Randles' men succeed; for if the regiment could hold and continue to cut the Neuhof Road the regiment's mission of preventing German reinforcements to travel north would be accomplished.

The march of Randles' company to their attacking positions was done through the deep snow measuring about two feet, contributing even more to the already sorry state of the men's frozen feet. Even with the greatest discipline, these hardships plague any unit.[705]

The men began to approach the Neuhof Road, and as Randles's men began to get ready to assault south in force, Lieutenant Reneau Breard's depleted platoon tried to patrol the contested road.

Battalion asked for a combat patrol from B Co. and Capt. Randles picked my platoon for the job. I don't think I had over 16 men at the time... It was a forested area. The platoon was supported by one tank destroyer. We were about 100 yds. out in front when we were hit by an enemy artillery barrage. The TD pulled back around a bend in the trail. Most of the platoon were wounded and one man was killed. I pulled the platoon back (only 4 men and myself). I put the 4 on outpost and reported back to Capt. Randles.

Time wise, my platoon was only out for less than 10 minutes. Capt. Randles reported the situation to Bn. and Lt. Col. Berry asked to talk with me. I told him what happened and he ordered me to take another platoon out. I told him that might not work and he asked if I refused a direct order. I said no. I would advance with another platoon but he would have to let him talk with Randles.

About that time the company was shelled again by artillery and Lt. Col. Berry cancelled the attack after talking to Capt. Randles.[706]

That evening, there was great confusion at both divisional and regimental headquarters as to the disposition of Lieutenant Colonel Berry's battalion. Berry called regiment at 1900 and told them that he was 200 yards short of where he originally said he was. Shortly after, Major General Gavin called and was told they were in a different spot, but this was later corrected when Colonel Tucker was better able to describe the situation.

Morris Holmstock watched as some of the men got their bayonets out and stabbed at a frozen pail of honey that night, their only rations. The men had been fed only a few K-rations, less than one per man, the past three days and the men were starving after marching most of the day on the flanking maneuver. Artillery continued to plaster Randles' exhausted men through the entire night. Holmstock was nearby Sergeant Paul Mann when he was sitting at the base of a tree when "a shell hit top of the tree and a piece of shrapnel hit him in the head." The wound was so severe that Holmstock thought that "it killed him."[707] This, fortunately, was not the case and Mann - one of the last remaining originals in the company - survived his wound. "The TD suffered a direct hit," Lieutenant Breard recalled, "and had 2 casualties as did B Co. from the treeburst. My 4 men were put on outpost all that night and fortunately were not in the shelling the company sustained."[708]

During the night, Lieutenant Colonel Wellems' 2nd Battalion informed regiment that they could hear small arms, artillery and machine gun fire in Berry's sector, and asked regiment about B Company's disposition of which there was little information. The following morning, a column of Germans was seen approaching the regimental area from the east. Lieutenant Colonel Wellems called Colonel Tucker at Regimental Headquarters to report that the Germans were moving against his 2nd Battalion in force. "Lay the leather to that column of Krauts," Tucker radioed Wellems. Soon, the machine gun, mortars and artillery plastered the column of Germans and drove them back into the woods. A few that were captured said they were to organize the high ground the paratroopers occupied.

Just south, B Company was still in the same position and continued to have artillery pounding down the forest around them. Large, mature trees were ripped apart and felled from the thundering barrages which could shake men's souls. "The area looked like a pine forest after a tornado," Breard recalled. "We were relieved early that morning and walked back some 5 miles to be picked up by trucks and taken to a Belgian village, issued snow pack boots and wool socks [and] fed overnight."[709]

For a few days, the men were given a respite from combat in the small Belgian village; but, as one lieutenant warned his men, they should not be too comfortable and pull out the makeup because they soon would be moving back up to the line.

Captain Irvin Bushman used the short respite to catch-up on his correspondence with friends back home.

Greetings from the Fatherland! What a muddy hole it is at this stage of things. Have meant to write you for several weeks but the tactical situation has been so hectic I just didn't find time. Not that I have a great many interesting things to write about, but I did want to apologize for having been a little abrupt in my last letter. I'm afraid it is equally as difficult for us over here to appreciate what you think about back home and vice versa. The main point is that fighting a war requires every bit of a man's time. True enough, we waste many hours in nothing, but that is one of the things that can't be avoided... In the meantime, we are slugging our way through the West Wall and arriving to find nothing but shot-up ruins. As one of our officers quipped, there aren't more than three walls standing in the town and not more than one on the same building, all of which makes for clean living.[710]

An Old, Worn-Out Combat Guy

On the afternoon of February 13, Lieutenant Colonel John Berry's 1st Battalion moved to the small German village of Bergstein, and began clearing the some 900-meter area between the village and the bank of the flooded, swiftly swirling Roer River. The first element to arrive in the village of Bergstein that afternoon was Company C. As the men had been given instruction and demonstration on river crossings before arriving, preparations were immediately begun for a forced crossing of the Roer. The battalion immediately got readings on the rivers flow: the water was up two centimeters, and had swelled to 30 yards wide with a 15-18 mile-per-hour rate of flow. Nearly hourly river readings were taken.

Lieutenant John Branca tried to cross the river that night with his platoon, but attempts to cross failed; and not just because of the German small-arms and mortar fire he received. Lieutenant Branca informed regiment that the river was too swift to launch boats, and too swift to swim. At the time Branca attempted to cross, the water reading was up 15 centimeters.[711]

On February 16, the 2nd Battalion began moving to the forward assembly in anticipation of the regiment's forced crossing of the Roer. "Got shelled the minute we got off trucks. Very good friend John Snow was killed," Kenneth Nicoll wrote in his diary. "Sun out beautiful day. Dug in on a shell torn hill to wait. Birds singing and everything seems so peaceful if you don't look around. There isn't ten feet of ground not dug up by shells."[712]

Between the 15th and the 17th of February, readings of the river's flows were taken almost every hour by Company C. Gilbert Dodd and the veteran Delmar Keefer were two of the troopers on outpost taking the speed readings of the swelling river. On their way back one day, they ran into German families trying to evacuate Bergstein, several with babies. For the first time, the men were interacting with German civilians, non-combatants. They were proceeding up a steep road covered with anti-tank mines. Although the mines were laid atop the road in plain view, it was sufficiently scary enough to frighten the ladies with children in their arms. Delmar Keefer, who had a profound hatred for Germans like many of the men, became angered. He ripped a child from the arms of a mother and threw the baby at a German man and leveled his M-1 rifle ordering the man to carry the baby across.[713]

Upstream, the Germans manipulation of the Stau-rur-see Dam threatened the feasibility river crossing; they had successfully flooded the Roer to the point that it was nearly impossible for an assault crossing by the paratroopers. When Lieutenant Branca attempted to cross the Roer on the night of the 14th, the water had increased by 15 centimeters. By dawn on the 17th, that change had more than tripled in depth, with a reading up to a 50 centimeter increase. The following day, the regiment began to be relieved. It was finally time for the men to rest; with no meaningful period of relief since they had left Remouchamps in January, they were exhausted and stressed, both physically and mentally. Gilbert Dodd saw one man just before they were to leave take his helmet off, sling it, and yell, "I don't like to wear those things!" By the 19th, the relief was completed and the men eventually settled in a former French military barracks in Laon, France.

When the veteran Sergeant Ross Carter returned to the unit in the French barracks at Laon from the hospital on February 24, after recovering from his wound at Cheneux, he found that his squad had once again taken a new composition, as it had several times since the night they parachuted into the Sicilian countryside over 19 long months ago. One of the new faces in Carter's squad was Gilbert Dodd. "They moved us to Laon, France for a few days to regroup," Dodd remembered, "and that's the first time I met Ross Carter, and we were staying in an old French fort, it must have been there before the First World War... Even the concrete steps were worn down real noticeably. We had double deck bunks we just made out of lumber. I was [laying down] on the top bunk and Carter was the O.D. – officer of the day – and his office was right around the corner and he was passing out mail or something." Carter, Staff Sergeant Frank Dietrich - who had returned from the hospital with Carter - and another trooper began talking. Inside the mail Ross Cater had was the general order awarding Dietrich his second Silver Star Medal. "Carter came out and he was carrying on a bit," Dodd recalled. "Back in those days they have newspapers and boys would be peddling them... He had this order giving Dietrich his second Silver Star so he was reading it out like a newspaper back home and he was saying, 'Read all about it! Frank Dietrich gets another Silver Star!'" Dodd watched as Dietrich angerly snatched the order out of Carter's hand.

At the time, Dodd did not know that Dietrich and Carter were really the most inseparable of friends, who had both been with each other since the company left the States. The two men were among the last of the originals, and Carter would become one of the most well-known veterans of the 504th Parachute Infantry Regiment to come out of World War II with the publication of his fictionalized memoir titled, *Those Devils in Baggy Pants*. The book, an artistic rendition of his service in the regiment - which he referred to as "The Legion" - would come to be a best seller with over a million copies sold.

Gilbert Dodd remembered that everyone admired Carter. "He was well respected. I didn't ever hear anyone downing Ross Carter." When they went back onto the line in Germany, Dodd was alongside Carter when they came under fire, and Carter was hugging a pile of rocks just above Dodd. "He really fit the picture of an old, worn-out combat guy," he recalled. Carter, as Dodd remembered him, was "gentle talking.

He had a little crooked stick pipe he got from somebody over there… He carried this book he read all the time, anytime he was in a foxhole he was reading it. He liked to read Homer."[714]

Gilbert Dodd of Company C (Gilbert Dodd)

25

SPIRIT, TONE, EFFICIENCY AND LETHALITY: WHAT MADE THE 504TH SO EFFECTIVE?

As the war begins to wind down, it will do currently serving officers and soldiers, and future historians, good to reflect on some of the lessons in leadership and combat effectiveness that have been woven throughout the service of the 504th Parachute Infantry Regiment from 1942-1945. These potential answers go beyond things like their physical prowess over-and-above their normal infantry counterparts; as has been evidenced throughout, the indomitable spirit of the men who served in the wartime 504th Parachute Infantry Regiment was something to beholden, and the pride with which they viewed their branch was a large derivative of their fighting spirit. Roy Hanna spoke of occasions of enlisted paratroopers out in town not rendering salutes to officers – even colonels – of traditional, non-parachute units; but when Hanna, a lowly lieutenant, walked by, the men would render the traditional military courtesy because he was a paratrooper.[715] Boiled down to its most simplistic terms: they truly believed they were the best, and on the battlefield they fought with the tenacity to match such self-imagery. After the invasion of Sicily in 1943, Jimmy Eldridge wrote:

I don't want you to think I am bragging, but we really are proud of our outfit. We have no way of knowing how people back home feel about what we did in Sicily, but we know ourselves what we did and what we went through. That's good enough for us. It's funny in a way, but this outfit seems more like a family now than it does a company.

I think it would break a fellow's heart to leave the paratroops now after he has gone as far as we have. Most all of us come into the 504th when it was first organized. We saw it start and we want to see it all the way through.[716]

It was this type of spirit and pride in the unit which allowed the regiment the ability to rapidly rebuild after the costly mountain campaign in December 1943, and the source of the spirit with which a 180-man company cut to 20 at Cheneux was able to continue on two days later with good morale and "very little bitching." This spirit saw themselves through at every turn: all the hard winters and long springs of campaigning throughout Europe. During the assault on the vaunted Siegfried Line after being exposed for months to the bitter elements of the winter of 1944, replacement officer Edward Shaifer observed that "the regiment was at what was popularly known as 'down to attacking strength.' Even with these deficiencies, however, the regiment was still a formidable group of fighters. Its morale was unshakable and its experience was broad."[717]

Captains William Sweet and Edson Mattice, both company commanders in the regiment during the war, described this spirit and morale simply as heart. As the unit was trying to rebuild itself from heavy casualties and extreme physical and mental exhaustion from the 1943 mountain campaigns – for the purpose of a planned parachute jump at Anzio – it was the pride in the unit which was played upon to its fullest extent. After a very hasty 'rebuilding' of the unit, they entered combat on the Anzio Beachhead for a just as hastily put together mission which turned into a 62-day long stretch of combat under the most austere conditions. Mentally, the men were not prepared to face these challenges. Yet, they overcame. "Despite the worst handicaps of bad weather which limited air support, physical and mental strain caused by terrific pounding by enemy artillery and generally unfavorable combat conditions," Captain Edson wrote, "this badly depleted Combat Team maintained such a stout-hearted spirit of aggressiveness and high order of combat efficiency that the enemy suffered enormous losses in its futile attempts to crack the line and vastly overestimated the number of the forces opposing them."[718]

In similar phrasing, when speaking of the same operation, Captain Sweet wrote that the men's "adaptability, initiative and understanding of the situation, along with great fighting heart, made the mission a success, as great as it was."[719]

These intangible traits which found themselves within the unit were weaponized on the battlefield through the leadership which found itself in the regiment.

For the duration of the overseas service of the 504th Parachute Infantry Regiment between 1943 and 1945, the regiment was under the charismatic leadership of Colonel Reuben H. Tucker. In his mid-thirties through the war, Colonel Tucker had commanded the respect of the men and created a great spirit of fighting within the regiment. Tucker demanded the world of his men and expected them to accomplish their mission at any cost, and expected them to act accordingly on the field of battle; but he loved his men both on and off the battlefield. Off the battlefield, he defended them: he defended them against Army courts and assaults on their reputation such as when he extended an invitation to a Woman's Army Corps unit for a 504 dance; when the WAC commander stated that she didn't "want my girls going out with underpaid killers," Tucker responded, "In that case I don't want my men hanging out with overpaid whores."

Major General James Gavin, the division commander, often spoke fondly of Colonel Tucker after the war to his family, and had a great fondness and respect for him and his abilities, although they often disagreed on methods with Gavin being more intellectual and Tucker being gruff. In the end, Gavin felt he could not promote Tucker because of his poor record-keeping, including a rumored incident where Tucker threw overboard the files of charges against some of his men while the regiment was traveling from Italy to England on the *Capetown Castle*.

On the battlefield, Tucker was often in the heat of the fighting, going places that no colonel had any business going. Lieutenant Roy Hanna had great respect for Tucker, like the rest of the men:

First, he carried himself like a soldier should. He walked around like he was the commanding officer, like he should. And just his stature alone - his little mustache, his square face - he looked like a soldier; he looked like a leader of soldiers and I think that was a plus to start with. And as far I know he was always fair.

He'd be on the front line when we were facing the Germans within rifle shot. He would come walking up. "Everything under control, lieutenant?" "Yes, sir." He had no business up there. He wasn't need up there. It was just to settle us down.[720]

Colonel Tucker helped to set the tone of 'leading from the front' for his junior officers. Bravery was a requirement, and any inclination towards cowardice or an unwillingness to charge first when required was met with immediate transfer out of the unit. During the Battle of the Bulge, for example, a patrol was moving through thick forest on a pitch dark night when it came under German fire. When one of the men yelled asking what they should do, the leader of the patrol, a brand new replacement lieutenant, yelled, "Get the hell out of here!" and ran off, leaving the men. So prompt was his transfer from the unit for his breakdown, that he was gone by the time the rest of the patrol got back and the men never saw him again.

And while their fearless regimental commander set the tone, the true executioners of the regiment's combat effectiveness were those lieutenants and captains – junior officers – and through their character traits, facilitated the true lethality of the regiment, which was found in its privates.

Formulating that relationship between the officer and enlisted man in the 504th PIR was not just found in their expected bravery, but in other traits as well. It can be described in a simple hypothetical situation set forth by Corporal James Gann: "All of our officers as far as I am concerned were the best. They were well-trained, they knew their business, and if my commander said, 'I want this mountain moved over on that side of the road,' I'd get my little shovel and start digging."[721]

Colonel Tucker, the athletic, demanding, and charismatic commanding officer of the 504th Parachute Infantry for its entire combat career in World War II. (Devils in Baggy Pants)

The trust the men had in their officers was multi-faceted. Private Francis Keefe's respect for his lieutenant, 1st Lieutenant Robert C. Blankenship, was undying even after the war. It was simply because he never yelled at the men when he asked for something to be done or when he was providing discipline, that he fought with higher headquarters on behalf of his men, and, perhaps most important of all, "he wasn't chickenshit."[722]

At every turn, the lieutenants were right along with the men. Lieutenant Roy Hanna would often share foxholes with privates; in the mountains of Italy Lieutenant Mearle DuVall gave his razor and soap for Private Fred Baldino - who called DuVall "a very caring lieutenant - to shave with.[723] This caring attitude taken up by many of the junior officers was something that endeared the men to their leadership, and its result should not be downplayed.

There may be no better display of this than in the letter which was written to the family of the late Lieutenant Charles Snyder. It covers the intelligence found in the junior parachute officers mentioned by Gann, which Snyder used "to benefit the soldiers" and made the men "fall out in force for his orientations or lectures." But perhaps greater was the fact of how Snyder cared for the men. Herbert Carney wrote, "He was the most conscientious man I ever saw. He tried so hard to be sure and positive that all his men were taken care of to the best of his ability…"[724]

Through the endearment of the men to their leaders, formed through that respect and caring attitude, and the tone set by Colonel Tucker, the lieutenants and captains were able to extract the highest levels of combat discipline and bravery from the men. That discipline was near suicidal. In situations where the men knew their leadership was utterly lost or had no knowledge of what they were facing, the men continued without hesitation or question because they trusted the ability of their officers to cope with the situation, act in the best interest of the unit and ensure the men were taken care of to the best of their ability. Most importantly, however, they trusted that the officer himself would be present with them no matter how bad the situation got.

All these things together: the spirt of the unit, the tone set by Colonel Tucker, the execution of the junior officers, and the lethality brought by the privates created, what Colonel Tucker wrote in the regimental history book printed the end of the war, "an unsurpassed spirit of cooperation, grim determination, and pride in the regiment [that] have written this story in blood and deeds on the pages of history."[725]

Their blood wrote and sealed history at places like Altavilla and Hill 1017 at Colli, where their actions at both engagements serve as examples of one of the things that made the regiment so tactically effective: initiative. It should not be lost that one thing which facilitated that initiative was mutual trust alluded to by Colonel Tucker. In the words of Captain Robert Halloran, a veteran of all the regiment's campaigns, "There was not only leadership at every level, but also tremendous appreciation of the leadership by those below in rank."[726] Mutual trust is the key to what the modern US Army has identified as the first guiding principle of mission command, and this trust paved the way for one of the largest traits which made the 504th successful on the battlefield.

It was not just the fact that leaders took initiative with groups of men – anywhere from two to hundreds – but it was something that was also ingrained into the privates; something necessary for airborne forces where a private may find himself alone or with just a handful of men behind enemy lines for hours or days at a time, and it this fact was not lost upon James Gavin in his theories of airborne warfare. As a member of the Regimental S-2 Section, James Gann often handled prisoners. One captured German officer explained to him that Germany would never win the war: "I had been up about 30 hours - boy, I was tired - anyway he was sitting on one side of the room… and I was sitting on the other side and I had a Thompson laying across my lap. I guess I [dozed off] like that, and I heard him move and raised up and he said, 'I think I could've made that door.' I said, 'You still wanna try it?' … He spoke good English and then he settled down and he said, 'Germany will never win the war.' I said, 'Well, I don't think he will.' He said, 'He won't.' He says the reason why is a German soldier, you want him to do something, you have to explain how, when, where and all of that."[727] This observation was not isolated. When Lieutenant Colonel Willard Harrison returned to the US after the war, he told a newspaper reporter that Nazis cannot fight without orders.[728]

In places like Altavilla, it was the initiative of every man, junior officers especially, in the absence of higher authority that turned the tide of battle and won the day for the Allies. At Altavilla, both Captain Albert Milloy and Lieutenant John Lekson displayed the initiative to move despite losing contact with their chain of command. Their decisions were two critical points in the battle: with their initiative to make decisions themselves, they gave commanders forces with which they could fight. When Lieutenant Lekson was lost on Hill 344 and the 2nd Battalion showed up, it would have been the easy thing for Lekson to sit and join his forces with those of the 2nd Battalion. This, however, was not what he did. Rather than 'wait and see', Lekson moved the force in search of his commander. When they finally reunited, Lekson's force gave his commander a way to properly defend terrain which was part of the key to victory. A similar decision that same night by Captain Albert Milloy, who had also become disconnected with the larger body, was met with the same result. In his decision to take initiative and continue moving, he denied the German's use of the dominating terrain feature while the rest of the battalion was still lost on the trails. This would become more consequential when the majority of the battalion began organizing on an adjacent hill which they incorrectly believed to be the objective. Captain Milloy's presence - only there, on the proper objective, through his initiative - provided a force with which the real objective could be denied to the Germans.

The fall of a corps objective to two companies of the 504th Parachute Infantry in November 1943 could also be pointed to as an example of the initiative which made the regiment so effective. In a similar instance, where the assaulting companies became disorganized, the men doggedly fought their way up the shrouded, tall mountain known as Hill 1017, near the village of Colli. Paratroopers like Lieutenant Henry Keep did not await reorganization, but continued on with the mission with just three or four men. They drove off a German squad on top, caught by surprise, and Keep did this because he thought that "it would be easier for our outfit to take the hill if there were already some of us on top." The speed with which they operated caught the Germans off guard, and Keep was able to hold the hill while the unit organized. His actions kept the Germans off balance.

There is a larger story at play with the fighting on this hill: it was really the initiative of the entire regiment which paved the way for its capture. As the men marched ahead of the Anglo-American armies in the mountains of Italy, an advance allowed because of their non-road-bound, light table of organization and physical prowess, they were moving so fast that the Germans were not yet prepared to defend the hill. Had the Germans been given more time, the dominating hill mass would have been extremely difficult to capture due to its heavy overgrowth and steep height. As Captain Fordyce Gorham stated to a newspaper reporter who did a story on the sacking of the hill, "We hit them before they expected us to make a try, and they did not have the positions manned as well as they would have had in a few days."[729] As a result, Headquarters, Army Ground Forces conducted a study on the 504th Parachute Infantry to collect the events which led up to the capture of the hill.

It was all those traits, and more, that saw the regiment through 21 months of trying overseas service. The regiment had chased the German out of Sicily, pursued him up the boot of Italy, terrorized his forces at Anzio, routed him out of Holland, destroyed his pride in Belgium, and blasted his impermeable wall on the Belgian-German frontier. As the spring approached, the Anglo-American army aligned on the Rhine River after getting back on its feet from the hard winter's fighting. Now, as the regiment began to be ferried deep into Germany, they were to take part in the final blow to the 1,000 year Reich. As Staff Sergeant Leo Muri would accurately observe later, the regiment remained in it to the very end.

26

GERMANY'S LAST STAND

A young, 17-year-old German boy, clothed in a German Labor Service uniform, was with a column fleeing from advancing American armor when the Allied planes came over strafing, showering bullets upon the road. The boy was separated from the column and decided to run home. As he ventured through the collapsing German lines near the Rhine, he almost ran into a column of British soldiers and fled in the other direction. Soon he fell into the hands of German Lieutenant Kohlgruber who handed him a *solbuch* and a rifle, and instructed him that he was on the path to die a hero's death for the Fuhrer.

Lieutenant Kohlgruber was the commanding officer of the 5th Company of the German 330th Infantry Regiment, which on April 4 came into the line along the Rhine River. Soon, Lieutenant Kohlgruber, his new 17-year-old recruit and the rest of his men would fight a brutal battle with the men of the 504th Parachute Infantry Regiment.[730]

After their rest in Laon, the regiment began closing in on the village of Longerich, Germany. From there, they went to Cologne, Germany, the site of the famous cathedral, and the banks of the Rhine River. The famous city, like many others in Germany, became the new battlefront as the Allies marched with one eye cocked towards Berlin. On the east side of the river lay a significant portion of Hitler's nearly defeated army, now forced to fight in their homeland, from within an encirclement that would come be known to history as the Rhur Pocket. Cologne was utterly destroyed by the war, with rubble piled high and craters deep in the streets. Buildings were a skeleton of their former selves, having been ripped apart piece by piece by bombs. It seemed the only thing standing in the city was the Ford factory and the famous cathedral. The Rhine, in all its glory, flowed through just as it had for centuries as one of the veins of German civilization, the same as peace and in war. On one bank, a nearly destroyed enemy sat waiting in a trap which they knew could collapse any day.

For Company G of the 504th Parachute Infantry, their first job when the regiment began assuming positions along the opposite bank of the river was to clean out the vacated Ford factory, which the Air Force had made a job of bombing. What the bombs could not get, however, were the underground tunnels and caves beneath the plant, which were in useful condition. The factory reminded some of the troopers from Michigan of the factories in Detroit, although on a smaller scale. There was still a sizable amount of raw materials around, and many abandoned typewriters, office furniture and other goods.

The men moved into air raid shelters and had nice bunks to sleep in at night while they were not patrolling or on outpost along the riverbank. The most luxurious feature of all, however, were toilets and washrooms.[731]

Colonel Tucker and his headquarters group moved into the basements and set up their typewriters, whose clicks and clacks, the sounds of conducting regimental business, began serenading the basement halls. At night, outside, the other sound of regimental business echoed the cool air: a German flak wagon sputtering, the sound of an MG42 zipping through the cool night air across the river and the slow rat-tat-tat of an M1. One of the German flak wagons across the river would often fire into the plant but it did little damage.[732]

Lieutenant Roy Hanna had missed out on the Battle of the Bulge, for he had been in the United States on leave, and had met his daughter - born while he was fighting in Italy - for the first time. Now, he was back in combat to finish what he started in Sicily many months ago.

He reported to the Ford factory and went down a few flights of stairs where he entered into a large room where some of the typewriters were clacking away on desks. After waiting a long time, Colonel Tucker came to see him and was asked to guide a new captain to the company which he was to take command of. After leaving, the two headed south along the river. A large amount of artillery was flying overhead, and with every overhead whistle the new captain would hit the ground. "Still hadn't learned the difference from 'outgoing' to 'in coming,'" Hanna remembered.[733]

With the dawn of April, spring was now in full blossom. Immediately upon the regiment's arrival at the first of the month, patrols began crossing the Rhine. By and large, the first few days passed quietly. Searchlights on the German side could be seen beaming into the cool night's sky. Occasional sniper fire came from across the river, but little of note. On the afternoon of the 5th, a colonel from a German medical unit came across the river under a white flag and requested to see the commander to get the bombing of his hospital ceased.[734]

Nearly immediately after arriving to their new positions on the line, the regiment continued their tradition of aggressive patrolling into the German lines. The darkness of the night which hid the grave dangers in the enemy's line were no different in Germany than they had been in Italy, Holland and Belgium. During their first few days on the line, Lieutenant Hanz Druener was commanding a patrol on the German side of the Rhine when he heard the sound of a scuffle emanating from the blackness ahead of him. He heard his lead scout Private Charles Katsanis say, "Okay, okay," and then heard a rifle drop to the ground. Katsanis disappeared, not to be found again by Lieutenant Druener.[735]

Soon after their arrival in the first days of April, a plan was hatched to send one company of the 504th to the east side of the Rhine and set up a base in the village of Hitdorf am Rhein. The operation was a "hurry up affair," Lieutenant Reneau Breard remembered. It was his company, A Company, which was selected to make the crossing and establish the base. The company had only been alerted of the mission that morning, and the paratroopers began crowding around the riverbank for the crossing as midnight neared on the night of April 5-6.

The Rhine, being extremely swift, meant the men would cross well up-stream and drift as they rowed the river. Lieutenant Reneau Breard was in the last boat with extra ammunition and other supplies; he had everything a force could need - except something to eat. Just as Breard was about to push off, a strange artillery officer came up to him. When Breard found that he could fire the whole division artillery from a nearby armored division, Breard immediately handed him a paddle. The two set off with their boat of ammunition to join the rest of the company, which was already across the river.[736]

The company had a quiet trip across despite their inexperience with navigating and rowing an extremely swift and powerful river. But by the time Breard landed, the company had already taken casualties. When the first elements reached the east bank of the Rhine, they landed in a minefield. Private James Emery tripped a mine, blowing off parts of his body before he rolled onto the second mine which ultimately claimed his life.[737]

After landing, Breard began to head for the command post. Breard decided to take a shortcut and made his way to the church, a centrally located place where most of the streets were easily accessible from the place of worship and its small park. When he arrived at the church he saw the body of Lieutenant John Spooner, who had been killed, laid out. Breard made it to the command post, located just one block north of the park on the second story of a building.[738]

Other than about 100 rounds of German artillery falling on the village, things were quiet in Hitdorf. In clearing the town, they had captured close to 50 German prisoners. Included in that group of prisoners was Lieutenant Kohlgruber, who just days earlier had instructed the young, fleeing 17-year-old boy a German Labor Service uniform that he was to die gloriously for the Fuhrer.[739]

From the perspective of other units of the regiment, the enemy seemed "very nervous," the regiment's situation report read. Along the river south of Hitdorf, the Germans set up a large searchlight in such a way that it would reflect off the river. Flares were being shot by the Germans, arching into the sky like white sparks. The Germans let the paratroopers know they were there by sending in a mortar round or two near the Ford factory. They were deeply unnerved about the crossing of A Company in Hitdorf.[740]

Breard noticed that by 10 AM the following morning, the Germans were beginning to work on their bridgehead in Hitdorf from two different sides, and realized that the enemy had become well-supported by artillery and tanks. In the area of Johannes Müller, to the northeast of Hitdorf, the Germans set up a fire direction center, and they continued to shell the village. At Johannes Müller a significant build-up of German forces, including armor and self-propelled guns, was occurring. Another build-up of tanks and German infantry was occurring just on the northeastern outskirts of the village.[741]

At noon, a large number of German prisoners were in the hands of the paratroopers. They were sent in the boats back to the western side of the Rhine, leaving A Company with no method to get back across the Rhine. By this time, Breard notes, they knew they had a fight on their hands.

At about 1330, the Germans laid down a blistering artillery barrage on the village which was directed against the church and other points. Wire communications with the platoons were cut.[742] The company's 3rd Platoon under the command of Lieutenant Richard Hallock held the southern end of town when the Germans laid a smoke screen across the horizon. Soon, the platoon was embroiled in a fierce fight with two tanks supported by a company of Germans. After approximately 30 minutes of fighting, Hallock's men were overrun. Hallock had sent a runner back to the company with a request for more Panzerfaust anti-tank weapons and neither he nor his men were ever heard from again. Hallock's men held up in the basement of a house, with a German tank dismantling the house over their heads. A German pulled out a loose stone from the foundation and threw a grenade inside.[743]

In the north end of town, a 200-man German attack soon befell the 2nd Platoon. While the machine guns were able to pin down much of the German force making a frontal assault, tanks soon made their debut as evening drew and the Germans found the flanks and began attacking them. The Germans soon began overrunning squads and as night fell, the situation became critical.[744]

"At dusk we heard tanks rumbling towards our road block and the biggest thing I've ever seen on tracks roared at us," related Sergeant Harry Smith. "Our gun position was in a strongly built basement of a stone house so we felt pretty safe; at 50 yards we opened up on its open hatch and vision slits. The bullets bounced off the sides like they were ping-pong balls. We gave a couple of sweeps at the infantry behind and after the tank blew down our house, we shagged back towards our main line of resistance. Our section chief picked us up; we fought our way a couple blocks towards the command post, but decided to take over a house and fortify it."[745]

Some of Captain Pease's A Company troopers in Germany. They are: Albert Sebastian, Joseph Gwiazdoski, John Isom, Mahonri Martin, Edward Mokan, John Mortzfeldt, Kelly, Fay Steger (taken prisinor at Hitdorf) and Frank Detrich of Company C. (Roger Mokan)

At the CP, Captain Pease had all but lost contact with virtually all of his company. With a general collapse of the company's lines, small groups of Germans swarmed in the streets like bees, running and gunning all over the place looking to fight small groups of paratroopers who, like Sergeant Smith and his cohorts, had taken over houses. Staff Sergeant William Bullock from the Battalion's Communications Section left his equipment behind to go try and contact the platoons. "Little groups of soldiers were walking all over town. I stepped over at least 50 dead men - only two were GIs - I came to a mangled pile of torn up Jerry corpses and as I was stepping over them I heard a cool voice ask, 'Is that a GI?' Two demolition men in the second story of a house had been up there since dark, letting small groups pass and dropping gammon grenades on every large bunch of Krauts that came within their range. We pulled back to the command post."[746]

There, the men who had been able to break out began to stiffen their resistance again around the CP. The men went into a horseshoe shaped defense with their backs to the water for the final stand. Colonel Tucker radioed the beleaguered men and told them to hold out - help was on the way.

Crowding around boats on the western edge of the Rhine River under the darkness of the night, in much the same way A Company had done the night before, was their salvation - the men of Company I. As they made their way to the crossing site, the engineers readied the boats for the trip. Jerome Unruh, one of the engineers who would paddle a boat, listened as Corporal Millson called back to headquarters and told them that they had been spotted by the Germans preparing to cross the river. Orders came back to proceed as ordered. "You're sending us on a fool's errand," Millson said to headquarters as Unruh listed.

Just before this, Fred Leys came up. "Hey, Unruh, I want to volunteer for your place," he said.

"Fred," Unruh replied, "I want to tell you something, I'm the last son-of-a-bitch that wants to go on this kind of a deal. If I let you go in my place and something happened to you, how do you think I could ever live with myself?"

Leys and Unruh went back to their second day in the Army when they met at basic training in Fort Belvoir, Virginia. The two had gone together through engineer training, infantry training and boarded the same ship to the same replacement depot in England where Leys decided to join the paratroops and told Unruh to come along. "I ain't committing suicide," was Unruh's response to Fred Leys, and there they parted ways for good - or so Unruh thought. After quite a long time of unhappily sitting in a replacement depot, Unruh found the paratroops his only way of escape and he was off.

As a new replacement to the unit, Unruh would go up and down the columns looking for a familiar face, like someone he went to jump school with, that he could relate to when all of the sudden there sat Fred Leys sitting on his helmet. Unruh had just been assigned to the same squad as his old friend from basic training.

Leys decided to take another man's spot in the boat, and Unruh, Leys and Millson grasped the gunwales and put the boat into the water. As Unruh was standing in the water, DeWitt Hamon came up and offered him a life belt. "Hey, I am going to put this on you," he said.

"No, no, no," Unruh insisted. "I'm a strong swimmer." Hamon walked out into the water and put it around Unruh while he was holding the boat.

The men piled in, and they were off. The clouds bounced off an illuminating glow over the river, from the German searchlights behind the IG Farben factory. Unruh could see driftwood floating down the river, and if he could see driftwood, he wondered, how the Germans could miss ten men piled in a boat rowing across the river. *How in the hell does them idiots ever think anybody's going to cross this river undetected*, he thought to himself.

Suddenly, the rapid zipping of the German MG-42 pierced the stillness of the night's air. The lieutenant yelled. Everyone jumped overboard, plunging into the cool German water.[747]

Company I Arrives in Hitdorf

Inside the final defensive ring at Hitdorf, it was quiet - too quiet - as Lieutenant Reneau Breard peered out of the second story window of A Company's beleaguered CP. Suddenly, a figure appeared on the street below him. The short, baby-faced figure was familiar to him: Bernard Karnap, his former platoon sergeant turned lieutenant, who earned his officer rank through a battlefield commission. As Breard would later come to find out, the platoon of Lieutenant Karnap was the only element of I Company to make it across the river to help, the rest of the boats shot out of the water by the Germans just like the one containing Unrah.

Breard watched as Lieutenant Karnap walked, tommy gun in hand, to the north up the street all alone. "I let him go by," Breard remembered, "and I didn't even wave at him because everything was quiet and I was happy."[748]

To link up with Breard and his beleaguered company, the men of Karnap's platoon had gone violently through the streets of town knocking out German flak wagons with grenades and moving down streets and alleyways shooting up Germans like they were in an old wild western TV show. They extracted the survivors in Hitdorf and made tail for the river.

Lieutenant Breard was helping James Kiernan, a replacement lieutenant who had only been with the company a few weeks, down to the river where the boats were awaiting them. Lieutenant Kiernan was severely wounded, and he had spent hours running amongst his men through hail storms of German gunfire, directing his men to keep up their fire against the German onslaught. He had personally killed six Germans and shot an untold number of others.[749]

Breard laid the brave lieutenant into the boat while the others poured in. The sound of a German tank rumbled and clanked. It rolled up to them at a short distance. At a near point-blank range, the tank fired and an ear-piercing *VRAARRACKKK* sounded overhead as the German shell angrily zoomed past them. Everybody spilled overboard and splashed into the Rhine's chilled water. Breard got up and heaved the wounded Kiernan, unable to move, out of the boat and into the water.[750]

Lt. James Kiernan was a recent replacement officer who earned the Distinguished Service Cross for his actions in Hitdorf. (James Kiernan)

The Germans remained restless and excitable the rest of the day, with the Germans continually shooting machine guns across the river, and throwing in artillery barrages on the paratrooper's positions. After making their getaway across the Rhine, a group of I Company men were crowding around a knocked out German halftrack, posing for Lieutenant Robert Blankenship who was snapping their picture. Just after the image was captured, the Germans began another light artillery barrage. Walter Hughes had just been posing for the photo when everything went black and woke up, with shrapnel in him, on a moving jeep which was heading to the aid station. Only a few days later he was back in action with the company, patrolling the Rhine.[751]

Life on the Rhine River

Donald Zimmerman, sitting in a cushy armchair, could look through a large hole in the wall, the result of the direct hit from an artillery shell, and could see a mile in each direction from his perch on the second story of the house. The small home had no roof, the result of still more artillery shells. In front of him, the Rhine majestically flowed north; it's commanding width and power a marvel of nature. The Rhine's waters became for the Germans a protector, but it could only do so much to protect them from paratroopers armed with a telephone, like Donald Zimmerman. Next to his armchair was a field telephone. The line ran directly to Sergeant Clem Haas and the platoon's 60mm mortar squad. Zimmerman was in a perfect position to view even the slightest movement on the other side of the river, as well as spot the fall of the mortar shells. The eastern side of the Rhine, being occupied by the German troops, was flat with the exception of heavy clumps of small trees and hedge resting atop high berms which bordered the rocky beach. If any movement, even in the slightest, was observed by Zimmerman he simply reached down and grasped the handset of the field telephone and spoke the range – all from the comfort of his ringside seat to the war.

Along the Rhine, troopers from I Company Headquarters pose by a destroyed German flak wagon. Pictured are Lee Johnston, Walter Hughes, Dominic LaFrada and 1st Sgt. Curtis Odom. (Richie Blankenship)

Not a minute too late, the faint thump of the mortar firing out of the tube could be heard in the distance, followed by its whistle, screeching over the head of Zimmerman. Then came the impact to the other side. Clouds of dirt, pebbles and molten shrapnel cascaded out of the ground, flying in all directions. Sometimes the fire would need to be redirected to the left or right, or forward or backward. "I would tell him two notches... but we got to the point where we could figure each other out. If he went left when I called him right, I called him all kinds of names: 'YOU DUMB ASS, GOD DAMMIT!'"[752]

As in the makeup of any battle, the moments of stress-filed terror and horror were interlaced with incidents of strange hilarity found nowhere but in battle, and nowhere was this more true than the sector of the 504th Parachute Infantry along the Rhine River. Company I seemed to be the source of may offbeat occurrences. Walter Hughes liberated a horse, on whom the company created their own mounted patrol tactics, which he named Fearless Fosdick after the Dick Tracy parody. In another incident, some men in the company discovered alcohol and became intoxicated and, placing their clothes in a neat pile, went for a swim in the Rhine River. When they returned, they discovered that a German had stolen their clothes. In another incident, Lieutenant Roy Hanna was walking around when he discovered about fifteen troopers who had set up their own private bar with kegs of beer they had liberated from the German side of the river and rowed back across the Rhine. Roy Hanna remembered, "The barrel was set up in a small two story house that faced a street – bar first floor and German owners lived on [the] second floor. They opened their bar for us and were pleased to be part of the fun. Can't remember any other officers... I think I got involved only because I happened to be passing by – [I] was not part of the patrol that brought the beer back. I remember the men... mentioned that the brewery or beer warehouse where they got the beer was guarded by just one elderly man that protested saying the factory was owned by Americans, not Germans, and so they shouldn't take the beer."[753]

Walter Hughes mounted atop their horse named Fearless Fosdick. (Walter Hughes)

Despite the hilarity, the daily transit of patrols - like the one which had supplied the beer for the private bar - made death continue to linger above heads of the men. Paratroopers were often preyed upon by silent German minefields. Lieutenant John Bigler, an engineering officer, was killed by a German mine while on patrol the night of the 9th. Hanna, whom had come to know Bigler through their years of combat together, heard that he was crawling on his belly through a minefield when he was killed. Hanna was greatly saddened by the news and was puzzled as to why he would have done such a thing.[754]

This photo shows Lloyd Gates of Company I on top of a halftrack he destoryed, probably in the village of Hitdorf. Walter Hughes remembered that Gates "climbed up on the front of the halftrack and threw a grenade in the front of the halftrack... and the explosion went off and one German ran out the back and I got to him before he got to the building and we didn't know it but we started taking pictures standing up on the thing but another German had got out the other side and he had his gun in his hand and we're standing there taking pictures! All the sudden somebody says, "Holy shit! There's another Kraut on the other side!" One of the other guys hot him." (Walter Hughes)

That same day, another offbeat occurrence happened when six men began rowing across the Rhine from Hitdorf in three small boats. They were escaped French prisoners of war. Seeing the low outline of the boats coming across the river, the paratroopers opened fire on them. One of the boats capsized into the water as the other two continued for shore. One of the Frenchmen was wounded. Another, once the shore was reached, stepped on a landmine before they were able to make their good intentions clear. One, it was found out in the conversations, had been sent to a concentration camp near Weimar and after a long odyssey escaped, and the other had been forced to work in a Bayer factory in Leverkusen which had been converted from making aspirin to making ammunition for the German army before escaping and hiding out in the woods. The two who survived were full of hatred for the Germans and asked to accompany the paratroopers on their raiding parties across the Rhine to get their retribution.[755]

Walter Hughes posing by the halftrack destoryed by Lloyd Gates. (Walter Hughes)

On April 13, contact with other Americans was made, and the Ruhr Pocket collapsed. The men were left on the line until the end of April, when they were trucked up near Hanover, Germany to cross the Elbe River to meet the eastern allies.

The Elbe and Beyond

Lieutenant Roy Hanna, riding in a jeep, was passing a house when he saw littered all across the ground the parts of jeeps and bodies; some body parts were even dangling from the trees. The culprit of this savage image was a German marine mine.[756]

At the time of the mine's detonation, the regiment was gearing up for its final attack of the war. A heavy engineer battalion had erected a pontoon bridge across the Elbe and tanks were beginning to flow over, poised to take on the paratroopers as cargo so they could ride gloriously into their final blow at the Germans of the war and link up with the Russians advancing rapidly from the east. In their last gasp of desperation, the Germans had planted these massive marine mines, big enough to blow trucks into oblivion and create craters that looked as if a meteor had impacted the earth from outer space, which had created the gruesome scene which was imprinted in Roy Hanna's memory.

Troopers of Company I found this abandoned Sherman tank and were able to get it running and firing again. Occasionally, they would run around the bank with it, out of view of the Germans, to make them think they were an armoured unit. They also fired tank shells at the German bank. Photographed on the I Company tank is Ed Utaski and Herndon. (Walter Hughes)

The mine was not isolated. Jerome Unruh remembers May 1, the day the regiment crossed the Elbe, and some of the final combat deaths of World War II.

We had one tank at the head of the column and when they got ready to move out they didn't go very far. All the sudden [there was] a terrible, tremendous explosion and the tank, it blew the bottom out of it and the top right off the top off of it. There was a six-by-six army truck right there by it and I never did see where the motor of that thing went to. But Joe Metcalf and I were two guys and we were back in the back of [the] column on foot and we went up there, [came] back and told Schmitty, our platoon sergeant... and he sent Max Albert, Rodney, and Prescott and Hurb Hurlbert to investigate it. The first three that I mentioned stopped at the first site and Hurlbert went up to the second site. And you could tell where the mines had been planted in the road because you could see where the dirt had been disturbed. So anyway, when they started digging in, there was another tremendous explosion and the first three that I mentioned – Max Albert, Rodney, and Prescott – all we ever found of them was just little tiny pieces of red meat no bigger [than] the size of golf balls. Blew them all to hell! And Hurlbert, he survived it; I guess a concussion messed him up. I used to call him about every Christmas and talk to him and he told me, he said that the three guys that were where the explosion occurred, he said they were using their medal entrenching tools. He was digging in the side of the embankment with his bare hands, what he told me, and we found out that they were magnetic sea mines...

Anyhow, when we went back and told Schmitty, our platoon sergeant, he called back headquarters and headquarters said, "Well, you got any PWs?" "Yeah, we got a whole bunch of them." They said, "Well, give them a choice. Let them go up and deactivate them, or disarm them or we're going to shot them on the spot."

Well, when the interpreter told them that they got pretty belligerent. And anyhow, he told them he said, well, up there, you disarm them you're prisoners of war. Back here, if you don't, you're dead ducks because we're going to put it to you right here on the spot. So they went up and disarmed them.[757]

The 504th Parachute Infantry Regiment climbed onto the tanks and proceeded in the attack; it was an attack in name only. Hardly a shot was fired. The Germans all gave up. They were overrunning the rear of a German corps, mostly service troops and some of the "poor front line troops," as one of the regiment's officers described them. There were generals, colonels, doctors, Bulgarian cavalry and isolated remnants of every other type of officer, man or unit that could be imagined.

The regimental CP opened up in the village of Eldena, just off a bridge crossing the Elde Canal, on May 2. For the next several days, the hordes and hordes of German traffic coming through the lines of the

82nd Airborne Division increased in near panic, all trying to be captured by the Americans rather than the Russians, brutal to Germans, who were giving chase to them.

While on the Rhine River, Walter Hughes and Ed Utaski used this captured motorcycle to run wire across exposed roads. (Walter Hughes)

The men stood along the road as the Germans streamed through, piling up their arms and equipment in large heaps along the way. Along the road came flowing the German army. The horse-drawn field kitchen and supply caravans of the beaten Wehrmacht, which looked like a scene straight from the First World War, flowing through the regiment's lines were in stark contrast to the GMCs and Ford trucks which the US Army had, a testament to the production power of the United States.[758]

Lieutenants Roy Hanna and Allen McClain were standing alongside the highway as the hundreds of German troops flowed through their positions. "Our men took their motorcycles and riding horses," Roy Hanna remembered. "Lt. McClain and I each took a beautiful riding horse… Mac and I took a short ride out of this small town on a cobble topped road. On the way back I was successful in getting the horse to run. Problem here was the horse didn't know what 'Whoa' meant and I went flying by the Mortar Platoon house and got a lot of 'Hold on cowboy,' etc. Don't know how I got the horse stopped, but walked him back to our barracks and gave him away to a civilian."[759]

Meanwhile, the procession continued. "Hell," Jerome Unruh told his comrades as the German surrendered, "they could beat us to death with sticks. They wouldn't need guns with as many of them as there are."[760] The scene was really something. Leading to this sight was a trail of the regiment's blood stretching all the way back to Africa. As with much of human history, those who had paid the most, those great men who had sailed the blue Atlantic in the spring of 1943, never got to see with their own eyes the completion of the undertaking for which they had struggled and fought so hard, and died for, for so long.

At the regimental CP in Eldena on May 3, Colonel Tucker was getting restless waiting for the Russians. Tucker's aid, Lieutenant Chester Garrison, remembered the day vividly. He later wrote:

The morning started well enough. Through my CP window, I could see that the number of surrendering German soldiers coming across the small bridge and towards our building was increasing by the hour. They were desperate to get behind American lines before the Russians overwhelmed them. By late afternoon, the Russians were reported to be just down the road.

Colonel Tucker soon could no longer bridle himself. The war was ending, and any good officer - particularly a West Pointer - would want his record to show that he had met the Russians first. The dim future would offer no such opportunities. He called to me to join him together with the two other officers standing by. We got into his command car and edged our way counter-current through the mob. We did drive over the bridge but not much farther. The oncoming traffic of horse-drawn carts, trucks, and humanity was too solid for the car to divide, and even Colonel Tucker was not Moses.

The four of us left the command car with the driver and started down the road as briskly as an opposition of shoulders and elbows would allow. Soon one officer disappeared in the crowd, obviously because he was a weapons addict and firearms were being discarded into the ditch alongside the road. Then the second officer evaporated, for whatever reason. That left me with Colonel Tucker in search of the Russians without our knowing a single word of Russian except for my, "Nyet!" I automatically became his aide as well as his adjutant and took proper positions one step to his left rear.

As we progressed down the swarming road, it became even more congested, almost solid. The oncomers, Germans, did attempt to make an aisle when they saw us. They might not have been able to interpret our insignia, but they immediately recognized us as Americans. In their thinking, once behind us they were captured - safe and secure. As we passed by, they threw their weapons in the ditch in a continuous thudding.

As we two continued on our way in full military stride, we passed the variety of vehicles loaded with German soldiers as well as more soldiers, and even camp followers, on foot. Most of the forbidding of all were the black uniformed SS troops, usually standing in the trucks. They were unsmiling; they glowered at us darkly for the indignity they were about to face. Eyeing us, many of them took their revolvers from their holsters and fired them into the air as a symbolic gesture of military leave taking and then threw them overboard.

This firing made me nervous. In the melee, an irate SS could easily have shot one or both of us and never been identified - two bloody bodies by the wayside. I slowly unbuttoned my holster, cocked the loaded revolver, and kept my hand on the butt. On going down, I would at least make some noise. My guess is we had walked at least two miles. Between us and any other Americans were thousands of German soldiers in many different moods. The afternoon was waning, and I preferred not to be in this situation in the dark.

Colonel Tucker's stride began to weaken. Even he realized that the Russians were much farther off than reported. Soon he decided to go into reverse. We turned and retraced our way through the moving river of human beings. We reached our CP safely - he disappointed and I relieved.[761]

Colonel Tucker was not the only man in the regiment to take a ride through masses of Germans to find the Russians first. Captain Burriss with a few others took a jeep and rode some 40 to 50 miles when they ran into the Russians; it was likely the first linkup with the Russians and troops from the 82nd Airborne Division. However, Burriss and his comrades decided they wanted to go sightsee in Berlin and took their jeep, along with a Russian colonel they had met, into the nearly-leveled capital of NAZI Germany where they posed for photographs.[762]

Another early linkup with the Russians involved two tank loads of I Company men. Dwight Boyce remembered, "Twenty of us loaded on two borrowed tanks and started through the Kraut lines but we hadn't gone very far when the dirty bastards opened up on us. The approaching Russians had no way of knowing who or what we were in that part of the lines so they opened up on us too. We dug in at a crossroads for the night, but at daylight we were able to get it across to the Russians that we were Americans and we made the link up. One of those guys kissed me."[763]

In short order, the whole regiment was soon in contact with the Russians. The first thing Lieutenant Reneau Breard recognized was the effect of the American lend-lease. The Russians were riding on brand new Studebaker trucks, while the regiment's Service Company was driving worn out GMCs and Fords. Breard, however, was likely one of the only men sober enough to make such an observation. The Russians wanted to party - Breard did not see a sober Russian soldier - and they found willing party partners in the men of the 504th Parachute Infantry.[764] The Russians soon proved to the paratroopers to be a brute-like group. One lieutenant remembered, "Shortly after we met the German forces, after we crossed the Elbe River and the war came to an end, a group of us (officers) met with a group of Russian officers for a vodka drinking party. It's unfair to judge an army by the stories I heard at that party, but I left with a very negative opinion. I've done a lot of traveling worldwide since the war and have not been to Russia and have no desire to go there. Enough said!"

I Company troopers Leo Muri and Ed Hahn pose with two Russian soldiers shortly after the linkup. (Walter Hughes)

Donald Zimmerman remembered that many of them were arrogant. We won the war was the sentiment many of them had - and they were under the modus operandi that to the victor goes the spoils. "They were looting everything they could take," Werner Speer remembered, "they were taking stuff out of the houses and taking it back to Russia, I guess. They were raping a lot of woman, that's for sure. They were pretty crude. They used to throw explosive into the water to stun the fish and pull the fish out. They thought that toilets, flush toilets, were for washing your feet or something. I don't think they had ever seen anything like it."[765]

The line of demarcation between the Russians and the American paratroopers was the Elde. Many times the paratroopers would cross the bridges of the canal and go to the Russian side to drink the copious amount of vodka that the Russian soldiers were supplied with, to the point that even the lowly private carried the beverage in their canteens. It was potent stuff, which even some paratroopers could not down. Sometimes during the parties there were incidences. One paratrooper tried to stop a Russian from raping a German civilian at one of the parties; the Russian tried to shoot the paratrooper, who took off running from the house and hid in nearby bushes until it was safe to swim the canal back over to the American side.

George Leolis and Walter Hughes with two Russian soldiers near the Elbe. (Walter Hughes)

At the bridges across the Elde, four sentries - two American and two Russians - were placed. There, casual conversation along with a little vodka drinking, sourced from the Russian canteens, also took place. The Russian had the idea that the paratroopers were expert knife-throwers, as many of the men had long, eight-inch field knives strapped to their belts or onto their shin over the boot. Since there was a language problem, one afternoon a Russian motioned to a paratrooper that he wanted to see him throw his knife. The trooper tried to tell him that he could not, but the Russian pressed so the trooper took his knife and threw it hard as he could at the wooden post on the bridge. The knife stuck, as if it has been thrown by a movie actor. The trooper looked at Charles Dodd with eyes as if he had seen a ghost and stuttered, "That was an accident!" Impressed, the Russian wanted to see it again, but the paratrooper reclaimed his knife and played it off like it was an everyday occurrence for the men of the 504th Parachute Infantry - just like it was nothing to see.[766]

The Wöbbelin Concentration Camp

If the ornate gold and crystal chandeliers dangling over cavernous rooms from high ceilings adorned by murals and gold tapestry did not make Ludwigslust Place seem as if it was the set of a romantic movie set in Europe where gaudy-dressed women were spun around by dashing men in tuxedos, the grounds on which the castle sat did. Across the wide cobblestone driveway was a large reflection pond followed by a long, narrow green space framed between two rows of mature trees. On May 7, that green space was a flurry of activity as German civilians pulled from the town, the women wearing their dresses and men wearing their suits, under the guard of Americans, dug 200 holes in the ground. There were representatives of every German occupation in the town, including shopkeepers, lawyers, doctors, mechanics and farmers - every foundation of German culture was represented in the diggers. The holes were graves for the victims of the nearby concentration camp, the victims of crimes done in the name of the German people.

The Wöbbelin Concentration Camp, liberated earlier in the week by the 82nd Airborne Division, was a sight of utter disaster, an icon of human callousness and brutality. In the midst of the surrender en-mass of the German army, a net call had gone out that every soldier in the 82nd Airborne Division should tour the camp; almost all men of the 504th Parachute Infantry Regiment had that opportunity. The sights they saw were incredible. Live human beings had disintegrated from bodies to figures; they were grotesque and contorted, withering away into dust before their very eyes. Donald Zimmerman remembers, "They were distressed, I will tell you that. It was difficult to tell [their nationality] because they had left them there and then it was awful. It was just a horrible thing. There were so many dead, they were just laying all over the place. It was – they had started to denigrate at all points."[767]

For Captain Robert Halloran, the regimental dentist, the lack of food was evident for those survivors. "To see a concentration camp first hand is an experience one could never forget. The smell of dead bodies, human excrement - starving bodies can't be adequately described," he would later write.[768]

Edward Mokan wrote that he "couldn't breathe the stink was so heavy. Dead, decomposed bodies, flies and maggots all over."[769] One paratrooper took a NAZI flag from the camp office, and it took years for the lingering odor to get out of the flag's cloth.

The sight was appalling, but two years of combat had hardened Lieutenant Chester Garrison so much that he was able to eat lunch afterwards; two years ago, before this war, that would hardy have been the case.[770] And it was likely not the case for the German civilians from the surrounding areas who were rounded up and marched through camp to view its atrocities. "Some of the women," Jerome Unruh remembered, "they'd put their hands up to their face and booo, they wanted to walk off. And we would put our arm out and stop them, point to our eyes and point to them and their eyes, and then to the figure [person] and when they looked at them we let them go."[771]

From the camp, the remains of 200 victims of the concentration camp were taken to Ludwigslust Palace and put in the graves dug by the civilians. German civilians and German soldiers who were taken under guard from the PW cage, including several general officers, were forced to attend the ceremony held on May 7. An account of the concentration camp was given by one of its survivors, Louis Camu who was transferred to the Wobbelin camp from the concentration camp Schandelah in April. The 82nd Airborne's report of the services summarized his account of the camp:

The following is a summary of testimony given by Professor Louis Camu, Professor of Administrative Law at the University of Brussels from 1936 to 1941. Members of this division and military authorities have already been witness to the evidence of his remarks. Professor Camu was Royal Commissioner of Belgium from 1934 to 1940. He visited the United States on two occasions; first, in 1930, a personal visit, and again in 1935 as a delegate of the Belgian Government for commercial negotiations between Belgium and the United States. Professor Camu was chief of the Underground Movement for the two provinces of Flanders. He was arrested on 18 July 1944 by the Gestapo. This was his testimony in substance:

At the Wobbelin Concentration Camp, s[outh] of Wobbelin, there were 500 persons working on the construction of the camp, in preparation for the reception of prisoners from the Schandelah Concentration Camp near Braunsweig. These workers received one-fifteenth of a kilo of bread in the morning, one-eighth in the evening, and one litre of soup made of rutabaga and carrots. This was their daily ration. They also received 25 grammes of margarine twice a week.

On 10 April 1945, 1200 prisoners arrived at the Wobbelin Camp from Schandelah, near Braunsweig, after five days of travel. On the same day, 2000 more arrived from Braunsweig. One week later, 1500 Jews arrived from Berlin. Their daily rations consisted of one-eighth of a kilo of bread with a teaspoonful of jam, and one-half litre of soup made of rutabaga and potato peelings. The potatoes were for the foremen and "Capos" who were put in charge of the prisoners. These men were German citizen prisoners with a criminal records, especially selected for their brutality and they made much use of it.

The total of prisoners at the camp was approximately 4500 and since the operation of the camp, 1200 to 1400 of them died of brutality and starvation. The foremen and Capos did not beat everyone the same way: the weak prisoner was beaten more often and mercilessly than the healthier one.

Also as a daily routine, they were beaten as they stood in line for soup; brutality was such that they came to look upon this as a trivial matter, compared with other sorts of brutality. Those whom the Capos disliked for having disobeyed them or for having rebelled against them were sent to work under an SS man. The latter would order the victim to go pick up a shovel or pick about 20 feet away. As the prisoner turned his back, he was shot. Such victims would be brought back as an example for the rest, they would be placed in latrines and urinals and other inmates were obliged to urinate and defecate on them. Any sign of reverence toward the dead resulted in 25 lashings on the bare buttocks with a thick cable.

Prisoners lay on the ground in the barracks without straw. The dead were left lying with the living for several days before being removed and buried. When removed, they were piled in heaps of five or six in a ditch. Sometimes there were some in the heap who were not yet dead. When the foremen were informed of this, they would beat the informant and go finish off the swing prisoner by kicking him to death.

The night before we arrived, prisoners were loaded into the trains to be reshipped to another camp away from the advancing forces. Weak persons who could not move quickly were beaten to death with clubs and cables. Approximately 100 were killed as a result. German SS men took all German citizen prisoners with them the day the Americans arrived and asked for volunteers to go with them. Some Russians, Belgians and Poles volunteered to go; these men had cooperated with the foremen and Capos against their fellow prisoners and consequently judged it best not to be left behind. They all took off towards the east.[772]

The following day, May 8, Germany official capitulated. The war was won.

The next several weeks, the men combed through the countryside to collect weapons and other contraband. Roy Hanna and First Sergeant Joseph Castellanos took 20 men to a small, nearby village to conduct a sweep. Hanna and Castellanos, standing at no more than five-foot-ten with thick black hair and an olive-toned round Italian face, immediately commandeered the nicest house they could find. The furnishings were beautiful, Hanna thought. It would do for their billet. It was an abrupt change from an exposed hole in the earth, exposed to everything from blistering heat to freezing rain, to a luxury most take for granted. Neither of them could bring themselves to sleep in the bed. "The beds too soft," Hanna said, "and the covers too warm." They had become paratroopers anesthetized to the feeling of basic luxuries.[773]

Just before the turn of July, the regiment was relieved and entrained on nice passenger cars and taken back camps near Epinal, France. "Our fighting was over," said Lieutenant Reneau Breard. "After a few days, it was spit and polish again."[774]

27

TRIUMPH

Following the route down New York City's 5th Avenue on which General John J. Pershing had paraded his victorious Doughboy's after the conclusion of the Great War, Major General James M. Gavin marched. Behind him, stomped the feet of 13,000 soldiers of the victorious 82nd Airborne Division - a unit he had helped led to victory in combat in Sicily, Italy, France, Holland, Belgium and Germany. Everything which they had fought for over two trying years became embodied in this one event.

As the 13,000 troops marched down 5th Avenue, the atmosphere was electric. Policemen struggled to keep the masses of excitable people, lining the streets for miles, at bay as the troopers stomped past. With wonderment in their eyes, hordes of people from all over the country came and waved flags and cheered at the top of their lungs, competing with the band whose drumbeat was pounding. People lined the rooftops over the route to observe the sea of paratroopers and glidermen as they marched in perfect sync with one another. Clouds of ticker-tape floated down onto the men of the 82nd and onto the crowd on the streets.

This was victory - total and complete - a celebration of the end of the worry and suffering, and a homecoming.

The celebrating crowds included people of all types, the young and the old, men and woman - and veterans whose grit, blood and bodies had made the 82nd Airborne Division into the renowned force which it had become, the result being this honor - marching in the New York City World War II Victory Parade. Out in the crowd, together, cheering on their former comrades was Fred Baldino, Joe Hirsch, and Bob Lowe. The three of them had known each other since 1942 when they arrived at Company A, 504th Parachute Infantry shortly after the unit's activation in Fort Benning. At the time, the outcome of the war was far from certain. The three of them had jumped into Sicily together, but their war wounds prevented their continuing on with the unit to Germany, and ultimately to march in the parade. Baldino was wounded in Holland, Hirsch in Sicily, and Lowe at Anzio. It was their blood which had made this moment a reality.

Lt. John Scheaffer, unknown, and Captain Adam Komosa pose with a captured German flag in Germany, around VE-Day. Both Scheaffer and Komosa survived all the battles of the regiment, stretching back to Sicily. Hundreds of their friends were not fortunate enough to see the end of the war. (Author's collection)

At 42nd Street, a special reviewing stand for the Gold Star Mothers - women who had lost children in the war - was erected. Sitting in that stand watching the spectacle was Mrs. Kennedy and her family, who had traveled from western Massachusetts to witness the division of her late son, Lieutenant Edward Kennedy, killed in Holland, march. The week before the parade, Lieutenants Robert Blankenship and James Megellas drove from New York to pick up their close friend and former comrade Lieutenant Richard LaRiviere, also a resident of western Massachusetts. The three of them went into Holyoke to the house where their late comrade Ed Kennedy grew up and personally invited Mrs. Kennedy, on behalf of the 504th, to have a spot in the reviewing stand for the parade.

Just two years earlier, her son and LaRiviere, the man who now stood before her, were together in a pitched battle when her son had watched LaRiviere get the seat of his pants caught on a barbed wire fence while attempting to lead a bayonet charge. The story, relayed by her son, was told to a reporter on the beachhead, and it was a tale which was turned into a cartoon that appeared in newspapers across the nation.

A week after the visit, Mrs. Kennedy was in New York City watching as the victorious company of her late, handsome son paraded by, being led by her son's friend Lieutenant Blankenship.

That night, after the parade was over, she went to the reception at the Waldorf Astoria as the guest of Blankenship, LaRiviere and Megellas, and met several other troopers who had known her son Lieutenant Kennedy, including Captain (Father) Edwin Kozak, her son's priest in the 504th, with whom she dined. Kozak, a longtime friend of Lieutenant Kennedy, had been alongside the table at the hospital talking to Lieutenant Kennedy as shock took its grip and Kennedy took his final breaths.

Lts. Robert Blankenship, Richard LaRiviere and James Megellas as the Waldorf Astoria after the parade. It would be the last time the three of them were togeather. (Richie Blankenship)

For those that participated in the parade, and those veterans of the unit such as Fred Baldino who attended, the celebration marked the last hoorah for the 504th Parachute Infantry in World War II and closed a chapter in the unit's history, and the men's lives. Once the ticker tape stopped flying and the Waldorf Astoria cleared out, the men parted ways, fanned out across the country to their homes, and began the process of building life anew. A few men, such as Father Kozak, opted to remain in the Army but his time with the 504th was complete. Fred Baldino had already been medically discharged, the result of his war wounds, when the parade took place. After a year back home in Pennsylvania, he moved to Burbank, California and bought a house on North Keystone Street - where he would remain with his wife Mary until the day he passed away at the age of 91 a proud veteran of the 504th - and spent a 32-year-career with the US Postal Service.

For Baldino, the biggest lesson he learned from the war was how much he wanted to live; others said they learned a lot about fellowship. "Knowing people like we talked about many times, Maggie and Rosenkrantz and different ones, you get to know people from all over the United States and you get the different opinions from them," reflected Donald Zimmerman. "We would sit around and talk about what home was like, what their home was like. It was interesting, but at the same time it was dangerous as hell. I found that out a few times. I did things that I shouldn't have done on my own."[775]

The road was long and the work hard. In reality there was little special about the men who made up the 504th. They were ordinary men who were thrown into extraordinary circumstances, who bore their share of the task with great heart, determination and self-sacrifice, and through those simple traits wrote a story that has come in contemporary times to be viewed as having the traits of military epics akin to the tales of the brave ancient Carthaginians fighting at Cannae. But, as Roy Hanna humbly says, "If I'm a hero, so are thousands of other WWII veterans. And I must add that I'm not fearless. It even scares me today to think of some of the episodes I was part of during WWII."[776]

~ THE END ~

LIEUTENANT JOHN S. THOMPSON'S SALERNO STICK

Shortly before midnight on September 13, 1943, 18 men of the 2nd Battalion's Light Machine Gun Platoon parachuted together out of the same transport plane and landed on the sandy beaches south of Salerno to turn battle's tide. Following this small sampling of men through the war gives an illustration of how commonplace attrition was for the men of the Regiment during the war.

2nd Lt. John S. Thompson	Transfered E/504 (WIA Anzio, 2/15/44)
SGT Alvin E. Tway	WIA Salerno, 9/18/43; **KIA Anzio, 1/30/44**
CPL Norman J. Patnaude	
CPL John E. Pillsbury	Transferred to States after Anzio
PFC Michael J. Buck	
PFC Floyd W. Durnil	
PFC James H. Roberts	WIA, 12/17/43; WIA, 10/14/44; WIA, 1/8/45
Thomas C. Considine	WIA Anzio, 1/25/44
PVT Albano Tassinari	
PVT Oliver J. Bohlken	**KIA Belgium, 1/8/45**
CPL Peter Plichta	WIA Hill 1205, 12/17/43
CPL Charles E. Dorrington	WIA Hill 1205, 12/17/43 (to States Jan '44)
PVT Harry E. Wilson	WIA Hill 1205, 12/17/43
PVT John W. Trevena	WIA Germany, 2/2/45
PVT J. Pisani	
PVT Harry A. Wensil	**KIA Salerno, 9/17/43**
PVT Salvador Rubio	WIA Hill 1205, 12/17/43
PVT Otis Page	WIA Hill 1205, 12/12/43; WIA Holland, 9/28/44

Pvt. Al Tassinari survived all the campaigns of the 504th PIR with the Machine Gun Platoon and was known to his comrades as "Trigger Tass." Tassinari saved his reserve parachute and copied the names of all the troopers who jumped in his stick, the source of this list. Tassinari was best friends with Joseph Jusek, and was with him during their fight against German tanks near Erlecom, Holland, an action for which Jusek would later receive the Distinguished Service Cross - only one of three awarded to a member of the 2nd Battalion during the war. (Jim Tassinari)

CASUALTIES OF THE 504TH PARACHUTE INFANTRY REGIMENT ON THE SALERNO BEACHHEAD, SEPTEMBER 1943

Last	First	Middle Initial	ASN	Rank	Company	Date	Status
Martinez	Joe	C	34025114	SGT	HQ-HQ	13	WIA
Newhart	Quentin	T	19140113	PVT	HQ-HQ	13	WIA
Pester	Frederick	J	13053832	1SGT	HQ-HQ	14	WIA
Pignatone	Vincent	J	32195925	PVT	HQ-HQ	15	WIA
Dubois	Billy	B	18117199	PVT	HQ-HQ	15	WIA
Richter	Forrest	E	O-456149	1LT	HQ-HQ	17	WIA
Freeman	Leslie	G	O-294314	LTC	HQ-HQ	17	WIA
Acheson	Robert	B	O-303279	MAJ	HQ-HQ	17	SWA
Dunham	Don	B	O-293927	MAJ	HQ-HQ	17	KIA
Masanlowski	John	A	6830325	PVT	A	14	WIA
Coppage	Ivan	L	19085662	T/5	A	14	WIA
Jackson	Harvey	T	14164730	PVT	A	17	WIA
Duvall	Mearle	D	O-463918	2LT	A	17	WIA
Whitman	Stanley	J	O-1295805	2LT	A	17	WIA
Olimpi	Ateo	NMI	13079718	CPL	A	17	WIA
Hauser	William	G	33081174	SGT	A	17	WIA
Munoz	Frank	NMI	18104622	T/4	A	17	WIA
Connolly	Peter	P	12085358	PVT	A	17	WIA
McCann	John	F	13152832	PVT	A	17	WIA
Bady	Charles	H	7084189	PVT	A	17	WIA
Carra	Anthony	T	12081345	PVT	A	18	WIA
Mokan	Edward	L	13079510	PVT	A	17	MIA
Wall	Ned	E	O-1283879	1LT	A	17	KIA
Rouse	Edwin	L	20402955	1SGT	A	17	KIA
Carter	Bernard	E	13086344	PVT	A	17	KIA

Young	Ralph	R	20312296	PVT	A	17	KIA
Jurewicz	Walter	A	32158374	PVT	A	17	KIA
Goodson	Thomas	J	34575051	PVT	A	17	KIA
Hesson	James	C	15013857	1SGT	B	14	WIA
Bagwell	James	H	18079670	CPL	B	14	WIA
Gerke	Julius	F	38074872	CPL	B	14	WIA
Craft	Benjamin	V	35123626	PVT	B	14	WIA
Suarez	Benjamin	C	39392995	PVT	B	14	WIA
Ott	Ray	A	13091600	PVT	B	14	WIA
Bates	John	R	35272394	PVT	B	14	WIA
Lennard	Lance	NMI	32580484	PVT	B	17	WIA
Carskadon	Robert	L	16084741	PVT	B	17	WIA
Scamihorn	John	E	35716229	PVT	B	17	WIA
Ferry	James	J	13029375	CPL	B	17	WIA
Favreau	Arthur	H	20110353	CPL	B	17	WIA
Nowotarski	Francis	L	32582488	PVT	B	17	WIA
Fuqua	Ivan	N	14097874	PVT	MED/B	17	WIA
Meerman	William	A	O-1296236	2LT	B	17	WIA
Zowacki	Joseph	N	O-1309472	2LT	B	17	WIA
Farrier	Clyde	A	39380352	PVT	B	17	WIA
Cleary	Francis	J	31049931	CPL	B	17	WIA
Robart	Kenneth	NMI	32070117	CPL	B	17	WIA
Dadasovich	William	NMI	39088290	T/5	B	17	WIA
Gensel	Ralph	C	33151543	PVT	B	17	WIA
Hixenski	Anthony	A	13055885	PVT	B	17	WIA
Charlton	Thomas	G	14099939	PVT	B	17	WIA
Meyer	George	NMI	32061170	PVT	B	17	WIA
DeCourcy	John	W	12033103	PVT	B	17	WIA
Clardy	William	W	19099477	SGT	B	17	WIA
Gonzales	Frank	NMI	38071677	PVT	B	17	WIA
Woodhead	Ivan	H	39018890	PVT	B	14	MIA
Klepacz	Emile	E	13056051	PVT	B	14	MIA

Paquet	Henry	P	36159242	SSGT	B	17	KIA
Weinberger	Emanuel	J	36103786	PVT	B	17	KIA
Hesselberg	Myer	T	33140720	PVT	B	18	KIA
Weeks	Vernon	A	37354425	PVT	B	19	KIA
Pate	Joseph	E	20811321	PVT	B	18	WIA
Montgomery	James	G	38065836	PVT	MED/C	14	MIA
Ownsbey	Arlie	J	20364865	PVT	C	14	WIA
Patrick	Lyle	B	13036552	PVT	C	14	WIA
Pelletier	Rene	R	31084963	PVT	C	14	WIA
Groover	Edger	S	13085999	PVT	C	14	WIA
Pease	John	N	O-416565	1LT	C	14	WIA
Namayeski	Frank	P	31007758	SGT	C	14	WIA
Conners	George	E	31039134	PVT	C	14	WIA
Guttry	Carlos	B	18109151	CPL	C	17	WIA
Divers	Peter	G	13036254	PVT	C	17	WIA
Henry	Arthur	W	16052714	PVT	C	17	WIA
Carr	George	O	38065037	PVT	C	17	WIA
Buscetto	John	J	31062780	PVT	C	17	WIA
Bulik	Wilfred	A	39105453	PVT	C	17	WIA
Clark	Joseph	E	19096204	PVT	C	17	WIA
Taylor	Joseph	A	33142998	PVT	C	17	KIA
Puhalla	Frank	A	13056153	PVT	C	17	KIA
Mattscheck	Gunter	P	12058862	PVT	MED/C	19	WIA
Drake	Oscar	S	14121626	PVT	HQ/1	14	WIA
Bradley	Robert	E	13069157	T/4	HQ/1	14	WIA
Mahoney	Charles	J	32156878	PVT	HQ/1	14	WIA
Bullock	William	W	14041375	PVT	HQ/1	14	WIA
Poitevint	James	C	20361304	PVT	HQ/1	14	WIA
Thurston	Paul	N	15090568	PVT	HQ/1	14	WIA
Tennis	Walter	J	13048955	PVT	HQ/1	14	WIA
Schwartz	Harry	W	19078995	PVT	HQ/1	14	WIA
Waters	Herbert	D	14123386	PVT	HQ/1	14	WIA
Brown	Thomas	NMI	33136327	SSGT	HQ/1	17	SWA

OHiggins	Donald	J	6873516	PVT	HQ/1	17	WIA
Hill	Edward	B	14097404	PVT	HQ/1	17	WIA
Wright	Arthur	M	35638819	PVT	HQ/1	17	WIA
Van Ackeren	Leonard	A	6934178	PVT	HQ/1	16	WIA
Brownell	Robert	NMI	36104665	PVT	HQ/1	17	MIA
Sawyer	Henry	B	20418075	PVT	HQ/1	17	MIA
Hepworth	Thomas	R	1904383	PVT	MED/HQ/1	17	MIA
Thomas	Aubrey	S	6968252	PVT	MED/HQ/1	19	WIA
Wall	Gerald	F	13151599	PVT	MED/HQ/1	19	WIA
Strayer	Arthur	D	15078955	PVT	HQ/1	14	WIA
Scheaffer	John	E	O-1309417	2LT	D	18	WIA
Lyness	Marvin	E	?	PVT	D	18	WIA
Sharp	Warren	D	15338646	PVT	D	18	WIA
Stokes	Ervin	W	12058544	PVT	D	?	WIA
Giananti	Ralph	NMI	12058447	PVT	D	18	WIA
DiRinzo	John	C	12073034	PVT	D	17	KIA
King	James	H	?	PVT	D	17	KIA
Lechner	James	E	?	PVT	D	17	KIA
Le Count	John	C	?	PVT	D	17	KIA
Monti	John	J	?	PVT	D	17	KIA
Misseres	Alex	NMI	39089362	SSGT	E	13	WIA
Anderson	Norman	N	35159231	PVT	E	13	WIA
Maney	William	A	15011495	PVT	E	13	WIA
Thompson	Richard	E	O-1302233	2LT	E	13	WIA
Tyra	Clifford	J	6235818	PVT	E	13	WIA
Kilpatrick	Robert	D	20421688	PVT	E	13	WIA
McKirdy	Cecil	D	20421688	PVT	E	13	WIA
Swinney	Larance	G	18086072	PVT	E	13	WIA
Cholka	Paul	G	13087080	PVT	E	13	WIA
Eason	William	D	34449455	PVT	E	13	WIA
Griffin	Henry	O	6379212	1SGT	E	13	WIA
Johnson	Floyd	A	37115402	T/5	E	13	WIA

Brinser	Harold	K	33238123	PVT	E	14	WIA
Madona	Vince	A	34152355	PVT	E	16	WIA
Satterwhite	John	L	38082776	SGT	E	14	KIA
Lalich	Dean	NMI	12158009	PVT	E	17	WIA
Smith	James	W	35150488	PVT	E	18	WIA
Frenning	Lawrence	O	37302433	PVT	E	18	WIA
Webster	Arvil	H	14121669	PVT	E	18	WIA
Gillilan	Thomas	T	18074876	PVT	E	17	KIA
Fulton	Curtis	L	13036734	PVT	F	13	WIA
Masel	Frank	NMI	15090505	PVT	F	13	WIA
Lisica	Krsevan	NMI	32533649	PVT	F	13	WIA
Serra	Laurence	NMI	20423182	PVT	F	13	WIA
Decker	Dale	E	39017143	SGT	F	17	KIA
Richie	Jesse	NMI	18096835	SGT	F	13	WIA
Latz	Peter	R	?	PVT	MED/F	13	WIA
Tess	Willard	G	06919906	PVT	F	13	WIA
Bagby?	?	?	?	PVT	F	13	WIA
Enoch	Joe	NMI	35591517	PVT	F	17	WIA
Lamance	Elmer	D	18068450	PVT	F	17	WIA
McAtee	Walter	M	15090579	PVT	F	18	SWA
Miller	Orval	L	18070182	PVT	F	18	WIA
Hall	Thomas	E	12131917	PVT	F	16	WIA
Moremand	Tommy	D	38082475	SGT	HQ/2	14	WIA
Thomas	William	C	20454122	PVT	HQ/2	14	WIA
Bandy	Robert	N	?	PVT	HQ/2	13 or 18?	WIA
Mahaney	John	M	33131147	PVT	HQ/2	13 or 18?	WIA
Wensil	Harry	A	14149069	PVT	HQ/2	17	KIA
Tway	Alvin	E	36152077	SGT	HQ/2	18	WIA

PARATROOPERS WHO JOINED THE 504TH PARACHUTE INFANTRY REGIMENT FROM THE 2ND REPLACEMENT DEPOT ON DECEMBER 10, 1943

Officers
- 1st Lt. Harry F. Busby
- 1st Lt. Bertram J. Dallas
- 1st Lt. Henry C. Dunavant
- 1st Lt. James D. Simmons
- 1st Lt. Hanford A. Files
- 1st Lt. Richard G. LaRiviere
- 1st Lt. Payton C. Hartley
- 2nd Lt. Arthur J. Lyon
- 2nd Lt. Robert J. Lyons
- 2nd Lt. Edward T. Wisniewski
- 2nd Lt. James Magellas
- 2nd Lt. Frank H. Breault
- 2nd Lt. Thomas A. Murphy
- Capt. Richard I. Manning
- Capt. Robert E. Kile

To Headquarters and Headquarters Company
- PVT William C. Kline
- PVT Clarence E. Hudson
- PVT Jack L. Bommer
- SSGT Myrle D. Olrogge
- PVT Max E. Pilarowski, Jr.
- PVT Heinz H. Plinzke
- PVT John L. Pingel
- PVT Harry L. Michael, Jr.
- PVT Daniel R. MacEwan
- PVT Anthony J. Sercel
- PVT Robert F. Schreiner
- PVT Donald L. Powell
- PVT Thomas J. Zouzas
- PVT William Zeller
- PVT Martin T. Whelan, Jr.
- PVT Edward O. Wetherell
- PVT Robert E. Tope
- PVT Robert M. Tambeaux
- PVT Andrew T. Swift

To Company A
- PFC Lacy E. Moore
- PFC Pedro N Whatley
- PVT Leo T. Bickham
- PVT William H. Consigny
- PVT Glenn M. Frew
- PVT Thomas L. Kelly
- PVT Arthur P. Mayard
- PVT Henry B. Millan, Jr.
- PVT Frank Pfeffer
- PVT James J. Musa
- PVT Homer G. Steepro
- PVT Junior H. Poor
- PVT Fay T. Steger
- PVT Robert C. Stester
- PVT William J. Rothweiler
- PVT Roger W. Smith
- PVT Richard R. Ranny
- PFC Peter Polifka
- PVT James H. Rosser
- PVT Alfred Hurtado
- PVT Edward E. Jackson
- PVT John J. O'Connor
- PVT Blair R. Carney
- PVT Edwin L. Zube, Jr.
- PVT Thomas Stead
- PVT Willard M. Strunk
- PVT Donald D. Weber
- PVT Ithel T. Wisham
- PVT William C. Wood
- CPL Clyde F. May
- PFC Eldon F. Young
- PFC Russell E. Stotler
- PFC Theodore W. Brown
- PVT Ignatius W. Wengress
- PVT Merwynn A. Tobias
- PVT John E. Wasielewski
- PVT Harland A. Tempel
- PFC Neil A. Wilson
- PVT Robert J. Yannuzzi
- PVT Charles A. Stankiewicz
- PVT Albert S. Sebasitan
- PVT John C. Parsons
- PVT Clyde T. Surrett
- PVT John P. Ternosky
- PVT Robert Washko
- PFC Lloyd V. Brandt
- PFC Vernon A. Roberts

To Company B

- PVT Frank W. Belfoy
- PVT Robert E. Cyman
- PVT Iver E. Johnson
- PVT Henry J. Klee
- PVT Henry McKnight
- PVT Robert P. Mielenz
- PVT Emilio J. Papale
- PVT Charles Piazza
- PVT Robert J. Sestric
- PVT Preston F. Pogue
- PVT Albert E. Ramsey
- PVT Joseph A. Sims
- PVT Robert D. Stern
- PVT Frank A. Svoboda
- PVT Herman C. Wagner
- PVT Carson L. Varner
- PVT George R. McCarron
- PVT Jack M. Eliphant
- PVT Fred W. Taylor, Jr.
- PVT Scott R. Rienschield
- PVT Leonard F. Kominowski
- PVT Anthony F. Zdancewicz, Jr.
- PFC James E. McManus
- PVT Epperson C. Maynard
- PVT Beppino DaGiau
- PVT John J. Skalican
- PVT Harris V. Duke
- PVT Harry B. Logan, Jr.
- PVT James M. McRae
- PVT Henry E. Moorhead

To Company C
- PVT Forrest L. Smith
- PVT Emil J. Segelstrom
- PVT Tom Zarro
- PVT Raymond R. Wilson
- PVT William J. Vorum
- PVT Benjamin F. Tedeschi
- PVT Harold D. Stevenson
- PVT Charlie L. Shipp
- PVT Albert J. Rowan
- PVT Donald E. Revard
- PVT Donald G. Pyper
- PVT Arden L. Peterson
- PVT Edward L. Partyka
- PVT John Styger
- PVT Elbert E. Winningham
- T/5 Donald R. Yurick

- PVT Duane E. Ralph
- PVT William N. Rowe
- T/4 Curtis L. Aydelott
- PVT Gene P. Frazee
- PVT Bernardo V. Jusaino
- PVT Wesley J. Groffen
- PVT Elmer W. Swartz
- PVT Norman L. Carroll
- PVT Harold R. Nigh
- PVT Charles P. Ornstedt
- PVT Milton J. Moore

To Company D
- PVT Walter C. Werth
- PVT Joseph Tyskewicz
- PVT Clarence A. Stough
- PVT Robert Shapiro
- PVT Robert W. Scott
- PVT Charles E. Savage
- CPL Kenneth F. Teats
- CPL Francis E. Wilson
- PVT Edward C. Rosella
- PVT Elton R. Venable
- PVT Juan M. Morales
- PVT Luther E. Krantz
- PVT Virgil A. Stavrum
- PVT Raymond Scott
- PVT Robert J. Reinarts
- PVT John D. Pritchett
- PVT Bernard L. Pestle
- PVT Ralph J. O'Neil
- PVT William S. Kendrick
- PVT Charles H. Samuel
- PVT Alfred J. Zurlino
- PVT Leebert L. Whitaker
- PVT Robert H. Walters
- PVT Harold L. Thomas
- PVT Eugene Sizemore
- PVT Richard W. Safrath

To Company E
- PVT George J. Simpson, Jr.
- PVT Constantine J. Pento
- PVT Robert M. Mic-Key
- PVT Maurice McSwain
- PVT Joseph S. DiSalvo
- PVT Robert P. Buchanan
- PVT Nelson L. Irvin

- PVT Orin Shirts
- PVT Ulysses G. Wismer
- PVT William D. Wilkerson
- PVT Patrick J. Travers
- PVT Eugene G. Strutzenberg
- PVT Hartsel H. Schoolcraft
- PVT Alfred C. Pontello
- PVT Samuel R. Shepler
- PVT Joe A. Placencia
- PVT George B. Modugno
- PVT Gerald R. Poehlman
- PVT Lyman K. Shawler
- PVT Kester C. Summers

To Company F
- PVT Henry D. Covello
- PVT John A. Patton
- SSGT Mark C. Williamson
- PVT Harold E. O'Brian
- PFC Charles R. Jacobsen
- PVT William L. Sandoval
- PVT Raymond L. Witter
- PVT Arthur C. Williamson, Jr.
- PVT Harry S. Rabb
- PVT Arch D. Williams
- PVT Robert C. Whitney
- PVT Joseph F. Tague
- PVT Edward C. Swanson
- PVT Harry J. Tebich
- PVT Elmer C. Stevenson
- PVT James H. Nunn
- PVT Philip H. Nadler
- PVT John L. Myers
- PFC Richard J. Martin
- PVT Anthony G. Marlow
- PVT Joseph R. Kurtz
- PVT John D. Kington
- PVT Alphonse R. Bourgoin
- PFC Albert A. Petrarca
- PVT George R. Sutor
- PFC James F. Stivers
- PVT Robert H. Shantz
- PVT Marvin C. Scroggins

To Company G
- PVT Joyce P. Brakken
- SSGT Albert M. Zardeneta
- PVT Stanley Hulkewiez

- PVT William E. Morphew
- PVT Anthony J. Petroziello
- PVT Robert J. Santucci
- PVT Jesse F. Philhower
- PVT Joseph Randazzo
- PVT John R. McLane
- PVT Eugene H. Scott
- PVT Robert B. Elliott
- PVT Ray H. Johnson
- PVT James E. McLeod
- PVT Leonard V. Modlinski
- PVT Clarence A. Rogers
- PVT Gonzalo C. Ramos
- PVT William A. Adams
- PVT Morris H. Zimmerman
- PVT Wesley R. White
- PVT Everett E. Smith
- PVT James J. Ward
- PVT Charles R. Mercer
- SGT Charlie B. Powell
- PVT Robert L. Amend
- PVT Vern L. Hutchcraft
- PVT John L. Burba, Jr.
- PVT Lester C. Burke
- PVT Ralph E. Simmons
- PVT Pius J. Miller
- PVT Homer L. Miller
- PVT Chester S. Kozinski
- PVT John R. Jasak
- PVT Raymond W. Holsti

To Company H
- PVT Fred C. Jarrell
- PVT Edward A. Kancir
- PVT Earl W. Keihl
- PVT Edward J. Kelly
- PFC Richard Rymer
- PVT Patrick Mickles
- PVT Vincent L. Vecchio
- PVT John O. Prieto
- PVT Malverne N. Moyer
- PVT John Shalonis
- PVT Edgar M. Stone
- PVT Edmund L. Quade
- PVT Douglas R. Reich
- PVT Kenneth H. Ristau

To Company I

- PVT Michael C. Valdes
- PVT Levi Simmons
- PVT Eugene B. Shaffer
- PVT Dante Sansiveri
- PVT Joseph R. Relac
- PVT Charles W. Pearce
- PVT Gerald E. Melton
- PVT Clyde C. McVinny
- PVT Edward D. Hermosillo
- PVT Arlen R. Greene
- PVT James G. Boetter
- PVT Leo Blanchette
- PVT Norland W. Allison
- PFC Julius M. Popp
- PVT Thomas D. Kasper
- PVT Howard L. Meeks
- PVT Ledlie R. Pace
- PFC Leonard G. Trimble
- PVT Orval R. Gilleland

To Headquarters Company, 1st Battalion
- PVT John J. Skrzynski
- PVT Russell C. Knotts
- PVT William A. Roth
- PVT Joseph Marks
- PVT Billie G. Howard
- PVT John M. Hughes
- PVT Thomas P. McDermott
- PVT Charles W. Bender
- PVT Glyn Ashmore
- PVT Andy Paul
- PVT Matt L. Boardman
- PVT Thomas J. Timone
- PVT Peter L. Ragolio
- PVT Eulan V. Layshot
- PVT Solon W. Whitmire
- PVT Fred H. Saar
- PVT Mathew W. Kantala, Jr.
- PVT Harry F. Roberts
- PVT Snowey T. Quick
- PVT Stanley J. Krokowski
- PVT Henry Phaneuf
- PVT Charles L. Ramsey
- PFC Donald E. Harden
- PVT Joe C. Spencer
- PVT Carl J. Sproles

- PVT Donald L. Simpson
- PVT Louis Ryoko
- PVT Norman O. Tarter
- PVT Rex D. Taplin
- PVT Vernon R. Sult
- PVT Charles Stiliha, Jr.
- PVT Frank Scherer
- PVT Arden P. Rohrer, Jr.
- PVT James J. Miller
- PVT Carl Anderson
- PVT Henry C. Marriner
- PFC Teddy L. Hunt

To Headquarters Company, 2nd Battalion
- PVT Robert E. McNally
- PVT Kenneth L. Kretsinger
- PVT Orie Nutter
- PVT Robert E. Snell
- PVT Raymond L. Rivers
- PFC William C. Ament
- PFC Harold J. O'Connor
- PVT Wallace R. Jones
- PVT William J. Mitulski
- PVT John J. Wasko
- PVT Wayne W. Tonningsmeyer
- PVT George M. Moran

To Headquarters Company, 3rd Battalion
- PVT Carl S. Swaggerty
- PVT Joseph V. Hamilton
- PVT Hubert L. Gafford
- PVT Donald G. Scallen
- PVT Harvey W. Schultz
- PVT Victor G. Rosca
- PVT Wallace J. Robinson
- PFC Robert G. Villareal
- PVT Martin M. DiFrancisco
- PVT Donald C. McLean
- PVT Charles V. D'Esposito
- PVT Robert R. Pettit
- SGT William J. Curtis
- PVT James J. Kilcullen
- CPL Martin J. Lofaro
- PVT Anthony P. Mann
- PVT Gabriel M. McNeel
- PVT Robert C. Ramsey

CASUALTIES FOR THE 504TH PARACHUTE INFANTRY REGIMENT FOR THE BATTLE OF MONTE SAMMUCRO

First Battalion – LTC Warren Williams
- 2nd Lt. Stanley J. Whitman, A/504, 20DEC
- CPL Carl E. Bales, C/504, 15DEC
- CPL Nicholas Moolick, B/504, 27DEC
- CPL Walter E. Smith, HQ1, 15DEC
- CPL William C. Johnson, HQ1, 14DEC
- PFC Amos R. Cundiff, A/504, 20DEC
- PFC Bennie H. Roach, B/504, 14DEC
- PFC Herald L. Rodman, A/504, 20DEC
- PFC Hugh L. Donnelly, C/504, 14DEC
- PFC Joseph J. Monte, C/504, 14DEC
- PFC Joseph R. Brain, Jr., A/504, 13DEC
- PFC Richard R. Glenn, HQ1, 15DEC
- PFC Roy Q. Hickman, C/504, 21DEC
- PFC Theodore J. Kowalski, HQ1, 14DEC
- PVT Arthur H. Farrell, C/504, 14DEC
- PVT Charles E. Nau, B/504, 28DEC
- PVT Edward L. Howard, B/504, 27DEC
- PVT Harry Gerahoff, HQ1, 14DEC
- PVT Ian G. McKee, B/504, 14DEC
- PVT Michael J. Komar, B/504, 14DEC
- PVT Stanley F. Szczebak, HQ1, 14DEC
- SGT John J. Mitek, HQ1, 15DEC
- SGT William J. Schlachter, A/504, 30DEC
- SSGT Robert J. Lowe, A/504, 22DEC
- SSGT William P. Walsh, C/504, 25DEC

Second Battalion – MAJ Daniel W. Danielson / MAJ Melvin St. John Blitch
- 1SGT Elbert Peck, F/504, 17DEC
- 1SGT Fredrick J. O'Brian, E/504, 16DEC
- 1st Lt. Herbert H. Norman, D/504, 16DEC
- 1st Lt. John L. Watson, HQ2, 16DEC
- 1st Lt. Joseph H. Boes, D/504, 15DEC
- 1st Lt. William P. Jordan, HQ2 (Medic), 13DEC
- 2nd Lt. Earl F. Morrison, D/504, 15DEC (DOW 18DEC)
- 2nd Lt. John H. Murphy, Jr., E/504, 16DEC
- 2nd Lt. Martin E. Middleton, F/504, 15DEC
- 2nd Lt. Partick C. Collins, E/504, 16DEC
- 2nd Lt. Richard A. Harris, F/504, 15DEC
- 2nd Lt. Richard E. Thompson, E/504, 16DEC
- 2nd Lt. Thomas D. Collins, F/504, 15DEC
- 2nd Lt. Virgil F. Carmichael, HQ2, 17DEC
- 2nd Lt. William L. Watson, F/504, 15DEC
- CPL Charles E. Dorrington, HQ2, 17DEC
- CPL Frank C. Waggoner, E/504, 19DEC
- CPL John F. Gumiela, F/504, 12DEC
- CPL John F. Schwindl, F/504, 16DEC
- CPL Joseph J. Jusek, HQ2, 16DEC

- CPL Peter Plichta, HQ2, 17DEC
- CPL Taylor Isaacs, E/504, 16DEC
- CPT Malcom A. Nicolson, HQ2, 17DEC
- MAJ Daniel W. Danielson, HQ2, 17DEC
- PFC Alvin Jenness, D/504, 15DEC
- PFC Burtis J. Fewox, E/504, 12DEC
- PFC Carolous O. Wessinger, D/504, 15DEC
- PFC Curits L. Fulton, F/504, 12DEC
- PFC Donald A. Head, D/504, 15DEC
- PFC Edward H. McFeeley, F/504, 16DEC
- PFC Edward J. Beaton, F/504, 15DEC
- PFC Edward P. Savage, E/504, 16DEC
- PFC Ernest L. Dixon, F/504, 13DEC
- PFC Frank Masel, Jr., F/504, 13DEC
- PFC George E. Armhold, E/504, 16DEC
- PFC Glennis V. Karns, F/504, 13DEC
- PFC Herbert C. Rosser, F/504, 15DEC
- PFC James C. Weidenheimer, E/504, 16DEC
- PFC James H. Roberts, HQ2, 17DEC
- PFC John D. Rupprecht, HQ2, 17DEC
- PFC Kenneth B. Thompson, E/504, 16DEC
- PFC Lars H. Nylen, D/504, 13DEC
- PFC Mathew A. Novak, D/504, 13DEC
- PFC Melvin C. Gentry, E/504, 14DEC
- PFC Michael J. Buck, HQ2, 17DEC
- PFC Phillip W. Hammond, D/504, 15DEC (DOW 20DEC)
- PFC Rocco F. Tripodi, HQ2, 16DEC
- PFC Walter J. Chmiel, E/504, 16DEC
- PFC Walter L. Rogers, F/504, 13DEC
- PFC William E. Grigg, E/504, 16DEC
- PFC William J. Garvey, Jr., F/504, 13DEC
- PFC William K. Pierce, F/504, 13DEC
- PVT Aaron I. Richards, D/504, 14DEC
- PVT Alfred L. Stone, Jr., E/504, 16DEC
- PVT Angelo A. Fiorentino, D/504, 16DEC
- PVT Burdell G. Miller, E/504, 16DEC
- PVT Charles N. Williams, HQ2, 16DEC
- PVT David Pogoloff, E/504, 16DEC
- PVT Donald Hiegel, F/504, 16DEC
- PVT Edward E. Renfeldt, E/504, 16DEC
- PVT Edwin E. Prescott, D/504, 15DEC
- PVT Elbert G. Stafford, E/504, 16DEC
- PVT Ellis L. Stewart, F/504, 13DEC
- PVT Elmer C. Guske, HQ2, 17DEC
- PVT Eugene W. Plonta, F/504, 13DEC
- PVT Frank Panjic, D/504, 15DEC
- PVT Fred Archer, Jr., D/504, 13DEC
- PVT George A. Ramentol, D/504, 15DEC
- PVT George A. Ruff, E/504, 16DEC
- PVT George M. Moran, HQ2, 17DEC
- PVT Gerald R. Poehlman, E/504, 17DEC
- PVT Harry E. Wilson, HQ2, 17DEC
- PVT Henry A. Bussiere, F/504, 12DEC
- PVT Jack H. Hinton, D/504, 16DEC

- PVT James A. Casey, HQ2, 16DEC
- PVT James D. Cummings, E/504, 16DEC
- PVT James F. Smoot, D/504, 15DEC
- PVT James L. Anderson, HQ2 (Medic), 16DEC
- PVT James W. Whitmire, D/504, 14DEC
- PVT Joe A. Plancencia, E/504, 24DEC
- PVT John C. Deldon, F/504 (Medic), 12DEC
- PVT John E. Boyette, D/504, 17DEC
- PVT John L. Nyzio, E/504, 16DEC
- PVT John M. Lawler, E/504, 16DEC
- PVT John W. Stier, F/504, 13DEC
- PVT Joseph Lynch, HQ2, 17DEC
- PVT Joseph P. Capobianco, D/504, 15DEC
- PVT Lathion L. Foster, F/504, 12DEC
- PVT Louis R. Segreti, F/504, 13DEC
- PVT Marceline R. Castillo, HQ2, 16DEC
- PVT Otis Page, HQ/2, 12DEC
- PVT Paul G. Cholka, E/504, 16DEC
- PVT Ray Carpenter, F/504, 13DEC
- PVT Robert Elsner, D/504, 17DEC
- PVT Robert J. Walker, E/504, 16DEC
- PVT Robert M. DeLaite, E/504, 16DEC
- PVT Robert W. Beggs, E/504, 16DEC
- PVT Roger S. Miller, HQ2, 16DEC
- PVT Salvador Rubio, HQ2, 17DEC
- PVT Shirley E. Addison, F/504, 16DEC
- PVT Stephen F. Drobnak, Jr., E/504, 16DEC
- PVT Thomas E. Bodiford, F/504, 15DEC
- PVT William A. Maney, E/504, 16DEC
- PVT William J. Zaremski, F/504, 16DEC
- PVT William P. Prodger, Jr., F/504, 16DEC
- PVT Willord C. Forrest, HQ2, 16DEC
- PVT Wilson C. Drinkuth, E/504, 19DEC
- SGT Blair B. Brumbaugh, D/504, 15DEC
- SGT Buell R. Snowden, D/504, 14DEC
- SGT Henry A. Duby, Jr., D/504, 15DEC
- SGT James B. Howard, E/504, 16DEC
- SGT John W. McGarrah, E/504, 16DEC
- SGT Raymond Gray, D/504, 15DEC
- SGT Simon T. Young, F/504, 12DEC
- SGT Stanley V. Wrocinski, F/504, 15DEC
- SSGT Esmer O. Partridge, F/504, 16DEC
- T/4 Antone Ozanich, HQ2, 17DEC
- T/5 Henry F. Hajdack, HQ2, 15DEC
- T/5 Stephen R. Suran, HQ2, 17DEC

Third Battalion – LTC Leslie Freeman
- 1SGT Mike Vincent, G/504, 12DEC
- 1st Lt. Charles A. Drew, G/504, 12DEC
- 2nd Lt. William D. Mandle, I/504, 12DEC
- CPL Arthur J. Flaherty, I/504, 11DEC
- CPL Norman H. Peppler, G/504, 12DEC
- CPL Vernon M. Evenson, I/504, 11DEC
- CPL William E. McGrath, HQ3, 12DEC
- PFC Albert Nesgoda, I/504, 11DEC

- PFC Edward C. Hoehle, I/504, 11DEC
- PFC Emil J. Mierzwa, I/504, 11DEC
- PFC Floyd E. Nusbaum, I/504, 11DEC
- PFC Frank G. Hatcher, I/504, 11DEC
- PFC Fred C. Stuckey, Jr., H/504, 11DEC
- PFC Glenn W. Foust, RHQ/504, 12DEC
- PFC James M. Haines, I/504, 11DEC
- PFC John B. Raulerson, RHQ/504, 12DEC
- PFC John C. Thiemann, G/504, 12DEC
- PFC Louis V. Whittington, H/504, 11DEC
- PFC Millard E. Mineer, G/504, 12DEC
- PFC Nicholas N. Stampone, H/504, 11DEC
- PFC Olin G. Marlow, G/504, 12DEC
- PFC Peter A. Caiello, G/504, 12DEC
- PFC Robert G. Anglemyer, H/504, 11DEC (DOW 15DEC)
- PFC Wiley L. Braddy, I/504, 11DEC
- PFC William J. George, G/504, 12DEC
- PFC Wilton Baker, RHQ/504, 13DEC
- PFC Zigmund J. Krajewski, H/504, 15DEC
- PVT Albert Weidner, HQ3, 12DEC
- PVT Alfred A. Carter, I/504, 11DEC
- PVT Alfred Hurtado, H/504, 23DEC
- PVT Charles W. Prichard, G/504, 26DEC
- PVT Clarence R. Stanford, I/504, 12DEC
- PVT Daun Z. Rice, H/504, 27DEC
- PVT David B. Cassetti, H/504, 11DEC
- PVT Edward M. Welsh, H/504, 11DEC
- PVT Edward P. Ustaski, I/504, 12DEC
- PVT Francis J. Bardon, G/504, 12DEC
- PVT Francis L. Campbell, H/504 (Medic), 13DEC
- PVT Francis W. McLane, I/504, 12DEC
- PVT Harold E. Bartlett, I/504, 11DEC
- PVT James E. McDonald, I/504, 11DEC
- PVT John F. McAndrew, 11DEC
- PVT John Galik, I/504, 11DEC
- PVT Laurence A. Allan, I/504, 11DEC
- PVT Leroy M. Simmons, I/504, 11DEC
- PVT Louis P. Holt, H/504, 11DEC
- PVT Oddie L. Berry, G/504 (Medic), 12DEC
- PVT Raymond H. Grummer, I/504, 11DEC
- PVT Robert Sullivan, I/504, 12DEC
- PVT Rubin McKay, I/504 (Medic), 11DEC
- PVT Samuel J. Garcia, G/504, 12DEC
- PVT Sylvester Larkin, H/504, 11DEC
- PVT Valentine Maliborski, H/504, 11DEC
- PVT William D. Willis, G/504, 26DEC
- SGT Albert L. Furman, I/504, 12DEC
- SGT David A. Johnson, H/504, 11DEC
- SGT Fred W. Thomas, H/504, 11DEC
- SGT James Allen, Jr., H/504, 13DEC
- SGT John D. Frantzen, I/504, 12DEC
- SGT Robert G. Dew, I/504, 11DEC

- SGT William L. Davis, Jr., I/504, 11DEC
- SSGT Edmund J. Burke, G/504, 12DEC
- SSGT Glenn A. MacDonald, I/504, 11DEC
- SSGT Lloyd V. Engelbretson, I/504, 11DEC
- T/5 Dominick P. LaFratta, I/504, 11DEC
- T/5 Henry C. Hoffman, G/504, 12DEC

Regimental Headquarters Company[1]
- CPT Francis G. Sheehan, 17DEC
- PFC Glenn A. Martin, 11DEC
- PVT Harry L. Michael, Jr., 16DEC
- PVT Leon T. Hold, 11DEC
- PVT William C. Kline, 16DEC

TOTALS:
First Battalion: 25
Second Battalion: 119
Third Battalion: 66
HQ-HQ: 5

Grand total: 215

---

[1] Attachments to rifle companies from HQ-HQ are listed with the battalions to which they were attached.

PARATROOPERS OF THE 504TH PARACHUTE INFANTRY ROTATED BACK TO THE STATES AFTER ANZIO TO FORM CADRE FOR THE 515TH PARACHUTE INF.

B Company

SGT Victor C. Ivey
CPL John Burns
PFC Jacob Cantelmo
PFC Clifford V. Cutrer

C Company

PFC Hugh L. Donnelly
SGT Ray U. Justice
SGT Jesse G. Smith
PFC Walter W. Gasiorek

D Company

CPT Andrew (William) Row

E Company

1SGT Kenneth O. Winn
PFC Glenn Anderson
PFC George A. Ruff

F Company

PVT Anthony G. Marlow
SSGT Henry P. Cody
SGT Stanley V. Wrocinski
PFC George S. Heffer
PFC Elmer D. Lamance

G Company

1SGT Mike Vincent
SGT Clyde B. Shoemaker
PFC Estle E. McCarty

PFC Charles J. Melle

H Company

PVT Patrick H. Mickles
1SGT Kello A. Goodner
SGT Shelby R. Hord
PFC George M. Harrison
PFC Pete F. Tkachyk

I Company

SGT Vernon M. Evenson
TECH4 E.J. Forshee
PFC Lawrence E. Gerry

Medical Detachment

PVT Edward R. Dinoski
TECH5 George P. Gardiner
TECH5 Leroy Munn
CPL Albert R. Creal
SSGT Ernest G. Crosby

Regimental Headquarters

PVT Eugene B. Vankirk
MAJ Henry B. Frank
1LT Edwin B. Bigger
MSGT Philip P. Byrne
SSGT Theodore J. Pozzi
PFC Roy H. Leaka
PFC William W. Bennett

Headquarters Company, 1st Battalion

1LT George A. Noury
SSGT Robert W. Lambert
TECH5 William M. McKinley
PFC Elmer A. Enos
PFC Leonard W. Wahl

Headquarters Company, 2nd Battalion

TECH5 Stephen R. Suran
MAJ Melvin Blitch
1LT Lewis P. Fern
2LT Russell V. Sisson
SSGT Stanley G. Smith
CPL Thomas C. Ereon
CPL John E. Pillsbury
PVT Maynard J. Kemble
CPL Wesley V. Holmes

Headquarters Company, 3rd Battalion

LTC Leslie G. Freeman
CPT Richard D. Aldridge
1LT Peter J. Eaton
SSGT Elbert L. Claunts
TECH5 John W. Colson
PFC James W. Robinson
PVT Edward E. McCrann

Service Company

1SGT Walter T. Carlock
SSGT Robert R. Davis
SSGT Wrensey A. James
SSGT Rossie J. Ross
PVT Warren E. Ricketts

Afterword

World War II veterans are an important part of the history of any unit, and the founders of most known mottos. For example, the 82nd Airborne Division, especially the 504th Parachute Infantry Regiment, is well known for their "Strike and Hold" motto and are called the "Devils in Baggy Pants." Both of these were assigned to the unit after events that occurred during World War II and they remain today. A First Sergeant that served in the 82nd Airborne Division for over six years stated: "The Devils in Baggy Pants: the most revered regiment in the greatest division in the Army."

I had the opportunity to serve in the 1st Brigade Combat Team (1BCT), 504th PIR for five years. Working as the Brigade Adjutant, I had the opportunity to participate, plan, and coordinate veterans' events and commemoration ceremonies. I was amazed by the history and the impact most of these veterans had over such a storied unit. War heroes like COL (R) James Kiernan, LTC (R) James Megellas, MAJ (R) Moffatt Burriss, CPT (R) Roy Hanna, PFC (R) Francis Keefe, PVT (R) Robert DeVinney… They fought over 300 days on the frontlines and some of them even wrote their memories in books that are used as tools for leadership development today.

The Netherlands celebrates Operation Market Garden every year during the month of September. Volunteers from all different communities come together to plan and celebrate commemoration ceremonies based on the impact World War II veterans had over each town. From all the commemorations I had the opportunity to be a part of, Sunset March is no doubt the biggest commemoration of them all. The Sunset March is celebrated every evening at De Oversteek Bridge, over the Waal River in Nijmegen. This bridge has 48 sets of lights that turn on as a veteran walks by them in remembrance of the 48 504th PIR paratroopers that lost their life crossing the river on 20 September 1944. In September 2018, 74 years after the crossing, two 504th PIR World War II paratroopers, LTC (R) James Megellas and CPT (R) Roy Hanna, had the opportunity to walk the bridge together. It was an honor to be part of such an amazing moment in history. Later that day, CPT (R) Roy Hanna was presented the Orange Lanyard which is the highest award in the Netherlands, equivalent to our Medal of Honor. CPT (R) Roy Hanna was not present the day the unit was awarded the orange lanyard back in 1945 and he finally received it 73 years later.

The active participation of the veterans and the keeping of history is felt throughout the 82nd Airborne Division to this day. Every year during All American Week, veterans are invited to different activities and are recognized by soldiers and families. The Division Hall of Fame, which had the first induction ceremony during AAW in 2018, has inducted three 504th PIR World War II paratroopers. These paratroopers are LTC (R) James Megellas, MAJ (R) Moffatt Burriss, and CPT (R) Roy Hanna. Also, during the 1BCT Change of Command in 2017, the 504th PIR Regimental Room was named after CPT (R) Roy

Hanna. These events, and others like the induction of Honorary and Distinguished Members of the Regiment, Prop Blast and Leadership Development Programs, always make veterans and their heroic acts a priority. The veterans have left a legacy for years on end and their history will forever be known as the "Devils in Baggy Pants."

Captain Wilmarie Flores Alvarez
Distinguished Member of the 504th PIR
Active Duty Historian of the 504th PIR Association

Acknowledgements

I want to open this text by, first and foremost, thanking the veterans of the 504th Parachute Infantry Regiment; and I specifically want to thank two groups of veterans. Firstly, those paratroopers who lost their lives fighting under the command. Their sacrifice wrote this story. Secondly, I want to thank the veterans who helped me compile and tell this story. Through their generosity, they have helped to ensure - at least I like to think so - that the story of those comrades who they left behind in Europe is preserved for further study and future generations.

There are four veterans who have been especially influential on this work. As with my first book, both Fred Baldino and Marvin Courtney were huge inspirations. Although they both passed by the time this work really took shape, the interest they fed and the inspiration they gave me were both large influencers and I hope I did them proud.

For this work in particular there are two veterans whose inspiration and input were absolutely vital: Roy Hanna and Francis Keefe.

Without Francis Keefe, this work would have looked much different. He has been among the most generous with his time and himself, always making himself available for questions or just to talk. We spent many, many hours on the phone and in person and he was always telling me the trivial details of life on the front. "Stuff like that is always left out, you know," he would say when he would tell me why they would throw their lemonade packets away under certain circumstances. Francis is without doubt one of the sweetest men I've ever known. To give an example, I was telling him that I was going to try and go to Italy and climb Hill 950 and Monte Sammucro, one of their battlegrounds, and he said that was a bad idea because he was worried I would step on a mine or on one of the many dud artillery shells that landed near their positions. If I really wanted to go, he volunteered to pay for a helicopter so I could fly over the mountain to observe. That is an example of the caliber of man Francis Keefe is.

Roy Hanna's support and contributions are almost too numerous to list. There are certain parts I submitted to him to review, and in those parts he even rewrote a few paragraphs and his rewrites appear herein.

There were many places where this book was written but one of them was in Roy's apartment. Roy graciously played host to me during my many visits to North Carolina, and my many memories at his dining table, of playing card games and talking, will accompany me to the grave. To many he will be remembered as a war hero, but to me he will be remembered as a close friend, and his friendship has been an honor.

There are many others throughout my life and research that have so freely given their time and knowledge, that have made it possible for me to write this, such as my parents for enabling me to do this by providing for me a blessed life. Naming all of these people would be a long undertaking and so in the interest of brevity I will only mention those who made this specific work a reality.

Interwoven into the regiment's story here presented, is the story is the story of one of its most cherished lieutenants. Throughout my years of research, the name Edward Kennedy often popped up. I heard stories of him from Moffatt Burriss and Roy Hanna, who as you will read are both valiant and respected combat leaders in their own right and men who I know and look up to. Both Burriss and Hanna thought very well of Kennedy, and when they hold someone else in high regard, I pay attention.

For two years, I searched off and on for the Kennedy's from Massachusetts. I found there to be no shortage of families with that name in the area. After a chance discovery, I finally found them.

In short order I came into contact with many Kennedy's; including Ed Kennedy, nephew of Lieutenant Ed Kennedy and his uncle's namesake. Ed graciously shared all the information he had with me. It was an appreciable amount, as his aunt Pat Cavagnaro - Lieutenant Kennedy's little sister - and her husband had assembled information about Kennedy's wartime service through the years. There were many photos, but through Kennedy's letters to the family which she saved, as well as through the stories I had heard from veterans, I felt that I got to know not "Lieutenant Kennedy," but "Eddie," a brave paratrooper, a devout Catholic, and a consummate gentleman - the exemplar of the citizen-soldier upon which our Army was founded.

Since the time I have been in touch with the Kennedy's, they have welcomed me both in person and on Facebook or phone, and I can now call some of the "Kennedy clan" friends. I am profoundly grateful and indebted to the entire Kennedy family for their assistance in helping me with my research on Eddie, and entrusting me with the story of their uncle.

The Kennedy's were not the only family to have significant contribution to this work. The family of the late Lieutenant Thomas Utterback contributed portions of their own family archives. Lieutenant Utterback was a faithful writer who vibrantly described his thoughts and feelings on the war and his life overseas through his letters virtually every day. Several have been quoted at length, and they provide a wonderful window into the thoughts of a parachute officer in WWII. We are also in great debt to Laurie

Utterback for sharing and allowing the use of her grandfather's historic remembrances which he wrote later in life.

Dale McOmber contributed valuable information about his uncle Lieutenant Marshall McComber, who was among the first 504th paratroopers killed in action. Dale provided many letters his uncle wrote home from training at Fort Bragg, many photographs and documents of McComber's life, and a few items of interest pertaining to McComber's best friend, Captain George Watts.

I am also deeply indebted to Dutch historian Jan Bos, who was introduced to me by WWII veteran Fred Baldino. Jan Bos has dedicated much of his life to the preservation of the history of the 82nd Airborne Division, and his guidance, advice and assistance have been greatly appreciated. He was also the one who provided copies of portions of Earl Oldfather's diary, and several excerpts appear herein.

History enthusiasts who read this book should owe a great debt to the families of Irvin Bushman and Alfred Landgraff. Both of these officers were attached to the 504th as the Officer in Charge of the secretive Interrogation Prisoner of War Team #45. One of the most unique things about this manuscript are first-person accounts of German soldiers who were fighting, and later captured, by the men of the 504th. These stories were sourced from the interrogation of these Germans by Bushman and Landgraff after their capture. Thankfully, the papers were saved by these two officers, and later preserved by their children, who were very gracious in providing copies of these unique intelligence documents.

There are dozens of others who did yeomen's work in getting information for me to put into this work, but you will soon read about them.

Tyler S. Fox
May 5, 2019

SELECTED BIBLIOGRAPHY

<u>Personal Interviews</u>

Baldino, Fred J. (A/504)

Bayley, Edwin R. (A/504)

Bonning, William L. (B/504)

Bramson, Robert E. (F/504)

Breard, Reneau G. (A; B/504)

Broadaway, Rufus K. (Service/507th PIR; Headquarters, 82nd Airborne Division; H/504)

Brooks, Jack (1st Infantry Division)

Burriss, Thomas M. (I; HQ3/504)

Courtney, Marvin R. (B/504)

DeVinney, Robert R. (H/504)

Dodd, Gilbert E. (C/504)

Edgren, Emil (US Army Signal Corps)

Fary, Raymond (C/80th ABN Anti-Tank)

Gann, James (G; RHQ/504)

Haider, Edward P. (I/504)

Hanna, Roy M. (HQ3; G; I/504)

Hannigan, William J. (H/504)

Holmstock, Morris (B/504)

Hughes, Walter E. (I/504)

Johnson, John R. Jr. (37th Troop Carrier Squadron)

Keefe, Francis X. (I/504)

Parker, Gerald A. (53rd Troop Carrier Squadron)

Sapp, James T. (HQ2/504)

Speer, Werner (F/504)

Tassinari, Albano (HQ2/504)

Unrah, Jerome (C/307 AEB)

Wallis, Hugh D. (H/504)

Wickersham, Ollie B. (C/307 AEB)

Zimmerman, Harry D. (H/504)

Books

American Forces in Action: Anzio Beachhead (22 January-25 May 1944). Historical Division, War Department (1948)

Antonaccio, Thomas E. *The Generosity of Strangers: When War Came to Fornelli.* Privately published (2014)

Blumenson, Martin. *United States Army in World War II, the Mediterranean Theater of Operations: Salerno to Cassino.* United States Army, Center for Military History (1993).

Burriss, Thomas M. *Strike and Hold.* Brasley's (2001)

Carter, Ross S. *Those Devils in Baggy Pants.* Signet Books (1951).

Churchill, Winston S. *The Second World War: Volume V Closing the Ring.* (Houghton Mifflin Company (1951)

Clark, Mark W. *Calculated Risk.* Enigma Books (2007).

Garland, Albert N., Smity, Howard M. & Blumenson, Martin. *Sicily and the Surrender of Italy.* US Army Center for Military History (1993)

Mandel, William D. and Whittier, David H., *The Devils in Baggy Pants: Combat Record of the 504th Parachute Infantry Regiment, April 1943 – July 1945.* Draeger Freres (1945)

Megellas, James, *All the Way to Berlin: A Paratrooper at War in Europe.* Presidio Press (2004)

Mrozek, Steven J. *Prop Blast: Chronicle of the 504th Parachute Infantry Regiment.* 82nd Airborne Division Historical Society (1986).

Nordyke, Phil. *More Than Courage: Sicily, Naples-Foggia, Anzio, Rhineland, Ardennes-Alsace, Central Europe: The Combat History of the 504th Parachute Infantry Regiment in World War II.* Zenith Press (2008).

Tregaskis, Richard. *Invasion Diary.* Random House (1944)

Van Lunteren, Frank. *Spearhead of the Fifth Army: The 504th Parachute Infantry Regiment in Italy, from the Winter Line to Anzio.* Casemate (2016).

Documents & Articles

504th Parachute Infantry Prop-Blast: Germany Edition. Monday, 23 April 1944. Volume II, Edition four. Personal possession of Roy Hanna.

Adams, Emory S. *S-3 Operations Summery.* Headquarters, 504th Parachute Infantry. 05 February 1944. Anzio Beachhead, Italy. Courtesy of the US Army's Combined Arms Research Library, Fort Leavenworth, Kansas.

Chapman, William E. "What is a Parachutist? Here's Their Version". *The Burlington Daily Times-News.* November 3, 1942.

Company I, 3d Bn, 504th Para Regt, 82d Abn Div. Document. Courtesy of Jan Bos.

Garrison, Chester A. *An Ivy League Paratrooper*. Unpublished manuscript (1996)

Garrison, Chester A. "Unit Journal of the 2nd Battalion, 504th Parachute Infantry." Courtesy of James Sapp.

Nicoll, Kenneth. Diary. Courtesy of the 2nd Battalion, 504th PIR, 1st Brigade Combat Team, 82nd Airborne Division.

"Narrative of Action on the Anzio Beachhead". Headquarters, 504th Parachute Combat Team, n.d.

Utterback, Thomas E. "Memories of World War II." Unpublished memoir. Courtesy of Laurie Utterback.

Whittier, David H. Private First Class. *Division Wants Prisoners: Patrol Along the Wyler Meer.* Article. *The Infantry Journal*. April 1945. Personal possession of Colonel Reneau Breard.

Whittier, David H. "Battle of Cheneux." Headquarters, 504th Paracute Infantry. Courtesy of Donovan Research Library.

<u>Letters</u>

Personal letters of David Rosenkrantz, C/O Phillip Rosenkrantz

Personal letters of Roy Hanna, C/O Roy Hanna.

Personal letters of Thomas Utterback, C/O Laurie Utterback

Personal letters of Edwin E. Decker, C/O Marcia Decker

Personal letters of Don B. Dunham, C/O Susan Murphy

Personal letters of Edward W. Kennedy, personal possession of author.

Notes & Complete List of Sources

[1] Mroso, John A. "Americans Watch Air Display, Then Move to Chosen Targets." *Poughkeepsie Journal*. Friday, July 16, 1943.
[2] Hanna, Roy M. Letter. May 17, 1943. Courtesy Roy Hanna.
[3] Zimmerman, Harry D. Interview with author.
[4] Hanna, Roy M. "My First Combat Jump". Written account. Courtesy of Roy Hanna.
[5] Green, Clinton. "Angeleno 'Captures' Captors – By Request". *The Los Angeles Times*. Friday, July 16, 1943.
[6] "82nd Airborne in Sicily and Italy."
[7] Vermillion, Robert. "Even a Million Cheers Won't Erase Memories of Dead Buddies as Famed 82nd Marches in N.Y. Parade". *Democrat and Chronicle*. Saturday, January 12, 1946.
[8] "Pvt. Pippen of Panama City Made First Combat Jump to Land on Sicilian House." *Panama City News-Herald*. Monday, August 30, 1943.
[9] "Dropping into Sicily". *The Gastonia Daily Gazette*. Wednesday, September 15, 1943.
[10] Courtney, Marvin R. Interview with author.
[11] Massaro, Chuck. "Now Franklinville Neighbors Veterans Recall Battle Blunder." *Olean Times Herald*. July 28, 1987. A copy of this article was kindly provided by Marcia Decker Ray.
[12] Decker, Edwin E. Letter to his father, Earl Decker. August 7, 1943. Courtesy of Marcia Decker Ray.
[13] Courtney, interview.
[14] Halloran, Robert M. "Army Service Experiences Questionnaire". 82d Airborne Division, Box 1. US Army Heritage and Education Center.
[15] Chapman, William E. "What is a Parachutist? Here's Their Version". *The Burlington Daily Times-News*. November 3, 1942.
[16] Brook, Jack. Interview with author.
[17] Tucker, Reuben H. Response to questionnaire. The Cornelius Ryan Collection, Ohio University. Courtesy Fred J. Baldino.
[18] Garland, Albert N., Smity, Howard M. & Blumenson, Martin. Sicily and the Surrender of Italy. US Army Center for Military History (1993). Page 179.
[19] Tucker, questionnaire.
[20] Komosa, Adam A. "Airborne Operation, 504th Parachute Infantry Regimental Combat Team (82nd Airborne Division), Sicily, 9 July-19 August 1943, Personal Experience of a Regimental Headquarters Company Commander." General Subjects Section, Academic Department, The Infantry School, Ft. Benning, Ga. Courtesy of the Donovan Research Library.
[21] Garrison, Chester A. "Army Service Experiences Questionnaire". 82d Airborne Division, Box 1. US Army Heritage and Education Center.
[22] Garrison, Chester A. *An Ivy League Paratrooper*. Unpublished manuscript (1996). Page 157-161. Personal possession of author. Note: a differing version of this manuscript was later published under the same title in 2002. It was privately published and then printed by The Franklin Press in Corvallis, Oregon.
[23] Sapp, James T. Interview with author.
[24] Levitt, Earl B. Interview. Earl Bernard Levitt Collection (AFC/2001/001/69249), Veterans History Project, American Folklife Center, Library of Congress.
[25] This story was relayed to the author by Jordan's two sons. Their father had told the story several times to them in his later years of life.
[26] Patrick, Carl. "Devils in Baggy Pants". *Static Line*. June 2000. A copy of this article was kindly sent to the author by Jan Bos.
[27] Mack C. Shelley. "Certificate". Headquarters, 61st Troop Carrier Group. August 21, 1943. Courtesy of Jan Bos.
[28] Parker, Gerald A. Interview with author.
[29] Mrozek, Steven J. *Prop Blast: Chronicle of the 504th Parachute Infantry Regiment*. 82nd Airborne Division Historical Society (1986).
[30] Joyner, James. Interview with author.
[31] Mark, Richard. Interview with author.
[32] Hanna, interview.
[33] Mrozek, Steven J. *Prop Blast: Chronicle of the 504th Parachute Infantry Regiment*. 82nd Airborne Division Historical Society (1986).
[34] "Paratroopers Borrow $1000 for DC Visit." *The Washington Post*, January 24, 1943.
[35] Decker, Edwin E. Letter to Alex Kicovic. Courtesy of Marcia Decker Ray.
[36] Komosa, "Airborne Operation".
[37] Hanna, interview.
[38] Hanna, interview.
[39] Moorehead, Edmond Q. Written account. Courtesy of Kathy Dasani.
[40] Komosa, "Airborne Operation".
[41] Moorehead, Edmond Q. Written account. Courtesy of Marilyn Mallow.
[42] Courtney, interview.
[43] Baldino, Fred J. Interview with author.
[44] Sapp, interview.
[45] Komosa, "Airborne Operation".
[46] "Louisville Paratrooper and Sailor Killed in Action". *The Courier-Journal*. Tuesday January 25, 1944.
[47] Sapp, interview.
[48] Thompson, John. "A Soldier Practices What the United Nations Are Preaching." *Detroit Free Press*. Sunday, August 22, 1943.
[49] Thompson, John. "Tells How 410 Paratroopers Died Off Sicily." *Chicago Daily Tribune*. March 19, 1943.

[50] Komosa, "Airborne Operation".
[51] Komosa, "Airborne Operation".
[52] Thompson, John. "A Soldier Practices What the United Nations Are Preaching." *Detroit Free Press*. Sunday, August 22, 1943.
[53] Sapp, interview.
[54] Courtney, interview.
[55] "The Castle". http://sicilia.indettaglio.it/eng/comuni/tp/partanna/turismo/turismo.html. & "Grifeo Partanna Castle Trapani City". http://www.sicily.co.uk/things_to_do/grifeo-partanna-castle/.
[56] Garrison, 168.
[57] Dunham, Don B. Papers. Courtesy Susan Murphy.
[58] Keefe, Francis X. Interview with author.
[59] Keefe, interview.
[60] Hand, Robert. "Operations of the 3rd Battalion, 143rd Infantry (36th Infantry Division) in the Attack on Altavilla, Italy, 13-14 September 1943 (Naples-Foggia Campaign) (Personal Experience of a Platoon Leader). General Subjects Section, Academic Department, The Infantry School, Ft. Benning, Ga. Courtesy of the Donovan Research Library.
[61] "Record of Events, 142d Inf., 36th Division: September 3d to September 20th, 1943." Headquarters, 142d Infantry. Courtesy of the Combined Arms Research Library.
[62] Levitt, interview.
[63] Gann, interview.
[64] Baldino, interview.
[65] Korman, Seymour. "Nightmare at Salerno: Yank Rifles Versus Nazi Artillery". *The Oregonia*. October 3, 1943. A copy of this article was kindly sent to the author by Susan Murphy.
[66] Lekson, John S. "The Operations of the 1st Battalion, 504th Parachute Infantry (82nd Airborne Division) in the Capture of Altavilla, Italy 13 September – 19 September, 1943 (Naples-Foggia Campaign) (Personal Experience of a Battalion Operations Officer)". General Subjects Section, The Infantry School, Ft. Benning, Ga. Courtesy of the Donovan Research Library.
[67] Breard, Reneau G. Interview with author.
[68] "Interview of Lawrence W. Stimpson". https://www.kued.org/sites/default/files/lawrencestimpson.pdf. Accessed 28 July 2018.
[69] Carter, Ross S. *Those Devils in Baggy Pants*. Page 41. Signet Books (1951).
[70] Courtney, interview.
[71] Lekson, "Operations of the 1st Battalion".
[72] Garrison, Chester A. "Unit Journal of the 2nd Battalion, 504th Parachute Infantry". Courtesy James Sapp.
[73] Garrison, "Unit Journal".
[74] Korman, Seymour. "Nightmare at Salerno
[75] Marino, Louis C. Interview with Brock Lucchese. November 9, 2004. Park Tutor School Worlds of War Oral History Collection. http://indiamond6.ulib.iupui.edu/cdm/singleitem/collection/ParkTudorLI/id/147/rec/1. Accessed August 19, 2017.
[76] "Interview of Lawrence W. Stimpson". https://www.kued.org/sites/default/files/lawrencestimpson.pdf. Accessed 28 July 2018.
[77] Marino, interview with Brock Lucchese.
[78] Tregaskis, Richard. *Invasion Diary*. Random House, 1944. Page 110.
[79] Korman, Seymour. "Nightmare at Salerno".
[80] Korman, Seymour. "Nightmare at Salerno".
[81] Korman, Seymour. "Nightmare at Salerno".
[82] Korman, Seymour. "Nightmare at Salerno".
[83] Carter, Ross S. *Those Devils in Baggy Pants*. Page 69-70. Signet Books (1951).
[84] Lekson, "Operations of the 1st Battalion".
[85] Huebner, Otto W. "The Operations of Company 'A', 504th Parachute Infantry (82nd Airborne Division) in the Defense of Hill 424 near Altavilla, Italy 17 September – 19 September, 1943. (Naples-Foggia Campaign) (Personal Experience of the Company Operations Sergeant and Acting First Sergeant)". General Subjects Section, Academic Department, The Infantry School, Ft. Benning, Ga. Courtesy of the Donovan Research Library.
[86] "From Sgt. Jimmy Eldridge". *The Gastonia Daily Gazette*. Wednesday, December 1, 1943.
[87] Hesselburg, Ethel T. Letter to Edwin E. Decker. April 10, 1944. Courtesy of Marcia Decker Ray.
[88] Lekson, "Operations of the 1st Battalion".
[89] *Salerno: American Operations from the Beaches to the Volturno 9 September – 6 October 1943*. United States Army Center for Military History, 1990. Pages 76-79.
[90] Blumenson, Martin. *United States Army in World War II, the Mediterranean Theater of Operations: Salerno to Cassino*. United States Army, Center for Military History, 1993. Page 136.
[91] "Record of Events, 142d Inf., 36th Division: September 3d to September 20th, 1943." Headquarters, 142d Infantry. Courtesy of the Combined Arms Research Library.
[92] Lekson, "Operations of the 1st Battalion".
[93] Hanna, interview.
[94] Hanna, interview.
[95] Keefe, interview.
[96] Courtney, interview.
[97] Lanning, Fred. Notes. Personnel possession of author.
[98] Baldino, interview.
[99] Levitt, interview.
[100] Levitt, interview.
[101] Hanna, interview.

[102] Keefe, interview.
[103] Boyle, Hal. "Steady Weakening of German Air Force Reveled in Italy." *The Plain Speaker*. Wednesday, October 13, 1943.
[104] Tassinari, Albano, interview with author.
[105] Hanna, interview.
[106] Zimmerman, interview.
[107] Kennedy, Edward W. Letter to sister. October 10, 1943. Courtesy of Ed Kennedy.
[108] Baldino, interview.
[109] Baldino, interview.
[110] Baldino, interview.
[111] Baldino, interview.
[112] Lekson, John S. *Major General John S. Lekson, United States Army*. Written account. June 19, 1981. Courtesy of the Lekson family.
[113] Garrison, "Unit Journal".
[114] Hanna, interview.
[115] Rosenkrantz, David. Letter to Harry Rosenkrantz. December 2, 1943. Courtesy Phil Rosenkrantz.
[116] Garrison, "Unit Journal".
[117] Sapp, interview.
[118] Garrison, "Unit Journal".
[119] Garrison, 195-196.
[120] Garrison, "Unit Journal".
[121] Garrison, "Unit Journal".
[122] "Episodio di Gallo Matese (Casterta)". http///www.straginazifasciste.it. Accessed August 19, 2017.
[123] Sapp, interview.
[124] Keefe, interview.
[125] Keefe, interview.
[126] Keefe, interview.
[127] Antonaccio, Thomas E. *The Generosity of Strangers: When War Came to Fornelli*. Privately published (2014).
[128] Keefe, interview.
[129] "S-3 Journal". Headquarters, 504th Combat Team. Entry for 2340, November 7, 1943 & Earl Oldfather Diary, entry for November 7, 1943.
[130] Nordyke, Phil. *More Than Courage: The Combat History of the 504th Parachute Infantry Regiment in World War II*. Zenith Press (2008). Page 113.
[131] Heinz Graalfs as quoted in "Nazi Strongpoint Taken by Platoon" by Don Whitehead. *St. Louis Post-Dispatch*. Monday, November 29, 1943.
[132] Hanna, interview.
[133] Whitehead, Don. "Nazi Strongpoint Taken by Platoon". *St. Louis Post-Dispatch*, November 29, 1943 & Nordyke, *More Than Courage*, Page 114.
[134] Heinz Graalfs as quoted in "Nazi Strongpoint Taken by Platoon" by Don Whitehead. St. Louis Post-Dispatch. Monday, November 29, 1943.
[135] "Biddle Family Papers," Finding aid prepared by the Historical Society of Pennsylvania's Hidden Collections Initiative for Pennsylvania Small Archival Repositories.
[136] "Biddle Family Papers: Finding Aid Prepared by the Historical Society of Pennsylvania's Hidden Collections Iniative for Pennsylvania Small Archival Repositories Using Data Provided by Andalusia Foundation." Andalusia Foundation.
[137] Hanna, interview.
[138] Keep, Henry B. Letter to Charles Biddle, November 22, 1943. Gertrude Sanford Legendre Papers, 1844-1996. Gertrude Sanford Legendre Papers: Correspondence. College of Charleston Libraries.
[139] "S-3 Journal". Headquarters, 504th Combat Team. Entry for 1600, November 18, 1943.
[140] Carter, Ross S. *Those Devils in Baggy Pants*. Page 69-70. Signet Books (1951).
[141] Fox, Tyler S. *Our Salvation: The 504th Parachute Infantry Regiment's Legendary Fight at Altavilla*. Createspace, 2016.
[142] Gann, interview.
[143] Gann, interview.
[144] Whitehead, Don. "3-Story House Scene of Wild Fight by Yanks." *The Longview Daily News*, December 7, 1943.
[145] Whitehead, Don. "3-Story House Scene of Wild Fight by Yanks." The Longview Daily News, December 7, 1943 & Garrison, "Unit Journal."
[146] Garrison, "Unit Journal"
[147] Whitehead, Don. "Peasant Woman Carry Supplies on Heads to Yanks in Mountains". *Lubbock Avalanche-Journal*. Sunday, November 28, 1943.
[148] Hanna, interview.
[149] Halloran, questionnaire.
[150] Gann, interview.
[151] Keefe, interview.
[152] Whitehead, Don. "Peasant Woman Carry Supplies on Heads to Yanks in Mountains". *Lubbock Avalanche-Journal*. Sunday, November 28, 1943.
[153] Courtney, interview.
[154] Zimmerman, interview.
[155] Utterback, Thomas D. Letter of November 17, 1943.

[156] Utterback, Thomas D. Letter of November 25, 1943.
[157] Garrison, "Unit Journal."
[158] Halloran, Robert M. "Army Service Experiences Questionnaire". 82d Airborne Division, Box 1. US Army Heritage and Education Center.
[159] Halloran, Robert M. "Army Service Experiences Questionnaire". 82d Airborne Division, Box 1. US Army Heritage and Education Center.
[160] Halloran, Robert M. "Army Service Experiences Questionnaire". 82d Airborne Division, Box 1. US Army Heritage and Education Center.
[161] Halloran, Robert M. "Army Service Experiences Questionnaire". 82d Airborne Division, Box 1. US Army Heritage and Education Center.
[162] Whitehead, Don. "Miracles of Surgery Performed by Front Line Physicians; Skill and Courage Save Many Soldiers." *The Bee*, December 2, 1943.
[163] *The Gazette and Daily*. January 6, 1945.
[164] Mandle, William D. and Whittier, David H., *The Devils in Baggy Pants: Combat Record of the 504th Parachute Infantry Regiment, April 1943-July 1945*. Draeger Freres (1945).
[165] Courtney, interview.
[166] Zimmerman, interview.
[167] Hanna, interview.
[168] "Interrogation Report No. 1" Headquarters, 504th Parachute Combat Team, December 12, 1943.
[169] Zimmerman, interview.
[170] Hanna, interview.
[171] Letter George Watts to Francis McOmber, October 10, 1043. Courtesy of Dale McOmber.
[172] Courtesy of Kathy Vargas.
[173] Earl Oldfather diary; Hanna, interview; "Miss Ramsey Weds Lieutenant Breathwit." *The Monroe News-Star*, March 1, 1943.
[174] Oldfather, diary.
[175] "Interrogation Report No. 4" Headquarters, 504th Parachute Combat Team, December 17, 1943.
[176] Zimmerman, interview.
[177] Garrison, Chester A. "Unit Journal of the 2nd Battalion, 504th Parachute Infantry". Entry for December 11, 1943. Courtesy James Sapp.
[178] "Interrogation Report No. 2" Headquarters, 504th Parachute Combat Team, December 12, 1943.
[179] Garrison, Chester A. *An Ivy League Paratrooper*. Unpublished manuscript (1996).
[180] "Windsor Man Home from Battles in Italy: Capt. Jordan Tells of Experiences with Parachute Outfit." *Bertie Ledger-Advance*. June 16, 1944.
[181] *Fifth Army at the Winter Line: 15 November 1943-11 January 1944*. US Army Center for Military History, 1990. Page 54.
[182] "Hoosier Paratroop Doctor Receives Purple Heart". *The Courier-Journal*. April 14, 1944.
[183] Carter, page 80.
[184] Pyle, Ernie. *Brave Men*. Henry Hold and Company, Inc, 1944. Page 151.
[185] Sapp, interview.
[186] Garrison, unpublished manuscript.
[187] Delbert Kuehl as quoted in T. Moffatt Burriss' *Strike and Hold*, Brassey's, 2000. Page 59.
[188] "Wounded Rescued by Army Medics in Daring Foray". The Indianapolis Star. January 2, 1944.
[189] "Wounded Rescued by Army Medics in Daring Foray". The Indianapolis Star. January 2, 1944.
[190] "Wounded Rescued by Army Medics in Daring Foray". *The Indianapolis Star*, January 2, 1944.
[191] Sapp, interview.
[192] Garrison, unpublished manuscript.
[193] Baldino, interview.
[194] Garrison, "Unit Journal"
[195] Shakespear's *Macbeth*. Scene 5, Act 5. https://www.sparknotes.com/nofear/shakespeare/macbeth/page_202/. Accessed 11 March 2019.
[196] Company morning reports for the 2nd Battalion, 504th Parachute Infantry.
[197] "Interrogation Report No. 11" Headquarters, 504th Parachute Combat Team, December 27, 1943.
[198] "Interrogation Report No. 5" Headquarters, 504th Parachute Combat Team, December 17, 1943.
[199] Utterback, Thomas E. "Memories of World War II." Unpublished writings. Courtesy of Laurie Utterback.
[200] "Interrogation Report No. 11" Headquarters, 504th Parachute Combat Team, December 27, 1943.
[201] "Interrogation Report No. 7" Headquarters, 504th Parachute Combat Team, December 20, 1943.
[202] Carter, Page 86.
[203] "Interview of Lawrence W. Stimpson". https://www.kued.org/sites/default/files/lawrencestimpson.pdf. Accessed 28 July 2018.
[204] Edward W. Kennedy, letter to Rose Pierce, December 24, 1944. Personal possession of author.
[205] Zimmerman, interview.
[206] "Christmas at the Front". Panama City News-Herold, December 26, 1943.
[207] William G. Brown as quoted in *the Democrat and Chronicle*, February 14, 1944.
[208] Keefe, interview.
[209] Sapp, interview.
[210] Edwin R. Bayley, interview with author.
[211] Garrison, unpublished manuscript & Garrison, "Unit Journal."

[212] Levitt, Earl B. Interview. Earl Bernard Levitt Collection (AFC/2001/001/69249), Veterans History Project, American Folklife Center, Library of Congress.
[213] "Marion Soldier Writes of Activities in Italy." *Asheville Citizen-Times*, January 27, 1944.
[214] Garrison, "Unit Journal"
[215] Garrison, "Unit Journal"
[216] Baird, Elizabeth. "The Service News". *Marine City Independent*, January 13, 1944.
[217] Hanna, interview.
[218] Kennedy, Edward W. Letter to Rose Pierce, January 14, 1944.
[219] Garrison, unpublished manuscript.
[220] "Narrative of Action on the Anzio Beachhead". Headquarters, 504th Parachute Combat Team, n.d.
[221] Sweet, William J. *Operations of the 2nd Battalion, 504th Parachute Infantry Regiment (82nd Airborne Division) on the Anzio Beachhead, 22January-23March 1944 (Anzio Campaign) (Personal Experience of a Battalion Operations Officer and Company Commander)* General Subjects Section, Academic Department, The Infantry School, Ft. Benning, Ga. Courtesy of the Donovan Research Library.
[222] Keefe, interview.
[223] "Narrative of Action on the Anzio Beachhead". Headquarters, 504th Parachute Combat Team, n.d.
[224] "Boat Loading". Headquarters, 504th Combat Team, 20 January 1944.
[225] "Sergeant Sends Lynd Neeley Story from Belgian Front." *The Liberty Vindicator*, January 25, 1945.
[226] Sweet, *Operations of the 2nd Battalion*
[227] Tessinari, interview.
[228] Breard, interview.
[229] Lekson, John S. *Major General John S. Lekson, United States Army*. Written account. June 19, 1981. Courtesy of the Lekson family.
[230] Zimmerman, interview.
[231] "Sergeant Sends Lynd Neeley Story from Belgian Front." The Liberty Vindicator, January 25, 1945.
[232] War Diary, USS LCI(L) 45. Entry for January 22, 1944.
[233] Keefe, interview.
[234] Sweet, *Operations of the 2nd Battalion.*
[235] Garrison, unpublished manuscript.
[236] Keefe, interview.
[237] Author's interview with daughter of Willis J. Ferrill.
[238] Keefe, interview.
[239] Lee, Clark. "Yanks Battle German Patrol". *Reno Gazette-Journal*, January 28, 1944.
[240] "Bullet Hit Ring on Hopkins Finger – Right Over Heart." *The Ada Evening News*, May 8, 1944.
[241] Keefe, interview.
[242] Hanna, interview.
[243] Zimmerman, interview.
[244] Keefe, interview & Lee, Clark. "Yanks Battle German Patrol". *Reno Gazette-Journal*, January 28, 1944.
[245] Lee, Clark. "Yanks Battle German Patrol". *Reno Gazette-Journal*, January 28, 1944.
[246] Keefe, interview.
[247] Hanna, interview.
[248] Megellas, James. *All the Way to Berlin: A Paratrooper at War in Europe*. Presidio Press, 2003.
[249] Keefe, interview.
[250] Garrison, "Unit Journal"; company morning reports; and Sapp, interview.
[251] "Paratrooper Rabb Makes First Jump". *The Daily Independent*, December 13, 1942.
[252] "S-3 Operations Summary." Headquarters, 504th Parachute Combat Team, February 5, 1944.
[253] Keefe, interview.
[254] Breard, interview & "S-3 Operations Summary." Headquarters, 504th Parachute Combat Team, February 5, 1944.
[255] Courtney, interview & "S-3 Operations Summary." Headquarters, 504th Parachute Combat Team, February 5, 1944.
[256] "Interview of Lawrence W. Stimpson". https://www.kued.org/sites/default/files/lawrencestimpson.pdf. Accessed 28 July 2018.
[257] "Interview of Lawrence W. Stimpson". https://www.kued.org/sites/default/files/lawrencestimpson.pdf. Accessed 28 July 2018.
[258] Fern, Lewis. Video interview. Witness to War. https://www.witnesstowar.org/combat_stories/WWII/4627. Accessed 25 January 2019.
[259] Sweet, *Operations of the 2nd Battalion.*
[260] Louis Bednar Collection (AFC/2001/001/04414), Veterans History Project, American Folklife Center, Library of Congress.
[261] Sweet, *Operations of the 2nd Battalion.*
[262] "Interrogation Report No. 2." Headquarters, 504th Regimental Combat Team, January 26, 1944.
[263] http://www.borghidilatina.it/borgo-piave-foto-storiche.htm. Accessed 13 August 2018.
[264] Sweet, *Operations of the 2nd Battalion.*
[265] "Comments and Lessons Learned." Headquarters, 504th Parachute Infantry Combat Team, February 5, 1944.
[266] Sweet, *Operations of the 2nd Battalion.*
[267] "S-2 Periodic Report." Headquarters, 504th Parachute Combat Team. 25 January 1944.
[268] "Narrative of Action on the Anzio Beachhead". Headquarters, 504th Parachute Combat Team, n.d.
[269] Baldino, interview.
[270] Sweet, *Operations of the 2nd Battalion* & Sapp, interview with author.
[271] Sapp, interview.
[272] Sweet, *Operations of the 2nd Battalion.*

[273] Tucker, Reuben H. Letter to Irvin Bushman, April 24, 1944. Courtesy of Robin Bushman. I am entirely grateful to the Bushman family for there great assistance in providing valuable historical data that would have otherwise been long lost and forgotten, if not for their great patience and generosity of time.

[274] "Interrogation Report No. 1." Headquarters, 504th Regimental Combat Team, January 25, 1944.

[275] "Interrogation Report No. 3". Headquarters, 504th Regimental Combat Team, January 26, 1944.

[276] "Interrogation Report No. 4". Headquarters, 504th Regimental Combat Team. January 28, 1944.

[277] "Interrogation Report No. 5". Headquarters, 504th Regimental Combat Team. January 31, 1944.

[278] Flamm, Paul F. *Combat History of the 84th Chemical Mortar Battalion.*

[279] Sapp, interview & "Officers Tell How Tampan in Italy Died". *The Tampa Tribune*, March 1, 1944.

[280] Company morning report for Company F, 504th PIR.

[281] Garrison, unpublished manuscript.

[282] Sweet, *Operations of the 2nd Battalion*.

[283] Company morning reports for Company F, 504th Parachute Infantry.

[284] Paul Hardy Pannell Collection (AFC/2001/001/29062), Veterans History Project, American Folklife Center, Library of Congress.

[285] Baldino, interview.

[286] Sweet, *Operations of the 2nd Battalion*.

[287] Sapp, interview.

[288] Paul Hardy Pannell Collection (AFC/2001/001/29062), Veterans History Project, American Folklife Center, Library of Congress.

[289] Milton Orshefsky as quoted in Flamm, Paul F. *Combat History of the 84th Chemical Mortar Battalion.*

[290] Sweet, *Operations of the 2nd Battalion*.

[291] Paul Hardy Pannell Collection (AFC/2001/001/29062), Veterans History Project, American Folklife Center, Library of Congress & "Narrative of Action on the Anzio Beachhead". Headquarters, 504th Parachute Combat Team, n.d.

[292] Baird, Elizabeth. "The Service News". *Marine City Independent*, March 29, 1944.

[293] Sapp, interview.

[294] Garrison, unpublished manuscript.

[295] "Narrative of Action on the Anzio Beachhead". Headquarters, 504th Parachute Combat Team, n.d.

[296] Garrison, unpublished manuscript & "Narrative of Action on the Anzio Beachhead". Headquarters, 504th Parachute Combat Team, n.d.

[297] Mokan, Edward L. "Army Service Experiences Questionnaire". 82d Airborne Division, Box 1. US Army Heritage and Education Center.

[298] Baldino, interview.

[299] Sweet, *Operations of the 2nd Battalion*.

[300] Baldino, interview.

[301] Baldino, interview.

[302] "Earl Morin". *The Bakersfield Californian*, April 13, 1944.

[303] "Home Folks Should Never Complain". Charlestown Currier, April 6, 1944.

[304] Halloran, Robert M. "Army Service Experiences Questionnaire". 82d Airborne Division, Box 1. US Army Heritage and Education Center.

[305] Garrison, unpublished manuscript.

[306] Baldino, interview.

[307] "Narrative of Action on the Anzio Beachhead". Headquarters, 504th Parachute Combat Team, n.d.

[308] "Narrative of Action on the Anzio Beachhead". Headquarters, 504th Parachute Combat Team, n.d.

[309] "Narrative of Action on the Anzio Beachhead". Headquarters, 504th Parachute Combat Team, n.d.

[310] "Narrative of Action on the Anzio Beachhead". Headquarters, 504th Parachute Combat Team, n.d.

[311] *The Infantry Conference, Report of Committee on Organization*. Fort Benning, Georgia (1946). Courtesy of the Combined Arms Research Library at Fort Leavenworth, Kansas.

[312] "Narrative of Action on the Anzio Beachhead". Headquarters, 504th Parachute Combat Team, n.d.

[313] von Clauswitz, Carl. *On War*. Translated by Colonel J.J. Graham. Kegan Paul, Trench, Trubner & Co., Ltd (1908).

[314] Baldino, interview.

[315] *Clarion-Ledger*, March 14, 1944.

[316] Mandel, William D. and Whittier, David H., *The Devils in Baggy Pants: Combat Record of the 504th Parachute Infantry Regiment, April 1943-July 1945*. Draeger Freres (1945).

[317] "Sergeant Tells Pfc. Robert Lanier Keep Nazi Sentry Covered with Rifle". *The Paris News*, April 17, 1944.

[318] "Tony's War." Written account. Courtesy of James Sapp.

[319] Sapp, interview.

[320] "Tony's War."

[321] Baldino, interview.

[322] Baldino, interview.

[323] Packard, Reynolds. "Daniel Webster, Pvt. Bachenheimer, Talks NAZIs into Giving Up." *Santa Cruz Sentinel*, February 17, 1944.

[324] "Private Argues Old Time Adage." *Linton Daily Gazette*, February 24, 1944.

[325] Baldino, interview.

[326] Gann, interview.

[327] Baldino, interview.

[328] Individual Deceased Personnel Field of Theodore Bachenheimer. A copy of this document was kindly provided to the author by Jan Bos.

[329] Baldino, interview.

[330] Keefe, interview.
[331] Edward W. Kennedy as quoted in "Yanks Battle in Sight of Eternal City" by Daniel de Luce. *The Escanaba Daily Press*, February 5, 1944.
[332] Kennedy, Edward W. Letter to Rose Pierce, February 4, 1944.
[333] Hanna, interview.
[334] Oldfather, Earl S. *I joined the Paratroops*. Unpublished manuscript. Kindly provided to the author by Jan Bos.
[335] Hanna, interview.
[336] Keefe, interview.
[337] Packard, Reynolds. "Office Hooked: Enemy Licked as Men Laugh." *St. Louis Star and Times*, February 7, 1944.
[338] War Diary, 1 Irish Guards. Entry for February 7, 1944. This document was posted on the ww2talk.com forums by user "DBF". http://ww2talk.com/index.php?threads/war-diary-1st-battalion-irish-guards-september-1939-july-1944.32054/page-6. Accessed 17 August 2018.
[339] War Diary, 5th Battalion, Grenadier Guards. Entry for February 7, 1944. This document was posted on the ww2talk.com forums by user "Drew5233". http://ww2talk.com/index.php?threads/5th-battalion-grenadier-guards-february-1944.61905/. Accessed 15 August 2018.
[340] War Diary, 1 Irish Guards. Entry for February 7, 1944. This document was posted on the ww2talk.com forums by user "DBF". http://ww2talk.com/index.php?threads/war-diary-1st-battalion-irish-guards-september-1939-july-1944.32054/page-6. Accessed 17 August 2018.
[341] War Diary, 5th Battalion, Grenadier Guards. Entry for February 7, 1944. This document was posted on the ww2talk.com forums by user "Drew5233". http://ww2talk.com/index.php?threads/5th-battalion-grenadier-guards-february-1944.61905/. Accessed 15 August 2018.
[342] Keefe, interview.
[343] Hanna, interview.
[344] Keefe, interview.
[345] Hanna, interview.
[346] Keefe, interview.
[347] Hanna, interview.
[348] Keefe, interview.
[349] Hanna, interview.
[350] Keefe, interview.
[351] Hanna, interview.
[352] Hanna, Roy M. Letter to family. February 17, 1944. Courtesy of Roy Hanna.
[353] Burriss, interview.
[354] Hanna, interview.
[355] This entire section was based off daily letters from Robert Utterback to his wife during the period. Copies of these letters were kindly provided to the author by his granddaughter Laurie Utterback.
[356] Halloran, Robert M. "Army Service Experiences Questionnaire". 82d Airborne Division, Box 1. US Army Heritage and Education Center.
[357] "Narrative of Action on the Anzio Beachhead". Headquarters, 504th Parachute Combat Team, n.d.
[358] Keefe, interview.
[359] Utterback, Thomas E. "Memories of World War II." Unpublished writings. These are used with the kind permission of Laurie Utterback, granddaughter of LT Thomas Utterback.
[360] Utterback, Thomas. Letter to wife, March 2, 1944. Courtesy of Laurie Utterback.
[361] Utterback, Thomas E. "Memories of World War II."
[362] Sweet, *Operations of the 2nd Battalion*.
[363] Baldino, interview.
[364] Garrison, Chester A. "Army Service Experiences Questionnaire". 82d Airborne Division, Box 1. US Army Heritage and Education Center.
[365] Mokan, Edward L. "Army Service Experiences Questionnaire". 82d Airborne Division, Box 1. US Army Heritage and Education Center.
[366] Baldino, interview.
[367] Sweet, *Operations of the 2nd Battalion*.
[368] Wickersham, Ollie B. Interview with author.
[369] Wallis, Hugh D. Interview with author.
[370] Stanford, David S. Letter to family, March 19, 1944. Courtesy of Rob Stanford.
[371] "Narrative of Action on the Anzio Beachhead". Headquarters, 504th Parachute Combat Team, n.d.
[372] Schwartz, John J. as quoted in the *Democrat and Chronicle*, October 2, 1945.
[373] "It Happened at the Front," *The Stars and Stripes*, January 11, 1944.
[374] Baldino, interview.
[375] Whitehead, Don. "Four Jumping Padres Carry the Cross with Paratroopers on Invasion Thrust," *The Cumberland News*, July 12, 1943.
[376] Gann, interview.
[377] Tucker, George. "Two Chaplains Are Decorated." *Cumberland Evening Times*, April 10, 1944.
[378] Sweet, *Operations of the 2nd Battalion*.
[379] Churchill, Winston S. *The Second World War: Volume V Closing the Ring*. (Houghton Mifflin Company (1951). Page 443.
[380] Churchill, *Closing the Ring*. Page 443.

[381] "Report by the Supreme Allied Commander Mediterranean to the Combined Chiefs of Staff on the Italian Campaign: 8 January 1944 to 10 May 1944." Page 10. Courtesy of the Combined Arms Research Library, Ft. Leavenworth, KS.
[382] "Report by the Supreme Allied Commander Mediterranean to the Combined Chiefs of Staff on the Italian Campaign: 8 January 1944 to 10 May 1944." Page 27. Courtesy of the Combined Arms Research Library, Ft. Leavenworth, KS.
[383] Churchill, *Closing the Ring*. Page 443.
[384] Churchill, *Closing the Ring*. Page 486.
[385] Clark, Mark W. *Calculated Risk*. Enigma Books (2007). Page 351.
[386] "Report by the Supreme Allied Commander Mediterranean to the Combined Chiefs of Staff on the Italian Campaign: 8 January 1944 to 10 May 1944." Page 12. Courtesy of the Combined Arms Research Library, Ft. Leavenworth, KS.
[387] Mandel, William D. and Whittier, David H., *The Devils in Baggy Pants: Combat Record of the 504th Parachute Infantry Regiment, April 1943-July 1945*. Draeger Freres (1945).
[388] "Narrative of Action on the Anzio Beachhead". Headquarters, 504th Parachute Combat Team, n.d. & company morning reports analyzed by author.
[389] Ridgway, Matthew B. Soldier: *The Memoirs of Matthew B. Ridgway*. Harper & Brothers (1956). Page 91-92.
[390] Stanford, David S. Letter to family, March 27, 1944. Courtesy of Rob Stanford.
[391] Front Row: McClain, Wilbur Clark, Norton Stevenson, Nick Esposito (KIA Holland), Robert Pears, Marvin Russell, Bill Vining, George Suggs. Second Row: Myron Bundrock, Winner Tims, John Turner, Edward Porebski, James Reed, Mike Zolvik. Third Row: James Perdott, Joe Hamilton (KIA Holland), Charles Lamberson, Ellsworth Sprinkle, Lester Oxford, William Hakeem. Fourth Row: Edward Collins, John Bryant, Bill Nichter, James Buskirk, Richard van Ort (medic), John McGraw. Fifth Row: William Altemus (KIA Holland), Paul Revere, Cecil Dodson.
[392] Keefe, interview.
[393] Hanna, interview.
[394] Freeman, Leslie G. Letter to Roy Hanna. April 8, 1944. Courtesy Roy Hanna.
[395] Keefe, interview.
[396] Hanna, interview.
[397] Steele, Robert H. Letter to Payton Elliott. April 17, 1944. Courtesy of Dwight Elliott.
[398] Hanna, interview.
[399] Garrison, unpublished manuscript.
[400] Garrison, unpublished manuscript.
[401] Campana, Victor W. *The Operations of the 2nd Battalion, 504th Parachute Infantry (82nd A/B DIV) in the German Counter-Offensive, 18 December 1944 – 10 January 1945 (Ardennes Campaign) (Personal Experiences of a Battalion S-3)*. The Infantry School, General Section, Military History Committee, Fort Benning, GA. Courtesy of the Donovan Research Library.
[402] Garrison, unpublished manuscript.
[403] Burriss, interview with author.
[404] Utterback, "Memories of World War II."
[405] Kennedy, Edward W. Letter to Rose Pierce, June 20, 1944.
[406] Keefe, interview.
[407] Utterback, Thomas E. "Memories of World War II." Unpublished writings. These are used with the kind permission of Laurie Utterback, granddaughter of LT Thomas Utterback.
[408] Gann, interview.
[409] Zimmerman, interview.
[410] "Britons Have Great Admiration for Boys from America". *Montana Standard Butte*, July 30, 1944.
[411] Gann, interview.
[412] Breard, Reneau G. Letter to Fred Baldino. March 4, 2004. Personal possession of author.
[413] Gann, James. Letter to Ollie Gann, August 24, 1944.
[414] Personal papers of Payton Elliott, courtesy of Dwight Elliott.
[415] Garrison, unpublished manuscript.
[416] Hughes, Walter E. Interview with author.
[417] Hughes, Walter E. Letter to Myrtle Selover, undated.
[418] Holmstock, Morris. Interview with author.
[419] Anderson, Peter & Jeramiah Murphy. "Remembering World War II: A Bridge Too Far". *Boston Globe*, September 10, 1984.
[420] Hughes, interview.
[421] Hanna, Roy M. Email to author. Date unknown.
[422] Kappel, Carl W. Interview. Box 103, Folder 1. Cornelius Ryan Collection of World War II Papers, Mahn Center for Archives and Special Collections, Ohio University.
[423] Wickersham, interview.
[424] Zimmerman, interview.
[425] Anderson, Peter & Jeramiah Murphy. "Remembering World War II: A Bridge Too Far". *Boston Globe*, September 10, 1984.
[426] Hannigan, William J. Interview with author. April 4, 2014.
[427] Wallis, interview.
[428] Zimmerman, interview.
[429] "Williams Sends Story on Holland Air Invasion". *The Republic*, December 27, 1944.
[430] Holmstock, interview.
[431] "Eldridge Captures Car". *The Gastonia Daily Gazette*, November 7, 1944.
[432] "Sergeant Sends Lynd Neeley Story from Belgian Front." The Liberty Vindicator, January 25, 1945.
[433] "Girls Helped Paratrooper in Holland". Review: Thomas M. England General Hospital, December 22, 1944.

[434] Wallis, interview.
[435] Zimmerman, interview.
[436] "Major Edward N. Wellems, CO 2d Bn, 504th Para Inf, 82d ABN DIV". Combat Interview. National Archives and Records Administration.
[437] Van Dreumel, et. all. *Bridge Eleven is Ours: de Bevrijding van Grave*. Private published book, Grave Kazematten museum.
[438] Baldino, Fred J. Papers. Personal possession of author.
[439] Van Dreumel, et. all. *Bridge Eleven is Ours*.
[440] Headquarters, 82d Airborne Division, General Orders No. 60 (November 30, 1944)
[441] Van Dreumel, et. all. *Bridge Eleven is Ours*.
[442] Headquarters, 82d Airborne Division, General Orders No. 60 (November 30, 1944)
[443] Van Dreumel, et. all. *Bridge Eleven is Ours*.
[444] Hughes, interview.
[445] Keefe, interview.
[446] Schama, Simon. *Patriots and Liberators: Revolution in the Netherlands, 1780-1813*. Alfred A. Knopf (1977).
[447] This letter is on display in the collection of the Graafs Museum in Grave, the Netherlands. The author and recipient cannot be determined.
[448] Keefe, interview.
[449] Wickersham, interview.
[450] Burriss, interview.
[451] Wickersham, interview.
[452] Wallis, interview.
[453] Zimmerman, interview; Hannigan, interview; James Megellas, *All the Way to Berlin*, Presidio Press (2003).
[454] Tison, Ralph N., Jr. "The Way I Remember It." Written account. Courtesy of Francis Keefe.
[455] Hanna, interview.
[456] Hannigan, interview.
[457] Zimmerman, interview.
[458] Hannigan, interview.
[459] Zimmerman, interview.
[460] Wallis, interview.
[461] Hannigan, interview.
[462] Zimmerman, interview.
[463] Keefe, Francis X. Written account. Courtasey Francis Keefe
[464] Keefe, interview; Burriss, interview.
[465] Keefe, written account.
[466] Hughes, interview.
[467] Keefe, written account.
[468] Hannigan, interview.
[469] Keefe, written account.
[470] Zimmerman, interview.
[471] Keefe, written account.
[472] Hughes, interview.
[473] Tison, Ralph N., Jr. "The Way I Remember It." Written account. Courtesy of Francis Keefe.
[474] Utterback, "Memories of World War II."
[475] Wickersham, interview. Three initials were engraved on the knife handle. They could be read either "NMH" or "HWM." Likely, they are "HWM" for Howard W. Morton, the first H Company parachutist killed in World War II on a training jump in North Africa. Apparently, the man whom Wickersham transported across the Waal had somehow bequeathed Morton's knife.
[476] Utterback, "Memories of World War II."
[477] Hanna, interview.
[478] Utterback, "Memories of World War II."
[479] Hanna, interview.
[480] "Sergeant Sends Lynd Neeley Story from Belgian Front." *The Liberty Vindicator*, January 25, 1945.
[481] Hanna, interview.
[482] Zimmerman, interview.
[483] Wallis, interview.
[484] Kappel, Carl W. Interview. Box 103, Folder 1. Cornelius Ryan Collection of World War II Papers, Mahn Center for Archives and Special Collections, Ohio University.
[485] Burriss, interview.
[486] Kappel, Carl W. Interview. Box 103, Folder 1. Cornelius Ryan Collection of World War II Papers, Mahn Center for Archives and Special Collections, Ohio University.
[487] Tison, Ralph N., Jr. "The Way I Remember It." Written account. Courtesy of Francis Keefe.
[488] Anderson, Peter & Jeramiah Murphy. "Remembering World War II: A Bridge Too Far". *Boston Globe*, September 10, 1984; Wickersham, interview.
[489] Utterback, "Memories of World War II."
[490] Zimmerman, interview.
[491] Serilla, Danny. "Mark XI – Tank Killer." *The Static Line*, August 1975.
[492] Burriss, interview.

[493] Hughes, interview.
[494] "Den Heuvel". Headquarters, 3rd Battalion, 504th Parachute Infantry. Courtesy of Jan Bos.
[495] "Den Heuvel". Headquarters, 3rd Battalion, 504th Parachute Infantry. Courtesy of Jan Bos.
[496] Headquarters, 82d Airborne Division, General Orders No. 61 (November 30, 1944)
[497] Tison, Ralph N., Jr. "The Way I Remember It." Written account. Courtesy of Francis Keefe.
[498] Individual Deceased Personnel File for Leon E. Baldwin. Courtesy of Jan Bos.
[499] Tison, Ralph N., Jr. "The Way I Remember It." Written account. Courtesy of Francis Keefe.
[500] Individual Deceased Personnel File for David S. Stanford. Courtesy of the Stanford family.
[501] Interview with Bud Kaczor.
[502] Oldfather, Earl S. Diary. Entry September 28, 1944. Courtesy of Jan Bos.
[503] Burriss, Thomas M. *Strike and Hold*. Brasley's, 2001. Page 150.
[504] Dew, Glen R. Letter to Robert C. Blankenship. July 29, 1945.
[505] Chapman, William E. "What is a Parachutists? Here's Their Version". *The Burlington Daily Times-News*. November 3, 1942.
[506] Hart, Scot. "Fling on Borrowed $1,000 Still Going Strong: 'At Ease, the Captain Said". *The Washington Post*, January 25, 1943.
[507] Front row: William L. Ford, unknown, Herbert H. Carney, unknown, unknown, Frederick M. Smits, Joseph Castallanos, James T. Ferguson, Francis Downs (KIA), Paul E. Mentzer, Edward P. Oleszek?, Unknown, Robert C. Ramsey. Second row: Donald H. Fox, Harvey W. Schultz (KIA), Unknown x4, Andew Demetras, unknown x3. Third row: Captain William Kitchin, Lt. Charles J. Snyder.
[508] Carney, Herbert. Letter to Snyder Family, March 23, 1945. Courtesy of the Snyder family.
[509] Hannigan, interview with author.
[510] "Two Soldiers Killed, One Missing in German Action." *The Evening News*, November 4, 1944.
[511] "Battle-Scared Veteran Home After Long Service in Combat." *The Courier-News*, February 24, 1945
[512] "Battle-Scared Veteran Home After Long Service in Combat." *The Courier-News*, February 24, 1945 & "Farrington Takes PCC Golf Crown." *The Courier-News*, July 8, 1946.
[513] "S-3 Journal" Entry for 1203, September 29, 1944. Courtesy of the Donovan Research Library.
[514] Kuehl, Delbert. Interview with Thomas Saylor, April 5, 2003. Minnesota Greatest Generation Oral History Project: Part 1, Minnesota Historical Society.
[515] "Pfc. Junior Posey May Be Liberated." *The Chillicothe Constitution-Tribune*. May 3, 1945.
[516] "Unit S-2 Journal." Entry for 2000, September 27, 1944. Headquarters, 504th Parachute Infantry.
[517] Fary, Ray. Interview with author.
[518] Garrison, Chester A. "Army Service Experiences Questionnaire". 82d Airborne Division, Box 1. US Army Heritage and Education Center.
[519] Mokan, Edward L. "Army Service Experiences Questionnaire". 82d Airborne Division, Box 1. US Army Heritage and Education Center.
[520] Tassinari, interview.
[521] Tassinari, interview.
[522] Headquarters, 82d Airborne Division, General Orders No. 60 (November 30, 1944)
[523] Tassinari, interview.
[524] Headquarters, XVIII Airborne Corps, General Orders No. 11 (1944)
[525] Headquarters, XVIII Airborne Corps, General Orders No. 11 (1944) & Headquarters, 82d Airborne Division, General Orders No. 60 (November 30, 1944)
[526] "Interrogation Report No. 7." Annex no. 2 to G-2 Report No. 103. Headquarters, 82nd Airborne Division, September 19, 1944.
[527] Hanna, interview.
[528] Oldfather, Earl S. Diary. Entry October 2, 1944. Courtesy of Jan Bos.
[529] Hanna, interview.
[530] "Girls Helped Paratrooper in Holland". Review: Thomas M. England General Hospital, December 22, 1944.
[531] Oldfather, Earl S. Diary. Entry October 2, 1944. Courtesy of Jan Bos.
[532] Hanna, interview.
[533] Oldfather, Earl S. Diary. Entry October 2, 1944. Courtesy of Jan Bos.
[534] Garrison, *An Ivy League Paratrooper*.
[535] Utterback, Thomas. Letter to family, October 10, 1944.
[536] Garrison, *An Ivy League Paratrooper*.
[537] Hanna, interview.
[538] Oldfather, diary & "Holland Campaign." Headquarters, 3rd Battalion, 504th Parachute Infantry. Courtesy of Jan Bos.
[539] Hanna, interview.
[540] Mandle, William. Letter to family, October 10, 1944. A copy of this letter was kindly provided to the author by Steve Mandle.
[541] Kennedy, Francis. Letter to Edward Kennedy, October 17, 1944.
[542] The artillery attack resulted in the death of his platoon sergeant Elmer O. Partridge, Sergeant John Duncan, and Privates Bernard M. McDermott and Joseph M. Smith. The wounded were Private James F. Lyons, Private First Class Albert Musto, and Private First Class Kelley W. Thurmond.
[543] "Paratrooper Now Missing." *The Altoona-Mirror*, November 16, 1943.
[544] Individual Deceased Personnel File of William Sandoval.
[545] Individual Deceased Personnel File of Robert Heniesen.
[546] Individual Deceased Personnel File of William Sandoval.
[547] Headquarters, 82d Airborne Division, General Orders No. 60 (November 30, 1944)
[548] Headquarters, 82d Airborne Division, General Orders No. 60 (November 30, 1944)
[549] "Unit S-2 Journal." Entry for 0025, October 7, 1944. Headquarters, 504th Prcht. Inf.

[550] Watson, William L. Letter to Maureen Wolf, March 1, 2009. Courtesy of Maureen Wolf.
[551] Baldino, interview.
[552] "G-2 Report". Headquarters, 82d Airborne Division. 27 October 1944.
[553] Sapp, interview.
[554] "Local Soldier Live 10 Days on Slim Fare." *Cumberland Evening Times*, January 19, 1945.
[555] Whittier, David. "Division Wants Prisoners: Patrol Along the Wyler-Meer," *The Infantry Journal*, April 1945.
[556] Burke, Mike. "City Playground Named for Hero." *Springfield Union News*, October 4, 2001.
[557] Hughes, interview.
[558] War Department, The Adjunct General's Office. Letter to Harry Kennedy, June 22, 1945. Courtesy of Ed Kennedy.
[559] Hughes, interview.
[560] Burriss, interview.
[561] Hanna, interview.
[562] Hanna, interview.
[563] Haider, Edward P. Interview with author.
[564] Keefe, interview.
[565] Hanna, interview.
[566] Burriss, interview.
[567] Madison, James H. *Slinging Doughnuts for the Boys: An American Woman in World War II*. Indiana University Press, 2007. Page 71.
[568] Hanna, interview.
[569] Kennedy, Edward W. Letter to parents, October 2, 1944.
[570] Kennedy, Edward W. Letter to sisters, February 15, 1944.
[571] Magner, John J. Letter to the *Holyoke Transcript-Telegram*, December 20, 1944.
[572] Magner, John J. Letter to Mrs. Harry Kennedy, December 15, 1944.
[573] Magner, John J & Eleanor Magner. Letter to Mr. and Mrs. Harry Kennedy, January 3, 1945.
[574] Kozak, Edwin J. Letter to Mrs. Harry Kennedy, December 13, 1944. Personnel possession of author.
[575] "Result of Patrol Activities for Night 1-2 November 1944." Headquarters, 504th Prcht. Inf., November 2, 1944.
[576] "Result of Patrol Activities for Night 2-3 November 1944." Headquarters, 504th Prcht. Inf., November 3, 1944.
[577] Carmichael, Virgil F. Questionnaire. Box 102, Folder 16. Cornelius Ryan Collection of World War II Papers, Mahn Center for Archives and Special Collections, Ohio University.
[578] Mokan, Edward L. Letter to Fred Balindo, undated. Personal Possession of author.
[579] "PW Interrogation Report." Headquarters, 504th Parachute Infantry, 17 September 1944.
[580] Bushman, Irvin. "PW Interrogation Summary." Headquarters, 82nd Airborne Division. 22 September 1944.
[581] "Interrogation Report 14." Headquarters, 504th Parachute Infantry. 10 November 1944.
[582] "Dutch Personnel Attached for Duty and Rations." IPW Team #45, 504th Parachute Infantry Regiment. 31 October 1944 & "Report on Civilian Petrus Dolmans from Hertogenbusch." Headquarters, 504th Parachute Infantry. 4 October 1944.
[583] Hughes, Walter E. Letter to Herb Brown, November 9, 1944. Courtesy of Walter Hughes.
[584] Breard, interview.
[585] Mandel, William D. and Whittier, David H., *The Devils in Baggy Pants: Combat Record of the 504th Parachute Infantry Regiment, April 1943-July 1945*. Draeger Freres (1945).
[586] Holmstock, interview.
[587] Bailey, Edwin R. Interview with author.
[588] Utterback, Thomas. Letter to family, November 27, 1944. Courtasey of the Utterback family.
[589] Hanna, interview.
[590] "Sky Fighter Home After Thrilling Battles Overseas." *The Ogden Standard-Examiner*, January 25, 1945.
[591] "News from the Men in the Service." *The Escanaba Daily News*, January 21, 1945.
[592] Flox, Seymour. Letter to mother. A copy of this letter was kindly provided to the author by Peggy Shelly.
[593] Sapp, interview.
[594] Benavitz, William. "Christmas Dinner 1944." Written account. Courtesy of the Benavitz family.
[595] Speer, Werner. Interview with author.
[596] Burriss, interview.
[597] DeVinney, Robert. Interview with author.
[598] Bramson, Robert E. Interview with author.
[599] Burriss, interview.
[600] Holmstock, interview.
[601] Speer, interview.
[602] Holmstock, interview.
[603] Boyle, Hal. "Slambang Battle." *Altoona Tribune*, December 23, 1944.
[604] McDermott, John. "Yank Retake Belgian Town in Fierce Fight." *The Brooklyn Daily Eagle*, December 23, 1944.
[605] McDermott, John. "Yank Retake Belgian Town in Fierce Fight." *The Brooklyn Daily Eagle*, December 23, 1944.
[606] Holmstock, interview.
[607] Headquarters, First U.S. Army, General Orders No. 34 (February 27, 1945)
[608] Holmstock, interview.
[609] Wickersham, interview.
[610] Hannigan, interview.
[611] DeVinney, interview.
[612] Burriss, interview.

[613] Bramson, interview.
[614] Speer, interview.
[615] Breard, Reneau G. Letter the author, date unknown.
[616] Holmstock, interview.
[617] Whittier, David. "The Battle of Cheneux." Courtesy of the Donovan Research Library.
[618] Holmstock, interview.
[619] Breard, letter.
[620] Holmstock, interview.
[621] Churchill, Winston. Speech to the House of Commons. 13 May 1940. http://www.bl.uk/learning/histcitizen/21cc/lang/persuasion1/bloodtoil1/bloodtoil.html.
[622] "To Whom it May Concern." Headquarters, 504th Parachute Infantry. 07 April 1945. Courtesy of the Deloris Branca.
[623] This previous chapter was constructed using correspondence with Edwin R. Bayley.
[624] Bach, Max. "The Glider War". Written account, 1988. Personal possession of author.
[625] Gault, Joe. *The Story of Company F, 325th Glider Infantry From Camp Clairborne to Holland, March 1942-September 1944.* Unpublished manuscript, 1989. Personal possession of author.
[626] Bach, written account.
[627] Haas, Bernie. "Roadblock Overrun 12 Hours into First Combat Mission." *The Bulge Bugle*, Volume XXIX (3), August 2010.
[628] Haas, "Roadblock Overrun 12 Hours into First Combat Mission."
[629] Unit S-1 Journal. Headquarters, 504th Parachute Infantry. Entry 23 December 1944 & O'Sullivan, J.F. "Interview with Colonel Charles W. Billingslea, Commanding Officer, 325th Glider Infantry Regiment, After the Battle of the Bulge. 24 March 1945. http://www.battleofthebulgememories.be/index.php?option=com_content&view=article&id=535%3Ainterview-with-colonel-charles-w-billingslea-325th-glider&catid=1%3Abattle-of-the-bulge-us-army&Itemid=6&lang=fr. Accessed 7 January 2019.
[630] Haas, "Roadblock Overrun 12 Hours into First Combat Mission."
[631] Haas, "Roadblock Overrun 12 Hours into First Combat Mission."
[632] Wilson, Louis E. Written account, 1988. Personal possession of author.
[633] Speer, interview.
[634] Garrison, unpublished manuscript.
[635] Zimmerman, interview.
[636] Unit S-3 Journal. Headquarters, 504th Parachute Infantry. 24 December 1944.
[637] Bramson, interview.
[638] Speer, interview.
[639] Wallis, interview.
[640] Speer, interview.
[641] Sapp, interview.
[642] Bramson, interview.
[643] Edgren, Emil. Interview with author. 22 February 2019.
[644] Hughes, Walter E. Written account. Courtesy Walter Hughes.
[645] Benavitz, George. "Christmas Dinner 1944." Written account. Courtesy Benavitz family.
[646] Nicoll, Kenneth. Diary. Entry for December 29, 1944. Courtesy of the 2nd Battalion, 504th PIR, 1st Brigade Combat Team, 82nd Airborne Division.
[647] Campana, Victor W. *The Operations of the 2nd Battalion, 504th Parachute Infantry (82nd A/B DIV) in the German Counter-Offensive, 18 December 1944 – 10 January 1945 (Ardennes Campaign) (Personal Experiences of a Battalion S-3)*. The Infantry School, General Section, Military History Committee, Fort Benning, GA. Courtesy of the Donovan Research Library.
[648] Nicoll, diary.
[649] Nicoll, diary & Sapp, interview.
[650] Sapp, interview.
[651] Sapp, interview.
[652] Nicoll, diary. Entry for December 31, 1944.
[653] Garrison, unpublished manuscript.
[654] Campana, *The Operations of the 2nd Battalion*.
[655] Bramson, interview.
[656] Campana, *The Operations of the 2nd Battalion*.
[657] Campana, *The Operations of the 2nd Battalion*.
[658] Sapp, interview.
[659] Burriss, interview.
[660] Breard, Reneau G., letter to author, March 21, 2014.
[661] Breard, letter.
[662] Thanks to Frank van Lunteren for assisting in identifying the name of this officer.
[663] Bonning, William L., phone interview with author, December 14, 2013.
[664] Holmstock, Morris, phone interview with author, February 13, 2014.
[665] Breard, letter.
[666] Holmstock, phone interview.
[667] DeVinney, Robert E., phone interview with author, January 23, 2014.
[668] Oldfather, Earl S. "Letters of the Editor." *The Bulge Bugle*, Volume XV, Number 2, May 1996.
[669] Headquarters, 82d Airborne Division, General Orders No. 119 (September 13, 1945)
[670] Headquarters, 82d Airborne Division, General Orders No. 21 (February 24, 1945)

[671] Bramson, interview.
[672] Sapp, interview. The four killed were members of Headquarters Company, 2nd Battalion, 504th Parachute Infantry. They were: Oliver J. Bohlken, George B. Ellzey, Wallace R. Jones, Paul R. Reynolds.
[673] DeVinney, interview.
[674] Bramson, interview.
[675] Holmstock, interview.
[676] Sapp, interview.
[677] Tarbell, Albert A. Statement. Encl. in Senator John Cornyn, et. all to The Honorable John McHugh, letter November 14, 2013. A copy of this letter and its enclosures were kindly provided by H. Donald Zimmerman.
[678] Sullivan, Harold J. Statement. Encl. in Senator John Cornyn, et. all to The Honorable John McHugh, letter November 14, 2013. A copy of this letter and its enclosures were kindly provided by H. Donald Zimmerman.
[679] Sapp, interview.
[680] Sullivan, Harold J. Statement. Encl. in Senator John Cornyn, et. all to The Honorable John McHugh, letter November 14, 2013. A copy of this letter and its enclosures were kindly provided by H. Donald Zimmerman.
[681] Crowder, Charles. Statement. Encl. in Senator John Cornyn, et. all to The Honorable John McHugh, letter November 14, 2013. A copy of this letter and its enclosures were kindly provided by H. Donald Zimmerman.
[682] Sapp, interview.
[683] Zucco, Peter. "Blow to Morale." *The Berkshire Eagle*, April 9, 1945.
[684] "From Sixteen Burned Up Joes". *The Tampa Tribune*, March 6, 1945.
[685] "Battle Experiences." Headquarters, European Theater of Operations, United States Army. 5 May 1945.
[686] Campana, *The Operations of the 2nd Battalion*.
[687] Gann, interview.
[688] Unrah, Jerome. Interview with author.
[689] Strutzenberg, Eugene. *Memoirs of World War II: February 12, 1943-November 26, 1945*. Unpublished account. Courtesy of the Strutzenberg family.
[690] "History, 504th Parachute Infantry: 1 February 1945 – 1 March 1945." Headquarters, 504th Parachute Infantry. Courtesy of the National Archives and Records Administration, College Park, MD.
[691] Shaifer, Edward F. *The Operations of Company B, 504th Parachute Infantry (82nd Airborne Division) in Piercing the Siegfried Line, Near Losheimergraben, German 2-4 February 1945 (Rhineland Campaign) (Personal Experience of a Platoon Leader)*. General Subjects Section, Academic Department, The Infantry School. Courtesy of the Donovan Research Library.
[692] Regimental S-3 Journal, various entries for November 2, 1945. Courtesy of the Donovan Research Library.
[693] Swenson, Richard W. Combat interview with Edward Wellems and Victor Campana. Courtesy of the National Archives at College Park, MD. Box 24058, RG407.
[694] Bramson, interview.
[695] Bonning, interview.
[696] Shaifer, *The Operations of Company B*.
[697] Shaifer, *The Operations of Company B*.
[699] Bayley, interview.
[700] Hallock, Richard R. *The Operations of the 3rd Platoon, Company A, 504th Parachute Infantry (82nd Airborne Division) in an Assault Across a Draw on the Mertesrott Heights, in the Siegfried Line, Near Neuhof, Germany, 2 February 1945 (Rhineland Campaign) (Personal Experience of a Platoon Leader)*. General Subjects Section, Academic Department, The Infantry School. Courtesy of the Donovan Research Library.
[701] Bayley, interview.
[702] Bayley, interview.
[703] Hallock, *Operations of the 3rd Platoon*.
[704] Shaifer, *The Operations of Company B*.
[705] Shaifer, *The Operations of Company B*.
[706] Breard, Reneau G. Letter to author. Undated.
[707] Holmstock, phone interview.
[708] Breard, letter.
[709] Breard, letter.
[710] Bushman, Irvin. Letter to Daniel Harris. February 9, 1945. Courtesy of the Bushman family.
[711] S-2 Unit Journal. Entry for 0400 hours, February 15, 1945.
[712] Nicoll, Kenneth. Diary. Entry for February 16, 1945.
[713] Dodd, Gilbert. Interview with author.
[714] Dodd, interview.
[715] Hanna, interview.
[716] Eldridge, James. "At Retreat." *The Gastonia Daily Gazette*, September 16, 1943.
[717] Shaifer, *The Operations of Company B*.
[718] "Narrative of Action on the Anzio Beachhead". Headquarters, 504th Parachute Combat Team, n.d.
[719] Sweet, *Operations of the 2nd Battalion*.
[720] Hanna, interview.
[721] Gann, interview.
[722] Keefe, interview.
[723] Baldino, interview.

[724] Carney, Herbert. Letter to Snyder Family, March 23, 1945. Courtesy of the Snyder family.
[725] Mandel, William D. and Whittier, David H., *The Devils in Baggy Pants: Combat Record of the 504th Parachute Infantry Regiment, April 1943-July 1945*. Draeger Freres (1945).
[726] Halloran, Robert M. "Army Service Experiences Questionnaire". 82d Airborne Division, Box 1. US Army Heritage and Education Center.
[727] Gann, interview.
[728] "Nazi Can't Fight Without Orders." *Nebraska State Journal*, April 11, 1945.
[729] Whitehead, Don. "Nazi Strongpoint Taken by Platoon." *St. Louis Post-Dispatch*. November 29, 1943.
[730] "Interrogation Report No. 3." Annex No. 1 to G-2 Periodic Report No. 191. Headquarters, 82d Airborne Division, 06 April 1945.
[731] Oldfather, Diary entry for April 4, 1945.
[732] S-2 Journal. Headquarters, 504th Prcht Inf. 05 April 1945
[733] Hanna, interview.
[734] Unit S-3 Journal. Headquarters, 504th Prcht. Inf. 05 April 1945.
[735] S-2 Unit Journal. 06 April 1945.
[736] Breard, interview.
[737] Kopfinger, Stephen. "Capture, Release, Return." *Lancaster Online*, September 28, 2008. https://lancasteronline.com/features/capture-release-return/article_322e6e09-5b68-5f5b-8c37-a2a9f96ea49d.html. Accessed 30 January 2019.
[738] Breard, interview.
[739] "Interrogation Report No. 3." Annex No. 1 to G-2 Periodic Report No. 191. Headquarters, 82d Airborne Division, 06 April 1945.
[740] S-2 Unit Journal. 06 April 1945.
[741] Breard, interview & Message from S-2, 504th Prcht. Inf. To G-2, 82d Abn Div. 062205 April 1945.
[742] Breard, interview.
[743] Kopfinger, Stephen. "Capture, Release, Return." Lancaster Online, September 28, 2008. https://lancasteronline.com/features/capture-release-return/article_322e6e09-5b68-5f5b-8c37-a2a9f96ea49d.html. Accessed 30 January 2019.
[744] "History: 31 March – 31 April 1945." Headquarters, 504th Parachute Infantry & W. Forest Dawson. *Saga of the All Americans*. 82d Airborne Division Association, 1946.
[745] Smith, Harry as quoted in W. Forest Dawson. *Saga of the All Americans*. 82d Airborne Division Association, 1946.
[746] Bullock, William as quoted in W. Forest Dawson. *Saga of the All Americans*. 82d Airborne Division Association, 1946.
[747] Unrah, Jerome. Interview with author.
[748] Breard, interview.
[749] Headquarters, XVI Corps, General Orders No. 55 (July 20, 1945)
[750] Breard, interview.
[751] Hughes, interview.
[752] Zimmerman, interview.
[753] Hanna, interview.
[754] Hanna, interview.
[755] "Special Interrogation Report." Annex No. 2 to G-2 Periodic Report No 194. Headquarters, 82d Airborne Division, 9 April 1945.
[756] Hanna, interview.
[757] Unrah, interview.
[758] Breard, interview.
[759] Hanna, interview.
[760] Unrah, interview.
[761] Garrison, unpublished manuscript.
[762] Burriss, interview.
[763] Dwight H. Boyce as quoted in *Connecticut Men of the United States Army: January 5 to 6, 1945*. State of Connecticut, 1945.
[764] Breard, letter to author. Date unknown.
[765] Speer, interview.
[766] Dodd, interview.
[767] Zimmerman, interview.
[768] Halloran, Robert M. "Army Service Experiences Questionnaire". 82d Airborne Division, Box 1. US Army Heritage and Education Center
[769] Mokan, Edward L. "Army Service Experiences Questionnaire". 82d Airborne Division, Box 1. US Army Heritage and Education Center.
[770] Garrison, Chester A. "Army Service Experiences Questionnaire". 82d Airborne Division, Box 1. US Army Heritage and Education Center.
[771] Unrah, interview.
[772] "Tombs of the Unknown." Appendix No. 1 to INT Notes No. 6. Headquarters, 82d Airborne Division, 7 May 1945.
[773] Hanna, interview.
[774] Breard, letter.
[775] Zimmerman, interview.
[776] Hanna, interview.

Made in the USA
Columbia, SC
03 November 2019